RELIGIOUS EDUCATION

RELIGIOUS EDUCATION

A Comprehensive Survey

Marvin J. Taylor, Editor

Abingdon Press
New York • *Nashville*

RELIGIOUS EDUCATION: A COMPREHENSIVE SURVEY

Copyright © 1960 by Abingdon Press

Library of Congress Catalog Card Number: 60-5477

SET UP, PRINTED, AND BOUND BY THE
PARTHENON PRESS, AT NASHVILLE,
TENNESSEE, UNITED STATES OF AMERICA

Preface

NOTHING IS MORE EVIDENT TO THE DISCERNING OBSERVER THAN THE FACT that religious education is a many-faceted part of the church's total program. The day when its boundaries could be encompassed within the phrase "Sunday-school work" has been past for several decades. As these multiphased emphases have emerged, each has tended to develop its own rationale, program, and leaders who become specialists. To the person entering the ministry of education this variety of much intertwined but equally distinct aspects is often too complex for easy comprehension. It has been our purpose to explore the field of religious education, elevating each important area for a brief survey, and thus to assist the reader in attaining broader understanding.

While this book is entirely new in outline and content, it is not devoid of heritage. Two previous volumes stand as its progenitors: *Studies in Religious Education* (1931) and *Orientation in Religious Education* (1950). It has been their rather wide acceptance and use, as well as the demand for a contemporary resource, which has motivated the preparation and publication of this third in the series. Perhaps the difference in intervals separating these symposia is indicative of the rapidity with which developments in this total field are occurring. Whereas the first book proved useful for almost two decades, the third has appeared only ten years after the second, reflecting the fact that the ever increasing tempo of modern times has profoundly influenced religious education just as every other phase of life.

The outline of the book has been arranged in a logical sequence for the systematic study of religious education. Beginning with principles, such areas as philosophy of education, psychology, theology, the use of the Bible, and objectives have been explored. All are foundational for an understanding of the nature of religious education. Part II considers programs, materials, and methods, with primary emphasis being placed on these as found in the local church. Part III gives attention to administration, including organization of the local-church program, leadership, buildings and equipment, evaluation, and the religious educational opportunities afforded college students. Part IV is devoted to summary descriptions of eight agencies which foster religious education both within and beyond the limits of Protestantism.

Each chapter has been written by a different contributor, one who is a specialist in the particular area. The major single purpose of each has been to present a broad description of the contemporary status within the assigned branch of religious education. While limitations of space have held all chapters to brief statements, authors have included bibliographies which will be useful to the person desiring more extensive data. There is also a Selected Bibliography of both the older standard and more recent works in all branches of religious education at the end of the book. The reader's attention is also called to the Biographical Index where additional information about the various contributors may be obtained.

The content and format of the book have been planned with the hope that it will have a number of different uses. It has been structured to serve the college or seminary class as an introductory survey textbook. The local-church minister, director, superintendent, and teacher will discover the major areas of their educational responsibility considered. And the general reader will find herein a ready resource for almost any phase of religious education in which he may be interested. To all of these the book is offered with the desire that it will be found useful.

I am deeply grateful to all of the contributors for their interest and courtesies extended during the preparation of the manuscript. Without their diligence in the midst of many other responsibilities, the volume could not have been completed.

MARVIN J. TAYLOR

Contents

I. PRINCIPLES OF RELIGIOUS EDUCATION

II. PROGRAMS, MATERIALS, AND METHODS
IN RELIGIOUS EDUCATION

III. ADMINISTRATION OF RELIGIOUS EDUCATION

CONTENTS

Part I

Principles of Religious Education

Chapter 1

A Historical Introduction to
Religious Education

Marvin J. Taylor

RELIGION AND EDUCATION ARE INEVITABLE COMPANIONS OF EACH OTHER; FOR wherever any religion exists as a living, vital experience, its adherents wish to guarantee its perpetuation. Education is the means most often utilized for initiating both the mature convert and the young into the practices and beliefs of the religious fellowship. This goal is partially—even though indirectly—reached as the community practices its religion; for the act of worship, the observance of ethical norms, and the like are themselves educational in significance for both participant and observer. In addition, religious groups have almost universally devised techniques, programs, and institutions for the direct pursuit of this objective. It is the purpose of this essay to survey historically the major ways that Christianity has endeavored to attain its educational goals.

Jewish Backgrounds

Christianity did not begin as a new religion devoid of antecedents. Rather, it was essentially a transformed Judaism retaining much of the Jewish heritage—a fact perhaps best illustrated by its continued use of Jewish scripture, the Old Testament. The educational practices of the early church reflect this influence. Although the entire Hebrew inheritance was subjected to reinterpretation in the light of the demands of the Christian gospel, particularly the lordship or messiahship of Jesus, the inheritance remained prominent in the new faith.

11

Three Jewish emphases stand out especially in assessing this educational heritage. The first is the concept of *Torah,* a term meaning (in one sense) "instruction." It may be used to refer to divine teaching, the occasion for designating the Pentateuch—or even the whole Jewish Bible—to be *Torah.* Much of Hebrew religious life was built around studying the *Torah.* The synagogue (which probably arose during the Babylonian exile of the sixth century B.C.) was essentially a teaching institution (cf. Mark 1:21 and Luke 6:6), with the scriptures given central place in the service because of their revelatory character. Here teaching became virtually synonymous with worship,[1] and religion and education were inextricably welded together. It was the synagogue that appeared wherever Jews lived and kept their religion alive amidst the myriad of wanderings to which they were subject at the hands of their conquerors. This same institution, with its central emphasis on teaching, provided the model for Christian worship.

The second influential, inherited pattern was the role of the family in Jewish nurture. From the earliest nomadic times the family was central, with the parents being the first teachers of the child. Starting at the son's fourth year, it was the father's duty to teach the Shema (Deut. 6:4-9) and to continue with instruction in knowledge and observance of the Torah. This function was accomplished both directly and indirectly through the use of ritual acts performed in the regular exercises of family worship. Until the appearance of the synagogue and formal schools, the family was almost the only agency of religious education for the great majority of Jewish children. It was thus that the high estimate of the family's importance developed in pre-Christian Judaism.

The third important educational emphasis was the emergence of formal schools. Though details remain uncertain, the *Beth Hassepher* (House of the Book) probably originated between 75 B.C. and A.D. 64, at which latter date the high priest Joshua ben Gamala decreed that every district and community should have one, with children entering by six or seven years of age. This was an elementary school, its rationale clearly implied by the title; the "Book" was the scriptures, the written Torah. It became customary for the school to be adjacent to or a part of the synagogue. Secondary education was offered in the *Beth Hammidrash* (House of Study) where the *Mishnah* (oral law) was the central element in the curriculum. Students usually entered this program at about ten years, continuing for various periods up to about fifteen years of age. Both institutions had been established within Judaism prior to the origin of Christianity in the first century. Thus, early followers of Jesus possessed this full inheritance of an educationally advanced religion as they carried on their ever expanding witness to the gospel.

Christianity to the Fall of Rome

In that spirit which referred to Jesus most frequently as a teacher, primitive Christianity accorded the ministry of "teaching" a prominent place. Its content encompassed several elements: the reinterpretation of the Hebrew scripture; the gospel of the life, death, and resurrection of Jesus; the meaning of the Christian's confession of faith in "Jesus as Lord"; the details of Jesus' life and sayings; ethical instruction regarding the "two ways," i.e., the ways of life and death; and the understanding of baptism and the Lord's Supper.[2] The agencies used were

---

[1] Lewis J. Sherrill, *The Rise of Christian Education,* p. 45.
[2] *Ibid.,* pp. 144-51.

to some extent borrowed and adapted from Judaism. The family continued to be the chief educator of children. Ignatius' words from the early second century illustrate this concern: "Fathers, bring up your children in the nurture and admonition of the Lord; teach them the Holy Scriptures, and also trades, that they may not indulge in idleness." [3] Worship and teaching also remained inter-mixed in function. At first services for the proclamation of the Word and the celebration of the Eucharist were united, but by the fourth century the expanding liturgy had produced two major divisions of the service. The *missa catechumenorum* came first and was primarily for instruction of the unbaptized. The *missa fidelium* followed with the Lord's Supper for the faithful.

Two major institutions emerged in the early centuries with fundamentally educational purposes. The *catechumenate* was essentially an adult education pro-gram, which arose in the second century and continued to grow until about A.D. 450, after which it gradually diminished in influence disappearing by the early Middle Ages. So long as Christianity's converts came from Judaism, less intensive instruction was required. However, non-Jewish adults came with deep-seated pagan influences which pervaded all of life and these *catechumens* were subjected to a period of moral probation during which instruction in scripture and doctrine could be accompanied with gradual induction into the fellowship and life of the Christian community. This probationary time usually extended from two to three years and through several distinct stages leading up to baptism and full membership. Patterns of instruction and content varied considerably, of course, throughout the widely scattered sections of the church.

The *catechetical school* was the second educational institution to appear in this era. Begun in Alexandria *cir.* A.D. 179, the school flourished under Pantaenus, Clement, and Origen, spreading to Antioch, Edessa, and Nisibis in Asia. Catecheti-cal instruction emerged chiefly because of the widespread influence of Greek thought and culture. From the late second century on, converts in increasing numbers were being won from the higher and better educated classes of people. Their background of Greek philosophy forced Christianity's most learned teachers to consider its implications. Hence, these schools, though limited in number, represent the first "advanced" or "higher" education carried on under the church's auspices. At Alexandria, a cultured city with extensive libraries and non-Christian schools, catechetical instruction was conducted in a wide variety of secular subjects, all being taught in relationship with Christian theology. Young Christian scholars were afforded the opportunity of studying in a Christian environment and exploring even secular truths from a Christian viewpoint. Perhaps the most significant result of these schools was their impact on Christian theology, for in the writings of Clement and Origen are seen the first efforts at the formulation of a theoretical and systematic theology, a careful and exegetical study of the Bible, and the production of scholarly theological works, whose influence was to last hundreds of years.

As the church became well stabilized in the Empire, particularly after the legalization and establishment of Christianity early in the fourth century, training for the ministry was a function performed in cathedral churches and the episcopal residences. Somewhat after the pattern of the Twelve traveling and

---

[3] *The Ante-Nicene Fathers* (Edinburgh: A. C. Coxe, 1899), I, 81.

living with Jesus, young men (and even children) were received and raised in the bishop's home, a practice made universally obligatory by the Council of Vaison in A.D. 529. Their instruction consisted of learning to read and write, in addition to studying the doctrines, liturgy, and scriptures of the church.

The Medieval Church

Following the fall of Rome and the collapse of imperial authority, the Church was the sole institution with continuing influence. This power vacuum inevitably produced increased ecclesiastical interest in the direction of all human affairs, secular and political as well as religious. The growth in the authority of the church spread over several centuries and reached its climax in Boniface VIII's famous bull, *Unam Sanctam* (A.D. 1302), which proclaimed that the ultimate jurisdiction in all of life's affairs belonged properly to the Church, under penalty of loss of salvation for opposition. This emerging dominance of life and thought had profound and far-reaching effects on medieval education.

Chief in importance as a medium of education was worship. This grew logically from the church's stress on "the vision of God" as a supreme goal in life. Although worship was directed chiefly toward God, the very richness of the symbolism used in the ritual was highly educative in result. Its elaborate character included the eight canonical hours and the Mass, each celebrated daily; the various Christian festivals associated with the liturgical calendar; and the religious drama of the mystery plays. These latter were built around the great themes of Christian tradition—the nativity, the Resurrection, the passion, and other subjects from the biblical era. Apart from occasional mention of the role of parents in teaching their children, these less formal means of worship and the sacraments were almost the sole education received by the masses of people through the Middle Ages, simultaneous with the Church's growth in power and importance.

Formal education was conducted in several schools which were reserved primarily for training a few young men for the religious life. The early education carried on in the episcopal residence was transformed into cathedral schools devoted to preparing priests for service in the diocese. Though narrowly religious originally, after about A.D. 800 some broadened the curriculum to include the seven liberal arts, and were the forerunners of later universities—for example, the University of Paris developed from the school at Notre Dame cathedral. From 500 to 1000 monastic schools were centers of intellectual activity. Inspired by the Benedictine Rule—Article 48 required reading—monasteries developed libraries by reproducing —hand copying—the Bible and other religious books. Their schools were chiefly to prepare novices for the monastic life, although limited numbers of boys from the community were also provided with instruction. As large cities grew after about 1100, collegiate church schools appeared. Their curriculum stressed the liberal arts chiefly, in addition to theology. Song schools were maintained by many cathedrals and other large churches for training boys to serve as choristers in the services of worship. In the later Middle Ages these offered elementary instruction in grammar and religion. Wealthy families frequently endowed private chapels with personal priests to "chant" masses for the family, and these priests customarily provided instruction for the children in what came to be known as chantry schools. As early as 800 the church expressed concern for parish schools and urged their development. There was no general compliance with this suggestion, however, at any time during the medieval period, though following 1250 some city parishes did begin to establish such schools for boys.

Beginning with the twelfth century, higher education came on the scene with the rise of the universities, many of which gradually emerged from cathedral schools (i.e., Paris and Oxford) as they expanded and elevated their curriculum. Their origin reflected the changing later medieval world—the growth of cities, the rise of a middle class, new intellectual interests stimulated by contacts with Moslems during the Crusades, and other such influences. When older educational patterns proved inadequate to serve these newer needs, the university appeared. Curriculums varied among the institutions, and some became noted for their specializations—Paris in theology, Oxford in the liberal arts, Bologna in law. Although their origin must be dated to the Middle Ages, there is one sense in which their spirit was foreign to the dominating motif of that era. The universities were not narrowly religious, and the majority of their students were enrolled in curriculums of law, medicine, and other secular areas in preparation for careers outside the church. While these often tended to be rigid and quite formalized, nonetheless these institutions as a whole maintained an intellectual environment in which the church, government, and even theology were subjected to ever-increasing critical inquiry.

The Renaissance and Reformation

Contemporaneous with the growth of universities was the rise of the Renaissance, a movement which produced a reawakened interest in the ideas, values, and literature of the Greco-Roman world. Often called humanistic, one major phase of this development was centered on man—his powers, nature, emotions, and goals. The resultant turmoil shattered the all-encompassing authority of the church. The educational results were focused primarily on new patterns of schools and broadened curriculums in the existing institutions. Perhaps no single facet of this movement was more important to Christianity than the rediscovery of ancient literature, for the Latin of the Vulgate was set aside and the study of the original biblical languages (Hebrew and Greek) produced a vast new interest in scripture for specifically religious reasons.

Luther's revolt and excommunication reflect this revived importance attributed to the Bible. Having sought and found his own personal salvation through intensive perusal of its pages, Luther made the authority of the Bible a foremost Reformation principle, replacing the priority of the church inherited from medieval centuries. Justification by faith in Christ as Savior also contributed to the diminution of ecclesiastical prominence wherein the sacraments and the role of the priest had held chief significance. Luther's third fundamental principle, the priesthood of all believers, further enhanced the importance of the individual believer.

The educational product of these precepts has been phenomenal. Having found a faith primarily through Bible study, Luther proceeded to translate it into the vernacular German. Since none could achieve faith for another, the instruction of the masses of people in fundamental literacy became essential, and herein emerged the principle of universal Christian education. Luther proclaimed that schools should be established everywhere so that every boy and girl might learn to read the scriptures and thereby be enabled to achieve a personal faith in Jesus as Lord and Savior. Municipalities were urged to assist in support and control of these institutions. In his famous sermon on sending children to school Luther described the Christian life as one of warfare with the devil and urged the conscription of youth for this battle—i.e., compulsory attendance.

These educational results were paralleled in other lands affected by the Reformation. The theocratic society in Geneva received Calvin's mandate for education in 1538. It included a system of elementary and secondary schools founded primarily to attain religious objectives but not confined to a narrowly religious curriculum. His influence spread far beyond Switzerland. In Holland church synods delegated educational responsibility to civil authorities, but the spirit guiding and permeating these schools was distinctively Calvinistic. Knox's plan for a complete system from the parish school to the university, while initially rejected by the Scottish Legislature and only partially and gradually accepted in later decades, partook of this same spirit. Thus, the Reformation on both the Continent and in a part of the British Isles established the principle of universal education, under governmental auspices to be sure, but with religious inspiration and for explicitly religious purposes.

Colonial American Religious Education

Education in the United States prior to 1787 took on three rather distinct forms. Each was characteristic of a particular geographical sector of the original colonies, and in a considerable measure reflected the circumstances of immigration and the religious factors influential therein.

1. With the notable exception of Rhode Island, all of New England was Calvinistic, and the Geneva ideal of state sponsored religious nurture prevailed. The 1642 ordinance of the Massachusetts General Court required that parents be responsible for their children's learning to read "and understand the principles of religion and the capital laws of this country." This religious motivation was even more explicit in the 1647 enactment—known ever since as the Old Deluder Act—which set forth the establishment of schools chiefly to thwart the influence of Satan, whose chief project was believed to be the keeping of men's minds in ignorance. These were state schools, but their goals were religious as well as civic, as is best indicated by the popularity and content of the New England primer. Published first about 1690, it sold thousands of copies annually for more than 150 years.[4] Even in teaching the alphabet, religion was foremost—i.e., "In Adam's fall, we sinned all" . . . down to . . . "Zaccheus he did climb the tree our Lord to see." This together with the Bible and the Westminster *Shorter Catechism* comprised the chief elements of the curriculum in colonial New England.

2. The Middle states possessed no such religious uniformity among their settlers. Variety of nationality as well as religion was their chief characteristic. Unlike New England no church was in a majority. Though many shared to some extent the Reformation-born interest in education, no central colony was able to follow the lead of Massachusetts. Hence, education became essentially a private matter under church auspices wherever sufficient interest existed. This produced only limited numbers of schools in Pennsylvania, New York, and New Jersey, confined to denominational sponsorship. Where they existed general and religious nurture were combined, but all too often few if any were established throughout these colonies.

[4] James Mulhern, *A History of Education* (New York: Ronald Press, 1946), pp. 279-80.

3. In the Southern colonies a third attitude prevailed. Their settlers were predominantly Anglicans who were loyal to the established church and had come to America for economic gain rather than religious freedom. Both the climate and the terrain quickly produced a plantation-structured society with various strata of social classes. Hence, though religious uniformity generally prevailed as in New England, democratic schools for all children were impossible. Further, reflecting the Anglican view that education was essentially a private matter, only a few "pauper schools" and some private, tuition schools emerged before the Revolution. The strong religious motivation inherent in the continental Reformation was notably absent from these ventures. Only those schools established by the Society for the Propagation of the Gospel in Foreign Parts—an English organization formed in 1701—provided a distinctly religious orientation.

In higher education, the colonial period produced several institutions, almost all under church auspices. Starting with Harvard (1636—Puritan), William and Mary (1693—Anglican), Yale (1701—Congregationalist), Princeton (1746—Presbyterian), King's College—now Columbia (1754—Anglican), Brown (1764—Baptist), Dartmouth (1769—Congregationalist) and Rutgers (1766—Dutch Reformed) were all established. Theology and the classics were at the heart of their curriculum, and all had as a primary goal the training of ministers for the new world churches.

American Religious Education to the Twentieth Century

Sunday-School Movement

Although originating in Gloucester, England, in 1780, the Sunday-school movement spread quickly to America and flourished. Similar isolated instances of these schools had existed in the colonies as early as 1669,[5] but no concerted movement appeared until the closing years of the eighteenth century. In 1790 the First Day Society of Philadelphia was formed to "instruct the rising generation by teaching them from the Bible and from such other moral and religious books as the society might from time to time direct."[6] In the same year the Methodist Conference meeting in South Carolina adopted the principle of Sunday schools in each church. As the religious content of public education was gradually eliminated during the pre-Civil War era,[7] interest in the church school grew. City "unions" were organized to sponsor them—among others, New York and Boston in 1816, Philadelphia in 1817. In 1824 these local unions formed the American Sunday School Union (A.S.S.U.), which identified its functions as: (a) to publish suitable materials for the Sunday school, (b) to select biblical outlines and teaching aids, and (c) to evangelize the nation by sending and supporting Sunday-school missionaries. Its program was promoted by national conventions beginning in 1832. Just as Robert Raikes, the English founder of the Sunday school had been a layman, the A.S.S.U. was largely a lay led organization. It is usually described by historians as undenominational rather than interdenominational, since it was composed of

[5] For details, see H. F. Cope, *The Evolution of the Sunday School* (Boston: Pilgrim Press, 1911), pp. 62 ff.

[6] Edwin W. Rice, *The Sunday School Movement and the American Sunday-School Union* (Philadelphia: American Sunday School Union, 1917), p. 45.

[7] See William K. Dunn, *What Happened to Religious Education?* (Baltimore: Johns Hopkins Press, 1958).

interested persons from many denominations but not acting as representatives of their communions. The nineteenth century witnessed the gradual expansion of this agency into all major cities with state associations also being formed, and by 1900 the nation was almost completely organized with city, county, and state Sunday-school unions throughout much of the land.

Sunday-School Curriculum

In its beginning years the curriculum material of the American Sunday school was chiefly confined to catechisms reflecting the Reformation heritage, when numerous catechisms were prepared to guarantee doctrinal understanding and purity. This technique of instruction prevailed until about 1810 to 1815. Under the influence of public education's abandoning of the catechetical methods, however, the Bible gradually replaced them as the major element in the curriculum. Between 1810-1815 and 1825 there was little systematic Bible study primarily because no system for its utilization had been devised. Stress was placed on memorization, and effectiveness of teaching was measured quantitatively. Pupils were encouraged to commit to memory vast amounts of biblical material, and contests and rewards were used to stimulate interest. The extent of this overemphasis is illustrated by the report of the 1819 New York City Sunday School Union wherein some schools reported an average of more than five thousand verses memorized per quarter, with numerous individual students reciting thirty or forty chapters at one time in public meetings. Widespread criticism developed quickly. Since such huge amounts of Bible were being mastered, no class time remained for consideration of meanings and values. Students often proved unable to discuss with understanding the very passages they had previously quoted. Hence, it became evident that some pattern of Bible study limited to comprehensible portions for each session was needed.

The first significant step was taken by the New York union late in 1824 when it issued a set of "selected lessons" for use during the early months of 1825. Selections were confined to fifteen to twenty verses, and while interest in memorization remained high, primary attention was given to instruction regarding the meaning of the passages being studied. This plan proved to be immediately popular, and it spread quickly. As an aid to teachers—who had previously only been required to keep records on their students' memory work—lesson helps were published. Judson's *Questions* were structured around the selections and provided both pertinent questions and assistance in finding answers in the biblical text. The A.S.S.U. issued its *Union Questions* in a succession of volumes covering several years. Others duplicated this approach with varying questions.

Unfortunately, these led to considerable competition in curriculum. Some denominations began to select and publish lessons for their churches. Independent, private publishers also entered the field until a considerable multiplicity of selections was available. Many series of question books were also marketed, and the resulting confusion was so great that 1830 to 1870 has been called by one historian the "Babel period of curriculum." [8] While variety itself was not deemed undesirable, the absence of any central or basic organizing principle added to this confusion which was further compounded with the passing of the years and the appearance of ever greater numbers of competing selections.

[8] Frank G. Lankard, *A History of the American Sunday School Curriculum*, p. 175.

The 1860's witnessed much agitation for reform, and it was finally accomplished at the 1872 A.S.S.U. convention at Indianapolis. Led by John H. Vincent, a Methodist minister, and B. F. Jacobs, a Baptist layman, the convention adopted the principle of complete uniformity. A lesson committee was created and instructed to select a series of Bible-centered lessons with the same lesson to be used in each class—regardless of age level—and in every Sunday school across the nation. Thus it was proposed that in one action all existing curriculum materials would be eliminated and replaced by a single set for universal use. The curriculum principle remained unchanged. A set of selected passages from the Bible for successive weeks was the plan, but only one group of selections would be made for utilization throughout the Sunday schools of the nation. The committee's first selections were arranged on a seven-year cycle, to run from 1873 through 1879, with the hope that this systematic approach would permit a complete survey of the Bible. In 1874 the still familiar practice of adding a golden text was begun. This curriculum scheme continues today in the International Improved Uniform Lesson series [9] issued by the National Council of Churches' Division of Christian Education, the organizational descendant of the American Sunday School Union.

Other Educational Developments

The early national period was characterized by increasing secularization of public education. The constitutional guarantee of religious freedom led to frequent conflicts over the religious content of the curriculum, and sectarian growth and strength were added factors of influence. Under the leadership of Horace Mann, Massachusetts banned the Calvinistic religious instruction which had been prominent in its schools for two centuries. Similar controversies around the nation contributed to this continuing secularization.

Confronted with public schools no longer providing for the teaching of religion, churchmen reacted to the challenge in at least two ways. First, the Sunday school was strengthened and extended throughout this century, as has been noted. Secondly, some groups gave serious consideration to parochial-type schools. The Presbyterian Church best illustrates this movement. In 1847 its General Assembly gave general approval to a plan for establishing a school in each congregation, and more than 250 were opened in the next twenty-five years.[10] Although the program was abandoned by 1870, other groups adopted this alternative and have continued to maintain day schools for their children.[11]

Numerous other agencies for fostering religious education also appeared during this century. Recognizing with appreciation the growth of the Sunday school, denominations began to establish boards of education for their promotion. The 1820's saw Methodist and Episcopal groups formed, the 1830's, Lutheran and Congregational, and the Baptist in 1840. While the immediate effect of these actions was limited, they do indicate the emergence and growth of denominational interest in and responsibility for the Sunday school, which was previously an almost totally nondenominational venture.

Leadership education also grew rapidly during the 1800's. One significant

---

[9] See ch. 9, p. 106.

[10] For a complete history see Lewis J. Sherrill, *Presbyterian Parochial Schools: 1846-1870* (New Haven, Conn.: Yale University Press, 1932).

[11] For current data, see ch. 22, pp. 236-46.

function of the A.S.S.U. program was the regular training of teachers, usually carried on through the city or county "unions." By mid-century Horace Mann's plan for public teacher institutes had been adapted to religious education, and normal classes were being held in various sectors of the nation. In 1874 the Chautauqua summer-institute program was begun for Sunday-school teachers, and within a few years the idea had spread to many local communities. Courses were offered for credit, with examinations being administered and diplomas awarded. Correspondence schools were also included in its program.

Finally, the nineteenth century also produced several of the agencies which developed into twentieth-century prominence. The Young Men's Christian Association started in London in 1844, with the Y.W.C.A. following in New York during the last quarter of the century. Youth work received its initial organized impulse through the nondenominational Christian Endeavor Society, begun originally in a Portland, Maine, Congregational Church. Its almost immediate success produced similar organizations and programs sponsored by the denominations. Church camping, in addition to the Chautauqua-type program and the predominately evangelistic camp meeting, is known to have begun as early as 1880, when a Rhode Island church used a site on Gardners Island, Wakefield, with its membership. In the last decade an Illinois minister's wife held what was probably the first vacation church school, a four-week program for children and youth in four departments. Thus, it is evident that by 1900 religious education's boundaries had been enlarged to include several of the agencies or their forerunners which have flourished during the past six decades.

The Twentieth-Century Scene

The development of religious education as a full-scale and many-faceted movement is usually traced to the turn of the present century. Prior to this time, except for a few preliminary and exploratory efforts as noted above, churches tended to confine their programs to Sunday-school work largely lay led and controlled. However, beginning with the 1900's the scope of the church's educational interest was widened to include the multiphased emphases evident to the contemporary observer. Only a few aspects of this expansion can be considered here.

Organizational Changes

The work of the A.S.S.U. had become international in the 1870's with the addition of Canadian representatives to its lesson committee and conventions. From this time on it continued to strengthen its local, regional, and national promotion of the Sunday school as a Bible-centered educational institution devoted to the use of uniform lessons under the leadership of interested, volunteer laymen. Simultaneously with these efforts, however, denominational concern for religious nurture was being heightened. Boards of education were establishing trained, professional staffs for the purpose of similar promotion within their communions. Since the framework of the International Sunday School Association (I.S.S.A.) provided little opportunity for the participation of these denominational leaders, in 1910 they organized the Sunday School Council of Evangelical Denominations. Tension between the two organizations mounted rather quickly both on the issues of educational policy and the control of the Sunday-school program. As these tensions grew in the years following 1910, the two became virtually direct competitors.

These problems were finally resolved by the complete merger of both in 1922 to form the International Sunday School Council of Religious Education—later shortened to International Council of Religious Education (I.C.R.E.). Here both lay and professional, denominational and interdenominational interests were combined in a flexible structure designed to meet the existing and newer needs of the churches and councils.[12] The I.C.R.E. continued in existence, frequently expanding as new educational emphases demanded, until its merger in 1950 with other interdenominational agencies to form the National Council of Churches.[13]

The twentieth century witnessed the appearance of numerous other organizations which have had significance for the expansion of the religious education movement. In 1903, under the leadership of William Rainey Harper, the Religious Education Association was organized to promote improvement in existing programs for religious nurture.[14] Weekday religious education—as now known—was begun at Gary, Indiana, in 1914, although a few ventures in North Dakota and Colorado had antedated it.[15] Within a few years the idea had spread to many states, and the I.C.R.E. recognized this prominence by the organization of the Department of Vacation and Weekday Church Schools. Similar developments occurred in youth and adult work in the 1930's, when both the United Christian Youth Movement [16] and United Christian Adult Movement [17] were organized. Both have been closely related to the I.C.R.E. and other denominational and interdenominational agencies from their beginnings. Other related organizational developments were happening on the world scene. Growing out of the world conventions which had been held since 1889, the World Sunday School Association was formed in 1907 at Rome. Recognizing the expansion of education to areas beyond Sunday-school work, its name was changed in 1947 to the World Council of Christian Education and Sunday School Association.[18]

Curriculum Developments

At the turn of the century uniform lessons had been in use for about three decades. They were still based directly on the Bible and issued for use throughout all departments of the Sunday school. Their acceptance had not been accomplished without criticism, however. The principle of age-level gradation was widely adopted in public education, and Sunday-school teachers of children were especially vocal in their demands for graded materials. Further, these decades had also produced marked advances in Bible study which were not being reflected in the uniform lessons. Such forces, as well as the appearance of competing sets of graded curriculum materials, such as the Blakeslee Series and the University of Chicago's "Constructive Series in Religion," compelled the I.S.S.A. to issue graded lessons beginning in 1908. Though originally closely graded, these were changed to group graded with six levels of materials in 1924. Uniform lessons continued to be issued and their popularity has diminished only very slowly.[19] Both the uniform

[12] For details see Bower and Hayward, *Protestantism Faces Its Educational Task Together.*
[13] See ch. 31, pp. 338-40 for details of this merger.
[14] See ch. 33, pp. 359-63.
[15] See ch. 21, pp. 226-32.
[16] See ch. 11, pp. 121-22.
[17] See ch. 12, pp. 132-42.
[18] See ch. 32, pp. 351-53.
[19] Bower and Hayward, *op. cit.*, pp. 77-78.

and graded lesson materials were based on the Bible and essentially content centered. They started with a body of subject matter which was to be mastered and then "applied" to the life situations of the learner. The only major difference between the two was the gradation of the content to the various age levels of the pupils.

The next major development was the International Curriculum of Religious Education, an entirely different approach to curriculum theory. Based on the premise that curriculum should be constructed around the learner's experience, its unit of learning was a "unit of experience moving from an identifiable situation to its outcome in a Christian response." [20] Thus, the traditional order was reversed. The curriculum consisted of a graded series of experiments in actual living. The full theory was presented in the *Curriculum Guide,* a document published to assist editors in the production of experience-centered curricula. While a complete international curriculum never appeared, the *Guide* has continued to influence curriculum developments by focusing attention upon the importance of the learner's experience in the educational process. The work of the Committee on the Study of Christian Education in the mid-1940's modified both the subject and experience-centered theories in a new synthesis discussed elsewhere in this book.[21] The most recent developments in curriculum have sought to preserve the values in both of these emphases.

Other twentieth-century occurrences in the historical flowering of religious education are considered at length in other chapters of this book. Only brief listing can be made here and the reader referred elsewhere for details. After several decades of gradually diminishing interest, the role of religion in public education has again risen to considerable prominence. Once again the possibilities are being actively explored.[22] Psychology's interest in religion, strong at the turn of the century, is again emerging as a significant guide to our growing understanding of the nature of religious experience.[23] The function of the counselor within the educational program has received corresponding attention during recent years.[24] Newer aids to learning now being adapted to religious education's program include the social scientists' insights in group dynamics,[25] the use of audio-visual materials,[26] and greater understanding of the values in the several creative arts for Christian education.[27] Summer camps and conferences are an ever increasing phase of contemporary programming in religious education.[28] To provide trained leadership, a new profession has arisen within the past forty years. No longer is the active local church willing to leave the program of education to volunteers. Where funds are available, the director of religious education is now a standard member of the church's professional staff, providing supervision and guidance for

[20] *Ibid.,* p. 71.
[21] See ch. 9, pp. 99-110, especially pp. 104-06.
[22] See ch. 8, pp. 87-98.
[23] See ch. 3, pp. 34-43.
[24] See ch. 15, pp. 162-72.
[25] See ch. 16, pp. 173-83.
[26] See ch. 18, pp. 193-203.
[27] See ch. 19, pp. 204-14.
[28] See ch. 20, pp. 215-25.

the varied phases of Christianity's educational ventures.[29] Few developments have rivaled this one in its phenomenal growth in the years since the early 1920's.

Conclusion

It is undoubtedly evident that this survey, of necessity, has been brief in its treatment of the subject. Similarly, it has been incomplete in its description of the past two or three decades, an era in which the religious education movement has expanded into numerous totally new patterns. However, this "historical introduction" has been included in this form for several reasons, chief among them being the writer's conviction that the present is seldom adequately understood apart from the conditions of the past which produced it. The remaining chapters of this volume are devoted to more intensive analyses of the many contemporary facets of the religious education scene. In almost every instance the authors have included the recent history for their subject areas. Hence, it is hoped that the reader will move from this survey with a generalized comprehension of the development of religious education into those specific areas which are of special and greatest interest to him; and further, it is hoped that this broad introduction will lend meaning to the study of these particular phases of the work of the church.

Bibliography

Bower, William C. and Hayward, Percy R. *Protestantism Faces Its Educational Task Together*. Appleton, Wis.: C. C. Nelson Publishing Company, 1949.

Brown, Arlo A. *A History of Religious Education in Recent Times*. New York: Methodist Book Concern, 1923.

Ebner, Eliezer. *Elementary Education in Ancient Israel*. New York: Bloch Publishing Company, 1956.

Eby, Frederick and Arrowood, Charles F. *History and Philosophy of Education: Ancient and Medieval*. Englewood Cliffs, N. J.: Prentice-Hall, Inc., 1940.

Lankard, Frank G. *A History of the American Sunday School Curriculum*. New York: Abingdon Press, 1927.

Sherrill, Lewis J. *The Rise of Christian Education*. New York: The Macmillan Company, 1950.

[29] See ch. 24, pp. 259-69.

Chapter 2

Philosophies of Education
and Religious Education

Albert E. Bailey

IN THIS CHAPTER WE WILL SEEK BRIEF ANSWERS TO FIVE QUESTIONS. 1. WHY study philosophy of education for light on *religious* education? 2. What are the major systems of philosophy and what are their educational concerns? 3. What influence have these systems had in recent educational practice? 4. How is this related to current trends in religious education? 5. What are some of the burning issues for a philosophy of Christian education?

Why Philosophy of Education?

Why bother with philosophy of education when our concern is with *religious* education? Is our religious, or "theological," perspective not the primary guide for religious education? Our religious convictions are indeed primary. Furthermore, a major assertion of most Christian educators today is that any education worthy to be called Christian must find its norms in a responsible theological discipline.

Philosophy also seeks answers to man's ultimate questions about reality, knowledge, and value, formulating these in logically consistent and comprehensive structures of thought which strive to discover the wholeness of existence. It also inquires into the truth and validity of beliefs. This concern for ultimate meaning which philosophy and theology share has given rise to various fact-finding sciences. Any valid theory of education must take all of these disciplines into consideration. No less is it the responsibility of religious education to call all of these processes into its service. Otherwise our religious education may at best be haphazard, and at worst, destructive of the values we seek.

Major Systems of Philosophy

Recent philosophies of education can usually be classified within one of two opposed streams of thought, progressivism and traditionalism or essentialism.[1] Nine approaches to philosophy of education were given expression in the Fifty-fourth Yearbook of the National Society for the Study of Education (N.S.S.E.).[2] The four major systems have been naturalism, idealism, realism, and pragmatism, and

[1] See Brubacher, *Modern Philosophies of Education*, p. 297. For comment on the Canadian scene, see Hilda Neatby, *So Little for the Mind* (Toronto: Clarke, Irwin & Company, 1953).
[2] Part I, *Modern Philosophies and Education*.

24

these will be summarized historically in this chapter. For a detailed treatment the student of religious education may consult J. Donald Butler.[3]

Naturalism

The most ancient form of Western philosophy is naturalism. The distinguishing mark of the naturalist is the belief that physical nature is all there is. Ultimate reality is found within a natural, physical order. Early Greeks sought for one ultimate substance common to all things. Various elements of nature were fastened upon—water, air, fire—and then the concept of atoms in space. Herbert Spencer (1820-1903) refined this somewhat by his concept of an underlying force or energy. This in itself is not perceivable but is revealed in the matter and motion of objects and in events.

From the time of Auguste Comte (1798-1857) there have been naturalists for whom the explanation of reality as substance was inadequate. Comte found the abiding reality of nature in its structure comprised of reliable laws and relationships. Thus positivism developed with an emphasis upon scientific investigation and description as the only reliable means of knowledge. A more critical naturalism defines nature as process, a continuous generative source from which all things or events emerge and in which they transpire. However, as naturalism becomes more critical it tends to change into forms of realism or pragmatism. Many realists and all present pragmatists have in common with naturalism a confidence in scientific method as the only valid source of knowledge.

Man is viewed as evolving from the process of nature, with no spiritual being such as a soul. Nevertheless there are high and varied refinements of the human self. The gaining of factual knowledge helps man to adjust to the laws and rhythms of nature, to preserve himself, and to discover his normal functioning in the processes of nature. If a naturalist speaks of God, it is that structure in nature that makes possible the realization of values and in which value inheres. Such a God is impersonal, wholly within the processes of nature, and therefore is finite.

Sheer naturalism is not a significant influence in education or religious education. But there are strong naturalistic influences in some forms of realism and in pragmatism. Similarities should also be observed between the all-encompassing physical nature of naturalism and the all-encompassing spiritual or mental nature of some idealism. In the latter, God is part of the spiritual process or becomes the process itself. Although personalized, he is often reduced to being the value-realizing structure in which selves or the society of selves inheres. In a specifically Christian idealism, such as J. Donald Butler's, this concept of God is rejected as inadequate.[4]

Idealism

The problem "How can we know?" is central in idealism. One can doubt the existence of everything except a mind which doubts. There is no external reality which can be known as such. There are only the ideas of reality which are in the mind of the knower, hence the name idealism.

From Socrates and Plato came the concept of an ideal world of forms of which the stuff of experience was only the shadow or image. There has been a persistent Platonic influence in Christian thinking, and many have read this into the biblical

---

[3] Four Philosophies and Their Practice in Education and Religion.
[4] Ibid., pp. 554-55.

record itself. The Hebrew tradition in the Old Testament, however, is realist in perspective. The New Testament, written in Greek to a largely Greek culture, has often been interpreted within the context of Greek ideas. Recent biblical theology, rediscovering the unity of the biblical witness, indicates rather that the New Testament message is cast in a distinctively Hebrew-Christian mould made relevant to the thought forms of the culture and language of the day. This is particularly true of the Gospel of John which, once widely viewed as thoroughly Greek because of its thought forms, is now generally recognized to be deeply rooted in the Hebraic viewpoint.[5]

From the time of René Descartes (1596-1650) one persistent problem of idealism has been whether all of reality is purely subjective—existing only in the mind of the perceiver—or whether it exists objectively. Objective reality is established by positing a universal mind in which everything exists. While this establishes an objective reality, such reality is not perceived directly in the external world. Universal Mind—God for the religious—emerges in man and is his inner essence. Reality then is beheld only in the inner experience of man.[6]

It is not merely ideas which exist, all of reality is mental process. To be known at all reality must in some sense be similar to our ideas of it and to the mind which knows it. This basically states a limitation of our knowledge. From this proposition the idealist deduces that therefore all reality is the expression of mind. This does not mean reality is limited by our ideas of it. Our ideas are imperfect formulations of the reality existing in Universal Mind.

The tension between potentiality and actuality has always loomed large in idealist thought. Only perfection is ultimately real, and only Universal Mind is absolutely good. Evil has no ultimate existence, but is the failure or refusal to realize full potentiality. In this sense a person participates in reality, or is "real," only to the extent that he or she has actualized potentiality, thus participating in the perfection of Universal Mind, or God. Falling short of his possibilities is "sin."

Education, then, is the leading and encouraging of free spirits to realize their full potentiality and find their completion in Universal Mind or the life of God. "Education is the eternal process of superior adjustment of the physically and mentally developed, free, conscious, human being to God as manifested in the intellectual, emotional, and volitional environment of man." [7] It is centered in the ideals which are to be realized; it is highly personal. It requires a teacher who personifies reality, who is a personal friend of each student, and who evokes a response in the student by which he is motivated to that self-activity by which he may grow. Imitation of the ideal personified in others or revealed in the work of others is a strong factor in idealist education.

Realism

The two earliest Western philosophies arose out of man's reflection upon his own experience. Beyond himself was a natural physical world of which he himself was a part. In accepting the physical as the basis of reality, naturalism rejects the spiritual and reduces mental activity to a process of the physical organism. But the

[5] See Edwyn Clement Hoskyns, *The Fourth Gospel*, ed. Francis Noel Davey (rev. ed.; London: Faber and Faber Limited, 1947), esp. pp. 154-62.
[6] Butler, *op. cit.*, p. 45.
[7] Horne, *The Philosophy of Education*, p. 285.

idealist says, "If there is anything 'out there' which corresponds to the ideas I have, it can exist only as the 'brain child' of a universal mind." Here the spiritual is identified with the mental and the physical reduced to expressions of thought.

These are the most naïve forms of man's rudimentary thinking but they indicate the setting in which most of man's philosophic thought has been developed. Later philosophies are largely rebellion against and/or refinement of these two. Realism, rebelling against the idealist theory of knowledge and the metaphysics it requires, affirms the *reality* of external phenomena. It does so with sufficient refinement of naturalism, at the same time, as to become a separate system of thought.

Naturalism and idealism appeared to be caught on two horns of a dilemma—the dualism of body-mind, physical-mental, resolved by subsuming either one as an aspect of the other. Realism champions the reality of both—and is thereby exercised to discover the underlying unity which would allow justice to be done to each, or that relationship which establishes harmony in a dualistic system. Some realists are naturalistic in their metaphysics, and some are idealistic, but all unite in affirming a "given" reality external to man and other than mind. The roots of realism can be traced back to Aristotle and many of its beliefs are found in various philosophers. Most notable among them was Immanuel Kant, the great watershed of modern thought, who viewed reality as a realist even though his theory of knowledge is the heart of idealism. Yet it was not until the twentieth century that realism emerged full-blown to affirm the reality of the external world and the validity of our knowledge of it.

How do we gain knowledge of what is "out there"? There are two main answers from realists. Objects may be presented or *re*presented in consciousness. In the first, there is a relationship between the subject and the object by which the actual object is presented in consciousness. There is a point of convergence of object and experience which is the point of knowledge. Mind is the relationship between the knower and the known and may also be external to the organism. Critical realists do not accept this, affirming the inner nature of mind. For them, external objects are *re*-presented in mind. The object exists "out there," but that which represents it in consciousness has no existence. For George Santayana and his followers the representations are essences—qualities—which subsist in themselves. The idealist holds a similar duality but insists that existence and essence are one.

Educationally, realists are inclined to place a high value upon content. Whether the pupil is viewed as having a brain to be trained or as being a self seeking meaning in life, the accumulated knowledge of the culture—the basic body of facts—is important.[8] The two extremes that may be held within the realist tradition may be seen in the naturalistic Russian education of dialectical materialism and the spiritualistic Thomism of the Roman church's educational theory. It may be surmised from this that a factor in the educational practice of realism is the formation of the pupil through an authoritative body of information.

Pragmatism

While pragmatism can trace roots back to the Greek Sophists and find forerunners in Francis Bacon and in Comte, it is peculiarly a child of modern America, a rebel child of idealism. Charles Sanders Peirce is credited with the central idea of

[8] Arthur M. R. Lower, "Education in a Growing Canada," *Canadian Education Today*, ed. Joseph Katz (Toronto: McGraw-Hill Company of Canada, Limited, 1956), p. 13.

pragmatism; William James popularized and developed it; but it was John Dewey who created the pragmatist philosophy.

In order to discover the meaning of an idea, put it into action in the stream of events and see what happens. This is roughly Peirce's criterion for knowledge. The central emphasis on experimenting has also led to the term "experimentalism." In Dewey's philosophy, hypotheses tested by experiment provide the nearest possible approach to knowledge. Such experiment is open to all and demonstrable to all. Therefore for Dewey the society of minds is of more importance than the individual mind. In other particular ways, however, the individual is very important.

Pragmatists are thoroughly naturalistic in rejecting anything beyond the natural world. However, they also reject substance, or a stable structure of laws and relations, as the basis of nature. All nature is process; ultimate reality is not one but many, not unchanging but in constant flux. Pragmatists are not overly concerned about a theory of how we know. Amidst the change and flux we cannot know with any certainty anyway, and it would be of little practical value if we could. What is important is how to use things. The value of knowledge lies in its capacity to help man adjust to and solve the problems of his continually changing environment.

While lacking a primary concern for a *theory* of knowledge, there is a keen interest in knowing. Only through knowledge can man take his proper place in the world process. But this is not knowledge in a general sense, it is the specific knowledge arising out of experience. Yet sense-perceptual experience itself does not yield knowledge. Sense perception is a two-way process of interaction with the world. The data of sense perceptions are not knowledge in themselves, nor does any body of proven facts constitute knowledge. Knowledge results only when data, or facts, are organized by a hypothesis which is put to the test in present experience and works.

Knowledge is not an end in itself, but an instrument in problem solving. The motivation for education is basically the seeking for solutions to problems, and the method par excellence is the scientific method. Furthermore, neither is man an end in himself; he is a part of the world, a product of the social process which is part of the flowing stream. He is a unique individual and must be viewed as such, but the meaning of his life and his development in life arise out of and flow into social experience.

Recent Educational Practice

With Dewey's active interest in education and the practical promise of his approach, pragmatism rapidly gained wide influence in America. It gave educational expression to the humanistic liberalism of the early twentieth century and suited well the temper of a nation born in the spirit of independence and rejection of authority. Allied closely with the social sciences it was quick to employ new insights which now form a valuable part of educational theory.

Often identified with pragmatism and holding many things in common with it, the progressive education movement arose from other sources. It was not a philosophy, but a practical revolt against cold formalism in teaching procedure. Dewey was quite critical of the movement at several points, especially its emphasis on the individual, its lack of social concern, and its failure "to recognize that the problem of selection and organization of subject-matter for study and learning is fundamental." [9] A combination of pragmatism and progressive education encouraged the decline of interest in philosophy of education and absorption in educational psychology that had begun in the nineteenth century. Methodology was of prime interest.[10]

Despite its good features, the new education has been deficient. Geared often to a naturalistic viewpoint, it has lacked the moral and spiritual strength to effect pragmatism's desire for a better society. Recent wars have disclosed that too few young people hold basic convictions worth fighting for. Extreme progressives have sometimes brought ridicule upon the movement. Even in its more restrained practices there has been a naïve confidence in the goodness of human nature. The human spirit needs freedom to grow, and self-motivation is a large factor in growth. But the human spirit must also discover the "boundaries" of life if the disciplined structuring essential to selfhood is to be achieved.

Increasing reaction to and enthusiasm for progressive education in recent decades have stimulated an unprecedented productivity in philosophies of education. Achievements of Russian scientists have led to a comparison of school systems. A spate of books is pouring out, each telling "what is wrong" with our educational systems. Growing public concern has prompted both the United States and Canada to hold government-sponsored conferences on education. Special studies such as James B. Conant's [11] are multiplying. Much of the hue and cry alleges that American education lacks essential content and fails to develop the discipline needed for pursuing education. It is "too soft," seeking primarily the pupil's adjustment to life. There has also been a demand for greater attention to "moral and spiritual values" in public education, largely from a humanistic viewpoint considered inadequate by most Christian educators.

Trends in Philosophy

With such a ferment about educational practice, there is little but confusion about educational philosophy. It has not been easy for educators to keep abreast of the expanding horizons in various fields of science, especially in the social and behavioral sciences. Furthermore, the findings from these sciences have tended to bring philosophers closer together on some points. John Wild writes as a realist, "to know something is to become *relationally* identified with an existent entity as it is," [12] while T. M. Greene, as an idealist, insists that knowable reality is "that which we encounter in primary experiences as having a character of its own, as impinging upon us coercively." [13] Thus, some realists approach the idealist emphasis on the primacy of the self and some idealists approach the realist emphasis on a reality external to mind. Efforts are being made to discover common points of agreement among the diverse philosophies.[14]

---

[9] Dewey, *Experience and Education*, pp. 95-96. For a summary of the relationship of Progressive Education to Pragmatism see Frederick Eby, *The Development of Modern Education*. (2nd ed.; New York: Prentice-Hall, Inc., 1952), pp. 629-31.

[10] Dewey, *op. cit.*, pp. 5, 6.

[11] James B. Conant, *The American High School Today* (New York: McGraw-Hill Book Company, 1959).

[12] Fifty-fourth Yearbook of the N.S.S.E., *op. cit.*, p. 18.

[13] *Ibid.*, p. 102.

[14] See Brubacher, *op. cit.*, chap. XV, "Consensus Among Philosophies of Education."

There is a growing tendency to try to deal with certain issues in education without setting them in the framework of a systematic philosophy. It is felt that the issues are distorted, and artificial controversies are engendered by dogmatic allegiance to systems of thinking.[15] Others view this as irresponsible, feeling that every issue must be examined at its deepest roots and set in the most inclusive perpective possible, allowing no level where principles can be discussed apart from their philosophic connections.[16] The problem lies in letting the various scientific disciplines speak for themselves on educational issues while still subjecting them to the critical examination required by a comprehensive system of thought.

Two recent developments in philosophy of education still in their early beginnings may have some relevance for religious education. One of these is an interest in analysis in educational philosophy. This interest is one of disinvolving meanings so that there is greater precision in what is said, but it does not go to the extent of using the mathematical signs of symbolic logic. It is an attempt at precision of meaning still depending upon the use of words. The other development is the growing interest of existentialism in education. A chapter on the existentialist approach to education was included in the Fifty-fourth Yearbook of the N.S.S.E. referred to previously. A book has now appeared showing more fully how existentialism might issue in educational practice.[17]

Religious Education

What is the relationship of all this to religious education? The religious education movement was strongly influenced by educational trends at the beginning of the century. It became, in effect, the religious counterpart of the "new education." It brought great advances in methodology and a deeper appreciation for the role of the pupils in learning. It rebelled against the imposed authority and transmission of content characteristic of traditional religious education. Emphasis came to be placed upon the development of the individual in terms of general religious experience. Indeed, every experience was religious, and each new insight was a disclosure of God. It soon became evident that "progressive" religious education was hand in hand with humanistic liberalism.

George Albert Coe gave a broad impetus in religious education to the social and democratic theories of John Dewey. When Shelton Smith launched his criticism against liberalized religious education in 1941, he devoted a section of his book [18] to "Religious Faith and the Democratic School," attacking the naturalism of pragmatic education. Many contended strongly for general religious experience, but the theological climate was demanding a new basis for specifically Christian nurture. Recent writers have sought to combine psychological and theological insights and to present principles and theories which could guide procedures and practice in specifically Christian ways. There remains a great need for a clearly articulated and systematic philosophy of Christian education.

There is also need for a Christian philosophy of education that will gain a greater hearing among public educators. Both humanism and supernaturalism oppose

[15] E. V. Sayers and W. E. Madden, *Education and the Democratic Faith* (New York: Appleton-Century-Crofts, Inc., 1959), p. vi.

[16] Butler, *op. cit.*, p. 43.

[17] Kneller, *Existentialism and Education.*

[18] Smith, *Faith and Nurture.*

secularism,[19] but the voice of humanism has been more influential. Perhaps the greatest issue in philosophy of education, both general and religious, is that of humanism versus supernaturalism, particularly in understanding the nature of man. Recently supernaturalism has been gaining strength, especially in religious education.

The same confusion reigns in religious education as in the field of general education. There is the same tendency to deal with issues and procedures rather than to develop a systematic framework within which the task of religious education may be viewed with integrity. Borrowings from psychology have been almost an obsession at the level of popular concern, but religious education has not been very thorough in its use of psychology as a science. A preoccupation with genetic psychology is slowly giving way to consideration of broader studies of personality. There is also a growing concern for adequate study in the field of communications, especially the function of symbols.

Part of the flux and confusion of the present stems from the desire to establish religious education on a sound theological basis while retaining the values and insights of the religious education movement. The integration of biblical theology with religious education continues to be an urgent problem. When the source of the biblical witness is found in the initiative and activity of God, there is a tendency toward realism; hence the parallels which may be drawn between neo-orthodox theology and realist philosophy.[20] When the reaching out of man toward God is stressed, there is a tendency toward idealism. The influence of existentialism and studies of the learning process have been leading toward what may be called a philosophy of encounter. This seeks to resolve the seeming contradiction between the otherness and the immanence of the divine, and establish a basis for religious learning, in understanding the media through which the divine enters the "life space" of the individual in continuing encounter. The initiative and freedom of both God and man are held in perspective.

Religious educators are placing strong emphasis upon the pupil as the center of learning, upon his changing needs, interests, and motivations, upon "experience under guidance" as governing teaching procedures. Problem solving, projects, experiment, creative activities, are to the fore in methodology. There is also a growing recognition among Christian educators that the essence of the Christian faith lies in something which is "given," so that a truly Christian education will include exploring and appropriating and being governed by that which is given. Religious educators are not so inclined to hold up a human Jesus as an example to be followed, or a nebulous Father as a supreme value to be sought. There is growing awareness of a living Christ, in whom God the Father and man are joined by the divine Spirit in a new community. There is a hunger for words which are not merely wisdom or reason, but which are Spirit and life. To that end, a new understanding is developing of the significance of the Bible as a "means of grace."

Social and democratic principles are being retained, but these are now largely viewed in terms of a divine community's being realized among men in the fellowship of the Spirit. It is in the witnessing community, where the "given"

[19] For a good summary of these influences see Brubacher, *op. cit.*, chap. XIII, "Religious and Moral Education," pp. 277-93. Discussion of "Public Education and the Teaching of Religion" will be found in ch. 8 of this book.

[20] Butler, *op. cit.*, pp. 382-83, 386-89.

becomes contemporaneous and dynamic, that religious nurture truly takes place. A happy wedding is sought between content and experience by insisting that content be experienced in the totality of life, and that experience be centered in a fellowship where the content of the faith is lived, studied, explored, proclaimed, where its meaning is sought and its teaching obeyed. Despite the church's imperfections, participation in its life is of prime importance.

There is strong feeling in some circles that the wedding of theology and the educational disciplines, of content and method, is not being effected too successfully. The findings of psychology and sociology are not taken seriously enough, but where religious educators do borrow from these findings there is a tendency to adapt understandings of theology and of the church to conform to them. This often results in the definition of religious education principles in humanistic and naturalistic terms while intending to confess a theistic and supernaturalistic faith. There is still danger that theology and the church will not be given their proper place and function. Part of this danger arises from failure to establish adequate norms and to test the validity of ideas systematically.

This problem has been a concern of D. Campbell Wyckoff.[21] He is insistent that both theology and the educational disciplines be taken seriously. But instead of philosophy's embracing the other disciplines in a comprehensive scheme which becomes educational "theory," he assigns it to a specific role among the disciplines.[22] The questions which must be answered to guide the practice of education are then put to all the foundation disciplines, among which theology is normative. From the answers elicited, principles (dependable guides to practice) are established which form a comprehensive theory of education.

The normative status of theology insures that none of the disciplines overrides the essentially Christian perspective, as psychology and sociology have tended to do. Yet theological answers are also examined in the light of answers from the other disciplines, giving promise of a more thorough integration than has heretofore been achieved. Seeing the total task "in the light of the gospel," while presenting difficulties for many, at least begins to take with seriousness the specific demands of the Christian faith. However, again the question is raised as to whether principles may validly be accepted as links between foundations and practice, or if the answers from the foundations must be comprehended in a consistent system of thought, a philosophy which then becomes a guide to educational practice.

Unitarians and related groups continue to follow a broadly humanistic and often naturalistic educational theory. Fundamentalist groups continue a largely transmissive and authoritarian education, although with greatly improved methodology in some areas. The trends described above are reflected by the majority of American Protestant churches, with wide variations throughout all groups.

Some Burning Issues

What is the role of philosophy of education? Does it have a limited function among the disciplines or is it the instrument for viewing things whole and entire? What faith shall undergird religious education, humanism or supernaturalism?

---

[21] *The Task of Christian Education.* This established a framework which is further developed in *The Gospel and Christian Education.*

[22] *The Gospel and Christian Education,* pp. 74-76.

Humanism has not experienced a Copernican revolution. Man is still the center of its universe. Therefore it cannot help man find his orbit. Supernaturalism holds promise of this, affirming a different center, but too often it has degenerated into mere rationalism.

A theory of knowledge is needed in which the categories of revelation are integral. What is the nature of religious knowledge? What is the function of the Bible and biblical theology in religious education? Is the Bible a source book of religious experience or a means by which God communicates himself? How does communication of this kind take place?

A theory of reality that is adequate for the biblical understanding of the nature of God, the world, man, and sin is needed. Are God and man essentially one? Are we all "children of God," begotten of his nature, needing education to lead us forth to our full potentiality, the fulfillment of our divine nature? Or are we "creatures" of God, who may receive the Spirit of adoption in the "only-begotten" Son of God and through that Spirit fulfill our humanity? Has man failed to achieve his essential divinity or has he perverted his essential humanity—a humanity which the descriptive sciences cannot discover, for they can only describe man as he is in the potentiality of his perverted nature?

Can religious education handle the categories of spirit without confounding them with either physical or mental processes? It has not done so. Yet it may be that herein lies the key to many of the paradoxes and problems that plague religious education.

Bibliography

Broudy, Harry S. *Building a Philosophy of Education.* Englewood Cliffs, N. J.: Prentice-Hall, Inc., 1954.

Brubacher, John S. (ed.). *Modern Philosophies and Education.* Fifty-fourth Yearbook of the National Society for the Study of Education, Part I. Chicago: University of Chicago Press, 1955.

————. *Modern Philosophies of Education.* Second Edition. New York: McGraw-Hill Book Company, 1950.

Butler, J. Donald. *Four Philosophies and Their Practice in Education and Religion.* Revised Edition. New York: Harper and Brothers, 1957.

Dewey, John. *Democracy and Education.* New York: The Macmillan Company, 1916.

————. *Experience and Education.* New York: The Macmillan Company, 1938.

Horne, Herman Harrell. *The Philosophy of Education.* Revised Edition. New York: The Macmillan Company, 1930.

Kneller, George F. *Existentialism and Education.* New York: Philosophical Library Publisher, 1958.

Redden, J. D. and Ryan, F. A. *A Catholic Philosophy of Education.* Milwaukee: Bruce Publishing Company, 1942.

Smith, H. Shelton. *Faith and Nurture.* New York: Charles Scribner's Sons, 1941.

Wyckoff, D. Campbell. *The Gospel and Christian Education.* Philadelphia: Westminster Press, 1959.

————. *The Task of Christian Education.* Philadelphia: Westminster Press, 1955.

Chapter 3

Psychology of Religion and Religious Education

Jesse H. Ziegler

IN OUR GENERATION IT IS ALWAYS APPROPRIATE TO STUDY THE PSYCHOLOGY OF salesmanship, of playing chess, of propaganda, of compromise—or of any more or less important subject in which we are interested. Our experience with ultimate reality or with God can profit from the same kind of study. If an understanding of the psychology of the teaching-learning process is relevant anywhere, religious educators will want to know what is most relevant to the teaching-learning process in religious education.

It is healthy for the psychologist and good for the relation between psychologist and theologian to draw some lines of responsibility at the beginning. The psychologist as psychologist cannot speak of the nature of God. He can speak of a person's experience of God. He cannot speak of the nature of guilt and of atonement. He can speak of the nature and sources of the feeling of guilt and the activities in which a person may engage to atone for it. He cannot speak of faith in terms of its meaning to God. He can speak of the roots of faith attitudes in the development of the child and the results of faith in the personality structure. What I am trying to say is that psychology has no tools for investigating the nature of God, the reality of guilt from God's view, the nature of faith from the view of the one in whom faith is placed, and therefore cannot properly speak of these matters. But all matters having to do with a person's perception of, evaluating of, having feelings about, and initiating action with regard to these same realities are proper subjects for the psychologist.

It is only fair to say that the main stream of psychology has had little concern about these matters. There is a distinguished group, however, who have written in the last fifty years about psychology of religion.[1] In the more recent period the writing has been quite strongly influenced by depth psychology and related to pastoral concerns.[2] Some have continued in the classic tradition although in more limited scope.[3] It is possible to see within the main stream of psychology, which tends to avoid study of religion, a smaller stream with continued research, theory, and writing. This stream has had its flood stages and its dry times but never dries up.

[1] James, Starbuck, Coe, Ames, Durkheim, Stratton, Pratt, Leuba.
[2] Stolz, Johnson, Oates, Ligon.
[3] Otto, Thouless, Josey, Clark, Wieman, Allport.

Because every man has a bias, and it is good for a writer and for his readers if this is made explicit, I will try to spell out my own at this early stage. In personality and developmental theory I lean strongly toward psychoanalysis. In the matter of social change and the climate of learning I may be seen as indebted deeply to Lewin and his disciples. I also must confess a strong religious bias rooted directly in the Christian tradition and in personal experience with God. Here my position may be seen as related to the current existential psychology, although I cannot hold these writers responsible for any of my thinking in this area since it had begun to take some form before becoming acquainted with their work. Indeed, although my own bias will be showing throughout this discussion, I cannot shift responsibility to Freud or Lewin or Rollo May for any error into which I may lead the reader but can only hope that in the intellectual encounter the readers will talk back until their minds really meet.

The idea of *encounter*, which is essential to any writing's being meaningful to a reader, has been chosen to integrate a number of ideas that are involved in the psychology of religion and religious education. This word has become significant in current religious thought. The ideas it embodies are not new ideas. It means "to meet." Sometimes the meeting is unexpected—sometimes to fight, sometimes to debate, sometimes in kindness. It implies face to face meeting. It may be the meeting of obstacles. It is this quality of experience or this idea of the nature of experience that will be very useful to us in considering the psychology of religion.

It is encounter with the objective world, with the world of culture, and direct encounter with God that contributes to the making of the person. It is encounter with obstacles and difficulties that provides the prodding necessary to development from one life stage to another. It is in situations that can best be characterized as encounter that there is the greatest opportunity for learning to take place—especially learning in which the learner is reaching far beyond himself.

The Subject in the Encounter

If we are to believe that religion is an aspect of normal development, as we do believe, then we need to assume that its form will be influenced by early experiences in the life of the child. Character is profoundly influenced—if not determined—by the experiences of the first several years of life. If character is so influenced, then we may assume that the form and bent of the individual's religion may be thus determined—or at least influenced.

We need to begin by asking about the nature of this being who is the subject in the early encounters of personal existence. What is a new baby like? We know that it is about twenty inches long, weighs six to eight pounds, can cry lustily when it feels discomfort, sleeps most of the time when it is not eating, engages when awake in quite diffuse and big movements, has the quite specific ability of responding to stimulation of the cheek by rooting and sucking. But what can we believe about the inner life of the baby?

He is concerned only to secure and to do what satisfies his needs. He needs primarily those things which preserve his existence as an organism. He needs oxygen; he needs food; he needs warmth; he needs care of his skin. He has no sense of time periods as we know clock time. He knows only personal time, time to suck, time to be held close to a warm object that makes soft sounds. He has no tools for testing external reality in the beginning; he only knows the reality of his own needs. There is no rightness and wrongness for the new born baby. What satisfies his need for food, for sucking, for being held close, for soft care of his skin—these are the right things. It makes no difference that mother, who must provide the food, feels as though she will never get enough sleep again.

At the beginning the need structure may be as simple as described. Within the first four months it comes to include a need for experiencing the tenderness and affection of a mothering person. There is a drive to express affection and to secure pleasure by the means at hand, chiefly through the mouth. Later, either as a part of maturing drives or because of frustration of drives toward tenderness, the child experiences the drive to master or even to be hostile. There is still no rightness or wrongness but only the drive to secure pleasure and satisfaction. In the shorthand of psychoanalysis what we have been describing as the inner life of the baby or of the growing child is spoken of as *id* functions. Such untamed, pleasure-seeking drives are characteristic of every age. They are the primitive and untamed drives in every person. This is the nature of the subject of the original encounter. But what is the nature of the encounter of this subject in his most primitive form?

Encounter With the Objective World

From the very beginning of his life outside the uterus the subject is in almost continuous encounter with a universe of objective reality. Indeed there is no reason to believe that this begins only after birth, but because the nature of objective reality to the child before birth is so limited and stable it does not seem to deserve time nor space for discussion here. Since the most primitive drives of the child are for direct pleasure and satisfaction, it is inevitable that these drives encounter the limiting, structured nature of external reality. The breast or nipple of the bottle yields milk only when taken in the mouth and sucked. Wet diapers get removed when one cries for a while. These acts are learned out of the encounter of drive with reality.

Ruth, who is nine months old, has learned to get fun from climbing up onto chairs. All goes well until she tries it on a chair at a table. She bumps her head twice, then sits down and looks the situation over, pushes the chair away from the table, continues her chair climbing fun. Her pleasure seeking activity "bumped its head" against the limiting structure of the reality of the under side of the table. Out of this experience Ruth built into her own psyche a cushion to prevent too painful head bumping. As this learning becomes a part of her psyche she is saved from pain from this sort of encounter.

In the repetition of this kind of encounter between basic drives of the id and the structured world of external reality there is built up a part of the psyche which attempts to secure the maximum satisfaction of the drive with a minimum of pain and a minimum amount of attempt at wrecking external structure. This encounter and its resultant building of psychic structure which is called the ego by psychoanalytic theorists goes on throughout life as the conscious intellect continues to develop. The functions of this part of the psychic structure are: (1) to provide accurate data regarding external reality through perception, (2) to make judgments about what is perceived so as to know what activity may be appropriate, and (3) to initiate appropriate activity as a result of the perception and judgment.

What we have suggested is that in the encounter between the most primitive part of the personality and the objective environment there comes into being the conscious intellect or ego. Without this part of the psyche man is not man but is more like a vegetable. With its development man not only perceives the universe around him but thinks about its origin, its meaning, its destiny. Thus from the encounter between the primitive part of man and his objective world emerges the growing ability to penetrate ever more deeply into the objective world by way of tools and instruments he makes to explore and manipulate his world.

Encounter With Culture

A second major encounter resulting in personality formation is the encounter of the drives of the id with the demands of the culture. In their earliest form these demands are represented to the child by the parents who are charged by the culture with bringing up a child in such a way that he will be an acceptable member of society. One of the earliest and most severe demands is that the child learn to restrain his primitive tendency to eliminate body waste anywhere and anytime. He is asked to engage in these activities only when in a place afforded by the culture. This is not easy since it involves achieving voluntary control over the sphincter muscles of anus and urethra. This control which is demanded by culture can be and is achieved, usually by the age of three.

The achievement of control over the elimination of body waste is just a symbol of the "no-saying" of culture to the primitive drives of the child and the child's response to the encounter. Mother says, "Don't wet our rug, go to the stool!" Daddy says, "Don't tear pages out of my new book." Both say, "Don't come out in front of company without clothing; don't hit baby sister over the head with a block of wood; don't turn the dial on the gas range; don't step out into the street; don't put nasty dirt in your mouth; don't play with your genitals; don't get the idea you can compete with your father to possess your mother." The culture does a lot of no-saying to the id drives of the child.

The child finds that the safest and most economical thing to do is to build this system of "noes" into himself. Then he will not be always faced with the danger of being punished or threatened by parents, teachers, policemen, judges, ministers. He can stop his expression of drives before they emerge as actions. This internalized no-saying of the culture is the basis of the negative part of what Freud called the superego. We have usually thought of this part of us as the conscience. It is the conscience that is the no-saying device inside us. It protests when there are tendencies within us to engage in behavior which is purely pleasure-seeking without regard to the limits imposed by our culture.

The encounter with culture may also be seen where the id drives come up against the ideals of mother, father, school, or church. "Be clean, share your toys, always tell the truth, play according to the rules, do gladly what your parents say, always be on time, make all 'A's,' make the team, practice your music every day, be a perfect little lady." These are the things that parents, teachers, and preachers hold up to children as ideals. To the extent that the child loves and admires the parent and sees these ideals in him, he will make these ideals a part of his own internal structure. This is what in psychoanalytic psychology is called the *ego ideal* which is a part of the control structure called superego.

Both the no-saying and the yes-saying parts of the inner controls result from the encounter of id drives with the culture. Once these are built into the personality, then that person will suffer guilt or shame when the controls are overridden. If the person engages in masturbation while having an internalized prohibition, then he will feel guilty for having been disobedient to his own no-saying. If the person makes all "C's" on his report card when he knew his parents wanted him to make "A's" and he wanted to, then he will feel ashamed. Feelings of guilt and shame are the internal experiences of frustrating conscience or ego ideal.

Encounter With God

Each person has that which for him is ultimate reality. To that ultimate he gives his complete devotion. The centering of his life on what is ultimate reality gives meaning to his life. Whether he calls it God or not, it is indeed his God. For those who are Christians this is the God who is most clearly revealed in Jesus Christ.

Ordinarily those of us who are Christians and happen to be psychologists do not talk much of the meeting of the central core of the personality with ultimate reality. It is not fair to leave this all to the theologian because there are data here that belong to the student of people. If there is encounter between the drives of the id and ultimate reality, we must ask ourselves about the nature of such encounter, the result in terms of personality development, and the function of whatever does develop within the person as the result of the encounter.

God meets persons through the objective physical reality that surrounds them on every hand. The vastness of the cosmos challenges one man to set down its description in mathematical symbols. For another man becoming aware of the same vastness becomes the holy ground on which he meets God. One man looks through a microscope at the structure of a leaf in order to understand the processes taking place within it. Another man looks at the same scene and is interested in the processes but also finds himself looking into the very nature of God. We cannot say that it is only the primitive savage who looks at the unexplained wonders of his physical surroundings and fears the gods. Many in more advanced cultures, both the simple and the sophisticated, have looked at the marvels of the physical world about them and have met God.

God also meets persons through culture itself. A brilliant science student in a university for the first time reads a Bible. In the witness of its writers he encounters a dimension of reality never encountered before. A little girl has the experience of a loving minister smiling at her and speaking kindly to her each Sunday morning. In his kindness she encounters God. A great nation meets God in the code of laws which is binding on it. Later it meets him in the judgment and disaster which comes upon it as a result of its disobedience.

From the beginning of man's writing about his own experiences up to the experiences of our contemporaries there is to be found an awareness of meeting the Almighty in the objective world surrounding or in the world of culture and people. The results of these encounters with God can be found in the shaping of ego or of superego. Through most of the years of the history of thought men have not assumed that God is limited to these ways of making himself seen, heard, and known.

God meets persons directly, speaks to them clearly, calls them out of their accustomed ways, invites them to become what they are not. Many of these meetings are in times of crisis. There is Abraham living comfortably in Haran but called by God to go out beyond into a life that is unknown (Gen. 11:27-13:18). There is Jacob in trouble with and fleeing from his brother Esau, falling asleep, dreaming, and waking up with the conviction that God is in that place (Gen. 27:46-30:24). There is Isaiah who has all the props pulled out from under his life and then seeing, "the Lord . . . high and lifted up" (Isa. 6). There is Saul of Tarsus, struggling desperately to find meaning in his own life, struck down and made blind on the road to Damascus and knowing that it was God speaking to him (Acts 9:1-31). Data of this kind do not vanish with the closing of the canon of the scriptures. Down to the present there are many people who bear witness to having experience in which they became aware of being in the presence of and in direct encounter with ultimate reality.

Shall we not say that all of this is delusion or hallucination and that at least at such times these people were mentally ill? If we insist on this it is necessary to press a basic question, What is mental illness, and who shall take the reponsibility for saying such experience is pathological? The unavoidable fact is that often it was precisely this experience of encounter with God, which someone may want to say is evidence of psychopathology, that made the person into the most creative and useful member of society. The decision cannot be made simply on whether the person "hears voices" or "sees things that are not there." The much more important question relates to what is heard or seen. And even more important is the question, what is the result in the life of the person? [4]

Is it not reasonable to assume that just as the encounter between primitive drives of the id and objective reality results in development of the ego, and as the encounter with the demands of culture results in the development of the superego, so the encounter of the primitive part of the personality with God results in the development of still another part of the personality? This might well be called the *spirit.* Just as part of the culture is internalized so that the person has the controls always with him, so in the encounter with God there is an internalization of the object. From that time on "God is in him," a part of him is spirit. He is never "far from God" because he has taken God within him (See Eph. 2:22).

In the immediate sense the development of the spirit as the result of the encounter with God seems to be due to a bipolar thrust. There is first the initiative of God in his approach to the person directly or through the physical universe and culture. There are also the thrusts of the primitive part of the person which come into encounter with the initiative-taking God. The person must deal with the God that is encountered. It is in this dealing that the spirit comes into being. Ultimately it may be necessary to say that God was taking the initiative much earlier in making a person with drives toward tenderness and mastery at the very core of his most primitive self.

Just as the ego and the superego have their own distinctive functions in the personality, so also does the spirit. It is the spirit in the person which gives the person a sense of destiny. This sense of destiny is perceived in two ways by the person. He now sees himself in the midst of a time-eternity continuum and not just half way through a life span of seventy-two years. This sense of destiny is also perceived in terms of vocation which gives significance to the most insignificant part of the total work he is doing. The spirit also gives the person a home base on which he

[4] Anton Boisen has made this point very well in *The Exploration of the Inner World.*

can feel secure. He is not just the pawn of chess-playing persuaders of his particular society. He has been face to face with the Eternal, and the Eternal has become a part of him. He cannot be "tagged out" when on home base. Finally, the spirit is the source of the courage *to be* and *to do*. Courage to exist at all and to do anything that is relevant to that existence requires meaningful contact with what is ultimate. The spirit is the representative of that ultimate right within the person where the struggles of his existence are worked out.

Encounter as the Basis of Human Development

A person does not become a human being just because he was born with a certain genetic structure that makes him a part of Homo sapiens. He becomes human as the result of encounter of quite specific kinds with various persons at the several stages of development. It is these encounters that cause him to move from one stage of development to the next. It is the nature of the encounter that rather largely determines the shape of development that takes place. We can only pick out certain significant types of encounter in the course of development and suggest something of the way in which this kind of encounter contributes to the development of the person. In the examples our specific interest will be the development of religious dispositions.

The first relationship for the child is with the mother. The very existence of the baby and its whole feeling about life depend on the kind of treatment received from the mother. Is there food when it is hungry, warmth for the body, gentle care for the skin, rocking and cuddling? In other words, is the universe dependable, is this person whom he experiences so much trustworthy? In the baby's experience of this relationship it may well be that the possibility of faith in God is rooted. When we remind ourselves that evidence shows that the experience of a loving relationship is even more important to the newborn than the most sterile care, we see that personal encounter is the essence of the first days of life, laying the foundations of basic trust.

During the second and third years the child is learning within this relationship with his mother that there are unlimited amounts of love but that there are also things that are expected of him. There is a firm but not rigid structure which helps the child to move into a stage of beginning to be a socialized being. It is not unlikely that here is laid the basis for a person's later conception of God not only as a trustworthy provider but also as the one who makes demands upon us.

In the years between three and twelve there is a significant encounter with the parents which establishes the gender of the child. The growing child finds from this encounter that he cannot possess the parent of the opposite sex in the way he may desire. All of the forces of society are represented by the father as he stands in the way of such desire. But the father offers a satisfying substitute. In effect he says, "You may not have your mother as other than mother but I offer companionship as part of being your father." A little boy does not find it too hard to give up his original desire when offered a chance to be with and become like his father. Here the encounter provides a basic frustration but an essential basis for becoming a man. It seems quite likely that during this time in an even more significant way is laid the basis for the conception of God as standing over against some of the things we think most desirable.

Encounter as the Basis for Religious Education

Education in religion takes place as there is significant encounter of religious ideas, values, and characteristics by a growing, questing person. It happens most effectively when such ideas, values, and characteristics are embodied in or associated with a person. This means that religious education may take place with deliberate intent or without conscious planning.

There is a sense in which learning of religion is like all other learning. It is changing one's potential for perceiving, handling ideas, feeling, and doing through experiences in which all of these steps are involved.[5] It may be held that the content of religious education is different and that the source of some of the content is thus different. The essentials in education are the same. Let us look at some of the implications of psychological theory specifically for religious education.

The earliest encounter that lays foundations for vital faith is the relation of the baby to mother. It is important that the child discover that the care of mother is completely dependable. In this discovery and its re-enforcement over and over by the provision of food for times of hunger, her presence in times of need, her care for his body, the baby develops an attitude of basic trust. This attitude not only is basic to healthy human relationships but may be at the heart of religious faith. The possibility of the idea of a God that is worthy of faith and trust becomes real in the first year.

A specific quality of encounter in the early years is another significant foundation factor for religious education. The young child sees the parents as both loving and frustrating. He sees love and structure represented in the same person. "Mother loves me but expects me to pick up toys." "Daddy loves me but will not let me tear pages from his new books." These are important perceptions and result in feelings of both love and resentment being simultaneously present in the child. In this way the child begins to learn of a God of love and of law, of mercy and of judgment. These learnings take place most significantly in the period of toilet training, in resolution of the Oedipus conflict, and in the relationship between parent and adolescent.

In general education it is well known that the climate and structure of the group deeply affect the learning process. A warm, permissive, democratic climate and structure make it possible for children to learn to be self-directing persons. A cold, critical, autocratic climate and structure develop great amounts of hostility in students and learning activity ceases in the absence of the teacher. In religious education the child is developing his concepts of the nature of the church as "family of God" primarily from his experiences of group life within the church. The kind of emotional climate pervading the class or group molds the learner's theology of the church.

One of the functions of education is to provide suitable words for referring to experiences. Because religion does not deal so much with concrete concepts as with abstractions it becomes necessary for the student of religion to have the experiences of meaningful relationships out of which religious symbols originally emerged. Forgiveness is understood by a child only as he experiences the continued

[5] Morse and Wingo discuss this matter with lucidity in their section on how learning takes place. Pp. 175 ff.

love and acceptance and even restoration of relationship with a group after he has done something to rupture the relationship. As the teacher supplies the word for the experience, the child learns a vocabulary with which to think and communicate. Only so did religious terms evolve, and only so can they be understood deeply in the development of the person.

Attitudes are learned chiefly through the process which may be called identification. As a younger or less mature person associates with one of greater maturity whom he admires and loves, without conscious effort to do so he takes into himself many of the characteristics of the other person. This process is seen most clearly in the taking on of sex roles by the child between six and twelve years of age as he identifies with the parent of the same sex. A person may become a religious person in the same way. This underscores the importance of the character of the teacher or group leader of children, since much learning will take place without conscious effort or plan.

An aspect of the encounter basic to religious education is the balance of anxiety in the learner with the feeling of safeness and security. A person learns nothing unless he feels some discomfort and need in his present condition. Even anxiety can be productive of learning. One must also feel secure enough in the encounter that he is not paralyzed by his anxiety, however. This balance seems especially important in the learning of youth and adults. Old assumptions and clichés must be challenged and the person made uncomfortable in the possession of untenable positions. It is then, if he feels safe enough in a group to explore and experiment with new ideas, that the way may be opened for significant learning.

For religious education, there will be conscious attempt by those responsible to provide the conditions for the God-man encounter to take place. This may be in planned or spontaneous worship experiences. It may be as child and teacher look together at some awe-inspiring part of God's creation. It may be as the class looks deeply into the meaning of the ministry of Jesus Christ. No teacher can make conditions which will guarantee the encounter; but the teacher will, with full awareness of the possibility, do what she can to make the encounter likely. She will do this in the knowledge that thus the life of the spirit in the child develops.

Issues for Further Study

There are several areas in which future research in the psychology of religion may be centered with profit. Little is currently known about the manner in which the spirit part of man is related to conscience, intellect, or the primitive urges of the id. Havighurst's educational theories [6] pose the interesting possibility that there may be similar developmental tasks of the spirit. If study should confirm this, then techniques for their definition, identification, and utilization in religious education are urgently needed. Further, additional understanding of the nature of the God-man encounter is required to aid in the development of conditions which are more favorable for the nurturing of religious experience. As a final suggestion, continuing study on the nature of the psychology of religious education is needed to discover whether it differs from the psychology of general education. These are among the more pressing problems of our day.

[6] See ch. 6, p. 68.

Bibliography

Cantor, Nathaniel. *The Teaching-Learning Process*. New York: Dryden Press, 1953.

Clark, Walter Houston. *The Psychology of Religion*. New York: The Macmillan Company, 1958.

Howe, Reuel. *Man's Need and God's Action*. Greenwich, Conn.: Seabury Press, 1953.

Johnson, Paul. *Personality and Religion*. Nashville: Abingdon Press, 1957.

Ligon, Ernest. *Dimensions of Character*. New York: The Macmillan Company, 1956.

Morse, William C. and Wingo, Glenn M. *Psychology and Teaching*. Chicago: Scott, Foresman and Company, 1955.

Oates, Wayne E. *Religious Dimensions of Personality*. New York: Association Press, 1957.

Sherrill, Lewis J. *The Struggle of the Soul*. New York: The Macmillan Company, 1952.

Wise, Carroll A. *Psychiatry and the Bible*. New York: Harper and Brothers, 1956.

Yeaxlee, Basil A. *Religion and the Growing Mind*. Greenwich, Conn.: Seabury Press, 1952.

Chapter 4

Current Theological Developments and Religious Education

Daniel Day Williams

THEOLOGY SEEKS TO INTERPRET THE FAITH OF THE CHRISTIAN CHURCH IN A systematic way with reference to all the areas of human knowledge and with special concern for the tests of truth. Thus the theology of the church offers to Christian education a perspective upon the nature of Christian faith, and guidance to the sources of Christian insight and values. At the same time the data for theology lie in part in the life of the church itself, that is, in its activities of worship, witness, action, and nurture. Therefore theology does not come to Christian education as a completely independent discipline. Theology must reflect upon those activities which involve Christian nurture. Christian education may, on its part, seek to define its goals and content solely from within the educational activities themselves. When this happens educational theory has itself become a theological doctrine. A serious separation of theology and education need not take place if it is recognized that all Christian practice must maintain its integral relation to the ultimate source of faith in the word of God made personal in Jesus Christ, and if in theology full weight is given to the special insight which comes from the appropriation of the word of God in the activities of Christian nurture.

It is the purpose of this chapter to indicate some major developments in recent theology which have a direct bearing upon Christian education, and in some cases upon any form of religious education. These developments have arisen from many sources both in the church's relationship to contemporary culture and in the exploration of its scriptural and theological heritage. A closer examination will reveal that there have been educational concerns which have influenced the theological development. Common insights have opened the way to a close relationship between theology and educational theory. While the tendency evident in the early part of the twentieth century for religious education to develop an independent doctrine of man and God drawn from pragmatic educational theory and the liberal doctrine of religious experience seems less in evidence at mid-century, there are developments in religious education, such as the exploration of group dynamics, which may produce an important and fruitful tension with the traditional practice of the church and with traditional theological doctrines.

In seeking to point out areas of concern in the relations of theology and Christian education we presuppose that there is no one-way influence confined to either side. We are dealing with a complex relationship which requires continual analysis from both sides. In the present chapter we shall examine three developments in theology which have special implications for religious education, and specifically for Christian education.

Three basic concerns shape the outstanding theological movements in Protestantism today. They are, first, the concern for the uniqueness and integrity of the Christian faith as it is rooted in the biblical witness to God's revelation in Jesus Christ; second, the concern to establish the Christian view of the uniqueness and value of persons and their relationships; and, third, the concern for the relevance of the Christian message to the radical questions, anxieties, and struggles of contemporary man. I shall characterize three theological movements which emphasize in turn one of these three concerns. It should be stressed at the outset that each theological movement exhibits all three of the basic concerns. They adopt somewhat different ways of interpreting the Christian faith so as to respond to the dimensions of the gospel and the contemporary need. It shall be suggested that each of these theological movements leads to a characteristic view of the goals and practice of Christian education. It should be clear, however, that no theology seeks to prescribe the modes of educational practice. At most it can be said to imply certain general directives and goals.

Biblical Faith

The concern for the uniqueness and integrity of the biblical witness to God's revelation in Jesus Christ has received perhaps its most powerful contemporary presentation in the theology of Karl Barth. The influence of Barth's "theology of the Word of God" extends far beyond the theologians who expressly follow his doctrine, for Barth has reasserted the structure of the faith of the Protestant reformers, especially of Luther and Calvin. The consciousness of the Protestant heritage is a major factor in the contemporary church. Man's works, however noble and inspired they may be, lead to idolatry and perhaps to futility. It is grace alone, the grace of the forgiveness and the power of God, which gives an indestructible basis for faith and hope.

What is most characteristic in Barth's theology is the affirmation of the absoluteness and exclusiveness of the biblical witness to God's grace in Christ. It is in scripture alone that the message of God's grace and reconciliation is given. Jesus Christ is the one man in whom we know the truth about all men and about God's will for men. All human philosophy, and all "religion" outside the biblical faith are seen by Barth as belonging to the sphere of the secular, the estranged, and the lostness of man without God.

At the same time Barth proposes to escape the legalism and literalism of traditional interpretations of scriptural authority. He does this by emphasizing the personal character of the revelation in Jesus Christ and the necessity for the openness of faith to the concrete word of God. The Bible "becomes" the word of God, Barth says, when its saving truth is made present to our faith. Everything in scripture must be understood from the center, and that center is Jesus Christ who can be known only in the response of faith.

This emphasis on the establishment of the biblical content in all Christian thought and life is manifest in recent developments in church-school curriculums. The curriculum of the United Presbyterian Church, U.S.A., shows the direct influence of theology informed by Barthian themes. Other curriculums, such as that in preparation for the United Church of Christ, show a concern to establish the biblical foundations of every Christian concept, while still incorporating values derived from the liberal interpretation of Christian experience.

At the center of the Barthian interpretation of scripture we have seen the theme of justification by faith alone. All Christian knowledge depends upon grace, and all Christian hope is dependent upon the action of God. We can indicate three special consequences for Christian education of this affirmation of the themes of the Reformation.

First, it is clear that this position asserts the foundation of Christian life in a relationship to God which transcends every moral achievement. A humanistic education is tempted to set up the specific results of religious inspiration and moral growth as fulfillments of man's need. It is possible thereby to lose sight of the ultimate estrangement between man and God which threatens all moral achievement with the corruptions of self-righteousness. The spiritual need of man transcends all particular moral requirements. It is need for the renewal of life at the personal center through the healing power of grace. An education rooted in this outlook would in principle place little confidence in moralistic injunctions or in efforts at producing specific types of behavior through controlled experience. It would rather seek to disclose the need of trust in God, and to communicate the present power of the divine spirit to renew and fulfill all of life.

Second, accompanying the assertion of the biblical rootage of faith there is the affirmation of the Church as the community of believers over against a purely individualistic conception of Christian experience. It is significant that Barth has called his monumental system of theology *Church Dogmatics*. It is as a participant in the community whose original witness is documented in the Bible, and whose faith is always a confession of solidarity in the new life made possible in Christ that the individual Christian lives and discovers the fuller truth of God. The deepening of the "confessional consciousness" in Christian churches is one of the marked tendencies of the mid-century era. Children and young people are to be brought up within the community and nourished by its heritage of scripture, liturgy, and thought. The word of God is not the possession of the church, but it continually creates the believing community. Christian education will provide an initiation into the historical content of the faith which may enable each one to make his own commitment. This point of view may be combined with a reliance upon the actual confessional statements and doctrines of the churches. Barth's theology has influenced both Lutheran and Reformed confessional groups. At the same time it does not encourage an absolute reliance upon any historic confession since the word of God judges all human expressions.

Third, the Bible is understood in its Protestant interpretations to stress the personal character of faith. "Each man must do his own believing as each man must do his own dying" is an often quoted statement of Martin Luther's. Since faith is personal trust and belief, it cannot be coerced or produced through the contrivance of certain methods of exciting emotional response. Thus biblical theology tends to view the pietistic emphasis on the experience of conversion with a certain skepticism. The faith created in the personal encounter with God transcends all private feelings and special emotions. It is therefore true to say that the emphasis on biblical faith can be accepted along with very great freedom for specific methods of Christian education provided always that the essential purpose of directing all people to the biblical message is kept in view.

Faith as Personal Encounter

The second major concern is that for the special character and religious meaning of personal existence. It has appeared in the biblical emphasis just discussed, and it has also been made the central theme of theologies which take a somewhat different direction from that of Karl Barth. There is the work of Emil Brunner, who has made the theme of the personal relationship between man and God the heart of his theology. In America H. Richard Niebuhr's theology, Reinhold Niebuhr's later writing, and many other theologies have stressed the meaning of the new personalism. We need first therefore to see what this position is.

The doctrine that there is a fundamental difference between knowledge of other persons and knowledge of impersonal objects was given its definitive modern statement by Martin Buber in his book *I and Thou*. As a philosopher standing in the Hassidic tradition of Judaism, Buber sought to give a general form to this distinction so that the nature of personal existence would stand out clearly. When I can say "I and Thou" I stand in a different relation to the other than when I say "I-it." In the I-Thou relation another person is addressed who is also a subject. He cannot be for me merely an object of use or external analysis. He is a free subject, with whom I am in communication.

For Buber the I-Thou relation discloses the nature of our human existence. It is the only way in which we can speak truly of our relationship to God. This is why the Bible has little to say about the philosophical problems of the "nature of being" or the structure of the cosmos. The faith of the prophets is concerned with the relationship in which man hears God speak to him and responds in obedience or unfaithfulness to the personal command. Thus the I-Thou doctrine may truly be called a "dialogical" view of human existence and of religious truth. The very structure of truth has this personal character. Religious truth is bound up with man's dialogue with God and with his neighbor.

Two developments are possible from this starting point. The I-Thou doctrine may be used in Christian theology to define the unique character of the Christian revelation. The Bible is taken as the source of the dialogical point of view with the New Testament conception of the word incarnate in the man Jesus as its final expression. The I-Thou doctrine may also be understood as a general philosophical truth which can be explored in various cultural situations without exclusive dependence on the biblical tradition. When interpreted in this more general sense, it is sometimes allied with existentialist philosophy. Kierkegaard himself prepared the way. The basic themes of the I-Thou philosophy were formulated by him, though he never gave them the systematic statement developed by Buber. In general, however, it is misleading to classify the dialogical point of view with existentialism since they have taken widely different paths in the twentieth century.

The Christian theologian who has most consistently built upon the I-Thou doctrine of religious knowledge is Emil Brunner. Associated with Barth in the early days of the break with liberal theology, Brunner came to sense in the Barthian development a tendency toward objectivism and a kind of scholasticism in theology. He found in the I-Thou doctrine a way of criticizing all impersonal elements in theology. For Brunner it is the Christian revelation with its climax in the incarnation of the word of God in Jesus Christ in which the real meaning of the I-Thou relationship is disclosed. All other human experience offers but vague and misunderstood analogies for the truth grasped in Christian faith. Only in Christianity is God known in the depth of the personal relationship constituted by his grace and forgiveness for estranged man. Brunner insists, however, that there is a point of contact between Christian faith and human culture. There are reflections of man's personal origin and need in art, politics, philosophy, and ethics. Brunner uses the dialogical point of view as a basis for the critique of culture, though he does not allow theology to become identified with a general philosophical outlook.

A considerable number of philosophers, psychologists, and cultural critics have developed the more general application of the dialogical philosophy. It appears in two primary contexts. First, it forms a basis for the critique of contemporary culture. The depersonalization, the pressures for conformity, the falsification of values in the "market personality" described by Erich Fromm, are themes which are developed in relation to the doctrine of the unique character of personal existence. Second, the dialogical philosophy can be used as the directing theory for the formation of communities of personal religious inquiry, for psychological therapy and counseling, and for the interpretation of group life within the church.

It is fair to say that most specific applications of the I-Thou philosophy to Christian education have come in forms which draw upon the general cultural interpretation of the philosophy. Ross Snyder, of the Federated Faculty of the University of Chicago, and his students have laid special emphasis on the Buberian outlook in dealing with the basic theory of religious education. The group dynamics movement has its origins in sources other than Buber's religious philosophy, but the goals and practices of the group life movement as adapted for religious education in the program of the Episcopal Church appear to have incorporated elements of the personalistic outlook.

The deepest problem in the educational use of the I-Thou doctrine seems to be inherent in the position. It is the problem of stating the conditions and content of a fully personal relationship. Even to specify such conditions would seem to be in some sense a violation of the point of view, since a definition of the personal relationship would seem to claim the very objectivity which the I-Thou relationship transcends. If no concrete characterization of the relationship can be given, then it becomes difficult to show how the personal relationship is relevant to the issues in the common life where persons have to deal with all sorts of technical, economic, and political structures. One can take the view that the I-Thou relationship is realized only in special circumstances, in groups which are able to maintain an independence of the technical aspects of the culture. They may hold the culture up to judgment, but they cannot tell a technical civilization how it can prepare for the fulfillment of personal life. It is difficult to show the relevance of the position to concrete issues. The religious educator is in a position to see this problem in its depth, and to explore the tensions it creates.

Theology in Correlation With Ultimate Questions

The concern for the relevance of the gospel to the questions asked by contemporary man finds expression in the theological thought of Rudolph Bultmann, Paul Tillich, and Reinhold Niebuhr. These three theologians can be grouped together though there are important differences in their views of how theology should solve the problem of displaying the relevance of its message in the modern world. Reinhold Niebuhr relies mainly on an analysis of political and ethical problems to give the setting for the message of grace which makes faith possible in the midst of the ambiguities of ethical experience. Bultmann and Tillich both rely heavily on existentialist descriptions of the human situation to display this revelance, but Tillich incorporates existentialism in the framework of the traditional search for "being-itself" in philosophy, that is in the ontological quest, and he develops his theology in a systematic correlation with questions asked in ontological terms. The search for God is the search for "being-itself."

The "method of correlation" which Tillich develops has implications for Christian education which go beyond the specific content of Tillich's theology. We may therefore summarize the method and note its implications.

Tillich sees man as the creature who asks the meaning of his own existence. What does it mean to be, and what threatens our being? As soon as we ask these questions we acknowledge the estrangement which all men experience. Life is threatened on every side. There is death; there is meaninglessness; there is the guilt incurred through the misuse of our freedom. All human life experiences ontological anxiety. When this anxiety leads to separation from the ground of our being, that is, when it leads to sin, we experience the threat of nonbeing. This is the plunge of our life toward destruction and meaninglessness.

What the method of correlation requires is that we see the message of the Christian gospel as an answer to our ultimate questions, and therefore as overcoming the threat of nonbeing. To show this is to correlate the gospel with the situation to which it is addressed. The Christian faith asserts that God has manifested his power and grace under the conditions of human existence and has shown his power to overcome the threat of nonbeing. This disclosure of God as being-itself is the meaning of revelation. There is preparatory revelation through all experience in which man finds himself receiving some answer to his ultimate concern about the fulfillment of his being. The revelation in Jesus Christ is final because it comes in a person who sacrifices everything finite, every claim for himself, to the one absolute relation between himself and God. The New Testament picture of Jesus as the Christ is the picture of a life in unbroken communion with God under the conditions of human existence.

When the Christian faith is interpreted by the method of correlation there are two consequences which have special implications for Christian education. These are, the possibility of interpreting the religious symbols, and the two-sidedness of the task of communicating the gospel. We shall say something about these two aspects.

The interpretation of the religious symbols has been given special attention by Rudolph Bultmann. His proposal has led to one of the most vigorous discussions in contemporary theology as he has asserted the need for a reinterpretation of the ancient mythological symbols in the scripture in order to show their relevance to modern man with his scientific knowledge of the world. Bultmann has called for what he calls the "de-mythologizing of the New Testament message." The necessity for this lies in the fact that the Bible was written at a time when the world was understood in the literal supernatural structure of a three-storied universe. Angels and demons invade the earth from a realm beyond it. God enters into conversation with Satan. There is a literal expectation of the apocalyptic overthrow of the world, and of a new heaven and a new earth. Salvation comes through the divine conquest of demonic powers. All of this, Bultmann says, creates an unbridgeable gulf between the biblical writers and ourselves so long as we try to fit its literal meaning into our twentieth-century understanding. What we must do is to keep the ancient myths, but discover the fundamental human experiences and questions which they expressed. We must interpret the message of scripture as an answer to the fundamental questions which we share with the ancient writers. We can then hear the gospel as the offer of an absolute and undisposable security in the midst of the anxieties and insecurities which are common to every life.

It will be seen that Bultmann's claim for the necessity of interpreting the ancient world view is more fundamental than any particular theory of how this interpretation is to be accomplished. In his own theology he has adopted the modern existentialists' analysis of man's condition. He has drawn heavily upon Martin Heidegger's philosophy with its description of man's insecurity in time, his attempt to escape from himself, and the burden of guilt which he bears for his failure to live "authentically" and with courage. Bultmann believes that the philosopher here raises the right questions, but only Christian faith sees the answer in the event of Jesus' life and death and resurrection. Jesus Christ is God's offer of his grace and eternal mercy to anxious man who discovers that he does not have to try to bear his own burden alone. God in Christ bears it with him. As man receives the new life offered by God he becomes open to the future. He can face whatever comes with joy and hope. Bultmann's interpretation of the meaning of faith is very close to Tillich's interpretation of faith as the "courage to be."

The principles established by Bultmann have application to the understanding of any traditional symbols, but of course their primary significance for Christian education comes at the point of the teaching of the Bible. An education following this method would present the biblical witness in its original form, but it would not leave the symbols uninterpreted and would acknowledge the necessity of their translation into terms related to contemporary experience.

The second implication of the method of correlation for education has to do with the two-sided task which is involved in the communication of the gospel. On the one side there is the task of drawing out from the person his questions in terms which are meaningful to him. This does not mean that Christian education will give its attention only to the specific ways in which modern man asks about the meaning of his life. It must dig beneath the surface formulations to discover the underlying anxieties, fears, and hopes which engage the person at the center of his being. This search for existential reality is relevant to every stage of the growth of the person. It demands a faithful attention to concrete experience, and the refusal to impose on any person at any stage of his development a purely formal analysis of his situation. It is the material content of what life really is felt to be by this person in this culture which must be faced.

The other side of the educational process follows from the second aspect of the method of correlation. The message of the Christian faith must be addressed to the person. In the view of Tillich and Bultmann the answers to our ultimate concern do not come from ourselves or our experience. They are given. Revelation means God's self-disclosure at the point of our human extremity. The word of God comes to us from beyond ourselves and can be received only by faith. Here then the givenness of the Christian revelation comes into view as it does in the first two theologies examined. Christian education prepares the way for the hearing of the gospel by those outside the Church and those inside, but the disclosure of the saving mercy and power of God is an act of God's grace. There is a point therefore at which all educational practice and all human effort come to their limits. Even our preaching and confession of faith can only present the realities as we see them. We depend upon the Holy Spirit for the renewing and vitalizing of faith.

It should be observed that the method of correlation does not imply the keeping of the Christian symbols and the existential questions in two separate compartments until they are finally brought together. There is a continual movement between religious faith and the asking of ultimate questions. We do not wait until we are sure we have adequately formulated our questions before we say anything about the Christian answer. Rather the faith itself and the forms of its expression help us to formulate the questions. One has only to look at the use of biblical symbols in the expression of the spiritual search of contemporary man as in William Faulkner's novels or Archibald MacLeish's play *J. B.* to realize that the expression of religious concern draws upon the substance of the tradition even when it cannot fully affirm the faith which underlies the tradition. For religious education this implies that part of the task is to provide in the Church and culture a knowledge of the heritage of insight out of which both a deepening of spiritual sensitivity and a positive response of faith may come. A continuing dialogue between questioning men and the Christian faith will be the goal of an education informed by this third theological standpoint.

Christian Education as Theological Inquiry

Whether or not any theological system can be considered as giving explicit directives to Christian education is a question which will be viewed differently by interpreters in both fields. There surely is a sense in which Christian education will accept as its norm and guiding principles a theological interpretation of the revelation in Jesus Christ which is the foundation of the Church; but this does not mean that it is for the "theologians" alone to say what the norm of faith requires. Systematic and biblical theology are technical attempts to deal with that question, and the Church cannot do without them. At the same time, the truth of the faith is deeper than any one route of approach to it. Every Christian must make his own decisions about the meaning of the faith, and he may always question the adequacy of any theological formulation.

There is always the possibility, therefore, that those who carry on the educational activity of the Church will develop their special perspective on the meaning of the gospel. This is not only legitimate, but should be encouraged as an enrichment of the theological work of the whole Church. The meaning of the Christian faith cannot be separated from the actual process of coming to understand how people at all stages of life do live and grow in the knowledge and service of God. It is appropriate therefore at the end of this chapter to indicate from a theological point of view three areas in which Christian education appears to have its positive word to say about the theological substance of the Christian faith.

First, in so far as we recognize the need for the correlation of the gospel with the existential questions, the Christian educator is in a position to develop the method of correlation at the vital point of the concrete experience of people. This means not only to discover the points at which there is openness to the gospel, but also the forms of resistance to it. It means to explore the situation of the unbeliever who does not accept the faith, and also that of the believer who takes it all too simply and finds religion a support to his complacency. No theological construction can exhaust the depth and nuance of man's spiritual need. The educator is in a position to point realistically to the actual need.

In the second place, the educator deals with the Christian life in its aspect of growth. He does not ignore the crises of conversion, of doubt, and of despair; but he must see them in relationship to a total life history with its dynamics, its internal connections, its relation to the social context in which it takes place. In dealing with this life history Christian education has the resources of the traditional patterns of the Christian life and also those of the modern psychological probing of the nature of the self. The concepts of sin and forgiveness, fear and hope, self-centeredness and love, must be theologically interpreted; they point to realities which must be grasped in the infinite variety of human circumstances. The knowledge of God's forgiveness on the part of a young man just awakening to his self-conscious independence may have dimensions far different from that of the mature person facing the crisis of the blasting of all his life plans. The educator can develop a knowledge of the values and goals of human living which will be brought within an ultimate theological perspective and which will be in itself an enrichment of that perspective.

Finally, the educator is in a position to contribute to the understanding of the nature of the church. The Christian community is a living organism. Its forms of thought and worship bear a heavy freight of traditional structure; but its life can never be wholly caught within the forms. The educator is continually exploring for every age and group the forms of congregational life and worship which may be genuinely fruitful in bringing people into a fuller participation in the body of Christ. At this point Christian education is in a strategic position to provide a material knowledge of the nature of personal existence, the possibility and character of the "I-Thou" relationship, and thus to throw light upon the nature of man's personal relationship to God. It may help to find the forms of congregational life which are appropriate to the nurture of persons as they seek to live in faith.

Since theology in the church is an interpretation of the Christian way of believing and living, all those who reflect critically upon Christian experience become theologians. Christian educators therefore not only draw upon theological insight provided by the tradition and thought of the church; but they help to create the body of materials and the reflective criticism which make a living theology possible.

Bibliography

Barth, Karl. *Dogmatics in Outline.* New York: Philosophical Library Publisher, 1949.

Bartsch, Hans W. (ed.). *Kerygma and Myth.* London: Society for Promoting Christian Knowledge, 1953. (This volume contains Bultmann's essay on the demythologizing of the New Testament message.)

Brunner, Emil. *The Divine-Human Encounter*. Philadelphia: Westminster Press, 1943.

Buber, Martin. *I and Thou*. Edinburgh: T. and T. Clark, 1937.

Niebuhr, H. Richard. *The Meaning of Revelation*. New York: The Macmillan Company, 1941.

Tillich, Paul. *Biblical Religion and the Search for Ultimate Reality*. Chicago: University of Chicago Press, 1955.

Williams, Daniel Day. *What Present-Day Theologians Are Thinking*. Revised Edition. New York: Harper and Brothers, 1959.

The Use of the Bible in Religious Education

Ralph D. Heim

Chapter 5

The Use of the Bible in Religious Education

Ralph D. Heim

No ONE WOULD VENTURE TO GUESS IN WHAT CENTURY MEN BEGAN TO USE sacred writing as resource material for religious education. In the Hebrew-Christian tradition the usage dates doubtless from the time when those components of our Bible now known as "literary fragments" appeared in the centuries before 1000 B.C. Today, of course, there is universal concern about the use of the Bible. For example, this topic appeared on the programs of both The First World Institute on Christian Education in Toronto, 1950 and the second in Nishinomiya, Japan, 1958. The Bible's high place in our educational work is evidenced also by the frequent mention of it in all statements of objectives such as those discussed in Chapter 6. Including Catholic, Jewish, Orthodox, and Protestant peoples, possibly a number approaching a billion have met the Bible in their educational experience.

Specific mediums in which the Book is used educationally can be classified in no less than eight areas: the arts, group study, mass mediums of communication, personal study, personal work, public address, worship, and "living epistle." In countless ways within so many fields we are seeking to accomplish the fundamental purpose of nurturing persons for individual growth and social reconstruction to the end of increased abundance within a maturing faith life.

Despite this universality and comprehensiveness of interest we find ourselves confronted by disquieting facts of no small proportions. For one thing, recognition of the Bible's significance in Christian education may not yet have reached the necessary level for the urgent and intelligent action required. There is considerable desultoriness and ineptitude about it all. Another reason for lively concern is the almost faddist popularity of theology at present. One can wonder whether this worthy derivative is to become a primary resource that will obscure the position of the Bible itself. Worst of all, the slightest acquaintance with our people's status regarding the Bible proves that we have much to accomplish before our work with it is adequately effective.

Types of Approach in Biblical Usage

Possibly there is promise in certain strong new trends, one of them the movement toward a particular type of approach to the use of the Bible. In a way there is nothing new about this for we find instances in which prophets, Jesus, and Paul were working by it. Perhaps, though, the present era may sometime be known as the one in which Christian education moved forward to use a functional approach instead of the prevalent factual one.

Factual Approach

Factual approach is that familiar way of looking at educational use of the Bible and going about it as if the teacher were to say to the pupils: "Here is the Bible. See what it says. Now master and remember that." Undoubtedly, an overwhelming proportion of church-school work is conducted in this manner. But we should be warned by the meagerness of satisfying results. Our success in securing biblical knowledge and comprehension is certainly not notable; witness the recurring lament, "They don't know their Bible." We are aware, too, that people's attitudes toward the Bible are often unwholesome. As for their living of the biblical message, experience shows that we even sometimes get negative reactions. Thus, while the cry for "more Bible in the curriculum" is comprehensible, possibly we should be making better use of a lesser quantity.

Functional Approach

In recent years leaders in religious education have been trying to win workers away from telling as a favorite method and memorization as a major measure of success. Meanwhile, they are developing various principles and practices to render biblical usage more effective in terms of knowledge as well as attitudes and especially in conduct. This other outlook and procedure is a functional approach. Doubtless some such concept has always been in the mental background, if no more, of many workers with the Bible. There is some justification for saying that the recent phase of its history got well under way in the period marked by the publication of such books as William C. Bower's *The Living Bible* (1926) and Ethel Smither's *Use of the Bible with Children* (1937).

Briefly, functional approach means using the Book purposively in relation to life's total activity, employing it primarily as a resource to effect actual adjustments of current personal and social living in some definite respect. With this outlook we proceed as if the learners and leaders were saying: "Here we are with this condition of life, asking, 'What shall we do?' Let us go to the Bible as our supreme resource for help. We shall be utilizing its message in action." Here the focus is upon the ongoing Christian faith lives of persons and groups in the process of being enriched and controlled by using the Bible to convey God's guidance, stimulation, and empowerment. Its substance is to enrich and control present experience—although this may be done with a view to future experience also. Its materials are to show people the kind of activities which are appropriate and move them to corresponding performance. Most noteworthy, its teaching values are to affect total personality and practice, not some facet such as the intellectual component.

To be sure, there is a secondary phase of the functional approach in which learners and leaders may work for a time at "content study" after the typical manner. Yet such study is to be done always with some total response clearly within sight; not chiefly for the result of "book-learning." The teacher's principal purpose is not to expound Bible or get people to master its content; the goal is to help people use the Bible so as to help themselves and others "live the Bible way" at some needful point of current experience. In such a way—the real way of balanced maturing in actual and immediate doing—functionalists believe the Bible will most readily promote growth toward the objectives of Christian education.

All in all, this is a way of using the Bible that reminds one of the naval craft sometimes brought alongside other vessels to render some special service—to put aboard a pilot; bring a doctor; supply food, water, or fuel; put out a fire; pass a line for a tow; ease the ship into a berth. Similarly, wherever life is most active and problematical, there the Bible belongs and, in functional approach, it is brought to that place and allowed to serve its intended purpose.

The Bible

Functional approach seems to be in harmony with the nature of the Bible itself. We may think of the Bible's essential character as to substance and function. Regarding substance, the Bible is the fundamental recital of man's discoveries about what God has been disclosing of his nature, work, and will for man. As to function, the Bible is an instrumentality for communicating the Word of God—really, the life of God—to man. This description is meant to include such other concepts as have been expressed in terms like "authority," "cradle of Christ," "drama of redemption," "gospel," and "revelation by inspiration." The many ideas can perhaps be combined best in the statement that the Bible is the Word of Life. Word came from the life of God, through human life into print; it is meant to go back into life again.

Christian education has been defined as a process in which learners and leaders work together at enterprises where God in his grace meets man in his need, so that persons are nurtured for development as more devoted disciples and apostles of Jesus Christ—while being blessed in this relationship. It seems proper that the Word of Life shall have the place of supreme "resource" toward such development. With the Bible persons meet Jesus Christ, commitment to his saviorhood and lordship is secured, continuance in growing faith and increasing good work is maintained. By the Spirit's agency in it, the Bible communicates to men the "heavenly information" of Christ *pro nobis* and fosters the growing reality of Christ *in nobis*. Thus it is the channel for the coming of the Spirit who changes spirits.

Teaching Values

The Bible is employed with some such understanding in Christian education according to the functional approach. Learners and leaders go to it as a storehouse of teaching values. A teaching value of the Bible is a utility with which to interpret, evaluate, and redirect human experience in the Christian way; a convincing effectuality for some type of functioning to change personal and social living; a means of transmitting and receiving a particular grace of God; a worth to be laid alongside some human aspiration, interest, or purpose and transfuse Spirit into spirit. The Bible has such potentialities resident in its passages to affect the objectives of Christian education; they are its teaching values.

The biblical teaching values can enrich life and control life, the latter by guidance, stimulation, and empowerment. They enrich life with interesting knowledge, experience of beauty, moments of pious feeling. In the area of control, they serve pupils by guiding them in the performance of Christian activities because they present examples in performance of activities (desirable or undesirable) and give statements of principles concerning them. Biblical teaching values also serve pupils by stimulating them in the performance of Christian activities. Here they show examples of the values and penalties associated with various possible activities and bring statements of sanction and dissanction to bear upon them. Finally, these teaching values serve pupils by empowering them in the performance of activities because the Bible as the Word of Life is a spring from which the life-giving power of God flows into the life of man.

Education and the Place of Content

The functional approach in educational use of the Bible is also in accord with a major type of education and with the proper use of content within it. Throughout the history of education there have been two chief constellations of theory and practice which may be called traditional and developmental—both of these, naturally, prevalent in church-school work with the Bible. The opposing types have been described briefly as follows: traditional education emphasizes transmissive preparation for life; developmental education concerns itself with creative experience in living. The former underlies factual approach and the latter is the basis for functional approach in educational use of the Bible.

Two Types of Education

Traditional education bears the name because it deals more largely in racial heritages than in pupil life. It is busy transmitting the achievements of the race in knowledge, practice, institution, and value—aesthetic, moral, and spiritual. It is striving to put oncoming generations in possesssion of these "traditions" so that the traditions will be sustained. It is striving also to see that each youth gets a grasp of them so that he may be a more competent adult.

In developmental education the focus is on the pupil's total, current development through interaction between his maturing personality and his environing circumstances, which include, of course, racial resources. According to this type of education, the pupil rather than the teacher takes the center of the stage in the classroom. The point of departure is the concern, curiosity, inquiry (need will be the favored term here) of a pupil rather than a portion of material to be mediated by the teacher. The basic purpose for the pupil is to learn, change, and grow at that critical point with the teacher as his helper. The basic procedure is pupil in performance guided by leader rather than teacher telling pupil. The basic unit of the learning experience is an activity moving toward an end rather than a "lesson" presented and learned. The basic outcome is not a textbook mastered; it is rather an activity completed—although the activity may well involve earnest dealing with knowledge. Meantime the basic control comes from the pupil himself and creativity is stressed rather than imitation.

Content in Education

These types of education differ most specifically as to the use each makes of content. Content can mean three things. One of these is material or subject matter —content outside the pupil. The other two meanings refer to content as psychological phenomenon; (a) intellectual content or knowledge and (b) total mental

57

content—that is, content aspects versus technique aspects of the cognitive, affective, and executive mental processes. A common denominator of the three meanings is "substance"—substance versus operation—content being the substantive component of educational experience with the operative as its counterpart. Simply stated, traditionalists deal primarily in substance; developmentalists are more concerned about technique or operative phases of the human process than content or substantive ones.

These outlooks on content determine procedure as well as objectives. In traditional education where content mastery is the purpose, that mastery is attempted by direct effort at it. The issues of life are to be solved as a by-product, perhaps somewhat automatically upon the attainment of the content mastery. In developmental education, where the solving of life's issues gets the spotlight among objectives, content is to be used as a resource for their management with content mastery being largely a by-product. Thus both traditionalists and developmentalists use content. Traditionalists use it in its logical form, to be mastered and later utilized when need may arise. Developmentalists use it in functional form, employing it when need has already arisen and it can become naturally a component of the pupil's total action system by more or less immediate utilization.

Similarly Christian educators according to either factual or functional approach to the Bible may use it as content with any of the three meanings. Factualist or functionalist may have in view its helpfulness for Christian faith living. Yet while the former depends upon the concept that biblical ideas can have consequence —hence the pupil should glean as many as possible and as soon as possible—the functionalist believes that the Bible serves best when it becomes internal by the means of utilization in an ongoing process of guided enterprise in the actual meeting of pupil's needs. The concentration is on the rounded growth of the whole learner in his current experience as he meets his issues well and in doing so grows ready to meet subsequent situations even more creatively and fruitfully for himself and society.

It has become obvious that this is "education as need-meeting activity," the kind in which felt need determines the purpose, the procedure, and the particular material to be used. Pupils learn most effectively when there is problem and quest, when a person or group cannot move forward and welfare cannot be served until help is available. A need, educationally speaking, is that kind of valid and important concern, not a superficial but a substantial one. Needs will be of innumerable sorts and conditions, arising within any of the categories of human-divine relationships. Whatever the case, the need is to be met at least to the degree that the crisis will have passed with larger understanding, changed attitude, or the beginnings of new habit patterns. Preferably, of course, there will be a more complete resolution of the issue with larger fulfillment as a result.

Procedure

Someone has said that the task of learner and leader in educational use of the Bible is the recovering and releasing into action of the Bible's teaching values. Perhaps the whole task is "release into action" with "recovery" as an essential phase. This phase requires that we go into the Bible and make ready the resident potentialities that are its teaching values so that these can be brought alongside some need experience. Thus recovering the teaching values of the Bible is somewhat equivalent to the subordinate tasks of selecting and interpreting scripture passages, a task described below. The release of teaching values into action is procedure, arranging the total enterprise in which potentialities become actualities in enrichment or control achieved, growth accomplished, need that has been met, along with an increment of enhanced abundance realized.

Learning in Living

The procedure of traditional education and so of factual approach in biblical usage scarcely needs to be described here. Its characteristic methods of story-telling, lecturing, drilling, questioning, and the like are familiar. The procedure of developmental education and so of functional approach takes on the character of "the workshop way" where learning is accomplished in actual doing under guidance. Such procedure can be understood most readily, doubtless, in contrast with its opposite number. In factual approach the purpose is that the pupil may know the Bible in the more complete aspect of intellectual mastery—understand the language, get the ideas, follow the history, recite the words, and state the ethical principles or the doctrines. To be sure the factualist hopes and even expects that this knowing of the Bible will have its salutary end results. Yet since that is not the focus of his intent, his manner of procedure is not in accord with that purpose; the center of his attention is on drill for memorization. The functionalist understands that knowing the Bible has a place, yet that is not the principal goal. It is rather a contributory and by-product phase of the process. His focus is upon the pupil's performing the activity, living the life, within the light of the Bible and under the power of its functioning. The procedure can well be described by the single word *utilization*.

In this type of Christian education the leader's task is to help pupils discover their needs, even when obscure, as they are often wont to be. Next, the needs must be clarified in some detail so that they can be attacked. Then the biblical resource is brought to bear. Sometimes the help can be quite direct; the answer is right there. More often the teaching values will be indirect so that the pupil must depend upon broad general principles or on examples in parallel situations which must be "applied."

A simple formula for conducting the procedure can be given:
1. Seeing the need (an anticipatory phase in which pupils discover and clarify the issue)
2. Understanding the scriptures (an ancillary phase in which the biblical teaching values are focused on the issue)
3. Living the message (the consummation, to be in view throughout the procedure as the principal thing)

Here we apprehend the major principle of procedure in the functional approach: *Use the biblical teaching values in actual experiences of living.* The work is to be done in units of human experience, not in units of biblical material. In units of that type we seek the creative reliving of the biblical experience that originated in the life of God and now issues forth in the new experience.

Selection and Interpretation

To recapitulate, Christian education is to provide the setting in which the Word of Life nurtures human beings within the new life in Christ. In that setting the

Bible is employed as the supreme resource to provide teaching values through which life is enriched and controlled by scriptural guidance, stimulation, and empowerment. In functional approach where life is the goal and growth the emphasis, teachers and pupils go to the Bible for help at points of felt need. The Bible, then, is material for educational process, material that can enter into learning as intellectual content and ultimately total content. Yet it is more, namely, a resource for total living. Through its utilization in a learning-by-doing procedure God communicates with man, and the original intent for which the Bible came out of the life process of the Judeo-Christian movement is served.

Such an educational use of the Bible, we have said, is equivalent to the process of recovering and releasing into action the Bible's teaching values. We have seen how these teaching values are released into action in a certain general procedure. There is that phase called recovering the values which, we saw also, requires the selection of scripture passages and their interpretation. We have now to consider these two processes which in practice interact, a certain amount of interpreting being needed while we select a particular passage, just as further interpretation is needed when selected scripture is being utilized.

Selecting Scripture Passages

Here we face the question: Which biblical passages are to be used in Christian educational units? The answer follows: *Select those that have the most potent teaching values for the need to be met* ("most potent" because we have too little time to deal with even the best; "for the need" because we can so easily get entangled with irrelevances).

The study of a comprehensive variety of curricular materials several years ago provided data on the biblical portions being used at that time.[1] Further, while we can hope that there has been some change in conditions meantime, present-day practice is surely not very different. A few of the major findings of the study can be listed as follows, mingling good and bad:

1. Old Testament books of history and law (Genesis through Esther) are used more frequently than the gospels. Old Testament prophets are used only a little more than one fourth as much as history and law. Exodus is the chief Old Testament book because the Ten Commandments are in it.

2. Matthew is the most frequently used book in the Bible, because its chapters include the Sermon on the Mount. One out of every fourteen references is to the sermon. Next in order, about one out of every seventeen references is to the passion narratives in the four Gospels. Miracle narratives are used more often than parables. Feeding the five thousand is first among miracles, the good Samaritan, among parables.

3. The Acts is used more often than any Old Testament book except Exodus and more than any New Testament book except Matthew. Among the remaining New Testament books, Romans ranks first and Revelation second.

4. The favorite Old Testament verse is Exod. 20:8, on keeping the Sabbath. In the New Testament the favorite passage is Matt. 6:25-34 and the favorite verse is from that passage, "But seek first his kingdom and his righteousness, and all these things shall be yours as well" (vs. 33 R.S.V.).

5. Age-group adaptation as commonly favored and supposedly practiced is largely a

[1] Ralph D. Heim, "The Bible in the Literature for Christian Education," *Religious Education*, XLVII, 6 (November-December, 1952), 402-20.

hallucination. We are employing essentially the same scripture across all age levels. Some of the things specified for preschool children are incredible. For example, the flood is used here more frequently than with any other age group.

6. For those whose major objective is Bible knowledge there is food for thought in the finding that the curricular materials examined cited 2,390 different passages for use. If a pupil studied one passage a week he would be approaching fifty years of age before he had covered all of it even once.

7. As a major deduction, amply supported by the data of the study, the paramount purpose of biblical usage now is transmitting the biblical facts. Many writers of curricular materials do not plan that we shall start with pupils' concerns and draw in relevant material as resource for functional results.

While there may be genuine satisfaction with some of those findings, broad change in our practice is eminently to be desired in other respects. As an example, we should move toward using biblical materials in such a way that the proportions among biblical sections would be somewhat more like this:

Old Testament

History and Law (now 31%)	15.0%
Poetry and Wisdom (now 10%)	7.5%
Prophets (now 9%)	17.5%
Total Old Testament (now 50%)	40.0%

New Testament

Gospels (now 29%)	32.5%
The Acts (now 7%)	10.0%
Pauline Epistles (now 9%)	12.5%
Hebrews through Revelation (now 5%)	5.0%
Total New Testament (now 50%)	60.0%

Some would likely wish to add: Let us use less Bible in total amount, so that it can be used in a better manner; also let it be adapted to individual as well as age group needs and be employed in a functional manner within developmental education.

Interpreting Scripture Passages

A passage selected for use in the program of Christian education must be interpreted as it is selected and utilized. In common practice an interpreter is one who stands between two other persons and explains each to the other so that there can be communication with response. No interpreter has any easy task, and the biblical interpreter has special difficulties because he deals with ancient Eastern writing, done chiefly by Hebrews within a thousand years of changing history and literary form. Besides, its subject is the complex field of religion, including morality. Thus we are not surprised when we find that there have been many types of interpretation in the long run of history. In fact the history of interpretation must be considered in the figure of several strands in a rope. These strands, with related ones, appear and reappear, never quite disappear as they enter the rope, are woven and interwoven into it, and emerge from time to time into prominence. They may be designated as allegorical, experiential, literalistic, predictive, rationalistic, realistic, and theological.

The strongest and most persistent strand in the rope that is the history of interpretation happens to be the one which seems to fit best the newer ways of Christian education. This is the one termed realistic. It means simply being realistic as to the original intent and present utility of the material being interpreted, letting reason and faith in all honesty and simplicity operate for truth in action. Interpreters with this outlook strive mightily to get at the real or actual sense of a passage so as to discover the original message of the author and recover what he wished his readers to receive of the Word of Life.

Two of the major concerns in such interpretation are first, historical, and second, literary. Summarizing the requirements of both these considerations that accomplish the total purpose of recovering the teaching value so that it can be released into action, the interpreter will:

1. Make use of the most exact text
2. Reconstruct the historical setting, especially the immediate situation
3. Know the author and his purpose
4. Recognize the literary type and form
5. Deal seriously with the language
6. Understand the historical process through which the text arrived

Half a hundred particular principles of realistic interpretation in general and for Christian education's various situations could be listed. However, only the over-all criterion can be stated: *Regard use, then and now, as the fundamental category of interpretation and find the ultimate significance of biblical material in its worth for utilization toward the moral and religious enrichment, guidance, stimulation, and empowerment of persons for creative and satisfying Christian faith living.*

Varied Views, Practices and Emphases

We can neither design nor evaluate an approach in educational use of the Bible without taking into account a wealth of writing during the last decade. The nature of this literature can be suggested by listing a dozen of its principal concepts:

church as "redemptive community" (and other definitions)
communication
confrontation with the gospel
covenant
education within relationships
group dynamics
images of man
interpersonal relationships
kerygma and didache
mighty acts of God
needs of persons (e.g., acceptance)
theology (biblical, dynamic, and other types)

Obviously the dominating motif is "theology." Within that emphasis the term most often used is gospel or perhaps redemption. For instance a recent volume dealing with "the guiding principle of religious education" enounces it as "the gospel of God's redeeming activity in Jesus Christ." [2] Much has been said, too, about the "drama of redemption," particularly in three volumes by Randolph Miller. He views the Bible as a record of God's activity in five acts—creation, covenant, Christ, Church, consummation—and says, "the keyword is redemption." [3] This drama is to be "made relevant" to pupils in Christian education. Allen Miller gives the matter a different turn. He regards the Bible as the script of "The Mystery of God and Man," a story in which "the meaning of our existence may be discerned by those who are willing to join the cast and accept a role in the Covenant of the Living God." [4]

Mention of these discussions necessitates a brief critique. The educator must continue to be educator, not evangelist—an educator whose focus is on the growth of persons in their new life of discipleship and apostlehood with Jesus Christ. He must maintain clearly his understanding that education basically is an inner experience, not an external institution. He will distinguish clearly between gospel as good news versus grace about which the gospel is the news; also between theology and religion, realizing that the former is only resource for the latter. Then the educator will be concerned not so much with God's mighty acts of the past as with God's quiet, present action for this inner experience of religious development. Our pupils—a majority of them—have already been "won" initially; they are the redeemed, the sinning saved, the reborn—though perhaps prematurely. Such are the sheep for whom the teaching shepherd cares and his particular type of care is leading them into pastures where they will be nurtured toward maturity in love of God and man. The nurturing itself is the creative, redeeming, sanctifying (not only redemptive) activity of God.

Here we are concerned with the manner of using the Bible as a means for mediating God's nurturing activity. How—exactly how—are the Bible and people to be related most effectually for growth toward Christian objectives? The writing under consideration contains little that deals precisely, rather than by possible implication, with this "how." Grimes has briefly stated, "Thus our teaching must move back and forth between the Bible and the living situation, sometimes beginning with one, sometimes with the other." [5] Sherrill is equally ambivalent although fuller in his treatment. He, too, says: "It is possible to start from human need and then move toward the Bible . . . it is possible to start with the Bible and move toward human need." [6] Sherrill clearly favors the latter; Grimes's brief treatment does not suffice to disclose his preference. Yet he joins Sherrill in negative reaction to need-meeting education while giving lip service to the theory that would favor it. Both writers fear fragmentary, superficial, and moralizing results from what is here called the functional approach. This is precisely the difficulty with the factual approach which the functional approach, broadly conceived and wisely conducted, is meant to cure.

Perhaps the writers cited mean to depend largely upon this variant of factual

[2] D. Campbell Wyckoff, *The Gospel and Christian Education* (Philadelphia: The Westminster Press, 1959), p. 92.

[3] *Biblical Theology and Christian Education.*

[4] *Invitation to Theology* (Philadelphia: The Christian Education Press, 1958), p. 8.

[5] Lewis Howard Grimes, "Christianity Is Learned Through Living Encounter with the Bible," in *The Minister and Christian Nurture*, Nathaniel F. Forsyth, ed. (Nashville: Abingdon Press, 1957), p. 162.

[6] Sherrill, *The Gift of Power*, pp. 106, 109.

approach which may be termed "applicational procedures": "Here is the Bible. Hear what it says. Believe, think, feel, do that." In practice such use of the Bible works out as primarily a hortatory transmission of ideas which are expected, more or less automatically, to fulfill our educational objectives. Experience suggests that there is a more effective type of education. Consequently, those who think the functional approach is in accord with current educational, psychological, and sociological findings and with Christian theology properly conceived doubt whether any other form of biblical usage will meet necessary standards and serve our purposes as fully. It is what one writer calls "the existential methodology" [7] we need.

Further Considerations

The full scope of educational use of the Bible includes additional concerns of varied importance and complexity. One of these is *promotion*. While people have been trying to force the Bible en masse into the curriculum for children—the sooner the better, as many work at it—we have relatively neglected youth and particularly adults for whom the Bible is best adapted. Adequate provision for a lifelong, expanding program of work with the Bible has not been made for even our Sunday church schools. *Evaluation* is another area in which we need to take steps. A generation ago there was considerable work with "tests and measures" particularly of biblical knowledge and comprehension. A reviving interest is promising. Simple and valid means of knowing exactly what we are doing should be available. The means of accomplishing *transition* from older materials and procedures into newer ones needs study, too. To be concrete, exactly how do you take leaders and learners over the bridge from factual approach into functional approach?

Another obvious need for study arises out of *age group adaptation*. Which teaching values are to be in readiness against the major concerns of children, of youth, of adults? Are there varieties of procedure that are most suitable at certain developmental stages? What are the foundation things to be favored today so that there will be greater readiness for what is needed tomorrow? A related area for research has regard for the *identification of teaching values* per se. Where do we turn for the most effectively relevant ones to match the more prevalent life experiences? Next, how do we properly handle these in view of the various types of literature and historical circumstance in which they appear? In short, who will give us definitive and ready guidance toward the most effective use of the best possible scriptural resources for our various units?

This field of educational use of the Bible seems to offer one of our paramount challenges to urgent next steps in study, research, experiment, and publication, as well as generally improved practice in Christian education so that we may rise to the high demands of this troublous time for the Christian community.

Bibliography

Bower, William C. *The Living Bible.* New York: Harper and Brothers, 1946.

Gettys, Joseph M. *How to Teach the Bible.* Richmond, Va.: John Knox Press, 1949.

Heim, Ralph D. *Leading a Sunday Church School.* Philadelphia: Muhlenberg Press, 1950.

[7] Iris V. Cully, *The Dynamics of Christian Education* (Philadelphia: The Westminster Press, 1958), p. 173.

Miller, Randolph C. *Biblical Theology and Christian Education.* New York: Charles Scribner's Sons, 1956.

Sherrill, Lewis J. *The Gift of Power.* New York: The Macmillan Company, 1955.

Smith, J. W. D. *Introduction to Scripture Teaching.* New York: Thomas Nelson and Sons, 1949.

Smither, Ethel. *The Use of the Bible with Children.* Cincinnati: The Methodist Book Concern, 1935.

The Objectives of Protestant Religious Education

Lawrence C. Little

Chapter 6

The Objectives of Protestant Religious Education

Lawrence C. Little

SOME UNDERSTANDING OF THE OBJECTIVES[1] OF EDUCATION IS ESSENTIAL FOR THE effective guidance of the educational process. Recognition of this fact has brought widespread interest in the formulation of statements of objectives in both general and religious education. Agencies such as the Educational Policies Commission of the National Education Association, curriculum committees of state departments of education, and local boards of education almost everywhere have attempted to state the aims of secular or public education. Catholic, Jewish, and Protestant leaders and agencies are giving increasing attention to the need for clarification and definition of their educational goals.

The Objectives of General Education[2]

The problem involved in specifying the objectives of religious education may be understood better, perhaps, if some preliminary consideration is given to ways in which leaders in general education have faced this task and some of the results that have followed their efforts. The limitations of space permit only a few illustrations of patterns that have been followed.

Early Statements

Most of the early attempts in general education to outline objectives were made by individuals (philosophers or administrators) or by committees representing educational agencies. They approached their problem from various angles.

CLASSIFICATION OF ACTIVITIES. Herbert Spencer held that the first step in determining "what knowledge is of most worth" must be to classify, in their order of importance, the leading kinds of activity which constitute human life—self-preservation, the "necessaries" of life, rearing children, social and political relations, and leisure.[3]

The "cardinal principles of secondary education" were based on an analysis of

---

[1] The terms aims, goals, objectives, and purposes are used almost interchangeably in current educational literature. They are used in this chapter without any attempt at sharp distinction.

[2] The term "general education" has come to take on a particular connotation in recent literature because of the controversy over the respective merits of "liberal" and vocational education. The term is used here to indicate a broad type of education considered desirable by society for all people, regardless of vocational or other special interests.

[3] Herbert Spencer, *Education* (New York: D. Appleton and Company, 1860), pp. 13-14.

the types of activity which enter into "complete living," as distinguished from mental discipline and the acquisition of knowledge. These were health, command of the fundamental processes, worthy home membership, vocation, citizenship, worthy use of leisure time, and ethical character.[4]

INDIVIDUAL RELATIONSHIPS. The Department of Superintendence of the N.E.A. in 1928 declared that "The individual self, nature, society and God—these four, and in particular the adjustments which the individual self must make—constitute the objectives of education." [5]

RECOGNIZED SCALE OF VALUES. The Educational Policies Commission of the N.E.A. in 1938 stated the purposes of education in terms of "American democracy," which was understood to include the general welfare, civil liberty, the consent of the governed, the appeal to reason, and the pursuit of happiness. From an analysis of these ideas, the purposes of education were defined as self-realization, human relationships, economic efficiency, and civic responsibility.[6]

As these and other statements were used in American school systems, it was found that they were too vague and general to be of much value in school practice. Although the seven "cardinal principles" were widely referred to, they had actually little direct effect upon school work because they failed to present clearly the divisions of "complete living" that might serve as focal points in instruction. The list of "purposes of education in American democracy" suffered the same limitations. Most schoolmen agreed, of course, that "self-realization" is a desirable outcome, but few were clear about the meaning of the term for education.

BEHAVIORAL CHANGE. As objectives stated in vague, general terms proved of little functional value, attention was turned toward individual and social needs. The President's Commission on Higher Education took into account the changing demands upon higher education made by recent advances in science and invention, diversity of population, the shift in orientation of American foreign policy, and the coming of the atomic age. The Commission stated that "The purposes of general education should be understood in terms of performance, of behavior, not in terms of mastering particular bodies of knowledge." [7] It selected "from among the principal goals for higher education, those which should come first in our time." [8]

The "Scientific" Approach to Objectives

In recent years there has been rapid progress in methods of analysis of human needs, abilities, and learning outcomes and, consequently, in the "science" of educational measurement. Departments of psychology and education in a number of leading universities have developed laboratories in which the observation and classification of behavior have been major concerns. Tests of a wide variety have been used in determining the proper content of instruction at various achievement levels and in improving methods of presentation. Such agencies as the Character

[4] U. S. Department of the Interior, Bureau of Education, *Cardinal Principles of Secondary Education.* Bulletin, 1918, No. 35 (Washington: Government Printing Office, 1918).

[5] National Education Association, Department of Superintendence, *The Development of the High School Curriculum* (Washington, 1928), p. 51.

[6] National Education Association, Educational Policies Commission, *The Purposes of Education in American Democracy* (Washington: National Education Association, 1938).

[7] *Higher Education for American Democracy* (New York: Harper and Brothers, 1947), I, 50.

[8] *Ibid.,* p. 8.

Education Inquiry[9] and the Character Research Project [10] have clearly demonstrated the possibilities of measurement even in such an elusive field as character development. It was inevitable that advances in the science of measurement would affect attitudes toward educational objectives. More and more the emphasis was shifted to desired changes in behavior in the light of the continuing needs of the individual. Only two examples of many current proposals can be given.

"PERSISTENT LIFE SITUATIONS." The Horace Mann-Lincoln Institute of School Experimentation at Columbia University based its curriculum design upon the "persistent life situations" which are met by individuals and groups in everyday living, "those situations that recur in the life of the individual in many different ways as he grows from infancy to maturity." The goals of education are defined in terms of growth in ability to deal with these recurring situations as the learners meet them in day-to-day experiences. A master list of types of situations is provided, each of which is outlined in great detail. Each item is illustrated by describing typical situations faced by individuals at the various age levels.[11]

"DEVELOPMENTAL TASKS." The Committee on Human Development, University of Chicago, has dealt with the objectives of education in terms of "developmental tasks," defined as "those things that constitute healthy and satisfactory growth in our society. They are the things a person must learn if he is to be judged and to judge himself to be a reasonably happy and successful person." [12] The Committee outlines these tasks at the various age levels and, in connection with each, analyzes its biological, psychological, and cultural bases and points out its educational implications.

A valuable part of the work of the Committee on Human Development has been its attempts to discover the possibilities of measuring achievement in the developmental tasks and the interrelationships between them. In seeking empirical data, the Committee defined certain tasks in terms of success or failure at several age levels and devised rating scales as instruments of measurement. It concluded that the several developmental tasks are highly interrelated. Good achievement on one task tends to go with good achievement in others. Poor achievement on one presages poor achievement in others. The relationships are undeniable, though they decline in strength with advancing age.[13]

The Collaboration of Groups of Specialists

The task of formulating a valid statement of educational objectives is now seen to be much too difficult and involved for any one individual, or even for a group unless this group includes individuals of a wide range of experience and competence. In recent years, leaders in general education have faced this problem by pooling the knowledge and understanding of groups of specialists in education and in closely related fields.[14]

ELEMENTARY EDUCATION. One attempt was that of the Mid-Century Committee

[9] Hugh Hartshorne, et al., Studies in the Nature of Character, 3 vols. (New York: The Macmillan Company, 1928-30).

[10] Ernest M. Ligon, Dimensions of Character (New York: The Macmillan Company, 1956).

[11] Stratemeyer, et al. Developing a Curriculum for Modern Living, pp. 115, 149 ff.

[12] Havighurst, Human Development and Education, p. 2.

[13] Ibid., pp. 325 ff.

[14] One example of this type of collaboration was that of the President's Commission on Higher Education, discussed earlier in this chapter.

on Outcomes in Elementary Education, a joint undertaking by Educational Testing Service, the United States Office of Education, and Russell Sage Foundation. The Committee attempted to describe "the measurable goals of instruction" and to "identify desirable attainable objectives so that they may be susceptible to measurement, evaluation, and critical philosophical analysis." It interpreted educational objectives in terms of "observable behavior—what happens to the child's way of reacting to his environment as a result of his school experience." The Committee published a list of "recommended goals," offered a detailed analysis of each of these, and discussed them with reference to the various age levels. The report concludes with an extended and helpful chapter on implications for educational practice, research, and measurement.[15]

SECONDARY EDUCATION. The last pattern for formulating objectives of general education to be reviewed here is the result of a study of behavioral goals in high school, conducted under the joint sponsorship of Russell Sage Foundation, the National Association of Secondary School Principals, and Educational Testing Service, with planning assistance from a number of other national educational organizations. The committee consisted of a number of consultants, who developed lists of behavioral outcomes and their "developmental equivalents" in the "areas of living in which they considered it important for all youth to be willing and able to behave appropriately and competently"; interested citizens who reviewed their work in the light of public needs; and reviewers (teachers, administrators, psychologists, and curriculum specialists) who were familiar with the work of young people in high school.[16]

This committee approached its task from the standpoint of "social expectations." It sought to provide "an organized consensus of the expectations that citizens and educators hold for the American high school" and "to help high schools develop what might be properly called behavior-centered general education programs which have as their goal building in youth the kinds of common competence they need to meet life's demands." The behavioral goals were stated in terms of "directions of growth involved in achieving maturity." A comprehensive list of "illustrative behaviors" was given under the headings, intellectual self-realization, cultural orientation, mental and physical health, and economic literacy and independence. The report concludes with a form for evaluating programs in terms of the behavioral outcomes desired.[17]

Trends

As the development of objectives for general education over the last several decades is traced, several trends may be noted. The focus of attention shifted from primary concern for knowledge and mental discipline to the "whole child" as he is engaged in "complete living." The content of statements of objectives changed from broad concepts, derived from philosophy, to emphasis upon the actual needs and capacities of individuals in a dynamic society. The individual is viewed in his cultural setting, and the importance of group relationships is recognized. The significance of cultural change is stressed. The developmental aspects of education are given emphasis, with an increasing concern for the relation of present behavior

[15] Kearney, *Elementary School Objectives*, pp. 7, 9, 37, 121 ff.
[16] French and Associates, *Behavioral Goals of General Education in High School*, pp. 16-18.
[17] *Ibid.*, pp. 14, 81, 88-89.

to past experiences and to future potentialities. "Operational" objectives in terms of behavioral change are of prime concern. Greater emphasis is placed upon the scientific approach, and much more extensive use is made of direct observation and classification of actual behaviors, experimentation, and measurement. The categories of classification are arrived at inductively. Objectives are stated in forms that make possible their use as instruments of evaluation. The task of formulating objectives is now regarded not as a job for single individuals or agencies but as necessarily a task for the collaboration of groups of experts in many fields.

The Objectives of Religious Education

Soon after its organization in 1922, the International Council of Religious Education established a Committee on the International Curriculum with instructions to undertake the construction of a curriculum that would provide an integrated program for Sunday and weekday church schools in the light of trends in general education.

Early Statements

"CHRISTIAN CHARACTER TRAITS." An early attempt of the Committee on the International Curriculum to specify objectives resulted in a list of twenty-two "Christian Character Traits," compiled by combining an existing list of the outstanding qualities in the character of Jesus, Bible traits "which seemed predominantly Christian," traits which thirty graduate students considered most representative of "the Jesus' way," and traits suggested by seventeen church leaders who were asked to state what they regarded as the marks of a Christian. This list was published in 1927. The following year the Educational Commission of I.C.R.E. was organized and the International Curriculum enterprise passed under its supervision. This Commission reviewed the instrument, "Christian Character Traits," in 1929 and approved it "for such use in the curriculum work of the International Council as may, through experience, be found desirable." [18] It has not played much part in the subsequent development of the curriculum.

COMPREHENSIVE OBJECTIVES. The Educational Commission recognized the need for a statement of general objectives as a basis on which curriculum construction might proceed. This responsibility was assigned to Paul H. Vieth, Director of Research for the Council and executive secretary of the Educational Commission. He made a study of objectives as a doctoral research project at Yale University, which he completed in 1928.[19]

Vieth's method of constructing this list was "to formulate and summarize the best thinking" of leaders in education. He analyzed the writings of ten "leaders of thought" in religious education, as selected in a referendum of college and theological seminary professors of religious education; twelve members of a Committee on Curriculum of the National Society for the Study of Education—who were found to have paid little attention to religious education; and statements of objectives issued by the boards of religious education of denominations having membership in I.C.R.E.[20] From this study a list of seven "Comprehensive

---

[18] Vieth, *The Development of a Curriculum of Religious Education*, pp. 64-74.

[19] "A Critical Study of Objectives in Religious Education" (an unpublished doctoral dissertation, Yale University, 1928).

[20] Vieth, *Objectives in Religious Education*, pp. 69-78.

Objectives" was compiled, having to do with the following areas: God-relationship, Jesus Christ, Christlike character, the good society, Christian life philosophy, the Church, and race heritage.[21] An eighth, the Christian family, was added later. The list was approved by the International Council in 1930 and was used subsequently by a great number of Protestant agencies as a basis for religious education curricula.[22]

SPECIFIC OBJECTIVES. Vieth pointed out the distinction between "comprehensive" objectives, which indicate the major purposes of education, and "specific" objectives, which he proposed as a next step. He wrote:

> Specific objectives . . . represent the meaning in Christian living of individual situations when seen in the light of the more comprehensive or general objectives. Their value lies in making the desired outcomes of the educational process more concrete, the procedure for achieving this outcome more definite, and the test of educational effectiveness more immediate. . . . This formulation of specific objectives may be approached through analysis of the comprehensive objectives, on the one hand, and through research in the actual experience of growing persons, on the other.[23]

"AREAS OF HUMAN EXPERIENCE." Two instruments were developed to aid in the observation and classification of experiences. The first contained an outline of significant types of experience, a discussion of principles to guide in observation, instructions to observers, and an observation record form.[24] The second was a list of eleven "Areas of Human Experience," which was intended to provide an outline for the preliminary analysis of experience, to serve as a check list in stimulating discovery, and to insure a proper spread of experience over all the areas of life.[25]

The Curriculum Guide

When the Educational Commission was established in 1928, it was decided to shift from the preparation of a system of lesson courses to the development of a *Curriculum Guide* and to leave the actual production of the curriculum to the participating denominations. The Guide was to include, among other things, a statement of educational principles, the list of comprehensive objectives, a description of experiences, and the specific objectives organized by age groups.[26]

Work on the *Curriculum Guide* was carried on for several years by committees of the International Council. A preliminary draft was presented in 1931, containing sections on children's work, young people's work, and adult work.

CHILDREN'S WORK. The section of children's work was divided into three parts, one each for the beginners', the primary, and the junior departments. Each part contained the list of comprehensive objectives, with attempts to adapt these to each of the age groups involved. Then followed analyses of each of the eleven Areas of Human Experience, under four sub-headings—experiences, needs, desired outcomes, and methods and procedures. The Committee on Religious Education of Children, which had been responsible for this section, expended a vast amount of

[21] This list of categories is taken from the chapter headings in Vieth's book.

[22] For the complete list, cf., *Christian Education Today*, pp. 16-17.

[23] Vieth, *Objectives in Religious Education*, pp. 282, 70.

[24] *Life Experiences and the New Curriculum* (Chicago: The International Council of Religious Education, 1929).

[25] Vieth, *The Development of a Curriculum of Religious Education*, pp. 47-57.

[26] *Ibid.*, pp. 59-60.

effort in assembling the report. A total of 752 "experiences" and 456 "needs" were catalogued.[27]

YOUTH WORK. The Committee on Religious Education of Youth presented a section on young people's work, divided into three parts, one each for intermediates, senior, and young people's departments. These also contained extensive analyses of the Areas of Human Experience under the headings: analysis of experience, age-group objectives, and curriculum units. The concluding part dealt with patterns and criteria for curriculum units, how to organize and carry out the program, techniques for discovering interests and needs, and testing results.[28]

ADULT WORK. The Committee on Religious Education of Adults presented a report which stated:

All the Committee has done . . . is to describe experiences in two major areas, "Citizenship" and "Specifically Religious Activities" on the basis of "general knowledge of leaders in religious education growing out of actual experience with growing persons." "Studies available in printed or manuscript form," and "new research studies," have not yet been used.

The report contained outlines of experiences and suggested specific objectives in the areas of citizenship and specifically religious activities, fairly complete outlines of five study units, a series of tests for use in discovering adult attitudes and interests, and blanks for reporting results in using the experimental units.[29]

The preliminary drafts were subjected to critical study by the age-group committees of I.C.R.E. over several years and were published in revised form at various times in the 1930's. These volumes of the *Curriculum Guide* are still a valuable source of information regarding the experiences of persons which have significance for religious education and give evidence of widespread participation in the curriculum enterprises of the Council during this period. The *Guide* had hardly appeared, however, before some of the age-group committees found it necessary to reconsider the objectives as they had been stated before they could be adapted for use in local church groups.

Revised Statements of Age-Group Objectives

CHILDREN. Soon after the *Curriculum Guide* appeared the Committee on Religious Education of Children began work on a new statement of objectives for work with children. Among the factors which prompted this effort were certain basic changes in theological, educational, and sociological concepts; awareness of the implications of current character education programs for religious education; a new understanding of the difficulty of using adult theological concepts with children; and a recognition of the importance of adult and parent education.[30] A new statement of objectives was published in 1945 and has since been used as a basis for the program in children's work.[31] This document begins with a discussion of the growing child and then proceeds to a statement of goals based upon understanding of the principles of child development. "Those who guide children," the

---

[27] *International Curriculum Guide, Preliminary Draft, Section I* (Chicago: International Council of Religious Education, 1931).

[28] *Ibid.*, Section II.

[29] *Ibid.*, Section III.

[30] Bower and Hayward, *Protestantism Faces Its Educational Task Together*, pp. 97 ff.

[31] *Goals for the Christian Education of Children.*

authors state, "recognize that all nurture, including religious nurture, must be based upon a sound, practical knowledge of how children grow. They recognize that goals must not be imposed from without, but must be integral to the child's wholesome growth." Emphasis is placed upon the various levels of maturity and upon definite limitations on the part of each child which must be respected. The goals suggested for achieving the purpose of Christian education were outlined under six headings: God, Jesus, Church, Bible, personal relationships, and social relationships.

JUNIOR HIGHS. The Junior High Subcommittee of the Committee on Youth Work and the Intermediate Subcommittee of the Committee on the Graded Series prepared a service bulletin on junior high objectives.[32] This bulletin begins with a brief introduction that stresses the rapidity and scope of the changes now taking place in the world, which is followed by a discussion of junior high experiences. These are analyzed under three headings—the self, other persons, the world. Six objectives are then listed under the headings, God, Jesus Christ, man, the social order, the Church, and the Bible. Each of these objectives was analyzed with respect to its component parts, and each subsection described the characteristics of incoming twelve-year-olds, the desired outcomes for fourteen-year-olds, and the implications for Christian education.

Thus the format was greatly simplified as contrasted with the complexity of the *Curriculum Guide*. Theological concepts still provided the organizing centers around which objectives revolved; but the original scheme of classification, "Areas of Human Experience," was completely abandoned. The focus of attention was the individual in his relationships to self, others, and the world.

NEED FOR RESTUDY. The foregoing has traced the continuing efforts of co-operative Protestantism to work out functional statements of objectives. The original statement was based upon careful research in the best literature on the theory of religious education available at the time. Efforts were made to refine it in the light of extended observation and descriptions of the actual experiences of growing persons. The list "has been used as widely perhaps as any other publication of the Council. It has profoundly affected the development of Protestant religious education in the United States and has enjoyed popular favor and longevity far beyond expectation at the time of its adoption. It has been truly one of the landmarks of our movement."[33]

No statement of objectives could be expected to last forever in the swiftly moving scene of modern education. As has been indicated, modifications were made in efforts to adapt the original list to the requirements of age-group and curriculum committees. These found it necessary to rearrange and to make various combinations of the original items. They sometimes reconstructed the statements entirely to make them better serve their purposes. Many of the constituent denominations formulated their own statements in the light of their conceptions of theology and education. Many changes have taken place in the "climate" of religious education since 1928. How far the original list had shifted from its dominating position in determining the format of the curriculum is illustrated by the fact that the latest edition of the *Curriculum Guide* makes no mention of the

[32] *Junior High Objectives.*
[33] *The Objectives of Christian Education: A Study Document*, p. 8.

list and bases its approach to curriculum production on other factors. This *Guide* states that "A statement of progressive goals for children, youth, and adults is not a part of this Guide. Statements of this kind may be obtained from the educational headquarters of most denominations [or] from the Division of Christian Education of the National Council of Churches." [34] With these changes and adaptations in progress, there was increasing recognition of the need for a restudy of the objectives.

The Special Committee on Christian Education Objectives

The Commission on General Christian Education authorized the establishment of a Special Committee on Christian Education Objectives in 1952. This committee, as originally constituted, consisted of twenty-one professional leaders in Christian education from local churches, denominational boards, theological seminaries, and the staff of the Division of Christian Education of the National Council. It worked steadily at its task over a period of five years and presented its report in 1958. The Commission on General Christian Education authorized publication of the report as a study document and referred it to denominations and agencies of the Council for suggestions and comments that would be helpful to the continuing work on objectives. [35]

The study document contains the following sections: (1) "Questions for Consideration"; (2) "Background Statement on the Development of the Objectives of Christian Education"; (3) "The Meaning of Christian Education"; and (4) "The Objectives." The background statement gives reasons for the restudy and a review of the work of the committee, including the types of exploratory studies made, further steps recommended, and a discussion of the relation of Christian education to public education. The section on the meaning of Christian education deals with the nature of the church, the mission of the church, and the relation of Christian education to the total task of the church.

STATEMENT OF OBJECTIVES. The statement of objectives released by the Special Committee is as follows:

The supreme purpose of Christian education is to enable persons to become aware of the seeking love of God as revealed in Jesus Christ and to respond in faith to this love in ways that will help them to grow as children of God, live in accordance with the will of God, and sustain a vital relationship to the Christian community.

To achieve this purpose Christian education, under the guidance of the Holy Spirit, endeavors:

To assist persons, at each stage of development, to realize the highest potentialities of the self as divinely created, to commit themselves to Christ, and to grow toward maturity as Christian persons;

To help persons establish and maintain Christian relationships with their families, their churches, and with other individuals and groups, taking responsible roles in society, and seeing in every human being an object of the love of God;

To aid persons in gaining a better understanding and awareness of the natural world as God's creation and accepting the responsibility for conserving its values and using them in the service of God and of mankind;

To lead persons to an increasing understanding and appreciation of the Bible, whereby

[34] *A Guide for Curriculum in Christian Education*, p. 31.
[35] *The Objectives of Christian Education: A Study Document*, p. 6.

they may hear and obey the Word of God; and to help them appreciate and use effectively other elements in the historic Christian heritage;

To enable persons to discover and fulfill responsible roles in the Christian fellowship through faithful participation in the local and world mission of the church.[86]

Recent Statements of Age-Group Objectives

SENIOR HIGHS. A Committee on Senior High Objectives was appointed in 1954, made up of members of the Committee on Youth Work and the Committee on the Graded Series. This committee made a report, which was received and authorized for publication by the Division of Christian Education as a service bulletin in 1958.[37] This bulletin begins with a discussion of "The Nature of Objectives" and, for its purposes, distinguishes this term from motivations, themes, and topics or problems. According to the committee, the objectives of Christian education

are conceived not as a list of tasks to be performed or relationships to be dealt with or areas of content to be covered, but as one end toward which the whole process is directed. Thus "objectives" become singular, that is the *objective* of Christian education. The value of one purpose or one end in view, i.e., a single objective, is that it provides direction and perspective for the entire process.[38]

The objective of Christian education is to help persons to be aware of God's self-disclosure and seeking love in Jesus Christ and to respond in faith and love—to the end that they may know who they are and what their human situation means, grow as sons of God rooted in the Christian community, live in the Spirit of God in every relationship, fulfill their common discipleship in the world, and abide in the Christian hope.[39]

Following this statement of objective, the bulletin contains a chapter on "Christian Education of Senior Highs," which deals with the nature and relationships of senior high young people; and a special chart, "Analysis of Learning Tasks."

ADULTS. A workshop on the Christian Education of Adults was held in the summer of 1958, under the joint sponsorship of the Department of Adult Work, Division of Christian Education, National Council of Churches, and the School of Education of the University of Pittsburgh. This workshop brought together ninety selected leaders who worked together for two weeks on the problem of formulating objectives for Christian adult education. These included some fifteen consultants who are nationally known specialists in fields other than Christian education (economics, political science, psychology, psychiatry, sociology, adult education, public education, journalism, and theology) and leaders in religious education (pastors, directors of religious education, editors, staff members of the National Council and of denominational boards, executives in men's and women's work, and professors of religious education in universities and seminaries).

The consultants summarized the findings and insights gained from study and research in their respective fields that seemed relevant to Christian education of adults and made such applications as they could to the programs of the churches. These presentations were followed by panel discussions, and then by study and

[86] Quoted from *The Objectives of Christian Education: A Study Document.* Published for the Commission on General Christian Education of the National Council of Churches. Used with permission.

[37] *The Objective of Christian Education for Senior High Young People.*

[38] Quoted from *The Objective of Christian Education for Senior High Young People.* Copyright 1958 by the National Council of Churches. Used with permission.

[39] *Ibid.,* pp. 14-15.

discussion groups, in which efforts were made to discover implications for the objectives of Christian adult education.[40]

The workshop adopted two "working papers": (1) "Basic Assumptions of Christian Adult Education" and (2) "A Tentative Statement of Purpose and Objectives of Christian Adult Education." These are being made the basis for continuing study by the Committee on Adult Work and the Department of Adult Work of the National Council, looking toward an eventual statement of the objectives of Christian education for adults that may be more useful than any which has been available before.

Future Tasks in Formulating Objectives

When its study document was released in 1958, the Special Committee on Christian Education Objectives outlined some further steps to be undertaken in formulating the objectives of Protestant religious education. It stated that

> The concern for an adequate statement . . . must be an interest shared by all who are engaged in Christian nurture. Board and staff members, pastors and directors, editors and field workers, theologians and research experts, seminary professors and church school teachers must consider what the objectives should be and what intermediate goals should be formulated to attain them.[41]

The further steps suggested by the committee were as follows: (1) *Study of educational and theological implications,* by each group using the statement of objectives "in the light of its own understanding of the Christian faith and valid insights regarding the nature of personality and the conditions which encourage its wholesome development"; (2) *Developmental goals,* adaptations of the general statement to various age groups and situations, by leaders in the various age-group divisions of the National Council and its co-operating agencies; and (3) *Specific aims.* "The determination of specific or immediate aims for the tasks of Christian education from week to week must be made by editors, writers of curricula, and local church workers, in light of their particular situations and resources." [42]

The task of formulating statements of religious education objectives must never be regarded as completed. As theological and educational concepts change, and as understanding of human nature and its potentialities is enlarged, the phrasing of statements of objectives must be altered in order to bring them into accord with current conceptions of the realities involved.

Bibliography

Bower, William C., and Hayward, Percy R. *Protestantism Faces Its Educational Task Together.* Appleton, Wis.: C. C. Nelson Publishing Company, 1949.

[40] Lawrence C. Little, ed., *Charting the Future Course of Christian Adult Education in America;* and *Formulating the Objectives of Christian Adult Education* (mimeographed documents published by The Department of Religious Education, University of Pittsburgh, 1958). The two working papers referred to are contained in the second volume, pp. 57-60. A revised edition of the first volume was published under the title, *The Future Course of Christian Adult Education.*

[41] Quoted from *The Objectives of Christian Education: A Study Document.* Published for the Commission on General Christian Education of the National Council of Churches. Used with permission.

[42] *Ibid.,* pp. 12, 14.

French, Will, and Associates. *Behavioral Goals of General Education in High School*. New York: Russell Sage Foundation, 1957.

Goals for the Christian Education of Children. Chicago: The International Council of Religious Education, 1945.

Havighurst, Robert J. *Human Development and Education*. New York: Longmans, Green and Company, 1953.

The International Council of Religious Education. *Christian Education Today*. Chicago, 1940.

International Curriculum Guide: Preliminary Draft. Chicago: The International Council of Religious Education, 1931.

Junior High Objectives. Chicago: Division of Christian Education, National Council of the Churches of Christ in the U. S. A., n. d.

Kearney, Nolan C. *Elementary School Objectives*. New York: Russell Sage Foundation, 1953.

Little, Lawrence C. (ed.). *The Future Course of Christian Adult Education*. Pittsburgh: University of Pittsburgh Press, 1959.

————. *Formulating the Objectives of Christian Adult Education*. Pittsburgh: The Department of Religious Education, University of Pittsburgh, 1958.

The Objectives of Christian Education: A Study Document. New York: Commission on General Christian Education, National Council of the Churches of Christ in the U. S. A., n. d.

The Objective of Christian Education for Senior High Young People. New York: Division of Christian Education, National Council of the Churches of Christ in the U. S. A., 1958.

Special Committee on the Curriculum Guide. *A Guide for Curriculum in Christian Education*. Chicago: Division of Christian Education, National Council of the Churches of Christ in the U. S. A., 1955.

Stratemeyer, Florence B.; Forkner, Hamden L.; McKim, Margaret G.; and Passow, A. Harry. *Developing a Curriculum for Modern Living*. New York: Bureau of Publications, Teachers College, Columbia University, 1957.

Vieth, Paul H. *The Development of a Curriculum of Religious Education*. Chicago: The International Council of Religious Education, 1930.

————. *Objectives in Religious Education*. New York: Harper and Brothers, 1930.

Chapter 7

Research in Religious Education

Walter Houston Clark

RESEARCH TAKES MANY FORMS WHETHER WITHIN THE FIELD OF RELIGIOUS education or outside it. However, rather than being concerned with more generalized studies such as those of a historical, biblical, or theological kind, this chapter will be confined mainly to empirical studies chiefly of a social psychological nature. Though relatively scanty as compared to research in other fields, there still are enough studies, of varying quality, so that considerable selectivity needs to be exercised.[1] We will try to suggest, through concrete example, how research may contribute knowledge and influence religious education.

History of Research in Religious Education

Considering the importance of the subject it is strange that so little thorough research has been attempted in the field of religious education. On the one hand, this is partly an expression of the feeling by social scientists that religion is too complicated a function for the application of such methods as they have devised up to the present. On the other hand, many pious church people resent the intrusion of social scientists into what they consider sacred precincts. Such influences have deprived the social scientists of important social and psychological insights, while the churches have failed to secure the aid for their educational programs that more precise studies in certain areas might have supplied.

Consequently when one surveys the field historically, he can see only two major efforts that stand out. The first was the Character Education Inquiry, suggested by the Religious Education Association and sponsored by Columbia University under the general direction of Hugh Hartshorne and Mark May. This was carried on in the 1920's but it still has its influence on the field. It consisted of an investigation into traits usually supposed to be cultivated by the churches, such as

---

[1] Each year the Division of Christian Education of the National Council of Churches compiles abstracts of dissertations in the total field of religious education. These are usually published in *Religious Education,* journal of the Religious Education Association, 545 West 111th St., New York City. Other listings of articles reporting research may be found in *Psychological Abstracts, Sociological Abstracts,* and the *Education Index.* The Religious Education Association maintains a Committee on Research to stimulate and give guidance in this area. Recently, in co-operation with the Character Research Project, the Association compiled information about such research, and it was published in *Religious Education,* May-June, 1959. It is expected that these reports will be continued, while the Association expects soon to publish a report outlining areas where research is needed and possible.

honesty, self-control, and co-operation, principally through the instrument of many ingenious tests devised to indicate these characteristics in simulated real life situations.[2] There has been wide criticism of the chief conclusion of the study,[3] namely that there is little evidence for the existence of consistent, generalized character traits. Rather, these only appear with respect to specific situations. Thus Hartshorne and May found that a child might be scrupulously honest, say in money matters or on the athletic field, but not in taking tests in the classroom. Despite questions regarding the conclusions drawn, the Hartshorne and May studies performed at least two important functions. First, they served as a model of precise study in the difficult field of character and so stimulated many lesser but still important studies in the field. Second, they directed the attention of religious educators to the importance of empirical as opposed to the merely verbal cultivation of character. This meant an increased emphasis on activities, participation, and personal relations in religious education, which is still with us.

The second major research effort in this field is the Character Research Project (C.R.P.) at Union College, Schenectady, New York, directed by Ernest M. Ligon. This has been operating over a number of years and is still in progress, generously financed by Lilly Endowment. Like the Character Education Inquiry (C.E.I.) it is concerned in large degree with traits, such as those reported by Ligon, who made a study of the Christian gospels to derive the characteristics of Christian personality.[4] The findings of C.R.P. were summarized by Ligon and published in 1956.[5] Since the studies have continued, however, C.R.P. is continually opening up new areas, so that one who wishes to keep abreast of its research is well advised to write to the project for the latest references.[6]

Among its many researches, C.R.P. considers its chief findings to have been in the areas of home dynamics, individual differences, and youth. In the first named area the basic question being studied is "What are the characteristics of homes which are most favorable for religious education?" Here the methods of factor and cluster analysis have been used to isolate the characteristics of homes in which lie the greatest potentialities. With this knowledge parents have been able to strengthen the favorable factors and weaken unfavorable ones to improve the climate of their homes for character development.

Under individual differences the basic question studied is, "How can the full spiritual potential of each child be realized by taking into account his unique personality and his possibilities for growth at each age level throughout his childhood?" Here reliance is placed on parent's reports and developmental studies. These studies have confirmed the concept of maturity as an integrative process. High ranking behavior items tended to be associated with other character traits, while low ranking items were not. The developmental studies yielded predictors of maturity at later age levels; for instance, the desire to grow up among kinder-

[2] H. Hartshorne and M. May, *Studies in Deceit; Studies in Service and Self Control;* and H. Hartshorne, M. May, and F. K. Shuttleworth, *Studies in the Organization of Character.*

[3] For example Gordon W. Allport, *Personality,* ch. 9.

[4] *The Psychology of Christian Personality.*

[5] *Dimensions of Character.*

[6] The following summary of findings was derived from information supplied by William A. Koppe, Research Associate at C.R.P., Union College, Schenectady, New York.

gartners and the questioning of parental authority among third graders. The studies of individual differences, largely through role playing, also developed methods for creating curriculums adaptable to children with a wide variety of characteristics.

In the area of youth the basic question is, How can youth be challenged to accept the responsibility for their own religious development? Through different methods it has been learned that attitudinal factors in the youth take precedence over other factors that might be thought to be equally important. Intelligence, teacher effectiveness, church denomination, and home town were found to be unrelated to religious learning and development. An active participation in the process was found to mediate growth in contrast to cases where the youth did not set goals.

The foregoing is merely a small sampling of the areas being studied and conclusions that have been arrived at in C.R.P.

Methods of Research in Religious Education

We would like here to make a few observations and to call attention to a few of the chief methods of research in religious education even though space limitations will allow us merely to mention these by name.[7] Religion itself involves values and aspects far beyond those accessible to social scientific study. Yet this does not absolve the religious educator from the duty of seeking exact answers when the questions asked are capable of being answered by precise study no matter how arduous. For example, it had always been assumed that Sunday-school instruction built character. When Hartshorne and May asked whether this was so and tested for the results, they found little evidence to substantiate it. Attendance at Sunday school did not seem to have much influence on such traits as honesty and self-control. It would seem self-evident that at least one of the pillars of the improvement of programs of religious education would be a sound program of research that would help sweep away some of the comfortable illusions of the church schools and point their programs in more creative directions.

Among the most frequently used devices are the *questionnaire* and the *interview*, both deceptively easy to construct when utilized by the untrained, whether *standardized* or *open-ended*. *Rating scales* have been used to measure religious traits and conditions, while properly devised *tests*, such as those used by Hartshorne and May, are among the more valid but correspondingly more difficult instruments of personality measurement. A test as well as other devices may be used in connection with an *experiment*, though experiments are particularly cumbersome in the field of religion, especially since it is difficult to provide for proper *controls*. Along with these methods the investigator needs to have some knowledge of *statistics*. Still other methods include the *developmental approach, projective techniques, the clinical method*, and the sociological *survey*, which may involve a number of methods. A recently developed statistical device for studying complicated aspects of personality is *factor analysis*.

It is quite obvious, even from this very incomplete list, that the religious educator interested in research requires considerable technical background and training.

[7] A survey of methods in the general field of the social scientific study of religion will be found in Walter H. Clark, *The Psychology of Religion*, ch. 3.

Religious Leadership as an Elite

In addition to the Character Education Inquiry and the Character Research Project, which have already been treated, there are a few studies of lesser scope deserving mention. Both C.E.I. and C.R.P. have addressed themselves to matters that almost completely inhere in religious education. The representative studies with which we will concern ourselves next either are extensive surveys, a part of which involve religious education and implications therefor, or are focused on the field but are much more limited in scope. They have been selected not only because they illustrate research in the field but also because their findings—as is true of any good research of this kind—seem to have important implications in practical areas.

In their book *Adolescent Character and Personality*, Havighurst and Taba report an intensive study of a few hundred adolescents by means of questionnaire, scaling techniques, case study, and other appropriate methods. As the result of this they describe five moral types into which their population seemed to fit, consisting of what they call *adaptive, self-directive, submissive, unadjusted,* and *defiant* persons. Of these the self-directive alone seemed predominantly creative and desirable. This category consisted of those adolescents who possessed positive standards within themselves and were not swayed by the prevalent standards of the group in working out moral choices for themselves. Furthermore, they often were found to be leaders and their example tended to have beneficial effects on others. Obviously this type of youth is of great importance to religious education. But, on the other hand, their numbers were proportionately very few within the total group.

One may ask whether the research has not simply confirmed what everyone knows anyway; namely, that leaders are always in the minority. The research not only described the type and gave case examples, however, but yielded quantitative estimates of the prevalence of all the five types. The issue it raises is whether or not religious education is making sufficient use of its self-directive youth. In its zeal for the democratic process, perhaps religious education has misconceived the duty of democracy to give scope to everyone. This should mean not merely the development of the majority but also increasing the scope of those who have within themselves the capacities to widen their abilities for the enrichment of all. We have no reason to doubt that the same conclusions would be reached if the spiritual as well as the moral function were considered. This might well be the subject of another piece of research. In a general way they seem to be confirmed by some of the findings of Murray G. Ross who, in *The Religious Beliefs of Youth*, reports that the overwhelming majority tend to think of materialistic and egocentric interests rather than religion when they are alone. Only a few think of religious and related problems.

Such findings point to the existence of a kind of moral *elite* and raise the question whether educational method in religion should not be less crassly "democratic" and more in line with what in the past has been excoriated as the aristocratic approach. Actually what we are suggesting is that the church concern itself not so much over the issue of democracy versus aristocracy as about that which makes for effective religious education, whatever its label may be. Building on Havighurst and Taba's conclusions, well-planned research might well provide direction to the church schools for the more efficient use of self-directive persons.

Another finding of this same study, somewhat related to the above and confirming observations of other investigators, is one to give serious pause to all religious leaders. This is that most of the youth studied seemed to be far more influenced by the behavior of their class than the teachings of their churches. At any rate their reputation for general reliability and co-operation could be more accurately gauged by their class status than by their association or nonassociation with a church. We have mentioned the fact that Hartshorne and May reported the same or very similar conclusions. This seems to indicate that for the average youth the urge to behave like his fellows in his social group is more fundamental than the urge to conform to the teachings of the church. When the *mores* of social class converged with church teaching, then behavior also tended to correspond, while when the two diverged church members were no more likely to follow the dictates of their churches then nonmembers.

An illuminating example is related in a comparison study to that of Havighurst and Taba, *Elmtown's Youth* by A. B. Hollingshead. A Methodist Church in Elmtown had two youth organizations for young women, one supported by higher and the other lower class girls. A new minister, sensitive to the very obvious denial of Christian principles implied in this arrangement, persuaded the groups to merge. In a few months the new organization was defunct through lack of attendance, and in order to revive any activity at all the traditional groups had to be reinstated.

Even when an apparent exception to the general findings was discovered, the researchers do not make it clear that purely religious considerations made the difference. A group of youth associated with the Norwegian Lutheran Church had higher reputations for desirable behavior than would have been predicted from their class status. This seemed to result in large part from the strict control of the local pastor and the high in-group morale of this church association. Social activities tended to be confined to contacts between members of the group and this exclusiveness was stimulated by activities arranged for by the church itself. Deviations from church-approved behavior were punished by sanctions which were no less severe for being social rather than always religious in nature. Deviants were ostracized by the group. Since the average church member depended so wholly upon the church for his social contacts, he had to be either exceptionally strongminded at one extreme, or else extremely weak in resolution at the other, to depart from this particular set of *mores*.

This is not to call in question the value of the service of this church to the community, which would appear to be very great. It is simply to point out that in large degree the motivations utilized are not necessarily religious but rather spring from the need for social interaction and the fear of rejection by the group. The Norwegian Lutherans in Prairie City were successful in utilizing in-group motivation to enhance moral behavior. In the other churches the youth identified themselves more thoroughly with the wider social class. The research as it is does not clearly point to the part played by religious motivation. Presumably it was there, and one suspects importantly so for certain individuals. But here is an area for further research with promise of much instruction both for the religious educator and the sociologist of religion. Otherwise the research as we have it seems to indicate the important debt that desirable behavior owes to purely social influences for which religion alone has often received the credit. A more precise understanding of the interaction between social and religious factors is needed in this area if the church is to improve its program of religious education.

The Harms Study

Still another piece of research with implications in this field illustrates the use of the projective method. This is a study by Harms [8] in which children of different ages were asked to draw a picture of God and to explain its meaning.[9] The results were then studied and classified. In brief, they indicated that children to the age of six made great use of fantasy; from six to twelve the ideas were more "realistic," being derived from what the children were taught; in adolescence they were much more varied, ranging from some ideas that were quite conventional to those of high originality. Some of the latter were surprisingly similar to esoteric religious ideas with which the children apparently had had no contact. The latter suggests the possibilities within adolescents for creative and original religious thought. The churches may well ask themselves whether they give proper scope for this creativity in the work with youth. Indeed this may be a clue as to why the youth program in so many churches seems to be missing the mark.

But perhaps an even more important aspect of Harms's study concerns the religious education of the young child. If Harms's findings are sound and religious nurture should be based on the natural bent of the child, it would seem that fantasy should play some part in religious education at the preschool period. This would call in question too much emphasis on the logical and factual at this early stage in favor of stories and myths that will appeal to the child's imagination. Certainly the exercise of this can bring a certain delight to the child at this age with an intensity he may never know again. This will help those favorable attitudes toward religion that may well prove lifelong. Another, perhaps most important consideration, is that through myths we may convey truths too subtle to be exactly described in words. This is the contention of C. G. Jung[10] and it may be questioned whether the rationalistic pendulum may not have swung too far in the cutting from many church-school curriculums the stories of religious wonder-working and marvels such as abound in the Old Testament. To delay until the child is old enough to understand the exact significance of myths may be to wait until their glory has departed. The eyes of the child grown too old may have lost their capacity to sparkle and his heart its ability to quicken. Without emotional arousal the deepest lessons of religion can never be learned. It is for this reason that the suggestive findings of Harms should be pursued with further research.

Sex and Religious Education

A very potent source of conflict among all American youth is the sexual impulse. We would expect this to be particularly keen among church youth because of the severe sanctions invoked through the agency of the church. The effects of these are variable, now strengthening the youth, now torturing him, now integrating

[8] Ernest Harms, "The Development of Religious Experience in Children," *American Journal of Sociology*, L (1944), 112-22.
[9] A summary of this study with illustrations may be found in Clark, *op. cit.*, ch. 5.
[10] *Modern Man in Search of a Soul* and *The Undiscovered Self.*

and maturing him, now overwhelming him with shame and self-doubt so that he remains a child. Rather than deal with the problem through inflexible edict, the church that wishes to participate in the moral and spiritual growth of its youth must somehow manage to understand and to steer a course between rigidity and license that will somehow allow natural potential its maximum growth. One study[11] indicated that a favorable or unfavorable attitude toward the Oxford Group (Moral Re-Armament) was linked to a favorable or unfavorable experience of the individual with respect to sex.

In general there is not very much precise information available regarding the exact scope of the problem, the extent to which the churches are or are not successful in dealing with it, or what procedures may be successful or unsuccessful in handling it. We do not know, for example, to what extent quality of leadership is a crucial element, or to what extent it is the way in which the leadership conducts itself, even though we may be reasonably certain that both of these factors deserve our attention.

What we do know is that at least some departure from approved sexual *mores*, particularly with respect to masturbation, afflicts a large majority of all youth and that intense guilt feelings are almost equally widespread. We also are quite sure that the church owes it to any particular youth to release him from an excessive amount of guilt by acquainting him with the fact that he is not alone in his struggle. By restoring him in this way to his sense of community, much like Jesus with the woman at the well, the church may free the youth from the preoccupation with thoughts of sex and the consequent distraction that robs him of his sense of purpose. At the same time the self-respect thus gained should free him from the compulsive urge to follow the crowd in everything it does and so allow him to develop his true moral and spiritual self.

Obviously research will be difficult in this area, but its importance is clear.

Crisis Conversion and Religious Education

Crisis conversion has alternately attracted and repelled religious scholars. A whole-hearted acceptance never has seemed quite respectable to them in view of the popularity of evangelistic excesses with certain lower class elements. Also the average middle- and upper-class religious educators do not know quite how to encourage conversion and at the same time to insure uniformly wholesome results. Hence gradual religious growth is assumed in most educational theory, and there has been little systematic investigation of sudden conversion in recent times that has made any impact on Christian education.

Yet the dramatic and effective changes in personality that occasionally occur, from early historical times to the present, compel some attention to the phenomenon. The last extensive study of conversion was undertaken by E. T. Clark and published in 1929.[12] This was a study chiefly of college students, of whom fewer than 7 per cent reported conversion of dramatic suddenness. Hidden away in the report, however, is the fact that sudden conversion is reported at least six times more frequently by religious workers than by others.[13]

[11] Walter H. Clark, *The Oxford Group: Its History and Significance.*

[12] *The Psychology of Religious Awakening.*

[13] See pp. 113 and 115; also see my commentary on Clark's figures in my *The Psychology of Religion*, p. 214.

This would seem to imply two things; first, that crisis conversion may often produce more permanent results religiously speaking; second, that more study of conversion is needed to see whether this is accurate. In the present state of dearth of religious personnel—particularly in the field of Christian education—if it is conversion that produces a large percentage of effective workers, it should be known, along with what other information we can gather as to the conditions under which conversion produces wholesome results.

United Presbyterian Family Research Project

In addition to the work in progress under the auspices of C.R.P. already described, there is one other important ongoing development in the field of research about which readers will wish to be informed. This is an extensive project of research into family religious education sponsored by the Board of Christian Education of the United Presbyterian Church in the U.S.A.[14] After thorough preparatory work, questionnaires were sent to pastors on their ministry to families, while interviews have been held with over a thousand parents, supplemented with questionnaires. To this information has been added interviews with psychologists, teachers, public health workers, and others who work in the field of family education. These data will lead to action research in pilot experiments to test program possibilities for a new kind of family education. A full report of the project is expected to be in print by 1960 or 1961.

Religion and Research

As a kind of footnote to this chapter we would like to finish with a few comments for the religious educator. The philosophy of the researcher has been that of positivism. In brief this assumes a strict cause and effect relationship between a phenomenon and that which originates it, the originator being tangible and usually measurable. The positivist emphasizes the point that nature is lawful and therefore completely predictable if all were known, so that free will is ultimately an illusion rather than a fact. For the purposes of research such assumptions often seem necessary, at least in the present state of social science.

The religiously committed investigator may not wish to carry such a philosophy over into other areas of his life. Furthermore, he may become concerned when he reflects that that to which a person gives the major portion of his energies may become his philosophy and his religion. The positivistic commitment, to many a social scientist, constitutes a kind of substitute for religion. That complete knowledge may lead to perfect prediction and therefore to perfect control is the faith that drives the latter to the discipline of many long hours of tedious and painstaking labor. It is to this labor that we owe much scientific advance, and religion will do well to make more use of it in the field of religious education.

At the same time that the religious educator does so he will want to guard against the danger of selling his birthright for a mess of materialistic pottage. Despite recent signs of improvement here [15] social science remains the least religious of all the academic disciplines. It is perhaps at this point that religion may be of

---

[14] Thanks are due to John Charles Wynn, Director of the Office of Family Education Research, Witherspoon Building, Philadelphia 7, Pa., for supplying information on the project.

[15] For example, see Gordon Allport, *Becoming: Basic Considerations for a Psychology of Personality.*

service to social science by remaining itself and in suggesting a richer concept of man that may ultimately lead to more productive science. Both social science and religion stand to gain from the closer contacts that expanded research in the field of religious education will involve. In the resulting interaction the religious researcher will wish to contribute his insights to the solving of mutual problems. This chapter has attempted to suggest some ways in which research has been and may continue to be of help.

Bibliography

Allport, Gordon W. *Personality*. New York: Henry Holt and Company, 1937.

————. *Becoming: Basic Considerations for a Psychology of Personality*. New Haven: Yale University Press, 1955.

Clark, Elmer T. *The Psychology of Religious Awakening*. New York: The Macmillan Company, 1929.

Clark, Walter Houston. *The Psychology of Religion*. New York: The Macmillan Company, 1958.

————. *The Oxford Group: Its History and Significance*. New York: Bookman Associates, 1951.

Harms, Ernest. "The Development of Religious Experience in Children," *American Journal of Sociology*, L (1944), 112-22.

Hartshorne, Hugh; May, Mark; and Maller, Julius B. *Studies in Deceit*. New York: The Macmillan Company, 1928.

————. *Studies in Service and Self Control*. New York: The Macmillan Company, 1929.

Hartshorne, Hugh; May, Mark; and Shuttleworth, F. K. *Studies in the Organization of Character*. New York: The Macmillan Company, 1930.

Havighurst, Robert J. and Taba, H. *Adolescent Character and Personality*. New York: John Wiley and Sons, Inc., 1949.

Hollingshead, A. B. *Elmtown's Youth*. New York: John Wiley and Sons, Inc., 1949.

Jung, Carl G. *Modern Man in Search of a Soul*. New York: Harcourt, Brace and Company, 1923.

————. *The Undiscovered Self*. Boston: Little, Brown and Company, 1958.

Ligon, Ernest M. *Dimensions of Character*. New York: The Macmillan Company, 1956.

————. *The Psychology of Christian Personality*. New York: The Macmillan Company, 1937.

Ross, Murray G. *The Religious Beliefs of Youth*. New York: Association Press, 1950.

Chapter 8

Public Education and the Teaching of Religion

Rolfe L. Hunt

PUBLIC EDUCATION IS IMPORTANT TO THE RELIGIOUS EDUCATOR. MORE THAN nine out of ten children attending a Sunday school or youth group sponsored by a church attend a public school. Nearly all Jewish children and more than half the children of Roman Catholic homes attend the public school. The religious educator must therefore be aware of the experience of the child in the public school as he makes plans for religious education. Further, because the public school serves also children of parents not interested in religion, it helps set a total community climate in which the children from the various denominational groups live and move. Nearly everything the church in the United States projects in the way of an educational program must be considered in the light of what has happened and will happen in the public schools.

The religious educator will therefore wish to attain familiarity with the public school curriculum, practices, and personnel to increase his efficiency in religious education. The religious educator further has an opportunity to influence public education in the direction of his purposes to the extent appropriate to his role as a citizen in the community.

Public Schools Serve Some Purposes of Religious Education

Public schools in the United States contribute to the purposes of religious education in many ways. Within the Jewish tradition, education is sometimes described as pursuit of truth as a religious duty to the God of truth. The teacher in the classroom is seen as a priest handling truth which is of God. The teacher is entitled to reverence, the pupil to respect, for these are religious roles. Christians share this tradition.

The Massachusetts State Legislature said in 1647:

It being one chief project of that old deluder, Satan, to keep men from the knowledge of the Scriptures. . . . It is therefore ordered, that every township within this jurisdiction . . . of fifty house-holders, shall . . . appoint one within their town to teach all such children as shall resort to him to read and write:

Then as now, Protestant Christians wished to make sure that every person learned to read, in order that each might read the Bible and know for himself the word of God which may reach him through the Bible. When a public school teaches a child

87

to read, it is serving one purpose of religious education. Still valid is the religious impulse to teach reading.

To the extent that a public school prepares a person to earn a living, it is serving a purpose of religious education. For our scripture says that he who eats must work. Because of our religious faith, we would prepare each person to contribute to the economic process more than he takes from it. It is more blessed to give than to receive. To the extent that public schools prepare a person to serve well as a citizen, they serve a purpose of religious education. Christians have a religious duty to be good citizens in the state. We are told to render unto Caesar that which is Caesar's. To the extent that public schools help children learn social skills, learn to live together, public schools serve a purpose of Christian education. For Christians are told to be a leaven in the world.

Our Christ said he came to bring life more abundant. As the body of Christ, the Church seeks to do the same. The public school serves this purpose of the Church by anything it does to awaken and enrich life, to develop for the common good any talent of any individual. Opportunities to develop the body and its muscles; to develop talents of art, music, academic or intellectual talents; or the genius of the kitchen stove and the hammer and the saw—all such opportunities in the public school are by so much a contribution to our religious desire to help each person become the best person he can be.

Ethics and morals are taught in good public schools, which is in keeping with the purpose of religious education for the growth of individuals toward worthy character. Good public schools provide an opportunity for students to learn something of the role of religion and religious institutions in our culture and history, transmit some information about religious ideas and institutions through the study of history, literature, music, and art. Good public schools do these things better than do poor public schools. The religious educator who is aware of such contributions as the foregoing of public schools to purposes of religious education will wish to make sure the public schools of his community are well financed, well equipped, well staffed.

A Child Has a Right to an Education

The Universal Declaration of Human Rights approved by the General Assembly of the United Nations in 1948 expresses ideals of the peoples of the world today. Article 26 is devoted to education, as follows:

1. Everyone has the right to education. Education shall be free, at least in the elementary and fundamental stages. Elementary education shall be compulsory. Technical and professional education shall be made generally available and higher education shall be equally accessible to all on the basis of merit.

2. Education shall be directed to the full development of the human personality and to the strengthening of respect for human rights and fundamental freedoms. It shall promote understanding, tolerance and friendship among nations, racial or religious groups, and shall further the activities of the United Nations for the maintenance of peace.

3. Parents have a prior right to choose the kind of education that shall be given to their children.

Christians, who see in every person one for whom Christ was willing to die, one whom God loves, agree that every child has a right to an education. Then comes the question, Who is to teach the child?

The Right to Teach

One answer to the question, "Who has a right to teach?" is given above: "Parents have a prior right to choose the kind of education that shall be given to their children." The insertion of this sentence into the Declaration came about partly as the result of experiences of parents under totalitarian governments. The Nazi government in Germany, for example, operated schools in which children were taught that their first duty was to the Fatherland and to the leader Hitler. Nazi teachers turned children against their parents and their churches, taught children to spy and testify against their parents to help send them to concentration camps and death.

A deeper experience lies under the truth that parents have a right to teach their children. The helpless infant comes into the home to the care of the parents. The law of nature supports the right and duty of parents to teach. The family, say Jews and Christians, is God's plan for the education of the child in his tender years. The law of Moses enjoined parents to teach diligently their children (see Deut. 6:6-9), with suggestions for method still useful. Christian parents are told to bring up their children in the discipline and instruction of the Lord (Eph. 6:4).

Both individual Christians and the Christian Church see as their own the charge of Jesus to "Go therefore and make disciples of all nations . . . teaching them to observe all that I have commanded you" (Matt. 28:19, R.S.V.). The Christian Church sees itself as commissioned to teach by its founder. All Christians, individually and collectively as a church, have a responsibility for the education of all children. The Golden Rule and the parable of the judgment reinforce this duty of the Christian. God sees as done to him whatever is done or not done even to the least of our brethren. If we love our neighbor as ourselves, we will seek for the child of our neighbor the good things we seek for our own.

Some parents are not able to take care of their children by reason of illness or death. Some parents fail to take care of their children's education through ignorance or indifference. On occasion, the right of the child to an education must be defended even against his own parents. Who then will pick up the responsibility? Individual Christians and the Church surely will, and the State will also.

In Christian doctrine, the State is of God as truly as is the Church. For the limited purposes which the State rightfully serves, it is entitled to obedience and co-operation from Christians. As the organized society for the maintenance of order, the State has a stake in the education of the child. Fellow citizens have a right to assurance that an elector will be qualified to cast an intelligent ballot to determine the welfare of all.

Society has a right to try to insure adult persons able to participate in the economic and political life of that society. The society has a right to survival, which means transmission of a culture and training of citizens in national defense. The State, meaning political organization at local, state, and federal levels, operates to meet these responsibilities, which spell out a right to teach for the State.

Parents, the Church, the State, all have a right to teach—a duty to teach. So is secured the right of the child to an education! In a democratic society such as ours, the right to teach is not limited to these, but is freely acknowledged to voluntary associations of all kinds and to business and industry. No one of these rights is absolute; each must take its place in relationship to the rights of others.

Can Teaching Be Delegated—Divided?

The Christian parent has a right and a duty to teach his children. Must he do the teaching entirely in person, or may he delegate part of his responsibility to others? May he participate in a co-operative endeavor in education, either in Church or State? Facing the responsibilities of making a living in our society, most parents see part of their tasks of education best done by co-operation and delegation.

The Christian Church has a duty to teach also. Must the Church do this teaching only through its own schools, or may it choose a co-operative channel for such parts of the task it thinks can well be delegated? In the United States most of the churches answer "Yes," and advise parents of their constituency to participate in support of public schools for all the children of all the community, for learning in tool skills. To these common schools also they have chosen to delegate shared responsibility for such things as ethics and manners, preparation for citizenship, and vocational competence.

The State also divides its responsibility. It permits its need for a trained citizenry, indicated by the laws for compulsory education, to be met by many children in schools not under state control but operated by private individuals and voluntary associations, including churches. The State requires that standards of health and safety be met in these schools and assurance of a curriculum adequate to meet its minimum needs and the basic rights of the child citizen.

The Christian parent and the Christian Church supplement the education of the common schools by teaching those things which cannot be taught in the school operated by the State and attended by persons of many faiths and no faith. Illustrative of these requirements are church doctrine and history and growing participation in the fellowship of the church. Churches attempt to do this teaching through parental instruction, through Sunday schools, weekday schools, children's and youth groups, and vacation schools and camps.

Can the educational task be thus divided, with literacy and civic training entrusted to one school and instruction in religion to home and Church? The question is sometimes reversed, to ask, "Is a monopoly in education anywhere good for the education of a child?" Since finite man can never fully understand the infinite God and his ways, is not that educational process best which permits growing persons to share and compare their respective insights?

Our wisdom is not sufficient to give adequate answers to these questions. To the extent that statistics of church membership and finances answer, note that all-time records in the United States have been reached for Protestant, Catholic, and Jewish religious institutions under a system by which children of all faiths attended a common school.

What May a Common School Teach?

When the legislature of Massachusetts passed the law of 1647 establishing public schools for religious reasons, it was acting in a theocracy, where Church was State and State was Church for most purposes. In a homogeneous community, all the members belong to the same church. In such a community, if control of the school is vested in the local community as was done in Massachusetts, the state school will not be aware of any problems in teaching religion. Teachers of the dominant faith will be chosen; the curriculum and textbooks, holidays and observances, will reflect the dominant faith. As the sociologist says, social institutions reflect the thinking of the majority of the population.

This simple society and simple community are no longer common in the United States. Thanks to technological inventions facilitating movement of people, big businesses requiring people to move, increases in population, larger school districts, and other such factors, it is a rare community today which includes representatives of only one church. Whether or not we like it, religious pluralism seems to be the prevailing condition in American society today.

The population diversity is accompanied by many other factors, such as increase in significance of government, wars, great advances in medicine, science, technology, bringing new tasks for the schools. If we grant as a given condition the expectation that the public school in each community must serve persons of more than one denomination and more than one faith, the task of the common school must be defined in terms which all can support. What does this mean for the common school's role in religious education?

Discussions of the subject, often in terms of bitter debates making newspaper headlines and court suits, show a great variety of issues. Shall the Bible be read in the common school? If so, what edition of the Bible is to be read? Shall the reading be accompanied by explanation and comment? Shall students participate in the singing of hymns, in prayer? If so, what hymns, what prayer? Does the common school appropriately mark by holidays or observances the festivals of the Christian religion while ignoring the Jewish traditions of Passover and Purim?

Just as the Bible gives little guidance on how Christians can meet their responsibility to teach, so old constitutions and old laws give little guidance on answers to such questions. Advocates find in the ancient writings evidence to sustain opposing views. Public-school systems developed long after the Constitution of the United States was written, yet that document must serve to determine policies for the public schools today.

The Legal Situation

"The Congress shall pass no law respecting an establishment of religion, nor prohibiting the free exercise thereof," says the First Amendment to the Constitution of the United States. This phrase must answer many questions about how public schools shall deal with religion, though its framers never thought of public schools in connection with it. At the time of its adoption, some of the states supported established churches with tax funds.

The United States Supreme Court for the past twenty years has made applicable to the states the restrictions imposed by the Bill of Rights upon the federal government. This has been done by the court's interpretation of the Fourteenth Amendment, which reads in part as follows:

No State shall make or enforce any law which shall abridge the privileges of citizens of the United States; nor shall any State deprive any person of life, liberty, or property, without due process of law, nor deny to any person within its jurisdiction the equal protection of the laws.[1]

What is meant by "establishment of religion"? By the term "respecting"? Does the second clause, by which the government is not to prohibit, have equal weight

[1] United States Constitution, 14th Amendment.

with the first, "respecting an establishment"? These difficult questions have occasioned many divisions among the learned judges of the United States Supreme Court.

In the case of *Everson vs. Board of Education* the Supreme Court was asked whether the Constitution of the United States permitted a state to authorize children bound for nonpublic schools to ride on school buses routed to public schools. The majority of a divided court said "Yes," and included in their explanation the following:

The "establishment of religion" clause of the First Amendment means at least this: Neither a state nor the Federal Government can set up a church. Neither can pass laws which aid one religion, aid all religions, or prefer one religion over another. Neither can force nor influence a person to go to or to remain away from church against his will or force him to profess a belief or disbelief in any religion. No person can be punished for entertaining or professing religious beliefs or disbeliefs, for church attendance or non-attendance. No tax in any amount, large or small, can be levied to support any religious activities or institutions, whatever they may be called, or whatever form they may adopt to teach or practice religion. Neither a state nor the Federal Government can, openly or secretly, participate in the affairs of any religious organizations or groups and vice versa. In the words of Jefferson, the clause against establishment of religion by law was intended to erect "a wall of separation between church and state." [2]

This line of reasoning was repeated in the McCollum case.[3] The Supreme Court there ruled the federal constitution was violated by the practice in the public schools of Champaign, Illinois, of holding religious classes taught by representatives of different faith groups in the school building during hours the school was in session. In the case of *Tessim Zorach and Esta Gluck vs. Board of Education of the City of New York*, the plan of released time for classes in religion taught away from the schools was sustained. Explaining, the ruling majority opinion said in part:

There cannot be the slightest doubt that the First Amendment reflects the philosophy that Church and State should be separated. And so far as interference with the "free exercise" of religion and an "establishment" of religion are concerned, the separation must be complete and unequivocal. The First Amendment within the scope of its coverage permits no exception; the prohibition is absolute. The First Amendment, however, does not say that in every and all respects there shall be a separation of Church and State. Rather, it studiously defines the manner, the specific ways, in which there shall be no concert or union or dependency one on the other. That is the common sense of the matter. Otherwise the state and religion would be aliens to each other—hostile, suspicious, and even unfriendly. Churches could not be required to pay even property taxes. Municipalities would not be permitted to render police or fire protection to religious groups. Policemen who helped parishioners into their places of worship would violate the Constitution. Prayers in our legislative halls; the appeals to the Almighty in the messages of the Chief Executive; the proclamations making Thanksgiving Day a holiday; "so help me God" in our courtroom oaths—these and all other references to the Almighty that run through our laws, our public rituals, our ceremonies would be flouting the First Amendment. A fastidious atheist or agnostic could even object to the supplication with which the Court opens each session: "God save the United States and this Honorable Court." We would have to press the concept of separation of Church and State to these extremes

[2] Everson vs. Board of Education, 330 U. S. 1 (1947).
[3] McCollum vs. Board of Education, 333 U. S. 203 (1948).

to condemn the present law on constitutional grounds. The nullification of this law would have wide and profound effects. A Catholic student applies to his teacher for permission to leave the school during hours on a Holy Day of Obligation to attend a mass. A Jewish student asks his teacher for permission to be excused for Yom Kippur. A Protestant wants the afternoon off for a family baptismal ceremony. In each case the teacher, in order to make sure the student is not a truant, goes further and requires a report from the priest, the rabbi, or the minister. The teacher, in other words, cooperates in a religious program to the extent of making it possible for her students to participate in it. Whether she does it occasionally for a few students, regularly for one, or pursuant to a systematized program designed to further the religious needs of all the students does not alter the character of the act.

We are a religious people whose institutions presuppose a Supreme Being. We guarantee the freedom to worship as one chooses. We make room for as wide a variety of beliefs and creeds as the spiritual needs of man deem necessary. We sponsor an attitude on the part of government that shows no partiality to any one group and that lets each flourish according to the zeal of its adherents and the appeal of its dogma. When the state encourages religious instruction or cooperates with religious authorities by adjusting the schedule of public events to sectarian needs, it follows the best of our traditions. For it then respects the religious nature of our people and accommodates the public service to their spiritual needs. To hold that it may not would be to find in the Constitution a requirement that the government show a callous indifference to religious groups. That would be preferring those who believe in no religion over those who do believe. Government may not finance religious groups nor undertake religious instruction nor blend secular and sectarian education nor use secular institutions to force one or some religion on any person. But we find no constitutional requirement which makes it necessary for government to be hostile to religion and to throw its weight against efforts to widen the effective scope of religious influence. The government must be neutral when it comes to competition between sects. It may not thrust any sect on any person. It may not make a religious observance compulsory. It may not coerce anyone to attend church, to observe a religious holiday, or to take religious instruction. But it can close its doors or suspend its operations as to those who want to repair to their religious sanctuary for worship or instruction. No more than that is undertaken here.

In the McCollum case the classrooms were used for religious instruction and the force of the public school was used to promote that instruction. Here, as we have said, the public schools do no more than accommodate their schedules to a program of outside religious instruction. We follow the McCollum case. But we cannot expand it to cover the present released time program unless separation of Church and State means that public institutions can make no adjustments of their schedules to accommodate the religious needs of the people. We cannot read into the Bill of Rights such a philosophy of hostility to religion.[4]

These decisions answered particular questions asked the Court in terms that seem still to leave for determination the next particular question. The divided opinions of the justices of the Supreme Court reflect divisions found also at the state level.

Since education has often been thought primarily a function of government at the state level, state constitutions, statutes, court decisions, rulings of attorneys general, regulations of state boards and superintendents of education, must also be taken into account. The wide variety of practice and opinion will be noted in the charted summary by Don Conway.

[4] Zorach and Gluck vs. Board of Education, 343 U. S. 306 (1952).

SUMMARY STATEMENT OF LEGAL REFERENCES RELATED
by Don Conway

Legal References	Alabama	Arizona	Arkansas	California	Colorado	Connecticut	Delaware	Florida	Georgia	Idaho	Illinois	Indiana	Iowa	Kansas	Kentucky	Louisiana	Maine	Maryland
1. States in which laws prohibit public aid to sectarian institutions.	C	C		C	C		C	C	C	C	C	C		C	C	C		
2. States in which laws prohibit sectarian influence in public schools.	C		C	C	E				C					S	S			
3. States in which daily readings from the Bible are required by law.	E		S			E	S	E	E						S			S
4. States in which daily readings from the Bible are specifically permitted by statute or judicial decision.				J							S	S	S					
5. States in which daily readings from the Bible are optional with the local authority, since no legal reference to this question exists.					2													2
6. States in which daily readings from the Bible are prohibited by state law, judicial decision, or Attorney-General opinion.	E	A									J				J			
7. States in which statute or judicial opinion permit pupils to be excused from religious exercises.				J					E					S	S			
8. States in which an elective high school course of Bible study is permitted by Attorney-General opinion.	A							A										
9. States in which constitutional articles specifically encourage moral improvement.					C					C								
10. States in which instruction in morals is required by law.	S	E			S			E	S	S								S
11. States in which statutes require that teachers are to be of good moral character.																		
12. States in which the displaying of the Ten Commandments is required by law.																		
13. States in which instruction in American ideals is required by law.	E	E			S					S					S			
14. States in which sectarian influence in textbooks is prohibited by law.									E		S							S
15. States in which teaching of the theory of evolution is prohibited by law.			S					6										
16. States in which law specifically prohibited the use of religious tests as qualifications for admission to public schools of students and/or teachers.	C			C				C										
17. States in which released time for religious instruction is permitted by law or by Attorney-General opinion.					E						7	S	A		S			S
18. States in which the use of public school property by religious groups is permitted by law.					9	10	E				J	S						11
19. States in which the use of public transportation to private and parochial schools is permitted by law.					A	12								S				
20. States in which statutes permit pupils to be excused from hygiene classes or physical examinations for religious reasons.					E			S										
21. States in which statute, judicial decision or Attorney-General opinion permit pupils to be excused from the salute to the flag for religious reasons.															J			
22. States in which judicial decision has stated that teachers are not public officers.	J										J				J			

Abbreviations used in the body of the chart:

C—Constitutional Article or Amendment, S—Statute, E—Educational Code, J—Judicial Decision, A—Attorney-General's Opinion.

The following notes refer to the footnote numbers in the body of the chart:

1. New Jersey statute requires daily reading from the Old Testament, permits daily reading from the New Testament, but forbids religious exercises other than reading from the Bible and recitation of the Lord's Prayer.

2. No legal reference exists in these states concerning reading from the Bible. Bible reading is optional with the local authorities.

3. Minnesota Attorney-General's Opinion permits the distribution of Gideon Bibles in the public schools.

4. Minnesota Attorney-General's Opinion permits displaying the Ten Commandments in public school classrooms.

5. Mississippi Educational Code requires instruction in the Ten Commandments.

6. Florida House Concurrent Resolution forbids instruction in the theory of evolution.

7. Illinois Judicial Decision permits released time for religious instruction, provided that the religious instruction is held apart from public school property.

8. This New York Statute was upheld by the decision of the United States Supreme Court in the Zorach Case, April 28, 1952.

TO PROBLEMS OF RELIGION AND PUBLIC EDUCATION[5]

Massachusetts	Michigan	Minnesota	Mississippi	Missouri	Montana	Nebraska	Nevada	New Hampshire	New Jersey	New Mexico	New York	North Carolina	North Dakota	Ohio	Oklahoma	Oregon	Pennsylvania	Rhode Island	South Carolina	South Dakota	Tennessee	Texas	Utah	Vermont	Virginia	Washington	West Virginia	Wisconsin	Wyoming
C	S	C	C	C	C	C	C	C		C	C		C	C	C	C	C		C	C		C	C		C	C		C	C
			E	C	C					C			C			C			S	C				C				C	C
S									1								S			S									
	J	J	J		J								S	J	S							J							
				2	2			2				2					2		2	2	2			2	2		2		
								S			S	C											C			C		C	C
S			E		C	J							S																
		3																											
			C				C	C						C			C									C			
C		S	E		S	S					S		S	S	C		S		S	S				S	S	S	S	S	S
S			E	S									S			S				S				S		S	S		
		4	5										S																
S						S	S										S							S	S	S		S	S
S						S	S	S					S									S							
			E																		S								
								C	C			S					S					S	C			S		S	S
S		S									8					S	S			S					S				
S											S	J		S	S	S										A			
	S		13					14	S			C			S														
									S																			S	
A																	S												
	J		15					J					J															J	J

9. Colorado Attorney-General's Opinion prohibits use of public school property for religious meetings.

10. Connecticut Judicial Decision permits use of public school property for religious meetings, but also permits injunctions prohibiting such use.

11. Maine Attorney-General's Opinion prohibits use of public school property for religious meetings.

12. Delaware Judicial Decision prohibits use of public transportation for private and parochial schools.

13. Mississippi Attorney-General's Opinion prohibits use of public transportation to private and parochial schools.

14. New Hampshire Statute permits public transportation to private and parochial schools through the ninth grade.

15. The Nebraska State Supreme Court reversed its former ruling (49 Nebr. 755) by declaring that teachers are public officers (111 Nebr. 288).

[5] From "Religion and Public Education in the States," *International Journal of Religious Education*, XXXII (March, 1956), 36-37. Used by permission.

Most of the states have conceived it to be sound public policy to keep power over public schools as close to the people as possible. Local boards of education have been given in most states large control over curriculum, personnel, and policies of the public school. Questions as to how public schools deal with religion have been most often answered by representatives of parents elected to the local school board.

What Is Taught in Public Schools About Religion?

The variety of controls just indicated makes it difficult to answer the question, "What is taught in public schools about religion?" The practice in one state may vary from that in the next. In one city, there may be differences among schools. It may even be true that what happens in a classroom in study of a given subject may be different from study of the same subject in the classroom next door with a different teacher. Only general answers can therefore be given.

1. By practices often antedating the writing of the United States Constitution, there are exercises in religion in many schools. Students and teachers frequently start the day with an act of worship, praying and singing together. Religious festivals are noted by observances or holidays.

2. Fourteen states require reading of the Bible daily, another two dozen permit it at the option of local district school boards. Bible memory passages are assigned at some grade levels in some schools. Credit is given for elective courses in Bible study at the high-school level in some schools.

3. Through teaching the regular school subjects such as history, literature, art, and music, a substantial body of information about religious institutions and ideas is transmitted to many students. Currently active in studies of how religion is relevant to the regular subjects of the public-school curriculum are professional bodies such as the American Council on Education and the American Association of Colleges for Teacher Education.

4. Ethical and moral values are taught in public schools, and in the judgment of some authorities, with some success. They invite comparison of the ethics and morals of the graduates of American high schools with the product of schools in lands where state schools teach an established religion, or with graduates of other kinds of schools in the United States.

The Educational Policies Commission, a representative professional body, says, "The American people have rightly expected the schools of this country to teach moral and spiritual values. The schools have accepted this responsibility." It suggests that public schools teach and teach well such values as:

Human personality—the basic value
Moral responsibility
Institutions as servants of men
Common consent
Devotion to truth
Respect for excellence
Moral equality
Brotherhood
The pursuit of happiness
Spiritual enrichment [6]

[6] *Moral and Spiritual Values.*

These are values common to the Judeo-Christian tradition. To the extent that they are well taught, public schools thus support church and synagogue in education. These efforts warrant support by the religious educator. The public school appropriately gives equal status to the sanctions for these values from human experience and religious faith. From our point of view, the sanctions from human experience are valid so far as they go; we do not wish to see denied other sanctions which to us are also valid.

5. The public school teaches respect for religious belief and practice. The public school encourages appreciative understanding of persons from different faiths and backgrounds, which is good preparation for life in the religiously plural American society. The varied religious backgrounds of the children provide an educational resource, as children refer naturally to different religious practices, opinions, and institutions.

6. The public school teaches the fact from history that American democracy is grounded in a religious tradition. In teaching the Declaration of Independence, for example, man is seen as a creature endowed with inalienable rights spelled out by later study of the Bill of Rights.

7. Many public schools co-operate in programs of released time,[7] enrolling as many as four million children annually according to some estimates. Such plans permit children to study sectarian religion in their normal working day, off campus, with teachers and textbooks supplied by a church or a group of co-operating churches. The principle of released time could be extended, it is suggested, to supply an hour a day for religious instruction if religious educators could use that time profitably. Perhaps school could be dismissed for an afternoon a week in certain grades. Public-school administrators have often been more willing than church authorities for such co-operative arrangements. In such situations, church educational programs must stand comparison with public schools in qualities of staff, curriculum, facilities, and equipment.

Each of the ways in which the public school deals with religion is appropriately under constant review. All policies of public institutions should bear such criticism, for eternal vigilance is the price of liberty.

Among the most cherished of our traditions are freedoms of conscience and religion. Our definition of the role of the public schools must always conserve these values. The compulsory powers of the State are not for religion to use. Our reliance upon the voluntary method has been proved wise by history.

The primary responsibility for teaching religion rests in the home, and some portions of that task can never be delegated. The family is the most effective teacher of religion. The church can help the home in its task of teaching religion, can supplement its efforts at some points. Again, portions of its task can never be delegated.

In the democratic society of the United States, governments exist to serve men. In such a society, Christians find it possible to co-operate as citizens with other citizens to achieve limited portions of their goals for the education of their children.

The Need for Further Study

Many difficult decisions on the role of the public school in religion are ahead.

[7] See ch. 21, pp. 226-32.

It would help to have objective evidence on which to base these decisions. It would help, for example, to know answers to questions like these:

1. What is the difference between the graduate of the American public elementary and secondary school and the graduate of other kinds of schools? Are there differences in command of tool skills, religious literacy, character, participation in church organizations, service to the community, success in later life, which can be attributed surely to the type of school attended?

2. What are the effects of religious exercises frequently practiced in the public school? What, for example, is the effect of hearing the Bible read daily without comment in terms of knowledge gained or other effects? What differences exist in states requiring and forbidding daily Bible reading?

3. How many children are currently enrolled in programs of released time? How do children who have had such instruction differ from those who have not? Are effects of religious instruction by released time comparable to effects of like hours of religious instruction in parochial schools and Sunday schools?

Summary

The public school is important to the religious educator. Its existence is a fact of religious significance, and as an institution it incarnates many ideals of religious faith. To the extent defined by the American people in a society including a wide diversity of faith backgrounds, the public school co-operates with home and church in their efforts to guide religious growth of children.

Bibliography

American Association of Colleges for Teacher Education, 1201 16th St., N. W., Washington 6, D. C. *Religion in Education: An Annotated Bibliography,* 1956.

———. *Teacher Education and Religion,* A. L. Sebaly (ed.), 1959.

American Council on Education, 1785 Massachusetts Ave., N. W., Washington, D. C. *Function of the Public Schools in Dealing with Religion,* 1953.

———. *The Relation of Religion to Public Education: Basic Principles,* 1947.

———. *The Study of Religion in the Public Schools, An Appraisal,* 1958.

Fairchild, Hoxie N. (ed.). *Religious Perspectives in College Teaching.* New York: Ronald Press, 1952.

The National Council of Churches, 475 Riverside Drive, New York 27, N. Y. *International Journal of Religious Education.* See special issues on this topic dated March, 1956 and May, 1958, and other articles appearing frequently.

———. *Report.* Committee on Religion and Public Education, 1959.

National Education Association, 1201 16th St., N. W., Washington 6, D. C. *Moral and Spiritual Values in the Public Schools.* Educational Policies Commission, 1951.

———. *Spiritual Values in the Elementary Schools.* Department of Elementary School Principals, Bulletin issued Sept., 1947.

———. *The State and Sectarian Education.* Research Division, 1957.

Stokes, Anson Phelps. *Church and State in the United States.* 3 vols. New York: Harper and Brothers, 1950.

Part II

Programs, Materials, and Methods
in Religious Education

Chapter 9

The Curriculum and the Church School

D. Campbell Wyckoff

THE CURRICULUM OF CHRISTIAN EDUCATION IS THE PLAN BY WHICH THE CHURCH
and home undertake to fulfill their obligations for the task of Christian nurture.
Much of education is unplanned, since its raw materials are gathered in all of
a person's relationships. Much of education is planned by the person himself, since
what he does with the raw materials, the way he educates himself, is largely a
personal and private matter. However, the schooling that a person receives helps
him to broaden his horizons, to find out what he needs to know, to learn how to
shape up his experience, and to develop the skills for effective living. Church
schools have been established because the church has such a deep interest in the
direction the person's education takes. Curriculums are developed and used by
the church to assist the person with his growth in the Christian life. The home,
where values are shared and attitudes are formed, shares responsibility with the
church school for the person's growth in the Christian life, thereby establishing a
partnership in the concern for the curriculum and its use.

The Curriculum and the Church

Christianity has a work to do, a mission to accomplish, with individuals and
cultures throughout the world in every generation. The Church, often spoken
of as the body of Christ, has responsibility for undertaking this work and mission.
The figure of the body of Christ suggests many important aspects of the
Church's life and relationships. Christ is the head, leading and directing the
Church and providing its will and purpose. Membership is of the utmost
significance, since it means being a part of the body, and at the same time indicates
the varieties of essential functions to be performed within and out from the body.

The work to be done is suggested, since the Church is Christ's body, responsible for carrying on his mission of preaching, healing, and teaching.

Christianity, then, is no impersonal force in the world, but a living body of persons—a church—undertaking a mission. In the study document *The Objectives of Christian Education*[1] the goal of the church is carefully analyzed:

> The mission of the church is to witness to the good news of God's redeeming love as revealed in the life, death, and resurrection of Jesus Christ; to hold out a continuing summons to the worship and service of God; to maintain and extend a fellowship in which persons, led by the Holy Spirit, may respond in faith to his transforming power; to help persons, both as individuals and in society, to develop such attitudes and relationships with God and one another as will lead to an increasing Christian witness through Christian life and service to human need, and to pray in word and deed, "Thy Kingdom come." [2]

The perpetuation and continuing effectiveness of a body of persons, a church, to undertake this mission requires unremitting educational effort. Part of the effort is directed toward the members, since their life of work and worship needs constantly to be renewed and strengthened. Part of the effort is directed toward the children of members, since they need to be brought up in the household of faith and attain Christian maturity. Part of the effort is directed toward nonmembers, both adults and children, so that they may come into a transforming and deepening relationship with the Christian fellowship.

The curriculum, the educational plan, is built to serve all three of these groups. The intention of those who build and use the curriculum is that members of all ages, the children of the church, and those who are not members, may become so thoroughly and effectively involved in the life, work, and mission of the church that they may have opportunity for full growth in the Christian life. The curriculum, then, not only provides instruction in the Christian faith, but is also a tool for the church to carry out its mission of communicating the gospel and making it relevant to all.

The Objective of the Curriculum

The objective of the whole educational effort of the church is also the objective of the curriculum. Indicating what most needs to be accomplished, it provides guidance on the criteria for the selection of the kinds of experience and learning activities to be included. To the degree that it is brief and to the point, it gives both the leader and the learners a clear sense of where they are going and what they ought to be doing. In retrospect, it serves as a key to the evaluation of the results that have been achieved.

Such an objective has been provided in the study document *The Objective of Christian Education for Senior High Young People*,[3] its use not being limited at all to the senior high group:

> The objective of Christian education is to help persons to be aware of God's self-disclosure and seeking love in Jesus Christ and to respond in faith and love—to the end that

---

[1] New York: National Council of Churches, n.d. See also ch. 6, pp. 74-75.

[2] *Ibid.*

[3] Quoted from *The Objective of Christian Education for Senior High Young People.* Published for the Commission on General Christian Education of the National Council of Churches. Used with permission.

they may know who they are and what their human situation means, grow as sons of God rooted in the Christian community, live in the spirit of God in every relationship, fulfill their common discipleship in the world, and abide in the Christian hope.

The Educational Plan

The educational effort of the church, bent on achieving its objective, requires a plan. The limitations of any plan for Christian education are quite obvious. We work with God in Christian education; we do not direct the effort and determine its end; our plans must serve God's purposes; the pupil himself does the learning, so that our plans must be devised in such a way as best to serve him; and our plan is a supplement to many other educational efforts that operate on behalf of the learner.

Nevertheless, the church has tried through the centuries to provide educational materials and institutions that could serve the purpose of Christian nurture. The writing and bringing together of the New Testament itself was largely for the sake of providing educational guidance for the church. The early church made much of the "catechumens"—those preparing for membership—and saw that they were given special schooling. The formation of the liturgy undoubtedly was undertaken in order not only to provide for worship but also for instruction. The annual recital of the great themes of the Christian faith in the church year has served through the years to bring these themes home to young and old. Schools for religious instruction have existed in many forms throughout the church's history. The catechisms were devised as aids for teaching the essentials of Christian faith and practice. The Sunday school, originally a school for general education with an emphasis on religious instruction, gradually became a school distinctly for Christian education. The major curriculum efforts of the recent past have been directed toward the provision of adequate Christian education materials for those of all ages (children, youth, and adults) mainly in the Sunday church school, but in many other settings within the program of church and home as well.

Current curriculum planning is being carried forward largely in terms of the "inclusive" church school. The idea of an inclusive church school is as yet in the early stages of development, but has proved to be important enough to command the attention of those responsible for curriculum. The inclusive church school incorporates in one co-ordinated plan all the educational work of the congregation for all ages, whenever it occurs. Thus it includes the Sunday church school, the weekday church school, the vacation church school, the youth fellowship, and adult groups. Protestant curriculum planning is, at present, as broad as the needs of such groups as these.

A careful distinction needs to be made at this point between curriculum and curriculum materials. The curriculum of Christian education is the church's educational plan. Curriculum materials are the resources and suggestions that are published or otherwise provided, from which that educational plan may be built in the local congregation and in the home.

Another distinction, a false one, is sometimes made between curriculum and program. The program of Christian education is, in fact, a large part of the educational plan, and is therefore indistinguishable from the curriculum of Christian education. Perhaps the most important point to be made in this connection, however, is that curriculum materials are program aids, and therefore do not stand alone.

The Scope of the Curriculum

The Christian education plan of the church and the home should be comprehensive, inclusive of the great concerns of the Christian faith and the Christian life. Any carefully conceived curriculum will attempt to state the elements of which it is built, these elements adding up to the scope of the curriculum.

Most Protestant curriculums in recent years have been built on the basis of the elements implied in the eight objectives of Christian education that emerged from the studies made by Paul H. Vieth and that were adopted by the International Council of Religious Education (now the Division of Christian Education of the National Council of the Churches of Christ in the U.S.A.). Briefly, they are God, Jesus Christ, Christlike character, Christian social order, churchmanship, Christian family, Christian philosophy of life, Bible and other materials.

Two more recent analyses have been made by denominations preparing their own Sunday church-school material. The Presbyterian Church in the U.S.A. (now the United Presbyterian Church in the U.S.A.) built its *Christian Faith and Life: A Program for Church and Home* on three themes—The Lord of Christian Faith and Life, The Scriptures in Christian Faith and Life, and The Church in Christian Faith and Life. The Protestant Episcopal Church, in the initial stages of planning for its *Seabury Series*, defined the content of its teaching in a series of books (*The Church's Teaching Series*), whose titles are indicative of the elements of the curriculum: *The Holy Scriptures, Chapters in Church History, The Faith of the Church, The Worship of the Church, Christian Living*, and *The Episcopal Church and Its Work*.

The church youth fellowships that join together in the United Christian Youth Movement generally build their programs on the basis of five themes that may be considered to be an attempt at comprehensive elements—Christian faith, Christian witness, Christian outreach, Christian citizenship, Christian fellowship.

In the search for a comprehensive curriculum for Protestantism, there seems to be a developing consensus that the curriculum shall be comprehensive (not narrow or limited), and that it shall thus take account of God, man, nature, and history. The fact is, however, that merely teaching about these matters of Christian concern does not guarantee a curriculum that is genuinely Christian. The curriculum of Christian education sees the area of God, man, nature, and history in a comprehensive way *and in Christian perspective.*

To see the whole field of relationships and experience in Christian perspective means to see it in light of the gospel of God's redeeming love and reconciling acts in Jesus Christ. To study about God is not enough; to study about man, nature, and history is not enough. The curriculum must be so constructed that the whole field of relationships is seen and experienced in light of the gospel.

The objective of Christian education cited above, used to guide the whole process of Christian education, requires a curriculum that embodies and seeks to develop this Christian perspective. The key to the objective is awareness and response, awareness of the gospel and response in faith and love, in order that all of life may be seen and lived in light of the gospel.

The scope of the curriculum of Christian education, then, is the great concerns of the Christian faith and the Christian life, the whole field of relationships seen in light of the gospel. This means experience of God, who makes himself known in the Word, the Word being mediated through the Bible and the church. As the Bible is studied, and as the church engages in the work and worship that are its mission, learners become deeply involved, and God calls them into a relationship in which they gain a new perspective on man, nature, and history.

In this new perspective, they see man as he is shown in the Word—created in the image of God, separated from God by sin, and redeemed by God's reconciling acts in Jesus Christ. This perspective on man enables learners to see the self in a new light, to understand the relationships of their common life and the responsibilities they involve, and to lay hold upon the human culture and heritage with deeper appreciation and meaning.

In this new perspective, nature is no longer seen as a purposeless mechanism, but as the cosmic setting created by God for the human endeavor. History is also viewed in a new light, not as cycles of more or less successful human effort at progress, but as a continuum in which God acts and man responds, moving from the first creative act to the consummation of God's purpose.

The curriculum for children, youth, and adults seeks to deal with these matters as completely as possible, and above all seeks to communicate the Christian perspective on the whole field of human relationships with God, man, nature, and history. This gives a unity to all that is done in the church and the home, through the whole Sunday, weekday, and vacation program.

Learning in the Curriculum

Christian education, like all of education, seeks to promote growth through learning. The educational plan, the curriculum, is thus grounded in the learning process, and is required to know and use it effectively.

On the surface there may seem to be something of a contradiction between an educational plan and the learning process, since learning is in essence an individual matter. The only really effective educational plan is the one that the learner adopts and uses as his own. As the person engages himself in finding out about his world, figuring out what it means, and adopting a stance with regard to it, he learns. Without the element of personal, existential involvement, there is no learning. This basic individuality of learning does not necessarily preclude, however, the use of some common educational plan. The curriculum stems from the attempt of the church and the home to introduce the learner to aspects of his world that he otherwise might miss. The experiences involved are definable, and the curriculum invites the learner to participate in them. Thus the integrity of his own learning is not violated, nor is the mission of the church or the message of the gospel watered down.

Actually, far from being exclusively an individual matter, the learning process is profoundly interpersonal. Learning requires that mind meet mind, and that spirits deeply interpenetrate. The fellowship of the church is an important factor in the effectiveness of Christian education. The give-and-take of groups is the heart of the matter. The sustaining solidarity of the home is a prime factor in the communication of basic life meanings. The communities in which we live influence us to adopt the values that undergird their common life. These are important factors in any education that seeks to transform attitudes and approaches to life as well as to develop concepts and skills. The curriculum of Christian education must recognize their place and include them in its plan.

The curriculum relies, then, upon the personal and interpersonal dynamics of learning. Discernible processes of learning are involved. Some learning takes place through the process of gaining insight into a problem or an area of experience. Some takes place through coming to recognize the determinative symbolic cues in a situation and finding out how to respond to them appropriately. Some learning occurs through rigorous practice of certain skills. Some comes through problem solving. Some results from association and identification with an admired person or group. The curriculum tries to use all these processes as appropriately and astutely as possible, for each of them is the clue to necessary kinds of learning, and each suggests appropriate methodology.

If learning takes place through personal effort in an interpersonal setting, then carefully defined learning tasks that stem from and are shared by the witnessing community are called for in curriculum. The curriculum consists of learning activities in which these tasks are undertaken by both individuals and groups.

In *The Objective of Christian Education for Senior High Young People* (see above), an attempt was made to define the learning tasks of the individual and the group out of which the learning experiences of the curriculum are constructed. The first learning task gives the curriculum its characteristic Christian orientation, and is directly suggested by the objective: "Listening with growing alertness to the gospel and responding in faith and love." The learning task that undergirds the curriculum with solid realism is: "Assumption of personal and social responsibility in light of the gospel." There is also a cycle of learning tasks through which the whole field of relationships is dealt with: "Exploring the whole field of relationships in light of the gospel, discovering meaning and value in the field of relationships in light of the gospel, and personally appropriating that meaning and value."

These are lifelong tasks, taking on different aspects as the person and the group grow and develop. In the curriculum the first task maintains priority, since without it the process loses its Christian focus. The curriculum, however, also seeks with the utmost seriousness to train persons to undertake the other learning tasks in light of the gospel. In this way, the curriculum seeks to drive home its essential point and at the same time seeks to influence the whole of life in the most pervasive way possible.

Organizing the Curriculum

One of the great contributions of The Study of Christian Education, summarized by Paul H. Vieth in *The Church and Christian Education*,[4] was its attempt at defining an organizing principle for Protestant curriculum. The need for an organizing principle is occasioned by the complex nature of the relationships between the scope of the curriculum and the needs of the person who is doing the learning. The task of an organizing principle is to show unmistakably how the whole scope of the curriculum may be dealt with so that the objective may be achieved. The organizing principle set forth in the study of 1946-47 may be stated in this abbreviated way: the curriculum of Christian education may be

[4] St. Louis: Bethany Press, 1947.

organized in terms of the changing needs and experiences of the individual as these are related to the scope of Christian education.

This principle served well for some years, and still contains two of the important insights on the problem. Recently, however, it has become evident that a satisfactory organizing principle for Protestant curriculum must come to grips with three factors—the developing life and responsibilities of the church as the witnessing community, the scope of Christian education, and the developing needs and capacities of the learner and groups of learners.

To the end of providing a principle that will deal integrally with all three factors, the following has been suggested in an unpublished working paper prepared for the curriculum study of the National Council of Churches of Christ in the U.S.A.:

> The curriculum of Christian education may be organized by planning to *involve learners*, with all their varied needs and developing experience, *in the church's ongoing study, fellowship, worship, work, witness, and mission*—in which they are helped to come face-to-face with the gospel through study of the Bible and through the life of devotion; see the relevance of the gospel to the understanding of all of life (God, man, nature, and history); accept the promises and implications of the Christian faith; and become committed to membership in the witnessing community and to full discipleship in the world.

The practical consequences of such a principle are that the curriculum will be rooted in the very life and work of the fellowship, while in no way neglecting the needs of the learner or the integrity of the message. Contrast this with the organizing principle of the study cited above, where the content of the curriculum is likely to be fragmented in terms of the need of the pupil, and in which the life and work of the church are by implication subjects of study rather than the organic heart of the process.

For more than three decades vigorous discussion has taken place on the basic orientation of the curriculum. Shall curriculum be subject-matter centered? Shall it be experience centered? Shall it be life centered? These and many other similar orientations have been suggested. Until the early years of this century, the curriculum had been almost exclusively content centered, and rather specifically Bible centered. Under the leadership of W. C. Bower, W. W. Charters, and Paul H. Vieth, the International Council of Religious Education in the 1920's undertook a full-scale restudy of Protestant curriculum, and began the development of an "International Curriculum of Religious Education." This curriculum never materialized, but it influenced the later direction of Protestant curriculum by establishing firmly the importance of the developing and growing experience of the pupil as the center of the process of religious education. The various curriculum guides that have been issued from time to time during the years since the abandonment of this project have kept before the churches the importance of this principle. The Study of Christian Education (1946-47) brought to the fore the issue of the relation of this principle to the church and to the Christian faith.

The present position in curriculum has been arrived at in an attempt to find an organizing principle that will do full justice to the developing needs and experiences of the pupil, the rich and normative resources of the Christian faith and the Christian life, and the dynamic and living reality of the community whose mission it is to live its life and make its witness on behalf of its Lord. Such a position attempts to catch up and integrate these ideas that have in the past seemed often to be in competition in curriculum theory and design.

Forms of Curriculum Materials

The curriculum is usually planned for specific agencies of Christian education—the Sunday church school, the weekday church school, the vacation church school, the youth fellowship, and other groups. Primary attention is given to the meetings and class sessions to be held, since it is here that the curriculum suggestions come to life. To achieve unity and sequence, however, these meetings and sessions are planned in units and cycles. The unit usually involves attention for several weeks to some one topic or problem or to some very closely interrelated set of topics or problems. The cycle is made up of from one to three years of work, devoted to several integral themes that seek to comprehend the scope of the curriculum for a given age or experience level.

The present plan for the *uniform* lessons centers upon the development of outlines which are used by denominational and other publishing houses as the basis for a "system of lessons, biblical in content, containing the principle of uniformity through including a core of common material and emphases to be developed in all age groups, but providing for a graded approach through supplementary materials and adaptations within the several age groups." [5] The outlines are developed in a six-year cycle, the major areas of biblical study being covered in each cycle. Each lesson is related to a unit that comes to grips with some portion of the Bible or some topic of biblical interest, and contains such standard material as the background scripture, devotional reading, a memory selection, and a careful development of the thought of the lesson. A church school using the uniform lessons is thus assured of consistent attention to the same biblical theme throughout the school on any given Sunday. Materials are provided for primary, junior, intermediate-senior, and young people-adult.

Closely graded lessons "are planned for those church schools which desire a program of Christian education correlated to the experience and religious needs of its children and youth, and paralleling their year-by-year growth and development." [6] Although practices differ somewhat, the most common mode of developing closely graded lessons is to provide a permanent curriculum which contains separate lessons for each grade, carefully adapted to the sequences of developing pupil need and capacity. Thus, first graders will on a given Sunday be using a different lesson from the second graders, and so on through the grades. Closely graded lessons as a rule are not prepared for groups above the junior-high level.

Cycle graded materials are prepared "for those Sunday church schools which desire lessons graded within the limitations of a brief age span." [7] A departmental basis for grading is used. A Sunday church school using cycle graded lessons will have all of its primary classes studying the same materials on a given Sunday, a different lesson for all the juniors, and so on through the departments. There is a two-year cycle for kindergarten, and three-year cycles for primary, junior, junior high, and senior high.

An interesting new development is the *broadly graded* material being prepared for

[5] *A Guide for Curriculum in Christian Education*, p. 115.

[6] *Ibid.*, p. 125.

[7] *Ibid.*

small churches, urban and rural, where there is a small enrollment with a limited number of classes. A church school having only enough members for about three classes may make good use of broadly graded material by grading according to such ages as younger children, junior and youth, and older youth and adults.

Although all denominations make their own arrangements for the production of curriculum materials, the National Council of Churches has given general guidance to the development of uniform, cycle graded, and closely graded material. It has also given attention to society topics for youth (using the themes of the United Christian Youth Movement), curriculum for older youth and young adults, weekday church-school curriculum, vacation church-school curriculum, adult curriculum, and home curriculum.

The Methodist Church provides a most interesting example of a church that seeks to meet the curriculum needs of its people in a variety of ways. Among other materials, it provides closely graded, cycle graded, and broadly graded materials from which the local church may select the most appropriate curriculum to meet its needs. Furthermore, youth fellowship materials and adult elective materials are available for use by churches in ways that fit into their particular requirements. Vast as it is, the Methodist curriculum is under constant revision to keep it up to date and vital. The published curriculum materials, as they go to the local church, are backed up by a program staff whose major task is to assist the local church in the creation of an educational plan that will be genuinely its own, and that at the same time will make the maximum use of the denominational resources at its disposal.

There are at the present time a number of noteworthy curriculum publishing enterprises. Among them are *Christian Faith and Life: A Program for Church and Home,* issued by the United Presbyterian Church in the U.S.A. The outstanding features of this curriculum are its attention to the home, and the use of uniform annual themes coupled with three-year graded cycles. Another outstanding experiment is the *Seabury Series* issued by the Protestant Episcopal Church. This series makes serious use of group processes of learning, stresses family worship services, and puts great responsibility for lesson planning upon the teacher-observer team in each classroom, while rooting itself in the Bible, the prayerbook, the hymnal, and the series of interpretative texts for adults and leaders whose titles were listed above.

The Presbyterian Church in the U.S. is presently engaged in formulating and experimenting with a curriculum that will take full advantage of the whole life of the congregation, as well as the various age groups, centering upon the principle of Christian education as an essential function of the church as the covenant community. Other denominational studies now being undertaken, which will eventuate in time in new curriculums, are those of several Lutheran bodies, the United Church of Christ, and the United Church of Canada. At the same time, the Division of Christian Education of the National Council of the Churches of Christ in the U.S.A. is studying the redesigning of Protestant curriculum, many of the results of the study to date being reflected in this chapter.

Mention should be made of a number of commercial and independent curriculums, most of which follow one of the curriculum patterns outlined above. Some of these curriculums are designed for churches of very conservative theological views, while others aim at extreme simplicity of design in order to be easily "teachable."

Using Curriculum Materials

If the curriculum materials available to the local church for use in its Christian education program reflect an educational plan that focuses upon a sound objective, uses the full scope of Christian education, involves basic learning experiences, and is organized to involve the learner's use of all the resources of the faith within the fellowship of the church as it lives its life and fulfills its mission, then the choice and use of the right materials is of the utmost importance.

How shall the church go about choosing its curriculum? How shall the curriculum be serviced? How may a full program of leadership education undergird its use? How may it be individualized, so as to meet each learner where he is? How may remedial work be accomplished? How may the curriculum be evaluated in use?

These are some of the important questions that the local church will deal with in devising its educational plan, deciding on materials, and putting them to use. What is clearly implied is the most careful and thoughtful approach to the matter on the part of responsible persons at the local level.

The local church's committee on Christian education will study and recommend curriculum materials on the basis of the degree to which they promise faithful implementation of the objective of Christian education, cover the scope of Christian education, are organized with the pupil's full involvement in the life and work of the church in mind, and promise effective results in the particular situation existing in the church. The committee usually gives priority to the curriculum materials of its own denomination.

Once curriculum materials are selected, officers, leaders, and learners must be helped to prepare for their most effective use. With their central purpose in mind, they will study the materials to see how the suggested educational plan is developed. Adjustments and adaptations will be discussed and decided upon. Changes in building and equipment that are needed for the chosen curriculum will be anticipated. Additional resources and supplies called for will be obtained.

Since most curriculums are planned on a departmental basis, the majority of churches will plan to meet in departmental groups to work out the specifics of their approach to teaching. A monthly previewing and planning session is ordinarily desirable, during which all teachers and leaders will come to see clearly the direction of their work for the coming weeks. Time ought to be spent in such meetings on review of the basic principles and foundations of Christian education as well as on the immediate task of getting ready to teach.

Groups using closely graded lessons find that departmental meetings may be easily adapted to their needs. Groups using uniform lessons sometimes meet together across departmental lines, although departmental meetings are preferable. Planning for the youth fellowship is usually done monthly in the age level cabinets of the junior and senior high fellowships. Monthly or quarterly meetings of parents are useful for helping them to plan for curriculum use in the home.

Back of this specific planning should lie conscientious and thorough use of other resources for leadership education.[8] Specific curriculum help is available in

---

[8] See ch. 25, pp. 270-80.

denominational schools, community schools, workers' libraries that are kept up to date and that are cared for by librarians alert to teachers' and leaders' curriculum needs, and magazines for the enrichment of Christian education workers.

One of the most important tasks of the teacher or leader is that of individualizing the curriculum. The suggestions that are included in the published material are necessarily somewhat general, although in most cases they are widely applicable to a variety of situations and needs. The individual teacher or leader, assisted by the appropriate supervisor, will want to study the individual needs of the members of his group carefully, and seek to adapt the specific goals, activities, and methods so as best to involve each one in the learning process. Emphasis on such individualization should be a part of every planning session.

In some cases remedial work is called for. The occasion may be the transfer of a pupil from one school to another or the enrollment of a new student in the church school. Most curriculums have certain materials for leaders that explain the chief aims and areas of content covered, so that the deficiencies in any individual's background may be easily identified. They also have certain key textbooks or reading books which may be used to bring a learner quickly up to the level of the group of which he is a member. Extra time and attention on the part of teacher, supervisor, and parents will reap a rich harvest.

Some curriculums suggest specific goals for various lessons and units. Others, while not setting them down in a definite way, give the leader help in setting such goals. The evaluation of results involves careful comparison of outcomes with these goals. Difficult as this is to do, it is important to work at it carefully and consistently. In the long run, however, the criterion for evaluation is the basic objective itself. Has growth taken place in awareness of the gospel and its specific relevance to life's concerns? Are there evidences of response to the gospel in faith and love?

Curriculum Problems

As Protestantism faces ahead, what are some of the chief problems that must be dealt with in the field of curriculum? One of the questions is that of the shape of the church school of the future. There is need for careful rethinking and redesigning of the church school, a further realization of the inclusive ideal, in order that it may perform the educational ministry of the church in a unified and integral way. This will not change the basic factors in the design of the curriculum, but will probably deeply affect the form that the curriculum takes.

As the design of Protestant curriculum is thoroughly studied in the future, the solutions to some of the problems discussed here will begin to appear. The matters of objectives, scope, learning, and organizing principle need constantly to be re-examined.

The question of methods has always been hotly debated. The debate for some time centered in the use of creative methods, while now it seems to focus upon the advisability of using "group processes" in the curriculum. In the future, studies should be made that would provide criteria for the selection of methods for curriculum that would retain the values in older methods, help to develop new methods in needed areas, and weed out methods that are nothing but fads.

Devising a curriculum that may be used in the home as well as in the church school has not as yet been very successfully done. Denominational studies and experiments are now being aimed at the solution of this problem, with the probable result that the approaches to the home may change somewhat in the future. Further painstaking work and experimentation will undoubtedly be called for before this problem is solved.

A new division of responsibility in curriculum is being sought between denominational and interdenominational agencies. While the denominations have always actually published the material, there has been co-operative development of outlines carried on through the National Council of the Churches of Christ in the U.S.A. The feeling is now current that there are even greater services that may be rendered interdenominationally in working on basic policy and design that, far from interfering, will greatly strengthen the denominations in their work.

Finally, there may come in the future a closer tie between the curriculum and the processes of leadership education that are needed to undergird it. It would be unfortunate if leadership education were to be geared exclusively to the demands of the curriculum, since leadership education has an integrity of its own in training Christian adults for intelligent and devoted service in the church's mission. Yet a more integral functional relationship that would result in practicality in leadership education and deeper understanding of the requirements for effective curriculum is urgently needed.

Bibliography

Bower, William C. and Hayward, Percy R. *Protestantism Faces Its Educational Task Together.* Appleton, Wis.: C. C. Nelson Publishing Company, 1949.

Cully, Iris V. *The Dynamics of Christian Education.* Philadelphia: Westminster Press, 1958.

Sherrill, Lewis J. *The Gift of Power.* New York: The Macmillan Company, 1955.

Vieth, Paul H. (ed.). *The Church and Christian Education.* St. Louis: Bethany Press, 1947.

———. *The Church School.* Philadelphia: Christian Education Press, 1957.

Wyckoff, D. Campbell. *The Gospel and Christian Education.* Philadelphia: Westminster Press, 1959.

———. *The Task of Christian Education.* Philadelphia: Westminster Press, 1955.

A Guide for Curriculum in Christian Education. New York: National Council of Churches, 1955.

The Objective of Christian Education for Senior High Young People. New York: National Council of Churches, 1958.

The Objectives of Christian Education: A Study Document. New York: National Council of Churches, n.d.

Chapter 10

Children's Work in the Church

Iris V. Cully

EACH INDIVIDUAL CHILD IN THE CHRISTIAN FELLOWSHIP IS COMMENDED TO THE care of the whole church, and upon all is laid the responsibility before God for his Christian nurture. Each child is called by his own name and must be seen as the unique person he is. The child is created by God and derives his personhood from this fact. He is made in the image of God and for this reason he is able to apprehend God. His freedom to grow into the fullness of himself is given by God. His choices, for good or for ill, are the gift of God who loves him and therefore frees him—for only one who is free can love and respond to the call of another. God speaks to each one, in his own time, calling him into a loving response to his holy purposes for each child's life. Each child is one for whom Christ was sent to seek and to save, one for whom he died and rose again. Sometimes a teacher looking upon a child has to remind himself of this fact. A child can cause a teacher so much trouble! Then one remembers the words of the Lord, "Take heed that ye despise not one of these little ones!" They are his and we members of his church are trustees and guardians of his own, each one infinitely precious in his sight.

The Child Himself

The child knows himself, and before he has lived very long, he is able to know other people—first those who immediately surround him—mother, father, brothers, sisters; then the occasional visitor, relative, and friend. Finally the neighborhood becomes his wider sphere, then the school, and later the whole world. He becomes able to transcend himself only because he has known himself. Those who are wise enough to help him truly know himself lay the foundations on which alone can come concern for the needs of others in the community as well as in the whole world.

The child has basic needs. This insight from psychology has become popular parlance among parents and teachers. The child needs to feel secure, but what does this mean? He feels secure only if his teacher accepts him as he is. Too often she is busy trying to make him over into what she thinks he ought to be. This does not work. If there is a person whom he ought to be, this can only be known through the growth of his own unique self in the way in which God purposes his growth. All the teacher can do is to witness to God's love through her life so that the child, seeing a Christian personality, will grow to love this person and

111

be drawn to love God. For the teacher is the mirror in whom the child sees God, the channel through whom the grace of God flows. The teacher needs to see the child himself apart from what he does—even admitting that his actions speak loudly of himself. Some actions speak of his joys, his aspirations and his loves. The teacher's sensitivity can relieve the pressures which cause the first kind of actions and strengthen the security which causes the second kind of actions. Here is the witness of Christian love, for love is the essential need of the child. The other needs spring from this prior longing.

Every child needs the assurance that he is loved, but not every teacher is able to give love all the time. Sometimes the block is within himself; sometimes it is in the child. The teacher needs to remember and to assure the child that God alone is love and that, while human love may fail and is always imperfect, God's love is our one sure hope. The child who knows this to be true will not despair even when parental love fails. He will not be disillusioned when friends turn against him. He will not forsake the church as "cold" even though the people seem indifferent. The love of God is the source of human love and God can make himself known to the child even when human beings fail to show his love.

The child also has certain developmental tasks upon which his growth depends. Only after he has learned to talk, can he make friends. Only when he has learned to walk, can he explore the neighborhood and widen his horizon. The child who is handicapped in his ability to learn these developmental tasks will have a more difficult time in his total growth. The religious life also has its developmental tasks. Only the child who has known the love of God can face the biblical view of his justice. Only the child who knows what it is to sin can have the experience of forgiveness—and be able to forgive those who wrong him. The child must first know Jesus—living, dying, rising—before he can surrender his life to him in loving obedience. The child must face the fact of death before he can know the good news that the Christian has eternal life. Meaningful research in the area of religious developmental tasks has just begun. This is an area to which more thought should be given. High school young people are confused and incoherent because the earlier tasks have not been accomplished. They have to do a lot of growing all at once and often they do not know where to begin.

The child has his own goals and purposes within which we must work. At present in almost every curriculum plan, each unit, as well as each session, begins with an explicitly stated purpose. This purpose is for the teacher. It is an illusion to suppose that this necessarily becomes the child's purpose. Even a teacher's skillful attempts to "motivate" the children in a class to accept the purpose may fail if the purpose is far from the needs, experiences, and goals of the children. This does not mean that the teacher should wander around looking for pupil goals on which to base a curriculum. It means simply that she should know the yearnings and aspirations of the children, working from that point and within that framework. The child who yearns for friends understands Zacchaeus; the young doubter echoes Thomas' question; the child with brothers and sisters understands the strivings of Jacob and Joseph.

The Child's Place in the Church

For many people the church is their only source of real community. The school is not a community to children. Attendance is required; the experiences with teacher, studies, and other children are sometimes good and sometimes dispiriting. The neighborhood is known only in terms of friends who are of the same age. The church alone links together whole families in the common bond of their allegiance to God through Jesus Christ. Whether they know it or not, people are in the church because they have been called of God and through their life in the church they are witnessing to the continuing work of his Holy Spirit.

In one aspect of its life, the church is a larger family. Those who have been members of a particular parish for many years know what this means. They have been conscious of the support of others in joy and sorrow—at baptisms, weddings, and funerals. They have worked together and prayed together. Children are a part of this fellowship and can only truly know the meaning of "church" when they feel that the adults welcome their presence in the midst. This is shown in the faces of the people whom they meet at the door. Are they greeted with a smile? It is shown in the accommodation for their classes. Are these light and attractive? It is shown in the willingness of those with special abilities to be the representatives of the whole church for teaching. These factors are more important in a child's view of the church than any visit to cellar or sanctuary or an examination of the organ and the stained-glass windows. The latter are interesting and useful, but they are not essentials of the church.

The child knows himself to be a part of the church as he participates in the worship of the congregation. The type of service is important. An elaborate liturgy holds the attention of the child through form, color, and motion. A simple service may be understood through its simplicity. The important fact is that the child is worshiping among adults and feels that he belongs here. The basic question is whether the Sunday service of worship is for the whole church or only for adult members. The child apprehends much that he cannot fully comprehend. Seated with his family or his teacher, taking part in the praise and prayer of the congregation he feels the spirit of awe and reverence which pervades the assemblage, and he knows in a new way what is meant by the word "church." Worship with his class or department may supplement this, but can never substitute for it. However, the opportunity for learning the materials and usages of congregational worship must be made in the age level class.[1]

The child also needs the opportunity of serving his church. This is difficult in a society in which so much is done for children and so little asked of them. They know the difference between "make-work" projects and meaningful activities. The small church can use the talents of children more easily than can the large one which has so many people to do its work. Children can plant seeds for a flower border or carefully raise bulbs either to beautify a room or to send to shut-ins. They can mount teaching pictures or make picture books. Juniors can plan attractive posters for entrance way or bulletin board. They can sing in a junior choir. Two or three calling on shut-ins with mother or teacher can brighten the day, making both child and shut-in know more clearly the reality of the church's fellowship.

The church lives today because it is part of a living past. The martyrs of the early centuries, the thinkers and builders of the Middle Ages, the reformers of the later centuries, all had a part in God's purposes for the life and growth of the

[1] For further discussion, cf. ch. 13, pp. 144-45 and ch. 14, pp. 157-59.

church universal. We are Christians today because they kept the faith and succeeding generations will know Christ as we keep the faith. The child needs to know these people who form the roots of the Christian community. He needs to realize that they faced problems similar to those which the Christian faces today—how to live the Christian life in a secular world, how to be faithful under persecution, how to believe in the face of doubt and skepticism. The example of those who, by God's grace, have triumphed is a source of strength to those now on the way. These are not dead, for God has given them eternal life, and they, with us, praise God who created and redeemed us all.

How wide is the church of Christ, covering all the earth and extending through the centuries! What more exciting privilege can a child have than to know that he belongs to this company!

Christian Living

Faith in Christ has always been shown through the way in which the Christian lives. For this reason training in the meaning of Christian living has been a major emphasis in the Christian nurture of children. This can only be understood in the context of "law and gospel." To be sure, the law preceded the gospel, and Paul says that the law was a schoolmaster leading him to Christ. Does this mean that we should begin by giving children the rules and helping them to keep the same? "John, it is Bill's turn with the truck now. We share our toys." "Alice, try to control your giggling. It is disturbing to the rest of us." Rules there must be, for they set the necessary boundaries within which alone real freedom can develop. The child who is given no boundaries feels lost. But we wrong the child if we give him only rules, however kindly we state them or however fairly we try to carry them out. The good news which Paul found was that Christ freed him from the demands of the Law. The Christian does not act in obedience to the Law (although this could be a joyous obligation). He acts in a freely-willed response to the love of God, shown to him in Jesus Christ his Lord. When we love a person, we do not have to be given a set of rules in order to know how to act toward that person. Love informs and teaches. When the love of God indwells the teacher, she is able so to act in understanding of the children that each knows himself to be loved. Then he does not need to get angry, to fight, to hoard toys, to make wisecracks, to pommel his neighbor—or to do any other of the hundred and one things which children do to turn a church-school class into one big discipline problem for a teacher. This change does not happen suddenly, but teachers who are patient see a change, sometimes in a few weeks, sometimes not for less than years. Occasionally outside factors preclude any permanent change, but the teacher can still surround the child with the loving concern of the church community, known through the life of a single class.

The child faces ethical problems in daily decisions. If spelling is difficult for him, should he cheat? Everyone else does. A friend asks him to whisper the answer. Should he do it? After all, this is friendship. The class is giving a substitute teacher a difficult time. Should he join the fun? What will the rest of the class say if he doesn't? Everyone avoids the new girl because she is fat. Dare someone befriend her—under threat of being labeled "queer"? When one fails to meet the deadline for arrival home, should he admit he forgot to watch the time—or lie out of it? After all, mother has ways of getting out of invitations she doesn't want to accept.

Some decisions affect only the individual's own peace; others might cut him off from the crowd of which he so desperately needs to be a part.

What answer can the church-school teacher give? How comforting it would be to rest back on the rules. "A friend loveth at all times" (shall I give my friend the answer?). "Love one another" (how can I love the child my father ridicules because of his accent?). "Be kind to one another" (but they won't let me be kind; they laugh and call me "sissy"). The Bible is not a rule book for all people. It is a guidebook for those who live under the covenant of God's redeeming love. Only the grace of God can enable one to act as a Christian under all circumstances. The child who is taught to try hard will only end by being discouraged. The radiantly joyous Christian life is for those who are indwelt by the Holy Spirit. The child needs the assurance that he is never completely alone, for God is with him. He can be encouraged to hope that usually his friends, seeing his faith and courage, will not cut him off forever but will recognize the justice of his actions when he stands up for that which he knows to be right. The insecure child needs the comfort of the crowd in every circumstance. The child who is loved can stand alone if necessary.

These are the elements involved in the child's witness to his faith in terms of everyday living. Another area is to be found in the invitation to others to participate in the life of the church. A teacher in a suburban Sunday church school made this suggestion to a class, only to be met with the puzzled reply, "But everyone in our school already goes to church!" There are, however, some areas in which this is not true; notably in rural sections and in the "inner" city. The Christian is eager to share the good news with others, and one way in which he can do so is to invite them to go with him to church. Teacher and children together can discover that the experience of welcoming the stranger and making him feel at home is not simply a theoretical matter to be explored in stories.

There is also the situation in which the child is rejected because of his faith. It is silly to go to church school; it is absurd to give up a ball game because one has choir practice; it is ridiculous to go to a weekday group instead of being on the playground. These pressures occur more often in the city than in suburbia. The child needs stories of Christians through the generations who have stood firm in the faith with courage and conviction, and he needs the surrounding understanding of a Christian community which upholds him and says "well done." For the child who is growing in his ability to practice his faith both in ethical example and in open loyalty is developing in the fullness of the Christian life.

The Child in Relationships with Others

The Christian faith has rarely been lived in solitariness. The child whom we meet in the church school apprehends the faith largely in terms of the people who make up the associations of his life. The most immediate relationships are those of his family. The family imagery is used often in the Bible and so we rightly use it within the context of Christian nurture. All children experience love (or rejection) first from their parents. Many children learn of God first from their parents. The church school builds on the knowledge and experiences gained in the home. The give and take of everyday living is learned as the child lives with brothers, sisters, or grandparents in his own home.

If these relationships are to be seen in Christian perspective, the church-school curriculum will need to reflect life as it is in the family. There are love and jealousy, unselfishness and selfishness, helpfulness and resentment. The hard necessity for understanding the reconciling power of the Christian faith in terms of repentance, forgiveness, and renewal must come through the work of the church. This suggests that curriculum units shall not confine themselves to such specific out-ward experiences as "helping at home," "the family worships together," or "mother works for all of us." Rather, the child needs to be able to explore, with teacher and other children, his feelings about the work he is asked to do, his attitude toward the younger child, and positive ways in which he can face the fact that sometimes we hurt the people we most love.

A fourth-grade class was asked in an introductory session, "Have you brothers or sisters?" Each one cheerfully enumerated the family connections, and it was universally apparent that older brothers and sisters could do no wrong—even when they imposed upon the younger one. Younger brothers and sisters were greatly resented because they were always "getting away with anything." Small wonder that in the biblical stories, they "sided with" the elder brother rather than the prodigal son, and with the eleven rather than Joseph. A realistic curriculum outlines units of study in terms of where the child is, rather than in terms of what it is hoped he ought to be.

As soon as he is old enough for church school, the child meets the teacher, and a whole new area of relationships is established. The teacher, like the parent, becomes the bearer of the Christian witness. This can be difficult for the teacher. It demands that he be loving, even when he has to be firm; that he continue to love the child even when he is frantic lest the whole class be disrupted; that he understand why a child acts as he does, even when he knows that the actions are wrong. He needs to have an understanding and love of children; an ever-increasing knowledge of material, methods, and resources for the class session; and a deep Christian faith which is affirmed by all that he does. This does not mean that he should be perfect, but rather that he should be able to admit without anxiety that he is not perfect. This in itself makes teaching less of a strain and gives the teacher more assurance. The Christian teacher is the one often privileged to lead the child to Christ. What he says about God can, by the grace of God, show forth the love of God. The teacher is the representative of the Christian community to fulfil the responsibility of the whole church for the nurture of the children. This is a difficult task, often enough, but a rewarding one, as thousands know. Ask any group of adults about their Sunday church-school memories and more often than not these are in terms of teachers.

The third group with whom the child forms relationships is that of other children. These include his brothers and sisters, his neighborhood friends, his classmates at school, and those at church school. He needs friends, and he is frightened when he feels alone. In the informality of the church-school class the concerns of these relationships can be explored, both in terms of being friends and of having friends. How do we feel toward a newcomer? Why do some children seem "odd," and what can we do for them? The child who has explored his own feelings is better able to reach out toward another child. Often enough the place where fewest personal relationships are experienced is in the church school. Here children meet once a week for only a brief period. Sometimes they come from many neighborhoods and many schools, with no further associations. They can be together for months without even knowing one another's names. The teacher finds it a perplexing task to make the meaning of Christian fellowship real within this framework. A constant use of names helps outward identification. Working in small groups promotes acquaintance. A free sharing of concerns, ideas, and attitudes brings an awareness of one another. The teacher's—and the class's—handling of difficult situations is an indication of the degree to which understanding and forgiveness and wisely channeled activities can help the child to grow in ways which will make clear to him the purposes of God and the reality of the Christian fellowship.

The Purpose of Methods

The teacher, having a practical necessity each Sunday morning, tends to see children's work largely in terms of the methods and materials through which she can put together her session. She is aware that her purpose is so to nurture children within the Christian Church that they will freely and joyfully accept the lordship of Christ in their lives and witness to this fact through daily living and their incorporation into the life of the Church. This is not necessarily the goal or purpose of the child as he comes Sunday to Sunday. He probably has no long-range purpose—he is sent by his parents. Only as he finds a meaningful place within the church will he have any inkling as to the existence of further goals or any desire to participate in them.

For this reason, the first step in teaching is to help the child to identify himself with the people who have been or are today participants in the saving grace of God. He needs to understand how Moses felt when he hesitated before the difficult task laid upon him; how Jeremiah felt, rejected by his people; the yearnings of the people who sat before Jesus as he taught or who beseeched him for pardon and for healing; the response of Andrew, called to be a disciple. Such participation comes largely through the arts. Storytelling is the one most universally used, and the teacher who increases her ability finds her class absorbed. The Bible itself, with its condensed storytelling often conveys its own message better than do our elaborations. Older children will enjoy books which introduce a fictional character who takes part in biblical events.

Drama[2] is another way of participation, for here the child actually takes a role. This may happen by reading "parts" from a story in the Bible. A story may be acted out, the children making up conversation. Play reading, taking an episode from a great religious play, is possible with older children. Role playing is a form of dramatics in which the children act out the possibilities in a contemporary situation. Sometimes an open-ended story introduces a situation but leaves the solution to the reader. The class proceeds to act out several different endings. An incident mentioned in class conversation may have possibilities. "What might you do if your younger brother took your favorite toy?" Sometimes the use of hand puppets is less "threatening" than direct role playing, for the child prefers to project himself into this simple figure. Even primary children can use stick puppets or bag puppets.

Poetry is a method of participation because it is always the personal expression of the experience of the writer. Great poets have written for children and the

[2] For further discussion, cf. ch. 19, pp. 205-9.

growing faith of today's children can be enriched through the hearing of their words. Similarly, music voices the deepest expression of the Christian faith. Often the hymn writer can say what we would like to say in words more satisfying to us than our own would be. It is his expression of the experience which helps us to speak. The child needs opportunities to learn and to use the great hymns of the church—both words and music—from the earliest years. Too much of the music written for children is vacant of true melody or meaningful words. Traditional carols and contemporary organ and cantata music are diverse and vivid expressions of Christian witness which should be used in the church school. Listening to music and making music are both useful methods.[3]

Although pictures—as well as projected visual materials—have been used for many years with children, the possibilities for the use of great art have hardly been explored. The artist sees deeply into life's experiences and conveys emotions more than facts in his work. The great photographer does this too, and the child who can look at such pictures has a realistic view of the Christian faith. The simplicity of early Christian art, the glowing colors of Byzantine mosaics, the richness of Renaissance detail, the subdued tones of Rembrandt's biblical canvasses, the starkness of contemporary art, point to many possible paths of exploration with children.

We cannot leave teaching simply in terms of participation, however. For what purpose is the child to participate in the experiences of those who are seeking faith or of those who are witnessing to what God has done for them? His participation is in order that he may see himself in their position and understand the decision which they have made. Through picture, music, drama, story, and above all through the words of the Bible, he encounters God. He hears himself called by God and is enabled to answer as each individual Christian has always answered, accepting the call and putting his whole life in the hands of God, his Savior. The outward manifestation of this action is to be found in confirmation, or being received into the membership of the church. Yet it can also be said that God calls the child in daily relationships and in everyday decisions—and, by his grace, enables the child to respond in Christian terms. His Christian faith ceases to be only a reflection of the religion of parents and teachers. He takes it upon himself and it becomes his faith.

Only at this point will the child be able to communicate his Christian faith to others. How can we express that which is not meaningful to us? This is why the kindergarten child cannot draw the pictures we ask of him, or why the primary child seems to have a distorted idea of the Bible. Let his work remind us of what he has not yet learned, as well as showing us what insights he has gained. "Creative" activities are an expression of the child's own understanding. He may paint a picture, draw a sketch, design a poster, write music, a story, a letter, a prayer, or express it in role playing. (We have tended to lay great stress on visual representation and very little on the written expression. Perhaps greater balance is needed here.) These suggestions do not preclude the use of constructive activities by which the child is helped to understand the environment of study—making scenes and dioramas, for instance. These serve another, and useful purpose. These activities give the child the opportunity to express what the Bible has said to him,

[3] For further discussion, cf. ch. 19, pp. 209-13.

what the gospel has meant to him, and how he understands Christian faith and action.

A Look Ahead

It cannot be said that every denomination and each local church is aware of all these facets in the approach to children. Although there is wide knowledge of the basic needs of the child—primarily those of love and acceptance—teachers, being human, still find it difficult to work with individual children. The curriculum may suggest methods that will bring satisfaction to some but only frustration to others. The unhappy depths of the child's life in crises are largely avoided. The stresses of the first year at school are mentioned only in the introduction to a teacher's guide. The tensions in changed (even temporarily) family relationships, the problems of adjustment in a new community, need to be explored in order to give support to some children. At the same time the rest of the group may have differing concerns.

Basic understandings about the relationship between law and grace and the application to children's work call for renewed thinking. Seldom does God treat anyone as he deserves, yet we guide children gently but firmly along the path of law. Relationships with other children are based on a sense of "ought," while psychological insights warn that changed behavior results only when the causes of hostility have been removed or the feelings channeled. Teachers who are sensitive to the working of God's Spirit and aware of the way in which children grow guide them through loving understanding.

A real effort is being made to relate the child to the whole life of the church. More churches are encouraging the family to attend at least part of the morning service together. There is a stronger emphasis upon religious nurture as the function of the whole parish. Yet children are often segregated so completely, whether in the new educational wing or in the basement, that the devoted work of many teachers goes unnoticed. Few churches have found meaningful service—apart from the choirs—through which children can express their part in the work of the church. At the same time, the teaching experiences are so rooted in the present that children rarely know their Christian past as "remembered history." The heroes of the faith and the climactic events of the past nineteen centuries are kept "in their place" and the child seldom realizes this is the story of his own family and that he is part of these happenings.

Methodology has come a long way in twenty-five years. It is now time to ask the difference in function between "creative" and "constructive" activities. When a class studies the surroundings of early Hebrew life, they "construct" a desert scene. This helps them to become involved in the situation in which Abraham lived. When they tell in word or picture what is meant by the New Testament comment, "By faith Abraham, when he was called to go out into a place which he should after receive, . . . obeyed," they are thinking of the meaning of these events. Such interpretations are their effort at communicating the Christian faith. Each type of activity is important in its own place in the learning process.

Every generation faces a somewhat changed context for living from that which preceded. Therefore although it may be safe to say that human nature does not change and that the gospel is always good news, children will be making differing responses within varied environments. This is why educational theories and practices inevitably vary. Past work met the needs of a particular generation, and gave insights on which to build for the future, but it cannot provide the entire framework.

Children's work today revolves around certain understandings in child development, the insights of contemporary biblical theology, and an awareness of the church as an environing fellowship. Thus the rewarding work of guiding the Christian nurture of children continues, ever-changing, and ever-renewed.

Bibliography

Bro, Margueritte Harmon. *When Children Ask*. Revised edition. New York: Harper and Brothers, 1956.

Brown, Jeanette Perkins. *The Storyteller in Religious Education*. Boston: Pilgrim Press, 1951.

Cully, Iris V. *The Dynamics of Christian Education*. Philadelphia: Westminster Press, 1958.

Hartley, Ruth E. and Goldenson, Robert M. *The Complete Book of Children's Play*. New York: Thomas Y. Crowell Company, 1957.

Heron, Frances D. *Kathy Ann, Kindergartner*. Nashville: Abingdon Press, 1955.

Hymes, James L. *Teacher Listen: The Children Speak*. New York: Committee on Mental Health of the State Charities Aid Association, 1949.

Jenkins, Gladys; Shacter, Helen; and Bauer, William. *These Are Your Children*. Chicago: Scott, Foresman and Company, 1949.

Keiser, Armilda. *Here's How and When*. New York: Friendship Press, 1952.

Lobingier, Elizabeth M. *Activities in Child Education*. Boston: Pilgrim Press, 1950.

Parkhurst, Helen. *Exploring the Child's World*. New York: Appleton-Century-Crofts, Inc., 1951.

Schultz, Florence. *Summer with Nursery Children*. Boston: Pilgrim Press, 1959.

Sherrill, Lewis J. *The Struggle of the Soul*. New York: The Macmillan Company, 1951.

Ward, Winifred. *Playmaking with Children from Kindergarten through Junior High School*. Second edition. New York: Appleton-Century-Crofts, Inc., 1957.

Whitehouse, Elizabeth S. *The Children We Teach*. Philadelphia: Judson Press, 1950.

Yeaxlee, Basil A. *Religion and the Growing Mind*. Greenwich, Conn.: Seabury Press, 1952.

Chapter 11

The Churches' Ministry to Youth

Donald O. Newby

WHILE THE CHURCH HAS ALWAYS MINISTERED TO YOUNG PEOPLE WITHIN THE framework of the family and society of the times, its ministry to youth as a distinctive group is a relatively recent development. As pointed out more fully in earlier chapters, a historic turning point in the ministry to this group was achieved in the founding and development of the Sunday-school movement with its special concern for children and youth.[1] It is also pertinent to note that the rise of youth organizations and movements coincides with cultural trends which include industrialization and urbanization. The role of young people in the culture of any given period is a strong factor in determining the approach which must be made by the Church in its effort to minister to them.

The impact of the earlier youth and student movements such as the Student Volunteer Movement, the Epworth League, the International Society of Christian Endeavor, the Y.M.C.A. and Y.W.C.A. cannot be measured. The boys camps and girls camps of the Sunday School Association and later the International Council of Religious Education were formative to youth work today.

Christian youth through these movements have always been in the forefront of the church's striving for renewal and its efforts in mission and unity.

In the past three decades many changes have taken place in organization for youth work largely because of the increasing assumption by denominations of responsibility for Christian education. New patterns of interdenominational cooperation have emerged. One evidence of this is seen in the common youth fellowship philosophy and commission structure developed by many of the denominations through formal and informal consultation since the 1930's. The establishment of the United Christian Youth Movement in 1934 and its subsequent development has served as a stimulant to and has been profoundly affected by the development of denominational youth programs.

The half truth that "youth today are the leaders of tomorrow" is demonstrated by the fact that a large proportion of the present local pastors, denominational executives, college faculty members, and executives of national and world councils of churches received their motivation and basic experience in churchmanship in youth movements. The other half of the statement is in many ways more important—youth today are leaders now! Young people are not merely, or from

[1] See ch. 1, pp. 17-23.

121

their viewpoint primarily, preparing to be leaders tomorrow. They are in any generation attempting to find answers to the problems of the world which they face and which shall become increasingly complex during the next decades. Their willingness and eagerness to "be the Church" has led to renewal of the churches' witness in such areas as race relations, voluntary service, world-wide Christian fellowship, missionary giving and service, economic and political affairs.

One of the most obvious weaknesses in the churches' ministry to youth brought out by several research studies has been the lack of provision for genuine responsibility and service.

Dual Approach in Ministry to Youth

The very nature of young people and their role in our culture require a dual approach unique to this age group. This is seldom understood and we often continue a given pattern simply because "we've always done it that way." This condition has been clearly stated in *The Objective of Christian Education for Senior High Young People.*

"The senior high lives in a world dominated by adults." "In the adult world the senior high encounters contradictory demands. Society frequently requires that he assume responsibilities of adult life and at the same time denies him opportunity for doing so. On his part, the senior high, because of his stage of development, both desires and rejects the responsibility of adult life. He fluctuates between feelings of self-assertion and self-distrust. At times he desires independence and at other times prefers to be dependent on others." He "is not alone in this adult world. He lives in intimate relationship with his peers. Group experience with peers is a major way . . . young people are helped to meet successfully the requirements of this stage of human growth." "This group life of the senior high is likely to have a clearly recognizable culture of its own." [2]

In every aspect of the church—local church, council of churches, denominational structure—two basic approaches are needed. An approach is needed which will capitalize on the peer relationship. Young people need to be helped to establish a fellowship through which they can grapple with all of the concerns of the church, especially those unique to their own age group, at the level of their experience. This youth fellowship has been well described as a microcosm of the church.

Another approach is also needed which will capitalize on their yearning for adult acceptance and status. They need to be helped to find their place as full "members of the household of God." This requires patience, understanding, acceptance, and encouragement on the part of all adult members of the church. It also requires careful guidance of dedicated, sympathetic, mature, competent adult workers with youth, working through a committee on youth work which attempts to see the total needs and relationships of young people and to provide necessary continuity and long range planning.

Changing Characteristics

Historically persons between the ages of twelve and twenty-four have been categorized as youth in our church programs. One of the basic changes in the past two decades has been the gradual lowering of the age of those youth actually

[2] Quoted from *The Objective of Christian Education for Senior High Young People.* Copyright 1958 by the National Council of Churches. Used with permission.

participating in youth groups and camps and conferences. There are several reasons for this. One is employment. Whereas in 1944, 17 per cent of teen-age boys eligible to work after school had jobs, in 1956, 36 per cent of them did. The contrast between 1934 and 1959 is far greater. Figures for those of nineteen to twenty-four years of age would show even sharper contrast.

The prosperity of these young people has made them the focus of commercial interests which have created many forms of entertainment that compete with church activities. Sixteen million teen-agers (13-19) in 1957 with a total income of nine billion dollars will increase to twenty-four million in 1965 with a total income estimated at fourteen billion dollars. The freedom and independence made possible by this prosperity and changes in our family life and society add to the increasing tempo of maturation. Undoubtedly, the impact on our culture of World War II and the Korean Police Action are also immense factors.

The earlier physical development due to improved nutrition and cultural stimuli adds to this earlier maturation. Studies of adolescent boys in 1957 in comparison to similar studies a decade earlier indicate that boys fourteen to sixteen years of age in 1957 are two years advanced in the pattern of dating and process of vocational choices than their counterparts in 1947.

Obviously, the mobility of population and the shrinking of the world by lines of communication and transportation have also contributed to the process.

The factors already listed have contributed to earlier marriages. Today's bride is a median age of 20 and her mate is 22½. In 1958 the largest number of women of any age to be married was eighteen years of age. In 1957, seven million youth under nineteen were married and one fourth of teen-age women were mothers.

The sheer number of youth is a major factor in the emergence of a youth culture and in the specialization of youth work at the junior-high and high-school levels. In 1945 there were 2,300,000 twelve-year-olds. In 1959 there are nearly 3,800,000. In 1966, 1967, and 1968 there will be 4,000,000 annually.

One can see clearly the implications for closer grouping and for special efforts to meet the increasingly varied needs of parents, students, service personnel, and workers in the older youth (18-24) age group. These changes also have profound implications for the number and role of adult workers with all ages of youth.

If we merely keep pace with the population, winning no larger proportion of youth to Christ and his Church, and if we maintain the present ratio of adult workers to youth—a ratio already too small—the 73,000 camp and conference leaders of 1956 must be expanded to more than 110,000 and the number of church-school teachers for youth (12-23) must be increased from 670,000 to more than 1,000,000 by 1965. The problems appear insurmountable when we realize that between 1959 and 1965 there will be no increase in the number of adults between the ages of 25 and 45, from which we have enlisted the vast majority of our workers with youth.

Their World

One writer, recently describing the current generation of youth, says they are "co-existing with chaos in a science-fiction-turned-fact world." This generation of young people in the United States has never known unprosperous times or a non-warring world. During their lifetime the world has entered the nuclear age and the space age and the United Nations has been established. Between 1945 and

1959 twenty-three nations were established, and more are already scheduled to be added to that number. The pressures of the arms race, the anxieties over nuclear fallout, the frustrations of oppressed peoples, the tensions in relationships between races, and the uncertainties related to the mobility of population exert pressures on youth, already overburdened by the problems which go with adolescence, far beyond those exerted on any previous generation of youth.

Presently more than 20 per cent of the families in the U.S.A. move annually. The significance of this for the teen-ager who is largely dependent upon acceptance by peers for security is immense. Between 1959 and 1975, thirty-two cities with less than 50,000 population in 1950 will become metropolitan areas. The two hundred metropolitan areas of 1975 may have as many people in them as all of the United States had in 1950—150,000,000. Many of these may have grown together into megalopolitan areas—strip cities as much as six hundred miles long by 1975 or 1980. This is one factor in the estimate that all other conditions being equal we may expect a 70 per cent increase in juvenile delinquency by 1975. The increasing complexity of our economic life is further evidenced by the fact that the 20,000 different job titles listed by the government in 1940 mushroomed to more than 43,000 by 1957.

The implications to be drawn from this information for the ministry of the churches to youth are innumerable.

Present Conditions

A very keen and forthright worker with youth in one of our denominations giving current observations on the churches' present ministry to youth said:

1. Our present pattern of local church youth program does not make enough of an impact to "touch and change" teen-agers.

2. Much of our so-called youth program is built on frills and froth; socials, business meetings, money-raising (has no content).

3. We fail to attract, hold, and cultivate the high quality adult workers, both for church school and evening fellowship.

4. Most often our churches are content to minister to the faithful few who "come to meetings."

5. The church is not the center of something tremendous. He continued by saying "we've got to come up with a daring formula, a new strategy, which will make the Gospel more relevant to the lives of our kids. . . . The traditional ways won't do it!"

This very negative observation can and will later be offset to some degree by some more positive observations, but there is much basic truth in it. It seems very strange that this should be true at a time when we have more youth workers (both salaried and volunteer), more and better program resources, and more financial resources for youth work than at any previous time in the history of the church. It is important for us to try briefly to assess this situation.

Lack of Objective and Conscious Group Goals

Perhaps the primary reason for any lack of effectiveness has been the limited understanding and conscious awareness of our basic objective. Many factors including the theological climate, educational philosophy, and the lack of adequately trained leaders, have made it possible in many instances for youth groups to become just another social clique or club without an awareness of any distinctive purpose. This is, of course, a reflection of the condition of the total church. We have operated largely on the assumption that learning is a conscious, overt act when in fact it appears that it may to a very great extent be informal, subconscious, and covert when most effective.

A great deal of help is now available to us in a statement of *The Objective of Christian Education for Senior High Young People* developed co-operatively by national youth workers. In summary fashion it states:

(1) *The objective of Christian education is to help persons to be aware of God's self-disclosure and seeking love in Jesus Christ and to respond in faith and love—to the end that they may know who they are and what their human situation means, grow as sons of God rooted in the Christian community, live in the Spirit of God in every relationship, fulfill their common discipleship in the world, and abide in the Christian hope.*

(2) *Christian education takes place in a setting that has natural, human, historical, and divine dimensions.* This setting, or field of relationships, is actually seen by persons in various ways, depending upon their experience and culture. We see it in terms of the world of persons and the self, the family, the community, the larger society, the natural world, history, and the church and the gospel. The essential character of this whole field of relationships is determined by its divine dimension, that is, by revelation and the gospel, as they relate to express themselves in various natural, human, and historical ways.

(3) *Christian education engages the person in certain learning tasks.* Throughout his life he is required to listen with growing alertness to the gospel and respond to it in faith and love as he undertakes the tasks of exploring the whole field of relationships in light of the gospel, and appropriating that meaning and value personally and assuming personal and social responsibility in light of the gospel.

(4) *The individual bears a responsibility for engaging himself in these learning tasks.* Others who are responsible for engaging him in them, thus sharing responsibility for the conduct of Christian education, are the home, various community agencies, and the church.[3]

In addition to some grasp of the basic objective it is essential that the adult workers and youth constantly, consciously establish intermediate goals in their unit planning.

Traditional Practices Still Prevail

A second likely cause of weakness in present efforts is well described in the words of a reporter speaking about some of our traditions in government, "We are traveling in Model T style in a jet-space age." For example, a decade or two ago when patterns for the youth fellowship were established, a youth group, morning or evening, of twenty junior highs and fifteen senior highs with a single teacher or advisor for each was a respectable sized group. A more homogeneous community in which they attended the same schools, went to the same social activities, and lived near the church made it more feasible for one adult worker to serve them. While it is true that many of our churches are still small and are located in small towns, it is also true that the majority of our young people today live in heterogeneous urban or suburban situations and are pulled every

[3] *Ibid.,* pp. 14-15.

direction by forces outside the church. In the face of this many of our larger churches continue with an obsolete pattern which does not meet these newer circumstances and needs of young people and which creates a frustrating, dissatisfying experience for adult workers already burdened with jobs requiring travel and/or commuting time away from their own families. This problem is further complicated by the fact that as adults we tend to try to re-create the programs and organization and experiences that were most significant to us as young people.

Another example of delayed reaction has been the lack of new approaches to interdenominational co-operation. Such co-operation in the small town or city is a relatively simple matter. The pattern long established of a council made up of representatives of each local church group can be effective if there is responsible participation and support of the adult workers in each church.

In urban areas, however, it is clear that new strategies must be developed by the churches in each city designed to provide for effective interchurch and church and agency co-operation to meet the needs of youth.

Current Varieties in Youth Programming

One description of the churches' programs for youth would stress their considerable variety. A listing of these numerous elements might be helpful: church-school classes; evening fellowship; agency clubs such as Boy Scouts, choir, girls guild; church worship services; camps and conferences; area denominational meetings; vacation church school; weekday Christian education courses; social affairs; committee planning meetings and many others which you can name. In addition there are occasional service projects, evangelism programs and summer voluntary service. A look at this list raises two questions: (1) Are all the ingredients necessary to meet the taste and needs of each person? and (2) How can we get the ingredients properly mixed?

It can be readily seen that the many facets of the churches' programs have many sources and the program has "grown like Topsy." One goal of the youth fellowship concept was to co-ordinate the many plans. The youth fellowship council recommended by many denominations is helpful but it is obvious that effective planning must be done by the adults working with youth in these many program phases and that they must do this planning in light of a common basic objective.

On the Positive Side

Never before in the history of the Church have there been resource materials comparable to those now available for youth work. It is equally true that the number of trained workers with youth, salaried and volunteer, has never been greater. Currently nearly every denomination is engaged in basic studies of Christian education objectives and curriculum. These studies are stimulating similar efforts in many local churches, and will have a profound effect upon youth work in the coming decade.

New approaches for recruitment and training of adult workers with youth are also being developed. Stimulated by facts of the present and future, some of which were given earlier in this chapter, those responsible for the ministry to youth in the denominations are consulting with one another through the city, state, and national councils of churches in an attempt to plan a long-range strategy for reaching and serving young people.

The Youth Worker's Kit made up of six sound, color filmstrips for use in the recruitment and training of adult workers for the first time provides co-operatively produced audio-visual resources for this purpose. Most of the approaches to recruitment and training of leaders described elsewhere in this book are applicable to the field of youth work. Recent experimentation, denominational and inter-denominational, with the laboratory school approach in training workers with youth indicates that this method can be highly effective and will be further developed. The changing circumstance and role of youth in our culture and the changing world itself require that we constantly evaluate and restudy the task and role of the adult worker with youth.

During the period when youth organizations included more older youth, the adult tasks often fell to officers who though they were young adults took the role of youth. In other instances the adult leader assumed that his role should be instructor, chairman, arbitrator, advisor, and director.

One distinctive change in the formation of the youth fellowship was the enforcement of upper and lower age limits for participants. This limitation, reinforced in the past decade by the dropping out of those in the eighteen to twenty-four age range, has clearly altered the relationship and roles of youth and adult workers with youth.

If we assume that the historic tasks of Christian education—to inform, to train, to nurture, and to evangelize—are valid today, we must also see that the approach is not one of adults putting young people "through the hoops." Nor is it merely adults sitting while allowing youth to do as they please. It is rather a responsibility that is shared by youth and their adult leaders at every point from initial planning, through the carrying out of those plans, to thorough evaluation and the planning of appropriate next steps. The active leadership is almost necessarily in the hands of the youth themselves. It is they who for the most part must do the informing, the training, the nurturing, and the evangelizing.

The adult stands ready to motivate, to support, to counsel, to guide, to suggest, to place resources at their disposal, and to help them evaluate and plan realistically. Often he has the information they need; the adult world he represents is the nurturing group they are gradually learning to participate in and in which they are being readily accepted; often he knows how to articulate the thoughts and feelings that they are groping for in their sometimes sure, sometimes fumbling, attempts to respond to God in Christ and become truly his disciples.[4]

One of the difficulties through which this process has gone is the concept held by many that youth programs, camps, and conferences are of, by, and for youth only. This has in some ways contributed to the barrier between youth and adults in the church. Many see the value of a larger ratio of adults to youth in planned activities provided that there is a genuine sense of partnership and fellowship which make both the younger and older learners as well as teachers. It has long been true and is coming to be realized more fully that in large measure Christian growth comes about through meaningful relationship with persons who have achieved significantly in the Christian faith. There are young people who have

[4] D. Campbell Wyckoff, "Some Observations on the Christian Education of Senior Highs," an unpublished study paper.

so achieved from whom many adults could well learn more of the Christian faith. This respect, understanding and acceptance is needed not merely between youth and those designated to work with youth but also between youth and all of the adult church membership.

Equally essential to the success of a church's ministry to youth is a committee or fellowship of adult workers through which new workers can be recruited, opportunities for personal enrichment and training can be provided, and a constant effort can be made to understand the young people and their problems. This fellowship of adult workers may well center in each church but because of the distinctive youth culture and the fact that youth more than any other age group live in the community as a whole, the church worker must consult regularly with those in the schools and agencies and other churches who also work with young people.

The necessity for continued training and study on the part of these adults cannot be minimized. While training in skills, techniques, and use of particular curriculum resources is essential, perhaps the basic need is that each person constantly strive for a personal maturity in the Christian faith which will be a source of informal—and sometimes subsconscious—learning on the part of the young people. The great demand is for adults, genuinely interested in young people who will take the time and make the effort to achieve a larger degree of personal faith and of professional competence in this field.

In the Local Church

Every week millions of young people in thousands of churches share in youth programs of great variety. In the majority of those denominations which cooperate in the National Council of Churches, there is a common youth-fellowship concept. This youth fellowship is intended to be inclusive of all experiences provided for youth by the given church. For most of them there is a common framework for program planning, sometimes referred to as commissions and sometimes as program areas. The basic framework includes the areas of Christian faith, Christian witness, Christian outreach, Christian citizenship, and Christian fellowship.

In many other denominations a different framework of committees or commissions is used and in several the youth program is based on the league or society concept. In virtually all denominations and structures, however, there is an attempt to provide an approach that includes some balance of experiences of worship, study, and action.

Whereas in the past it has been customary to have one person or a married couple serve as advisor to a Sunday evening fellowship, with this same person or another teaching morning church school, we are now faced with more varied programs and the need for new kinds of adult participants. In many churches the number of youth requires several morning classes and in many instances, Sunday evening is no longer the best possible time for the "evening fellowship meeting."

Much experimentation is being done to meet these changing needs. One proposal is the "cube group" plan[5] which provides for several smaller fellowship groups constituted on the basis of interest, age group, geographical area of residence,

[5] See Henry Tani, *Some Ventures in Youth Work.*

availability for meeting on program design. Adult leadership may be provided for each cube on the basis of skills or information needed. In such a proposal the entire youth group may meet in total fellowship on alternate weeks or once each month. The task of planning and co-ordinating such an approach is quite different and not without its difficulties.

Whatever the organizational approach may be, an encouraging trend is to be found in the year-round planning that is done by many local church groups. Spring or fall week-end planning retreats where adult workers and youth together review their objective, state their goals, and outline their plans for the year are contributing to a more effective ministry to young people.

The units included in the outline are characterized by much greater variety than ever before. New curriculum materials of many denominations suggest study or action units in keeping with the problems and opportunities of the world. Today within easy transportation of most churches there are persons who through study, service, or travel are qualified as resource leaders for international concerns of the outreach commission. Availability of adequate, speedy transportation make "go-and-see tours" more possible and worthwhile. Thousands of young people in this age of mobility have opportunity for travel, seminars, study abroad, and voluntary service which qualifies them as resource leaders for their study units. Communication lines have so reduced the size of the world that it frequently requires little imagination to see the need for Christian response to events all over the world.

One significant new understanding of the task of the church youth program is related to the fact of availability of information. In another time a study unit on missions in Africa would have required some searching for information about the economy, culture, politics, and geography, as well as information about how we relate the demands of the gospel to those conditions. Today with young people constantly pressured by experiences of and news of significant events of the world, the responsibility of the church youth programs comes more clearly to focus on the interpretation of these events in light of the gospel and the guidance toward assumption of responsibility in light of the gospel.

Evangelism

In isolated instances denominations and local churches separately or in co-operation have, with some success, carried out programs of youth to youth evangelism. When we consider the vast majority of present church members who became Christians before they were twenty-one, the importance of this concern is evident. It would appear that currently many youth programs are being carried out on the assumption that it is our responsibility to provide Christian education for "our own."

A resurgence of concern to "go into all the world" has led in recent years to a careful examination of the youth world or youth culture and to consideration of the most effective means of communicating the gospel. There are many efforts emerging including an increasing participation of young people in evangelism efforts of the Church as a whole. If we are to minister to many young people, it will require that the Church in some way go to them. The many excellent youth meetings in the churches, while nurturing those present, must also help them to share their growing faith with others. Another possibility is represented by the action of one church which has called a minister to youth, who instead of filling his schedule to overflowing with class and group leadership responsibilities within the church building, will roam the streets, cover the youth "hangouts" and minister and evangelize by first being available to the youth where they are.

The medium of religious television has also been used successfully in reaching and stimulating unchurched youth through dealing realistically and entertainingly with the real issues of their culture.[6]

Extensions of the Local Church Program

As a part of their life as Christians, every year hundreds of thousands of youth in thousands of communities across the country participate in voluntary service projects—caravaning, tours, seminars, and work camps here and abroad every summer. During the past decade thousands have given at least one full year of their life to voluntary service through their churches here and abroad.

Millions of dollars are given annually by these young people, much of it to youth mission funds. Through denominational youth programs and the United Christian Youth Movement, they share with Christian youth throughout the world in a mutual program of world youth projects. This includes the sharing of thousands of dollars annually for support of ecumenical youth programs in dozens of countries.

Space does not permit the description of efforts in political responsibility and international affairs, the use of arts in religion, the involvement in concerns of faith and order, and many other aspects of the current efforts in the churches' ministry to youth and the witness of Christian youth.

Unmet Needs

Lest we allow all this good news to allay the fears and challenge of the first section of the chapter, let us consider several areas in which much work must be done. One recent report indicated that nearly 45 per cent of our young people do not finish high school. Very few of these "drop outs" are reached by the churches' ministry. The proportion of youth among those in institutions (medical, penal, and the like) is staggering. Provision for their participation in meaningful Christian experiences is very inadequate. The isolation of young people in neighborhoods, communities, and suburbs from persons of other nationality, race, economic, and religious groups is more extreme than in earlier stages of our economy. If they are to know the Church in its wholeness, they must have opportunity for meaningful relationships with persons of different groups.

The changing world makes other demands as yet unmet. The cold war and the world expansion of American businesses have created congregations of American Christians in hundreds of cities and armed forces bases all over the world. The need for an adequate ministry to the youth of these families is one of which we have been unaware and which promises to explode in the coming years. The needs of those persons, especially nonstudents, in the older-youth—young-adult age group require continuing research, experimentation, and specialized ministries.

Basic to the churches' ministry to youth in the present and future is a constant

---

[6] An example is "Look Up and Live," a CBS-TV network program produced in co-operation with the National Council of Churches.

evaluation in light of our objective of Christian education, bold experimentation, new strategies in interdenominational co-operation, and long-range planning.

Bibliography

Bowman, Clarice M. *Ways Youth Learn*. New York: Harper and Brothers, 1952.

Cummings, Oliver DeWolf. *The Youth Fellowship*. Philadelphia: Judson Press, 1956.

Gesell, Arnold; Ilg, Frances L.; and Ames, Louise B. *Youth: The Years from Ten to Sixteen*. New York: Harper and Brothers, 1956.

Griffiths, Louise. *The Teacher and Young Teens*. St. Louis: Bethany Press, 1954.

Harner, Nevin. *Youth Work in the Church*. Nashville: Abingdon Press, 1942.

The Objective of Christian Education for Senior High Young People. New York: National Council of Churches, 1958.

Tani, Henry. *Ventures in Youth Work*. Philadelphia: Christian Education Press, 1957.

Wattenburg, William W. *The Adolescent Years*. New York: Harcourt, Brace and Company, 1955.

Wittenberg, Rudolph. *On Call for Youth*. New York: Association Press, 1955.

Wyckoff, D. Campbell. *In One Spirit*. New York: Friendship Press, 1958.

Chapter 12

The Christian Education of Adults

Paul B. Maves

IN MANY WAYS A NEW EMPHASIS UPON ADULTS IS THE MOST OUTSTANDING development of the present decade in Christian education. In fact, it could be said that whereas the first half of the twentieth century was devoted to child study and the development of programs for children and young people, the second half promises to center around the study of adulthood and the development of programs for the Christian nurture of adults.

Of course, adult education has always been a part of the ministry of the Church. Perhaps what is happening now is a return to a concern that the Church has always held central. As a missionary and evangelistic movement the Church proclaimed the gospel mainly to adults. For centuries the Church assumed that the family was the primary agency for the Christian nurture of the children, and therefore it concentrated upon the nurture and training of the adults. The Reformers depended upon the sermon, catechetical instruction, and the distribution of printed materials for the edification of adults. The Pietistic movement in Germany and the Methodist revival in England developed small cell groups for the mutual care of souls. In the nineteenth century the organized Bible classes came into existence, and women's groups were formed for the study and support of missions. In the first half of the twentieth century the standard leadership training schools were developed for the training of the adult teachers in the Sunday schools.

Causes of the New Concern

The contemporary renaissance of concern for adult education in the churches reflects a new understanding of adulthood and a realization of the mounting need for continuing education throughout our whole society. It is estimated that about fifty million persons are currently enrolled in some form of adult education in the United States. Polls reveal that nearly half of all adults want to further their education. Fifteen million persons are in organized church programs of adult education. The rising interest in and the significance of adult education can be explained by a number of factors.

First, there has been a marked and rapid lengthening of the duration of life, adding twenty years to the life span of the average person since 1900. This means that for the first time in human history most persons will live on past the time when they have responsibilities for child rearing so that they will have to find new interests to replace those supplied by growing children. This means also that most persons will live on beyond the time of retirement so they will have to reckon with the prospect of fifteen to twenty years of leisure, for which very few have been prepared, at the end of the life span.

Second, this lengthening duration of life means that there is a larger proportion of adults in our population. Moreover, these persons are the persons who make the decisions which mold the characters of the young and shape the world in which the coming generations must live.

Third, we have become aware of the fact that the aging process brings changes just as crucial, if not as noticeable, as those brought by growth. These changes indicate the need for a continuing education which will prepare us for each new phase of life. Out of the observation of these changes are coming increasing efforts to chart the developmental tasks and change gradients of adulthood. These should enable us to plan better curriculums.

Fourth, in a rapidly changing society the realization that adults need to continue to study and to learn has been forcefully impressed upon us. Changing technologies now make occupational skills obsolete about every twenty years unless there is continual learning and retraining on the job. Rapid transportation, new means of communication, and expanding populations have brought the peoples of the world closer together and raised new problems of adjustment, realignment, and accommodation, as old patterns of human relations are being shattered.

Finally, no one doubts any longer that adults can learn if they want to learn. The research studies on adult learning which began with those of Thorndike in the 1920's have been extended so that we know how adults learn as well as how much they can learn.

Within the churches themselves new developments are taking place which increase the need for adult education and at the same time make clear that it is an essential aspect of the Christian life. The clarification of the concept of the Church as the covenant community with a mission to perform, the rediscovery of the Protestant doctrine of the priesthood of all believers in which every Christian is a minister of Christ, the growing understanding of Christian vocation as laying upon every man the responsibility for serving God in his whole life and work, the new concept of revelation as the encounter with the living God in the events of history, the new approach to the Bible as the witness of the apostolic community to the event of the Incarnation, which is the norm for our faith and practice and a medium of revelation for us, all point to the need for a theological re-education of the laity to close the gap between people and pastor. In his covenant relation with God it is the responsibility of each Christian to study to know God's will and purpose for him and to prepare himself to carry it out as efficiently as possible.

It seems clear that the first part of the decade of the 1950's saw the passing of some significant milestones in the history of adult education. In 1950 the First White House Conference on Aging was held in Washington; it brought together about a thousand of the nation's leaders in this field to attempt to stimulate, establish, and co-ordinate programs in this area. As a result the National Committee on Aging was formed within the National Social Work Assembly to act as a clearinghouse and co-ordinator of voluntary agency programs in this field. Also a council on aging was formed within the federal government with a special staff on aging to direct it. A Second White House Conference on Aging planned for 1961 will see committees and commissions and conferences organized on the state, county, and community levels. The significant thing about this development has been its interdisciplinary character and the attempt to co-ordinate health, welfare, recreational, and educational programs which affect a particular segment of the population. Most important, interest in gerontology has illuminated the whole life span.

In 1951 the Adult Education Association of the United States of America brought together in a unified movement the American Association for Adult Education (founded in 1926) and the Department of Adult Education of the National Education Association to co-ordinate the work of many organizations engaged in adult education. The National Training Laboratory in Group Development (organized in 1947) is a significant part of the program of the N.E.A.

In 1957 there was an expansion of program within the Division of Christian Education of the National Council of Churches of Christ in the U.S.A. by separating Family Life and Adult Education into two departments. The Workshop on the Christian Education of Adults held at the University of Pittsburgh in 1958 was an event of real importance for the Christian education of adults in the Protestant churches.

Within the denominations there has been a significant focusing upon the development of new programs of family life and parent education. The Methodist Church has held two national conferences on family life, publishes a magazine called *The Christian Home,* and through its Department of Family Life stimulates and guides the development of parent groups, marriage counseling, and family life education. The Southern Baptists' magazine, *Home Life,* and the new *Faith and Life* series in the curriculum of the United Presbyterian Church, U.S.A. give a central place to home and church co-operation, providing church-school materials for the family to use at home. The new *Seabury Series* of the Protestant Episcopal Church's curriculum makes parent education central to its program.[1]

Approaches to Adult Education in the Churches

In the light of this growing concern for adult education in the church, what has happened to the organization and method within the church?

Doubtless it is safe to say that, other than incidental teaching done through the sermon, the organized adult Bible class is still the primary agency relied upon by the churches for adult education. These groups generally have a name and officers. Frequently they have constitutions and bylaws. Usually they meet on Sunday morning for Bible study and monthly for a social affair. Typically there are separate organizations for men and women, and the teacher is some prominent layman who lectures on the Bible. However, in small churches members of the class often take turns in reading the lesson from a quarterly. Usually the International Uniform Series provides the structure for their approach to the content of the Bible. Probably this movement reached its peak in the 1920's when large classes often met in auditoriums in the community with attendance, stimulated by contests, running into the hundreds or even thousands, and with programs frequently in competition with the churches. Sunday-school conventions, rallies,

[1] See ch. 13, pp. 143-44.

and parades no longer figure largely in programs of these classes. Not only has there been a dwindling of attendance and a disbanding of many classes, but also more classes are made up of both men and women, and often they branch out to deal with topics other than Bible study. In some cases they use materials and approaches other than the International Uniform Series such as those which make an intensive study of a single book or theme. The denominations usually provide for the use of elective or undated units of this type.

Within the past decade attempts have been made to improve the effectiveness of the Bible class, even when led by a teacher who lectures and when using the International Uniform Series. Audio-visual aids to the lecture, panel discussions, debates, reports of member research, and dramatic skits or role playing have been suggested. It has also been suggested that the large class can be broken up into small discussion groups for a few minutes to talk about specific questions and then to report back to the total group. In one church a large class of about two hundred persons, while retaining its organization, has a period in the year when it divides into several interest groups of an elective nature.

To some extent the separate groups for men and for women have been superseded among younger adults by couples clubs. More recently many couples clubs have been opened to unmarried persons and made into age-group classes in order to provide for all, regardless of marital status.

In contrast to the organized Bible class we find an emerging interest in small-group Bible study which involves participation and sharing by all members of the group. For example, one church has a policy of limiting membership in these groups to twenty. When additional interest is generated, new groups are started so that more than a dozen of these Bible study groups meet in the church. The method used is sometimes called "Depth Bible Study" in which each person attempts to rephrase in his own words what the writer of the passage under consideration said, to understand what the writer was trying to convey through it, and then to share with others what he feels God is saying to him through the medium of the passage. Some small groups study theology and Christian ethics intensively. One church has a group of its leading laymen which meets every Tuesday evening for a discussion of theology based on a textbook.

Closely allied to the small-group Bible study movement is the increasing number of Christian nurture groups. These are intentionally kept small so there can be face-to-face interaction between all the members. They meet regularly at any time convenient to the members. They include prayer, discussion, Bible study, and testimony or whatever kind of sharing seems to be indicated by their need and interest. One large suburban church has its entire adult constituency organized into small Christian growth groups limited to about fifteen or twenty persons which meet in homes, usually during the week. Another large church has a more varied and voluntary group program with some units meeting for breakfast, some for a coffee break in the morning, some in the afternoon, and some in the evening.

In a real sense this is a recovery of a movement which has often stimulated or accompanied a revival of religion. It has affinities with the monastic movements of the Middle Ages, the Brethren of the Common Life of the fifteenth century, the *collegia pietatis* (associations of piety), the Wesleyan class meeting in the eighteenth and nineteenth centuries, and the Utopian communities of the nineteenth century. They are deliberate attempts to recapture the feelings of intimacy, commitment, comradeship, and mutual support which characterized the early Christian communities and which are no longer possible in large urban congregations or in churches where so much membership is social and nominal.

Next in importance to the organized Bible classes, and perhaps surpassing them in effectiveness, come the women's societies of the church. Their original concern for missions has branched out to include almost all of life in all countries. Consequently mission study groups have expanded their interests to include Bible study, the study of social issues, and leadership training. The typical woman's group has a monthly meeting for all the women in the church. Part of this meeting may be given over to an address or some type of presentation on topics of current interest to women. In addition most of these organizations encourage and stimulate the formation of study groups focusing more intensively on a variety of topics related to the Christian mission. Furthermore these organizations have regional and national conferences and assemblies enrolling thousands, which are mainly educational in nature.

In addition, it must be kept in mind that various types of leadership education have been a significant aspect of adult education, whether it be the Standard Leadership Training School, correspondence courses, worker's conferences, supervision on the job, week-end retreats, or laboratory-demonstration schools.[2]

Special mention must be made of the parish life conference. Originally designed by the Protestant Episcopal Church for the training of its leaders, it suggests a way whereby the religious experience of all adults can be enriched and their theological understanding deepened. This is essentially a week-end retreat in which the participants are led to raise fundamental questions about what they believe and to share their understanding of the Christian faith. It includes worship, Bible study, meditation, and discussion. The main thing is that it tests their statements of belief by focusing them first upon their immediate experiences in relationship to each other and then upon the life situations of the parish. This is an adaptation to the parish of the laboratory in human relations developed under the auspices of the Adult Education Department of the National Education Association and the Research Center in Group Dynamics founded by Kurt Lewin. The wider use of this approach depends upon the recruitment and training of persons who may be qualified to direct such conferences.

Another notable form of adult education in the churches is the School of Christian Living or Institute. These are similar to and are sometimes organized in conjunction with the Standard Leadership Training schools. Characteristically they meet for a series of evenings, either Sunday or week night, and include a number of elective courses. If they meet on a Sunday evening they often begin with an informal period of fellowship and a simple supper, followed by a period of worship. Then persons go into groups of their choice. Six evenings seems to be a popular length. The fall and Lenten period are popular seasons. One large church has a long tradition of a Lenten school which meets for six Wednesday evenings and enrolls from six to eight hundred persons. Each adult may elect one of four or five courses in each of two class periods, the first from eight o'clock to eight-fifty, the second from nine o'clock to nine-fifty. One of the courses is designed for

[2] See ch. 25, pp. 270-80.

mass interest and meets in the sanctuary of the church. Usually one course is designed for a specific leadership group. A course on the Bible is always a popular feature. The evening concludes with a coffee hour.

Another straw in the wind is the emerging interest in the use of fine arts in the church.[3] Many churches are developing dramatic clubs and producing more and more drama. In the new understanding of drama, religious plays are defined as those which have an ultimate concern or raise questions about man's ultimate destiny as well as those which have biblical themes and characters. Some churches are developing rhythmic choirs and choral dance groups to interpret religious themes. A New England group of churches holds a choral dance festival annually. This new interest in art, architecture, and drama is pressing for more courses in art appreciation and workshops in creative art. The Department of Worship and the Fine Arts of the National Council of Churches is spearheading this renaissance of interest in the use of symbols in Protestantism. New interest in liturgy and the liturgical heritage is leading to more courses on worship and hymnody.

The new emphasis upon family life has been mentioned above.[4] This emphasis includes not only family oriented programs but also premarital counseling and courses to prepare for marriage and home life. The current tendency is to set up separate departments of family life as distinct from those for adult education in the organizations of the churches. This may represent a problem of overlapping and duplication. It also illustrates the way in which adult education is carried forward by many agencies so that the total extent of it is easily overlooked.

Camping for adults is just beginning to be developed by the churches. With the shorter work week and the longer vacations, camping—along with retreats, workshops, seminars, and laboratory schools—has real promise for the future.[5]

The new emphasis upon adult education is logically reflected in the development of curriculum materials. Notably several denominations are now producing books on theology, Christian ethics, the Bible, and kindred topics which can double as individual reading books or texts for discussion groups. Many of these are in paper-back editions. Along with these is a wider use of Bible dictionaries, atlases, and commentaries. The reading table and the church library are assuming increasing importance in the Christian education of adults. The Methodist Church has produced a set of brief guides for Bible readers. Generally the curriculum of the adult department shows a trend toward materials with more substance designed to be used for more intensive study.

Mention must be made of men's clubs and brotherhoods. While it is probably fair to say that they in no way match the women either in numbers involved, in the significance of the topics dealt with, or in the intensity with which members go at it, nevertheless they do make a contribution to adult education. The typical men's club program is primarily social and recreational in nature. Occasionally they deal with topics of crucial concern such as social issues, political issues, and new developments on the world scene. Perhaps one of the great challenges to the church in our time is how to win and hold the interest of men to a religious concern

[3] See ch. 19, pp. 204-14.
[4] See also ch. 13, pp. 143-44.
[5] See ch. 20, pp. 220-21.

when men have abdicated so much of responsibility for the creation and cherishing of any aspect of our culture except the technological. Perhaps the few attempts to bring together persons in particular occupations to study how they can bear Christian witness and fulfill their Christian vocation in their work bears the most promise of making religion relevant to the men's world.

Rapidly growing in significance are the Golden Age clubs, as they are often called, for older people. Typical of all club programs, they have varied activities including recreation, fellowship, worship, and informational and entertainment programs. In addition they also have hobby and craft programs and occasional field trips.

It should be mentioned that there seems to be increasing interest among the clergy in making the sermon more effective as a means of Christian nurture by having sermon committees working with the minister in planning and evaluating them, by having forums or question periods following the service, by printing and circulating the sermon, and by having two persons engaged in dialogue in the pulpit.

Influences upon Adult Education in the Churches

New approaches to adult education are being developed on the basis of the insights emerging from the social sciences. These are affecting both method and content.

To begin with knowledge of the relation between culture, society, and personality is helping us to understand better human behavior and the factors which influence it. This means that in education our concern is shifting from learning in the sense of acquiring knowledge or skills to learning as change in behavior and relationships. For a long time we have been aware that persons had knowledge upon which they did not act, that they held attitudes which did not affect their practice, and that they possessed skills which they did not use. The social sciences are making us aware of how cultural patterns and social pressures color our perception of a situation, dictate our attitudes, and shape our actions. Therefore, if we are concerned to change human behavior we must attempt to deal with the social pressures and influences within a situation as well as the individual's perception of it, and as well as his actual knowledge and skill.

New understanding of the characteristics of social systems, such as groups, organizations, and communities, helps us to analyze a situation and to forecast what is to be expected from particular persons within that situation. An analysis of the power and authority structure of the community enables us to discover the centers of major influence which affect the outlook and behavior of many persons. A recognition of the existence of particular social status structures, role patterns, symbols, standards, values, goals, and means of operating enables us to diagnose difficulties, estimate openness to change, find points of entry into the social system, and to set realistic change goals.

The new studies in group dynamics and leadership help us to understand the importance of interpersonal relationships for both learning and living, and to provide a more helpful kind of leadership education.[6]

[6] See ch. 16, pp. 173-83.

Principles of Effective Adult Education

Out of these studies we can discern a number of emerging principles which must be observed in adult education if it is to be most effective.

First, we cannot change persons. Persons change only when they want to change themselves. This means that for adult education to be effective the learners must be personally involved in the formulation of the objectives and methods of learning and committed to what they themselves have helped to bring into being. In the development of adult education the students must be consulted about their needs and interests, participate in working out the plans for program, and be drawn into the responsibility for what takes place. Such involvement usually means that a planning group surveys the adult constituency through interviews, questionnaires, interest finders, and problem-census discussions to get definite information on their needs, interests, time schedules, talents, and concerns. It means that individuals must take responsibility for active participation in study rather than being passive recipients of presentations by others. It means that students are involved in the evaluation of their learning and of the process of teaching.

Second, persons learn most when they experience what is being taught as directly as possible. If experience cannot be immediate and direct, then it will include observation, dramatic participation, and laboratory types of experience. For example, in addition to hearing a Bible student expound the results of his study, they will themselves engage in Bible study and share with others what it means to them. Instead of talking about the applications in general terms, specific applications will be tested out and evaluated in experience by case examples, role playing, and experimental or pilot projects.

Third, persons are freed to learn, stimulated to learn, and supported in using what they have learned when learning takes place within the context of a learning fellowship. Within such a fellowship freedom of expression is essential so persons can ask questions, voice doubts, admit ignorance or bewilderment. There needs to be encouragement to experiment, to make mistakes, and to try again. There must be a mutual sharing of meanings as well as of information. In the main, a group will be kept small enough so that members can get to know each other and interact in face-to-face relationships and so each person will have opportunity to participate in the discussion. At the same time it will be large enough to have in it the resources needed to perform its task. It will be diverse enough to be stimulating and to have a fruitful sharing of differences, and yet there will be enough in common to hold it together. The group will have concern not only for the content of its study but also for the relationships between the members of the group.

Fourth, because of the highly individual character of adults, an adult-education program in a local church must include a variety of methods, approaches, time schedules, and subjects. No single, monolithic program can ever meet all the needs of all the persons. There is a place for organized and for informal groups, for presentations by authorities and for sharing by members of the group of their own tentative explorations of a subject, for long-term and short-term courses, for Sunday and for weekday activities. Such a program will be continually evaluated and constantly evolving in response to changing conditions.

Fifth, leadership will be shared as widely as possible among all the members of

139

the group so each person can assume some responsibility for contributing to planning, working, and evaluating. This means that generally instead of an authoritative teacher and a large group of passive pupils, many will help in the teaching. Often teaching will be done by a team.

Problems in the Christian Education of Adults

At the end of the decade the Christian education of adults in the church is still faced with problems that have plagued it for many years. For one thing, it is extremely difficult to get adults in the church to break away from a reliance upon a single method of education, that is, from dependence upon the lecture by a so-called expert. This is the concept of education that stands in the forefront of their minds and almost automatically blocks out any other picture of education. This tradition is supported by the fact that it protects persons from exposure to embarrassment, from real involvement in any process which would demand effort or energy or anxiety, by fear of asserting independence of powerful persons and by lack of confidence in their own ability to assume any leadership. In many churches there is no awareness that any other method exists. Even where such groups are aware of the discussion method, it seems to them to be merely a pooling of ignorance, probably because they are not able to involve members in preparation outside of class or to find persons who can lead a discussion. Most persons do not know how to participate fruitfully in discussion or conversation.

It is hard to persuade adult classes to attempt any other approach to Bible study than that of the International Uniform Series. This approach is closely tied up with the dependence upon the lecture method or upon a printed quarterly which outlines the lesson in such a way that it can be read aloud. This is a long-established pattern re-inforced by most of the factors which re-inforce the lecture method.

It is difficult to establish other patterns of program than that of the organized Bible class which meets on Sunday morning. Short-term elective units do not seem to meet the need for a continuing personal relationship and involve a great deal more continuous planning. If resistance to elective courses is overcome it will be because the needs for an intimate continuing relationship are met by nurture groups which free persons to take specialized courses and when the success of a program can be evaluated in terms of personal change rather than in terms of the size of the group.

In many churches it is difficult to overcome the pattern of separating men and women. This problem, like the ones named above, represents a carry-over from the Sunday-school movement of the nineteenth century, and probably is experienced more intensely in rural areas.

Too often adult-education programs in the church do not deal intensively enough with a subject to provide any thorough understanding or mastery. Study tends to be too sporadic. Too frequently churches shy away from significant areas of study because of their fear of controversy.

A problem of a different order is that of finding and training leaders for carrying on an adult education in the local church. As education has become more professionalized in the sense that it is based upon rather technical principles, insights, and sensitivities, requiring special skills, it becomes more and more difficult for laymen to feel comfortable in assuming leadership in education.

Education, like medicine, is becoming the domain of the specialist. Doubtless, trained leaders too often unwittingly have sapped the confidence of lay leaders by communicating to them their awareness of the gap between high professional standards and actual practice, by attempting to start on too advanced a level, by expecting too much, or by being impatient with growth.

Areas for Additional Study

There are many areas in adult education which demand continuing study and research. Only a few can be suggested here. The social sciences have been producing many data with pertinent implications for the churches, and techniques for the widest communication of these are urgently needed. Studies in theories of personality should be continued to identify the best frame of reference for understanding adults. The analysis of adult needs must be extended to all the various stages of adult development and related to the gospel of Jesus Christ. This study of needs should include those with special problems—such as blindness, deafness—and the church must learn to serve more effectively those in special circumstances, such as the aged, working mothers, one-parent families, and the like. Exploration designed to aid the transcending of class, cultural, and language barriers is equally necessary if adult Christian education is to approach its potential.

Continued research on the curriculum should also have a high priority. The adaptation of centrally planned materials to regional or local differences remains unsolved. The relative value of dated versus undated study units has not been established. In fact, the measurement of effectiveness of the entire educational program requires unremitting attention. As criteria for evaluation are selected and established, care must be given to their being structured in such manner that relatively untrained persons in local churches may find them helpful.

Leadership in adult education—as in other phases of local-church work—continues to be crucial. The church will need to create designs for more effective recruitment and training of lay leaders. The church must also devise new techniques for alerting clergymen to advances in this area which they may share with their congregations. Further study is also required on the function and value of the sermon as a means of adult education. These are but a few of the immediate problem areas confronting adult education at the present time. Hopes for its improvement will in large measure be realized only as their solutions are found and utilized by the church.

Bibliography

Bergevin, Paul, and McKinley, John. *Design for Adult Education in the Church.* Greenwich, Conn.: Seabury Press, 1958.

Casteel, John. *Spiritual Renewal through Personal Groups.* New York: Association Press, 1957.

Clark, Burton R. *Adult Education in Transition.* Berkeley: University of California Press, 1956.

Clemmons, Robert S. *Dynamics of Christian Adult Education.* Nashville: Abingdon Press, 1958.

Havighurst, Robert J., and Orr, Betty. *Adult Education and Adult Needs.* Chicago: Center for the Study of Liberal Education for Adults, 1956.

Kempfer, Homer. *Adult Education.* New York: McGraw-Hill Book Company, 1955.

Knowles, Malcolm S. *Informal Adult Education*. New York: Association Press, 1956.

Lentz, Richard E. *Making the Adult Class Vital*. St. Louis: Bethany Press, 1954.

Lindhorst, Frank A. *Teaching Adults*. Nashville: Abingdon Press, 1951.

Little, Lawrence C. (ed.). *The Future Course of Christian Adult Education*. Pittsburgh: University of Pittsburgh Press, 1959.

Little, Sara. *Learning Together in the Christian Fellowship*. Richmond, Va.: John Knox Press, 1956.

Lowry, Louis. *Adult Education and Group Work*. New York: William Morrow and Company, 1955.

Maves, Paul B., *Understanding Ourselves as Adults*. Nashville: Abingdon Press, 1959.

Sheats, Paul; Janye, Clarence; and Spence, Ralph. *Adult Education: A Community Approach*. New York: Dryden Press, 1953.

Thelen, Herbert A. *Dynamics of Groups at Work*. Chicago: University of Chicago Press, 1954.

Zeigler, Earl F. *Christian Education of Adults*. Philadelphia: Westminster Press, 1958.

Chapter 13

The Role of the Home in Religious Nurture

Wesner Fallaw

WITHIN THE JUDEO-CHRISTIAN TRADITION THE HOME IS EXPECTED TO NURTURE the young in the faith. Since Old Testament times, in principle, parents have been responsible for both religious ceremony and direct teaching, but in modern society Protestants have tended to neglect religious nurture. Among other things, a diminished faith—in part due to the scientific era and the hurried pace at which people live—undermines family worship, Bible reading, and explicit teaching of scripture and the heritage. For the past two decades, however, strenuous effort has been made by certain denominations and local churches to restore nurture to the home. Books, curricular series, departments of family life, institutes, and workshops in great variety remind the churches that the home is of fundamental importance in the child's spiritual development. Just how effective all these efforts are in convincing Christian parents that they are primarily responsible for the child's faith and conduct remains in doubt, but there is no doubt that parents are to be regarded as "the first and foremost teachers of religion."

In many churches there is no lack of activities designed for the enlightenment and enjoyment of parents and children. These range from Sunday-morning family worship services and parents' classes to fun nights and summer camping for families. Indeed, the volume of church-sponsored programs appears to be about as great as the flood of pamphlets and other printed matter aimed at the home.

Perhaps religious educators and pastors are baffled by the multiple possibilities for uniting church and home for effective Christian nurture. What are some of the major aspects of current "church-family education"? [1] More particularly, what is the place of the home in the nurture process?

Church-Family Education Today

1. CURRICULUMS. Most church school curriculums expect less than a fully co-ordinated program of church-family education, but denominations commonly seek parental backing for the teaching of the Sunday school. To this end leaflets are issued bearing "a message to parents"; visits to the home, parent-teacher teas,

---

[1] Though not widely used the term refers to an educational program which co-ordinates the teaching of the local church and the "nuclear family" (comprised of a mother and father and their children). For fuller treatment of church-family education, see Wesner Fallaw, *The Modern Parent and the Teaching Church* and *Toward Spiritual Security*.

and demonstrations of classroom work are recommended, and more. Implicit in these practices is the idea that religious education is the task of the church, carried on through the Sunday school. So ingrained is this viewpoint that parents grow uneasy when the newer curricular developments suggest that the home should carry major responsibility for Christian nurture. Even when curriculums and local church leaders attempt to distinguish between the respective tasks of the home and the church uneasiness is slow to vanish, for large numbers of mothers and fathers know themselves unready for guiding the religious growth of their children, notwithstanding the help available in denominational materials.

The Presbyterians' venture in their 1948 launching of a curriculum for church and home has stimulated other denominations to follow. The more recent *Seabury Series* of the Protestant Episcopal Church challenges families to join with the church and be the nurturing, redemptive community.

Of assistance to church families are such publications as *The Christian Home* (Methodist), *The Hearthstone* (Baptist-Disciples), Family Resource Books (Congregational), and Family Kits (United Church of Canada). These and similar materials are less demanding on the home than are curriculums which integrate home and church nurture.

2. PARENTS' CLASSES. It is widely recognized that parents' classes are needed to assist fathers and mothers in taking their place alongside church teachers. In some instances local churches have tried to make the parents' class mandatory but usually voluntaryism and persuasion are relied upon. Generally classes deal with questions of child guidance, the aims and scope of the church-school curriculum, the Bible and Christian doctrine on an adult level. Courses are sometimes formal—with more or less straight content teaching—sometimes informal, with a steering committee to locate parents' interests and build the study program accordingly.

Parents' classes have at least two aims: first, to bring the family unit into a continuing relationship with the church, the nurturing community; and second, to help mothers and fathers become competent religious mentors of the child. Some groups specify that the teaching of content is mainly the church's responsibility, while development of Christian attitudes is the home's responsibility. It is recognized that overlapping occurs as both church and home interpret biblical, doctrinal, and ethical issues.

A variant of the parents' class is the parent-teacher conference in which an attempt is made to unify church and home teaching and harmonize conflicting viewpoints that may arise. There is reason to believe that the conference is more productive of church-family education than are the more popular church parent-teacher associations that have sprung up in recent years. At any rate, either in the parents' class or in some variation of it, adult education takes place as a by-product of concern for children's Christian nurture.

3. FAMILY WORSHIP. Increasingly churches are holding family worship services. The Episcopal curriculum stipulates a weekly service in which the principle of graded worship in the church school is abandoned in favor of the regular liturgy conducted in the sanctuary, with all members of the family present. Proponents of this practice argue that beyond verbal concepts there is a "language of relationships" which conveys meaning to children no less than to adults. Possibly the pageantry of the liturgical service binds the young to the worshiping

community, but in churches which rely mainly on verbal symbols to communicate the gospel message the principle of graded worship is not soon dismissed.[2]

Nonliturgical churches ordinarily conduct family worship led by the minister, assisted by young people in the pulpit and by children's choirs. But much remains to be accomplished before mastering the problem of creating worship forms suitable for young children and adults alike. Meantime most churches adhere to the graded worship idea, with a growing number alternating age-level services with family worship on a monthly or quarterly basis.

4. FAMILY NIGHTS. Of the many steps currently taken toward drawing the church and home more closely together, family nights are perhaps most widely observed. A typical plan calls for supper—often pot-luck—fun songs and hymns, and special entertainment features followed by brief worship. Sometimes there are movies for the children while parents listen to an address or take part in a discussion dealing with the Christian family. Adjournment comes early in the evening, so that the children can get to bed on time. It is interesting to note that the family night may be held quarterly, monthly, or even weekly. Any night—including Saturday and Sunday—seems to attract people, helping them establish their identity both as kinship families and as members of the people of God, the local church family. To anyone privileged to participate in a number of these in various communities, the impression is strong that the popularity of the family night is deserved, for it serves the cause of Christian nurture of family groups.

5. AUDIO-VISUAL AIDS. Stimulated both by organized religion and commercial enterprises, radio and television offer occasional programs which reach the home with the claims of religion. Drama on family life themes is fairly common, but hardly a rival for Western movies pouring into the living rooms of America. However, the mass media are of sufficient importance to claim the attention of the several responsible church commissions. Nor are we lacking for filmstrips and movie-shorts devised to educate persons for Christian family living.

The International Journal of Religious Education and other publications of the Division of Christian Education of the National Council of Churches provide periodic evaluation of audio-visual aids that deal with the family.

6. NURSERY AND HOME GUIDANCE. In recent years weekday nursery classes have been adopted by churches which seek to engage young families in a co-operative educational venture. Beyond conducting a good nursery school, the church purposes to guide mothers and fathers in making the home Christian. In some instances parents must agree not only to help with the class but also to participate in study groups. The school may be financed by tuition fees and grants from the sponsoring church. Care is taken to secure a head teacher competent in child and adult education. A few professional workers devote themselves entirely to weekday and Sunday nursery education and its counterpart, parent guidance. Occasionally seminaries and neighboring churches collaborate in establishing nurture programs for young families.

Where public schools do not provide kindergartens, numbers of churches have done so for some years past. Their programs appear to be less specifically directed

[2] Cf. ch. 14 for additional discussion of family worship.

both to parents and children than are those of the more recent church nursery school.

7. PASTORAL CARE. In addition to all the new and not so new work being done in Christian family life education, formal and informal, the steady task of pastoral care continues. The past decade has seen a notable advance in equipping ministers for marriage and family guidance, and recent graduates of seminaries appear more interested in this phase of Christian nurture than in any other. Those pastors concerned to counteract the mass-mindedness infecting the churches may well view their role not so much as counselor—after the pattern of the consulting psychologist—but as pastor-educator, serving families rather informally as friend and spiritual guide. Be this as it may, the pastor rightly has the single most influential position with respect to nurturing the home in Christian faith.

From this sketch of church and home relations, we turn now to the question, What is the proper role of the home in religious nurture?

Toward an Understanding of the Family's Role

1. THE FAMILY MATRIX. Somewhat as the mother provides the prenatal matrix to enable the embryo to come to birth, the kinship family serves as the postnatal matrix, providing essential nutriment for personality development. At birth the child—in Horace Bushnell's phrase—is a "candidate for personality," and both hereditary endowment and relationships experienced during infancy and early childhood within the family contribute to the child's development. He is completely dependent upon others, and the growth process requires interrelations if human personality is to be achieved.

A sensory being, during the first three years or so of life, the child is predominantly emotional, relying on feeling for communication with others from whom he is learning, whose attitudes and care for him are directing him toward the sort of person he is to become. Parents or parent-surrogates inevitably contribute ingredients used by the child to fashion his emergent self through responses to the human environment. There can be no question but that the child senses whether he is wanted, accepted, loved. By the tone of the parent's voice, especially by physical contact with the mother, he is learning to trust or mistrust the world. If he learns trust, senses that he is ministered to by trustworthy persons, he is predisposed to be confident and enjoy emotional and physical health, the first condition denoted by his relatively placid reactions, the second by proper intake of food and gain of weight. Contrariwise, a rejecting parent or a home marked by parents at war with each other, implants mistrust and dis-ease reflected in the child's emotional stress and bodily disfunction. An infant who displays chronic irritation for no discernible physical cause may be signalling for help in finding needed ingredients with which to grow a healthy personality. The home, therefore, is to offer the child patient, loving care and provide a milieu suffused with affection which parents have for the child and for each other. On these points there is no deceiving of the child, and his behavior shows it.

In summary, the home is responsible for starting the child off in an atmosphere of interactive love. Closely allied with this trust-producing quality is the parents' task of disposing the developing person to respond to authority.

Though personality is not found at birth it emerges during the first year of life.[3] Within another year the child is likely to assert himself by means of resistance to parental treatment. Granted that negativism manifests the child's growing individuality, his proper growth requires a blend of permissiveness and restraint by his elders, for otherwise he is denied requisite limits, a structure of relations, and opportunity to learn to respond to authority. Not merely parental authority but also—where there are older children in the family—corporate authority of the household is to be exercised for the sake of the child's development as a social being. Excess of either permissiveness or restraint is to be avoided, but absence of authority gives a dubious bent to personality development and may cause malformation of the person. Hence it should be the concern of church educators to help parents fulfill their responsibilities for providing the young child with these ingredients; love and restraint—grace and "the law"—for spirituality in later years depends on these.

It is the young child's nature to copy and identify with persons who in his eyes are significant. Normally he invests both of his parents and his older siblings with significance. They have power over him; he wishes to possess this power and be like Mother and Dad, big brother or big sister. Identifying with them he comes to identify himself. Experiencing his elders' love-nature, he can later experience the love of the unseen heavenly Father.

Basil Yeaxlee[4] has traced the stages of psychological and religious nurture and indicated the role of the home in fostering spiritual growth. Suffice it to say here that before school age the child's imagination and growing experiences within the family lead him into an enlarging world wherein the quality of his earliest relations remains dominant. During middle and older childhood his parents serve as his guides and interpreters of life, as he learns to question and distinguish between the real and the imaginary, develops a conscience, and shows concern for others, in contrast to his natural self-centeredness.

2. THE SELF THROUGH INTERACTION. A person hopefully spends a lifetime trying to know himself, yet he can achieve a valid conception of himself in mid-childhood. Because a self-image simply cannot come out of a social vacuum, the home rightly becomes the ground against which the individual sees himself as the figure. Individuality always connotes community, and it is in the structure of family relationship that sustenance and freedom are provided for the person to be himself, an individual, unique, yet bound to other persons with whom to interact and develop selfhood. Interactive love is the essence of familihood by means of which both young and old gain personal, social, and spiritual growth. Luther speaks of persons within Christian fellowship being Christs one to another—an ideal for the home to ponder, but seldom possible for it to attain, for human love is imperfect. Reuel Howe tells of a group of parents worrying because they could not give enough love to their children and describes their relief when they realize that only God can give children what they need.[5]

Both parents and children lack the love that bears all things—all frictions, abuse, heartlessness, neglect. Adults must be clear about their frailties and sinfulness, realizing that only through the sufficiency of God can love govern the home. Happily the realism of the school-age child enables him to accept parents'

[3] See Gordon W. Allport, *Personality: A Psychological Interpretation*, pp. 129, 130.
[4] *Religion and the Growing Mind*.
[5] *Man's Need and God's Action*, pp. 90-92.

fallibility. Being a child he is quick to forgive parental transgressions—provided emotional health and spiritual integrity mark family relationships. If there is emotional illness or religious shallowness, the child is destined to be confused if not blighted in some measure. Accordingly, doubts plague him about the merits of religious avowals. Moreover, where parents are found to be spiritual frauds, the child's capacity for realism may be strained to the breaking point, leaving him bereft of a model for guiding his growth. As Richard V. McCann's researches[6] show, the child without a worthy parent-model has a serious problem in relating himself either to persons or to God. This plight bodes ill for the person on the threshold of adolescence.

3. ADOLESCENT AND FAMILY DEVELOPMENT. Early adolescence has been called the graceless age.[7] Certainly the years from twelve to fourteen represent a struggle of the individual to discover himself. It is not uncommon for him to shift abruptly from one interest to another, one passion to its opposite, his feelings erupting much as though he had reverted to age four. Emotionally he is flighty, socially uncertain, but intellectually he is something of a thinker inclined to challenge the adult world. The child has become the father of the man, his sentiments reaching out for new objects of devotion. By turns aggressive and withdrawn, hostile and tender, rebellious and conforming, he is in quest of new and more personal values. Parent-models suffice his needs only in part, even in homes where formerly the best of interpersonal relations were enjoyed. During this period an older admired brother or sister may exercise a more stabilizing influence than the parents, but a hero figure beyond the family circle is needed to embody the youth's aspirations and anchor them in reality.

Religiously, the adolescent seeks a master devotion and the best contribution of parents is made in the measure that they, like John the Baptist, are ready to decrease while Jesus Christ increases in the life of the youth. By mid-adolescence commitment of the self to God in Christ means the difference between finding the self one is created to be and remaining lost both from the self and God.

It is a truism that families, like individuals, differ, yet Christian families are likely to hold this experience in common—the spiritual health of their young adolescent is somewhat in proportion to the emotional and religious condition which all along has characterized the family. The family may be an inadequate religious influence, however, especially if it is not an authoritative guide for the adolescent in ordinary affairs.

Gibson Winter[8] has emphasized the necessity for the family's exercising leadership aimed at counteracting the dangerous drift of American society. He charges that parents have abdicated; the home is disordered, caught in a cold war and marked not by liberty but license.

Assuredly the shift from a patriarchal to a democratic family has deprived some homes of leadership. Consequently, individuals—adult and child—do that which is right in their own eyes. Alone, without the help of the supporting, guiding family of God—the Church—few families can develop authority and leadership requisite for passing over the shoals of pagan values and practices into the deep

---

[6] *Delinquency: Sickness or Sin?* Especially pp. 55 ff.

[7] Cf. Emmanuel Mounier, *The Character of Man,* p. 269.

[8] *Love and Conflict: New Patterns in Family Life,* pp. 39 ff.

waters of Christian living. Confused by conflicting claims of child-guidance specialists, psychologists, and educators, modern parents are torn between desire to give their young enough latitude in which to grow and a suspicion that by the time the child reaches high school he is seriously in need of counsel and control which now it is too late to give. The very practice of companionship between husband and wife—plus excessive permissiveness of the young child—appears to have first divided then weakened the home's authority.

This is no argument for a return of authoritarianism to the home, nor for repudiation of democracy in family life. What is indicated, however, is the definite need for parents and children together to establish corporate control not within the framework of materialistic but of spiritual values, not of an other-directed but an inner-directed order of human existence, not of social conformity but of Christian transformation. Toward this ideal, parents and religious educators together need to make a realistic approach to the problem of developing strategies for enabling families to be so unified with the church that they shall seek first the kingdom of God and his righteousness, subordinating the kingdom of things and its welter of deceptive values and activities. To put the matter somewhat differently, on Christian authority—articulated by word and deed of responsible parents—the home and church together ought to essay the task of empowering young and old to overcome modern modes of personal and social living. From this perspective, a home fit to guide the young is necessarily Christian.

Yet, no matter how excellent a home may become, it cannot escape problems, frictions, and sins.[9] Nevertheless, Christians have a faith that fortifies them for right handling of error and sin. It is the mission of the home no less than of the church to be a redeeming fellowship in which persons are reconciled with one another and God. In some respects, it is more dangerous for the family to aspire to be Christian than unchristian, precisely because Christian relationships are costly to pride. The will to forgive those in the family who despitefully use us is but a degree less difficult than the will to forgive one's self for despitefully using them. Furthermore, one may be called upon to go more second miles with his adolescent child, or his parent, or his marriage partner, than with persons less close to him. In other words, either the youth or the adult may find it is easier to be loving and forgiving outside the family. So it is that the home is the crucible in which personal worth is most severely tested.

4. LIMITATIONS OF THE HOME. The home is not the supreme value which the youth or adult is to serve. In our society, even as in other cultures and in New Testament times, a person growing in Christ sometimes finds that he has to break with the standards and values of his family. Perhaps more often than is realized, the individual ought to forsake what his parents stand for in order to follow Christ. This is indeed a hard saying, but how else can the Buddhist become Christian—or a person in a pagan American family forsake Mammon for God?

Basil Yeaxlee is correct in pointing out that in mid-adolescence an individual is ready for something to do, something to worship. A hero-worshiper, the youth looks for a person outside the family who seems to incorporate the kind of values he regards most highly. Currently American adolescents are speeding up the rate of social living, their behavior at sixteen resembling that of college-age people

[9] In his *Pastoral Ministry to Christian Families*, J. C. Wynn presents an enlightening discussion of this issue.

a few years ago. Close attachments are formed with a member of the opposite sex, and marriage comes at an earlier age.[10] Between the ages of sixteen and twenty-four the individual reaches his full intellectual and physical maturity and it is in the late adolescent period that economic, occupational, and romantic concerns tend to crowd out religious and social devotions. Marriage, possibly further schooling, his new home, and his job come first. He depends on the increment of religious values derived from his childhood home far more than he realizes. Yet the instability of childhood homes—with about one out of every five families broken in some way,[11] and an unknown percentage marred by tensions and sins—transmits something of the same instability and sickness to the newly founded home.

Nor is the situation in the young couple's home helped if the husband idealizes the "organization man" and his habit of conforming to the various security gods; or if the girl-wife idolizes the movie star or copies the artist's model. Success and glamour shroud spirituality, and youths lose sight of heroes worthy of emulation, unaware that a young family cannot live unto itself or its members develop productive lives by identification with unworthy figures. Yet authentic direction for growth inheres in Jesus Christ, and fortunately the first-born child may lead the family to the church, a community wherein Christian relations nurture persons and the family unit. Separated from the church, the family has no role in Christian nurture. Linked with the larger family—people covenanted together with God—the kinship family can fulfill its role as the spiritual matrix of growing persons, adults as well as children.

For Further Study

Family-life education has by no means solved all of its existing problems, and the rapid pace of contemporary living adds new ones each year. The following are among the more important which will demand the church's attention in the immediate future. Population in the United States increases by more than 8,000 every twenty-four hours. In 1957 a total of 4,302,000 babies were born, and by 1958 the figures showed over 173,000,000 Americans. By 1975 it is expected that there will be 225,000,000.[12] In addition there will be another 10,000,000 married couples and a total of about 55,000,000 families—the latter comprised of two or more related persons living together.

At both ends of the age span there has been sharp increase in population. By 1975 it is probable that we shall have close to 21,000,000 people past the age sixty-five. With increased life expectancy and marriage partners spending more years together, families pass through more stages than formerly. These present both opportunities and difficulties to which religious educators are wise to address themselves.[13]

The United Presbyterian Bulletin of Family Education Research [14] has raised a recurring issue concerning the effect on children of homes disrupted by any of the usual causes—death, illness, desertion, divorce, men away on jobs or in the armed

[10] Paul Glick, *American Families*. In 1950 the median age of first marriage for men was 22.8 and for women 20.1, p. 54.

[11] Edward V. Pope, Department of Agriculture. Lecture at Andover-Newton Theological School, August 1958.

[12] *Ibid.*

[13] See Evelyn M. Duvall, *Family Development*.

[14] Board of Christian Education, United Presbyterian Church in the U.S.A.

forces. Citing various studies and authors, the bulletin serves to remind us that findings are inconclusive and that additional studies are needed to determine wherein mental illness, delinquency, and other behavior problems may be related to disorganized and broken homes.

Despite extraordinary increase in the divorce rate during this century, marriage remains popular and perhaps a half to three fourths of the divorced persons remarry. Opinion is general that courses of study and counseling on marriage and family problems strengthen the home. Further investigation in this area is desirable, as is a study of content and method used by youth fellowships to prepare their members for marriage. It is noteworthy that this preparation is now given to youth in mid-adolescence or even younger years.

A survey of local churches around the country would evaluate the existing impression that weekday nursery classes are among the most effective ways to reach parents and educate them for their role in Christian nurture. Because of the decisive increase of working mothers and of fathers engaged in more than one job, children are left much to their own devices. Local churches might well experiment with ways to give special attention to such children, and undertake to provide mothering and fathering needed by the young for various reasons.

Parents can unite in church and neighborhood groups to devise means for establishing a better balance between the claims of the school and the church on the child's time and interest. In so doing, effort could be made to subordinate social and cultural standards and values to Christian ethics and theology.

Bibliography

Allport, Gordon W. *Personality: A Psychological Interpretation.* New York: Henry Holt and Company, 1937.

Duvall, Evelyn M. *Family Development.* Philadelphia: J. B. Lippincott Company, 1957.

Fallaw, Wesner. *The Modern Parent and the Teaching Church.* New York: The Macmillan Company, 1946.

————. *Toward Spiritual Security.* Philadelphia: Westminster Press, 1952.

Glick, Paul. *American Families.* New York: John Wiley and Sons, Inc., 1957.

Howe, Reuel. *Man's Need and God's Action.* Greenwich, Conn.: Seabury Press, 1953.

McCann, Richard V. *Delinquency: Sickness or Sin?* New York: Harper and Brothers, 1957.

Mounier, Emmanuel. *The Character of Man.* New York: Harper and Brothers, 1956.

United Presbyterian Church in the U.S.A. *Bulletin of Family Education Research.* Philadelphia, n.d.

Winter, Gibson. *Love and Conflict: New Patterns in Family Life.* Garden City, N. Y.: Doubleday and Company, 1958.

Wynn, J. C. *How Christian Parents Face Family Problems.* Philadelphia: Westminster Press, 1955.

Yeaxlee, Basil. *Religion and the Growing Mind.* London: Nisbet and Co., Ltd., 1956.

Chapter 14

Worship in the Educational Program

Kendig Brubaker Cully

ONE FUNCTION, CERTAINLY, CAN BE SEEN TO CHARACTERIZE ALL BODIES OF Christians across the years—their worship. To be sure, there has been a considerable variety of understandings as to the meaning of worship; forms of worship have differed widely among the various groups. Yet there never has been any serious debate as to the primary role of worship in the life of the church.

An interesting and a most significant development of recent decades has been the effort to re-examine the nature of worship as it is understood in the major traditions within Christendom. This effort has been encouraged by the ecumenical movement of our time. Practically every church body in non-Roman Christendom has been asking itself basic questions about its own life and worship in order that out of its self-understanding it might interpret its most commonly held positions to its sister denominations. The World Council of Churches, through its Faith and Order Division, has spurred such efforts.

The fruits of extensive international conversations were embodied in studies of a theological commission of faith and order, which published its findings in 1951 under the title *Ways of Worship*.[1] In that volume are contained statements concerning liturgy, word, sacrament, and devotion by representative theologians of many traditions—Orthodox, Anglican, Lutheran, Reformed, Baptist, Congregational, Methodist, Friends, and Old Catholic. There are also fraternal contributions by two Roman Catholic scholars.

The commission's report asks the question, "What *is* Christian worship?" In reply to that question it states:

Whilst we are actually worshipping the question does not arise, or if it does has to be banished again. For the essence of worship is that it is the concentration of all faculties on corporate self-giving to God in response to his love and in praise of his glory. All is centered upon him, and we only come into the picture at all as living recipients of his living self-communication. That is the heart of the matter. In practice, of course, individuals fall far short of this, but inasmuch as they do so, they have in that moment ceased to worship. But once the question has been raised as to the nature of what we do, we cannot go back to those times and places of worship without having at least begun to meet that question with answers which satisfy all that we know of the God and Father

[1] Pehr Edwall, Eric Hayman, and William D. Maxwell (eds.), (London: Student Christian Movement Press).

152

of our Lord Jesus Christ, and which make clear what it is he asks of men if they are to "worship him in spirit and in truth." [2]

In that statement a hint is given as to the increasing recognition of certain elements in worship which the church as a whole is coming to emphasize. Since the church's educational work must of necessity include a consideration of worship, it is important that we should look at several of these emphases in order to see what they have to say about worship in relation to Christian nurture.

The Corporate Character of Worship

Although individuals can come into God's presence privately, in accordance with Jesus' own urging (cf. Matt. 6:6), the worship of the Church is always first and foremost a corporate matter. This has been true of the Church as the body of Christ from the earliest days of the Church's life, from Pentecost onward. "They were all with one accord in one place" (Acts 2:1). The Christian does not know God in a vacuum; he knows God through Christ. To be in Christ is to be in the fellowship of Christ. The fellowship derives its meaning, its purpose, and its power from Christ. As the commission of the World Council of Churches indicated, "This *koinonia* is not something added to our private devotion, a coming together of privately saved souls: it is the way in which God reaches man." [3] In so far as the fellowship is really of Christ, it will of necessity express its action in terms of the whole body of Christ, or that segment of the whole gathered in one place at one time. Even though quantitatively the individual congregation may be relatively small, worship is possible whenever those two or three come together to invoke his Spirit and adore him for his own sake. "For where two or three are gathered in my name, there am I in the midst of them" (Matt. 18:20).

There is a sense in which we can say that the chief purpose of the Church is to draw all men reached by the gospel into a response to God through Christ. This is the Church's primary work for Christ in the world. Whenever that work is effected by the guidance of the Holy Spirit, people of all ages will be ingrafted into his body and will become worshiping members of the community. The very word "liturgy" is derived from the Greek *leitourgia*, which means a public service.

This emphasis on the corporateness of the Christian community has far-reaching implications for Christian nurture. It means, with reference to our present discussion, that although individuals will be encouraged to pray to God and adore him in their personal living, every possible effort will be made to relate such private devotion to the worship of the whole body of believers. This task will involve a number of aspects which we shall examine below.

The Heritage of Worship

The congregation's habits of worship will need to be communicated to the children and adults who are admitted into the fellowship of the Church and who participate in the life of the Church. The Church has a heritage of worship linking the present congregation with the vital past of the whole Church. Some elements of the Church's worship come from the earliest sources of our faith and

[2] *Ibid.*, pp. 17-18. Used by permission.
[3] *Ibid.*, p. 25.

are preserved in the Bible itself. When we read the Psalms responsively, we are sharing in the identical words used by God's people in the worship of the Temple at Jerusalem hundreds of centuries ago. When we read or sing a canticle such as the Magnificat or the Nunc Dimittis, we are using hymns of praise that came into existence not very many years after Jesus' earthly life. When a person was received into Baptism in the early church, he was to ask a simple question, such as "What is to prevent my being baptized?" To which the reply was made, "If you believe with all your heart, you may." Then would follow the candidate's confession of faith, "I believe that Jesus Christ is the Son of God," [4] or the simple affirmation, "Jesus Christ is Lord." Some scholars have pointed out that brief statements like these marked the beginning of the use of creeds, eventually elaborated into the Apostles' and Nicene Creeds and the later confessional statements of the various Reformation churches.

The hymnals of every denomination contain words and music taken up and incorporated into the public worship of the church, even though first written by individual poets like Clement of Alexandria (third century), Isaac Watts or Charles Wesley (eighteenth century), or John Greenleaf Whittier (nineteenth century), and composers like Giovanni Palestrina (sixteenth century), Johann Sebastian Bach (eighteenth century), Sir John Stainer (nineteenth century), or Ralph Vaughan Williams (twentieth century). This, furthermore, is a process that has continued even to the present time. Every new revision of a hymnal contains hymns that have recently achieved a place in the life of common worship along with the continuing classics for past centuries.

Likewise, in the dominical sacraments (called "ordinances" by some Christian bodies) of the church—the Lord's Supper and baptism—Christians have an especially meaningful corporate expression of their closeness to Jesus Christ. In baptism they are identified with Christ's dying and rising again to newness of life, and by this symbolical participation they are dedicated to unending faithfulness to him. In the Lord's Supper they remember him in the symbols of bread and wine which he himself indicated as the means whereby his followers might find his presence and continue their expression of relationship to him in faithful, living response. Long ago Augustine called the sacraments "visible words." These sacraments constitute a very special language of faith for the Christian community, a language fully understood only by those who participate in the corporate life of the church.

It is apparent that an important aspect of Christian education will be to introduce each new Christian into the forms and patterns of worship in order that he might enter into his heritage as a living mode of expressing faith. Worship in the church school is never an isolated phenomenon. As William Temple once wrote, people need to be trained in worship in order "to quicken the conscience by the holiness of God, to purge the imagination with the beauty of God, to open the heart to the love of God, and to devote the will to the purpose of God." [5] Individual Christians can enter into the fullness of faith only in so far as they are introduced into the church as a divine, redemptive fellowship, "the blessed company of all faithful people," as it is called in one of the historic liturgical prayers.[6]

[4] Cf. Acts 8:35-37. Note that in the R.S.V. vs. 37 appears in a footnote only.
[5] William Temple, *The Hope of a New World* (New York: The Macmillan Co., 1943), p. 30.
[6] *The Book of Common Prayer*, p. 83.

The question arises, Is the worship of the church only for the believers, or are the nonbelievers, the pagans, also to be included? George Laird Hunt has analyzed this question significantly:

The service should . . . not be built around the assumption that the congregation is composed of pagans but around the assumption that they are Christians. It should speak to growth in the gospel and not to ignorance of it. If this is done, if the service is an expression of common faith, the unbeliever will want what the believer has and the Holy Spirit will speak to him out of the witnessing of the congregation. Christian worship is a witness to our Baptism, not an evasion or denial of it.[7]

Whenever a person responds to God in awe, wonder, love, and a yearning to be one with these others who, before him, have been drawn to God in worshipful response, at that point he becomes a sharer in the worshiping community. He is no longer an onlooker but is drawn into the circle.

In those churches which practice infant baptism, the child is acknowledged as a member of Christ's flock at the time of his baptism. Even among bodies which do not admit children to baptism there is normally practiced a dedication service, one meaning of which is the congregation's recognizing the child being dedicated as a part of the community, for whom it has a nurturing responsibility. Hence we can say that as soon as a child is admitted into the congregation by name—even though he may be a baby in arms—his training has begun. Certainly if he is to grow up into the full meaning of membership in the church, it will be in terms of taking his part, according to his developing understanding, as a worshiper.

The Explaining of Worship

The religious education program will differentiate between actual worship—an objective action of the congregation—and the analysis of worship. This differentiation may be compared to the difference between religion and theology. Religion refers to the community's or the person's realized encounter with God—the actual meeting of the souls of men with the Holy Spirit of God. Theology is the explication of the experience, the logical analysis of what the experience entails. So it is with worship. It is the living relationship between God and his people. But the forms in which that worship is couched, the expressions it involves, are teachable and can and must be learned. As one interdenominational study committee stated, "The teaching program must assume as a major responsibility the teaching of young and old in the meaning and forms of worship. . . . Christian education involves practice in the act and instruction in the meaning of that act as inextricably woven." [8] The act will take place whenever the children, youth, and adults truly gather for worship; the analysis of the act properly belongs to study. The latter will be done through curriculum units on the church's worship. It will be accomplished as the teacher gives incidental instruction week by week, relating the classroom discussion and activity to what has transpired in the worship services, whether of the whole congregation, the department, or in an individual class.

The possibilities for study of the meaning of worship forms are illimitable and

---

[7] *Rediscovering the Church,* p. 136.

[8] *The Study of Christian Education,* Part III, "The Local Church Program." (Chicago: International Council of Religious Education, 1947), p. 9.

infinitely rich. The whole body of materials, actions, and symbols constituting the ingredients of worship services is available to the teacher and pupils, according to the age capacities of the pupils to respond to such analysis.

What does prayer consist of? Why are certain types of words used rather than others? What is the difference between the invocation (or collect) and the so-called pastoral prayers? In what sense is the Lord's Prayer the prayer of the whole church? How does it serve as a model of prayer, as Jesus taught? What is a litany? Why do we read the Psalms responsively, and use them so frequently? What are the sacraments? Why are they especially precious in Christian worship? What symbols do we use in our worship? Why do we sing? How do we open and close our services, and why? Why does "teaching" in the form of a sermon come in a worship service? These are a few of the more important kinds of questions that come to mind as one thinks of the range of the instructional approach to the understanding of worship.

Learning to Worship Through Worshiping

Furthermore, this approach is an excellent example of "learning by doing." The questions arise out of the act participated in or the action witnessed. The type of teaching suggested grows out of worship and prepares the pupils for more meaningful participation in worship, both at the same time. As the report on *The Study of Christian Education* stated:

> The church will never be stronger in any of its aspects than it is as a center of worship. Unquestionably worship is a function that is widely diffused, integrating itself with every activity that a Christian undertakes. But formal worship is of prime importance and liturgical education is indispensable. The symbols of worship have a potency that transcends intellectual formulations, and nothing can take the place of corporate repentance, aspiration and praise. And, as is true of all other learnings, we learn to worship by worshipping.[9]

We might say that participation in worship is the basic, foundational raw material of the Christian life. In the teaching and learning process we enrich the participation itself in so far as in the classroom we analyze and examine the nature of that worship in which we have shared.

The ecumenical temper of our day has vastly enlarged the scope of the teaching about worship. Whereas in former times many churches were quite content to make sure that their people knew the practices of their own denomination, or sometimes merely of a local church, now it is quite customary to encourage people to see the relation of their own forms to the ongoing developments in the Christian Church as a whole. We have been discovering that Christians of many traditions share with one another in the basic ingredients of worship, and that all of us represent in some measure a modification or development of the patterns of common worship that started with the earliest church of New Testament times. This is especially true when we consider the place of the sacraments in worship. Names of the Lord's Supper vary—Eucharist (thanksgiving), the Holy Communion, the Liturgy—the manner in which it is celebrated, observed, or interpreted will differ from denomination to denomination. The fact is that all Christians

---

[9] *Ibid.*, p. 36.

have taken seriously the commandment of Jesus, "This do in remembrance of me" (cf. I Cor. 11:23-26).

Grading Church-School Worship

Not only shall we want to train pupils to appreciate the forms of worship, but also we shall want them to grow in their understanding of the phenomenon of worship itself. This is something that can only be perceived by conscious incorporation into the curriculum—by talking about worship, thinking about it together, sharing in ideas as to what it means.

The value of graded departmental or class worship lies in the fact that it can contribute to this end. If a regular period of worship for the department or class is included as a part of the Sunday morning schedule, there can be a close correlation between what the children and youth are studying and their experience of worship. When the pupils themselves are involved in the preparation of departmental worship, they can examine the ingredients of the service while they plan it in the light of what worship itself really is—a coming into the presence of God, who, in the community of the faithful, speaks his word to those who truly seek after him.

When departmental or class worship is a part of the regular program, there will be an opportunity to relate the children's worship to the type of worship they will later be experiencing in the adult congregation, as well as to select materials for inclusion that are definitely related to their own present experiences, as to vocabulary, emotional range, and idea content.

Considerable work has been done across the years on the matter of planning and carrying out departmental or class worship services. Readers of *The International Journal of Religious Education* will be aware that each month suggested "Worship Resources" are published for teachers and leaders in the primary, junior, junior-high, and senior-high departments. These constitute a rich body of resources.

Marjorie Haynes has suggested that there are four basic principles around which every good worship service is constructed:

1. A central idea around which to build. 2. Parts of the service planned to bring the children step by step closer to that period of communication with God. 3. A leader using creative imagination in planning a service that takes into consideration the needs of his group. 4. The anticipation of the children built on the knowledge that part of the service will contain songs and scripture they love, but that part of it will be "different."

She does not think that a story should always have to be included. Instead, there may be used a carefully thought-out discussion, an explanation, visual material (such as slides), or dramatization.[10]

Most writers agree that formal worship is not possible on the kindergarten level, although primary and junior children are quite competent to participate in a more structured worship service. On the junior level, certainly, a careful correlation of the ingredients of a worship service with the children's study can be made. For example, in selecting hymns, a junior department worship committee might well be helped by the teacher's advising them to ask such a question as "What hymn will best illustrate the theme of today's lesson"?[11]

[10] *When We Teach Primary Children*, p. 64. See pp. 66 ff. for a specimen service.

[11] This suggestion is offered by Jane Bowerman Harris in *When We Teach Juniors* (Philadelphia: Presbyterian Board of Christian Education, 1957), p. 58.

Ralph D. Heim suggests criteria for choosing material to be used in a departmental worship service, as follows: adaptation (as to age interests and experience of the children involved), completeness (in relation to the thought or theme for the day), familiarity plus variety, fitness, participation (are the children given an adequate opportunity to share in responses, e.g.?), and unity.[12]

Less emphasis is being placed today than formerly on the "beauty corner" or "worship center" in the classroom. More use is being made of the main church or chapel, according to a definite scheduling arrangement, oftentimes even the kindergarten children being taken to the church for a brief period, though normally their worship moments would be centered in the classroom itself. Churches with separate chapels can use those for children's services even when the sanctuary is occupied. Some years ago it was popular to create "children's chapels," which were an attempt to imitate the adult church by reducing the size of furnishings and altar to what was considered appropriate for children. Many church planners in recent years have deemed it a wiser use of space to think of a chapel as a room large enough to accommodate whatever worshiping groups might need to use it, whether for a funeral, wedding, or a church-school class or department on Sunday morning.

The Place of the Family

The role of the family in worship is extremely important to recognize. A great deal of rethinking has been taking place regarding the place of family worship in the educational program of the church. One denomination has gone so far as to say that the effective use of its extensive new curriculum materials will be dependent on the seriousness with which children and adults worship together in some part of the church's worship schedule.[13]

It will be remembered by older readers that the pattern in the early part of this century was for children to attend Sunday-morning worship with their parents. The "family pew" tended to fall into disfavor with the advent of the newer age-level emphases during the religious education movement of the 1920's and beyond. It was argued that because children cannot "understand" the adult worship, they should be segregated for their own worship. Commenting on this, David R. Hunter has said:

If understanding is the primary objective of worship this argument has great virtue, but to make understanding a prerequisite for being a real participant in an act of worship is to permit secular standards of education with their supreme emphasis upon the intellectual to extinguish that which is uniquely Christian about Christian education. One grows and develops in the Christian faith not by understanding a mass of facts and propositions, but by entering into a relationship within which alone the facts of our Christian heritage can be understood.[14]

It cannot be said that there is any widespread consensus of opinion about this matter of family worship in the church as a regular practice. Many denominational

---

[12] *Leading a Sunday Church School* (Philadelphia: The Muhlenberg Press, 1950), pp. 219 ff.

[13] "The family pew also furnishes church school classes with one of their liveliest accesses to the resources of the church." *Right or Wrong* (Teacher's Manual, Grade 4, the *Seabury Series*, Protestant Episcopal Church; Greenwich: The Seabury Press, 1958), rev. ed., p. vii.

[14] "Families at Worship," *Religious Education*, LII (March-April, 1957), 98-102.

departments of Christian education would hesitate to recommend it very strongly. The weight of tradition is oftentimes arrayed against having children included in what has long been conceived as worship for adults alone. Although an occasional child visitor certainly would cause no lifted eyebrows, whole classes suddenly being distributed over the congregation with parents or teachers might incite a definitely negative reaction. Clergymen often hesitate to make modifications in the service (content or structure) which the presence of large numbers of younger children would necessitate.

Nevertheless, even when there is no strong disposition to welcome children to stay with their parents or teachers for the entire service, there is a marked tendency in many parishes to recognize that it is good to have the children visit the service for part of the hour, departing for their classes during the singing of a hymn. Or, sometimes the schedule is arranged so that children can be included on festival days in order that they might experience what it means to be a part of the large worshiping congregation on such joyous occasions as Christmas and Easter. Many churches are increasingly reversing this matter, also, urging that there is no valid reason to assume that study is for children only while the adults "major" in worship. The ideal seems to be moving in the direction of a totally worshiping and studying community within the church, people of all ages being engaged in both types of interrelated activity. Worship leads to study, and study is incomplete without worship.[15]

Informal Worship Times

The emphasis on formal corporate worship is not meant to minimize the occurrence of informal "moments of worship," more properly to be thought of as moments of devotion. These, too, are suitable for inclusion as a part of the church-school session routine. Such insightful moments of inspiration or closeness to God are perfectly legitimate and indeed to be encouraged. One might say that they will always emerge in a class where effective interpersonal relationships exist between teacher and pupils, and where God is the background and the foreground of the class discussion and activity.

This is the kind of experience of "awe and wonder, joy and thankfulness, love, aspiration and purposefulness" which "all come from within," as Jeanette Perkins Brown has suggested.[16] As she explains, this type of experience arises when a sensitive teacher plans, beyond mastery of subject-matter, to "create an atmosphere in which discoveries may make a truth apparent; in which a child's insight may emerge and ripen. When this has happened, she knows that in that moment of awareness the child is having a religious experience and is close to worship." [17] Although distinct from formal worship, such worshipful experiences are indeed enriching for the children, and the encouragement of them in their religious growth through such means is enhanced by the use of relevant poetry, art, storytelling, conversation, and song. Here would belong such a valuable activity as the formulating of a litany. The children talk about matters for which they feel grateful. The teacher then arranges these thoughts into a form resembling versicles and responses for the class to use in unison, or perhaps to include in a devotional service shared

[15] For further discussion, cf. ch. 13, pp. 144-45.
[16] *More Children's Worship in the Church School*, p. 17.
[17] *Ibid.*, p. 22.

with another class or department. This kind of activity may serve the useful purpose of helping children become familiar with forms such as they will encounter in adult services all their lives.

The question arises, Should children be taught to lead in worship? The theory underlying their doing so is that by taking part they will more deeply penetrate into an appreciation for worship. That there are advantages and disadvantages in this few would deny.[18] In so far as they take a responsible share in worship now, for their own church-school group, they may be learning how to conduct worship at some future time when they will have to do so if they occupy positions of leadership in a church men's or women's group, or as advisers to youth societies. It is even possible that by becoming involved in the conduct of worship, some children might be given their first encounter with the possibility of choosing to prepare for a church vocation. On the other hand, most children will grow up to be adult participants in worship that normally will be conducted by a clergyman. It may, therefore, be more important to train them in the various aspects of participation in worship under the direction of adults who can execute the service in a manner befitting the exalted mood of worship. Whenever possible the minister himself should be drawn into situations where he can be seen by the children in his role as one who leads in worship. They will be seeing clergymen in that role during all their years ahead.

The Christian Year

Finally a word should be said about the rediscovery of the church year. The Christian year commemorates the rhythm of the church seasons from Advent through Christmas, Epiphanytide, Lent, beginning with Ash Wednesday and culminating in Good Friday and Easter, Ascension, Pentecost, and the long Trinity season. This pattern has been deliberately followed by churches that have stressed the historical continuity of worship. In some measure all Christian groups have remembered at least parts of the Christian year. Although it was illegal to celebrate Christmas outwardly in colonial Massachusetts Bay, the Resurrection Day (Easter) was not forgotten. Today all churches have been showing a new interest in this ordered approach to the celebration of God's redemptive activity amongst men, which has been called "the drama of our salvation."[19] One writer addressing primarily ministers from a nonliturgical background, has suggested, "Those who will give the Christian year a fair trial will wonder why they ever became slaves to a series of unrelated free texts!"[20] The church year has a particular appeal to children and provides leaders and teachers in the church school with yet another fertile mine of resources whereby to relate the children's studying to the central life of the church's worship. Thus a skillful teacher is assisted in his task when the church focuses its attention in divine worship on the major themes in the redemptive faith of our fathers.

[18] See Paul H. Vieth's discussion in *The Church School* (Philadelphia: The Christian Education Press, 1958), p. 117.

[19] Cf. Bernhard W. Anderson, *The Unfolding Drama of the Bible* (New York: Association Press, 1953), p. 12; also G. Ernest Wright, *God Who Acts* (Chicago: Henry Regnery Company, 1952), pp. 112-16.

[20] F. R. Webber, "The Revival of the Christian Year," *Christianity Today*, III (January 5, 1959), 6.

Bibliography

Abba, Raymond. *Principles of Christian Worship.* New York: Oxford University Press, 1957.

Bowman, Clarice. *Restoring Worship.* Nashville: Abingdon Press, 1953.

Brenner, Scott Francis. *The Way of Worship.* New York: The Macmillan Company, 1944.

Brown, Jeanette Perkins. *More Children's Worship in the Church School.* New York: Harper and Brothers, 1953.

Davies, Horton. *Christian Worship: Its History and Meaning.* Nashville: Abingdon Press, 1957.

Edwall, Pehr; Hayman, Eric; and Maxwell, William D. (eds.). *Ways of Worship.* London: Student Christian Movement Press, 1951.

Haynes, Marjorie. *When We Teach Primary Children.* Philadelphia: Presbyterian Board of Christian Education, 1957.

Hedley, George. *Christian Worship: Some Meanings and Means.* New York: The Macmillan Company, 1953.

Hunt, George Laird. *Rediscovering the Church.* New York: Association Press, 1956.

Kerr, Hugh Thomson. *The Christian Sacraments.* Philadelphia: Westminster Press, 1944.

Martin, A. W. *Worship in the Sunday School* (Revised by O. W. Moerner). Nashville: Abingdon Press, 1943.

Shepherd, Massey H., Jr. *The Living Liturgy.* New York: Oxford University Press, 1946.

Sherrill, Lewis Joseph. *The Gift of Power.* New York: The Macmillan Company, 1955.

Towner, Vesta. *Guiding Children in Worship.* Nashville: Abingdon Press, 1946.

Williams, John G. *Worship and the Modern Child.* London: Society for Promoting Christian Knowledge, 1957.

Chapter 15

Counseling and Religious Education

William E. Hulme

THERE IS A GREAT DIFFERENCE BETWEEN WHAT IS UNDERSTOOD AS RELIGIOUS counseling today and what would have been understood by this term in a former age. Religious counseling in the old sense of the word meant an imparting of spiritual and moral wisdom in which the counselor did the imparting and the counselee the receiving. The process was simply a one-to-one extension of either preaching or teaching or both. The fact that we can speak of it in the past tense is due to its failure to fulfill its purpose. Because it was coercive in nature, people were afraid to submit themselves to its obligations. Because of its redundant relationship to the pulpit, people saw little advantage in availing themselves of it. With all the advantages of hindsight we see that its failure was also due to the fact that its methodology structured the process at a level where it could not meet the real need.

Religious counseling in its contemporary sense is something quite different. Its origin can be traced to Freud as much as to anybody. Out of his revolutionary discoveries about the *modus operandi* of human nature, modern clinical psychologists have perfected methods of counseling. So far as religion is concerned it was the clinical pastoral training movement founded by men such as Anton Boisen in institutions such as mental and general hospitals that incorporated the new approach into a religious context. From this hospital clinical setting religious counseling spread to the classrooms of theological seminaries. Today both seminary and clinical institution work together for the effective training of religious counselors.

Basic Principles

The new idea of religious counseling differs from the old in the direction of communication. We have moved from a counselor-centered approach to a counselee-centered or at least a relationship-centered approach. The process moves from counselee to counselor. The counselee's need is to communicate his problem. This means good listening on the part of the counselor. It is particularly important that the counselee give expression to his negative feelings. This means the counselor must be alert to respond to whatever indications the counselee may give to the presence of these feelings. When the counselee is relieved of the pressure of these emotions, his mind is better able to function. He gets insights into his problem which heretofore have been beyond his range of vision. It is the task of the counselor verbally to recognize these insights as the counselee gives expression to them so that they may become fixed in his mind and so serve as a foundation for further insights. The most significant insights are those that expose the ambivalent nature of our motivations and the rationalizations that have concealed it. While this intimate communication takes place between the counselee and the counselor, a relationship is being established between them that becomes the enabling factor for growth. It is this interpersonal matrix of the communicating process that makes it possible for catharsis and the achievement of insight to become maturing experiences. These same principles govern the process of group counseling as well as of counseling on a one-to-one basis with which we are primarily concerned.

Modern religious counseling asks less of the counselor than did the old. In line with its principles the new stresses that the counselor should do no harm, while the old asked that he be an expert in the wisdom to diagnose the ill and to prescribe the remedy. The new centers in helping the counselee to help himself; the old centered in the counselor's taking over responsibility for the counselee. The new emphasizes a relationship to sustain one over a period of time; the old was content to do it all in one interview.

The contrast is due to the new understanding that we have from the personality sciences concerning the operation of negative feelings. Where formerly we thought it best to suppress the counselee's expression of these feelings by some sort of reproof, we know now that this simply causes them to increase. It is the opposite approach that is needed. The more these emotions are allowed to be expressed in an atmosphere of acceptance, the more they are likely to decrease. We have always known this about the destructive emotion of guilt and have made use of it in the custom of confession, but so far as applying this knowledge to the feelings of discouragement and anxiety and especially resentment, we found it beyond our comprehension. Yet we should have known. The heroes of the faith in both the Old and New Testaments expressed these negative feelings freely to God and their fellows with what would appear to be the same results as are now verified in the clinical setting.

These same sciences have also helped us to a better understanding of the role of the relationship itself in counseling. Where formerly the counselor thought his contribution centered in what he said and how he said it, he now realizes that his own interest and attitude and patience toward the counselee may mean more over a period of time than his advice. As a result he is less anxious about what he should say and more concerned that he show understanding toward what is *being* said.

Religious counseling has its own techniques of procedure with which it attempts to realize its aims. Dictated by the theory behind counseling these methods emphasize *reflection*. By this we mean that the counselor responds to the counselee in a way that shows the counselee that he understands, and at the same time clarifies what has been communicated. Perhaps the best way to describe this technique in this survey chapter is by way of example. We shall take an excerpt from a counseling interview with a young lady whom we shall name Anna.

ANNA: I love the Lord more than anything I could mention and I know it must grieve him when I have the feelings I now experience.

COUNSELOR: These feelings seem to contradict your love for the Lord. (*He tries to reflect her inner conflict.*)

163

ANNA: Lately I haven't been able really to feel close to God. I haven't been able to pray and feel that he honored my prayers. I realize this must mean sin in my life but I just can't seem to be able to put my finger on it.

COUNSELOR: You feel there is something wrong about you that is interfering with your prayer life. (*He responds to the indication of guilt to encourage her to continue.*)

ANNA: Ever since my early teens I've been feeling sorry for myself. I lost my father then. Mother divorced him. Our home hasn't been the same since. I'm always asking the question, why did this have to happen to me! I sometimes think it's no use to go on—that no one really cares for me anyhow.

COUNSELOR: When it seems that no one cares it is pretty hard to keep going. (*There were all manner of significant things to which he could respond in this statement of Anna's. He chose to concentrate on her feelings and explore the family problems later.*)

ANNA. I'm ashamed to admit it but I've even thought of suicide. It seems that in being so much in despair I've failed God. I know it says in the Bible, "I can do all things through Christ which strengtheneth me." I've tried to claim this verse when I begin feeling sorry for myself, but it just doesn't work. I'm so unhappy I just don't know what to do.

COUNSELOR: On the one hand you feel you have failed God by your behavior, and on the other hand it seems that your religion has failed you. (*He tries to capture her ambivalence in her feelings toward God without going beyond what she herself has communicated. To prevent a premature rejection on her part he used the word religion instead of God in reflecting the more negative phase of the ambivalence.*)

ANNA: Yes. What worries me most is the fact that I don't want to go out with anyone. It seems I imagine people are always talking about me when really they aren't. I've given up going to the church youth group and practically everything I have ever been in. I really don't want to be this way because I know I could be a lot worse off, but I just can't help it.

COUNSELOR: You are becoming a lone wolf, I take it.

ANNA: I guess I should explain something else. I had been pretty good up until about six months ago. That's when my boy friend broke up with me. (*Would this have come out if the counselor had chosen instead to offer advice on her previous communications?*)

COUNSELOR: This was a pretty hard blow. (*He shows he understands the trauma.*)

ANNA: I was so sure he was God's choice for me. I prayed about it and the Lord seemed to give me the go-ahead signal. Why did the Lord lead me to believe he was the one for me, if he wasn't? (*The real basis for her resentment toward God now comes out and illuminates her inability to communicate with him.*)

COUNSELOR: You are wondering why God would treat you in this way—which doesn't seem to you to be exactly fair or kind. (*He is able now to respond to the full import of the ambivalence toward God. Notice how his expression of understanding is based upon her feelings and not on his own opinion about the actual trauma.*)

Religious Problems

What kind of problems come under the scope of religious counseling? The old tradition would say religious or spiritual problems and by definition would mean those problems that the counselee consciously associates with his religion. The new discipline makes no such line of division. Life cannot be so rigidly categorized. Beside having many different interests and activities, each person is a unit. His various roles and activities have an interdependence for the simple reason that they all influence and are influenced by this one person. We can see this in the case of Anna. She first expressed her problem in religious concepts. As the counseling progressed she was able to relate this problem to her unhappy home life, her feelings of rejection by her peer group, her broken romance, and finally returned at a much deeper level to her religious problem. She might have begun with her family problem or her feelings of rejection by her group, or even with her broken romance. In any case the counselor would have been dealing with the same basic problem. Problems in these other areas of life have a two-way connection with religious problems: on the one hand they directly influence a person's religious life and on the other hand the person's religious life influences his role in these other areas.

If we understand a person's religion as that which helps him to see his life as a meaningful whole, then all problems that disturb his personal equilibrium have a religious dimension, even though he may not consciously realize this. This needs to be said in the modern scene also, for there is a growing tendency to categorize again. This time the term *psychological problems* is used to distinguish from religious problems, the implications being there is no connection between the two. By psychological problems is meant those emotional disturbances brought on apparently by conflicts inherent in the culture. Yet wherever a counselor is confronted by the emotions of guilt, anxiety, or moodiness, regardless of their apparent cultural causations, he is confronted also by problems that have a potential religious depth. Anton Boisen's pioneer work in the clinical aspects of religious counseling was inspired by his conviction that even mental illness is a potential for religious growth and therefore of great religious significance. The divine-human encounter is relevant to all human problems. It is this which constitutes the challenge to the religious counselor.

This does not mean that the religious counselor envisions himself as the counselor for everything. He envisions himself as a member of a healing team and he relies heavily on the members of this team as he pursues his own task. This team includes the physician whose healing emphasis is on the body, but the body as it is related to the total person; it includes the psychiatrist whose emphasis is in mental illness; it includes the clinical psychologist whose efforts center in emotional disturbances; it includes the social and family caseworker whose work centers in family relationships; it includes those professions whose advice and co-operation is often needed, such as the lawyer, the economist, and the vocational guide.

Even as he sees the work of each member of this team contributing to the religious development of the people for whom he has a responsibility, so also the religious counselor sees his own work contributing to the ends desired by the other professions. Because he realizes that others have skills and abilities different than his, he works with these experts as their skills are required. Because he realizes that human problems have a religious dimension, he knows that he too is needed, for he contributes in an area to which the other professions are not oriented.

How Different?

In what way is religious counseling different from some of these related fields such as clinical psychology? Because of what appears to be a similarity of approach some might conclude that the only difference is that the religious counselor is less qualified. Because of the interrelatedness of all of life and the concern of religion for all of life, it is important to emphasize that God can and does work through both the therapist and the process representing these other healing professions, not only in terms of their professionally prescribed goals, but in terms of the growth in wholeness of the person in his totality. The difference between religious counseling and other fields such as clinical psychology is not that God works through one and not the other, or that the one therapist is religious and the other is not, but that the nature of each profession constructs a difference in perspective for each task, so that although some methodology is held in common, the perspective within which this methodology is used is different and therefore the results achieved may differ in emphasis if not always in kind.[1]

This orientation about the God-man relationship is specific in religious counseling. This does not mean that it must be acknowledged verbally or even that the vocabulary used must be religious terminology, but it does mean that both the counselor and the counselee are aware that the orientation is there and because of this it is natural on the part of both counselor and counselee to refer the problem to its God-relatedness. Not that this referral will always take place. The dynamic of each interview is unpredictable. But the fact that this referral lies within the concept of the profession and that both counselor and counselee are aware of this, is indicative that normally this referral will be made and consequently influence the direction of the counseling.

Tension over Communication

Like any new discipline religious counseling has its areas of tension. The most critical of these is whether or not the counselor may verbally communicate religious truth without departing from the process of counseling. Some of the tension over this question comes from the remnants of the old tradition still asserting itself among those who have not had a clinical orientation to the new approach. But there is also a genuine disturbance over this question among those who have no brief for the old ways. These people react negatively primarily to the idea of a *nondirective* counseling. Actually the reaction is chiefly against the *word* nondirective. (Because of this the word *client-centered* has been substituted, but the old name continues to be a label.) *Nondirective* implies that no authority other than the conclusions of the counselee exists in the counseling process. In tension with this is the Christian belief that authority resides in the word of God. Although a small minority of Christians would have no problem in identifying the Word of God with the insights of the counselee—namely the Society of Friends in their doctrine of the Inner Light—the majority of Christians associate the authority of the Word of God with the Bible or the Church or the denominational confessions. This authority pertains both to articles of faith (dogmatic theology) and of life (moral theology).

Part of the tension is caused by the failure of critics to recognize the value of nonverbal communication. Christendom is relatively unanimous in believing that the Word of God was made man in Jesus Christ. Jesus however not only revealed the Word of God by what he said but by what he was and by what he did. So the counselor's communication of love, acceptance, understanding, and faith may be chiefly manifested to the counselee by his attitudes and over-all bearing rather than by anything specific he may say. If this is the case then God may use such a relationship to communicate his word or at least to create the receptivity to his word.

The Church as a fellowship of believers is necessary for the communication of the Word of God. Without it the Bible or the Sacraments or the ecclesiastical

[1] Cf. William E. Hulme, *Counseling and Theology*.

decrees are incomplete so far as communication is concerned, for it is through the fellowship that the Word of God is realized. It is through the experience of love among Christians that the love of Christ is made comprehensible enough to believe. The religious counselor represents this fellowship of the Church in his relationship to the counselee.

In spite of the significance of a nonverbal communication of the spirit of the gospel, there remains the suspicion that the nondirective approach is based on humanist in contrast to theist assumptions. The counselor himself may interpret his methodology in terms of activating resources inherent in the human personality. This may mean that he believes in the sufficiency of human nature itself without any reference to God other than that the word "God" may serve as a symbol for these natural human resources. On the other hand, he may look upon the whole process as an example of how God operates and heals. Another counselor who uses the same methods may believe that the process opens the way for God to give *his* resources. Because individuals may have different theoretical frameworks from which they operate does not necessarily mean that they must adopt radically different methods of operation, no more than because they use similar methods must they arrive at the same results. Because one person interprets in one way why his methods work as they do, this does not mean that another who uses the same methods may not interpret this differently. Take Freud for example. When he secured his data from the laboratories of psychotherapy, he was functioning as a clinician. When he interpreted these findings from a naturalistic and mechanistic point of view, he was functioning as a philosopher. When he tried to corroborate his philosophy by recourse to primitive customs and myths, he was functioning as an anthropologist. In the opinion of many Freud was a good clinician—due to his training as a medical scientist—but a poor philosopher and an even poorer anthropologist. It does not require a Christian to find out how nature functions, even human nature; it requires an acute observer. How one interprets the findings depends on his own attitudes and creed. Therefore it is only logical that the Christian would have a different interpretation of the laboratory data and methods based upon these data than would one with some opposing viewpoint. It is a Christian conviction that without this Christian interpretation, therapy may never move into its fullest significance for the whole person, since it is religion which is the integrating power.

Actually the nondirective approach properly understood does not mean that the counselor cannot give direction to the counselee. We have already seen that through his approach the counselor communicates understanding and acceptance to the counselee which certainly give direction to the interview. Nor may his direction be strictly in the communication of attitudes. He often finds it necessary verbally to describe the structure of their relationship to the counselee, and to offer suggestions on how best to proceed in the interview. All of this is directive in nature. He may when he deems wise focus the interview on a certain area by asking the counselee to elaborate further on what he has said. Although he knows the danger of overdoing its use, he will occasionally direct the course of the interview by asking a question, even though the motivation for the question came from the counselee's communication. Also as a religious counselor he may show the counselee how the experience he has been through together with the subsequent insights correspond to certain biblical illustrations or Christian teachings.

Nor is it beyond his role for the counselor to communicate a helpful insight to the counselee. In doing so he must be confident that there is some identification with this insight within the counselee enabling him to receive it. This is a wise caution because it is based upon the necessity of keeping the initiative and responsibility with the counselee where it must remain if he is to grow in his own maturity rather than become dependent upon the counselor.

Communication of insight on the part of the counselor is a matter of timing so that the communication fosters rather than hinders the growth of the counselee. Such timing requires skill in apperception. The problem in religious counseling lies in precisely how far one can carry the verbal communication of religious truth on the part of the counselor without violating the fundamental principles upon which the new counseling rests. Some would answer that these communications have no place at all in religious counseling. They maintain that these insights should develop within the counselee himself without any suggestive verbalizing by the counselor. Others would say that they are in order and even helpful so long as they are timed to identify with insights already emerging within the counselee. Still others say that if timed in accordance with the dynamics of the moment, the presentation of these truths may even stimulate the counselee to develop the corresponding insight as his own. This much is sure—the further the counselor goes in his presentation of religious helps to the counselee the more skill he needs in terms of timing and manner of presentation. Consequently for beginners and learners in the art it is best to master the basic fundamentals which are guided by the principle "do no harm." The question now before us is whether these verbal religious communications from the counselor are a part of religious counseling or of religious education.

Counseling or Religious Education?

Strictly speaking the functions of religious communication center in preaching and teaching. The occasional communication of religious truth by the counselor in the counseling relationship could scarcely fit under the principles governing either of these circumstantially differing functions. Seward Hiltner has attempted to clarify this by making a distinction between counseling in its client-centered interpretation and whatever communication of religious truth the counselor may give in the counseling interview. The difference between such counseling and communicating is not one of categories by which we classify different religious activities, but of perspective on the part of the counselor whereby he determines his approach on the basis of the dynamics of the interview. Both the perspective of counseling and the perspective of communicating may be involved in the same interview, one perspective being dominant while the other is recessive and vice versa.[2]

By allowing for a possible shift from one perspective to another during an interview, Hiltner has helped us to see the whole activity as a unity without having to resort to a rigid interpretation of the function. We can call the entire operation religious counseling whether or not the perspective of communication is involved, because the circumstances of the activity belong to the counseling relationship and setting. On the other hand one may also consider the communication part of the interview as teaching on the basis that the counselor is communicating the needed

[2] Seward Hiltner, *Preface to Pastoral Theology* (Nashville: Abingdon Press, 1958).

religious help at the right moment. If we call it teaching, however, we need to take into account the counseling milieu which makes such teaching unique. It is teaching existentially—communicating the gospel when the dynamics of the interpersonal relationship suggest that now is the time. It is bringing religious truth out of and into the very moment where the counselee is doing his living, not by any projected anticipation of this moment by the "teacher," but by the counselor's actual participation in the moment with the counselee. The result may be an appropriation of the truth that makes of it an essential characteristic of future living.

There is a mutuality of support between teaching as such and counseling. It was my experience as religion teacher and religious counselor at a church-related college to observe many times the manner in which the events of the classroom led students to desire religious counseling, and of equal importance, the way in which religious counseling contributed to the learning potential of the student as the insights of the counseling experience aided in receiving with affinity the teachings of the religion classroom. The one negative factor in this mutuality between the two disciplines in an academic setting is the necessity for grades. The fact that the religious counselor is also the religion teacher who grades the student adds a complication to the counseling relationship. But this complication is missing from the church congregational setting. Here teaching and even preaching have a decided reciprocity with counseling. This leads us to a consideration of the role of religious counseling in congregational life.

Counseling in the Congregation

The first question that confronts religious counseling in the congregation is, who does it? Normally religious counseling is called pastoral counseling, because of its association with the role of the pastor of the congregation. May it also be associated with the directors of religious education or other teachers and workers on the church staff? So far as knowledge and preparations are concerned the answer would be yes, for the opportunity to learn is open to all in many theological schools and clinical centers. For some churches, however, the office of the ordained minister has more ecclesiastical significance than for others. For the former such things as confession and absolution belong to the office of the ordained ministry. Since religious counseling often leads to confession, the problem in these churches would have to be worked out in some way that preserves the prerogatives of this special office of the ministry. For other churches the problem primarily is the necessity of both the unordained religious counselor and the ordained pastor working out each other's roles so that no disturbing questions of authority or responsibility need arise.

The second problem in this area of congregational life was voiced by the English Puritan divine Richard Baxter some three hundred years ago when he said, "Because the people are grown unacquainted with the office of the ministry, it belongeth to us to acquaint them herewith, and to press them publically to come to us." [3] The same problem exists today although the recent emphasis on religious counseling in America has helped matters. The point remains that many church people are still afraid to bring their problems to a religious counselor, and either keep them to themselves or rely solely on the other healing professions. In confronting this

[3] *Ibid.,* p. 17.

problem we are working against the secularization of our society. The question before us is how to encourage the people in our churches—and outside as well—who need religious counseling to come for it.

The answer lies in education. It is the task of religious leaders to explain the counseling opportunities to their people in a manner that helps them to see the wisdom in securing this help when it is needed. This should be followed by the invitation to come for this help and an explanation of how to make the contact. Youth are particularly in need of this explanation and invitation as well as the counseling itself and are most likely to take advantage of the opportunity. If we succeed in educating the church's youth to the opportunities of religious counseling, we are influencing the attitudes of the next generation.

If this program of education is to be successful in encouraging people to seek religious counseling, the counselor needs to bring order and system to the opportunity. This means first of all a place in which to counsel. In the congregational setting the best place for counseling is a room in the church which is both private and attractive. Next of importance is the time. If there are regular times set aside for religious counseling and announced as such, it is a help to people in making the contact, and a help to the counselor in being prepared to receive them when they do.

Cautionary Measures

Because counseling has its methods, there is always the danger that the learner will concentrate on methods and lose sight of the theory behind the technique. The result is a mechanical and impersonal caricature of counseling. Normally this is only a passing and perhaps even a necessary stage in learning. However the danger remains that technique even after it becomes second nature may be separated from spirit. Counseling methods are, among other things, intelligent means for communicating a spirit. When they are used as ends in themselves they destroy the counseling relationship. Simply allowing a person to get things off his chest is not enough. Listening is no substitute for caring, but rather a vehicle for it. Religious counseling in all its methods should communicate to the counselee the assurance that the counselor is concerned about the problem and intends to work with the counselee toward its solution under God.

Those who treat counseling as a mechanical technique are usually those who lack an affinity for it. Those who seem to have a talent for drawing others to them for counsel, have need for caution in the opposite direction. Subconsciously they may enjoy the fact that others come to them—even though they complain about it—and in order to keep them coming may encourage a dependent relationship. There is always a danger that counseling may lead to exploitation. For the counselor it may be a fad that temporarily augments his sense of importance. For the counselee it may become more a means for getting attention than for getting help. So each may exploit the other as both exploit the opportunity. In this avenue of service as in others it is important for the servant to know himself.

Since people whose problems are beyond the scope of counseling will come to the religious counselor, it is very important that he recognize his limitations. Foremost among these are people with psychotic tendencies. These people are mentally disturbed to the point where they have difficulty distinguishing reality from their own distorted imaginings. Naturally when their contact with reality is this tenuous they are unable to respond to a conversationally oriented therapy like counseling. If in this state of distorted perception negative emotions should overwhelm them they may do harm to themselves or to others.

While all of us are neurotic to a degree, people with decided neurotic tendencies may require a more intensive therapy than many religious counselors are prepared to give. The problems of the neurotic seem simple as he relates them, but this is only because the things he believes are causing them are so small and insignificant. That they are not simple is shown by the fact that they persist in spite of all the supposed progress of the counseling. Actually the real causes are deeply repressed—often centered in buried hostility—with many defenses erected to keep them repressed. It is possible for counseling to unearth them but it requires more understanding and skill than for emotional problems whose causes are more easily discerned.

The fact that people with these psychotic and neurotic disorders come to the religious counselor makes his position strategic for referral. It is necessary for him to have working arrangements with competent representatives of the other professions of the healing team so that he can quickly make the necessary transfer. It can be a delicate situation to suggest to a person that he see a specialist, particularly when the specialist is a psychiatrist. Often the religious counselor is able to do this better than others. By introducing the subject in a way that reduces its threat and by offering to accompany the person to the psychiatrist, he gives him the support he needs. Once the transfer has taken place, he is not thereby out of the picture. He should keep in touch with the doctor and with the patient. Although religious counseling is not what the person needed in his illness, there will undoubtedly come the time when he will need it for his full recovery, for the religious counselor belongs in the healing team and no other can take his place.

Conclusion

The principles of contemporary religious counseling in contrast to those of a former day are based on the insights from dynamic psychology in which the counselee is helped to work out his own solution to his problem. Although all disturbing problems have at least a potential religious dimension, the religious counselor does not see himself as the only counselor, but as a member of a professional healing team. It is important for him to recognize his limitations and to make much use of his strategic opportunity for referral. As a member of this healing team his is the unique contribution of a therapy structured unapologetically upon the God-man relationship. This therapy has its basis in a nonverbal communication of God's love through the counselor's attitudes. Though there is admittedly some tension over the point, it is the opinion of many that this nonverbal communication may assume verbal form as the counselor senses the proper timing. This fact brings religious counseling into close relationship with religious education, and the two disciplines have a demonstrable mutuality. Religious counseling's opportunity in the Church depends upon the encouragement people within the congregations receive to utilize this ministry when they need it. The almost phenomenal increase in its role in American congregations shows that it is both being accepted as a legitimate ministry and being used. Whether it will continue to grow or even to hold its own depends upon whether its advocates can refrain from overemphasizing its importance to the de-emphasis of its interdependence on the other ministries of the Church, and whether it is viewed primarily in a theological dimension rather than a psychological one.

Bibliography

Doniger, Simon (ed.). *Religion and Human Behavior.* New York: Association Press, 1954.

Hiltner, Seward. *Pastoral Counseling.* Nashville: Abingdon Press, 1949.

———. *The Counselor in Counseling.* Nashville: Abingdon Press, 1952.

Horney, Karen. *The Neurotic Personality of Our Time.* New York: W. W. Norton and Company, 1937.

Hulme, William E. *Counseling and Theology.* Philadelphia: Muhlenberg Press, 1956.

———. *How to Start Counseling.* Nashville: Abingdon Press, 1955.

Johnson, Paul E. *Personality and Religion.* Nashville: Abingdon Press, 1957.

Kunkel, Fritz. *In Search of Maturity.* New York: Charles Scribner's Sons, 1943.

Wise, Carroll A. *Pastoral Counseling: Its Theory and Practice.* New York: Harper and Brothers, 1951.

Chapter 16

Group Dynamics and Religious Education

C. Ellis Nelson

THE WAY IN WHICH PEOPLE LIVE AND WORK TOGETHER IN GROUPS HAS INTERESTED the social scientist for a long time. Prior to World War I, leaders in social thought speculated on problems such as the proper size of a group for effective work or the effect of one person on another in their group life. In the 1920's, the social scientists began to gather information about group life—size, ability to solve problems, and group factors in worker productivity. In the 1930's, research projects were designed to test theories about groups; one of these grew out of the work of Kurt Lewin at the University of Iowa. Lewin, a social scientist refugee from Nazi Germany, was concerned with the problem of how the social atmosphere would affect individuals in a group. With Ronald Lippitt and Ralph K. White a research project was designed whereby democratic, authoritarian, or *laissez-faire* leadership was arranged for groups of eleven-year-old children; and the result of the different types of leadership could be studied in terms of productivity and interpersonal relations. The democratic type leader, who helped the group organize itself and make its own decisions, proved to be the most productive and provided for more personal growth and group maturity than the other types of leaders. Since that experiment the group has become the object of careful observation, measurement, and experiment.

Almost all human activity is done in groups. Because the person in a group represents the interests of sociologists, psychologists, educators, and psychiatrists, the study of groups branched out rapidly in all directions and became a recognized field of study and work. Most of the research has been done in large universities, such as The Research Center for Group Dynamics at the University of Michigan, The Human Development Laboratory at the University of Chicago, The Department of Social Relations at Harvard, and The Human Relations Center at Boston University. Training of leaders in group dynamics, in addition to research, has been the major function of the National Training Laboratories in Group Development, which is related to the Division of Adult Education Services of the National Education Association.

Interest in group dynamics spread rapidly because this subject had immediate practical implications for almost everybody. Psychiatrists have been interested in supplying theories on the kind of needs that a person has satisfied when he participates in a group, and they have also developed techniques of group psychotherapy and psychodrama whereby individuals act out their hostilities, fears, or other emotions. Sociologists have been concerned with the sociogram, whereby the relation of one person to another is charted, and with sociometrics, which is the measurement of various relationships within the group, and with the "role" that is played by persons in groups. Psychologists and educators have been concerned about learning in groups, about leadership of groups, and about the practical application of group dynamics to the school, industry, adult education, camping, government, recreation, and social agencies. Perhaps the next phase of research will harmonize the important findings from the various social scientists and will provide the church with a more complete understanding of the group. At the present time, however, we must be content with information from a variety of sources that was not developed with the special needs of the church in mind.

The term "group dynamics" has been applied loosely to all kinds of group activity; but it should be restricted to a study of the forces at work within a group of people who are engaged in a common task. In this sense, all groups with some degree of stability have dynamic factors at work—an interplay of personality upon personality. Techniques such as "buzz groups" do not constitute group dynamics but are methods of stimulating participation. "Group process" is a more restrictive term denoting the interaction as it takes place at a particular time or a pattern of interaction that is taking place in a group. Sometimes the term group process is used for the known patterns of interaction that take place—the predictable and, to a certain extent, controllable processes of the group that can be seen and assayed.

Group Dynamics and the Church

Although the church exists in a relation to God who uses and yet transcends all methods of communication, and although group dynamics exists in a scientific orientation that is indifferent to values beyond what can be measured and controlled, there are three important places where underlying assumptions of the church and group dynamics have general agreement. In each case the reason for these affirmations may differ; yet, the two find common interest in the following areas:

1. Every individual has dignity and worth in himself. This affirmation, the basis of our political democracy, is reflected in phrases such as "endowed with certain inalienable rights—life, liberty and the pursuit of happiness," or "government of the people, by the people, and for the people." Although people differ in ability, personality, and interests, they have equal rights and deserve equal respect. Each individual is free to participate according to his ability; each person is expected to respect the feelings of others and to work co-operatively with others for the common good. Individuals are not sacrificed nor manipulated; rather, individuals are expected to grow in a permissive atmosphere and to enter responsibly into decision making. Group dynamics affirms this principle and the democratic method.

The church likewise upholds man's dignity. Man was made in the image of God and one person cannot violate another, not even King David when he had his friend Uriah murdered in order to get his wife. The mature theology of the New Testament is represented in John's Gospel in the famous verses (John 3:16-17) that interpret the life and mission of Jesus as a demonstration of God's saving love for anyone who believes in him. This conviction that each person is valuable in the eyes of God is a central affirmation of the church. We find it repeated by Karl Barth (*Church Dogmatics,* Volume II, Part 2) where he insists that man is elect in Christ, that the sum of the gospel is that God is for man, and that we must look at man as a person and not as persons.

2. Man has the capacity and responsibility to plan his corporate life. Group dynamics proceeds on the assumption that man can apply his intelligence to the problems at hand and create a better life for himself and that he can increasingly control his environment, even his human relations. Basic to this assumption is the idea that government and laws are to be created and re-created by man and that he is not to be governed against his will. People must have the opportunity to participate in organized social life whether it be government, labor union, management in industry, lodge, or church in order to learn how to control their affairs. This is the motive behind group dynamics; it gives a sense of direction and urgency to the leaders who would awaken people to their opportunity and responsibility.

The church is not so optimistic about man's ability to create the good life, especially after the devastating wars of the immediate past or the threat of future wars. Yet the church works to bring about a better social order. The major portion of Jesus' teaching was of a prophetic nature in which he sought to expose greed, power politics, and the tyranny of spiritual leaders. This prophetic element has always been active in the church and today it works for a just and durable peace, better race relations, and for a more equitable distribution of our nation's wealth. The church today would not imply that these activities are the gospel, but they are the places where Christians work to demonstrate their responsibility to God for a better social order.

3. Man finds his deepest satisfactions and develops his finest potentialities in a group. Group-dynamics theorists find a secure foundation at this point, for the social scientist and psychiatrist are in general agreement that the individual comes to selfhood as a result of interaction with other persons in the family and community. Man is a social animal and his satisfactions come from life in a group that shares his common purposes, hopes, and problems. Furthermore, the healing of man's fears, anxieties, and frustrations comes about more adequately in a group where he is respected and accepted. An illustration of the curative power of a group is Alcoholics Anonymous. People who were confirmed alcoholics are able to salvage their life and redirect their energy by the support, understanding, and guidance of a small group of people who shared the same problem and struggled with the same foe.

The Church, likewise, is confident of the transforming and transmitting power of the group. Matthew's Gospel says the Church is "where two or three are gathered together" with Christ (18:20). We conceive of the Church as a demonstration of the work of the Holy Spirit, and biblical theologians say that we have no account of the Holy Spirit apart from the Church. Although the Spirit comes to an individual, he causes the person to work for, or in, the body of believers. The Church is the body of Christ and the place where the new life is born and nurtured. A *koinonia*, which is inadequately translated "fellowship," is formed. The idea is really sharing, joint possession, or joint participation. The fruits of this relationship in the group of believers are "love, joy, peace, patience, kindness, goodness, faithfulness, gentleness, self-control" (Gal. 5:22-23, R.S.V.). These fruits can be enjoyed and can be communicated only as one experiences Christ in a group of believers. The church, therefore, affirms that the best she has to offer is found in her corporate life and worship.

The Use of Group Dynamics in the Church

Although leaders of the group-dynamics movement and of the church might agree on the above areas of common affirmation, each group has its own separate reasons for doing so. The affinity is there, and that is why the church has so quickly responded to the group-dynamics movement. Its utilization by the church can be seen in four major areas.

1. TEACHING. Many of the methods of teaching that grew out of a knowledge of group dynamics are not new, but they are used with a clearer understanding of why they are used, and the conception of learning is broadened to include the students' attitudes, values, and behavior. There are three major principles underlying any utilization of group dynamics in teaching. (1) The group (class) should participate in deciding on the curriculum, that is, what is to be learned. The leader (teacher) needs to help clarify the group's thinking about its needs and interests and to help work out a plan for study and work. This might be done by a check list, group decision, or interview. A church-school class might do this by looking over the prepared curriculum, gauging its usefulness for their situation, and then altering its scope to fit their needs or abandoning it completely. (2) The group should participate in the teaching. After needs and interests have been determined and agreed upon, the group should take responsibility for deciding the course of the educational experience. The appointed teacher may be asked to take certain responsibilities; the group may divide into smaller work committees to do research about topics or problems and bring their findings back to the group. (3) The group maintains itself. The teacher is a stimulator, guide, coach, and friend. One of the major responsibilities is to achieve an atmosphere in which learning can take place; to accept the individuals as they are with their fears, frustrations, and criticisms; yet to see in them, and help them see in themselves, possibilities and opportunities for mental and emotional growth. The teacher does this by the way he handles himself and the group so that a feeling develops that they are all engaged in a common task which has its own rewards, where failure is not met with blame but with an honest facing of the situation so that new plans and efforts can be started afresh. Members of the class are helped to feel relatively secure so that they can progressively drop their false faces, see themselves at a deeper level, and respond more creatively to the realities of life. The group takes responsibility for maintaining its own active participation and attendance.

The specific methods used for teaching with an understanding of the dynamic elements in a group will vary considerably according to age, social class, maturity, educational goal, and educational attainment of the class. The most frequently used techniques can be classified in two major categories.

Methods related to formal presentation. A lecture does not allow for overt participation but it can create a mental and emotional participation on the part of the audience. A lecture has certain advantages—well-thought out material, efficiency in covering a wide area of thought quickly, ability to articulate and give data for problems a group faces. A forum, film, debate, play, symposium, or group interview are variations of a formal presentation with limited group participation. Group dynamics does not abandon formal presentation but it provides for ways the group can quickly interact with material that is presented. Buzz groups present one of the widely used methods whereby the group is divided into smaller groups, usually six to eight people, for discussion of a topic or to formulate questions or to provide next steps for the group to consider. After a short time in a buzz group, usually ten to fifteen minutes, a reporter from each group gives his group's thinking on the matter at hand. These reports become the basis of further work or discussion. Listening teams can be selected in advance of a formal presentation in such a way that one listening team will give special attention to one aspect of the topic, another team to another. The teams will then report to the whole group, indicating their reaction to the presentation. Role playing is not so much a reaction to a formal presentation as it is an informal presentation to the group of emotional content, of a point of view, or the acting out of attitudes in a common life situation. Without script or rehearsal, individuals are asked to assume a role. Usually a situation is sketched in rough outline form that fits the concern of the group. For example, a group concerned with juvenile delinquency may, from its knowledge of a home that produced a juvenile delinquent, enact a home scene that brings out the tension between boy and parents. The whole group will then discuss the scene, its adequacy or shortcomings, and gain an understanding of the emotional factors that underlie delinquency.

Methods related to group process. When Harrison Elliott introduced group discussion to religious education in the 1920's, he had in mind a problem-solving process whereby the group defined a problem, explored and experimented with possible solutions, and finally developed an adequate solution. That method is still widely used today, but studies in group dynamics have opened up important new areas—such as the interrelation of individuals in the group during discussion and a more profound understanding of the individual as he participates in group discussion. The term "group process" is coming to connote this newer perspective. Group process is quite different from teaching with group techniques as explained in the section above, although some of the group techniques may be utilized in a group process situation.

Group process is task oriented. The group is expected to move ahead in planning or discussion. The task may be suggested by individuals in the group or by the leader; but in any case, members of the group start the discussion about the nature of the task or problem by defining or redefining it in their own terms. They then work on the problem, contribute their own experience and knowledge, explore ways to work, and define areas where they need more help or information. The role of the leader is different from that of the traditional teacher. The leader is sensitive to the total group situation; he rephrases questions; he helps modest persons break in; and, when things are going well, he lets the group develop its own ways of working. This means that the leader cannot have a fixed agenda; in a church-school class it can easily mean that the curriculum topic for the day simply gets things started, but the real problems of the class will lead elsewhere.

One important characteristic of group process is the group observer. The observer seldom enters the group discussion. His task is to sit aside to figure out what effect the leader's action is having on the group and how the individuals react to one another. He is not greatly interested in the content of the discussion but how it is developing, the atmosphere within the group, the roles people are playing, and the factors that are helping or hindering discussion. Often the observer uses a check sheet to help him evaluate these points and to plot the interaction that takes place. The group may ask the observer at any time to report and often will expect him to do so at the end of the session. The report is to help the group face its problems in a responsible way, to help the group become more mature. Therefore, the observer must be careful not to use his position in a way that will increase anxiety or conflict. In his first reports, he should be factual and informative; later when the group is ready, he may be more interpretative in his comments.

A special form of group process is the workshop. A workshop, as the name implies, is a place where something is made. Those who come together are peers, each with talents and a common interest in the work to be undertaken. A workshop group meets daily for a period of several weeks. Although some planning is done in advance, the group takes charge when it meets, sets a schedule, plans its work, and evaluates its progress as it proceeds. Library, films and other resources are available and are used as needed. Although some formal presentations or lectures may be scheduled, most of the workshop time is spent in small work groups seeking to develop various facets of the total task.

2. GROUP WORK. A second major contribution of group dynamics is related to program groups such as a youth fellowship. Normally called group work, this is a guided interaction wherein the participants plan and lead their own activities. There is a leader, usually called the worker, who guides the interaction of the group. Group work is a method of conducting group activity. The worker guides the interaction to help the individuals become more mature and responsible, but it is always within a group setting and about group activities.

The worker is the key to the group work approach. He is to help the group develop—to do things with, not for, them. He works by suggestion indirectly. He helps the group clarify its purposes and goal. He helps the group understand the church as an institution and the group's capacities, opportunities, and limitations as they function in the church. The worker has to make judgments about the maturity level of the group—how much anxiety they can handle and under what circumstances he must offer rather clear-cut suggestions. The worker must be sensitive to the changes that take place in and between individuals and must plan his participation according to the needs and the development of the group.

Since groups differ in many ways, principles have to be adapted to specific conditions. However, the group must be small enough so that the members know each other well and have a chance to participate in the activities; it probably should not have more than twenty members. Organization is held to a minimum with great informality and spontaneity in planning. Good group work is held together and given its enthusiasm by the interaction between individuals functioning within the group's general purpose. The worker encourages this process, helping the group to harness its own energy and helping to give it direction and meaning. Individuals participate at the level of their capacity and receive from the group the satisfactions that come with status and a growing sense of personal competence. At times, the worker helps the group evaluate its own progress by the questions he raises and by the goals which the group has agreed to work toward.

3. LEADERSHIP. Group dynamics in its modern phase began with studies in leadership of a group as indicated earlier in this chapter, and research in this aspect of group dynamics has continued. Leaders of the group-dynamics movement seem to agree that leadership is not a trait or a set of traits; it is not inherited; nor is it a function of the well-educated person. Various studies have been made of traits that were supposed to indicate leadership such as health, physical vigor, intelligence,

confidence, will power, enthusiams, but no distinct pattern of these traits emerges which clearly indicates the characteristics of a leader. Studies of leadership have led to the conclusion that leadership can be learned and that it is a set of functions related directly to the group in two ways. Ross and Hendry in *New Understanding of Leadership* summarized the two ways leadership can be related to the group. The first is that leadership is a function of the group. With this notion, leadership is something in which many members participate. One member will be a leader in suggesting an idea that others agree to; another member will conceive of a better way to perform a task; someone else will provide enthusiasm and personal interest in others that keeps the group relations pleasant. By this definition, all partake of leadership. Leadership is a role that is played by many at different times for the welfare of the group. From this standpoint, the most effective group would be the one in which there is no status leader, that is, no one who is the head of the group—a situation in which many group members could slip into the role of leader as the occasion demanded and the needs of the group emerged. In fact, the word leader is considered archaic, and a term such as "central person" would more adequately represent the newer concept.

A second way leadership is related to the group is to see leadership as a function of the situation. That is, a certain person is the leader when a group is discussing business, but when they stop for dinner and enter a social situation, a different person may emerge as the leader. Studies have shown that a group will often change leaders as the group changes from a task that requires reasoning to a task that requires mechanical assembly of parts.

To utilize the newer concepts of leadership, some leaders in religious education have done two things. First, they have sought to interpret leadership in terms of a group-defined function rather than personal characteristics, thus taking over the group-dynamics conception of leadership. This necessitates a different training experience; to adequately understand group-centered leadership one must participate in the group and see what shared leadership is like. A second way some religious education leaders have responded to the newer concept of leadership is to develop teaching teams consisting of a leader, a recorder, and an observer, each of whom will fill a role in the group process. Some have proposed that formal leadership should always be set up in terms of pairs of people so that a genuine dialogue gets started from the outset.

4. EVALUATION. Although evaluation is not new to religious education, it is a phase of the educational process that is left to the last or is rejected as improper for the spiritual life. Group dynamics, on the contrary, has insisted on evaluation as a part of the group's experience; and it is included in every phase of group life. This comes about because, when the center of gravity moves to the group, the group becomes the authentic voice for direction and correction.

In teaching by formal methods the group techniques are in themselves a type of evaluation. The buzz session, like the other devices for developing participation, gives the group an opportunity to judge what is said and to direct the discussion to the most profitable channel. More precise and formal methods of evaluation will elicit from the group, by means of a questionnaire or further discussion, information about how much was learned, whether the object of the group was met, or specific suggestions as to how the group can improve or alter its program.

In teaching by group process, the use of an observer is the most widely employed method of evaluation and his work has already been described. Often the group observer will make his work more objective by diagramming the individual participation in the discussion and noting the number of times each person participates with some indication of the role each person plays, noting whether the participant's comments tend to clarify, elaborate, analyze, belittle, distract. The use of a team of leaders is an evaluation device if the leaders keep notes, compare them, and proceed according to their joint judgment. The individuals in a group are often requested to write out their reactions to the group in addition to the rather constant evaluation that takes place in the group's discussion.

In group work, evaluation is more difficult because the group is often made up of adolescents who respond on the basis of the personality of the leader or their need for friendship with certain members of the group. However, the worker can keep an anecdotal record of events that affect the life of the group and the way the group responds. A similar record can be kept regarding individuals in the group. The worker can make some evaluative judgments about the growth of maturity in the group by their appearance on time, enthusiasm for their projects, their development of a sense of responsibility for each other and the common task, and by their venturing into new and more complex programs.

Limitations of Group Dynamics in the Church

Although the assumptions of group dynamics about the work of the individual, his responsibility for properly ordered society, and the creative results of good group experience are likewise affirmed by the beliefs of the church, the church has her own unique reasons for these affirmations. Furthermore the church has other beliefs, such as man's tendency to be sinful, which cause the church to understand these assumptions differently. Therefore, the utilization of group dynamics in the church is surrounded with certain limitations, some of which would be the following.

1. The norm for the Christian life, although cultured by and expressed in the group, is not the group; it is a person's relationship to God. Biblical illustrations of men who have lived lives of faith show that they were often in conflict with their society, even with the religious groups that nurtured them. Although some writers in the field of group dynamics vigorously oppose the idea that their method is adjustment minded, it is fair to say that group dynamics developed in America during the period when many sociologists were concerned about "the resolving of social conflict." Kurt Lewin proceeded on the basis that social conflict was disintegrating, whereas today some sociologists, such as Coser in his book *The Foundations of Social Conflict,* find that social conflict has a necessary functional value in a democracy. Floyd Hunter's *Community Power Structure* shows how powerful are the informal lines of control that regulate a community; group dynamics does not have a philosophy of power adequate to combat selfish force.

Certainly within the church the only norm of the Christian life is the will of God, however difficult it may be to ascertain his will for a given situation. Disagreement within the church is not in itself bad or even undesirable. The Christian's task is to so relate himself to the God of the Bible that he can live and work, confident of God's leading, and can conduct himself with a generous and open attitude toward others with whom he disagrees. In this way he learns, has his beliefs clarified, and is able to share his knowledge of God with those among whom he lives. Perhaps we can say the Christian life is a handling of tension between his life situation and God's leading rather than a reduction of tension or adjustment to a group pattern of behavior.

2. There is little doubt that many of our most creative and rewarding experiences come in groups of congenial people with a common cause. Experience alone is not enough, however. Research conducted by the Continental Army Command has shown that an army unit that was good at one activity was not necessarily good at another. Men who were very companionable on off-duty activity and had many of the basic qualities of a cohesive, well-integrated group could perform more poorly when operating equipment than crews which were limited in their association to duty hours. This is not to deny that group experience is a powerful agency for learning, but it is to deny that a group which works together harmoniously, effectively, and with growing group maturity and responsibility is necessarily Christian. After all, such a group could be bank robbers! Group process should be subordinated to the purpose of the church when it is used in the church.

3. The concept of leadership as group centered, as a role that is passed around and performed by various persons in the group, does not give a satisfactory explanation of leadership. It is true, of course, that some people can do certain things better than others, and that a person skilled in leading folk games may not be able to lead a discussion. But leadership in the sense of guiding and inspiring a group, anticipating unseen difficulties, adventuring into new areas of thought and work, or a capacity to develop and articulate a worthwhile program is more complicated. Group dynamics leaves one with a very elusive leader, and to call him a "trainer consultant" or "central person" doesn't change the situation very much. Although the trainer consultant may successfully demonstrate that he doesn't qualify as a leader, his position as trainer shows that he has more know-how and prestige fastened to that facet of his personality. Group dynamics has probably overplayed the idea of group-centered leadership; for, taken literally, the most successful group would then become the one in which the fewest leadership roles were found in one person. Yet our common experience with groups does not support that assumption. Almost every human group with a measure of stability has some recognized leadership. Newer studies in leadership, such as reported by Ross and Hendry in *New Understanding of Leadership*, show that leadership is very complex. Although certain aspects can be learned, there is still a personality factor that is too elusive to be domesticated within a fixed theory and too obvious to be dismissed.

4. Group dynamics has rightly insisted that the group is a powerful agency for education, especially in the formation of attitudes and values and for developing emotional health in a group atmosphere of acceptance and mutual concern. However, we must be careful not to assume that the permissive group situation will necessarily cause a person to share his deepest problems or, indeed, that he will even be more aware of his real situation. We must be even more cautious about one's spiritual experience; for when we speak of one's relation to God, we are discussing something that is essentially private and mystical although it may take various overt characteristics. We cannot say, therefore, that group dynamics is a preferred way of learning about God or having an experience with God. It is one method. We must realize that it focuses attention on the personality traits of people in the group and the relationship of people in a group, with a reduction of interest in the quality of ideas being discussed. Jacob in his *Changing Values in*

College surveyed the various teaching methods used in college, including group process, and came to the conclusion that no one method was best. Rather, it seems that learning is more related to the learner and his personality structure than to any one method of teaching. Therefore, the teacher should be prepared to use a variety of teaching methods, including group process, on the basis of the type of pupil, his life situation, and the purpose of the educational experience.

5. Group dynamics proceeds on the basis of the needs and concerns of the group and it can logically produce no other data for consideration. This process is excellent for the emotional development of the group, especially where group dynamics is considered to be a process to help people achieve mental health. Moreover, this method gives motivation to learning for problems which are local, which are real problems, and whose solutions have an immediate utilitarian value. However, one can question the wisdom of using only local problems and concerns for the educational task. One important task of education should be to expand the area of awareness, to develop wider concerns. After all, parochial loyalties are already rather well established, but to create a sympathetic and intelligent understanding of the needs of people elsewhere is difficult yet urgent in our threatened world. Often these wider areas of concern do not have a clear-cut local application, and some methods other than group process are necessary to bring them into focus.

6. Leaders who have fostered group dynamics in the church report that several practical problems often emerge. There is a danger that the group may become too intrigued with analyzing the process going on within itself and lose sight of worthwhile achievement. Sometimes a group probes too deeply into a person's inner-self and the person freezes up, or contrariwise, a person finding a friendly group may reveal an acute personal problem that the group can't handle. The group will, then, feel chagrined about its impotence, and the individual will feel a deeper sense of failure and frustration.

Summary

Since almost all religious education is done in groups the study of the dynamic interaction of individuals within the group is of paramount importance. Some of the beliefs of the church about man coincide with beliefs that underlie group dynamics and, therefore, the church can share some of the techniques that make for a good group process and use the knowledge of group behavior that is developing. Theories of learning that have emerged from a careful study of group process are of special importance to the church. However, religious education is a servant of the church and therefore has a different purpose from the intent of group dynamics. Religious education must adapt rather than adopt the methods of group dynamics.

Bibliography

Adult Leadership. A magazine published monthly except July and August by the Adult Education Association, 743 N. Wabash Ave., Chicago 11, Ill. This magazine deals with various practical problems of leadership in small groups. The Association has also published Adult Education Leadership pamphlets such as: 1. How to Lead a Discussion; 2. Planning Better Programs; 4. Understanding How Groups Work; 5. How to Teach Adults; 6. How to Use Role Playing and Other Tools.

Cartwright, Dorwin and Zander, Alvin. *Group Dynamics: Research and Theory.* Evanston,

Ill.: Row, Peterson and Company, 1953.

Douglass, Paul F. *The Group Workshop Way in the Church*. New York: Association Press, 1956.

Douty, Mary Alice. *How to Work with Church Groups*. Nashville: Abingdon Press, 1957.

Gordon, Thomas. *Group Centered Leadership*. Boston: Houghton Mifflin Co., 1956.

International Journal of Religious Education. Special Issue on "Christian Growth in Dynamic Groups," XXXIII, No. 9 (May, 1957).

Little, Sara. *Learning Together in the Christian Fellowship*. Richmond, Va.: John Knox Press, 1956.

Religious Education. See issues for January-February, 1951, XLVI, No. 1; November-December, 1951, XLVI, No. 6; November-December, 1952, XLVII, No. 6.

Ross, Murray G. and Hendry, Charles E. *New Understanding of Leadership*. New York: Association Press, 1957.

Sullivan, Dorothea F. (ed.). *Readings in Group Work*. New York: Association Press, 1952.

Thelen, Herbert A. *Dynamics of Groups at Work*. Chicago: University of Chicago Press, 1954.

Trecker, Harleigh B. *Social Group Work*. Revised edition. New York: William Morrow and Company, 1955.

Chapter 17

The Church School and Techniques of Teaching

Howard M. Ham

SPIRITUALLY CLUMSY INDIVIDUALS STRUGGLE AND SEARCH FOR MATURITY IN religious living. Often unaware of what they seek, these unfulfilled ones pursue the meaning of life, the experience of redemptive relationships, the affirmation of being. In every mood and temper they come to fill the classrooms of the church each Sunday—eager and indifferent, rebellious and searching, serious and playful. They come, willingly and unwillingly, to discover the resources of religion, and perhaps a new life, through the church school. It is an enduring tribute to the church-school teachers that considerably more than half of the church's members have entered the church through their classes.

Church Schools Find New Ways to Serve

Recent years have brought major changes in the patterns of church-school teaching. Prior to the early 1930's, church-school teaching was largely devoted to the mastery of biblical knowledge. Two developments in fields outside of the church school resulted in major modifications of church-school practices. The discovery of the educational values of activity and experience units by the public schools was a major break-through at the frontiers of learning.[1]

At about this same time, the five-year Character Education Inquiry, conducted by Hugh Hartshorne and Mark A. May at Teachers College, Columbia University, made available research findings [2] which raised serious questions about the character building effects of biblical knowledge and other standard methods of religious and moral education.

Under the weight of these research findings, the church schools had moved almost entirely into life-situation teaching by the early 1940's. Along with this, student-teacher co-operation in planning and carrying out the learning activities was highly valued.

---

[1] One of the most influential early treatments was *Principles of Unit Construction* by Arthur J. Jones, E. D. Grizzell, and W. J. Grinstead (New York: McGraw-Hill Book Company, 1939). The trend, first reported in 1927, was furthered significantly through the suggestions of Hollis Caswell and D. S. Campbell, *Curriculum Development* (New York: American Book Company, 1935). By 1940 the movement was so widespread that a survey of the literature was felt to be needed by James A. Michener and Harold M. Long, *The Unit in the Social Studies* (Cambridge: Harvard Graduate School of Education, 1940).

[2] Hugh Hartshorne, Mark A. May, *et al., Studies in the Nature of Character* (3 vols.; New York: The Macmillan Company, 1928-30).

During World War II, military experiments to test the possibilities of accelerating learning through the use of audio-visual techniques proved highly successful. Beginning with the establishment of the Division of Visual Aids for War Training in the U. S. Office of Education in 1941, the experimental program moved so rapidly that by 1945 articles reporting the successful application of audio-visual techniques in every conceivable kind of educational situation were appearing in educational journals of all types. In 1946, the appearance of Edgar Dale's definitive book, *Audio-Visual Methods of Teaching,* marked the maturation of this trend in teaching techniques. During the 1950's the use of audio-visual materials and methods became almost universal in the church schools of America.

Accompanying the enthusiasm for audio-visual techniques was a growing interest in the educational possibilities of new understandings of group processes. A challenging world of knowledge had been opened up for exploration by the establishment of a Research Center for Group Dynamics at the Massachusetts Institute of Technology in 1945. This center was soon moved to the University of Michigan, where it has remained since that time. Tremendous amounts of information concerning group processes have been made available by this center. The impact of these findings upon the teaching techniques in the church school became increasingly apparent during the later 1950's.[3]

More recently, another distinctive body of research evidence has been stimulating new developments in church-school teaching procedures. The knowledge concerning processes of motivation has grown so rapidly during the 1950's that annual volumes [4] have been required to make this information generally available to the public.

At approximately the same time, intensive government-supported research has been concentrating on a study of the processes of leadership. During the late 1950's, the initial results of this research began to make its appearance in an impressive stream of books and articles. One important insight for church-school teachers in these research findings is that the function of any leader—including the teacher—is that of helping the group achieve its goals.

Along with these two rather fully developed bodies of knowledge, a third type of knowledge has reached the stage of very promising beginnings. This is the measurement of the changes which occur in the personality processes as a result of educative efforts. Processes which were once thought to be unmeasurable qualities are now measured.[5]

As a result of these recent developments, the newer techniques of teaching reflect a concern for the ways in which students can be challenged to enter actively into the learning process, and with even greater emphasis, a concern for the ways in which teachers can help the learners to achieve the purposes to which the group is committed.

Techniques of Preparation for Teaching

The responsibility of the teacher for challenging students sufficiently to involve

---

[3] Cf. ch. 16, pp. 173-83.
[4] *Nebraska Symposium on Motivation* (Lincoln: University of Nebraska Press), annual volumes since 1953, ed. M. R. Jones.
[5] Cf. ch. 29, pp. 316-25.

them in the processes of learning, requires a greatly increased emphasis upon the teacher's preparation prior to his actual encounter with the students.

The older techniques of teaching were primarily performances by the teacher. Thus, preparation for teaching consisted primarily in deciding in advance what would be done when one faced the class.

In the newer approaches to teaching, the bulk of the classroom time is used by the students in the pursuit of their own educational purposes. Consequently, the teacher has the responsibility of anticipating the needs of the learners and of giving on-the-spot help and guidance when the students encounter obstacles in their attempts to learn. Such responsibilities require extensive preparations before the class assembles.

Intelligent preparation requires more than just the expenditure of adequate time and thought before meeting a class. At least the following preparations must be made if teaching is to be as effective as it can be.

1. DEFINE THE TASK. Before anything else is done, the teacher should write down a brief, clear-cut statement of what is to be accomplished through the activities of the class. Until the teacher has clearly in mind the precise nature of the task to be attempted, it is pointless to start assembling materials, selecting methods, or visualizing possible activities of the class. One does not normally look around for his golf clubs or his paint brushes in preparation for a game of tennis. It is equally absurd to assemble materials, methods, and planned experiences which are inappropriate for the class activities in which one will be engaged.

Once the basic task has been defined, it is well to list the four or five central learnings which are inherent in this task. Such anticipated learnings may be basic principles which are to be comprehended, essential skills which are to be mastered, attitudes which are to be developed, and so on.

When the total preparation has been accomplished, the teacher may return to the task definition as a means of checking the adequacy of the preparation. By asking in relation to each activity, reference book, or piece of resource material, "How will this help us to accomplish the learning task as we have defined it?" the non-essential ideas, activities, and materials may be eliminated and the class time devoted to the essential learnings involved in the purposes of the class.

2. DISCOVER THE LESSON'S RELEVANCE. Unless the teacher has a clear understanding of the value of each lesson or learning task and can see its relation to the unit as a whole, he will not be able to help the students to see the relevance of what they are doing. And unless students can see that learning is worth the time, thought, and energy required for it, they are not likely to put forth the necessary effort to learn.

As a technique of discovering the relevance of a specific learning activity, some teachers have found it helpful to ask themselves, "What will the student be able to do, as a result of this learning, that he could not do as well before?" Other teachers stimulate their thinking at this point by asking, "How will Student X be different from what he now is because of what he is about to learn?"

Regardless of how small the results of a specific learning experience may be, the teacher should be able to see the way in which it contributes significantly to the long-term development of the student. If the learning cannot be seen as a link in a long chain of development, the activity may not be worth the time of either the teacher or the student. Morale is difficult to maintain on the part of both the teacher and the student unless they can see the significance and relevance of each activity in which they engage.

3. LOCATE THE NECESSARY RESOURCE MATERIALS. When students are vigorously engaged in pursuing their educational purposes, it is important to have the resource materials readily available at the time they are needed. Resource materials are those reservoirs of help to which the student can turn for specific types of assistance in accomplishing his learning tasks. For example, one type of resource material might be an encyclopedia or a documentary film. Here the student could obtain information that he needs to carry on his learning activity, if he wished to do so.

In order to anticipate the needs of the class for resource materials, it is helpful to have a list of the more common barriers to learning which the class is likely to encounter. Such a list might include, in addition to the types of important information with which the students cannot be expected to be acquainted, such items as the areas of prejudice and misinformation most frequently encountered when dealing with this subject, issues about which it is difficult to do objective thinking, experiences and skills which the students could not be expected to have, and the sources of dependable information which are likely to be unknown to the students. The important items will vary according to the ages of the students, the nature of the lesson or unit, the cultural backgrounds of the students, and the individual differences present in the group of learners constituting the class.

Anticipation of class needs becomes easier as the teacher's experience increases. There is no reason, however, why each teacher should have to work at this task alone. Teachers in the public schools have found it desirable to combine their efforts in developing libraries of resource units that deal with the more common topics, projects, and units. Church-school teachers might profit from the example of their public-school friends and develop such resource libraries in the church school.

4. PLAN THE SEQUENCE OF LEARNING EXPERIENCES. A growing body of research seems to indicate that there are at least three steps in a normal learning process. First, there is a vague, undifferentiated perception of what is to be learned. This learning task is seen in terms of its massive wholeness, challenging the student to track its mysteries to their sources. Next, there is a progressive differentiation of the learning into its component parts with an accompanying sharpening and refinement of the perception. Finally, the specific, differentiated learnings are integrated into a highly complex understanding or mastery, which is progressively related to all the other learnings which have been accumulating in the life of the person.

The church-school teacher who is attempting to follow this three-stage sequence of learnings will select a different type of learning experience for each of the stages. The initial learning experiences will be designed to enable the learner to perceive the lesson or unit in a somewhat oversimplified but meaningful unity. Perhaps the central thesis or organizing idea of the unit will be lifted up for attention, or the over-all situation with which the lesson or unit deals may be presented vividly. Next, the basic issues or problems inherent in the thesis or situation can be made the focal points of attention in a series of learning experiences. Finally, experiences will be provided which are designed to gather up all these separate learnings into a single, comprehensive understanding, viewpoint, or orientation.

Teachers will find it helpful to experiment with variations in this psychological organization of learning experiences until they find the sequence that is most effective for them.

Young children and difficult learning tasks demand a psychological organization of learning experiences. As the learners become older or as the learning tasks become less difficult, other types of organization may be used effectively.

Fairly well developed space-time orientations are necessary before students can work meaningfully in learning situations which are organized in terms of chronological sequences, or in terms of widening concentric circles of relationships. The child of nine or ten years of age is usually able to comprehend historical developments and geographical relationships, at least in their larger outlines.

A logical sequence of learning experiences can be utilized effectively with youth and adults, providing the logical connections do not exceed the learner's powers of relational thinking. It should be realized, however, that if the student's mental powers are not sufficient to grasp the complex logic of the lesson or unit, his interest in the learning process can be expected to diminish rapidly.

Where possible, the students and teacher should plan the sequence of learning experiences together in relation to the needs and backgrounds of experience of the group.

Techniques of Classroom Leadership

A major responsibility of the teacher is that of helping students to define their purposes in learning and to formulate efficient ways of achieving those learnings. The carrying out of this responsibility is a basic element in the newer techniques of teaching. Some of the factors which are involved in the efficient discharging of the teacher's responsibilities should, perhaps, be viewed more closely.

1. THE MOTIVATION OF LEARNING. It is only the very inexperienced or unobserving teacher who can assume that all students will enter wholeheartedly into the learning of any lesson or unit, no matter how interesting, important, or relevant it may be. As a general rule it is necessary to make deliberate plans for the stimulation of learner interest in any unit or lesson that is studied.

However, no learner is completely inert. He is in process of coping with the problems of living at every moment of his existence. Consequently, one of the simplest techniques of motivating learners to enter enthusiastically into the learning activities of the class is that of tying the lesson or unit directly to the coping behaviors in which the members of the class are currently engaged. Thus, the adolescent youth who is trying desperately to formulate a satisfying understanding of what it means to be a man in the fullness of manhood in relation to a woman in the fullness of womanhood (or vice versa), can be easily motivated to study a unit on Christian courtship and marriage. All that is necessary is to show him how this study can help him to work through the problem of defining sex-appropriate development in which he is already involved.

Each stage of maturation has its appropriate developmental tasks [6] which must be accomplished before the person can move on freely to the next stage. Each developmental task is a potential source of motivation available for use by the church-school teacher.

[6] The classic statement of this viewpoint is provided by Robert J. Havighurst in *Human Development and Education* (New York: Longmans, Green and Company, 1953).

2. THE CONTROL OF CLASSROOM CONTAGION. Most teachers discover at one time or another that the contagion of classroom interest can operate in either of two directions. Interest in a specific type of learning activity on the part of one student tends to stimulate interest on the part of other students. On the other hand, interest on the part of a student in disrupting the learning situation can have an equally contagious effect. It is critically important, therefore, in a class divided between those who are interested and those who are disinterested to make certain that the interested group has every opportunity possible to infect the classroom with the contagion of their interest.

The contagion of interest in the classroom may be encouraged by giving interested students opportunities to express their interest publicly and enthusiastically. For example, in planning the consideration of a mission study unit, the teacher might be aware that a member of one student's family had traveled in one of the countries which might be included in the study. In such an instance, it might be desirable to let this student know in advance that the possibilities of studying such a unit will be discussed at the next session of the class. A casual suggestion that he might like to bring some samples of interesting objects or ideas connected with a mission area should result in an enthusiastic participation by this student at the appropriate time. If two or three respected members of the class are prepared to sponsor a unit enthusiastically, the contagion of their interest can be expected to spread to the other members of the class.

Where prior knowledge and interest cannot be used because the area of study being considered is either unfamiliar to all members of the class or has been covered so frequently in the church-school classes of previous years that the students assume that everything worth knowing about the subject has long since been learned, a different technique has to be used. In such a situation, the teacher may find it desirable to select certain interesting but unfamiliar items from the potential unit of study. By suggesting to selected individuals that they might be interested in using the class period to do some research on the items selected for attention, all of the members of the class can be gradually involved in the study without allowing their lack of knowledge of the area or their preconceptions concerning it to deprive them of the potential values of the study.

3. CREATING A CLIMATE FOR LEARNING. No single factor is so important in the creation of a classroom climate favorable to learning as the feelings of the teacher toward his students. By every act, movement, gesture and facial expression, the teacher communicates to the class his feelings toward them. In this connection, it should be noted that although the teacher may feel that his hostility or aggression is directed against a specific member of the class and not against the class as a whole, the students feel the hostility or aggression as directed against the class as a whole.

Because the classroom climate is formed out of very small happenings, the teacher who would increase the effectiveness of his classroom leadership will need to pay close attention to the small details of his relations with the students. For example, it becomes apparent only after long experience in the leading of discussions that the freedom with which students offer ideas depends upon how the previously expressed ideas have been received. If the teacher uses the chalkboard to record ideas expressed in a discussion, his control of the chalk may have more influence than he realizes. It can be readily observed that ideas flow freely where the teacher writes down each idea expressed in the words of its formulator. On the other hand, ideas are slow in coming when the teacher stops to dispute a proffered idea, rewords the contribution into his own language, or refuses to list some of the ideas expressed. Attention to the small details of interpersonal relations is critically important in the creation of a warm, accepting classroom climate that is productive of learning.

Some Specific Techniques of Teaching

The variety of teaching techniques available for use by teachers in church schools is almost overwhelming in its richness. There are at least fifty major techniques of teaching commonly in use in church schools in America today. In the remainder of this chapter, some of the more recently developed techniques which reflect the contemporary trends in teaching are described and illustrated. Teachers are encouraged to use their imaginations freely in developing variations in these methods which are especially appropriate for the age levels and topics with which their teaching is primarily concerned.

1. THE CASE METHOD.[7] After a long and respected history in the fields of law and medicine, the case method has become popular in recent years in many other areas of education. In essence, this teaching technique has three basic parts: (a) description of a typical and meaningful problem situation; (b) student research and discussion; and (c) effective leadership by the teacher in enabling the class to make progress toward its goal.

The teacher or some other qualified person selects an actual situation as the basis for the case presentation. Care must be used in making sure that the situation is typical of those which the students must learn to handle. The full context of the situation is described. Every attempt is made to make the case as realistic, as vivid, and as demanding of responsible research as possible. Having been confronted with the case through a verbal description (oral or written), the students proceed to deal with it. The students consult reference books, do individual and group thinking, and use every means at their disposal to gather all of the relevant information that they can find, as a basis for handling the case. They talk with each other, sharing their findings and ideas, and evaluating the several alternative approaches which seem promising. During all of this time, the teacher helps the group to keep addressing its efforts to the handling of the case, keeps track of ideas coming out in discussions, summarizes the progress made to date when the group feels a need for this information, and helps the group to culminate its research and discussion in a firm decision as to the most appropriate resolution of the case. Where it seems to the teacher that some aspects of the case are being ignored, he probes with pointed questions until the neglected aspects are being given attention.

2. THE IN-BASKET TECHNIQUE. Developed initially as part of a military training program by the Educational Testing Service, this technique was adapted to industrial situations as a training device, and was then tried on an experimental basis in the teaching processes of Columbia University. The essence of the method is that persons are asked to function in fictional but realistic situations as well as they can. As they carry on the normal activities of the situation, suitable ref-

[7] Kenneth R. Andrews, *The Case Method of Teaching Human Relations and Administration* (Cambridge: Harvard University Press, 1953).

ference materials and supervisory evaluations and suggestions are provided for the use of the learner in improving his performance. Actual materials normally present in such situations, movies, flat pictures, recorded noise or other sound patterns, and any other devices which can give the illusion of reality are used to provide the setting for the learner's practice in functioning.

For example, the situation might be that of a teen-age youth preparing to lead a portion of a youth fellowship service. The student would begin with the sorts of performances in which he normally engages when involved in this task. At those points where the teacher can see opportunity for improvement, he places his evaluations, suggestions or relevant reference materials on the student's desk. The student makes whatever usage he can of these helps in improving his functioning. The process continues until the learner is able to perform the activity with the desired degree of efficiency. Other members of the class may take turns as assistant teachers, as group evaluators, look up helpful references, obtain needed materials, handle the stage settings, and such other activities.

3. THE HELPING-GROUP TECHNIQUE. Arising initially in the area of mental health, this technique has become popular in a wide variety of educational settings. The essence of the technique is that a situation is developed to a critical point and the class is then expected to provide helpful suggestions as to ways in which the situation might be terminated successfully. For example, in a parents' class, a tape recording might be played of a parent's attempt to deal with a problem of discipline in the home (film clips, excerpts from novels, or other sources of situations might be used). After telling the parents the situation they are observing, and asking them to help complete the situation constructively, the recording is played. At the critical point the recording is stopped and constructive suggestions are elicited by the teacher. Much self-help normally results, also.

4. THE PLAY-A-STORY TECHNIQUE.[8] This technique was developed in the primary department of Riverside Church in New York. In this technique, the children give creative expression to the ideas and feelings which are stimulated by stories and experiences. There is no script or rigidly defined "right" way of doing the informal dramatization. However, the children and the teacher do plan the story playing together to make the experience enriching and releasing. The children give their own impressionistic version of a story they have heard or read, or act out experiences which have remained vividly in their minds from encounters with adults or other children.

Conclusion

These are but a few of the many techniques which have been developed within recent years. Actually, a whole resource notebook on creative techniques of teaching religion can be developed by scanning the successive issues of only a few of the journals devoted to helps for teachers. However, it should be recognized that the teaching technique is exceedingly rare which can substitute for good preparation on the part of the teacher combined with an understanding of the purposes to be accomplished through the teaching, and a genuine concern for the individual learners in the class. Techniques of teaching should be selected and used to supplement and increase the teacher's effectiveness, not to replace the teacher.

[8] Elizabeth Allstrom, *Let's Play a Story* (New York: Friendship Press, 1959).

Skillful teaching must accompany personal adequacy and appropriate techniques if effective education is to occur in the church school.

Bibliography

Bergevin, Paul and McKinley, John. *Design for Adult Education in the Church.* Greenwich, Conn.: Seabury Press, 1958.

Grambs, Jean D., *et al. Modern Methods in Secondary Education.* Revised edition, New York: Dryden Press, 1958.

Hanna, Lavone A., *et al. Unit Teaching in the Elementary School.* New York: Rinehart and Company, 1955.

Hilgard, Ernest. *Theories of Learning.* Revised edition. New York: Appleton-Century-Crofts, Inc., 1958.

Hunnicutt, C. W. and Iverson, William. *Research in the Three R's.* New York: Harper and Brothers, 1958.

Muldoon, Mary. *Learning to Teach.* New York: Harper and Brothers, 1958.

Reed, W. W. *Teaching the Church's Children.* New York: Morehouse-Gorham Company, 1958.

Strang, Ruth M. *Group Work in Education.* New York: Harper and Brothers, 1958.

Chapter 18

The Use of Audio-Visuals in the Church

Howard E. Tower

THE USE OF AUDIO-VISUALS IN THE PROGRAM OF THE CHURCH HAS BEEN GREATLY accelerated recently. This acceleration has given rise to considerable literature on the subject. A current listing of research and study projects done by graduate students notes over two thousand doctoral or masters dissertations and theses dealing with communications.[1] Many texts on radio, television, and films in education have appeared. Several of these deal exclusively with the church field.[2] These books outline quite adequately the principles of use, the types of materials, the program functions to be served, and the church organization needed to make for effective use of audio-visuals and other newer mass media in the program of the church.

Therefore, it is not the purpose of this presentation to restate or condense these materials. Rather, this chapter will seek to evaluate the experience of the church in the past decade in order to assess more adequately the part mass media holds, or should hold, in the total program of Christian education.

We will seek to interpret some significant developments in Christian education that have recently emerged in relation to the use of audio-visuals, radio, and television. Against this analysis we will attempt to outline some persistent and unsolved problems which impede the effective use of the media. Finally we will discuss the need to understand what the implications of the new communications situation are for the total program of Christian education, including the implications for the ecumenical movement.

This evaluation is predicated upon two assumptions. First, both by extensive research and practical usage in the church, the effectiveness of the visual method has been adequately demonstrated. We no longer need to ask whether visual presentations add a new dimension of effectiveness to our teaching. Rather, we ask what medium is most effective for what teaching task. Which tool should we choose to use with this particular group to bring to them the most telling learning experience?

The second assumption we make is that when we speak of audio-visuals, we are thinking of vastly more than motion pictures. The types of visual presentations,

---

[1] Robert J. Golter, *Bibliography of Theses and Dissertations* (Nashville: Department of Church School Curriculum, The Methodist Publishing House).

[2] See Bibliography; note especially Parker, *et al.*, Tower, and Rumpf.

or tools, that are used in the church include the whole catalogue of visual media—flat pictures, diagrams, charts, chalk boards, flannel boards, objects, slides, film-strips, films, recordings, recorders, radio, and television. These types of media are discussed in a number of texts[3] and therefore will not be described here, but as we survey the road traveled and evaluate the skills and understandings achieved, it is assumed that we have this wide range of media in mind when using the shorter term audio-visuals.

Significant Developments

It can be said that the experience of the church in the use of audio-visuals, not to mention radio and television, is so limited and has spanned so brief a period of time that one can hardly claim that any permanently significant developments can be identified with certainty. There is much truth in this assertion. But any method that has been used for more than ten years warrants an attempted analysis even if such a study is inconclusive. It is hoped that the following will be helpfully suggestive to the leader or student who has surveyed the audio-visual literature and who wants to better understand a potentially powerful tool.

Few leaders today, either at the general church level or in the local church, question the validity of the use of audio-visuals. It is safe to say that audio-visuals have now earned a significant place among other resources for Christian education. They have been accepted in the family.

Discrimination in Use

A very encouraging development in the past few years is a new and controlling interest in and concern for discrimination on the part of the user. The first evidence of this is to be found in a study of the rental records of distribution libraries. Most libraries show an increased over-all volume and an increase in the number of churches who order materials, but a decrease in the amount of materials ordered or used by each church. When this fact is compared to surveys made of local churches,[4] we discover that there is a decrease in showings to large or mass audiences and an increase in use with limited audiences.

Another trend which is evidence of discrimination on the part of the user is the trend toward the production of much shorter materials that can be used as a part of a teaching situation rather than as the principal feature of a program. Likewise, the film or filmstrip that is produced for a specific church-wide program or age group gets wider use than the film produced for a general purpose, but unrelated to program.

The most significant result of this developing concern for discriminating use of materials is the evaluation program of the Division of Christian Education of the National Council of Churches. Between 1949 and 1959 this program has increased from a reviewing and evaluating service supported by seven regional committees to the current use of more than fifty committees.[5] There is, of course, a sense in which this evaluating service contributed to or helped develop this concern, but without the broader base of interest in what should be used and for what purpose, such a wide program of evaluation could not be supported.

[3] See Bibliography; Dale, Tower, and others.
[4] The Presbyterian U.S. and The Methodist Church.
[5] *Audio-Visual Resource Guide.*

Integral to the Learning Experience

Since the program of Christian education began to take seriously the use of the newer media of communication, there has occurred an interesting evolution of terminology which reflects the developing underlying philosophy of the function of these media. In the mid-forties we referred to various types of visual resources as audio-visual aids. The philosophy behind the use of this vocabulary was born chiefly of fear. Leaders were afraid that pictures, particularly those that moved and talked, were so glamorous that they would become "ends in themselves." Hence, every *proper* teacher carefully referred to picture materials as *audio-visual aids* to learning. They were to be thought of as "tools" which brought "vicarious" and never "real" experience, to use only a few words from the vocabulary of that period.

Soon it began to be clear that the word "aid" was gradually being translated "crutch" in the thinking of many leaders. This gave rise to the realization that audio-visual resources were aids only in the sense that any other resource is an aid. Therefore, leaders began to refer to pictures, records, and films as audio-visual materials as contrasted with printed materials. It was natural to shorten this terminology to audio-visuals.

Concurrently with and underlying this changing vocabulary, a change in the philosophy of the use of audio-visuals was taking place. Essentially it was this: instead of the audio-visual being brought in as a special resource, it was included as a significant and integral part of the learning experience. A film not only provided a vicarious experience of something that happened some other place, some other time, and to some other person, but the seeing of it was an experience of immediate significance to the viewer.

This change of philosophy has had a number of important results in relation to the use of audio-visuals in the program of Christian education. First of all, it has caused the careful teacher to ask what experience within the continuum of learning experiences can be provided by an audio-visual that it is impossible or difficult to provide in any other way. The answer to this question has resulted in some very interesting uses of audio-visuals—notably the tape recorder. The inexpensive tape recorder has made it possible for small groups to share experiences and thinking and to keep a record of this shared experience for both their own and their leaders' later study and evaluation. Although this use is not universal, it does play an important part in the curriculum of at least one major denomination.[6]

If audio-visual resources are thought of as an integral part of the learning experience, it follows that they should be created integrally to other materials provided for the curriculum. This is what is happening. True, it is not being done on a major scale by any denomination, because of many unsolved problems, but the fact that the curriculum bodies of many denominations are seriously at work toward this end is a significant new development for both the use of audio-visuals and for the program of Christian education. No major new curriculum is being developed without careful consideration being given to the place of audio-visuals.[7]

Denominational Production

In the 1940's, church leaders concerned with audio-visuals generally agreed that

[6] Protestant Episcopal.

[7] United Church of Christ, Methodist, *et al.*

the production of these resources would need to be done co-operatively. Few denominations had either sufficient interest or funds to produce these expensive and still unproved resources. A few pioneers—notably the Reverend James Frederick, an Episcopal clergyman—risked not only their personal funds but their professional standing as well, to develop films for church use. Frederick, through Cathedral Films, focused the attention of the church on the potential of the film. Others, some related to the church and some not, saw the church as a potential market and entered the field of church production.

The first decade in the audio-visual movement saw the organization of the Protestant Film Commission and the production of many good missionary and stewardship films. Only one project of three films, *Birthday Party*, *A Job for Bob* and *What Happened to Jo Jo*, was done within the framework of the International Council of Religious Education (I.C.R.E.). But the curriculum committees of I.C.R.E. had audio-visual committees and prepared many production outlines. In 1949, the last year of I.C.R.E., it was confidently expected that audio-visuals for the curriculum would be done co-operatively through the regular curriculum channels and produced by the Protestant Film Commission.[8]

In spite of these expectations and the earnest efforts of leaders from many denominations, the fact is that the most significant development in the 1950's in the area of production was the move toward denominational production. Eastman Kodak Company's 1957 survey of church use of audio-visuals showed that an overwhelming volume of these materials was produced by denominations as over against either independent producers or B.F.C. A second evidence of this development is that three major denominations have production studios and producing units.[9]

Leadership Training

At the beginning of the audio-visual movement the training of leaders in the local church was related to the pressing needs of the new media—skills in operation, sources of materials, and how to relate the materials that could be found to important purposes of the church. And an important factor to keep in mind is that the beginning use of films, in particular, was largely in situations outside the formal program of Christian education while the work of leadership training was largely within the framework of that program. Another factor to note is that in the beginning, training in the use of audio-visuals had of necessity a large element of promotion in it. Hence, the training sessions in the early days consisted largely of short workshops or conferences in which equipment was demonstrated, new materials previewed, and some attempt made to interpret principles of use and to demonstrate the appropriateness of the materials reviewed for some phase of the church program.

During the first decade of the church's use of audio-visuals the important development was the regularizing of these spontaneous efforts at leadership training. At the top this regularization was guided by the International Audio-Visual Workshop begun by I.C.R.E. in 1945. Soon the departments of leadership education of I.C.R.E. and of the denominations saw the need for an audio-visual course in the leadership curriculum and such was developed [10] and used rather widely in both

[8] Now Broadcasting and Film Commission (B.F.C.).
[9] United Church of Canada, Southern Baptist, and Methodist.
[10] "Audio-Visual Leadership Course" (Course 141.1b), National Council of Churches.

co-operative and denominational schools. All too often this course was taken by persons who had a special interest in audio-visuals but no responsible place in the teaching program of the church.

The above brief analysis describes the leadership situation that developed in response to the demands of an emerging area of interest. The significant development in recent years has been the integration of training for use of audio-visuals into the total program of leadership training. The audio-visual co-ordinator is a term now used to designate the person who in a leadership school or on a conference or synod staff is responsible for integrating the use of audio-visuals into all the courses of the school or all the programs of the conference or synod. The extent to which audio-visuals are now being used with greater educational soundness is largely due to this new leadership emphasis. This new stress upon integrating training in the use of audio-visuals with the regular leadership program of the church has tended to lessen our efforts to provide workshops and institutes on the local church level. The total effect has been to provide a general church leadership which is better trained, but to narrow the base of well-trained local leaders.

Better Local Church Organization

In the early days the use of audio-visuals in the local church depended largely on an interested pastor or layman. This meant that the use of films usually was as a "special program" outside the regular functions of the church. However, guidance has been given to local churches concerning the need to have the use of visual materials related to the total program of the church. General boards of education of the denominations have recommended the establishment of an audio-visual committee in the local church representative of the various programs of the church and related administratively to the local church board of education, official board, or other responsible body. This guidance has been effective to the point that it can be said that generally speaking the local church has a more adequate organization for the effective use of audio-visuals.

Emergence of Television

While Christian educators have been rethinking the approach to Christian education in the light of the new theological emphasis, television has become the most pervasive influence in the lives of the people for whom the program of Christian education is intended. For the most part, the emergence of television is a factor outside Christian education. In reality it may well be the most significant development of the 1950's so far as the future program of Christian education may be concerned.

Some Persistent and Unsolved Problems

Let us now turn our consideration to some problems that still perplex us. Of these, perhaps none is more persistent than those related to distribution.

Distribution: Still a Problem

The distribution pattern adopted by the churches was a combination of that used by the motion picture entertainment industry and that used by the public school. In a word, it consisted of established libraries, independent or owned and controlled by the church, and patterned after those serving secular education.

Coupled with the libraries which did the physical handling and mailing of the films was the concept of the entertainment theater—namely a particular film being reserved for a definite showing date in a specific place.

So long as the primary use of films in the church was a special program use with a large audience, this pattern presented no particular problem. A church could easily decide when it would schedule a film program and reserve the needed film long in advance, and obtain sufficient offering from the viewing audience to pay for the rental. When the church began to think of the film as an integral part of a stream of learning experiences, however, it became increasingly difficult to forecast at what point in that stream the group would be ready for the film. Also, if the group having the series of experiences was a small one, how could the cost of the rental be met? In short, though leaders have been aware of this problem for many years, no satisfactory answer has been found. The problem of getting the film to the using group when it is needed and as often as it is needed remains unsolved.

Related to rental-distribution considerations is the problem of producing short audio-visuals, including sound motion picture films, in such quantity and at such cost that a church can afford to purchase them for their permanent library. This is related to the problem of providing audio-visuals as an integral part of curriculum. The key to its solution is partly technical. The cost of production of a particular resource must be amortized over the total volume of use. For example, if a ten-minute sound motion picture costs $10,000 to produce and it can be sold to 1,000 users, then the cost per use for production is ten dollars. If it can be sold to 10,000 churches, the cost is reduced to one dollar per user. It is easy to see that the cost of production can be reduced to a negligible amount by volume. But the cost of printing this film can never be reduced below the cost of the raw film stock or about two cents per foot. Many experts believe the cost of printing can be reduced by technological advances. As yet, it has not been. The whole difficulty of producing materials in such a way that they can be distributed by direct sale is a significant unsolved problem.

An Integrated Curriculum

As stated earlier, an important development in recent years is the growing conviction that audio-visuals make their greatest contribution when they are prepared as an integral part of the curriculum. This viewpoint has general acceptance in theory but only slight support in practice.

There are several practical problems that contribute to the generally unrealized good of effective integration. First, there is the matter of buildings. Few, even recently built educational plants, are equipped for using audio-visuals in the regular sessions of the church-school group, class, or department. Second, most church schools are scheduled for only one hour, often with less than half of this free for group work. The effective use of even a ten minute film requires more time than is here available. A third practical factor is the inflexible nature of the established curriculum, calling for a specific lesson on a particular Sunday. Fourth, there is the factor of the customary practices of local churches in reference to curriculum selection and purchasing. These patterns often do not allow for extras outside the "regular quarterlies."

If audio-visuals are to be effectively integrated into the curriculum, here are some necessary innovations: some radical changes in buildings, more realistic scheduling of the time needed for Christian education, the development of a more flexible curriculum, and a more vigorous dealing with the problem of distribution.

Research Needed

Perhaps the most pressing and perplexing problem is that of developing skills in testing the validity and effectiveness of the materials we are using. Actually, this is not peculiar to the area of audio-visual materials and method. Christian educators are now asking very basic questions: How do persons become mature, committed Christians? Which experiences contribute what, and how can these experiences be provided with assurance? There is a difference in the problem as it relates to the creation of audio-visual resources and at two points. First, the newness of the field means we need to study our experience more carefully and secondly, the cost of any adequate development of a curriculum that makes any primary use of audio-visuals is so great that we cannot afford to move without definite study. A number of experiments are being conducted and studied, but many more are needed before we can go forward with any degree of confidence toward an integrated curriculum.[11]

Visualizing the Bible

It is generally accepted that the Bible is basic to any program of Christian education. The feeling also weighs very heavily on the conscience of the Christian educator that the Bible is not very well understood by many Christians. Furthermore, research in the use of audio-visuals indicates that one of the prime functions of these resources is to help the learner bridge time and distance. These two generalizations would seem to point to the fact that Bible interpretation should be a key area for the audio-visual media. A very great amount of audio-visual material on the Bible has been produced and is being used by the churches.

In spite of this fact, there are a whole cluster of questions which have not been satisfactorily answered relative to the visualization of the Bible. What happens when nonbiblical materials are dramatically portrayed along with biblical materials? What happens to the growing child's concept of Jesus when he sees him portrayed again and again on the screen by the same actor and by different actors? Do spiritual truths suffer when they are confined within the boundaries of a literal visual transliteration of the text? Would we accept a portrayal that honestly seeks to interpret events in the Bible as they probably happened? Has the visualization of the Bible to date deepened our appreciation of it, or limited our understanding and imaginations? All these, and others which could be named, are questions that need to be answered before we can very confidently apply the power of the visual media to the interpretation of the message of the Bible. Some studies are currently in process and others should be undertaken with careful planning and adequate financing. No area of research promises more for sound investments for individuals, denominations, or foundations.

Christian Education in a Visually Dominated Culture

Thus far we have discussed the use the church has made of audio-visuals in the program of Christian education as it is carried on within the four walls of its building. We have seen that though there are many unsolved problems, some

---

[11] Audio Visual Study Project, Editorial Division, Methodist Publishing House.

significant developments have occurred in relation to the place audio-visual materials and methods hold in present-day Christian education. We now turn our thinking toward the effect the present mass communications situation has had and may have on the developing program of Christian education.

From Words to Pictures

The story of man's communication with man is the story of human history. In that story the first important event happened when the first vocal sound was uttered and a listening person responded with meaning, using a second vocal sound that was received by the first person. How long it was before the next step in communication was taken we can only guess; perhaps centuries. One day one man made a mark in the sand or the wet clay, and another man understood. When that second man used the same mark to convey to another the same meaning, the art of writing began. The means for a continuing communication from man to man and from generation to generation was realized. Again we cannot precisely date when this communications event took place, but we do know that the spoken word and the handwritten word remained the basic tools of communication until the invention of movable type about five hundred years ago.

Then the accumulated communications of the centuries became the property of an increasing number of mankind. The Holy Bible, the literature of the Greeks and the Romans, the current writings of every people, these not only became readily available, but they became the dominating and controlling factor in Western culture. For more than four centuries, ours was a word-dominated culture.

In the early twentieth century three inventions took place that have brought about a veritable revolution in communication. These were the motion picture, radio, and television. With the coming of television, which has built upon the impact of forty years of motion pictures, we can now say that our culture is more picture dominated than word dominated. Take into account two factors: the amount of time the average person watches television, and the early age at which the child begins watching. Today an average two-year-old child has seen more places than his grandfather saw in his whole lifetime. The same grandfather made up his vocabulary meanings in relation to the word spoken by someone in relationship to the real thing or experience, supplemented by words read in the reader and later the newspaper, magazine, and classic literature.

Now the two-year-old grandson sees visual images on the television screen to which meanings are attached which are often unrelated to his actual experience and sometimes unrelated to the corresponding words. On television, Mickey Mouse is a man with big black ears. Certainly this visual image bears no conceptional relationship to the dictionary definition of the word mouse, or to the little animal that may have run freely in and out the baseboard hole in grandfather's boyhood bedroom. We have experienced a communications revolution. Our culture is visually perceived if not so dominated. What has this new situation to say to the Christian educator?

The Changing Attitude of the Church

To attempt to answer the above question, let us examine the attitude of the church toward the communications changes of the past five hundred years. The Bible was the first book printed by movable type. Although there was resistance from time to time to putting the Bible in the vernacular of the church, and some branches of the church consistently have sought to control the printed word, the outstanding fact is that the printed word has become, during the past five centuries, the primary tool of communications for the church. Every great reform and revival has been undergirded by the printed word.

The story is quite different in respect to the other recent communications inventions. When the motion picture became a factor in our culture, the first response of the church was open opposition. With notable exceptions, church leaders denounced the motion picture as the work of the devil and the good church member didn't attend the movies. Gradually this attitude changed from one of opposition to one of acquiescence and acceptance. The last two decades have seen the church accept the motion picture as a legitimate medium for the proclamation of the gospel.

When radio came into common use there was no open opposition on the part of the church. There was in fact general recognition that radio could be an effective tool of communications and on the local level many ministers became radio preachers. But measured by annual denominational and interdenominational budgets, radio as a powerful tool of communication has never been taken very seriously.

Now television in one short decade has slipped up on the church. There is little opposition to it per se. There is much criticism of what it does, and a deep feeling that the church must take hold of this newest tool of communication, but no one seems to know just what to do next. What should be the approach of the Christian educator to this new communications situation?

Awaken to an Awareness

The least we can expect of persons who have leadership responsibility in Christian education is that they be aware of the present communications situation. It is not unusual to hear a minister or lay leader say with just a tinge of pride that they never watch television and what they have seen of it leads them to feel that they are not missing very much. This attitude may be justified on the basis of their need for television, but it cannot be justified if they profess to be planning for and carrying out a program of Christian education. Their unconcern or lack of experience does not alter the fact that Zoro is more real to their juniors than Paul; that space travel is more in their consciousness than the travels of Paul.

This awareness is called for at every level of leadership. Certainly the teacher in the local church must have it if he is to know the vocabulary of his students, not to mention knowing what they are thinking. Likewise, the leader at the general church level must be aware of the changed communications situation if an adequate curriculum is to be planned.

A New Orientation

The first result of an awareness on the part of the leader will be a new orientation of the total program. Much thought has been given to the preparation of materials for use in the program of the church. When we become acutely aware of this visually dominated culture, we will see with new vividness how inadequate our program of Christian education is unless it is carried forward in the context of the kind of world in which we live. What are some of the characteristics of this communications situation that are of primary concern to the Christian educator?

First, the impact of mass communications is toward uniformity and conformity while Christian education is concerned with individuality and self-fulfillment. Second, much of the entertainment fare of radio, television, and films places a high value on the things we possess and position or status we hold, while Christian faith is concerned with inner personal values and the loss of self in the service of others and God. Third, mass communications are often used as a means of manipulation of persons to the end that they buy or do what the program wants. Christian education must not manipulate, but must provide opportunities for free growth.

On the positive side of the ledger, mass communication today brings a knowledge about and an awareness of the peoples of the world that can be a real asset to the developing faith that calls all men brothers.

The focus then of Christian education is not to be oriented toward the in-church experience of persons only, but also toward the total experience of all persons.

Putting the Communications Media to Work

When leaders in Christian education are aware of the present communications situation and when they plan and carry out their program in the context of a visually dominated culture, they still feel uncomfortable. They have a feeling that these various powerful media of communication should be used directly in the task of communicating the Christian gospel. They feel that if films and other audio-visuals can be used in the program of the church, radio and television can also be so harnessed. Of course, this feeling is right. The fact that there are many problems, not the least the high cost of effectively using them, should not deter the church and will not. When Jesus said, "Go ye into all the world," he was speaking vertically as well as horizontally—go into every area of human experience by every means of communication.

The Communications Media and the Ecumenical Movement

One of the trends of the past decade, as noted, is the move toward denominational production of audio-visuals. This would seem to indicate that the use of audio-visuals in the program of the church has contributed to the rise of denominationalism and militated against ecumenicity. This is hardly a warranted conclusion, for there are many other results of the audio-visual movement that have laid and are laying a better ground work for the growing ecumenical movement.

Perhaps the most significant by-product of the development of audio-visual materials has been its demand for careful thinking and analysis of the message to be visualized. Whether within a denomination or within co-operative groups, the preparation of any particular facet of the Christian message for visual presentation has forced us to do very careful thinking and re-evaluation of that message. This very process has made for new discoveries of the reasons we hold for the faith that is within us. More often than not, the area of common ground has been found to be greater than the area of difference. The more this procedure is followed, the better will be the ground of understanding between groups, which is the very basis of intergroup co-operation.

When we consider the use of radio and television as media for the proclamation of the gospel, we discover that we are dealing with a medium that belongs to all the people, and therefore must be used for the common good. This means that programming, whether prepared by general church agencies or local groups, when placed on the air is directed to the entire community. The only effective approach to these media is a co-operative one. We are finding that such co-operation affords a very practical exercise in ecumenicity.[12] For the first time in its history the church has the means to go into all the world and to confront all peoples with the gospel of Jesus Christ.

Bibliography

Audio-Visual Resource Guide. Fourth edition. New York: National Council of Churches, 1958. Annual supplements are usually published between the various editions.

Bachman, John. *How to Use Audio-Visual Materials*. New York: Association Press, 1956.

Dale, Edgar. *Audio-Visual Methods in Teaching*. Revised Edition. New York: Dryden Press, 1958.

Parker, Everett C., *et al. The Radio-Television Audience and Religion*. New York: Harper and Brothers, 1955.

Rumpf, Oscar J. *The Use of Audio-Visuals in the Church*. Philadelphia: Christian Education Press, 1958.

Tower, Howard E. *Church Use of Audio-Visuals*. Revised Edition. Nashville: Abingdon Press, 1959.

Wittich, Walter A. and Schuller, Charles F. *Audio-Visual Materials: Their Nature and Use*. New York: Harper and Brothers, 1953.

[12] *Annual Report 1958, Broadcasting and Film Commission* (New York: National Council of Churches).

Chapter 19

The Creative Arts in the Church

James H. Warren and Rosa May Butler

THERE ARE TIMES WHEN A MOMENTARY GLANCE AT A CATHEDRAL OR A CHANCE hearing of a hymn can suddenly reveal the essence of a faith far more vividly than a statement of creed or theology, for the arts have a unique way of expressing the impact of religious experience on life. Furthermore an examination of the history of religions reveals that the arts have always played an integral part in the expression and development of a faith, because they show its dynamics in everyday living. Great Christian artists have always particularized the Christian faith for their age and epoch.

Just as the arts reveal the essence of a religion, so also do they create the experience of that religion, for they are living media that surge forth from the deep wellsprings of the artist into the hearts and minds of the receivers. Since we believe that the Christian faith is the answer to life itself, we can discover meaning and purpose for our times in the work of a Christian artist, just as we can find strength and direction in devotional and theological books. In the great works of artists of former times we relive life's glories and dilemmas and find a greater impetus to live a God-directed life. The creations of a painter like Roberto Salvini Giotto, or of a musician like Johann Sebastian Bach, or a sculptor like Michelangelo Buonarroti bring us closer to God. Thus art is no mere entertainment for the passing pleasure of a moment, but a means by which we can enter into the very presence of God himself.

Our age, like earlier ones, is expressing the dynamics of the Christian faith in its own art forms and styles. Some of these are being created independent of the church's program, yet much of the movement is coming from an earnest desire of the church to witness to Christ in our modern culture. For example, worship in the church has new depth and dimension in contemporary architecture, music, and drama. More than this we note that modern painting, sculpture, dance, choric speech all find their place in a forthright, contemporary witness to the Christian faith.

In so far as the arts involve the total personality—body, mind, and spirit—Christian education has a unique ally in these media. Modern Christian education does not seek solely to transfer a body of knowledge about the faith, but also to bring its members into a deepening experience of that faith. Christian education is exploring every available way to bring people into the dynamic of its way of life, and when the arts are a part of its program they become a powerful force in extending the outreach of the church. Creative dramatics, creative movement, and educational painting are but a few avenues of art that will make God a reality among us.

Although each art medium has its distinctive nature, they all are dynamically related to one another. A production of the old medieval trope, "Quem Quaeritis," is in reality a synthesis of music and drama; creative movement often uses music as its source of inspiration; painting often depends upon architecture. So we see that the arts are all close kin, each having relationship one with another. The more the church envisions the arts emphasis as a total and unified one, the greater and deeper the effect upon the congregation, for when all of these media are used together they can produce new and deeper experiences of Christian living and a sharper awareness of Christian truth.

Drama

Each age must have its prophets to make God's word real for its own time. In dreaming of a spokesman for God in our own age Dean Inge wrote: "When this new prophet comes, I think he will choose to speak to his generation not from the pulpit, nor from the platform, nor from the printed page, but from the stage. A great dramatist might help us find our souls." [1] Inge's words have the ring of truth about them, for drama has the power to influence and change life. Among the arts drama comes closer than any other to representing the experiences of living, in that it uses the substance of life itself—character (or personality), dialogue (or conversation), and conflict (or problem). In the hands of a master dramatist these elements are fused into a compelling story or plot that intensifies, sharpens, and illuminates the struggles of life. When audience and actor are drawn into the "dramatic moment," they enter into an experience that changes their thinking and living, for they become "involved" in the conflicts, defeats, and victories of others. Involvement is the secret of the power of drama, and if the playwright, actors, and audience are concerned with the realities of Christian living in a world of tension and chaos, then there can be genuine revelation of God's word for our times.

Drama has always been closely related to the worship life of the church. For example, interpretive reading, choric speech, artful pageantry, dramatic movement, tasteful decor, and imaginative lighting are but a few techniques that can bring a congregation into a mood of worship. Drama is not only to be found in these recognizable techniques, but it can be discovered as an impetus in liturgical worship (i.e. when a service of worship steadily progresses toward moments of adoration and commitment).

Yet the relationship of drama to worship is not merely confined to techniques or liturgy, but may also be found in the experience of a sanctuary play, which has the "awareness of God" central in its meaning. The beauty of sanctuary drama is that it uses the church on its own terms, for it fits into the setting of the building, using limited, if any, properties or scenery. Instead it calls on the imaginations of the congregation to envision whatever backdrop is needed. The use of curtains and elaborate sets belongs in the theater not in the sanctuary, and actors should be cautioned not to disturb the chancel furniture. Actually the sanctuary

[1] Fred Eastman, *Drama in the Church* (New York: Samuel French, Inc., 1942), p. 20.

setting does not limit staging opportunities but offers great flexibility in the use of aisles, choir loft, balcony, and chancel area. In past years there has been increasing use of sanctuary drama, and one may conjecture that future Christian playwrights will write more plays distinctly for the house of worship.

As drama can be closely related to worship so can it also be an integral part of the church's educational program. To be arbitrary it might be said there are two major categories of educational dramatics. The most widely known one is called "formal" drama, which is the presentation of a fully produced script. Yet another category is called "informal" drama or the use of the dramatic method in classroom or fellowship activity.

When members of a church-school class or classes or a drama interest group within the church produce a play, they should work for the unique goals and aims of the church. In order that their production bring actors, staff, and audience into an awareness of the Christian way of life, they should strive for the highest artistic standards; in this way they can truly make their play an offering unto God. It is of course essential that they choose a director with thorough technical training and deep Christian commitment, for he will shoulder a great deal of the responsibility in making the production a success. The producing group should relieve the director of all technical responsibilities—scenery, lights, and costumes—so that he may have ample time to help the actors create their parts. The success of a well organized, thoughtfully produced drama can be wonderfully satisfying and produce a deep attitude of respect for the church.

Choosing a play can often be as exciting as producing it. Play reading committees will enjoy ordering, reading, and selecting scripts for the group that is planning the production. Sometimes they may select a beautifully written play that is directly related to the heart of the Christian faith; for example, a biblical play, or a drama concerned with a great Christian personality. On the other hand they may want to choose a script that involves audience and actors in the perplexities of modern living so that they may seek some Christian resolution to life's dilemmas. Or it may be that the committee will favor a play that simply enriches fellowship through comedy and delightful entertainment. To guide them in their selections they should ask themselves the questions, "Does the experience of the play lift and illuminate life that is Christlike? Or does it present living in such a way that one is deepened in his sensitivity to others?"

Drama as it is produced in the church is many times radically different from the productions of other groups. Often school, community, college, or commercial theaters produce plays of religious and even Christian significance. If their leaders and participants are earnestly seeking for Christian values in their venture, the end result may be genuine religious experience. Generally speaking, however, the church and all its various agencies have this as their unique aim and goal.

In order to help people achieve an abundant, released life, plays are best chosen to fit the needs of actors and audience. A church that has a tendency to be complacent, smug, or self-centered needs drama which will awaken it to its danger, just as a church that is spiritually alive yet lacks social concern needs a play of world vision. Throughout the year a rich variety of plays should be presented, keeping a balance between dramas for worship, education, and recreation.

Dramatics belongs not only upon a stage but in a classroom, whether it be for children, youth, or adults. "Informal" dramatics, which encompasses many creative techniques, can be used with all age groups.

For example, everyone has observed how children are so spontaneously dramatic. Many times their keen imaginations shame adults, who often unfortunately let their own imaginative powers die as they face the hard realities of living. There can be little doubt that children are "naturals" for the informal dramatic method. Creative dramatics, creative movement, choric speech, puppetry, and creative writing are only a few techniques that delight a child. Children and intermediates (junior highs) are not ready to form organized groups, but they can find great joy in various creative drama activities.

Anyone who has watched intermediates involved in creative dramatics will easily recognize that this is the best drama technique for them. Yet they will enjoy forming short-term groups built around interests like choric speech, creative movement, and creative writing. Sometimes these interests involve building scenery, costumes, or lights, but they should never be stretched over too long a time span, since intermediate interest wanes quickly. In their dramatics activities, intermediates will need the guidance of a skilled adult sponsor.

Within recent years informal dramatics has been in widespread use with youth and adult groups. When informal dramatics is employed in classroom or fellowship activities, it is used not primarily for performance but for stimulation. For example, role playing has been used increasingly to expose youth and adults to social and religious problems. In role playing a group struggles with an individual or social problem by "acting it out," creating its own characters, dialogue, and situation. As the members enter into their parts they "feel" themselves into the minds and hearts of others.

Sometimes a class will hear a play reading and then discuss the characters and issues in the play. This method, called "discussion drama," vivifies units of study and makes issues and ideas personal and real. The same method can be applied to a fully produced play. After attending a performance, audiences enjoy sharing ideas and feelings that they have received from the play. Discussions of this sort should be led by a leader or panel that is well acquainted with the script.

The method of play reading, when actors read from a script, may be employed in various ways. By adding action and imaginative pantomime the reading may become a "walking rehearsal." Because it uses no technical aids (scenery, lights, and the like) it may be given anywhere at any time. It requires only a few rehearsals depending upon the reading and interpretive ability of the performers. Play reading techniques may be applied also to the broader field of religious literature. Scenes from great novels, plays, narrative poems, and other literary forms may be arranged for group reading, each character in the work being enacted by a reader. Often one person can read the narrative, tying the story together and setting the scenes through a few well-chosen words.

If drama is to have permanency in the life of the church, it needs to be well organized in order that its impact may go deep into the fiber and character of the congregation. One way to insure having these results is to put central control and planning in a supervisory drama committee, whose duty it is to make these aims a reality. The committee may be comprised of a representative from each church department, a representative from a drama interest group (if one is formed), and other people with special training and interest in the art of drama. It may be desirable also to have a representative from the church organizations for men and women. Naturally the minister, director of Christian education, and church-school superintendent should be welcomed to each meeting as ex officio members. The educational commission of the church should be encouraged to appoint a drama supervisory committee and should invite the chairman to attend the commission's regular meetings. At first the committee probably will explore the field of religious drama, giving them background knowledge on which to build a program. The vast number of projects and activities which the committee can promote will include planning workshops and training sessions for church-school teachers and workers, supervising and co-ordinating drama activities in various church departments, sponsoring church drama festivals, and adding drama resource books to the church library. It can easily be seen that an adequate budget will be needed to make the committee's work effective.

One of the goals of a supervisory drama committee may well be to create and nurture a religious drama interest group that will gather together church members interested in the field. Some controversy has been raised as to whether there is a place for a group of this nature, the chief objection being it tends to become exclusive. These objections can be avoided if a few basic principles are observed. For example, a church-wide religious drama organization will want to include members from several age groups—mature youth, young adults, and adults. In some cases there may be definite advantage in forming separate organizations for each age group, but this will not usually be true. Another principle is that the fellowship group should plan its programs to encompass the vast range of life as revealed through drama and the arts. Finally a fellowship of this type should look upon itself as an arm of the church's outreach to humanity. It should be a service organization which willingly offers help to the various classes and fellowships of the church. Some of its members may offer aid in role playing, creative dramatics, or play readings. If there is an attitude of wanting to serve, the group will become an integral and much needed part of the church's life.

The health of a drama fellowship group stems from its balance between study and production. Regular play productions keep the fellowship growing, but in addition there is great need for programs that lift the members' horizons. The group will need to hold regular meetings in which the members discuss their purposes, enlarge their knowledge of great dramatic literature, and develop techniques. At all times they must avoid overemphasis on producing plays which can so easily exhaust their time and energy.

Perhaps the chief problem in church dramatics is the developing of leadership. Workers with children, youth, and adults need first to see the possibilities of drama in their instruction and, second, to learn how to do it. Experts in the various areas of creative dramatics, creative movement, play directing, and oral interpretation can be brought into training sessions where teachers and workers can be taught these techniques. There should be an adequate period of time for training leaders before they try these new ways of teaching in classroom situations since failure in a new method can easily dishearten the novice. Workers should be encouraged to read books in respective techniques and fields before they plan to use these methods. Above all a teacher must use them for their unique value, and not rely upon them solely for novelty or variety. Workers should also be counseled against overuse of the dramatic method. Too great a use of it may cause a group to become highly stimulated and emotionally exhausted. Drama should be brought in where it can make a real contribution to a study unit—where a great Christian personality or story is being explored, and adequate time must be allotted to the use of drama if it is to be truly effective. Careful exploration of leadership possibilities in nearby community theaters, colleges, and public schools will often reveal a person who is willing to instruct church leaders in the methods of using drama.

In order to train workers effectively churches should send members with drama potential to regional and national religious drama workshops. They may also hold drama workshops of their own using local talent for faculty or staff; or perhaps they can secure a special resource person in the area of religious drama to guide them in their endeavor.

The future of religious drama seems to offer two opportunities for full-time vocational service. One opportunity can be found in church-related colleges which need capable, well-trained teachers to develop drama programs which adhere to Christian principles. Another opportunity is opening in local churches where a full-time religious drama director is employed as a member of the educational staff. Though there are relatively few churches that are employing directors of religious drama at the present, it is hoped there will be more openings in the future.

In conclusion let it be said that drama in the church must have a unified approach. It must be seen as something that can lift and deepen the lives of the entire congregation. It is multiform and each avenue must lead toward developing a unified Christian personality, helping the member grow from childhood to old age in a free and imaginative way. Then, and only then, will drama be central in the life of the church.

Music

Most of us have had at least one experience of being "turned into another man" (I Sam. 10:6 R.S.V.) by the emotional impact of music. Such has been the power of music since the beginning of recorded history. How much do we need to understand this power today!

The secular world is aware of the potency of music. Witness, for example, the widespread use of singing commercials, of musical therapy in mental hospitals, of music by industry to speed up production. The increasing number of school and municipal orchestras, the growing demand for the best in recorded music, the emphasis that educators place upon music education all point to recognition of the fact that music is an essential part of the growth of persons. Alice Lee Humphreys, in her inimitable style, declares that "musick should be scattered abroad and gathered up in some way by every creature." [2] Should not Christian educators, along with other educators, join in providing the many experiences of music which enrich life, nurture religious growth, and often let the face of God shine through?

Since all do not respond to music alike, a balanced program of Christian education will contain a variety of music experiences. Such experiences may include singing, listening, playing instruments, rhythmic expression, and creating music. While these are not separate experiences apart from one another, each one finds a readier response from some persons than from others.

Singing is the musical experience most readily available to everyone. The only

[2] Alice Lee Humphreys, *Heaven in My Hand* (Richmond, Va.: John Knox Press, 1950), p. 34.

instrument necessary is the human voice. Many and varied are the ways of using singing experiences in a program of Christian education. The joyous singing of folk and other fun songs can contribute much to the spiritual quality of group relationships. Such fellowship singing may often be a means for breaking barriers of timidity, social status, language, and culture. It can bring a feeling of oneness or togetherness to a heterogeneous group.

The most basic experience of singing, however, from the viewpoint of Christian education, is to be found in singing the great hymns of the church. Beginning with children of junior age, church-school members should know and use the hymns of our Christian heritage. "Praise to the Lord, the Almighty" by Neander, "All Creatures of Our God and King" by Francis of Assisi, "Now Thank We All Our God" by Rinkart—these are but three of the many beautiful hymns of our Christian heritage which have meaning today for juniors and intermediates as well as for older youth and adults. Kindergarten and primary children would find it difficult to grasp the theology, imagery, and symbolism in such hymns. In order that their singing experiences may be meaningful songs containing concepts within their understanding should be chosen for use with these younger boys and girls. Songs addressed *to* Jesus should be avoided. Songs *about* Jesus will help young children begin with a simple but sound theology on which more profound concepts may be built later.

"The Bible and the hymnal stand together as witnesses to God's continued communication with men." [3] To appreciate the hymnal in its historical perspective is one of the most rewarding approaches to the study of hymns. Only when read with a historical background in mind is an adequate appreciation of the Wesley hymns, for instance, possible. How much can be learned of the Christian witness through the centuries when the hymns of such writers as Nicolaus Zinzendorf, Isaac Watts, Charles Wesley are studied! The witness continues as the tradition of hymns "through every land, by every tongue" [4] is kept alive by Christians of all cultures.

A wealth of beautiful hymn tunes is available in the quest for greater appreciation of hymns and hymnals. There are chorale tunes, psalm tunes, Welsh tunes, tunes by the masters, and the incomparably beautiful plain song melodies. What treasures of music the hymnal reveals to those who seek!

Inherent within a rightly directed choir program is tremendous potential for Christian education. The minister of music who counsels with teachers of preschool and primary children, who integrates junior and youth choirs with the programs of their departments, who interprets to youth and adults the opportunity each choir has to lead in worship, who plans with the pastor and other leaders concerning the meaningful use of music, becomes one of the key persons in a program of Christian education. Here music has its greatest opportunity to lead individuals into an actual experience of our faith. A director of music, however, "cannot share what he does not have. One cannot lead others into the presence of God through music, unless he has been there himself." [5] The minister of music must have, therefore, a depth of commitment just as great as that of any other minister of the church.

[3] Morsch, *The Use of Music in Christian Education*, p. 115.
[4] Isaac Watts, "From All That Dwell Below the Skies."
[5] Morsch, *op. cit.*, p. 129.

Listening is a part of good singing, but for some who "cannot carry a tune in a bucket" the experience of pure listening may be the only experience of music that is meaningful. Recall the parts of a service of worship which, for members of the congregation, are entirely listening experiences—prelude, choir responses, anthem, offertory, postlude. These must be carefully planned if they are to be vital experiences of the presence of God. Music which does not attract attention to itself either by its ornateness or by its unworshipful associations will more likely be conducive to worship.

A well-planned visit to the sanctuary to see and hear the organ can have great educational value. The organist may demonstrate the varying sizes of pipes and corresponding qualities of tone and pitch. Compositions may be played to illustrate the range of contrasts possible. So are appreciations and understandings developed that lead to the deeper meanings of music.

The use of recordings with all age groups has unlimited possibilities. An obvious use of recordings is to increase appreciation of hymns. For example, the hymn "Joyful, Joyful, We Adore Thee" may be used with juniors and older age groups. The tune, "Hymn to Joy," is adapted from the last movement of Beethoven's *Ninth Symphony*. An exciting experience can result from the combination of listening to the symphony and singing the hymn. Never underestimate the listening potential of young children. With primaries, for instance, an ingenuous teacher can use "Pastoral Symphony" and "He Shall Feed His Flock" from Handel's *Messiah* in connection with the shepherds' story at Christmas.

The person who is familiar with the masterpieces of sacred music will find it an exciting venture to plan experiences which will relate them to the materials contained in the curriculum. There is, for instance, Mendelssohn's *Elijah*, parts of which could be used in a study of this Old Testament prophet. There are also such compositions as Honegger's *King David*, the many settings from various masses of the ancient words of Isaiah known as the "Sanctus" (Isa. 6:3), and the innumerable psalm settings of great beauty. For those who would delve into this exciting realm the possibilities are unlimited.

The values of using musical instruments may not be as obvious as those of singing and listening but they are nonetheless real. Experiences with instruments help individuals find new ways of expressing themselves and thus contribute to growth in poise and maturity.

For the preschool child music should be an informal, exploratory experience. The home offers an unlimited environment for exploring with tone and pitch. There are percussion instruments which have no pitch or tone—fingers which may tap on a table, the fist which may hit the open palm or table top. Glasses of water may be tuned by pouring varying amounts of water into each one so that a melody may be played upon them. So also may tone and pitch be discovered by hitting flower pots that are hanging upside down or by striking a silver spoon hanging upon a string. We strum the strings of an autoharp and are pleased with our discovery of tone.

The ancient art of hand-bell ringing has an appeal for young and old; so, too, does the making of simple instruments—a tambourine made with a paper plate and bottle tops, a triangle made by bending a length of brass curtain rod. The shepherd's pipe made at home or in vacation church school may give children an experience akin to that of David when he played for his sheep on the hills of ancient Palestine.

Thus do we draw the instrumental experience into our curriculum teaching, enriching its scope and appeal.

In both the home and the church school, experiences with instruments may appeal to some from whom neither singing nor listening have elicited a response. Wherever there is opportunity for self-expression, guided rightly, there is opportunity for Christian growth.

Historically rhythmic expression has always been a part of religion. From the dignified processional of a choir down the center aisle toward the altar to the informal hopping and skipping of kindergarten children, rhythmic movement has an important part to play in the growing toward maturity. Not all rhythmic experience is confined to physical expression. The majestic singing of a great hymn, the sensitive performance of a beautiful anthem, the coming and going of the seasons and of night and day—these and many other experiences involve the experience of rhythm. To be sensitive to it is to perceive anew the myriad ways God's wonders are made known to the children of earth.

The experience of creating usually is a combination of some or all of the other four experiences of music, and it may take place on different levels. For youth and adults the creative experience is involved, for instance, when music suitable for use with a particular drama is selected. The need for melodies for hand bells may stimulate the creative impulse, for there is little or no music for those ancient instruments now enjoying a revival in many churches. Another experience of creating may occur as individuals express in finger painting what a particular piece of music says to them. The making of a musical instrument is also a creative effort.

Primaries and juniors may respond to the idea of creating their own melodies to passages of scripture. Many verses from the psalms lend themselves to this treatment. Nursery and kindergarten children will respond with uninhibited rhythmic movement to such music as Stravinsky's *The Rite of Spring* and Debussy's *Afternoon of a Faun*. Here often is creativity of pristine purity. Let it be encouraged and nourished!

One of the most exciting experiences is the creating of both words and music. This will happen most readily with children, for they are less inhibited than youth and adults. Such an experience takes time and should never be hurried or forced. It is most appropriate, then, in sessions longer than the usual Sunday morning session. Take children to see a beautiful garden, to visit a lovely chapel unfamiliar to them, or to see a new building in process of construction. Encourage discussion about the experience, and let the words of their song grow out of the expressions of their own feelings. The kind of melody they will want will be determined by the kind of words they have created. Thus has taken place the exciting experience of creating something that has never before existed in quite that form. In such manner do children begin to sense the wonder of what persons have created and of how God works in human hearts and minds.

Perhaps we are never closer to the heart of God than when we ourselves become a conscious part of creation. The richer are our experiences of God's world the more naturally do our hearts yearn to express this richness—that is, when those who believe in the hidden potential within us are there to guide and direct us.

The unprecedented demand for ministers of music in churches of this country and for missionary teachers of music in other countries, the development of multiple choir programs, the widespread use of choir clinics and training classes, the stimulated interest in congregational singing—these are but a few of the indications that the place of music in Christian education is approaching maturity. This is not a new emphasis. It was King David who appointed the Levites to be ministers of music in the ancient Temple worship of the Jews. It was the apostle Paul who wrote to the Christians at Colossae that they should "teach and admonish one another in all wisdom . . . as you sing psalms and hymns and spiritual songs with thankfulness in your hearts to God" (Col. 3:16 R.S.V.). It was Martin Luther who said, "I would fain see all arts, specially music, in the service of Him who made and created them." [6] This is our heritage. Let us lay claim upon it.

Conclusion

The challenge before us is how the arts may genuinely create and re-create the experience of the faith. They do communicate the meaning of our faith, but the creative arts in Christian education must be more than instruction. They do express great beauty at times, but art is more than entertainment. It is not enough that a sanctuary be beautiful; it must somehow express the needs and yearnings of those who worship within it. It is not enough that religious drama be well executed; it must also stir participants and audience to deeper awareness of what Christian living means. It is not enough that an anthem please the worshipers; it must be an experience of worship.

Somehow Christian educators must lead churchmen to a new understanding of the purpose and function of the arts and of their interrelatedness. To say that a church has a multiple choir program, one or more drama interest groups, certain masterpieces of painting, and a beautiful sanctuary is not necessarily to say that the arts in that church are deepening the experience of the Christian faith.

What then is our criterion? Only when worship becomes more real, commitment deeper, social outlook more discerning, the distinction between right and wrong sharper; only when persons have taken another step along the road to Christian maturity may an experience of art be said to have been within the purpose of Christian education. The experience of the faith which the arts make possible is more than instruction, more than the sum total of words, paint, music, and acting. They bring to hearts ready to receive the impact of the experience of God himself and the good news he sent his Son to proclaim.

Bibliography

Drama

American Theater Wing Community Plays. The National Association for Mental Health, Inc., 1790 Broadway, New York 19, N. Y.

Eastman, Fred. *Christ in the Drama.* New York: The Macmillan Company, 1947.

Ehrensperger, Harold. *Conscience on Stage.* Nashville: Abingdon Press, 1947.

Enterline, Mildred Hohn. *Best Plays for the Church.* Philadelphia: Board of Christian Education, 1958.

Hicks, H. G. *The Reading Chorus.* New York: Noble and Noble, 1939.

Plays for the Church. New York: National Council of Churches, 1958.

Siks, Geraldine. *Creative Dramatics: An Art for Children.* New York: Harper and Brothers, 1958.

[6] C. S. Phillips, *Hymnody Past and Present* (New York: The Macmillan Company, 1937), p. 109.

Music

Andrews, Gladys. *Creative Rhythmic Movement for Children.* Englewood Cliffs, N. J.: Prentice-Hall, Inc., 1954.

Bailey, Albert E. *The Gospel in Hymns.* New York: Charles Scribner's Sons, 1950.

Benson, Louis F. *The Hymnody of the Christian Church.* Richmond, Va.: John Knox Press, 1956.

Cantate Domino. Hymnbook of the World's Student Christian Federation, Geneva, Switzerland, 1951.

Davison, Archibald T. *Church Music: Illusion and Reality.* Cambridge: Harvard University Press, 1952.

Morsch, Vivian Sharp. *The Use of Music in Christian Education.* Philadelphia: Westminster Press, 1956.

Shields, Elizabeth McE. *Music in the Religious Growth of Children.* Nashville: Abingdon Press, 1943.

Stevenson, Robert M. *Patterns of Protestant Church Music.* Durham, N. C.: Duke University Press, 1953.

Thomas, Edith Lovell. *Music in Christian Education.* Nashville: Abingdon Press, 1953.

———, (ed.). *The Whole World Singing.* New York: Friendship Press, 1950.

Chapter 20

Camps and Conferences

Maurice D. Bone

THE STORY OF CHURCH CAMPS, CONFERENCES, RETREATS, INSTITUTES, AND ASSEM-
blies at the mid-century is one of rapid growth and expansion. Today, people of the
church have before them a cafeteria offering a wider variety of programs than
has ever been true in the history of the church.

The summer-conference program of the church, which has made limited use
of the out-of-doors for the past fifty years, has broken many bonds and is now
finding expression in such new and interesting adventures as canoe conferences,
trail conferences, trip conferences, pack conferences, "go-and-see" conferences,
and the like. While a generation ago, the summer program of the church was
largely limited to a few weeks "for the young people," today the entire summer,
including late spring and early fall, is finding church groups making use of camp
and conference settings for highly concentrated, intensified, enlarged, and varied
experiences to serve the deeper needs of people of all ages in the church.

The camp-conference-retreat center is now thought to be a necessary part of
the Christian education of persons growing up in the church. In a very real sense,
the camp has become an extension of the educational arm of the church. Every
group that builds a new camp is building an additional education wing to its
present facilities.

The camp pattern, as distinct from the summer-conference pattern, is emerging
as a new opportunity for Christian education. Defined simply as an experience of
living in the out-of-doors in the Christian community, the camp tends to emphasize
the living together, while the conference tends to emphasize study. The camp
makes greater use of the situation in which the camp is located, involving boys
and girls, families, and adult groups in exploration, trips, discoveries, camp fires;
while the conference tends to concentrate on classes, study, the use of visual-aids,
and the relationship of its experience to the local church, with an emphasis on leadership training in many areas. Obviously conferences are being held on many college
campuses quite effectively, while more and more camps are being held in a camp
situation with as great a degree of isolation as is possible from the typical accelerated
pattern of living in the urban community.

Some of the differences between the camp and the conference are reflected
in the daily schedule, as can be observed in the following:

A Day at Camp[1]

7:30 Rising
8:00 Breakfast
8:30 Dining room work
        Cleaning and putting camp in order
9:15 Discovery group activities—planning for the day, exploration, discussion, work projects, worship, play, craft activities, swimming
12:15 Lunch
        Dining room work
1:30 Rest
2:30 Discovery group activities, as suggested in morning
5:00 Return to shelter to get ready for evening meal
5:45 Evening meal
        Dining room work
6:45 Evening activities; occasional all-camp event, such as campfires, games, worship; otherwise, discovery group or intergroup activities
7:45 Return to shelter
        Bedtime preparation
        Talk-it-over time, closing with brief worship
8:30 Lights out

A Conference Schedule[2]

7:30 Rising time
7:50 Morning watch
8:15 Breakfast
8:45 Cleanup time
9:15 First period
10:45 Assembly
11:15 Second period
12:30 Lunch
1:30 Quiet hour
2:30 Committees meet
3:00 Activities time
4:00 Active recreation
5:00 Conference cabinet, the program areas, evening program preparation
6:00 Dinner
7:00 Advisers' meeting
7:40 Vespers
8:15 Evening program
9:15 Relax (snack time)
9:45 Call to quarters
10:10 Fellowship groups
10:30 Lights out

Camping, as such, is no longer an extra or an alternative. It is no longer for the select few. Camping, in its own right, is becoming an integral and important part of the Christian growth and development of the individual.

Camping provides opportunity for:

[1] Quoted from *Planning the Church Camp* by LaDonna Bogardus. Copyright 1955 by The National Council of Churches. Used by permission.

[2] *Westminster Fellowship, Summer Conference Advisers' Handbook* (Philadelphia: Board of Christian Education, Presbyterian Church in the U.S.A.), p. 41. Used by permission.

1. An experience of relationships with persons of the peer group, as well as with other age groups, which are essential to the Christian growth and maturity of every individual.

2. Small intimate face-to-face groups to live on a twenty-four-hour basis in an atmosphere which is conducive to Christian growth, an atmosphere in which the individual takes his own share of responsibility for the life of the group.

3. The individual to gain or regain a sense of Christian perspective in which he brings to bear the teachings of the church, which he has learned through his educational experience, upon the actual problem of living the Christian life.

4. The individual, who is pushed about, highly stimulated, and sometimes over-stimulated in the busy rush of urban life with all of its artificialities, to establish himself in a new community quickly and to find persons who are concerned about him and his welfare.

5. The family as a unit to strengthen and enrich relationships between its members in a new and vital way.

6. A new dimension to living, not usually found in our normal day-by-day existence.

Camping by Age Groups

The typical pattern of camping, conducted by the church, follows age group lines.

Day Camping with Juniors

While many private and agency camps accept children five years of age and younger, the church-sponsored camps take the position that children under ten years of age, in the fourth grade in school generally, can best be served by the day-camp program sponsored by the church within the local community. This means that the leadership is indigenous to the community. Boys and girls may go home at nights. The camp makes use of the city park, a small adjoining farm or some natural setting within easy reach of the children. It adds additional experiences whereby the teachers and pupils may establish and deepen their relationships. The program of the day camp is quite different from the program of the daily vacation church school. The camp is a living situation and not intended to be a school.

The length of the camp period varies from one to two weeks, with a minimum of six days. Children are transported by buses often leased from the public-school system. The time is arranged to suit the climate and the availability of leadership and facilities. The distance from the local church should not require more than a thirty-minute ride on the bus each way. The children are involved from about 9:30 A.M. to 3:30 P.M. each day that they are in camp, and the program during this part of the day is almost identical with that in any good resident camp for children of the same age.

While camping by the day has been carried on by the Girl Scouts, Y.M.C.A., Y.W.C.A., and other agencies as well as private groups for many years, camping by the day is just beginning to emerge as a specific pattern for church groups. The development of guidance materials following experimentation during the 1950's provides a background of experience and guidance for churches interested in this phase of the program.

Some groups carry on a day camp on alternate days. Many of them are using a two-week period as the minimum and finding this a splendid preparation for the individual's participation in resident camping at a future time.

Resident Camping for Juniors

Resident camps for juniors are being sponsored by the church in increasing numbers. The juniors are so available. There is often the temptation to fill an empty period on the summer schedule with another junior camp period, just to keep the camp filled. Actually great care and concern should be given to camping with juniors, in everything from recruiting, relationships with the home, preparation of leaders, selection of a proper site, and so on.

Camping with juniors in many areas of the church tended at first to follow a reduced edition of the summer conference for senior-high young people. During the 1950's however, there has been a swing to an actual experience of living in the out-of-doors in what some call "real camping."

Church leaders believe it is important for the child to have an experience in a group which in many ways is similar to his own family in which a family group lives in the camp in association with other family groups. Here there is a minimum of stimulation and a maximum of responsibility and freedom for the family group to plan its own life and interests.

Church leaders are studying the effect of the size of the group upon the individual child. Standards indicate that the maximum size group in which a junior participates should not exceed sixty, including leadership. In such a group, the junior camper would find himself in a smaller nucleus of boys and girls together with two leaders so that the total would not exceed ten. Camps are increasingly providing facilities which permit each family group of this kind to live in the same general location and to prepare some of their own meals and take responsibility for the camp life as well as planning their own activities for the duration of the camp.

Camps providing facilities like this are multiplying the number of groups of sixty to allow for as many such groups as are needed to serve the number of boys and girls who are available for this type of experience. This is called a decentralized camp. One administrative group can plan for several decentralized groups of sixty, provided the camp property is sufficiently large to permit these groups to be located in such a way that each has its own privacy from the others, and there is adequate room for exploration, hiking, and trips to places of interest for the campers.

Camping with Junior Highs

Camping with junior highs follows somewhat the same plan as camping with juniors. Junior-high boys and girls, in a "real" camp, live in quarters so each family group can be housed in a specific area and each family group can then be given the responsibility for planning its own life and activity.

Standards indicate that the family group should not exceed twelve, including leaders, and the total camp maximum should be seventy-five, including leaders. In the same way as planning the junior camp, the numbers served in a decentralized camp depend upon the persons available, the facilities, and the leadership.

Church camping is following the great move to the out-of-doors. The availability of canvas shelters in many types and designs is making camping more interesting to the child. It also brings camping within the reach of many groups who do not have the resources to build more permanent shelters even if that were desirable. It is evident that there is emerging a specific pattern of camping as a part of Christian education. Christian educators believe there is more potential for real Christian learning in the experiences of the small group than in any other kind of experience which can be provided by the church for persons in the summertime in the out-of-doors.

Senior Highs

The church-sponsored experience for senior highs in the summertime usually follows the conference-institute-assembly plan. Each year, however, has brought a new crop of interesting variations to the main theme which now finds senior highs actually going camping, taking trips to visit mission stations, engaging in work camps in nearby and distant places, taking pack trips along some of the famous trails—such as the Appalachian Trail, holding canoe conferences for two-week periods in Minnesota with its ten thousand lakes, and taking pack trips into the Rockies and Southern Mountains, where senior highs pack-in all of their gear and stay for a week or more. This is also accomplished by a number of senior-high youth groups on week ends throughout the summer as well as in fall and spring. All of this indicates that approaches are constantly changing to meet new needs and present times. The objective is to provide the type of experience which will be most fruitful in terms of Christian education.

The conference-institute-assembly began with the Chautauquas bringing several hundred people together in one place. The average number of participants in the conferences held across the country would approximate one hundred. This was not true a generation ago.

Even in the larger conferences and annual youth assemblies, which bring several hundred and sometimes thousands of young people together, Christian educators are using small study groups. When these large numbers are broken down into smaller groups in which the individual is not lost, more effective use is made of the time and more effective relationships between persons are established. One assembly involving sixteen hundred young people operated on the basis of one hundred groups of sixteen each. The core of the assembly took place in the life of these small groups of sixteen which included two leaders. The platform presentations were designed to contribute to the conversation, discussion, and study that was going on in the small units.

All of this leads to certain observations. Increasingly, Christian educators, in using the patterns of both the camp and the conference, are becoming more concerned about the individual person—his welfare, his well-being, his relationship to others, his participation in a group small enough so that he has a sense of belonging and will be missed if he is absent and small enough so that he will feel the concern of the others of the group for him, yet large enough to offer challenge and variety. These groups are almost universally coeducational and usually provide two leaders, a man and a woman. Sometimes a delegate and an adult adviser share the responsibility for the leadership of these groups.

The second observation is that these small study groups in the conference pattern have more time together. The time allotted them is long enough so that they can have a variety of experience—sometimes in worship and play as well as study. This means the addition of other dimensions to the life of the group.

The youth fellowship concept appeared in the 1930's and has had almost universal adoption in some form or another by the Protestant denominational groups in America. With it came an increasing awareness that the young person involved in the youth fellowship of the local church, in the youth rally of his area or district, and in the summer camp or conference is the same person. These events are planned by the major committee, which is generally the youth-work committee, rather than by having some of the events planned by one group while others are planned by a separate conference committee.

This has produced a closer integration of the conference experience with the life of the local church. The conference is planned to meet the needs of the young people in the churches served. Leadership for the conference is now selected on the basis of service to existing youth groups.

In 1954 and 1957, the National Council of Churches experimented with different patterns of the summer conference, attempting to help the summer conference relate more specifically to the local church. The outcomes of this experiment were evident. The young people who participated in the conference along with an adviser from their own local church had a much more effective carry-over of the experience of the conference into the life of the local church than those young people who came from churches where there was no adult person from the same congregation at the conference. This seemed so obvious that educators wondered why they missed it before. Increasingly, administrative committees planning summer conferences with senior highs include the advisers and young people from local churches on these committees.

Administrative and guidance materials for the senior-high conferences are planned by the denominations. Conference planning groups are increasingly making use of program guidance materials for young people in the Sunday church school and the youth fellowship as well as those provided specifically for the summer conference.

Family Camping

The church program of family camping grew very rapidly during the 1950's. In 1940, the church-sponsored family camp was a rarity in America. By 1950, properties owned by the church were beginning to serve programs of camping with families. In addition, in keeping with the trend for the greater use of the recreation facilities provided by national and state parks, many church groups began to use these facilities for camping with their families. By 1959, it had become the standard procedure for each organization of the church, thinking in terms of developing facilities for camping, to include somewhere in the program facilities that will accommodate families.

The family-camping program includes a wide variety of program elements. At the moment it has been influenced by the summer conference, and many so-called camps are an adaptation of a conference pattern and really might be called "family conferences." A few groups are experimenting with the church's responsibility when it takes its families camping. Some local churches are providing family camps for the families of their own congregations, making use of public facilities and state and national parks, as well as renting other camp facilities.

Programs for family camping usually stress an opportunity for all the members of the family to be together in an experience in the out-of-doors. The family referred to is the family unit, whatever that may be, and includes families with only one parent as well as families with both parents.

The program seems to highlight the experiences that families can have as a group. This means giving each family freedom each day and during the total camp period to plan some things to do as a family—fishing, hiking, getting up early for an exploration trip of some kind, going on an overnight hike, cooking their own meals, painting, following a hobby, rock collecting, hunting arrowheads, wading in the stream, swimming, and everything and anything which comes within the range of the normal interest of a family and which can be done in the out-of-doors.

The leadership in a family camp is built-in. Persons invited to serve as leaders come with their families. The rest of the leadership is found among the persons who come. Parents are encouraged to share their hobbies; children, their interests. Groups develop on the basis of interests, hobbies, and likes. All in all the program is designed to give the family opportunities to do things as families. These include worship, play, study, work, leadership in the total program, and other such experiences.

Family camps are becoming smaller. Christian educators are discovering that when more than twelve to fifteen families come together, the group tends to lose the individual and is less mobile, less functional. Children find more security in a group which does not exceed fifty or sixty whom they can come to know at least on an acquaintance basis within the span of the camp period. There seems to be better adjustment, less homesickness, less frustration, more flexibility, and a happier time throughout when these numbers are served in a family camp situation.

Ministers are finding that when the pastor takes ten of his families to a family camp each summer for four or five years, the experience gradually revolutionizes the life of the church. This is done not through preaching at the families, but by simply living with them and giving them an opportunity to learn to know each other on a person-to-person basis and to share experiences which include play and work as well as worship and study.

Camping With Young Adults

Camping with young adults, both single and married, is being done on a special interest basis, and the program varies from the experiences of living in the out-of-doors—as is typical of camping—to the conference-study-seminar-consultation type of program.

Summary of Camping by Age Groups

Important in all that has been included in these observations about types of programs are the elements of participation as far as the person is concerned. Included are study and group life that will allow the individual freedom and yet permit him to take responsibility on his own initiative and to exercise it in his relationship to others as far as group life is concerned. All is done within the context of the Christian church and in the light of the gospel.

Camp Site Development

The rate and the rapidity with which church groups have entered into the purchase of property for church camp-conference-retreat purposes has been amazing during the 1950's. Actually it seems as if the church-camp movement has grown "from rags to riches" when some one hundred to one hundred fifty million dollars is being spent during this decade in the securing and developing of facilities for the use of the church camps, conferences, and retreats.

In trying to meet the demands and in trying to assure the facilities being developed to serve educational needs, seven of the major denominations participating in the National Council of Churches have employed national staff personnel to give guidance to this movement. These persons work together through the National Council and also serve denominations which do not have full-time staff in this field.

Increasingly, church groups entering into the ownership of property and its development for camp purposes are securing the services of nationally-known camp planners and architects. This is a highly-specialized field. The church has concern for its educational program. Program determines facilities.

The types of development range from the very simple to a few which are quite elaborate. The experience of the American Baptists with the Assembly Grounds at Green Lake, Wisconsin, consisting of eleven hundred acres with some eighty buildings, is an example of property to serve a wide range of groups throughout the nation. The experiences made possible by individuals and families coming to Green Lake from all parts of the American Baptist Convention have helped to unify the denomination. The program gives persons training in the various aspects of Christian education. Significantly enough, the church has developed on this property demonstration centers, which are in use during the summer for teachers of children in the Sunday church school. Other demonstration centers are to come in the future. A model camp has been developed and is served by the central kitchen, by using thermal containers and transporting the food. A number of other organizations in Wisconsin make use of these assembly grounds as a meeting place because of their accessibility and beautiful setting in which to meet and plan.

As the camping movement has increased, the camp grounds are being secured closer to the place where the people live. Some groups are finding themselves with three types of property—one property that is used for retreat centers only, a second for conference purposes primarily, and a third for camping. Where such is the case, the property is generally administered by one board of directors or commission for better administration and better relationship to the total Christian education program. Other groups are uniting all of these functions on one or sometimes two properties. This means that when all are combined on one property, the acreage must be sufficiently large to make possible the operation of these groups simultaneously. Architects and planners serving with the church groups now say that they cannot draw the plans for church camp facilities all on one piece of drawing paper. A generation ago this was possible; now it takes at least two and sometimes three. Groups are buying sites by the hundreds of acres— two hundred, three hundred, four hundred, six hundred, one thousand—all in an attempt to get sufficient space to serve the program needs.

Camp groups are not the only ones seeking open spaces of land in large acreage in our country. The extension of our metropolitan areas into the suburbs, the linking of large cities along routes of communication, and the development of super highway systems all require great land areas. In addition, the extension of industry, the moving of industry from one section of the country to another for reasons both of transportation, labor, and operation closer to the source of raw materials is a part of the same picture.

The National Park Service, which has traditionally and historically set apart certain public lands for use of the public for recreation, has to struggle continually to retain these lands for such use. These and other factors have prompted the National Park Service to conduct a survey attempting to discover the facilities now available for use of persons in the out-of-doors and, second, to see what additional facilities may be needed to serve the public in the future. All of this raises the question of stewardship on the part of church people. It suggests the wisdom of securing sufficient acreage when a site is purchased in order to insure privacy, isolation, and accessibility to the churches being served.

The Small Group in the Camping Program

The term "small group" in the camping program refers to a group of boys and girls with two leaders—the total group not to exceed ten for juniors, or twelve for junior highs and older. The idea of the small group is to provide the opportunity for each individual to find his place in a unit which includes his own peers on a coeducational basis together with two counselors, a man and a woman, in such a way that the total group experience involves the normal situations of living together.

The experiences of living include eating together, working together, worshiping together, studying together, working together for others, and suffering together. The authors of *Recreation and the Local Church* [3] call these "levels of communication." Christian educators are discovering that when a group of people is involved in the experience which includes all of these elements that the whole round of the experience is deepened and more complete.

Each small group in a camp takes responsibility for planning its own life. This is an attempt to bring about conditions for learning in which the individual will find the best opportunities for learning. Christian teaching takes place in relation to the day-by-day living situations. A vital part of each small group's experience is the "talk-it-over" session which is planned around the campfire, usually, before going to bed at night. In these intimate discussion sessions there is perfect frankness about the relationships that have existed during the day, the significant things that have happened to individuals, the concern of each individual for the others, and other matters related to the spiritual development of the individual.

The significance in the small-group experience is the factor of responsibility. Christian educators believe that in camping as in other situations a person matures as he is able to take increasing responsibility for his own actions. The small group in a camp gives each individual the opportunity to accept his fair share of responsibility within the context of the total group.

The operation of the small group makes important demands upon leadership. This means a careful selection, preparation, training, guidance, and supervision of leadership all through the camp experience.

The Use of Group Work Techniques

The camp and conference of the church is definitely being influenced and strengthened by the insights made available through the social scientists working

[3] Clemens, Tully, and Crill (Elgin, Ill.: Church of the Brethren Press, 1958).

in the field of group dynamics.[4] The fifties marked the period when the group work principles and patterns found their way into the actual planning for and conduct of church-camp and conference experience. Note for example the use of the small group. This is group work at its best when leadership is adequately prepared. Many camps are using "talk-it-over" sessions, "live feed-backs," and "post-meeting reaction reports." Also leaders in camps are using the aids of group work, such as the role of the observer. Camp administrators are giving help in this field to counselors under their leadership.

A specific "design" for training has also emerged. This "design" for training leaders on the national scale, developed by the National Council of Churches for the training of church-camp leaders, is a case in point. Reference books such as Sara Little's *Learning Together in the Christian Fellowship*,[5] *Together We Grow*[6] by Sweet and Arnim, and Bonhoeffer's *Life Together*[7] are found regularly on the bibliography for leadership in preparation for the camp and conference program.

A Look at the Future

The church's use of the out-of-doors for the program of Christian education will likely proceed at an increasing degree of acceleration for the next decade. The church is just beginning to discover the use of the rural setting in the real sense of the word and on a wide scale. The shortened work week, the hot crowded cities in summertime, the lure of advertising of vacation lands with all the comforts of home, and the wholesome desire of many people to get their feet on the ground are contributing factors.

Increasingly local church groups will be finding experiences which will add a new dimension to the life of groups that already exist. This means that families, youth groups, men's groups, women's groups, will make use of the summer for their own purposes. This does not imply that each church will have to own its own property—far from it. Rather properties being purchased by area organizations of the denomination will be able to serve local church groups on this basis for some time to come. It also means that state, city, and national parks will be increasingly used by local church groups for such experiences.

The big factor in all that has been said is the responsible role of the leader. The next great move will be in the direction of providing more adequate training for church leaders who take groups into the out-of-doors.

Christian educators are discovering that present methods are not adequate. It is no longer held by the majority of research leaders that training which lasts only a few hours is adequate for a full-time job in a camp setting. This is true for all types of experiences—camps, conferences, and retreats. Along with the search for ways to better use the out-of-doors for Christian education is coming the search for better ways for training leaders to help others have a satisfactory and rewarding experience in such situations.

Bibliography

Bogardus, LaDonna. *Planning the Church Camp*. New York: National Council of the Churches of Christ in the U.S.A., 1955.

[4] Cf. ch. 16, pp. 173-83.

[5] Richmond, Va.: John Knox Press, 1956.

[6] Philadelphia: The Board of Christian Education of the Presbyterian Church in the U.S.A., 1958.

[7] New York: Harper and Brothers, 1954.

————. *The Church Day Camp*. New York: National Council of Churches of Christ in the U.S.A., 1955.

Davis, Louise. *Juniors in God's World*. Philadelphia: Christian Education Press, 1954.

Ensign, John and Ruth. *Camping Together as Christians*. Richmond, Va.: John Knox Press, 1958.

————. *My Camp Book—Stewards in God's World*. Richmond, Va.: John Knox Press, 1953.

Goddard, Carrie Lou. *Learning to Live with Others*. Nashville: Abingdon Press, 1953.

Objective of Christian Education for Senior High Young People. New York: National Council of Churches of Christ in the U.S.A., 1958.

Venable, Mary. *God at Work in His World*. Nashville: Abingdon Press, 1955.

Chapter 21

Weekday and Vacation Church Schools

Alice L. Goddard

MANY CHURCHES CONDUCT RELIGIOUS EDUCATION PROGRAMS THROUGH THE WEEK but much of this work has little common pattern excepting the weekday or the vacation church schools. The former provide for Christian teaching during the school year, the latter, when boys and girls are free from public school responsibility. The first section of this chapter will concern itself with the weekday church school and the second portion with the vacation church school.

The Weekday Church School

The weekday church school is "a school set up by the churches in co-operation or individually, in which the attending pupils are excused from the public school at the written request of parents to go to a church or other building to receive religious education." [1]

The weekday church-school movement in the Protestant churches celebrates its fiftieth anniversary in 1964. It began as an experimental venture in Gary, Indiana. A survey by the U.S. Office of Education in 1941 showed 488 school systems in 38 states releasing pupils with an additional 126 school systems spread over 32 states with plans to release pupils. [2] Due to several reasons, recent statistics are not available, nor are they easy to obtain. Data which are available, although very incomplete, show that the program is most extensive in the northern area of the United States east of the Mississippi River. The work is carried on in scattered communities between the Mississippi River and the Rocky Mountains and in several areas along the west coast.

The community school is the prevalent pattern and is generally assumed in this material. In it Protestant, and sometimes Orthodox, churches unite in conducting classes. Other faiths may co-operate in general planning and in approaching the school board. Los Angeles, California, is representative of this type of system. The Church Federation of Los Angeles administers the program for the co-operating Protestant churches, selects and trains leaders who teach the children released to the church buildings the Federation secures to house the classes. The Federation also represents these co-operating churches on the interfaith committee which includes among its members representatives of the Roman Catholic Church, the

[1] Shaver, *Remember the Weekday to Teach Religion Thereon*, p. 5.
[2] *Weekday Classes in Religious Education*, Bulletin No. 3 (U.S. Office of Education, 1941), p. 17.

Association of Evangelicals, and the Christian Science Church. All contacts with schools are made through this interfaith committee.

In the semicommunity school, co-operating churches plan together and approach the school board unitedly, but each teaches its own pupils. Many of these schools exist, for example, in Minnesota. This school requires more leadership than the community type, supervision is difficult if not impossible, and the value of peer group participation is decreased. In the parish type, a single church carries its own program completely independent of other churches. This is more apt to occur in a one-church community, or where only one church is interested.

In the Zorach versus Clauson case, April 28, 1952, the United States Supreme Court declared release of pupils from public school during the day for religious education legal when parents request it. One condition of this case was that no school machinery was being used in conducting classes. Records state,

> When the state encourages religious instruction or cooperates with religious authorities by adjusting the schedule of public events to sectarian needs, it follows the best of our traditions. For it then respects the religious nature of our people and accommodates the public service to their spiritual needs. To hold that it may not would be to find in the Constitution a requirement that the government show a callous indifference to religious groups. That would be preferring those who believe in no religion over those who do believe.[8]

The church cannot dictate to the public school regarding the work given to pupils who remain, if any, when others are released. Public school leaders frequently use this time for review, study, or personal assignments. Many are careful to avoid introducing new work which would make later learning difficult for those who missed it.

In spite of the Zorach case decision, some still oppose the program as being divisive because pupils separate by faiths to go to various churches or to remain in school. Those who support the weekday church school accept religious differences as a recognized part of our culture and believe that our children and youth should be taught to respect these differences. Certainly neither pressure nor discrimination should be brought to bear on any pupil or his parents because of lack of participation in these classes.

A very few state constitutions raise questions in the minds of its opponents as to the legality in their state, regardless of what the United States Supreme Court may say. For this reason, church leaders in some states have sought the opinion of their attorneys general or the passing of a permissive act by the legislative bodies to assure their rights to released time.

Several denominations, including as examples the United Presbyterian Church in the U.S.A., and the Board of Education and Publication of the American Baptist Convention, have published statements or otherwise indicated their support of the weekday church school when conducted as recommended by the National Council of Churches. They urge their churches to participate actively in its administration and leadership. This program was also given a priority rating when member units of the National Council recently studied its Christian education activities.

Most denominations do not write the weekday school into their Christian educa-

[8] Zorach and Gluck vs. Board of Education, 343 U. S. 306 (1952).

tion materials to any extensive degree. One reason may be because the co-operative nature of this work necessitates considerable local planning. Consequently patterns vary and ways have not yet been found to relate them in a satisfactory way to national denominational efforts. This matter requires careful study in order to bring about desirable program co-ordination.

Other faiths also recognize the values in the weekday church school and provide released time classes for their boys and girls. This is especially true of the Roman Catholic churches. Many of the Jewish bodies are opposed to it for a variety of reasons although some hold classes or co-operate in interfaith committees in a few communities.

Many public-school leaders are strong supporters of the weekday church school and welcome its contribution. Others are less enthusiastic if they are active in groups which oppose it or if the work is not of standard quality.

Release of Pupils

In some states the time of day pupils are released is governed by laws which permit excusal at certain periods only; in other places boys and girls from various classes are released at various times throughout the day. Information regarding state laws is available from the state board of education or from the National Council of Churches' Department of Weekday Religious Education.

Excusal during only one period a day for all pupils is known as simultaneous released time; excusal throughout the day as staggered released time. Staggered time allows for employment of full-time professionally trained teachers, for whom weekday church-school teaching becomes a vocation.

A few communities operate on dismissed time when all pupils are excused from school during the first or last period of the day, to go to weekday church school or do anything else they desire. This puts the work on the same basis as any other after-school activity and, since all are excused, removes it from the workday.

Every child who is excused must have a request card signed by his parents and indicating the faith of the class he is to attend. Some schools have meetings in which the work is interpreted to parents, their suggestions heard, and their support enlisted. Some invite parents to be sponsors and to interpret the work to others. Others prepare materials for home use on special days or include at least one family activity during the year. Community planning is necessary among the churches so that the weekday program supplements and does not duplicate the rest of the family-life program.

Leadership and Curriculum Materials

The key to an effective weekday church school is primarily leadership. Springfield, Findlay, and other cities in Ohio; some areas of Massachusetts; and Virginia, which has several county as well as local systems, are illustrative of many communities with a staggered released-time program employing professional teachers with special training for their work. Teachers are generally employed for the school year with salary and benefits similar to those of the public-school teachers in the area. State councils and the National Council of Churches recruit these teachers through seminaries and other schools, send information to prospective teachers, and serve as placement centers.

A larger number of teachers is needed in communities with the simultaneous released-time program, such as Scranton, Pennsylvania, or Buffalo, New York. They are chosen from church-school leaders who have had public-school experience or laboratory school and other Christian education training beyond that generally required of leaders in the Sunday church school. Securing enough qualified teachers demands constant effort and training of recruits as well as in-service training.

Many councils provide training opportunities in leadership schools, special conferences and workshops, retreats and institutes—as for instance, Oregon, with a laboratory school, and Indiana or Northern and Southern California, with teachers' fellowships or associations for enrichment and special training. The National Council has an annual meeting of weekday church school leaders where new insights are gained, problems discussed, and experiences shared. Continuing fellowship on the state and national level is maintained through newsletters, visits, and correspondence. Several state and local councils employ a staff member who assists local communities.

Supervision is essential to maintain a desirable quality of leadership. Some person needs to be available for teachers and churches to turn to for help, support, inspiration, and the maintaining of standards. Waterbury, Connecticut, is typical of one type of situation where a council staff member trains and supervises a large group of leaders, each of whom teaches only an hour or so a week; whereas in a city like Dayton, Ohio, the supervisor is responsible for a staff of full-time professional leaders.

The minister or director of Christian education is an important person in the weekday church-school system. He has responsibility for the quality of work done with pupils in these classes and must make sure that the Christian education forces of his church are officially represented on the sponsoring body. Directors of Christian education sometimes teach in the classes or act as supervisors. Not all ministers are trained to do so. Many with some Christian education background teach, for example, in Pittsburgh, Pennsylvania, where the pupils are senior-high-school students. Unless there is more than one on the local church staff, ministers often find regular attendance difficult.

Denominations working together through the Cooperative Publication Association have produced texts for the weekday church school in the areas of the Church, the Bible, the universe, and Christian living. They are graded on a two year basis from the first through the twelfth grades. In developing these, the denominations have taken into account what is taught in the Sunday and vacation church schools and in the public school, in order that what is included might supplement and complement the rest of the pupils' educational experiences.

Materials are also published by several state and local councils of churches. These follow a variety of patterns and are sometimes used beyond the boundaries of the councils which prepare them. The United Lutheran denomination also publishes its own texts, one of which is used as a co-operative text. There is need for further study and evaluation of all available curriculum material.

The sponsoring body is responsible for deciding what curriculum material will be used and its sequence. Many councils such as Cincinnati, Ohio, or Chicago, Illinois, have curriculum committees which study materials regularly and select what is to be taught, thus assuring order and progression in teaching. In deciding on texts, consideration must be given to the recommendations of the denominations of the co-operating churches, to the curriculum of the local churches, the public-school social studies for the various grades, and any other pertinent information regarding the boys and girls being taught.

Organization and Administration

Where there is one, a council of churches as the established interdenominational body is the desirable sponsoring group for the weekday church school. A ministerial association, council of church women, or a laymen's group is not generally representative enough of the Christian education forces of the churches to be responsible for an educational program which reaches out to the community's children or youth. Most councils establish a committee to carry detailed responsibility, but this committee's plans and policies are subject to action by the governing body the same as those of any other committee.

When there is no council of churches, interested individuals or groups often invite all of the churches to send representatives to a meeting to consider the weekday church school and to sponsor any program which the churches may agree upon after careful study of the community and the plan. Churches are cautioned to make certain that their Christian education leaders are active in any group responsible for this work.

Classes are housed in churches, buses or trailers, converted recreation rooms in homes, and in buildings which have been erected for this purpose. The use of school buildings was a major factor in the Supreme Court decision against the plan as conducted in Champaign, Illinois. The McCollum case was the occasion for this decision. This is a reason why the National Council of Churches does not approve the use of public-school buildings for classes.

The budget should include supervision and teaching costs, materials, transportation if required, and other necessary items. The participating churches approve and underwrite the proposed budget. Funds are handled through a central treasury in most weekday systems although communities have various fund raising patterns, as for instance, Rochester, New York, where neighboring churches unite to underwrite the program in their own area and to care for their share of the over-all costs, including work in less privileged areas; or cities such as Indianapolis, Indiana, where sponsors are invited to increase the budget beyond the amount the churches contribute. All costs of the program are borne by the churches with no involvement of public funds or resources.

Establishment of weekday church schools in a community requires at least a year of careful planning. Those interested should know the reactions of the churches to the idea, the approximate number of unchurched boys and girls in the area, possible housing facilities, leadership, and financial support as well as the community's readiness for this program. Interfaith co-operation in planning and in approach to the school board is important to community good will and is generally sought, with the establishment of an interfaith committee resulting.

Although the church is responsible, the school board has a right to expect high standards and needs to know what will be done to maintain them if the plan is carried out. Agreements with the school board must be carefully spelled out in writing to avoid questions as personnel changes or policy matters arise.

The state councils of churches and the National Council are sources for guidance materials and counsel for communities contemplating this program.

Distinctive Values of the Weekday Church School

Growth has occurred because the weekday church school, properly organized and conducted, has distinctive values and a unique contribution. It enables the church to include Christian teaching in the pupil's work week and in his weekday teaching-learning program. Although many of its leaders recognize the importance of spiritual values and endeavor to foster them in their work, the public school cannot provide specific religious training. This is the task of the church.

The weekday church school as part of the general study schedule offers opportunities to give public-school work religious interpretation and meaning. Weekday teachers hear many questions carried over from public school. For example: "How can nations that love God carry on wars?" "Does God want us to do all this exploring of the universe?" "Did the early churches have any influence on the Roman empire?" "If God loves everyone, why do some people have so many more opportunities than others?"

The weekday church school reaches the pupil in the peer group with which he associates five days a week. Boys and girls know the strength that comes from each other as school friends receive the same Christian teaching. The grouping for the rest of the church's program is usually not the same as that of the public school.

The weekday church school is often the pupil's only opportunity to share religious ideas and concepts across interdenominational lines under leadership dedicated to help him at the same time to move into closer relationship with his own church and its teachings. In his weekday class he increases his respect for the beliefs of others and comes to accept differences in beliefs and values.

Under the trained leadership in many weekday systems, pupils find their learning experiences equal in quality to that of their public school. Respect for religion and the church increases along with learning. Regularity of attendance also allows for more sustained work than is generally possible on Sunday, with its interruptions of family activities, late rising, or other competing demands.

Parents, pupils, ministers, and others testify to the amount of work that pupils accomplish in this additional period of religious teaching. A national youth leader said recently, as have other church leaders, "It was in the weekday church school that I really came to know what was in the Bible and what it means."

Reports from across the nation show that from 10 to 70 per cent of the pupils in these classes are without any other church connection at the beginning of the school year. Many weekday pupils and their parents are received each year into the fuller program and ultimately into membership of the church as a result of the weekday church school.

A weekday church school is as strong as its leadership, which begins with the sponsoring body. Here are the people who must provide direction and guidance for the program; keep it closely related to the total church program of Christian education; assure a high quality of trained Christian leadership with sound theological and educational background; and provide curriculum materials, housing, and working tools adequate to the task. Then the weekday church school becomes a strong arm of the church's Christian education program for its boys and girls.

Conditions indicate that some opposition is likely to continue and that the desirable way to meet it will be with increased efforts of good will and respect for differences. In some states, legal difficulties may still be encountered due to the nature of the state constitution or its interpretation, but the many states where legality is established far outnumber these. Rapid expansion is neither anticipated nor encouraged. Rather the continued emphasis will be on improving the quality of work through thoughtful planning and careful administration and on tying the weekday church school more closely into the total Christian education program of denominations and councils, locally, regionally, and nationally.

The Vacation Church School

The vacation church school provides boys and girls with joyous Christian education during vacation from public school. It is filled with many learning opportunities through Bible study, dramatics, creative writing, rhythmics and music, play, hand activities, choral reading, trips, and explorations. Everyday clothes and weekday time allow for work and play not always suitable for Sunday. Service enterprises rank high in the activities which center around the purpose of the school and its program.

Schools vary in length from one to four weeks or longer. The vast majority, however, last for only two weeks, although the longer school offers many advantages. A reason frequently given for the shorter period is the lack of qualified leadership for the more extensive time.

In 1924, twenty-four denominations reported 5,411 schools with 161,735 pupils enrolled. Churches have now come to accept the vacation church school as a more important element of Christian education, as indicated by 1956-57 reports of 98,160 schools in Protestant and Orthodox churches in the United States and 935,916 pupils.[4]

Most boys and girls have more time with fewer competing demands during the vacation period. Although various character building agencies plan summer programs, there are many places where no such program is offered; or if it is, it is for a brief time only and the rest of the summer is left open.

Consecutive daily sessions allow for continuing work and sustained effort. This makes possible study and other activities which require more than one period for completion but which could not easily be spread over sessions a week apart without considerable loss of interest. Each daily session can be from two and a half to three hours long and includes a variety of related learning opportunities. Older boys and girls especially appreciate this chance for depth study and purposeful work and service.

The vacation church school can double the time given to Christian education. A four-week school meeting for two and a half hours a day five days a week is equivalent in time to another year of work in the time ordinarily used on Sunday.

Types of Schools

Many local churches conduct their own schools. Others unite with neighboring churches of different denominations in a community school. In an individual church school, curriculum and teaching are easily correlated with the rest of the

[4] *Facts for 1959 Planning in Christian Education* (New York: National Council of Churches, 1959), p. 2.

program. The local church often feels a greater responsibility for its own pupils and takes its own school more seriously.

On the other hand, because of a pool from which to draw, better leaders can often be secured for the community school. The pupils join in work and study with their friends and playmates from other churches. Reports would indicate also that local church schools do much less about outreach in comparison with the community school.[5] This may be because the local school reaches out largely to its own people whereas the community school puts serious effort into enlisting boys and girls from the entire neighborhood.

Churches occasionally show some real imagination in planning the vacation church school. Some now meet during spring vacation. Families in a rural church held a school recently early in the evenings which both parents and children attended. Junior-high-school groups often meet in the late afternoon or early evening rather than during the morning when most of the children's schools are held. Some schools meet for three days a week over a longer period of time to secure better leadership not available for every day in the week. Other churches follow their regular school with weekly or biweekly sessions throughout the rest of the summer. Churches, especially in crowded areas, occasionally provide a full day's session with a wide variety of activities out-of-doors as well as indoors. Some with adequate facilities do most of their work outside.

Organization and leadership

The vacation church school is one unit in the total educational program. The board or committee on Christian education is, therefore, responsible for its administration, leadership, and general supervision in the local church or appoints members to the community school administrative body. In either case the responsible group can secure more qualified leadership and develop a more adequate plan when, as soon as one year's school closes and is evaluated, plans are begun for the next one.

The leadership and physical facilities usually determine the age groups that will be included. Few schools include pupils beyond the junior-high age. Many include nursery-age children, but this is not recommended unless mature leaders trained to work with this age group are secured, health standards met, and the children ready to be away from parents for the long periods of time the school requires.

The Christian education committee selects curriculum. The denominations working together have developed vacation church-school co-operative texts in six areas of work which are studied in cycles, one area being recommended for each year. Several denominations also publish their own materials which they endeavor to correlate with their ongoing program of study. Catalogues and further information regarding texts are available from denominational publishers or the National Council of Churches.

Important as curriculum is, the key to the quality of a vacation church school is its leadership. The first requisite is a sound Christian faith and the ability to communicate this faith to boys and girls through living as well as through planned teaching. The supervisor or director needs to be able to inspire and to work well with adults and children. Age group leaders should have had experience in teaching the particular group which they are to lead. Helpers are also needed. The younger the children, the fewer there should be in proportion to the number

[5] *Study of Vacation Church Schools* (New York: National Council of Churches, 1951), p. 26.

of adults, and the more maturity is required of the leader who works with them.

Resource leaders are often recruited to give special help, but it is recommended that whatever they do should fit into the purposes and plan of work and not be substituted for the continuing program.

When leadership is enlisted from the teachers who serve the rest of the year, the total program can be easily unified. Relationships are already established between leaders and pupils. They carry memories from the school into their later experiences together. This continuing service is not always possible for some teachers, however. Consequently churches often recruit and train leaders to work primarily in the vacation church school, with another group carrying the load at other times. These recruits are sought from among parents, college or seminary students, public-school teachers, weekday church-school teachers, and other church members. Their training and experience condition the role they will take as leadership assignments are determined.

Denominations offer training through literature and conferences. Many councils of churches send teams throughout their areas to train prospective leaders. Leadership schools frequently include vacation church-school training in their age group courses or as a special subject. Even though a person may teach regularly in the Sunday church school, additional training is desirable for this work with its longer daily sessions, its freer type of activities, and its concentrated period of time. One means of in-service training is the regular staff meetings which are a part of every well-planned school.

The budget of the vacation church school is a part of the educational budget of the church. Most churches now include it in their regular financial structure. Funds are needed for any remuneration paid to leaders, for curriculum materials and teaching supplies, fruit juice or other light refreshments for younger children, postage and promotional materials, and incidentals. Costs vary with the number of pupils and the program as well as with the amount paid to leaders. The co-operating churches each carry a proportionate share of costs for a community school.

The Role of the Minister or Director of Christian Education

The minister of a church carries the same responsibility for the vacation church school as for the rest of the program of Christian education, and relates to it in much the same way. Ministers with Christian education training often like to teach in their own local school or in a community one, when they can plan it so that this responsibility does not keep them from other church demands or from showing active interest in the rest of the school. The minister is usually responsible for the service of dedication of the leaders and for giving them spiritual guidance and assistance throughout the entire school.

The director of Christian education, where there is one, may decide to direct the school or to teach in it, especially if there seems to be a particular need for a good teacher in one of the classes. Many directors, however, feel that they can make a greater contribution if they can be free from any direct leadership responsibility to train others, to give support, encouragement and guidance, and to work to improve the general quality of the school and its leadership.

The vacation church school has established itself as a vital and worthwhile part of the program of the church. Denominations and councils will continue to seek for new ways to plan for the summer, with the vacation church school taking its place in a total program which will also include camping, family events, and other activities especially suited to the season.

Bibliography

Weekday Church School

Introducing the Weekday Church School. New York: National Council of the Churches of Christ in the U.S.A. A pamphlet giving guidance regarding the organization and administration of the weekday church school.

Shaver, Erwin L. *Remember the Weekday to Teach Religion Thereon.* New York: National Council of Churches of Christ in the U.S.A. A pamphlet of forty-five questions and answers.

Shaver, Erwin L. *The Weekday Church School.* Boston: The Pilgrim Press, 1956.

Weekday Church School Texts. Denominational publishers or National Council of Churches of Christ in the U.S.A. A descriptive catalogue of available co-operative texts.

Vacation Church School

Bogardus, LaDonna. *Let's Play.* New York: National Council of the Churches of Christ in the U. S. A. A guide on using the out-of-doors in Christian education.

Butt, Elsie Miller. *The Vacation Church School in Christian Education.* Nashville: Abingdon Press, 1957.

Rippy, Leo Jr. *Let's Go Exploring.* New York: National Council of Churches of Christ in the U.S.A. A guide on using the out-of-doors in Christian education.

The How of Vacation Church School. New York: National Council of Churches of Christ in the U.S.A. A practical guide for planning and administering the vacation church school.

Chapter 22

Protestant Full-Time Weekday Schools

Raymond S. Moore

IN THE SHIFT OF EMPHASIS DURING THE LAST HALF OF THE NINETEENTH CENTURY from church-controlled education to free public education in the United States, many church-education groups were forced to a re-evaluation of their programs and their goals. Tax-supported free public elementary and secondary education for the masses, they realized, was no doubt one of the answers to the demands of an accelerating democratic civilization.

What of the distinctive religious values that were the center of their lives? Doctrinal teachings of the churches were not likely subject matter for state-supported education in a democracy. Should parochial or weekday church schools bow out to free public schools? Would Sunday schools suffice to inculcate in their children the principles and doctrines of the church? If not, how should the churches proceed without appearing to be antidemocratic—against the public spirit? Was it worth this risk to maintain their schools in view of growing public sentiment for public education?

Historical Perspective [1]

In attempting to understand the issues and prospects of Protestant day-school education it is helpful to briefly review certain well-established facts:

1. An influential number of those immigrating to North America in the seventeenth and eighteenth centuries sought freedom of religion. Communities, therefore, were usually church centered.

2. During this period, virtually all formal education was assumed to be within the province of the church. The State recognized this prerogative and assisted the church financially. That this close tie between church and State was fraught with some danger to the freedoms of prospective democracy was apparently realized by the framers of the United States Constitution. Yet, state-subsidized church schools prevailed until well into the nineteenth century.

3. It was not until about 1825 that strong public interest was stirred for systematic free public education. Some had now become convinced that the miscellaneous religious and private school groups were not meeting the needs of state or nation. Thus was triggered one of the great controversies of United States history. Factions developed; churches were split; there was strong feeling within

[1] The information contained in this section is obtained from a number of historical sources, the more prominent of which are listed in the bibliography.

and between denominations. "Excepting the battle for the abolition of slavery, perhaps no question has ever been before the American people for settlement which caused so much feeling or aroused such bitter antagonism." [2]

4. Inasmuch as Roman Catholic parochial schools as such were almost unknown in the United States until the middle of the nineteenth century, the great conflict centered in Protestant circles.

5. Reactions varied, however, with greatest resistance to public education apparent in those areas where church-controlled education was most deeply entrenched. Diverse situations existed in the Northern, Middle, and Southern colonies. The Calvinists of New England had long controlled both state and religion there. The schools in this area were therefore primarily Calvinistic, usually one to a town.

In the Middle colonies where there was considerably more religious freedom than in New England, the variety of church schools reflected the denominational differences. Here a given town often had several parochial schools within its small limits.

In the South the Anglicans maintained a control of church and state similar to that of the Calvinists in New England. There were few weekday church schools as such, however. Private schooling and the use of tutors was the rule for the well-to-do. Formal education for the less privileged was generally limited to apprenticeships.

By 1850 public education had become established, displacing some of the church schools. This was particularly true in the towns where the formal educational program had been centered in one school. A number of the early denominations have since concentrated their support on the public schools. Probably foremost among these are the former Presbyterians, U.S.A., and the Methodists.

Others of the early churches, while agreeing in principle to the vital role of the free public school in a democracy, have chosen to retain and advance their own systems. These include the Mennonites and the Friends. The courts have upheld this right, recognizing education first as a parental right and responsibility. In this climate a number of Protestant systems have subsequently flowered, including the Missouri Synod Lutherans, Seventh-Day Adventists, Christian Reformed, Protestant Episcopal, Joint Synod of Wisconsin, the National Association of Christian Schools, and others.

Objectives, Issues, and Rationale

Sponsors of parochial schools believe that daily religious instruction should be given their youth, not just as an added class, but as the central theme and focus of instruction in all disciplines. This is a weakness of public-school instruction as far as they are concerned; yet they believe that the public schools must not attempt to provide this instruction, for that would lead to a union of church and State.

The attitudes and objectives of Protestant elementary and secondary education are, however, almost as varied as the denominations, and sometimes even the individual churches themselves. These abruptly merge into two camps, however, when the question is asked, What is the effect of the church-related school upon the public school?

[2] Elwood P. Cubberley, *Public Education in the United States* (Boston: Houghton Mifflin Company, 1934), p. 119.

The first camp includes a number of large and influential religious bodies who warn that the growth of parochial education brings with it a "very real danger that . . . the public school system may be reduced to a second-rate institution." [3] They also fear a weakening of the body politic, diminishing of community freedom, social cleavage, inferior education, and inroads into the functions of the Sunday church schools and of youth organizations. Some of them hold that church money is better used for church extension. Desirable religious principles and requisite character qualities may be developed, they say, through released-time instruction, Sunday schools, and youth organizations.

Principal spokesmen for this group appear to be Methodists and the United Presbyterian Church, U.S.A. Taking similar positions in creed or in practice are the Congregational and Christian churches, some Baptist communions, the Anglicans, Nazarenes, Universalists, Unitarians, Latter-Day Saints, and others.

The most frankly and frequently expressed fear concerns the historical Protestant-American position of separation of church and State. More specifically it involves use of tax monies for the support of parochial education.[4] This has been due to the effort of some church groups to urge the expenditure of tax monies for their educational programs. This, they affirm, would most certainly mean the weakening, if not eventually the total ruin, of the American system of free public education.

The second camp is in generally strong agreement with the doctrine that holds for the maintenance of a strong system of free public schools. It subscribes almost without exception to the principle of church-State separation. In fact some of its members are the most militant in supporting this program. There the difference ends. This camp includes among its chief members the Missouri Synod Lutherans, Seventh-Day Adventists, Protestant Episcopal, Joint Synod of Wisconsin, Christian Reformed, and Mennonite movements. Prominent in the drive for Protestant parochial education is also the National Association of Christian Schools. Nearly all of these have one hundred or more schools providing elementary or secondary instruction during the same weekday periods as the public school.

Authorities of these groups point out that they are not in competition with the public schools, but that their schools are established to provide a Christian education which cannot and should not be provided by tax-supported schools. Most of the churches in this camp consider their schools as evangelistic agencies for their own children. They make no secret of their desire to indoctrinate their students with the beliefs of the church. They feel, in view of the preoccupation of the modern family with many interests often to the exclusion of family worship, the day school must absorb more of the responsibility for Christian character education. They maintain with the Roman Catholics that the first road to church extension is through education of their children—to hold those which they have. Therefore, Christian day-school education is essential. The public schools, they aver, cannot fulfill the educational prescriptions implicit in the scriptures.[5]

Lutherans in the United States early in their history desired to establish "a

[3] *The Church and the Public Schools*, pp. 18, 19.
[4] *Ibid.*, p. 19.
[5] See Isa. 54:13 and Deut. 6:6-9.

distinctively Lutheran Church separated from all who were of a different spirit." [6] But they give not only religious reasons but also those of language for the establishment of their early schools in the United States.[7] Most early Lutheran schools were conducted in German. The Lutherans teach "Word and Doctrine" to lay a sound foundation "for practical Christian living—helping the child to relate his life to God." [8]

"The harmonious development of the physical, the mental, and the spiritual powers" is the historical aim of Seventh-Day Adventist education. This group holds that the true objective of life should be "To restore in man the image of His maker" in keeping with an ultimate goal of heavenly citizenship.[9]

"Similarly the Mennonites desire to shield [their] sons and daughters from harmful moral and spiritual influences" in the "greatly secularized" public schools.[10] By "secularism" the Mennonites specifically mean atheism.[11] This appears to be a general concern among the groups of this second camp. The National Association of Christian Schools describes the condition of "some public schools" as "materialistic and anti-God." [12]

Other principal reasons listed by the N.A.C.S. include:

1. Overcrowded conditions in public schools.
2. The need for Christian training for students from Christian homes.
3. To counteract immoral influences in high delinquency areas.
4. To provide adequate training for underprivileged youth, particularly in mountain areas and among diverse nationalities.[18]

Both privately and sometimes in print they point to the Roman Catholic school system (approximately 12,000 schools with more than 4,000,000 enrolled) as a prime agency in maintaining church loyalty.[14] Our first camp answers this argument with its fear that such a powerful, growing church system may overwhelm and to a greater or lesser degree control the State, as it has in a number of countries. The second camp in rebuttal says in effect, Let us keep church and State separate. Restrict tax monies to public education. We will finance our own schools and develop stronger Protestant churches. We are not against public education. In fact, we willingly and diligently support it. However, "the Christian school is the link which unites the home with the Church. If we take this link out, we destroy both the home and the church, but if we maintain this link, we save both." [15]

---

[6] *My Church: A History of the Missouri Synod for Young People*, pp. 38 ff., cited by Albert G. Merkins, "Origin and Development of Lutheran Schools of the Missouri Synod in Northern Illinois," p. 8.

[7] *The Church and the Public School, op. cit.*, p. 8.

[8] Letter from W. A. Kramer to Raymond S. Moore, February 3, 1959 (St. Louis: The Lutheran Church-Missouri Synod), p. 2.

[9] White, *Education*, p. 13.

[10] Fretz, "Report on Day School Education in the Mennonite Church," p. 1.

[11] Graybill (ed.), *Christian Day Schools for Mennonite Youth*, p. 20.

[12] Banta, "The Status and Quality of Education in the National Association of Christian Schools," pp. 55, 56.

[13] *Ibid.*

[14] Graybill, *op. cit.*, p. 32.

[15] *Ibid.*

The Present Situation

In certain respects the differences between the Protestant camps may currently be said to concern method more than principle. Both sides in the main are concerned with the preservation of the historic American posture of separation of church and State. As already shown, however, the historic Protestant position has not always been one of church-State separation. Some do not believe others to have as clear an understanding as they, of the transcendent principles of freedom.

Presently the leading exponents of the Protestant full-time weekday schools unanimously hold that: (1) They are in no way interfering with the optimum development of the free public school system; (2) Their consistent refusal to accept government subsidies should be more carefully acknowledged and credited by their opponents; and (3) Their programs should neither be confused with nor impugned because of the prominent efforts of the Roman Catholic hierarchy to secure state and/or federal funds.

They readily answer the expressed fears of some large Protestant groups that parochial schools constitute a threat to community freedom and political welfare.[16] Their consensus might be stated this way: On the basis of Holy Scripture we recognize our high responsibilities as citizens of our country. We are also aware that our ultimate goal is citizenship in heaven.[17] In the process of preparing our children for that greater citizenship we are determined to insure to the best of our ability that they are the best citizens here.

The public-parochial school issue however is incidental to a number of denominational goals. There are many who believe that the spiritual strength of the church lies largely in the broad early religious education of its youth. They believe that this preparation is not adequately supplied by Sunday schools, "released time" education, or Bible reading in public schools.[18]

One researcher pictures the current Protestant denominations in five groups.[19] First are those who have operated broad church-school programs over many years. These include the Missouri Synod, Joint Synod of Wisconsin, and Norwegian Synod Lutheran Church, the Seventh-Day Adventists, Christian Reformed, Mennonite (including Amish), and Friends.

Second are the churches "that for many years had no elementary schools, but that in the last decade have shown an interest in the establishment of church kindergartens and nursery schools. Among these are the Southern Baptist Convention, The Methodist Church, the Presbyterian Church, U.S., and the Presbyterian Church, U.S.A." [20] It should be noted, however, that the Southern Baptists and the Presbyterians, U.S., are currently operating a number of parochial schools, although in general they have not developed as diocesan or denomination-wide systems.

Third, "are the long-established denominations that have had relatively few parochial schools for many years but have in recent years encouraged their establish-

---

[16] *The Church and the Public Schools, op. cit.,* p. 19.

[17] See Rom. 8:16-17, Heb. 11:13, and Phil. 3:20. (Cf. original Greek.)

[18] Nelson, "Diagnostic Survey of Certain Attitudes and Values Related to the Development of Day Schools in the Presbyterian Church, U.S.," pp. 4, 21, 22, 243.

[19] Blair, "Church-Related Elementary and Secondary Schools in Continental United States," p. 1.

[20] *Ibid.,* p. 5.

ment—the American Lutheran, Evangelical Lutheran, and Protestant Episcopal Churches." [21]

Fourth, are the associations of schools recently organized by "evangelicals." These include The National Association of Christian Schools, the Los Angeles Baptist Mission Society, and the New England Association of Christian Schools.

Fifth, are the denominations with but few schools for many years, none of whom show present interest in developing their school systems to any great extent. These include the American Baptist Convention, Evangelical Mission Covenant, Latter-Day Saints, Moravians, Reformed Church in America, Wesleyan Methodist, Unitarian, and four Lutheran bodies—the Slovak Evangelical, Augustana, National Evangelical, and the United Lutherans.[22]

The number of elementary and secondary schools of these Protestant churches, with enrollments, is presented in the following Table. It should be noted that these figures do not include overseas enrollments, which with some denominations are noteworthy. "Everywhere that the Mennonites have gone from their original countries . . . They have very early after their settlement established their own schools." [23] The same can generally be said for the Missouri Synod Lutherans, Seventh-Day Adventists and others maintaining strong overseas mission programs. The Adventist figures for the United States, in fact, approximate less than one fourth of that church's world enrollments.

Also omitted here are the practices of these churches in preschool education. The Southern Baptist, Presbyterian, U.S., United Presbyterian, U.S.A., Methodist, and Protestant Episcopal denominations in that order are leaders in kindergarten and nursery-school programs.[24]

Control and Organization

Throughout this chapter the terms *parochial school, church school, Protestant weekday school,* have generally been used synonymously. Some however, divide these institutions into two broad categories, *private schools* and *church schools.* Some private schools are classified as *parent-society schools.* Church schools in turn may be classified as either *parochial* or *diocesan.*

The private school is usually maintained by an individual or group independent of any church, parish, or diocesan control. Friends' schools generally fall in this category, as do many of the Episcopalian institutions. The parent-society school is usually controlled by a group of parents of a given church or group of churches, not necessarily of the same denomination. Although there is some church relationship, there is little or no church control. A number of Methodist, Mennonite, and N.A.C.S. schools and a few Seventh-Day Adventist schools fall in this category. The difference between private and parent-society schools is sometimes obscure, depending chiefly on the degree of church influence in the school.

Of the two church-school categories, the parochial school is usually sponsored by a local church group or parish. The diocesan or conference school on the other hand is controlled by the diocese, conference, or larger organization. Both church-

[21] *Ibid.*
[22] *Ibid.*
[23] Fretz, *loc. cit.*
[24] Blair, *op. cit.*, pp. 3, 4.

NUMBER AND ENROLLMENT OF CHURCH-RELATED *
ELEMENTARY AND SECONDARY SCHOOLS IN THE UNITED STATES [25]

10 Principal Protestant School Systems (listed by enrollment)	Elementary [1]		Secondary [2]	
	Schools	Enrollment	Schools	Enrollment
Missouri Synod Lutheran	1,175	130,124	13	7,022
Seventh-Day Adventists	825	42,069	290	13,380
Christian Reformed [3]	160	31,874	26	6,664
Protestant Episcopal [4]	128	12,028	104	17,900
Joint Synod of Wisconsin	208	21,901	n.r.	
Nat'l Assoc. Christian Schools [5]	77	8,960	49	7,492
Friends	15	4,978	22	4,940
Mennonite (including Amish)	54	[6]	38	5,870
Southern Baptist Convention	78	2,000	12	3,606
The Methodist Church	2	244	17	5,063

Other Protestant Denominations with Schools (listed alphabetically)				
American Baptist Convention			5	968
American Lutheran Church	38	2,765		
Augustana Lutheran Church	2	259		
Council of Liberal Churches			2	126 [7]
Evangelical Lutheran Church	9	1,151 [8]	3	692 [9]
Evangelical Mission Convent			2	944
Latter Day Saints (Mormons)			1	324
Los Angeles Baptist City Mission	19	2,949		
Moravian Church			2	574
Nat'l Evangelical Lutheran	1	38		
New England Assoc. Christian Schools	3	218	2	173
Norwegian Synod Lutheran	14	379		
Presbyterian, U.S. [10]	21	1,130	2	970
Reformed Church in America			1	62
Slovak Evangelical Lutheran	2	147		
United Lutheran Church	18	625		
Wesleyan Methodist Church	n.r.		1	72

* Figures generally are for those of the school year of 1957-58. Kindergarten and nursery school enrollments not included. It should be observed that this listing is according to number of schools and enrollments. The fact that a church is listed with a substantial number of schools and enrollments does not necessarily indicate that it supports the philosophy of the parochial or diocesan education. Some of these schools are church-related, but tend primarily to be private schools available for those who do not want to send their children to public schools.

[1] Includes schools with kindergartens but no schools with grades above grade 8.

[2] Includes all schools with one or more grades 9-12, including schools with elementary grades also. Does not include junior colleges or other institutions of college level that offer precollege level courses.

[3] The schools sponsored by this denomination comprise the National Union of Christian Schools.

[4] Enrollment figures for this denomination were for 85 nursery-kindergartens, 112 elementary schools, and 84 secondary schools.

[25] Blair, op. cit., pp. 3, 4; adapted.

[5] A few schools and their enrollment are not included in the figures shown in order to eliminate duplication of schools reported by another denomination.

[6] Included with figures for secondary schools.

[7] One school only reporting enrollment.

[8] Eight schools only reporting enrollment.

[9] Two schools only reporting enrollment.

[10] Not to be confused with communions of the United Presbyterian Church in the U.S.A. which does not sponsor elementary and secondary schools as such.

school categories are explicitly church affiliated. The guidance and control of the parochial schools stem essentially from the local congregation. The diocesan or conference school on the other hand is, by nature, under the broad direction of diocese, conference, or other higher denominational echelon. It should be observed, however, that regardless of this broader control, these diocesan schools are often locally initiated and more often than not are essentially under local operational control.

By far the largest and by nature the best-integrated groups are the diocesan or conference schools. Usually they are guided in varying degrees by broad policy emanating from a general education board of the parent denomination. Prominent in this category are the Missouri Synod Lutherans, Seventh-Day Adventists, the Los Angeles Baptist City Mission Schools, and about a third of the schools of the N.A.C.S.[26]

In the church-school groups elementary and secondary education are frequently administered by separate groups. The Missouri Synod community high schools "are in most cases maintained by groups of congregations in the area" while their "elementary schools are in most cases maintained by individual congregations." The trend toward central schools is gaining favor in the Missouri Synod. Nearly forty such central schools, though usually elementary, are maintained by groups of congregations after the manner of the high schools. [27]

The Missouri Synod educational program is headed at the policy level by a denomination-wide Board for Parish Education. Actual supervision of elementary and secondary schools is accomplished by District Boards of Education, which have in most cases full-time superintendents of education.[28]

The Seventh-Day Adventist school organization is similar to that of the Missouri Synod. Local churches are assisted by the local conference in the establishment of their elementary or intermediate schools. These congregations are responsible to the local conference for salaries of their teachers. Thus the teacher has the security of being a conference employee in event of breakdown in local church finance. Local church-school boards nevertheless guide the affairs of the school, with assistance from the local conference educational superintendent or supervisor. Adventist secondary schools or "academies" not only have local conference subsidy and supervision, but also are financially aided and professionally assisted by the union conference—the organizational center of a group of local conferences.

[26] Ibid., p. 3.

[27] Kramer, op. cit., p. 2.

[28] Ibid.

Generally the parochial schools are smaller than public schools and include many one-room elementary schools. This is considered by many to be closer to the original family school planned by God and therefore desirable from a character-education standpoint.

Many of the Friends' secondary schools include the elementary grades, as do most of the Seventh-Day Adventists'. The Missouri Synod usually begins its high schools with the ninth grade and builds up to the twelfth. This seems to be a typical pattern. Some denominations operate elementary grades from one to six, and secondary as seven to twelve; others, one to eight or nine, and nine or ten to twelve. Because of the nature of their organization the schools of the National Association of Christian Schools also present a similarly varied organizational expression. The parochial pattern further varies depending somewhat on state and local situations.

Financial Structure

Methods of financing vary widely. Most private schools depend for their operation upon direct tuition and endowments. Strong alumni ties are encouraged in these schools and many times become their life blood. The day-to-day operations of parent-society schools are similarly financed, except that their closer church ties tend to give them a more stable financial base.

The parochial schools might be said to be financed wholly or in part in at least five major ways or combination of these ways: (1) *Straight tuition,* paid directly to the school. Tuition charges vary widely. (2) *Indirect tuition,* paid to the church as a pledge or offering; the church in turn is responsible for the school. (3) *Offerings or tithes* of the local congregation with no amount, or tuition as such, specified. (4) *Operational subsidy* and/or *capital donation* from higher church organization such as diocese or conference. (5) Payment of *tuition* and *offerings through local church to diocese or conference,* which in turn pays the teachers. In this case, however, certain funds are generally retained by the local church organization to meet nonsalary expenses.

Teachers in the parochial schools traditionally work for subsistence wages. Their motive is often defined as evangelical or missionary. Their salaries vary as widely as the tuition charges, but are usually below public-school levels in a given community. In the more highly organized denominational systems, however, definite salary bases are established.

Capital expenditures for lands, buildings, and equipment are usually derived from the same general sources and in a similar manner as the operational funds. The principal difference between operating and building church-related schools lies in the likelihood of higher echelons of the church or of interested groups to contribute more heavily for the more urgent or exciting initial building program than for the less-colorful day-to-day operation.

Some churches, including nearly all of the leaders in the table, page 242, seem to regard both building and operation of these schools as evangelistic or mission projects. Financing therefore would have a church-extension motive. Other communions operate their schools more because of "lack of confidence in some aspects of the public school, because of desire for exclusiveness of schooling or for reasons of race." [29] These latter motives do not dominate the financing and operation of church-related schools.

[29] Nelson, *op. cit.,* pp. 237-47.

Among Protestant educational programs there is virtually complete unanimity in the refusal to accept government monies. Occasionally there is a difference in application of this aspect of church-state separation. Some parochial schools will not accept government surplus foods for their students nor encourage government scholarship programs. Others insist that there is nothing harmful in this practice, for they are simply acting as social-service agencies without pay. Some accept government surplus materials, equipment, and even lands for negligible cost, pointing out that it is a business transaction involving properties of no further use to the government or its free public schools and therefore is not inviting government control. However, a generally cautious demeanor obtains mutually between the denominations and the governments, both state and federal.

Distinctive Characteristics

There are a number of distinctive ways in which the Protestant full-time weekday schools are presently serving their churches and their country:

1. They are less inhibited by state and local relations, and therefore have certain advantages in experimenting with new educational concepts. They are less bound by selection of textbooks; they have greater flexibility in development of schedules; they have considerably more liberty in the formation of their curriculums, including the teaching of religion. In other important aspects they have freedom which does not obtain in the public schools. Although they are usually supervised broadly by government agencies, these nonpublic schools are not subject to the close scrutiny which the taxpayer demands, and for this reason many educators have used them as laboratories in developing educational concepts which have later been adopted by public education.

2. A substantial number of these systems operate boarding schools. These are particularly appreciated by isolated families, or families broken by death or divorce, for they can provide a more nearly complete education than a nonboarding facility.

3. These nonpublic schools also have a freedom of organization which, for example, permits a given school to operate in one plant all grades from kindergarten through high school, and thus more readily adjust to the personality of the church and the community.

4. The Methodists, and some others, operate a number of separate schools for boys and schools for girls, feeling that this plan affords an opportunity for education in a formative period, without the distractions of the opposite sex. With rare exception, coeducation is the rule in public education.

5. A number of boarding schools provide systematic daily physical work experience to balance the mental application. Inculcation of such character qualities as industry, order, integrity, and dependability are important motives in such programs. The Seventh-Day Adventists hold this method as fundamental in their educational philosophy.

6. Most distinctive in the operation of Protestant full-time weekday schools is their freedom to develop religious attitudes of their choosing and throughout the entire curriculum to indoctrinate their students in the tenets of the parent faith.

Bibliography

Banta, Forrest Dean. "The Status and Quality of Education in the National Association of Christian Schools." Unpublished Doctoral Thesis, the University of Buffalo, 1953.

Blair, Bertha. "Church-Related Elementary and Secondary Schools in Continental United States," *Information Service*, XXXVIII (January 3, 1959).

Brinton, Howard H. *Quaker Education in Theory and Practice.* Pendle Hill Pamphlet, No. 9. Pendle Hill, Wallingford, Pa., 1940.

Christian School Directory for the School Year 1957-58. Chicago: National Association of Christian Schools.

Corwin, Edward T. *A Digest of Constitutional and Synodical Legislation of the Reformed Church in America.* A Report Prepared by the General Synod, 1906.

Counselor's Guide to Methodist Schools, Colleges and Universities. A Report Prepared by the Board of Education of The Methodist Church. Nashville: Board of Education, 1958.

Fretz, Clarence Y. "Report on Day School Education in the Mennonite Church." Harrisonburg, Va.: Eastern Mennonite College, December 9, 1958.

Graybill, Paul J. (ed.). *Christian Day Schools for Mennonite Youth.* Lancaster, Pa.: Lancaster Conference Schools, Inc., 1945.

Lutheran Schools. A Report Prepared by the Board for Parish Education of the Lutheran Church—Missouri Synod. St. Louis: Concordia Publishing House.

Merkins, Albert G. "Origin and Development of Lutheran Schools of the Missouri Synod in Northern Illinois." Unpublished Master's Thesis, the University of Pittsburgh, 1934.

Nelson, Carl Ellis. "Diagnostic Survey of Certain Attitudes and Values Related to the Development of Day Schools in the Presbyterian Church, U.S." Unpublished Doctoral Thesis, Teacher's College, Columbia University, 1955.

Stellhorn, A. C. "Lutheran Central Schools." *A Manual of Information and Guidance for the Establishment and Administration of Central Schools.* St. Louis: The Board for Parish Education of the Lutheran Church—Missouri Synod, 1957.

The Church and the Public Schools. A Report Prepared by the Board of Christian Education, Presbyterian Church of U.S.A. New York: Presbyterian Distribution Service, 1957.

White, Ellen G. *Education.* Mountain View, Calif.: Pacific Press Publishing Association, 1903.

Part III

Administration of Religious Education

Chapter 23

The Local Church Organized for Christian Education

Paul H. Vieth

THE CHURCH, WHETHER SMALL OR LARGE, IS A COMPLEX BODY. IT HAS ONE
purpose but many activities. Its purpose is to be a divine-human community in and
through which the grace of the Lord Jesus Christ, the love of God, and the
fellowship of the Holy Spirit may work in persons for their salvation and spiritual
growth, and which may be a witness to the world to call it to repentance and faith.
Its activities—such as worship, preaching and teaching, fellowship, and missions—
are the means through which this purpose may be achieved. The total of such
activities, properly conceived, interrelated, and conducted, constitute the church's
program.

Christian education is a spirit and method which permeates the whole program
and at the same time is a specific function of the church among other functions.
Spiritual growth, which is the aim of Christian education, results from both
nurture within group relationships so that God's own spirit may be communicated
and teaching so that they may be confronted by God's word and acts, in history
and now, and understand the meaning of Christian faith and life as experienced and
believed by God's people.

The purpose of organization for Christian education is to provide a planned
structure for program. It is a means whereby program may be ordered, and all
the people of the church may be drawn into activities for their nurture, discipline,
and participation in mission. Administration is the process whereby the functioning
of organization is facilitated, to the end that a fruitful and effective program
may emerge.

Organization exists for the sake of program, but it also is program. Participation
in organization and administration results in educational experience for the
participants. The ways in which persons are organized and administered are factors
in their experience of the Christian fellowship.

247

Principles of Organization

Organization for Christian education will be guided and judged by certain basic considerations. These grow out of the nature of the church and the way in which persons respond to the gospel and develop in spiritual maturity.

1. UNITY IN PURPOSE AND FELLOWSHIP. The church as a whole is the community in which God acts. It is an organic unity, variously referred to as the Body of Christ, the community of the Holy Spirit, the redemptive fellowship. It is the church which is the Christian educator. Organization for Christian education must provide the means whereby the purpose and nature of the church itself can inform and guide all that is done and guard against independence and separateness resulting from necessary diversity in structure and program. It must provide for enough togetherness of constituency so that the sense of belonging to and acceptance by the Body will be experienced by all. It must assure that the resources of the church in personnel, equipment, and budget are administered in equity and in consideration of the needs of the whole program and each individual in the constituency— whether child, youth, or adult.

These ends of organization are achieved only when each person stands in saving relationship to the whole redemptive fellowship, all groups within the fellowship are representative of the whole in purpose and program, and the insights of Christian education are available to and utilized by all aspects of the church's program.

2. DIVERSITY WITHIN UNITY. The church includes persons of all ages and of many interests and needs. This involves the obligation to serve each in accordance with his needs. Within the comprehensive Christian fellowship, organization for Christian education needs to provide for grading which makes possible adapting program to maturity levels, varieties of activities which appeal to a broad range of interests, and groups which are of proper size to permit intimate face-to-face relationships.

A graded program is made possible through organization of the constituency by age-group divisions, departments, and classes. Varying interests are appealed to by the special program emphases of the several agencies which together make up the church school. These agencies, such as Sunday church school, youth fellowship, vacation church school, clubs, and adult groups, came into being independently in response to needs. The process of bringing them into a single, unified, comprehensive church school is a persistent problem of organization.

Diversity of organization is necessary and need not serve to atomize program, so long as each group and agency recognizes its place within the church's whole purpose and mission and sustains its dependence on and loyalty to the whole. Good organization will provide the means for desirable diversity which does not destroy essential unity.

3. COMPREHENSIVENESS—CONGREGATION-WIDE AND PERSON-WISE. Organization is properly comprehensive when it embraces the whole church constituency in its provision for Christian education, and when it makes possible the utilization of all church activities for their maximum contribution to spiritual growth.

Christian education is not confined to particular agencies whose primary responsibility is the teaching ministry, but permeates every aspect of the church's work. Worship, evangelism, missions, stewardship, and other functions not usually classified as educational nevertheless participate in education in two important ways: (1) They depend for their effectiveness on being supported by understanding and commitment which comes from teaching; (2) Their effect on participating persons is a contribution to the same ends of spiritual growth for which Christian education is conducted. For example, the call to conversion, to "accept Jesus as Savior and Lord," can have little meaning to one who has not learned who this Jesus is whom he is to accept. Conversely, the climactic experience of conversion results in a reorientation of the whole life, which is one of the highest aims of Christian education.

With respect to each person, organization is properly comprehensive when at the program planning level he may be seen as a whole person, and provision made for his total Christian education. Individual persons will usually be related to more than one agency. For example, a junior-high-school boy may be in the Sunday church school, the vacation church school, Boy Scouts, junior-high fellowship, church membership class, and attend the church service of worship. Good organization should make possible planning for the total interests and needs of this boy and should help each agency contribute its share without conflict or overlapping with others.

4. WHOLE CHURCH RESPONSIBILITY. Since Christian education is a vital part of the whole mission of the church, responsibility for it rests on the whole congregation. When a person is received in baptism and the affirmation made "to bring up your child in the nurture and admonition of the Lord," it is not just the parents, but all the people of the fellowship, who assume this obligation. While necessity requires that some be selected to represent the church as officers, committee members, and teachers, ways must be found whereby the whole church can share in this responsibility, not only financially, but by acceptance and support in every possible way.

5. FUNCTIONAL AND FLEXIBLE. Since organization exists to achieve a purpose, it follows that its quality is to be judged by the extent to which it achieves this end. What happens to people is important, not perfection or complexity of structure. A functional approach will seek a minimum of structure to achieve its purpose. Any organization which exists for its own sake and does not contribute to better program is superfluous.

6. REPRESENTATIVE AND SHARED LEADERSHIP. Some persons must be chosen to serve the church as administrators, teachers, and other leaders. Since these persons have the most intimate contacts with the learning constituency, it is essential that in character, maturity, and spiritual insight they truly represent the whole congregation at its best as a redemptive community. It is their opportunity to witness to their faith and to answer their call to the priesthood of believers. Service in the church's program of Christian education should not be a burden for a few, but a privilege of many. Hence leadership responsibility should be widely distributed, with some plan for rotation in office.

Persons called to positions of leadership should regard themselves as servants, not as masters. They will seek to lead others as co-workers, not to direct them as subordinates. They will seek to draw as many as possible into participation in program planning and strive together to find the will of God for the church. It is one of the problems of organization to make this kind of shared leadership possible.

Participation in the leadership of Christian education may itself be one of the most fruitful means of spiritual growth for those participating. Every office, board, and committee offers an opportunity to come to a better understanding of God's will and the nature and work of the church, and for better understanding of and interaction with others. "The face-to-face relationships of people working together on a problem in purposeful, God-related groups provide experiences which contribute to personal maturity, the development of participant skills, and the attainment of spiritual poise." [1] Those responsible for organization and administration will seek to achieve these spiritual values as well as the accomplishment of specific tasks.

7. CHANNELING THE MINISTER'S LEADERSHIP. The minister of the church is not only its spiritual leader but also its chief Christian educator. While it is traditional in practice and sound in policy that most of the work in Christian education be done by members of the congregation, lay workers need the minister's leadership and guidance. In most churches he is the only person who is professionally trained for the Christian ministry. A plan of organization must provide the channel through which he may contribute his leadership, without assuming duties which laymen can perform, and without seeming to interfere with the work of others.

In the vast majority of churches, the minister must of necessity include the ministry of Christian education among his responsibilities. Larger churches can have a group ministry that will usually include a minister or director of Christian education. This does not mean that the senior minister can eliminate Christian education from his responsibility. It does mean, however, that someone with more specialized educational training will be recognized as the Christian educator on the staff. Again, this requires organizational strategy which will relate the minister of Christian education to the whole program in such ways as to free him to perform his function most effectively, enhancing rather than diminishing the place of lay workers. Such problems as his relationship with the minister, his relation to the committee on Christian education, his relation to the general superintendent, his supervisory relation to all the other workers, will need to be solved. [2]

How may these principles of organization be expressed in a church structure for Christian education? This will be the concern of the rest of this chapter. Fortunately it is not necessary to approach this problem without precedent. Denominations and many local churches have dealt with it. The plans which have been evolved are largely in agreement on principles and general patterns. At some points alternative patterns of organization are acceptable. At other points program policy is undergoing changes which need to be reflected in organization. These will be pointed out in their proper places. Our concern is not so much with a standard pattern or organization as with principles of good organization and illustrative ways in which these may be expressed in practice.

Within the Church

The concern in this section is with organization of the church which will properly provide for Christian education in a comprehensive and unified program. While the whole congregation is responsible for the whole program, the actual work

[1] Paul F. Douglass, *The Group Workshop Way in the Church* (New York: Association Press, 1956), p. 3.

[2] See ch. 24, pp. 259-69, for discussion of the role of the minister-director of Christian education.

of program planning and review will be delegated to a smaller, representative body.

Plans for the organization of the local church in most denominations provide for a central body to initiate, direct, and review the whole program. Various names, such as official board, church council, consistory, session, are given to this body. We shall call it simply the general board. This general board needs to be both prophetic and practical—prophetic in ever seeing and proclaiming more clearly the will of God for the church; practical in devising ways and means for so ordering the life and work of the congregation that all may participate in this vision and work toward its realization. While its functions will vary in different churches, it provides the organization which is necessary and adequate for comprehensive program planning. The difficulty is not usually with lack of organization at this level, but with getting existing boards to work seriously and comprehensively at the task.

The general board cannot do the whole work of program planning and administration. It will need to assign specific functions to committees under its direction. Thus there may be committees responsible for evangelism, worship, membership, finance and stewardship, missions, community relations, Christian education, and so forth. Some denominations designate the number and define the functions of such committees. In others this matter is left to the local church.

The total program cannot be divided into such neat packages that each committee can operate in its own field without to some extent overlapping the functions of others. For example, the committee on Christian education may derive important support and program content from committees on worship, missions, and social action. In turn, Christian education contributes to the work of such other committees. This illustrates the need for co-ordination at the whole-church level, so that the program impact for any person may be unified and effective. This is precisely the reason for the general board's assuming the over-all function of initiation, authorization, integration, and review. It must take its task of program planning seriously, and constantly hold before all committees the major purposes and thrusts of the church's work.

Committee on Christian Education [3]

The committee on Christian education has responsibility for the whole educational program of the church, subject to authorization, review, and co-ordination by the general board. Various names have been given to this committee—committee or board of Christian education, commission on education, board of parish education. The name is not important, but it is very important that its functions be clearly defined and understood. In broad terms, it is the function of this committee to put an educational emphasis into the spirit and life of the whole church, and to plan and maintain an educational program within the church, generally called the church school.

Within the broad scope of its work, this committee will undertake many specific tasks which are suggested by, but not limited to, the following: (1) educating the whole congregation in awareness of the importance of Christian education, (2) developing educational policies and building a program which is consistent therewith, (3) evaluating and selecting curriculum materials,

[3] The organizational plans which follow have been more fully developed by the author in his book *The Church School.*

(4) mobilizing the resources of the church for its educational work, (5) providing for and recruiting workers, (6) studying the needs of the constituency to be educated and co-ordinating the contributions of the church in meeting the needs of each person and group, (7) maintaining relationship with homes, (8) maintaining effective relationships with educational agencies in the denomination and community, (9) hearing and considering reports from officers and making reports to the general church board and the congregation, (10) making and recommending a budget for Christian education.

The members of this committee should be interested, competent, and representative. Election of members will be by the congregation or the general board, as may be specified by the church's polity or bylaws. The number of members will vary with the size of the church and the varied educational interests which should be represented. A minimum of five and a maximum of fifteen to twenty is suggested. The term of office may be two or three years, with expiration of terms so arranged that not more than one third or one half the members will be new in any year.

In selecting members, care will be taken to assure a committee which can competently deal with the church's whole educational program. Membership should include some from the church at large, selected for their competence in this field, some who are active in the church school, some who are parents, and some who are closely related to other agencies with which interrelations should be maintained. If this suggests an overly large committee, it should be remembered that frequently there are persons who fall into more than one of these categories. The pastor, director of Christian education and the church-school superintendent will usually be ex officio members.

The chairman of this committee is usually designated by the appointing body. He should be a person who can give spirit and direction to meetings, and utilize procedures which will bring all members into full participation. He will represent this committee in the general church board. It is usually best to have a layman or woman in this position rather than the minister, director of Christian education, or church-school superintendent, so as to leave the latter free for active participation in the meetings. A committee with such broad responsibility will need to meet at least every month.

Many churches experience difficulty in keeping this committee broadly concerned with Christian education in all its aspects, and not just the Sunday church school. This difficulty is largely avoided when provision is made within the committee for three divisional subcommittees, to deal with the total program of Christian education for children, youth, and adults.

Do small churches need a committee structure such as has been recommended? The answer must be that the tasks which this committee assumes exist in small churches as well as large. A concession is sometimes made in favor of simplicity by combining the functions of the committee on Christian education and the workers' conference. When this is done, it should be borne in mind that the two have different functions, and meetings so planned that proper attention will be given to both.

The minister, director of Christian education and the church-school superintendent sustain relationships of peculiar significance to this committee. In addition to being regular participants, they should give two important services. (1) Because of their close relationship to the operating program, they are in a position to co-operate with the chairman in determining what are the most crucial items of concern for the agenda; and (2) they, especially the director and superintendent, will assume executive responsibility for implementing the actions of the committee.

Organizing the Constituency

This section will be concerned with grouping the people of the church for nurture and teaching. The plans presented will illustrate ways in which principles of grading have been worked out in practice. No standard pattern is recommended as equally well-suited to all churches. Local church committees must do creative work in evolving an organization which best fits their situation, but whatever is done should be done with an understanding of the principles involved.

The name "'church school" is generally used for the total program of Christian education. Within the church school there is a complex of agencies, each with its own structure and leadership and each seeking to contribute to the spiritual growth of its members. These agencies include the Sunday church school, the vacation church school, youth fellowships, adult groups, clubs, camps, and conferences. Many persons are related to two or more of the agencies. Having these several agencies may be good from the standpoint of a multiple approach to the interests of people, involving them in church activity for more hours than any one agency can command. It is often disastrous, however, from the standpoint of serving the whole person with a unified, all-church program which ministers most effectively to his spiritual growth.

A radical solution to this problem of fragmentation would be to wipe the slate clean and start over with a single agency which would provide a whole-church educational program. If this could be done in a way which would conserve all the time, interest, leadership, and contributions to spiritual growth now available through the several agencies, it would greatly facilitate planning a program which meets the needs of persons and has comprehensiveness, balance, and desirable sequence. It would also simplify the problem of planning for home participation in Christian education.

It is doubtful whether such a radical procedure would be practical in many churches. It is to be questioned, also, whether any single agency could conserve all the values of pupil interest and program impact now contributed by different agencies, each created in response to specific needs. It is not so much the existence of the several agencies which constitutes the problem, but their tendency to function independently, with resulting overlapping, omission of important elements, lack of balance and continuity of activities, and fragmentation of what should be a unified program.

The organizational approach to this problem, then, becomes one of providing a structure through which unity of purpose and program on a church-wide basis can be achieved, while at the same time conserving the particular contributions which any agency can make. Can they be co-ordinated in a unified whole, the church school, which at the planning level achieves unity of purpose and integration of program, with each agency made responsible for its own best contribution to the whole?

This is in effect what is happening in many churches. The first step toward this is taken when the committee on Christian education becomes in fact the planning center for the whole program. By definition of function, this committee is authorized to consider the total needs of each person and to plan a whole educational program. It is responsible for co-ordinating and guiding the work of all the educational agencies toward common objectives. Hence this committee must see its work from two perspectives: (1) age-wise, so that for any division, department, or individual total needs for Christian education may be considered and a balanced and co-ordinated program planned to meet those needs; (2) agency-wise, so that each agency may function most effectively in performing its own particular tasks within the whole. A way of accomplishing this is to constitute three subcommittees, responsible respectively for work with children, youth, and adults, and to appoint a superintendent for each of these divisions.

A second step which needs to be taken is to bring into relationship all the workers in each division in a council of workers, for fellowship and planning. Its relation to the committee on Christian education, through the division committee and superintendent, will enable such a council of workers to receive guidance, review plans and make recommendations. The purpose of such a division council has been aptly stated by Robert R. Powell in the following quotation:

A junior-age boy, for example, might be in a junior Sunday-school class, the junior choir, the Boy Scouts, in a junior class in the vacation church school, and go to a church camp. If these activities are related to one another, if the adult leaders in each activity know the adult leaders in the others, if each of these leaders knows what the others are doing, if they understand one another's purposes and have worked out a central core of purpose that they hold in common, if these several methods of work fit together sensibly, if interrelatedness of this kind exists, then the church is making a concerted effort to meet the needs of this junior boy. [4]

The following chart shows the organization into nurture and teaching groups which has become traditional through long experience, though there may be variations from it as will be noted.

CHILDREN'S DIVISION
    Nursery Department—birth to 3
    Kindergarten Department—ages 4-5
    Primary Department—grades 1-3
    Junior Department—grades 4-6
YOUTH DIVISION
    Junior High Department—grades 7-9
    Senior High Department—grades 10-12
    Young People's Department—post-high school to about age 23
ADULT DIVISION
    Young Adults
    Middle Adults
    Older Adults

It is considered better practice to classify pupils of school age by grades than by chronological age. The transition points between divisions, and in some cases between departments, coincide with similar transitions in school and life. Most

[4] Robert R. Powell, "The Minister as Teacher," *The Minister and Christian Nurture,* ed. N. F. Forsyth, p. 42. © 1957 by Abingdon Press. Used by permission.

published curriculum materials follow this general plan of grading. With young people and adults it is difficult to fix exact dividing lines between divisions and departments. Practices differ widely, and much depends on local conditions.

While the three-grade department is the most common, some churches prefer the two-grade department, and some are making the single school grade the unit without combining grades into departments. Such variations from the standard pattern are made in the interest of getting more homogeneous groups than is possible when three grades are combined. Some curriculum materials are now organized on the basis of two-grade departments, and churches using such material will normally organize the church school on the same basis.

Since organization must facilitate program, changes in educational policy usually need to be accompanied by organizational changes. It has been customary to conduct church-school worship by departments, and this is still being done in most churches. There is, however, an increasing conviction on the part of workers with children that worship should be integrated into the teaching session, and should, therefore, take place in the classroom. It is not our purpose to evaluate the merits of this as compared with department worship. Much could be said in favor of each. We are concerned only with its organizational implications. If the church-school class is to be the unit for all activities, departmental organization will be less necessary and may become obsolete. This will also affect building and equipment, thus making it essential that an educational policy be established before a new building is planned. Conversely, an existing building with a fixed number and size of rooms will to an extent determine the organization which is best suited to these facilities.

Desirable size for church-school classes is another problem on which there is difference of opinion. Some leaders maintain that classes of eight or ten pupils are ideal for assuring maximum participation of each pupil, enabling the teacher to give individual attention to each and maintaining home contacts, and minimizing discipline problems. Others hold that classes of twelve to eighteen pupils are not only practical, but lead to greater interest and better group response. Two related developments have led to the recommendation that classes of grade-school age and older have as many as twenty-five or thirty pupils. The first is the plan for having all educational activities unified in class groups, including worship, story, discussion, creative activities, and whatever else is done. With this plan the class as such is usually broken down in the course of the period into several activity groups. The second is the plan for having not just one adult teacher for a class, but a group of teachers associated together in teaching.[5]

Size of classes will to an extent be controlled by church-school attendance, since it is desirable to have pupils of only one school grade grouped together in a class, and by classroom space available. However, when a new building is being planned, it is essential that a policy be established on this important problem before plans can be drawn.

Another problem in organization of classes concerns the question of whether they should be coeducational or segregated. It is now fairly common policy to combine the sexes in church-school classes, as well as in most other groups except clubs and similar through-the-week activities. There are many advantages in this, and few arguments against it.

[5] For further discussion, see ch. 25, pp. 270-80.

Some of the foregoing applies more particularly to the organization of children and youth than to adults. Problems of adult organization are more complex because of the wide ramification of adult activity in the church. Adults will be found in church-school classes, men's and women's organizations, weekday study groups, parents' meetings, and on boards and committees. Any or all of these may contribute to their Christian education. The adult division of the church school embraces all these opportunities for adult education. What is happening to the spiritual growth of adults is more important than where it is taking place. Adult activities should be graded so as to take account of changing interests and needs with advancing age.

A major problem in organization is that of bringing each person into saving relationship with the whole church community. The sense of togetherness, of acceptance and belonging, is an important factor in Christian education. In the church where it is the practice of whole families to attend the church school as well as the congregational service of worship this is no problem. It can be argued that this is possible in any church, except those who have church school and church worship at the same hour. But this wholeness of experience in the church is not likely to eventuate unless it is planned, and unless organization provides the channels to make it possible.

There is increasing recognition of the desirability of persons of all ages having some experience in the congregation as a whole, particularly in worship, but no common plan has emerged. A good beginning is made when the whole church program is considered as a unit, some phases of which require being together, and others, separation into graded groups. Some churches provide a service of worship for the whole family, preceded or followed by graded groups for more specifically educational activities for all the members of the family. Others on occasion have family services which children attend with their families. Still others have younger members attend a part of the service only.[6] No one has yet spoken an authoritative word concerning this problem except to emphasize its importance. It is a matter which cannot be ignored when planning the organization of Christian education in the church.

Organization of Staff

The effective functioning of an organization requires executive and administrative leadership. A complex organism like the church school involves many leadership functions, performed by many persons, who together constitute the staff. Within the staff will be included general officers, divisional and departmental officers, agency officers and counselors, class teachers, and group leaders.

Three principles will guide staff organization: (1) clear definition of function for each leader, (2) freedom and authority to perform his function, (3) communication and fellowship within the staff so that co-ordination of effort may grow out of mutual respect and sense of worth, and that the highest leadership potential of each will be released.

Under the direction of the committee on Christian education, there will be general officers whose concern is with the whole church school. These will include the minister (in his capacity as minister, not usually as executive or administrator),

[6] For further discussion, see chs. 13 and 14, pp. 144-45 and 157-59.

the director of Christian education, the church-school superintendent and assistants, and the general secretary. If the church has a unified financial plan, there is no need to have a church-school treasurer; an assistant church treasurer may be assigned to work with the church school.

Ideally, the superintendent should exercise his function in relation to the whole church school. However, since he is usually a layman or woman, it may be impossible for him to assume such wide responsibility. His work may be limited to the Sunday church school, with others as heads of other agencies co-ordinate with him. In the latter case it is essential for the minister and the director of Christian education to assume the function of general direction and co-ordination. Since, if educational records are to assist in program planning for whole persons they need to be unified for the whole church school, the general secretary should serve all educational agencies, with assistants as needed.

General officers are responsible for maintaining an effectively organized and smoothly running church school. This does not mean that they are to direct others with a heavy hand. The popular notion of the efficient executive is out of place here. Leadership and direction there must be, but the church is not the place for some to lord it over others. Better and more permanent results will be achieved when the general officer assumes the role of servant and, through good group processes, encourages the members of his staff to adventure with him in maintaining the finest possible church school.

Division superintendents are next in the panel of organization. There will be three, one each for the children's, youth, and adult, divisions. They are in responsible relationship to the general officers on the one hand, and the workers in their respective divisions on the other. Each will work in close relationship with the subcommittee in the committee on Christian education for that division. Each is responsible for the administration and supervision of the total program of his division. It is through them that effective co-ordination of program and interrelation of workers in their respective divisions will be achieved.

Within each division, the organized departments will be under the leadership of department superintendents or principals, and such other department workers as may be needed. A department principal should embrace in his work all the educational activities of pupils in the age group of his department. Department principals stand in direct relationship with the division superintendent of their division, and are immediately responsible for the guidance and supervision of the teachers and group leaders within their departments. Co-ordination of work is achieved through departmental or divisional planning conferences which include all the workers in such department or division.

Conclusion

This chapter has sought to deal broadly with organization of the church for Christian education, and the organization of Christian education in the church. The concern has been more with principles of organization than with specific practices. A church is a living organism, and does not yield readily to being straight-jacketed into a preconceived mold. Church-school members are unique human beings, children of God whose spiritual welfare must always have priority over the mechanism by which organization-minded men are prone to manipulate them into neat packages of program. Churches differ from one another, and each has its unique problems with which organization must deal.

Yet a church school must have organization. In the final analysis, the local committee on Christian education is responsible for determining what organization is best for achieving the purposes for which it is responsible. The principles and possibilities which have been outlined in this chapter will serve as basic proposals with which such committees may work.

Bibliography

Forsyth, Nathaniel F. (ed.). *The Minister and Christian Nurture.* Nashville: Abingdon Press, 1957.

Foster, Virgil E. *How a Small Church Can Have Good Christian Education.* New York: Harper and Brothers, 1956.

Gable, Lee J. *Christian Nurture Through the Church.* New York: National Council of Churches of Christ in the U.S.A., 1955.

Grimes, Howard. *The Church Redemptive.* Nashville: Abingdon Press, 1958.

Heim, Ralph D. *Leading a Sunday Church School.* Philadelphia: Muhlenberg Press, 1950.

Lobingier, John L. *The Better Church School.* Boston: Pilgrim Press, 1952.

Miller, Randolph Crump. *Education for Christian Living.* Englewood Cliffs, N. J.: Prentice-Hall, Inc., 1956.

Vieth, Paul H. *The Church School.* Philadelphia: Christian Education Press, 1957.

Chapter 24

The Director of Religious Education

William F. Case

THE CONCERN OF CHRISTIAN EDUCATION IS WITH THE TOTAL RESPONSE OF WHOLE persons to a saving relationship with God through Jesus Christ in the fellowship of the church. In attempting to respond to this concern, the church has developed a system of education that permeates its entire life. To help make this education most effective, a new profession—the director of religious education—has developed. It is our purpose to examine this profession in order that we might understand what contribution it may make to the church as it attempts to fulfill the ministry for which its Lord called it into being, "Go therefore and make disciples of all nations, baptizing them in the name of the Father and of the Son and of the Holy Spirit, teaching them to observe all that I have commanded you; and lo, I am with you always, to the close of the age."

A New Profession

The profession of director of religious education is a relatively new one. It got a rather vigorous start in the 20's but with the depression of the 30's, few within the ranks were able to withstand the drive to economize. In recent years the profession seems to have developed more soundly and has deeper roots in the life of the church.

As churches have expanded in size and complexity, it has become increasingly difficult for one person to provide all the professional leadership. Further, Protestants are taking their educational tasks with ever more seriousness and are looking more critically at what is being done in this field. In response to these situations the new profession has grown very rapidly. All schools training directors for work in this field report many more requests for trained persons than they can provide. Most denominations report the demand for directors is so great that churches are often forced to turn to persons who are ill-prepared for such responsibility. In the long run this creates ill will and a lack of respect which must be overcome.

Since many churches are hiring directors for the first time, the job is often poorly defined. A church senses that the work load is too heavy for one professional leader. The natural step is to survey the work and discover those aspects of the job that are least pleasant, that require little specialized skill, or that lie outside the competence of the pastor, and assign them to a second person. This well may include responsibility for secretarial work, calling, playing the organ, directing the choir, and running the Sunday school. All or any combination of these jobs may fall to the director.

With no developed set of professional standards and no clear definition of job, the director is subject to frequent moves. If his training and skill is inadequate for the multifaceted job, he is asked to find another position. On the other hand, if he is successful, greater opportunities quickly open to him. Short tenure is one of the real problems of the director. He works in a job that involves long-term human relations, but all too often he is able to work at it for only a short term.

Because of the nature of the job and the long history of lay responsibility for the church's educational work, both the director and the church are often confused as to whom the director is responsible. Is he a junior member of the church staff and, consequently, responsible to the pastor? Is he responsible for a special area of work—education—and, therefore, responsible to the body in charge of that work —the board of education? Is he a minister and, therefore, responsible to the governing body of the church as any other minister? Confusion at this point leads to difficulty for all who are involved.

The denominations are just beginning to assume their responsibility for defining the new profession. In the past the director was often uncertain of his relationship to the larger church. He seemed to have no place as a professional worker in the organization of the church. He owed no responsibility to any denominational group, and no denominational group owed any responsibility to him. He sought and found his job on his own, and if he lost it he was still on his own. This pattern is changing, however. Many denominations are developing standards for the profession, providing for professional recognition, and assuming some responsibility for helping directors and churches seeking directors to get together.

The director is a member of a new profession. As such he is a part of the process of defining the standards and role of that profession. At the present it is rapidly growing. One who enters it will be in great demand. But one who enters it has a responsibility to help integrate the profession more completely and more soundly into the church.

The Job of the Director

The job of the director is defined by the nature and mission of the church. With all members of the Christian community—lay and clerical—he is concerned with the church's fulfillment of its basic mission in the world. He shares with the pastor the responsibility for helping all within the fellowship to come to a clear understanding of this mission, to develop an ever more compelling commitment to it, and to discover more effective means for carrying it forward. However, in the fulfillment of this basic ministry of the director, there are special responsibilities that fall within the definition of his job.

1. As EDUCATOR. The director functions first in his role as an educator. This means that he helps the church develop an educational point of view in all its work. Everything the church does teaches something to everyone who comes into relationship with it. The church does not teach just by its organized educational program. The worship, the preaching, the administrative groups, the women's organizations, the relationship among members—everything that happens in the

fellowship teaches. As a trained educator the director interprets this to the church, helps it evaluate the teaching it is doing in its total life, and guides it in improving its teaching ministry.

Of course, the teaching responsibility is most directly fulfilled through the organized educational program. So the director helps the church develop an understanding of its goal and purpose which in turn determine and control its policies. As it comes to understand its goal all other decisions become easier. What to do about curricular materials, leadership, and the host of other matters that must be dealt with in carrying on an educational ministry can now be faced from a perspective. The director is responsible for the development of an educational approach in the total life of the church.

The educational approach is basically concerned with persons. So the director is always helping the fellowship to evaluate its life and work in terms of persons. What is a nursery child like and how will the family night program affect him? In family worship, how can the needs of a primary child be met most helpfully? How are the practices of the men's club helping the youth group to understand Christian vocation? What is the meaning to the older members of the Christian community of enforced retirement from official positions in the church?

There are, of course, certain skills and techniques that facilitate learning. These the director is responsible for making available to all who need them. As a professional educator the director serves as a resource person for every person who carries any educational duty in the church. Much of his work is directed to this end.

2. As ORGANIZER AND ADMINISTRATOR. In any attempt to provide a structure through which goals may be reached, there is need for organization and administration. The director will find that much of his time and energy will be spent in these areas. The wise director will understand that these channels are ways by which the church fulfills its purpose and that through them he has direct opportunity to minister to persons. Consequently, he will not chafe at these duties but will use them as opportunities to fulfill his ministry. This, of course, means that he uses the structure to open communication between himself and persons and not to block it. It also means that all organization is evaluated in terms of what is happening to persons. It means that organization is flexible and responsive to changing conditions and needs.

As an administrator the director is in a service role. The administrator is responsible for providing the setting and the resources by which the goals of the organization may be reached. Groups are often frustrated because they are unable to accomplish the goals they have set. The director as administrator is there to help groups find the structure and resources by which they can achieve their purpose.

Most denominations provide for an organization of the educational program. This organization usually requires adaptation to the special requirements of a particular congregation. The director, seeing the need for adequate organization and understanding these special requirements, helps the local congregation adapt the provided organization to meet its needs. The wise director will not ignore the structure the denomination provides but will use it creatively as the situation in which he works requires.

Organizing for education has been discussed in detail earlier.[1] The director has a responsibility to see that the necessary structure of organization is provided and to serve as administrator so that the organization functions to fulfill its goal.

3. As SUPERVISOR. Perhaps the most creative and distinctive function of the director is that of supervisor. In this role the director serves to help leaders be more effective as they carry out their responsibilities. Years ago George Albert Coe defined supervision as "sharing the burden." Probably this is the best definition we know. This defines the supervisor as one who shares with another whatever skill and resources he has in order that the other person might do a better job. Often teachers and other leaders in the church are bewildered and frustrated by their jobs. The skillful supervisor relieves this bewilderment and frustration by making available to the teacher or leader the skills and resources he needs to fulfill his job effectively. No teacher should feel that he is tackling an impossible job alone, but he should be made to feel that there is a skilled and friendly supervisor, lay or professional, standing by to "share the burden."

Quite clearly the role of the director in supervision is a job in human relations. Here the greatest skill in understanding and working with people will be required. A teacher is most vulnerable when he is having difficulty with a class. No one likes to admit defeat or that he is unable to cope with a situation. To be able to help, the director will need real understanding and skill.

The director is usually able to help most effectively, through supervision, if the help is sought by the teacher. The relationships the director establishes in his regular work with individuals and groups are therefore very important. If he is warm and accepting, quick to praise and reluctant to criticize, if he is able to contribute fruitful ideas and useful resources without insisting on his own way, teachers and leaders will naturally turn to him for help. He will be invited to observe in the class that is having difficulty. The teacher will seek a conference for help with a difficult student. The director will not have to force himself on teachers but will be actively sought by them if he has proved that he is truly concerned about them and is able to help.

Supervision of individuals will be carried on through observation, conferences, providing resources, and in countless informal ways. Many of the most creative and satisfying relationships of the director will develop in his work of supervision.

However, not all of the director's work in supervision will be on an individual basis. Many of his most fruitful opportunities will be in group situations. As he meets with the boards and committees, with the departmental organizations, with planning sessions, and with the many other active groups, opportunities for group supervision will arise. Consequently, he will not only need great skill in working with individuals but in working with groups as well.

It is often almost impossible for the director to give as much time to individuals as he would like. So he tries to make help available to a larger number by working with them in groups. As he guides a group of primary teachers in an evaluation of a unit of learning just completed or as he plans with a group of junior-high counselors for a coming camping experience, he can do effective group supervisory

[1] See ch. 23, pp. 247-58.

work. Any time he is making available to leaders new skills and resources so that they can do a better job, he is fulfilling a supervisory role.

In recent years directors have been led to realize more completely the importance of their ability to work with groups. Skill in understanding and freeing groups for creative work is an important part of the director's job as a supervisor.

4. SECURING A POSITION. In looking at the work of the director it is important for us to ask how the director secures his appointment. Naturally there are variations from denomination to denomination, but there are some common practices that it is helpful to understand. At the present the director is in a favored position for the demand for trained persons is great.

The individual who is interested in securing work as a director or in changing positions would probably start by consulting the national staff person responsible for such placement in his denomination. Almost all the denominations have someone responsible at the national level for such placements. In many denominations there will be a person responsible for smaller geographic areas—conference, synod, diocese, association—that can be consulted. Although there is no national interdenominational agency that functions in this role, state or city councils of churches often serve informally in helping churches and professional leadership to get together.

The director will also usually find the school at which he received his professional training a source of help in securing a job. Almost all schools operate some placement service and they are all beseiged by churches.

When the director is approached by a church for a position, there are a number of questions that need to be faced. One of the most crucial is the definition of the job. Many times a church is securing a director for the first time, and they are not quite sure what they want. At other times there is a difference of opinion between the pastor and the lay people as to what is wanted. Occasionally the job will cover other areas—music, parish visitation, business administration—as well as Christian education. The prospective director will want to strive for as careful an understanding of the job as is possible with both the pastor and the responsible laymen. It is true that there are times when this definition will evolve as the director works in the situation. It can be a real educational experience for a church and a director to work together in coming to an understanding of the role of the director in its life. However, when a director enters a situation with this task before him, he needs to be certain that the pastor and laymen understand and are committed to this experimental approach.

Another question that will need to be answered is, To whom is the director responsible? In some denominations this may seem clear, but in actual practice it can often be a source of trouble. Many denominations assign the task of hiring a director to the responsible lay bodies. At times in practice, however, the pastor regards the director as his assistant and therefore subject to his direction. Always there is a sense in which this is true. At the same time it is true that the director is a responsible professional leader who has a task to perform. It is important for the director to be clear as to whom he is responsible for the fulfillment of his job.

There are numerous other questions that are of minor significance but may prove to be very trying if they are not clearly worked out. One of these is the matter of an expense account. Is the director to have an expense account? What are legitimate items to be included in it? Who is to verify the director's account? Another has to do with the director's free time. Some pastors work without any set time off from their responsibilities and may expect the director to do likewise. Is the director willing to accept this arrangement? If not, what time is he to have off? What adjustment in schedule is to be made for evening meetings? Are a certain number of hours to be spent at the job each week, and is the director free to arrange these or is he expected to follow a fixed time schedule?

The question of the director's vacation needs to be determined. What will be the length of the vacation? Upon what will the time when he takes his vacation be dependent—the pastor's plans, the needs of the church school, or his own personal desires? Will participation in summer programs away from the local church but sponsored by the denomination or co-operating interdenominational groups be taken from vacation time?

A further question has to do with the attendance at professional meetings. Will the director be encouraged to attend professional meetings sponsored by the denomination or by interdenominational groups? How many will he be expected to attend a year? Will the church pay his expenses?

The director will also want to know of any expectations the church will have in terms of his personal habits. Expectations here may vary from one part of the country to another and the director should understand these so that they do not become a source of embarrassment.

Since the profession is so new, plans for supplemental benefits—pensions, hospitalization, insurance—are not always clear. The director will need to know what the church is going to do in these areas so that his total planning can take this into account. It is never wise to leave these matters to chance.

As a member of a new profession the director has a challenging opportunity to help define the role the profession will play in the life of the church. He may have a part in setting standards that will direct the future of the profession. At the same time he will often be frustrated and confused as he helps work through this process in a local church. He will lack some of the security of an older, more stable profession, but he will be challenged by the opportunity to help establish and define a new profession of service for Christ, his church, and those both are called to serve.

The Relationships of the Director

1. To THE CHURCH. As a servant of the church the director must think of himself first in relationship to this institution he is called to serve. Although he is certainly committed to the Church of Christ, he will have some relationship to a denomination as the particular branch of the church through which he ministers. This relationship will vary from denomination to denomination and will be confused in almost all of them.

In some denominations the director will be regularly ordained and fulfill his special ministry as a member of the clergy. For other denominations this will be a choice the director may make depending on a number of factors, perhaps, whether the director is a man or woman. At times the relationship of the director to his denomination will be much less clear and will be only as strong as he works to make it. In general the denominations are beginning to face more seriously their relationship to directors and are searching for ways to relate them more closely to the life and structure of their church. Among other things this means that the director is getting a little more security in his job and a little more assurance of some retirement support.

The director will also be related to a local church. This relationship will also vary from denomination to denomination and, perhaps, from local church to local church within a denomination. Organizationally the director should be related in some direct way to the structure of the church that is responsible for its over-all life—the quarterly conference, the session, the annual meeting, or whatever. Further, of course, he should be responsibly related to the group carrying forward the educational program—the board of education, commission on education, religious education committee, or whatever. It is to this group that he will be directly responsible and this group will supervise his work.

The church itself will provide the most significant and meaningful relationship of the director's life.

2. To THE PASTOR. The relationship of the director to the pastor also will be determined in part by the denomination. However, the more important level of his human relationship to the pastor will be determined by the qualities that both possess as persons.

It is important for the director to remember that in the eyes of his church, the pastor is responsible for the well-being of the total life of his congregation. Therefore, he must not expect the pastor to be able to adopt a "hands-off" policy concerning education. The pastor will need to be informed about all that is going on and a participant in making policy decisions as they affect the church.

On the other hand the director has special training and experience that has led the church to set him aside for this ministry. Ideally the pastor will free the director to do this job as effectively and creatively as he can, at the same time giving him understanding support. Each should see the other as a responsible minister fulfilling his unique role in the total ministry of the church. Each should feel the responsibility to sustain and strengthen the ministry of the other.

For this kind of relationship to develop, there must be adequate channels for continuing communication. Regular staff meetings and frequent consultations are essential if each is to understand the other and be able to contribute most effectively to the total ministry.

3. To MEMBERS OF A MULTIPLE STAFF. While relatively few churches have a multiple staff, an increasing number are served by more than two professional leaders. In this situation there are many opportunities for misunderstandings of job assignments to arise and for other disruptions in human relations to develop. Here again each staff member needs to see his own job as clearly as possible, and yet understand it within the context of the total ministry being carried out by other staff persons and lay members.

For this to be possible there must be opportunity for the staff members to spend sufficient time together to come to a mutual sharing of purpose for their combined ministry. As they come to respect each other and to appreciate the concern of each for this ministry, they will be strengthened in their own work and will sustain each other.

In working with a staff, lines of communication must be kept open. Perhaps the most useful way to accomplish this is by regular meetings of the entire staff. Further consultations with individual staff members are important both for helping to clarify job responsibilities and for building strong personal relationships. Working on a staff can be a very creative opportunity as each is mutually stimulated and encouraged by the total group.

4. TO THE SUPERINTENDENT. The director will probably have his closest working relationship with the superintendent of the church school. The superintendent is the lay person assigned the task of being the executive officer of the group responsible for the church's educational program. As such, it is his duty to see that the policies and decisions of this board, commission, or committee are carried out. The director is the professional person selected by this responsible group to provide the guidance, skill, and resources to assure that their goals are achieved. As such, the director works closely with the superintendent to see that whatever he needs— skill, organization, or resource—is made available so that he might effectively fulfill his job.

Since the superintendent and the director work so closely together and both share responsibility for the over-all task of education, there are many opportunities for friction to develop. The superintendent may resent the director and feel that he has had his job taken away. At other times the director may feel that the superintendent is assuming his prerogatives. As in every situation where persons are involved, the most effective way of dealing with this is by improving the relations between the persons through more effective communication. If the director honestly sees himself in a service role of helping the superintendent do a better job, he will usually find himself well-received and welcomed by the superintendent.

Usually the division of responsibility between the director and superintendent calls for the superintendent's handling most of the administrative functions of the church school. The director serves as resource person for the entire staff. He attempts through his supervisory role to help the church and each individual worker understand its purposes and discover ways of reaching its goals.

5. TO TEACHERS. The director works closely with the teachers and bears a responsibility for the quality of teaching they do. His working with the teacher may be in group situations or with the individual teacher. He constantly strives to build such relationships with teachers that they turn to him whenever he can help them to be more effective. Together the superintendents, teachers, and director form the working group that provides Christian education for the church of which they are a part. Each must fulfill his role, and each must help the other if the education is to be most effective.

6. TO THE COMMUNITY. The director is a citizen of a community as well as a servant of the church. As such, he has a responsibility to the community in which he lives. In turn the community will sustain him and provide for many of the needs he and his family share with the rest of the community.

As a professional person concerned with the community, the director will take an active part in its life. The schools will be of special interest to him. At every point he will seek to improve them. He will be helpful in interpreting what they are trying to do and will strive to assist them in doing well their assigned task. At the same time he will be constructively involved in every effort to increase their effectiveness.

The Training of the Director

1. PRESENT CONFUSION. At the present time standards for the training of the

director are in confusion. As a new profession tries to define its role and establish standards this is almost certain to happen.

Almost all denominations now expect that the director shall be at least a college graduate. Others insist that the director shall have graduate training. A few denominations are encouraging their directors to finish a regular seminary course leading to a B.D., or equivalent degree.

There is almost equal confusion as to what the training of a director shall include. Some training programs place great emphasis on educational theory and methods. Others give major attention to the content of the Christian faith as the basic requirement. Still others try to combine these emphases, since the professional competence of the director should include both of these areas.

2. CURRENT TRENDS. The person seeking training to become a director is most likely to find it in one of three places—a college, graduate school, or seminary.

Several colleges, usually church-related, have attempted to provide training for directors on the undergraduate level. Most colleges working in this area recognize that graduate training is desirable for the director. However, with so many churches needing directors they feel that it is better to give them some training than to permit them to drift into the profession with no special preparation. Further, many young women enter the profession for a few years prior to marriage, and they can scarcely be expected to enter a long period of professional training. Although some of these colleges are doing admirable work, they face the inevitable problems of attempting to do professional training at the undergraduate level. Most directors who are expecting to devote a lifetime to the profession feel the need for graduate training.

In some universities professional training is being provided for directors at the graduate level. This may be related to the school of education, the department of religion, or organized in a separate department of religious education. Although this was formerly one of the most popular ways of training directors, it is not as widespread as it once was. Some universities are doing excellent work in providing this professional training but many of them sense some problem here. If the work is carried on in a school of education, courses in the Christian heritage—Bible, theology, church history, and the like—are apt to be very limited. Often in a graduate department of religion, it is difficult for the student to secure adequate help in understanding human learning and how it may be guided.

Perhaps the greatest number of directors are now being trained in seminaries whose responsibility it is to provide professional leadership for the church. In the seminary the director studies in the same classes and is introduced to the same material as are the pastor and other professional leaders of the church. Most seminaries that train directors have provided specialized programs that lead to a professional degree, usually an M.R.E. or M.A. with a major in religious education. Several seminaries are now encouraging persons training to become a director to follow the regular B.D. program.

The place to secure professional training to become a director will need to be decided by each person on the basis of his own background, needs, and professional goals. Each type of training institution has certain advantages and certain limitations. These need to be evaluated and each person will decide which best meets his needs.

3. THE DIRECTOR'S TITLE. Just as there is uncertainty as to the training the

director should receive, there is confusion concerning his title. In the past anyone who was assigned responsibility for the educational program was given the title of director. Recently, as the profession has matured, there has been an effort to set some standards for those who carried the title. Several denominations have made proposals on this subject and it has been referred to the Division of Christian Education of the National Council of Churches.

Most of these proposals suggest at least three different titles. The college graduate who begins work without further professional training might be called an educational assistant. The person who meets more rigid professional standards, including at least one year of graduate study, might be given the title of director of Christian education. The person who has met the standards of his denomination and has been ordained but who serves in a specialized ministry, might be called a minister of education. These may not be the final titles accepted by the churches, but certainly some standards will be set for the professional title of persons working in the educational field within the next few years.

The Growing Director

One of the criteria of the effective director, as for any other professional person, is that he be a growing person. This growth for the director will include professional growth, personal growth, and growth as a Christian.

There are many opportunities for the director to grow professionally. Of course the most immediate and probably the most important opportunity is the growth that comes out of his experience as he attempts to do his job. He grows and learns in the interaction of meeting with teachers and staff in his own church. He grows as he works with committees and groups to improve the educational program. He grows as he reads and studies to find answers to develop his own competence, and to keep abreast of the many fields to which he is related. The numerous training schools sponsored by his denomination and by the interdenominational agencies give opportunity for professional growth. The specialized courses conducted by seminaries and graduate schools either in evenings or summers are excellent opportunities for professional growth.

In his professional growth the director will be stimulated and helped by professional groups. Almost every geographic area has such a group organized on a denominational or interdenominational basis. The major denominations also have nationally organized professional groups meeting on a regular schedule. There are at least two interdenominational groups to which the director should belong for his own professional growth. The Religious Education Association is an interfaith organization that will contribute much to the director. It has local and regional chapters as well as a national organization. Its publication *Religious Education* is the most important professional journal the director will have. The other organization is the Director's Section of the Division of Christian Education, National Council of Churches. This group is one of the associated sections of the Division and meets annually, usually in February. The director who wants to grow professionally must relate himself to his professional groups as fully as possible.

The director must also grow personally. To do this he must protect himself so that he has time to grow. Time for family, friends, creative leisure, and needed rest is as necessary as time to do the job. The director who allows his social relationships to dwindle and become dull is apt to be a dull person and so a dull director. All of the interests and enthusiasms that he brings to the job ought to be stimulated and nurtured by the job. As he becomes a richer, more creative, and more interesting person, he becomes a richer, more creative, and more interesting director.

It is hardly necessary to say that one who has responded to the call of Christ to serve his Church must grow as a Christian. Yet the director may become too familiar with Hcly things and may become a professional Christian. As he works with others devoted to a common task and as he shares in the growth of others toward God, he has the fullest opportunity to grow himself. Paul, writing to the Thessalonians, says, "We were ready to share with you not only the gospel of God but also our own selves, because you had become very dear to us." So the director as he shares, not only the gospel of God but also his very self with those who have become very dear to him, will find himself growing in his faith and in his relationship to God—growing as a Christian.

Bibliography

Gable, Lee J. *Christian Nurture Through the Church*. New York: National Council of Churches of Christ in the U.S.A., 1955.

Gwynn, Price H. *Leadership Education in the Local Church*. Philadelphia: Westminster Press, 1952.

McKibben, Frank M. *Guiding Workers in Christian Education*. Nashville: Abingdon Press, 1953.

Miller, Randolph C. *Education for Christian Living*. Englewood Cliffs, N. J.: Prentice-Hall, Inc., 1956.

Munro, Harry C. *The Director of Religious Education*. Philadelphia: Westminster Press, 1930.

Additional resources

Denominational boards of education frequently publish reports and pamphlets on the director of Christian education.

The Division of Christian Education, National Council of Churches of Christ in the U.S.A. is an additional source of information. See especially, BB06-554, "The Local Church Director of Christian Education."

Chapter 25

Selecting and Training the
Local Church's Educational Staff

Lee J. Gable

EVERY CHURCH SHOULD GIVE SERIOUS ATTENTION TO SELECTING AND TRAINING
the persons on whom the effectiveness of its program depends. They are the teachers
of its classes, the officers and members of its committees and commissions, the
advisors and officers of its fellowship and service groups, the administrators of its
various organizations and activities.

At the outset, three assumptions need to be recognized: (1) Each congregation
is responsible for selecting and training its own educational staff. It may use
persons and programs provided by its denomination, council of churches, or another
agency, but the church itself is responsible. (2) The church relies on the volunteer leadership of laymen for most of its organized group activity. (3) The
church looks to such professionally trained leaders as the pastor and director of
Christian education for inspiration and co-ordination of effort, but it does not
expect them to replace the layman.

Some Basic Considerations

Before dealing with the things a church should do to assure for itself an adequate
staff, several basic considerations should be examined. They affect virtually everything a church should do and the way it will proceed.

1. The educational staff should accept and practice the best available knowledge
regarding leadership. These concepts have been changing. Among the many insights which studies in group dynamics and human relations have given us[1] two are
especially important in the concept of leadership. *Leadership is shared.* It belongs
not exclusively to the person who has been elected or appointed to office. Rather,
it belongs to the person, elected or not, who can best help the group accomplish
the task before it at a given time.

Leadership represents power released in a group, not power exercised over a group.
The best church leader, therefore, is not the person who knows how to get his
way or how to get the group to accept a predetermined goal or program. The best
church leader is the one who makes it possible for a group to set up its own goals
and to work toward these goals, always in the spirit of the Christian gospel. The

[1] Cf. ch. 16, pp. 173-83.

leader does not allow the group to go on its own uncontrolled way; rather, he keeps people confronted with their Christian responsibility, and he encourages them to exercise their own responsible churchmanship.

2. Each child and young person in the church should be growing in Christian faith, life, and service in preparation for leadership. The church should encourage persons of every age to accept as much responsibility in learning, worship, service, and fellowship as their stages of development will permit. The junior, for example, should occasionally help to plan and conduct the worship service in his church-school department. A teacher should work with him to aid in developing his understanding of worship and to be certain that the resultant worship service will be well-conceived. The teacher coaches him in reading scripture and in praying. If he has leaders who share with him in this way as he grows through youth into adulthood, he will be ready to be selected for mature church leadership. He will need further specific training, to be sure, but a solid foundation will have been laid.

3. Sound Christian motivation is essential. If it can be assured, the problems of finding and training staff members will be greatly reduced. Some of this motivation should result from lifelong participation in the life and work of the church. It should be deepened as the worker participates Sunday after Sunday in the worship of the congregation. It should be sharpened in the worship periods of the workers' conference and in such special occasions as the service of installation. It should be given warmth in fellowship at the workers' banquet and in the give-and-take of discussion and planning. It should be confirmed through the personal "thank you" and the public recognition which every church should give to its faithful workers.

4. The church should develop a long-range program for selecting and training its educational staff. While details will be considered later, here it is sufficient to point out the folly of trying to work without a plan. Where there is no program, each position is filled as the vacancy occurs by securing the best person who is available. If there is training, if there is evaluation, if there is improvement, it is largely accidental. The chief victims are the children, the youth, and the church of the future.

5. The training program should foster readiness for change and a willingness to accept change. It is the purpose of any training program to help persons to improve in the task for which the training is given. If there is no improvement, the training program is open to serious question.

Research and experience combine to suggest that four conditions should be provided in a training program if it is to result in constructive change.

a. *Relevance.* The program must promise help that the worker needs and knows he needs. A program that is geared to a curriculum which the worker is using or to an age group with which he is concerned is likely to appeal to him.

b. *Breadth.* The program that includes a number of insights or procedures is more likely to produce change in the worker than the one that is limited to a single insight or procedure. For example, it is doubtful whether monthly church-school conferences with talks on such general subjects as the Christian faith, understanding persons, group dynamics, lesson planning, and teaching techniques will produce much lasting change. From month to month the worker is not likely to relate one of these to another and to put the insights into effect. However, suppose his church sends him to a laboratory school. He will see a counseling teacher use all of these insights in work with a group. He will discuss these insights with that teacher both before and after he sees him at work. He will read, study, worship, and discuss for a week or two, with these insights clear and fresh in his thinking. Then he is sure to make some changes. Thus, the good training program is broad enough to bring many insights together.

c. *Depth.* The word "depth" is much used, and often with widely varying meanings. It is used here to suggest that training should go beyond the general to the specific applications of the general; beyond superficial activity to the objectives, causes, and effects of the activity; beyond human interest and "felt need" to ultimate purpose and divine will. Concern for this kind of depth suggests a number of implications for the training program. It should involve the trainee in study as well as in discussion, in personal use of the Bible as well as in reading books about the Bible, in worship as well as in study about worship, in guided practice as well as in classroom study and discussion.

d. *Interaction.* The conclusions which a group reaches for itself are much more likely to be accepted and used than those which a leader presents. In one experiment leaders trained in discussion and those untrained worked with different groups dealing with the same problem in industrial relations. "The important gain was that the trained leaders almost completely avoided failures and in their stead obtained alternate solutions, some of which might have been of higher quality than the solution established as the satisfactory one." [2] The implications for work with church groups and for training for that work are obvious.

A Plan for Selection and Enlistment

As in all phases of church work, no one plan is best for every church. Much depends on the unique situation of the church with respect to its community, people, background, resources, and opportunities. It is possible, however, to suggest some elements which each church, in its own way, should incorporate into its own program for enlisting workers.

1. ASSIGN RESPONSIBILITY. A board or committee, often the committee on Christian education, should have general responsibility. Much of the detailed work will need to be assigned to a personnel committee for the church. Pastor, director of Christian education, and church-school superintendent should work closely with this committee.

2. ESTABLISH PERSONNEL POLICY. The church should decide on the general principles and procedures according to which people will work in its program. It should develop job descriptions so that persons who hold positions, or are asked to assume them, may know precisely what is expected. Each person should thoroughly understand his duties, to whom he is responsible, what resources and facilities are available, and what help the church can provide.

Definite terms of office should be set, and some form of rotation system established. Because the rotation system is by no means commonly accepted, it may be well to note certain of its advantages and disadvantages. Some advantages are that it cultivates leadership by distributing responsibilities and opportunities, it enriches the church program by bringing different persons with their varying contributions into office, and it spares both churches and people from terms in office which are

[2] Norman F. Maier, "An Experimental Test of the Effect of Training on Discussion Leadership," *The Study of Leadership,* ed. C. G. Browne and Thomas S. Cohn, p. 463.

too long but cannot be terminated gracefully. Two disadvantages stand out—rotation may lead to loss of interest on the part of the person leaving office, and the church program may suffer by replacing a person who is more capable than his successor. In experience, the advantages usually outweigh the disadvantages.

With the exception of some children's and youth's offices, the term should not be less than one year nor exceed three years. There should be clear understanding regarding the possibility of re-election. However the system is established, provision should be made for overlapping terms of office. In any organization there should be some officers from a previous term and some new ones, so that new and experienced persons are always working together.

3. ESTABLISH A PERSONNEL FILE. A record which shows the service each person is willing to render in the church is necessary, even in a small church. The nature of this file depends on such factors as the size of the church and the availability of employed or volunteer persons to create and maintain the file.

Information to be recorded in this file should be secured by some form of Christian service registration in which members of the church indicate the types of service they are prepared to give as the church may need them. For this purpose blanks can be purchased from several sources, but it is more effective for each church to prepare its own, including services that fit its program and people. The blank should name specific types of service, including such variety that every person will find at least a few that are within the range of his interest and abilities. The following list is offered as suggestive:

Church School
  Teacher
    Children
    Youth
    Adult
    Older adult
  Superintendent
    General
    Children's division
    Youth division
    Adult division
    Vacation church school
    Weekday church school
  Group Leadership
    Camping
    Scouting
    Youth fellowship
    Hobby groups
    Men's groups
    Women's groups
  General Church Service,
    Ushering
    Finance
    Home visitation
    Baby sitting
    Public speaking
    Publicity

Telephoning
Correspondence
Typing
Mimeographing
Cooking
Nursing
Audio-visuals
Decoration
Work with families
Pianist
Librarian
Secretary
Music
  Directing
  Instrumental
  Singing
  Organist
Community Service
  Community welfare
  Industrial relations
  Intergroup relations
  Radio-Television
Interest Group Leadership
  Art
  Crafts
  Photography

Dramatics	Church Program
Athletics	Missions
Folk games	Evangelism
Nature lore	Interchurch co-operation

People may be given opportunity in a number of ways to check these blanks. In a series of church worship services stressing stewardship two offerings may be received, one of money and one of services. In the every-member canvass people may pledge both money and services. Each new member, at the time of his reception into church membership, may register for service.

The minimum file should include two sections. One contains the completed blanks, filed in alphabetical order. The other contains a card or sheet of paper for each type of service and lists the names of persons who showed interest in that particular service. Though it may be argued that the leaders of a small church know what the people can and will do, there are two reasons why such a file is desirable. One is that no person or committee can be sure that he knows what each member of that church is able and willing to do. The other reason is that the act of registering for service can be a significant part of a person's churchmanship, and it should not be denied to him.

4. DEVELOP A PLAN FOR ENLISTMENT. Most of the changes in volunteer personnel in the church take place at the time when officers are elected and at the time when a new program year begins. A plan for enlistment should acknowledge this and operate on a time schedule that provides the worker with sufficient time to prepare for his responsibilities.

In most churches, the program year begins in September or October. Enlistment of workers for that date should begin not later than April, with a listing of the positions which will probably be vacant in the fall. If a worker leaves office by rotation, or if a teacher should be given a chance for personal rest and renewal after a reasonable term of service, that fact can be established as easily in April as September. If there is to be a change of program that will involve new leadership needs, that too can be determined in April. The plan for enlistment, then, should begin with the discovery of all the positions for which persons will be needed.

The next step is to select the persons to be invited to assume these positions. What are the possible sources from which the needed workers may come? Here the personnel file is invaluable. It will be helpful too to think of the personal talents and training required for each position. Keep in mind those who have served as apprentices to educational staff members, former workers who may again be ready for service, business and professional leaders with related backgrounds, parents (preferably not for the particular groups in which their children are members), newcomers to the church or community, couples whose interests might lead them jointly to assume one of these positions.

The next step is to invite each person to accept the task to which the church is calling him. The invitation should be extended in the most direct and personal way possible. Appeal by general announcement is the poorest of ways. A letter is little better. The potential worker should be visited and informed of what is involved in the task he is being asked to accept, what materials and facilities are available, how the church will help him, why he is "the man for the job." These enlistment interviews should take place in May for work to be begun in September.

This is not unreasonably early if the new worker is to make proper preparation. Let him have these three months to become familiar with the materials he will use, the age level of the group, and individual members of it. Let him read some good books. Let him observe others working in the same general type of program and with the same age group. Let him attend a summer conference or workshop. For the worker who undertakes this kind of preparation, the time he can give to it in three months will seem all too short.

Remember the place of prayer in the plan for enlistment. Each step in this process will be the better if it is undertaken against a background of sincere prayer. A director of Christian education once had to deal with a junior-high teacher who was upset about an especially difficult girl and wanted her removed from the class. The director asked the teacher first to pray five minutes each day for that girl. When the teacher found that she did not know enough about the girl to pray five minutes, she visited the girl's home. Then began a series of events that changed the teacher, the girl, and the class. At their conclusion the teacher said, "I want you to promise that whenever you ask a person to teach a class you will ask that person to pray as you did me." This true incident has been made basic to the filmstrip, "The Growing Teacher." [3] Prayer should not be used to make a person feel obligated to accept an invitation to service, but its power should be released sincerely at every stage in the enlistment plan.

The Church's Training Program

The church that would develop an educational staff must provide the training needed to help the members of that staff do justice to their tasks. Some of this training should be "pre-service," that is, it should take place before the person undertakes his responsibilities. Some of the training should take place during the person's term of work—"in-service" training. Logically, it would seem that most training should precede the assumption of responsibility, for a person should receive training prior to the actual work. In experience the reverse is often true, and there is reason for it. A person who is teaching a class recognizes his needs more clearly and feels them more sharply than one who is preparing to teach a class "some time." In-service training, therefore, has relevance and motivation that can seldom be achieved in the pre-service program. A church should make provision for both kinds, and often a particular training class will involve some people who are now in active service and others who are preparing for it.

What kind of training program should a church have for its volunteer workers? How much of that program should the local church provide by itself, and to what extent should it rely on co-operative enterprises, either denominational or interdenominational? There is, of course, no easy answer to these questions. Experience suggests, however, that every church, either by itself or in co-operation with other churches, should provide at least six major kinds of training opportunity: the leadership training class, the workers' conference, the workers' library, supervision, observation, and apprenticeship.

1. THE LEADERSHIP CLASS. One of the best-known forms of training is the leadership class or school. The major denominations, working together through the Division of Christian Education of the National Council of Churches, have

---

[3] In the *Leadership Education Audio-Visual Kit.*

developed the Standard Leadership Education Curriculum. This curriculum offers a large number of courses dealing with Bible, church, Christian living, the different age groups, and administration. Textbooks and leader's guides, frequently revised to keep them up to date, are provided. Each year tens of thousands of men and women enroll in these classes. The values that result depend almost entirely on the seriousness with which instructors and students undertake their work. This, in turn, depends on the extent to which churches support the schools and encourage their people to put their learnings to subsequent use. The closer the relationship between the leadership class and the church work of students, the better the chance that significant change will take place.

Many churches make such classes a regular part of the Sunday church-school program. These classes are free from the competition for time which makes it difficult to schedule weekday activities. They are usually open to older youth and adults who are interested in training. It is unwise, however, to recruit for such classes by general announcement. It is preferable to issue direct invitations to those whom the personnel committee may have singled out as especially promising. This Sunday morning class should meet in a separate room if at all possible, utilizing the entire church-school period for its work. On some Sundays its members will observe the church-school program. Sometimes they may act as substitute teachers. These visits or teaching experiences serve as laboratory periods for the class.

2. THE WORKERS' CONFERENCE. One of the best means of in-service training is the workers' conference, "a meeting where church school workers confer about their work with a view to improving it." [4] Normally such conferences are held for the workers of one church alone, for only so can they deal with their particular problems and opportunities. Occasionally a group of neighboring churches may hold joint sessions. This is especially valuable when they use the same curriculum materials and meet regularly to plan their use of successive units.

Some conferences include all the workers of a church, regardless of the age group with which they work. These general conferences deal with concerns of the whole church—building and equipment, evangelism, church-family partnership, observance of special seasons, or the church's community responsibility. Sometimes each department meets separately, in order to deal with its own problems, or to plan its work for the coming weeks. In the course of a year a church should have conferences of both kinds. Their frequency will depend on the need and interest in the individual church. As a rule, however, general conferences should be held from two to four times a year and departmental conferences at least quarterly, or even better, prior to the beginning of each new curriculum unit. Attendance is often a problem. To improve it, base the program on the needs of workers, give publicity that is clear and personal, demonstrate month after month that the conferences are beneficial, and keep business and detail to a minimum.

3. THE WORKERS' LIBRARY. Books and their use confront us with a strange contradiction. They have been published on every subject that bears on the work of a church. In conferences, conversations and correspondence, church workers show that they are looking for answers on these very subjects. Yet how hard it is to bring the books and the workers together!

The workers' library is by no means an automatic solution to the dilemma,

[4] Vedia Burke, *The Workers' Conference*, p. 9.

but it helps. Every church should provide a minimum library for its workers. This library should include basic reference books—commentary, concordance, Bible dictionary—and also reliable books on the church, Christian beliefs, Bible, children, youth, adults, and ways of teaching. Each department should have the background books which are recommended in the current curriculum materials. In addition, the best denominational and interdenominational church-school magazines should be given regularly to teachers.

To establish such a library is a costly project. Each annual budget should include an item for the library. Most denominational book stores have library suggestions for their churches, and often a library discount. Community libraries always have religion sections and are usually willing to set up special reference shelves for churches that will make use of them. The chief problem seems to be to get the books actually used. The closer the relationship between the library and the church work, the better the chance that the library will be used. Many departmental superintendents can testify that the books that are used in department planning sessions are used later by individual teachers. The church that will buy duplicate copies of basic reference books, so that a teacher may have one for use through the week, has solved the problem of getting that book used.

4. SUPERVISION. The very word "supervision" arouses resistance in many teachers, for it puts them on the defensive. Visions arise of an expert watching us at work, seeing our faults, and waiting for a chance to take us to task. This is unfortunate, for supervision can be one of the most effective tools for improving the leadership of a church. The kind of supervision that churches need is "a plan whereby an experienced leader counsels with and makes suggestions to a less experienced worker as they work together on problems." [5] This kind of supervision does not put people on the defensive. The terms "helping teacher" and "teacher consultant" point the direction that churches should take.

This type of supervisor meets with the teachers of a department as they plan. He works as a member of the departmental team, making his suggestions when they are appropriate in the planning process. He is ready to talk with teachers about their questions, accomplishing most when they come to him rather than making him seek them. They are likely to come to him if first they have planned their work together. He checks with teachers to see how the plans they have made are working. If they feel unsure about a plan, project, or way of teaching, he coaches them in its use until they feel more secure in undertaking it. He gives special attention to new workers, being certain that they understand their duties, introducing them to future co-workers, checking with them occasionally, and being ready to help as needed.

Supervision, in the form of coaching, should especially take place in the children's and youth's programs of the church. Its purpose is to help children and young people prepare for the various responsibilities they are asked to assume. If they are ill prepared for these duties, mistakes and embarrassment will usually result. When this occurs, they will often refuse the next invitation to do something special. On the other hand, if they receive sufficient help to perform a function well, they remember it with satisfaction and are likely to accept the next request also.

[5] *And Gladly Serve*, p. 28.

5. OBSERVATION. The too-ready reply to a new suggestion is that it may work some places "but not in our church." This often means that the objector does not understand this new suggestion and is afraid to try it. Or perhaps he feels that the current program is reasonably effective. If he could observe someone else using the new suggestion, he would be more disposed to adopt it.

At least three provisions should be included in a plan for observation. There should be some assurance that the program to be visited is good, otherwise the visit may be wasted. Occasionally one finds a church or a council of churches that keeps a list of programs that have been observed and found to be good. Also, the church should arrange for substitute teachers, thus encouraging the conscientious worker to take advantage of the opportunity and also insuring that the group he serves does not suffer. When the visit has been made, there should be opportunity to discuss it. What was effective in the program observed? What could we do differently, and how should we go about it? With this type of follow-up procedure it is almost certain that some desired changes will take place.

6. APPRENTICESHIP. Many of the skills any person has acquired have come through a form of apprenticeship—swimming, driving a car, baking a cake, leading a discussion. Regardless of the amount of theory a person may know, he has not mastered the skill until he has practiced it. Trial and error will lead to mastery—ultimately. This will proceed more rapidly, however, if one already skilled stands beside him, watches, notes effective and ineffective performance, and makes suggestions.

Many churches aim to have leaders "two-deep" at many points in their programs. Wherever there is a leader who is capable, mature, and willing is a good position in which to place an apprentice. The apprentice, or "cadet," is present for planning, observes the regular leader at work and helps as he can. In the process he learns a great deal, and becomes more capable of doing the work himself.

Each of the training enterprises here described can be provided by a congregation for its workers, either within its own program or in co-operation with other churches. Each of them should be provided, for otherwise a portion of the training that workers need is neglected. In addition, there are some opportunities that can seldom be provided by individual churches, but which the local church should make available to its people. Of these, three are dealt with in some detail: the laboratory school, the conference or institute, and the services of staff members or field workers.

7. THE LABORATORY SCHOOL. The training program that is most uniformly considered helpful is the laboratory school. By definition, it is a form of training that involves counseling teachers working with pupils to help them have a genuine learning experience, with student teachers observing and assisting in order that they too may learn. The church worker who attends a laboratory school for one or two weeks has, in the course of a typical day, such experiences as these: group worship, a training class in such a practical subject as understanding the pupil or ways of teaching, observation of a skilled teacher at work as he prepares for a session and works with pupils, evaluation of the session, planning and preparation for the next day, classes or discussion groups for personal enrichment, fellowship with other students, opportunity to talk and share with others who are also lay workers in the church. The laboratory school compresses all these types of leadership training into a short period of time. It has an unusually good chance of

producing change in the concepts and procedures of those who enroll in it. Good laboratory schools, unfortunately, are scarce. However, the church that wants its workers to have this experience can provide it. Denominational Christian education departments and councils of churches will have information as to when and where such schools are held.

Few individual congregations can develop their own laboratory schools. They can, however, provide parts of the laboratory experience. Some of the elements of the laboratory program are present when a supervisor works with the teachers of a department or when an apprentice and an experienced teacher work together. A still better opportunity can be provided through the vacation church school. It is usually possible to secure a good faculty for the two or more weeks of a vacation school during the summer. If new teachers or prospective teachers are assigned to them as helpers, and if they plan and evaluate together, the church can have some of the values of the laboratory school within its own program.

8. THE CONFERENCE OR INSTITUTE. Conventions, conferences, and institutes have long been used for training. Though the form of these meetings changes from time to time, the general pattern remains. The church sends delegates to receive inspiration and information. The value to the church and its workers depends in part on the quality of the program and its leaders. It also depends on the use the church makes of the experience. The church that would really benefit from conference attendance of its workers should take these steps: (1) Carefully choose the persons whom it sends, including several so that they may supplement each other during the conference and when they return. (2) Prepare the delegates in advance by helping them to understand the program to which they are going and to identify the kinds of learning they should try to bring back. (3) Give the delegates the opportunity to report their findings to the committee or group that can best weigh those findings and act on them.

9. STAFF AND FIELD SERVICE. Increasingly, denominations and councils of churches are making the services of staff members and field workers available to their member churches. These staff members distribute materials, conduct conferences, answer inquiries, consult with persons on request, and, as their schedules may allow, conduct intensive visitations to individual churches. These services vary too widely for accurate description here. Suffice it to say that some churches seek these services and benefit from them while others do not. The church that would develop its own educational staff will miss no opportunity to secure for its staff the best counsel available from the experienced persons whom the councils and denominations can offer.

Continuing Christian Growth

Perhaps the most perplexing problem confronting church administrators is that of continuing growth. It is so easy to work hard for a time, to develop new ways, and then to settle back in the conviction that this church or program has achieved its destiny. That is the moment of failure, for to stop growing is spiritual death. How can the church administrator promote continuous growth?

One is tempted to write in terms of evaluation, with plans for improvement and then further evaluation in an unending cycle. One is tempted to urge the continuing creativity that leads one to expose himself again and again to the new and the untried, never settling back into contentment. The repeated setting of goals, ever higher, is another way of continuing to grow.

The last and best word, however, is not on this level of human aspiration and effort, but on the level of dedication to the Divine. We worship a God who is infinite, who always has more truth waiting to break through into our laggard experience. More than anything that human planning can devise, we need to keep ourselves continually open to the God and Father of us all, that his Spirit may flow through us and lead us, not toward our goals but toward his.

Bibliography

And Gladly Serve. New York: National Council of Churches of Christ in the U.S.A., 1949. Revised, 1957.

Browne, C. G. and Cohn, Thomas S. (eds.). *The Study of Leadership.* Danville, Ill.: The Interstate Printers and Publishers, 1958.

Burke, Vedia. *The Workers' Conference.* St. Louis: Bethany Press, 1954.

Church School Administration Audio-Visuals. Especially the filmstrips entitled "Mirror to Myself" (supervision) and "Together We Grow" (workers' conference). New York: produced co-operatively through the National Council of Churches of Christ in the U.S.A., 1955.

Crossland, Weldon. *Better Leaders for Your Church.* Nashville: Abingdon Press, 1955.

Frank, Lawrence K. *How to Be a Modern Leader.* New York: Association Press, 1954.

Gwynn, Price H., Jr. *Leadership Education in the Local Church.* Philadelphia: Westminster Press, 1952.

Haiman, Franklyn S. *Group Leadership and Democratic Action.* Boston: Houghton Mifflin Company, 1951.

Leadership Education Audio-Visual Kit. Especially the filmstrips entitled "Leads to Leadership," "The Great Adventure," and "The Growing Teacher." New York: produced co-operatively through the National Council of Churches of Christ in the U.S.A., 1950.

Leadership Education Curriculum Handbook. New York: National Council of Churches of Christ in the U.S.A. Usually revised and published biennially.

McKibben, Frank M. *Guiding Workers in Christian Education.* Nashville: Abingdon Press, 1953.

Ross, Murray G. and Hendry, Charles E. *New Understandings of Leadership.* New York: Association Press, 1957.

Chapter 26

Educational Facilities: Building and Equipment

C. Harry Atkinson

THE WIDE, DEEP CHANGES WHICH HAVE SO SWIFTLY ENGULFED US IN RECENT
years are spurring our churches to re-evaluate their educational procedures and to
adopt new teaching tools. Serious efforts are being made to relate Christian education more intimately to the religious needs of sensitive, developing personalities and
to give religious teaching a more varied and effective impact. These carry important
implications for those persons who design and equip our church-school buildings.

Pertinent Questions

If our buildings are to meet the needs of growing personalities, set as they are
in communities with social involvements, we ought to know the answers to certain
pertinent questions before we proceed with building plans: (1) Who are the
people we are to serve? How many are in each age group now? How many will
there be in the future? (2) What are the general and the special needs to be met at
each age level? (3) How do we propose to meet these needs? What teaching
methods should we adopt in view of the great changes which have overtaken the
Christian educational movement in recent years? (4) How many pupils of a given
age provide the best learning situation in a classroom? What teaching procedures
bring the largest measure of desirable learning results? How many teachers are
needed in that room? (5) How large should each room be to provide the adequate
space to implement the teaching procedures we adopt? (6) What furnishings,
equipment, and teaching tools most effectively implement the learning process in
each age group? (7) What factors, physical and psychological, tend either to lower
or heighten pupil levels of interest and attention? (8) Do we propose to make
multiple use of space? If so, have we carefully evaluated such procedures? (9)
Have we organized a study or survey group made up of competent persons to get
the needed information and to interpret it to the church constituency so they
will be disposed to support a reasonably conceived program designed to meet the
educational needs of their church?

Right Answers

Getting the right answers to such questions is the first order of business for the
church. Until the church knows what her job is and how it should be done, the
architect cannot be expected to design the facilities and to create the environment

which furthers the creative communication of the mind of Christ to developing personalities. For the want of adequate pre-building research, far too many educational buildings are poorly planned; others are already outmoded; and some of them defeat the very purpose for which they were erected. To avoid such mistakes, we must train better church building leaders.

Practically every church has the human resources needed for a thoroughly competent building study or survey group. A vast amount of excellent written material and trained personnel is available in most of the major denominations to help churches prepare a thoroughgoing statement of building requirements. There is a considerable accumulation of educational experience in both secular and religious fields which can be adapted to the use of each particular church. The building-planning committee should be selected and organized to do the needed research. Their findings must be communicated in writing to the architect in such exact terms as to enable him to translate them into a structure which is functionally adequate, economically feasible, and aesthetically befitting its redemptive purpose.

A Co-operative Effort

A church-school building program should involve a great number of people. They must be carefully selected, organized, trained, and directed or the operation gets out of hand and bogs down under its own weight. Wisely directed, such a group makes possible the enlisting of new personalities, new ideas, and utilizes persons with special skills and aptitudes who may have been inactive previously. Awareness of needs and exposure to new ideas tend to widen the vision, to lift the standards of education, to prepare the people of the church for the sacrifices necessary to finance the building program, and to give the church members a new sense of responsibility. So conceived and carried out, the building program becomes a meaningful and rewarding project in Christian education.

The following chart suggests the kind of organization needed to draw up a program of church building requirements. This can be expanded by adding sub-committees or contracted by combining two or more committees and their functions.

Generally Speaking

There are many requirements which should characterize the educational building as a whole:

1. OPENNESS. The day of the grim, fortress-like church-school buildings with their formidable façades is, fortunately, disappearing. The same is true of forbidding, dark brown corridors through which sensitive little children so often are herded into uninviting classrooms or musty basements. Today's classrooms are livable and more intimate in feeling and proportion. Generous window areas and the openness of inviting doorways give pupils a sense of being welcomed into a cheerful, colorful, and pleasing place of many interests. Once inside, the pupil becomes aware, through wide window expanses, that the out-of-doors is visually, at least, another interesting dimension of his classroom. Young children in particular are relieved of any feeling of being fenced in.

Good landscaping will permit children to look out upon the objects that the God of growing things has brought into being. A secluded play yard or an open

The Building Council

```
Executive Committee or Cabinet

Comprising:
General Chairman of Council
Chairman of Working Committees
Pastor, ex-officio
```

```
Working Committees

1. Survey                          5. Administration and Special Facilities
2. Worship and Arts                6. Plans and Construction
3. Rooms and Equipment             7. Finance and Promotion
4. Fellowship and Recreation
```

```
The Church Constituency
```

Committees 2, 3, 4 will need to work together to avoid cross purposes.

court can be designed to be reached directly from the children's classrooms. Flowers, shrubs, bird feeding stations, and other out-of-door features add to the further delight and development of growing children. Such physical features favorably condition the attitudes of children and elicit desirable responses.

2. LIGHT AND COLOR. The sense of well-being, the desired levels of attention, and the conduct of pupils are conditioned by the use of light and color. Meaningful religious experiences are more likely to be engendered in surroundings that are comfortable, cheerful, elevating, and aesthetically pleasing. The use of light and color should be carefully considered together by persons with more than a casual understanding of their use. Color should be chosen in terms of the prevailing and required light intensity needed for all of the various wall areas and work areas of each room. Changing the color value on the wall surfaces and floors of a room modifies the quality of the light. Likewise, when we change the light intensities we modify the color values.

Soft, cheerful, pastel shades are usually preferred to the very strong overstimulating colors. If flat paint is used in predominantly neutral shades, walls will serve as pleasing backgrounds against which to place accents of color and beauty such as pictures, works of art, window draperies, vases of flowers, and objects of interest to children. Strong brightness and darkness contrasts so tiring and sometimes injurious to sensitive eyes should be avoided. It is important that light of adequate intensity reach all working surfaces in all parts of each room. Someone has rightly said, "No nerve can relax if the eye is not comfortable."

In order to get even, adequate light intensities throughout a classroom, it is sometimes necessary to use a combination of electric lighting and daylight to reach the areas farthest from the windows. Otherwise, some areas may be too bright and others so lacking in proper light intensities as to cause eyestrain, inattention, and discipline problems. In some instances, it is necessary to control the light from out-of-doors by the use of light-diffusing glass blocks, sheet glass designed to filter intense sunlight, or by use of properly installed venetian blinds, outside canopies or other window shades.

3. VENTILATION AND TEMPERATURE CONTROLS. Our concern for the physical well-being of pupils and for the high levels of interest and attention we strive to elicit from them, makes adequate ventilation and properly controlled temperature essential. Educationally speaking, little is accomplished where air is foul or temperatures cause physical discomfort. Discipline is difficult to maintain. Regular attendance drops, due to the absences arising from the high incidence of infectious illnesses prevailing where classrooms are not properly ventilated. Drafts which impinge directly upon pupils or lower or raise temperatures too suddenly are also hazardous to their health.

The increasing use of projected visual materials calls for the use of opaque window covering to control unwanted outside light. These shades should be installed in such a way as to assure good ventilation in those rooms which must be aired through the window openings.

Air conditioning is now looked upon as a wise investment in practically all parts of our country. Where budgets do not permit its immediate installation when new buildings are being erected, provision should be made in the construction for later installation of the conditioning system. We emphasize the importance of adequate ventilating, heating, and temperature regulating systems in all buildings used for educational purposes.

4. SANITATION. It is advisable to have toilet facilities for preschool children accessible directly from the room they occupy. If junior fixtures are not installed, a movable step should be placed in front of each fixture to permit use by smaller children.

Church-school buildings which are occupied for shorter periods of time, do not need as elaborate toilet installations as the public schools. They do need readily accessible separate toilet rooms for males and females. Doors leading to these facilities should preferably not be in close proximity to each other. An opaque screen should be placed in each toilet room to shut off any view of the interior from the hallway. Each toilet room should also be equipped with one or more hand basins, soap, and towel dispensers. All floor surfaces should be covered with materials that are waterproof and impervious to strong soap and disinfecting solutions. Adequate ventilation is also required by law and should be maintained at all times. Walls, ceilings, and dividing partitions should be painted with a high gloss enamel paint or its equivalent. Glazed tile provides a durable sanitary surface which is easily cleaned and maintained.

Sinks with drain boards are now being installed in classrooms occupied by children up to and including elementary school age. Such installations permit preparation of materials used for handicrafts, for cleansing dishes and implements used in the classroom, and for the washing of hands, thereby avoiding staining clothing or soiling objects in the classroom.

Accessible splash-proof drinking fountains in close proximity to classrooms are needed for the well-being and comfort of those occupying the educational building. Where needed, a low step should be placed by each fountain for the convenience of the little children.

Where food is handled, every precaution should be taken to provide an adequate supply of hot water, heated to such temperatures as will insure that all hands and dishes are perfectly sterilized. This is a very important but often neglected requirement.

Churches should maintain the highest standards of sanitation and safety. Regrettably, many of them take advantage of the leniency extended by public officials and fail to maintain sanitary standards. Constant inspection to maintain sanitary standards should be the responsibility of the properly constituted boards or committees of the church. The church should safeguard the health of the community and respect the sensibilities of those who are rightly offended by the lack of good housekeeping.

It is particularly incumbent upon those churches providing child care for very young children that all facilities and personnel adhere to the highest sanitary measures. Very special care should be exercised in areas where children's food is stored and served. All toys, dishes, and objects handled by little children should be thoroughly cleaned after each use. The same applies to bedding, resting pads, floor coverings, and floor surfaces. Where church facilities are used on Sundays and for weekday nurseries, good sanitation is particularly important for the welfare of children.

5. SAFETY. Tragic happenings in public and religious school buildings emphasize the urgent need for adequate protection against fire hazards. A solemn moral responsibility rests with churches whose buildings do not afford the needed protective installations. Even new buildings that have merited a low insurance premium rating are often found to be unduly hazardous for human beings. Restricted exits, inaccessible stairwells without fire resisting doors at all floor levels, and long corridors finished with inflammable materials are exceedingly dangerous. Deadly flash fires sweep swiftly through these areas. Many times children perish from smoke, fumes, and excessively hot air even though flames have not actually reached the rooms in which they are at work.

Church boiler rooms and stairways should not be used for storage purposes but kept free from inflammable materials. Adequate storage should be provided for such materials.

6. STORAGE SPACE. Many of the fire hazards to which we have made reference are the result of inadequate storage space. Most church buildings lack proper storage facilities. Such space should be carefully designed for the tools and materials needed for the teaching procedures in each specific area of the building. The so-called catch-all "walk-in" storage closets are no longer recommended. It is far better to have the storage cabinets built to order. The same is true of open shelves. These need to be designed for ready accessibility and carefully geared to the requirements of each age group.

Many materials in constant use, particularly for children's rooms, can be stored in low space dividing cabinets mounted on casters and readily moved from place to place. They are used to divide floor space, to control teaching procedures and/or to bring teaching accessories to the area where they are needed. Storage walls can be built between classrooms. Provision should be made for books, pictures, maps, handicraft material, audio-visual equipment, papers, pencils, crayons, and a great variety of other objects. In some instances, cabinets should be designed to take a few extra folding chairs and even a small folding table or two so they can readily be put into use when occasions demand.

In many of the newer buildings an additional 10 per cent is added to the recommended floor space per pupil per room to insure that there is plenty of storage area without encroaching upon the teaching space. Convenient storage eliminates hazardous objects from hallways and other places where they endanger human welfare, and prevent unnecessary marring of the building. It contributes to the safety, convenience, neatness, time-saving efficiency, and to the flexible, multiple use of space.

7. Acoustics. Despite the great variety of corrective materials available and the accumulated knowledge governing their effective use, churches continue to erect buildings that are acoustically deficient. In some instances, the reverberation of sound within the classroom makes good teaching almost impossible. In other situations, distracting noise emanating from outside the classroom comes in through the heating or the ventilating system or from corridors which have not been acoustically treated. The extensive use of glass, high-gloss enamel paints, polished terrazzo or cement floors, hard plaster ceilings, and cement blocks or other hard surfaced masonry in our modern buildings tends to accentuate acoustical difficulties unless given proper care. In many instances, the natural sound absorbing qualities of the fabrics of the building are ruined by the application of too much of the wrong kind of paint. This paint closes the pores of the fabric and thus shuts off its sound absorbing values.

Attempts at economy that dispense with soundproof walls and doors, good acoustics, or which invite distracting noises from improperly installed mechanical equipment are unwise. Churches need to realize that there is a point beyond which they cannot economize, if they are to produce a building suitable for the Christian education of their constituency. A building can be made too dead as well as too lively as far as acoustics are concerned. This is particularly true in rooms where musical instruments or choirs need the extra lively quality which makes for good music. Both extremes should be avoided.

The sound of joyous, happy children engaged in purposeful activity, while it may be a bit distracting to adults, is music to the children. The intensities of such sound need not be bereft of their liveliness.

8. Circulation. A well-planned building makes ample but not extravagant provision for safe, ready access to each room or facility without the necessity of passing through other rooms. Some of our older buildings are very deficient at this point. What could be good classroom floor space is often tied up in assembly rooms which are used for but brief periods. Otherwise, this valuable space is little less than a glorified hallway.

In most communities, the building codes dictate the width of corridors in relation to the pupil loads of the rooms which open into the corridors and also the number and the sizes of the entrances and exits from the building to the out-of-doors. Codes or no codes, our buildings should be designed so people can move about in comfort and without loss of time. Handrails, wide stair treads, low risers, and well-lighted stairwells will prevent accidents and facilitate movement through the building.

Where classroom doors open into the corridors from both sides, such doors should not be placed opposite each other. A staggered arrangement eliminates traffic congestion and prevents accidents where children tend to rush from classrooms to corridors. Long hallways often become raceways where boisterous children endanger themselves and others. These hazards can be overcome by placing double hung doors at intervals. Reception areas where adults can be placed will serve to control traffic problems occasioned by the exuberance of the younger generation.

Access and egress for parents with their preschool children should be away from the heavily traveled corridors. The newer buildings provide separate entrances for the very young children and their parents. Ample reception areas are essential if we are to keep parents from the classrooms. These areas can be equipped with informal furniture, a reading table, a bulletin board, appropriate literature, and a display of books dealing with the religious nurture of children.

Overcrowded corridors invite accidents, raise disciplinary problems, and are extremely hazardous in times of emergency. On the other hand, ample corridors make access to the building pleasant and provide space enough for social greetings and for brief conferences with pupils and teachers.

9. FLEXIBILITY. The change from the passive "sit and listen" classroom methods to the permissive type of teaching with its group learning situations, its greater variety of teaching techniques, less formality, and more pupil participation in the purposeful activities provided calls for fewer but larger classrooms. These classrooms are manned by a team of teachers who, while they do not have any more pupils per teacher, work together in promoting a planned, co-operative and co-ordinated program for the whole group. Pupils may at times divide up into small units within the same room to participate in purposeful learning activities in keeping with their aptitudes and interests. This calls for "types of activity space," movable furniture, functional space dividers, and, perhaps, portable screens with ample surfaces for displaying materials relevant to the class procedures of the day. Such classroom floor areas can be adjusted to the requirements of the particular group and to the program agreed upon for the particular occasion. This type of flexibility is needed. It stands in striking contrast to the more arbitrary arrangement of space where small, cell-like rooms are clustered as satellites about a large assembly room.

Today, many church educational buildings are erected with nonload bearing partitions between classrooms. These curtain walls of masonry or other sound resisting, durable materials can, if occasion demands, be removed without appreciably marring the building or incurring great expense. Moreover, partitions can readily be installed when it is necessary to divide a large area. This gives the building a considerable measure of flexibility. The flexibility recommended for each classroom should characterize the building as a whole. It is important that the building site be large enough, and that provision be made in the master plan for additional units to be readily added to the original building as needed. Such flexibility permits caring for increased attendance and provides for such changes in teaching procedures as may come because of population changes or by the adoption of different teaching methods.

Churches frequently insist upon a specified style of traditional architecture. This may often arbitrarily dictate that the arrangement of interior space conform to a predetermined spacing of windows or doors. While the desire to build a church "that looks like a church" is commendable, it may handicap the architect in working out an effective floor plan. The building should be planned from the inside out. The wise church will work closely with the architect to make certain that the religious functions of the building are adequately provided for and are not restricted by some predetermined pretty form of ecclesiastical architecture.

10. SPACE. Adequate space—more and more space—is the urgent demand of the Christian educational leaders. Lack of space can be a serious handicap in all teaching situations, particularly where children are concerned. Certain standards of square footage per pupil per age group have been agreed upon as essential for the experimental learning in relationships which make religion most meaningful. These will be set forth specifically later in this chapter. We shall now deal with those considerations which apply generally to the educational building.

Classrooms which are practically square in shape or approximate the dimension ratios of five feet to six feet are recommended. Such rooms permit interest and work groups to occupy each of the four corners. The center can be kept open for use of the group as a whole and as a vantage point from which supervision and ready communication from the leader to the several work groups are facilitated. Wall spaces are also important. They provide areas for displaying many kinds of valuable visual materials and background for worship settings.

Floor space gives character to a room. For this reason materials and colors should be chosen with care. Floors can refract a considerable amount of light coming in through windows. Light colors best serve rooms where light intensities are low. In no case should floor coverings be dark and forbidding. Floor areas should be kept sanitary and should be given particular care in rooms where the little children sit and play upon such surfaces during most of the time when in the building.

Learning spaces for Christian education need to be adequate in area but also— and this is often forgotten—they need to carry a qualitative character befitting their sacred purpose. Religious educators, building committees and architects ought to give far more attention to making our religious buildings less barren and cold and institutional in feeling and more pleasing and distinctly spiritual. Too much emphasis cannot be placed upon the importance of providing a suitable environment for each learning situation. This does not necessarily mean added expense. In most instances, skillful handling of fabrics, colors, and materials by the architect, will suffice. A great deal has yet to be done in interpreting to the architect and to the churches themselves the fact that Christian education calls for distinctive treatment of space within each room in keeping with its aims and procedures.

Financial limitations—some real and some imagined—and the urgent need for space lead churches to resort to multiple use of facilities or to reduce room areas to meet a budget which is sometimes predetermined without a proper sense of meeting critical needs. The latter alternative should be strenuously avoided. Let us build what we do build in keeping with the recommended standards. We must not overcrowd and over-stimulate our children and reduce the spiritual effectiveness of our teaching methods. Multiple use of space has a great many problems connected with it, yet it is far better that a church in its beginning resort to multiple use of its facilities rather than erect a functionally defective building. True, multiple use calls for very exact programing, good administration of teaching time, and the skillful handling of traffic in and out of the building. Otherwise, the time devoted to education will be interrupted, teaching periods shortened, and the effectiveness of the program impaired.

In many instances, if the program had been adequately conceived in the beginning and the needs communicated intelligently to the constituency of the church as a whole the requisite facilities would have been provided. In instances where financial resources are not available to provide all the space needed, we again emphasize the importance of doing what we do in keeping with the recommended standards. Resort to multiple use of space will serve until such time as the building can be completed and the needed teaching equipment furnished.

Space and Equipment for Each Age Group

The following recommendations governing space and equipment are generally accepted by the Division of Christian Education of the National Council of Churches. They are presented in detail in *Building and Equipping for Christian Education,* a normative book recently published by the Council.

Preschool Children

There is a difference of opinion among Christian educators as to whether or not children of less than two years should be brought to the church-school building. Where the church encourages parents to bring such children, child care should be under the provision of trained personnel. Every sanitary precaution should be exercised to assure the safety and well-being of these children. Rooms occupied by children of the preschool age are rated as follows: thirty-five square feet per pupil is rated good; thirty square feet per pupil is rated fair; twenty-five square feet per pupil is rated poor. The latter is rated poor for the reason that children are overcrowded and overstimulated, and teaching procedures suffer seriously as a consequence. Pupil loads per room vary as follows: Where cribs are used they should be spaced at three-foot intervals and not more than eight to ten cribs in a room. For two-year-olds, eight pupils per room is considered good; ten fair; and twelve poor. For three-year-olds, up to fifteen pupils is considered good in a single classroom; fifteen to eighteen fair; more than eighteen poor. Pupil loads for ages four and five years, up to twenty is rated good; twenty to twenty-five fair; and over twenty-five pupils poor.

Furnishings and teaching tools for children should be selected piece by piece with great care by competent persons. Churches should confer with their denominational leaders and read the literature provided by them when planning the furnishings and equipment for the preschool children. It is very important that all toys and other materials handled by these children be kept sanitary, that they shall be free from sharp edges or injurious substances such as paint or dye.

Elementary School Children

Here the floor space required per child is reduced slightly and the pupil load per room is increased: thirty square feet per pupil is rated good; twenty-five square feet per pupil is rated fair; twenty square feet per pupil is rated poor for children of this age. Twenty-five pupils per room is considered good; twenty-five to thirty fair; thirty to thirty-five poor.

Furnishings, display areas, and teaching aids should match the needs and capacities of this age group. Visual materials need to be placed on the walls at eye level of this particular age group. Every care should be exercised to assure the needed flexibility in each room so variety and interest can be achieved and an interesting and challenging curriculum can be brought to the physical, psychological, and spiritual development of these children.

The energetic, highly imaginative children of this age, conditioned as they are by their public-school experiences, associate modern teaching facilities and modern teaching tools with education. The church cannot afford to suffer too greatly by comparison if she expects her efforts in the religious field to be effective. Environment is an often neglected but very important consideration, especially where sensitive children are involved. The great variety of materials and the several items of equipment which are needed in the classrooms used by elementary school children are detailed at great length in *Building and Equipping for Christian Education.*

Youth

Special needs confront us at each of the several age levels within this age group. Program facilities and equipment should be very closely related to their problems and capabilities. Admittedly, our youth programs are the weakest link in our Christian educational system. As a consequence there is at present less to offer in the way of recommended building and equipment standards than for other age divisions of the church school. A great deal of study is now in progress looking to the improvement of our youth programs. Churches should give critical attention to the successful procedures being developed co-operatively at both denominational and interdenominational levels, while seeking to improve their own programs.

In a recent article Hamlin G. Tobey says, "The key word to successful work with young people is 'involvement'—making certain youth are so involved in the life of the church as to participate enthusiastically in its activities." [1] Such involvement affects our buildings and equipment at two points. First, there will be less demand for formal worship centers in the rooms used by youth groups in the Sunday church school. Youth are now encouraged to participate in the regular Sunday worship services of the church. Large assembly rooms for departmental worship will no longer be called for. Training in worship can be conducted occasionally in the church chapel or in the nave of the church at such times as it is not otherwise in use. Sunday evening youth fellowships can also devote time and use to such suitable rooms as are available for conducting their own worship services.

Second, the successful involvement of youth requires rooms and teaching tools geared to a meaningful program which includes many creative, purposeful activities. Role playing, handicrafts, group service or study projects, buzz discussion groups and other similar forms of procedure are suggested. These can supplement and enhance the teaching impact of other teaching procedures.

Youth classes need to be large enough to afford the learning values of group relationships and group participation, and yet they should not be so large as to prevent careful guidance or to relegate the less aggressive members of the class to a passive, non-participating status. Junior-high-school groups of fifteen to twenty pupils with two or three adult leaders present and working as a team within the same classroom are recommended. Rooms should provide approximately eighteen square feet of space per pupil. Pupil loads per room should not exceed

[1] "The Church and Our Youth," *Protestant Church Buildings and Equipment* (February, 1958), p. 91.

twenty persons. Some leaders now propose twenty-five square feet per pupil to assure plenty of space for flexibility of use and for the variety of teaching procedures carried on in their classrooms. Much the same provision should govern the classrooms assigned to high-school students with the exception that the pupil load per room is increased to twenty to twenty-five persons, presided over by a lead teacher and two or three co-operating associates.

Youth by virtue of their natures and needs should be provided with attractive, informally furnished rooms which can be used as classrooms and as socially inviting meeting places. A fireplace, easy chairs, pleasant surroundings, a kitchenette or kitchen privileges, the use of the church social hall, and ample, conveniently accessible storage space, will add to their effectiveness. Detailed lists of equipment and teaching materials for youth rooms may be found in the publications of most major denominations. A complete statement is included in the youth section of *Building and Equipping for Christian Education.* In his article, "The Church and Our Youth," appearing in the pamphlet entitled *Christian Education Today,*[2] Hamlin G. Tobey offers further helpful suggestions on providing facilities and equipment for young people.

Adults

The rapid growth of the adult constituency and the newer approaches to Christian education call for a restudy of the church facilities assigned to this age group. There is a shift away from the large adult classes and their passive lecture teaching methods to smaller groups where active participation by all class members in study, discussion and research are the order of procedure. Audio-visual techniques, buzz groups, role playing, discussion groups, as well as the lecture method, now characterize adult learning.

Adults meet on Sunday and during the week to participate in a great variety of creative activities which are meaningful to them. Adequate space for these various teaching methods requires from eighteen to twenty square feet per person in the classroom instead of ten to twelve square feet usually assigned where the lecture method is the only teaching system employed. A room measuring 18x25 feet or 20x30 feet will amply care for twenty-five adults and at the same time provide the flexibility required for the newer concepts and the great variety of activities needed for a well-rounded educational program. Adult rooms should be attractive, well-lighted, and cheerful in their decor. Light intensities within adult classrooms should be adjusted to adult requirements. Informal furniture, floor lamps, tables approximating 4x4 feet in area, some comfortable straight-backed chairs to use with these tables or to provide seats for those who find difficulty in using the lower upholstered chairs, portable chalk boards or turnover charts, attractive window shades or other means for controlling the light when projecting audio-visual materials, appropriate pictures for the walls—these are some of the useful items needed to furnish and equip the adult classrooms.

Adult facilities should preferably be placed on the ground floor to assure easy access from outside and to eliminate climbing stairways. All areas traversed by older persons should be equipped with nonskid floor materials. Passageways should be well-lighted, and hazardous features, if such there must be, should be clearly defined. Preparing and sharing food with those of their own age is a happy

[2] New York: Christian Herald Association, Inc., 1958.

experience for older persons, particularly for those who do not have access to kitchen facilities. The church kitchen or a conveniently placed kitchenette should be made available for their use. Access to suitable books in the adult section of the church library, craft rooms equipped with tools, table games, a quiet chapel affording privacy for religious devotions, add much to the church's ministry to these people. There should be a place for recreation and for social affairs planned by the adults themselves.

Other Considerations

We have, for the most part, been dealing with the requirements of the Sunday church school because of its very large demand for space and its call for a great variety of equipment. There are many other features which ought to be included in the church building. We will mention but a few. First, there is need for well-planned and well-equipped office space from which to effectively administer the church's program as a whole and its educational procedures in particular. Provision should also be made for an accessibly located library attractively furnished and equipped and stocked with carefully selected books for all ages. Today's church needs a library for audio-visual materials and for curricular materials. Counseling rooms, recreation facilities, choir rehearsal and dressing rooms, place for a music library—all these and many more should be in the purview of the planning committee. Music, the arts, drama, choral speaking and such other activities as can be cared for budgetarily and in terms of leadership, should also be included.

To make certain that all requirements are met and that multiple use is made of space wherever feasible, the planning committee should first list, age group by age group, all the facilities and equipment needed for the Sunday church school. The committee should then list the other Sunday activities and place them opposite the group upon which they impinge. A similar listing of the many weekday activities and their requirements should also be prepared. If this material is assembled in three perpendicular columns and all activities are placed opposite the Sunday church-school age groups upon which they impinge, it will then be possible to design each room to meet most, if not all, the requirements of each particular group.

Each function has many ramifications, structurally speaking, and involves certain mechanical implementation which must be included in any well-planned effectively functioning building. We stress the importance of thoroughly studying and reducing to a clearly written statement what the church plans to do and how it plans to do it, the quantities of space required, and the qualities which should characterize the teaching environment. Such a program is the backbone of a successful building program. It is from such conceiving that the competent architect can proceed to create a building which will be an adequate tool for the teacher and an environment for the pupils—"sensitive to their emotional needs and conditioning their responses."

Churches, which of necessity have to carry on their educational programs under far from ideal conditions can, until such time as better facilities are made available, apply the principles and approximate the ideal methods which characterize all good Christian education. This may call for many adaptations of both space and methods, but let us be assured that, according to Virgil E. Foster's very helpful book *How a Small Church Can Have a Good Christian Education.*

In the words of Lawrence B. Perkins, "To design for learning is to seek fitness, order and beauty, and to place them in the service of those who learn as well as of those who teach."

Bibliography

Atkinson, C. Harry. *Building and Equipping for Christian Education.* New York: National Council of Churches of Christ in the U.S.A., 1956.

Department of Health, Education and Welfare. *Designing Elementary Classrooms.* Washington: U. S. Government Printing Office.

———. *Planning and Designing the Multipurpose Room in Elementary Schools.* Washington: U. S. Government Printing Office.

Flexible Classrooms. Detroit: Carter Company, 1953.

Foster, Virgil E. *How a Small Church Can Have Good Christian Education.* New York: Harper and Brothers, 1956.

Gable, Lee J. *Christian Nurture Through the Church.* New York: National Council of Churches of Christ in the U.S.A., 1955.

Perkins, Lawrence W. *Work Place for Learning.* New York: Reinhold Publishing Corporation, 1957.

Planning Schools for Use of Audio-Visual Materials, Book No. 1. *Classrooms* (1953); Book No. 2, third edition. *Auditoriums* (1953); Book No. 3. *Audio-Visual Instructional Materials Center* (1954). Washington: National Education Association.

Using Audio-Visuals in the Church. New York: National Council of Churches of Christ in the U.S.A., 1950.

The reader's attention is also called to the numerous guidance manuals and pamphlets issued by the various denominations. Inquiries regarding these should be directed to the board of education of the denomination from which additional information is desired.

Chapter 27

Religious Education in Church-Related Colleges and Universities

J. Edward Dirks

THE INSTRUCTION OF CATECHUMENS IN CHRISTIAN FAITH DURING THE FIRST centuries of the church's history was broadened by the time of Augustine to include an interest in the larger task of education in the liberal arts. In the early Middle Ages the desire to consecrate the humane learning of Greece, to secure the assistance of the liberal arts for biblical studies, and to express the theological idea that (in Anselm's words) "we believe in order that we may understand" combined to place an increasingly higher value on the tradition of learning within the church. The resulting synthesis of Christian faith and rational learning, identified primarily with Thomism, became the foundation upon which many of the earliest Western universities were established. They were "communities of scholars" whose rational pursuit of truth embraced the heritage of human knowledge, and they carried on their pursuit within a Christian framework.

Some of the limits imposed by ecclesiastical bounds were broken in the period of the Renaissance and Reformation, but even where much of the scholastic philosophy was rejected the churches of the Protestant tradition continued to place higher learning within a Christian context. Many leaders of the Reformation contributed heavily to the continuing educational tradition which related classical learning and religious instruction.[1] Some of the centers of learning which combined humanist and Protestant influences also encouraged new developments in the natural and social sciences. The scriptures and the natural world were viewed as two related sources of true knowledge, and the mind engaged in seeking precise knowledge was believed to render an acceptable service to God.[2]

The basic substance of the tradition of higher learning had been provided, as we can see, by the medieval university and the Reformation academy before it was transferred to the shores of the New World. As soon as the early settlers had

[1] E. Harris Harbison, *The Christian Scholar in the Age of the Reformation* (New York: Charles Scribner's Sons, 1956).

[2] See J. W. Ashley Smith, *The Birth of Modern Education* (Naperville, Ill.: Alec R. Allenson, Inc., 1955); Also, Howard V. Hong (ed.), *Integration in the Christian Liberal Arts College*, pp. 6-36.

cared for immediate needs—the securing of their livelihood, the founding of civil government, and the worship of God—they attended to the advancement of learning. Alongside the church and the State, the college served as the third primary institution in "one seamless garment of responsible democracy." [3] A major theme, closely related however to a number of theological motifs, undergirded the development of most American higher education throughout the period from the founding of Harvard in 1636 to the Civil War. George H. Williams states it as "that of the co-ordinate authority and the relative autonomy of the University in respect both to the Church and to the State." [4] Nevertheless, this segment of history shows that higher education's internal relations were closest to the church, whereas it depended upon the State for its exterior forms and privileges.

The westward movement of higher education was, therefore, carried out under religious auspices and directed by a Christian philosophy. Intellectual efforts united with evangelical fervor established new colleges in great profusion along the advancing frontier. During the early decades two main lines were dominant; one emanating from Congregational New England and the other from Presbyterian centers in New Jersey and Pennsylvania. With the migration of Lutherans into the Midwest, colleges patterned originally after the *gymnasium* began to appear. Soon thereafter, other advances were under way; the larger and fast-growing Methodist and Baptist denominations took up the challenge, along with many of the other churches and religious groups. Several hundred permanent institutions reflecting a "theological idea of the university" had been founded on the edges of the wilderness by the time of the Civil War. They mark a steady academic procession expressive of a persistent concern of the church with higher learning.

Most of these institutions were, in varying ways, church-related. Some of them, having had no direct denominational ties, became privately endowed and affirmed a status similar to such institutions as Harvard and Yale. Still others became the foundations of state-supported universities. A large number, however, have continued an identification with the denomination which founded them. Though many differences mark their relationships, these institutions constitute the present group of more than 450 church-related colleges and universities in the Protestant tradition.[5] In general terms, the following characteristics apply to them, though not uniformly: (1) The board of trustees, though self-perpetuating, will include a certain number or proportion of members of the denomination; (2) Financial support of the college is provided, in part, by the denomination; (3) The make-up of the key administrative officers, and sometimes of the faculty, reflects the denominational relationship; and (4) Requirements in religious education, and sometimes in worship, are included in the total college program.

---

[3] George P. Schmidt, *The Liberal Arts College* (New Brunswick: Rutgers University Press, 1957), p. 29.

[4] *The Harvard Divinity School* (Boston: The Beacon Press, 1954), p. 311. His development of this theme and the related motifs is available also in the booklet, *The Theological Idea of the University*.

[5] The United States Office of Education in 1959 reported the existence of 771 church-related colleges and universities, of which 486 were Protestant, 280 were Roman Catholic, and 5 were Jewish. *Education Directory, Part 3: Higher Education*, edited by Theresa B. Wilkins (Washington: U. S. Dep't. of Health, Education and Welfare, 1959), p. 11.

Some Current Problems and Issues

Since the middle of the nineteenth century complex problems and issues have marked not only higher education's general growth, but they have arisen with peculiar urgency and relevance for Christian colleges and universities. Denominational ties tended to weaken under the dual pressure of the reaction to sectarian religious influences in a society of increasing pluralism and the pervasive impact of secularism within the larger cultural context and especially within higher education. Such pressures as these tended, moreover, to reinforce a major shift which was taking place in relation to the earlier theme of co-ordinate positions for State, church, and college. No longer was it being assumed that the church and the college should maintain close, internal relations, while the exterior form and privileges of higher education would derive from the State. The roles of church and State tended to become reversed as the major developments of colleges and universities became increasingly the province of the State. With changes such as these, institutions which had been founded with a local community or a denominational constituency in mind were either forced to become larger and more cosmopolitan, serving a wider national constituency, or they were superseded by institutions which had the capacity to fulfill such a mission.

Within the Western academic tradition a historian can readily delineate some of the major changes which brought into being the "modern" university. Technological and democratic motifs assume the primacy once ascribed to the liberal arts within a Christian framework. The emphasis upon specialization, technical mastery, and ongoing research derives inescapably from the importance of the sciences and the lesser values attached to the arts, and utilitarian aims which view higher learning as the avenue to reach for more desirable work and greater economic security provide little incentive for intellectual reflection or spiritual growth. One writer summarized his analysis of the changes in the following statement: "Within the universities as without, these two influences, the technological and the proletarian, are in course of producing a new culture; and this differs sharply from that in which universities originally were nourished and took their shape." [6] A similar type of evaluation is expressed in the concern that over the past decades "the pursuit of knowledge and the training for function in society have been falling apart; we have irresponsible learning on one side, and, equally irresponsible, technical competence on the other, with disastrous results to our culture; [this] has happened because they have been no longer held together in the context of Christianity." This same writer goes on to say that, "for the saving health of our education and our culture, we must bring them together again into a fruitful relationship . . . This is the task of the Christian college." [7]

A third general area of problems for church-related institutions arises from an altered concern of the churches with respect to higher education. Most of the denominations related to colleges continue to affirm educational objectives; they maintain their defined responsibilities; and they understand higher learning to be the child of religion. But at the same time these are the same churches which have undertaken the additional responsibility of providing their ministry and outreach to

[6] Sir Walter Moberly, *The Crisis in the University*, p. 49.
[7] Marjorie E. Reeves, "The Christian College in the Western World," *The Christian Scholar*, Supplement Issue, XXXVII (Autumn, 1954), 189.

students and faculty members in many other, most of them larger, institutions. These extensive responsibilities are part, moreover, of a religious program which can frequently be supported, provide facilities, and employ personnel far beyond the scale which is possible in a smaller church-related college. At the same time, though such a college's constituency may also have become extremely diversified and though it may reflect the pluralism of society about it, the assumed unity of its program and objectives in Christian terms may make it extremely difficult for the college to provide a diversified religious approach. This problem may in turn be reflected in its denominational relationships, since a unified theological perspective may not encompass the churches' divergent responsibilities in church-related higher education and in privately endowed or state supported universities.

Problems of these dimensions and issues of these kinds are a large part of the background of the church-related institutions' recent attempts to reconsider and restate the particular and essential characteristics of their nature and purposes. These problems and issues have been faced with greater urgency than ever before in the years since the end of World War II. It is still too early to indicate the nature of the results which are emerging from the many studies which are taking place. But, it can be noted that churches, faculty members, administrative officers, and also students have engaged together in extensive self-examination. Between 1950 and 1954 some 350 institutions engaged in a national self-study project, which was entitled, *What Is a Christian College?* [8] The gradual identification of several common concerns has led to a large number of continuing studies, to faculty retreats and conferences, to the organization of laymen for a better understanding and support of these institutions, and, perhaps most important of all, to two national conferences of representatives of church-related colleges and universities, one in 1954 and the other in 1958.[9]

Recent Restatement of Educational Objectives

Some of the distinguishing characteristics of church-related institutions of higher education have already been noted. They, for the most part, maintain particular and definable types of relationships, through trustees, administrative officers, faculty members, or student constituencies, with their parent denominations. They provide a program of religious instruction and observance, frequently requiring some fulfillment of religious obligations as a normal part of the academic and extracurricular program. They are usually small, residential colleges, giving emphasis to close personal relationships as an essential ingredient of higher education. Though these are important marks which reflect the nature of the college, equally important has been the emphasis upon certain distinctive educational objectives.

Perhaps the most prominent traditional objective has been the affirmative and consistent attitude toward the place of religion in higher education. The energies of these institutions have been devoted to religion on the basis of the view that the spirit deriving from religious sources should underlie and motivate the entire life of the institution. While this has been a consistent interest, a number of

[8] This project was conducted under the auspices of the Commission on Higher Education of the National Council of Churches; a report of the project is available.

[9] Both convocations are fully reported in supplement issues of *The Christian Scholar*, the first in a supplement for autumn, 1954, and the second a supplement for the autumn, 1958.

writers have noted significant shifts. One such writer, treating primary historical sources, has noted the following changes: (a) "A gradual shift from a defensive to a more positive attitude"; (b) "The progress from a sectarian to a nonsectarian emphasis or spirit"; and (c) "The distinction between mere interest in, and self-assumed responsibility for, the religious life of the students." [10] In summary he goes on to say that "the interest of the church-related colleges in religion has proceeded to the recognition of their own obligation to function." [11]

The recognition of the centrality of a religious objective has also tended to focus more specifically upon Christian faith itself. During recent years studies of these institutions have tended increasingly to use the term "Christian Colleges" to identify not only their nature but their aims. One of the early self-study guides prepared by representatives of these institutions states that, "A Christian college is . . . separated from other institutions of higher learning only by its faith. . . . It is the Christian's ultimate educational philosophy that the search for and transmission of truth are processes most effectively carried on within the framework of a dynamic religious conviction." [12] The concern these colleges have recently given to the need that they occupy a distinctive role in American higher education undoubtedly accounts for the renewed emphasis upon their Christian character. This is made explicit in the report which reads, in part, "if these church-related colleges have no distinctive educational or religious function, then it may be objected that the Church has no business (theologically speaking) maintaining colleges." [13]

Closely related to the restatement of religious objectives is the renewed emphasis which has been given to academic and educational objectives. If educational excellence is to be measured in relation to endowment figures, extent of buildings and equipment, size and adequacy of resources, it is objected that these standards do not readily fit the way of determining quality in church-related institutions. The most useful field of educational service has been found by these colleges in the type of program which emphasizes the liberal and cultural studies, offers small but often excellent basic courses in the sciences, and generally aims to give a broad, fundamental outlook on life based upon not only a selective undergraduate curriculum but upon the quality of the community engaged in it. As colleges of the liberal arts they seek to develop attitudes toward truth from all the humane sources of knowledge, stressing the belief that openness to truth is a Christian characteristic in itself.

While it is true that an increasing number of these colleges acknowledge the way in which tensions arise from their desire to give attention equally to their Christian and their academic objectives, it must also be noted that there has been a twofold development in this regard. First, there has been less tendency than was formerly true to assume that piety would in itself be a value for such a college apart from high standards of excellence. Though high standards could not always be achieved and maintained, these were less often due to the greater interest in

[10] Merrimon Cuninggim, *The College Seeks Religion* (New Haven: Yale University Press, 1947), pp. 51-63.

[11] *Ibid.*, p. 62.

[12] *What Is a Christian College?* A Summary Progress Report, December, 1951, p. 266.

[13] "Theological Foundations of the Christian College," *The Christian Scholar*, XLI (Autumn, 1958), 274. Used by permission.

religious concern. Secondly, the demands for excellence were increasingly interpreted as implications of the Christian claims of the colleges; that is, the
Christian faith, more theologically understood, has been an incentive directly
related to the aim of educational quality. The interrelated aspects of the challenge
are well-stated in the following passage:

> The Christian college as it ought to be would be in essence a two-fold reality: an
> academic and a Christian community, at once restlessly searching for truth and resting its
> life in the worship of God who has disclosed himself in Jesus Christ. It would give through
> its faculty an example of high intellectual competence and concern. It would expect of its
> students, as they lived in fellowship of the Christian community, a life of intellectual
> excitement, endeavor and achievement. It would manifest in its life an attitude of free
> and open respect for ideas. It would, again in freedom out of the richness of Christian
> community, scrutinize the social, political, economic, and intellectual dimensions of our
> common life. As a part of the Christian community of faith it would dare to be a college,
> a part of the Western tradition of the University. As a college it would dare to be a
> Christian community.[14]

Three "dimensions" are treated, therefore, in the interrelation of Christian
and educational objectives: (a) Openness in attitude toward knowledge and truth;
(b) Sense of community with respect to relations among persons; and (c) Ac-
knowledgment of responsibility with respect to society. These summarize the ways
in which in recent restatements of objectives distinctly Christian and educational
concerns have been brought into mutual relationship.

In a statement which sets forth a broad area of minimum goals and purposes
which are believed to be common to both Roman Catholic and Protestant institutions of higher education, and for the achievement of which both groups can
work together, the Christian college is defined in functional terms.

> [The Christian college] . . . is a community of teachers and students seeking to know
> the nature of the universe created by God and the kind of society in which man can live
> according to God's will. Education in this context enables a student to learn and grow
> within a framework of a meaning and purpose that unifies and orders his knowledge,
> illumines his appreciation, and gives direction to his existence. The Christian college offers
> to our generation an interpretation of the whole of knowledge, a way of life and learning,
> and a sense of earthly vocation and eternal purpose, without which the sciences and arts,
> inventions and technology may enslave and destroy mankind.
>
> This Christian conviction of the unity of truth, of the love of God, and of man's
> nature as a child of God is the surest safeguard of freedom, high ethical and moral
> standards, and social responsibility. Further, we affirm this commitment to the freedom
> of our colleges and universities under God is the ultimate safeguard of these institutions
> against domination by the state or by other forces within our culture.
>
> For these reasons church-related colleges—upon which this Christian higher education
> depends—must be maintained at all costs.[15]

In the pursuit of these goals and purposes more than financial support in increasing
amounts is needed. A Christian philosophy of higher education which is both
theologically oriented and can guide practical developments is called for. A redis-

[14] *Ibid.*, p. 284.

[15] *Information Service*, Bureau of Research and Survey of the National Council of Churches,
XXXVII (March 8, 1958), 4. Used by permission of the Association of American Colleges.

covery of the distinctive place of the liberal arts and sciences within the academic and cultural context is needed. The importance of a responsible academic community needs to be more widely acknowledged if intellectual quality and fundamental human freedom are to be interrelated in the way suggested above. The restatement of educational objectives, which has been moving along at a rapid pace in these institutions, must still find secure foundations and a reinforcing environment.

Religious Education in the Curricular Program

General statements of objectives have their significance. However, these must be translated into particular terms in order to assess the programs of religious education in church-related institutions of higher education. We shall include reference here to (a) course offerings in departments of religion or Bible, (b) provisions for college worship under the direction of the institution itself, and (c) the role of "religious perspectives" in various fields of study and in the concern for integration within the educational program.

Curricular offerings in the study of religion are provided in all church-related colleges; students are normally required to either take certain prescribed courses or to elect a minimum number of courses to meet standards set for graduation. The extent of course offerings and of required work varies greatly among the colleges, but two general statements can be made. (a) At least a full academic year of study is the average requirement, according to a recent study of selected institutions, and (b) the extent of course work offered in religion is normally inclusive enough to realize the following major objectives:

1. To develop a student's knowledge of the contents of the scriptures, providing some acquaintance with critical problems concerning the text and problems in biblical interpretation; in addition to the development of knowledge, as such, the aim is that of having the Bible's contribution to a Christian philosophy of life made vivid.

2. To provide a factual background study of various living religious traditions through historical and comparative study of literary resources, in order that the kinds of insights which educated persons should have into the whole of man's religious experience may be discovered by the student.

3. To consider the history and contemporary issues of Christian thought, so that the ethical, psychological, and intellectual problems raised by religion may be understood, that interests and skills essential for effective participation in the Church may be developed, and that foundations for further study may be provided those who plan to enter professional Christian vocations.

4. To stimulate a critical approach to religious faith, on the grounds that such a faith adopted after careful intellectual scrutiny is more wisely and firmly held than if it is adopted apart from critical studies.

5. To understand and appreciate the variety of man's religious experience, and to deepen an awareness of the relation of religion to other areas of culture and to various academic fields.

Course offerings in the area of Bible and religion are usually of four distinct types. The first, and often the basic, type of course work is biblical, using survey approaches in introductory courses and more intensive and limited aspects of study for advanced offerings. The second type of course work is historical and comparative, and, though it is usually elective, attempts to examine the general phenomenon of religion in human culture and thought or to give attention to the various specific religions. The third type of course work is more philosophical, dealing with problems of an intellectual order; the relation of religion to ethics, to philosophy, to science, or to other areas may be found to be stressed; or the more analytic type of critical reflection upon religious problems is pursued. The fourth type of approach is with respect to practical courses, primarily those designed to develop skills for leadership in the Church or in Christian education.[16] The discipline of religion is therefore conceived so as to include work in Bible, history of religion, religious thought (philosophical and theological), and applied religion (religion in personal and social life).

The development of studies in religion, when this is related to the concern for liberal learning, is designed not only to provide resources in the area of faith. Together with the pursuit of other disciplines, the study of religion may be said to serve as a means to develop students' abilities to think clearly, to enlarge individual intelligence, to cultivate sensitivities and sharpen moral judgment, to understand the world of human affairs and ideas, and to relate the intellectual endeavor to the ultimate questions of human existence. These are therefore studies intimately related to the liberal arts, joining other disciplines to bring students face to face with "the issues of truth, values, and faith as they arise in human experience." [17]

Two primary groups of persons are related most directly to courses and requirements in the area of religion in church-related colleges. The role of administrative officers is large because they influence the way in which religion is emphasized through published statements, guidance and selection of faculty members, decisions in matters of policy and educational program, and the admission and orientation of students. More directly involved are those members of the faculty who are appointed to teach the courses in religion. A recent statement indicates the kind of aims which are stressed: "Because there is no teaching area in the church college more important than the area of religion, attractive, capable teachers who will be at least the equal of teachers in other disciplines should be secured." [18] A list of desired achievements and qualities is given as follows:

The religion teacher should possess a Ph.D. degree or equivalent in the appropriate field. In any case, academic qualifications should not be less than those expected of teachers of like standing in the institution.

He should be a person of unquestioned Christian commitment.

He should be committed to teach, and trained specifically to teach Bible and religion to undergraduates.

He should be able to win students to an intelligent understanding of the Christian faith, rather than confuse or repel them through an unwise use of the all-too-familiar "shock treatment."

[16] Many of the findings with respect to course offerings in religion are based upon a survey done by the author; the report in full was published in *Religious Education*, LIV (March-April, 1959).

[17] H. Richard Niebuhr, Daniel D. Williams, and James M. Gustafson, *The Advancement of Theological Education* (New York: Harper and Brothers, 1957), p. 91.

[18] *Religion in the Church College* (Nashville: Board of Education, The Methodist Church, 1953), p. 11.

His academic effectiveness should be enhanced and encouraged by limiting his extra-classroom assignments on the basis of his teaching load.

He should have good rapport with the churches served by the college, and should be in sympathy with the program of the Church.[19]

These requirements provide occasion to point out that church colleges conceive of the study of religion as being important in relation not only to the liberal arts, but in direct relation to the perspective of a Christian commitment and with reference to the church.

Closely connected with curricular courses in religion, the provision by church-related institutions for services of worship is also distinctive. During recent years two problems in this area have received extensive consideration. The first has had to do with the problem of "required chapel," this having been subject to question with increased pluralism in the student and faculty constituencies. Recent studies have shown that requirements are in general maintained, though they have been greatly modified to allow for needed flexibility. The other problem has centered on the issue of "the college church," which as a "congregation" served by a chaplain has raised certain theological and ecclesiastical questions.[20]

Church-related institutions normally provide for worship, pastoral care, and religious counseling through an administratively appointed chaplain or director of religious activities. In addition to official duties and frequently some teaching, such a person usually also provides the co-ordination of extracurricular religious activities. The broad way in which these tasks are usually defined is a source of both strength and weakness, according to a recent study.[21] The primary tasks include these: (1) Preacher and Teacher; (2) Director and Counselor; (3) Faculty and Administrative Functions, including relationships to student organizations, activities in the Church and the wider community.[22] With the increasing demand for development of religious programs for the campus, the numbers of officially designated college chaplains have grown and the range of their duties has been enlarged. With increased specialization of functions, they have been called upon to direct and express the college's religious outlook and to represent it in its relationships.

Religious Perspectives and Curricular Integration

In addition to course offerings in religious studies and provisions for worship, church-related institutions have been concerned also in exploring the relation of religion to other studies, religious perspectives in all teaching and study, and the integration of the curriculum around a Christian philosophy of education. This wider interest in religion indicates the desire of these institutions to assign the responsibility for developing religious interest and knowledge throughout the whole academic program; it reflects the assumption that, from a Christian stand-

[19] Ibid.

[20] See published pamphlets by the National Association of College and University Chaplains on this subject, 1955-57.

[21] See Seymour A. Smith, The American College Chaplaincy (New York: Association Press, 1954).

[22] Ibid., pp. 47 ff.

point, truth is a unity and interrelationships of knowledge can be stated. The vocation of the Christian teacher or student is seen to be limited not to the area of religious studies alone but to all aspects of knowledge.

In these broader discussions of religion in higher education there is an increasingly wider recognition of the role that presuppositions have in the pursuit and the transmission of knowledge. Knowledge in various fields is being viewed more generally as having sociological and personal reference; it is less widely claimed that knowledge is wholly objective and that its transmission must be undertaken with academic neutrality.[23] This does not reduce all knowledge to purely subjective terms, nor does it seek to diminish the proper role of objectivity in all intellectual inquiry. Instead, religious affirmations are acknowledged as being among the kinds of presuppositions which are essential to the enterprises of human knowledge; the perspectives that are inherent in the historical religions can be explored in relation to the fields of inquiry.

In the conservative statement of the positive role of religious perspectives, four assertions are made:

1. A religious perspective requires the teacher to give due weight to the religious facts which are relevant to his field.

2. A religious perspective enables the teacher to recognize the limitations of the method used in his field.

3. A religious perspective affects profoundly the interpretation of facts in a field of study.

4. A religious perspective may often be expressed more effectively through the personal qualities and attitudes of the teacher than through anything else he says.[24]

The acceptance of such a perspective in the academic community provides Christian teachers and students a point of relation between their work and their faith; it can also guide students in religious interests and values in ways integral with their so-called secular studies.

What is more, a church-related college is provided a new opportunity to examine its religious center as an integrative focus for the program of study. The fragmentation of higher education has been widely acknowledged, and the concern intelligently to reintegrate the areas of study has been persistently expressed. Additional courses and programs of general education have been seen as having only limited values. What is being sought is more in the area of integrative perspectives and qualities; the education offered by the church-related college is being relocated within a context which is at once organic and rooted in the Christian identification of the institution. In a study devoted to this specific topic, the central thesis is stated as follows: "the Church has a definite stake and a special interest in liberal education. Since the liberal studies deal with the central powers and the core studies of human knowing, they constitute the unique and decisive area of education where the Christian viewpoint can and must make its impact." [25] Some experimentation in curricular interrelationships and the exploration of the

---

[23] For a fuller discussion of this theme see Arnold S. Nash, *The University in the Modern World.*

[24] Hoxie N. Fairchild (ed.), *Religious Perspectives in College Teaching* (New York: Ronald Press Company, 1952), pp. 32-36.

[25] Howard V. Hong (ed.), *Integration in the Christian Liberal Arts College,* p. 68.

meaning of knowledge from Christian perspectives are the forms in which church-related institutions are seeking to be colleges of liberal education with a Christian philosophy radiating from their center.

Extracurricular Religious Programs

Classrooms, libraries, and laboratories are not the exclusive centers of education. The campus in its community life, its ethos, and its co-curricular program, also contributes decisively to the college's total educational program. Concern is, therefore, often expressed by administrations and faculties for the college's promotion of an atmosphere favorable to the intellectual, spiritual, and moral growth of its members. Only as a campus is conducive to study and promotes a Christian spirit does it surround the curricular and official provisions for education and religion for their maximum effectiveness. The Christian spirit in college life may be defined as humility, unselfishness, helpfulness, generosity, objectivity, and freedom from envy in personal relations among both students and faculty.[26]

Church-related institutions tend to give special emphasis to the way in which the college as a whole must accept responsibility for the moral, the spiritual, and the intellectual formation of its students. Dormitory life, social functions, eating places, and the like, are viewed as contributing to such development of integral persons. More particularly, a program of religious activity is provided; it consists of organized groups, such as a Christian association, a series of addresses on issues of religious interest, discussion groups on topics of Christian concern, and others. These are usually co-ordinated through a council of students, sometimes including faculty members, and through the work of the chaplain.

During recent years interest has been expressed increasingly in developing ways which would help to realize two expressed needs—(1) That the ministries of the churches would themselves be more effectively represented than they are in church-related institutions, comparable to the way in which they serve students and faculty members in larger private or state-supported universities; and (2) That there should be closer intercollegiate, interdenominational, and international relationships provided for the Christian groups in church-related institutions. These are closely related. The major Protestant churches have expanded their college and university ministries greatly during the past several decades; their efforts have given rise to student Christian movements, many of which work closely together at regional and national levels, and all of which are related through the United Student Christian Council [27] to the World's Student Christian Federation. Yet it is often true that such ministries have not been effectively expressed in relation to colleges and universities of the type we have been describing. Hence, the experience of conferences, of the use of study resources, and of the sense of common fellowship which they have provided have not been extended to church-related institutions. Several new developments are currently taking place to remedy this situation. At the level of faculty interest and work, it is important to note that the program of the Faculty Christian Fellowship has been strong in church-related institutions as in other types of colleges and universities.

We can bring our review of the situation in these institutions to a close with

[26] See A. John Coleman, *The Task of the Christian in the University* (New York: Association Press, 1947), pp. 19 ff.

[27] The United Student Christian Council became the National Student Christian Federation in September, 1959.

some comments about the way in which they have been important to the church's rethinking of its attitude toward the academic enterprise. Many factors have contributed, but most important are three. First, the development of the "ecumenical movement" in recent decades has recalled the church to its unity and its mission in the world; it has challenged the churches to deepen their reflections about the nature of their identification with higher education. Secondly, recent Christian thought has been described as evidence of a "theological renaissance" in both the quality and quantity of scholarship in this area. This has required new understandings of the essential content and relevance of Christian faith; it has called for the recognition that theology is properly, not queen, but servant of the sciences.

Thirdly, the relation of the church to human culture has been brought into clearer focus, through a more penetrating delineation of the alternatives than was true in the nineteenth century,[28] and a more realistic understanding of the challenge to the church when it is called upon to participate in culture with critical discernment but with affirming responsibility. The consequence for education of the view that the church is faithful to its mission only when it participates beneficially in cultural life is a basic reaffirmation of the significance of academic inquiry, a concern to see the total unity of truth and the wholeness of being beneath all the contradictions and uncertainties, and a primary rediscovery of man's intellectual creative world as the heart of the cultural context. As this development enriches the intellectual and the spiritual life of the colleges their relations to the church may come to be defined not by historical and organizational ties alone, but they will give emphasis instead to the view that the nurture of the community of faith within the community of learning is a basic Christian responsibility, shared both by the church and the institutions of learning.

Bibliography

Brown, Kenneth I. *Not Minds Alone.* New York: Harper and Brothers, 1954.

Espy, R. H. Edwin. *The Religion of College Teachers.* New York: Association Press, 1951.

Ferré, Nels F. S. *Christian Faith and Higher Education.* New York: Harper and Brothers, 1954.

Fuller, Edmund (ed.). *The Christian Idea of Education.* New Haven, Conn.: Yale University Press, 1957.

Hong, Howard V. (ed.). *Integration in the Christian Liberal Arts College.* Northfield, Minn.: St. Olaf College Press, 1956.

Moberly, Sir Walter. *The Crisis in the University.* London: Student Christian Movement Press, 1949.

Nash, Arnold S. *The University in the Modern World.* New York: The Macmillan Company, 1944.

Von Grueningen, J. Paul (ed.). *Toward A Christian Philosophy of Higher Education.* Philadelphia: Westminster Press, 1957.

Williams, George H. *The Theological Idea of the University.* New York: Commission on Higher Education, National Council of Churches of Christ in the U.S.A., 1958.

---

[28] See H. Richard Niebuhr, *Christ and Culture* (New York: Harper and Brothers, 1951).

Chapter 28

Religious Education in
Public Higher Education Institutions[1]

Robert Michaelsen

PUBLICLY SUPPORTED INSTITUTIONS ARE PLAYING AN EVER LARGER ROLE IN higher education in the United States. Today more than 50 per cent of the students in colleges and universities are in public institutions. In all likelihood this figure will continue to increase. These facts have much significance for religious educators. Religious groups can no longer rely on their own colleges and universities to educate their members in "the faith" or even to train their future leaders.[2] These facts are also of significance to the welfare of the nation as a whole. We cannot be sanguine over the prospect of a religiously illiterate people.

Variations in Religious Education

Practices in religious education at publicly supported institutions of higher education in the United States vary widely. There is no single common pattern. Some state or public institutions are very little different from many private or church institutions in their approach to religious education. Most of the state colleges and universities in this nation grew up in a predominately Protestant atmosphere. In many instances this meant the carry-over of patterns followed by Protestant institutions of learning. Courses in religion have frequently been a regular part of the curricula. Compulsory chapel was at one time a common feature among state colleges and universities. It has almost ceased to be so today, but there are still many publicly supported institutions of higher learning that have a chapel on the campus, and some sponsor regular worship services—usually of a Protestant nature. A number of such institutions employ chaplains.

Some state institutions, established in a more secular atmosphere, have **not**

[1] This chapter concentrates on the state universities and colleges of the United States.

[2] In my own state (Iowa) there are, for example, twice as many Methodists enrolled in the State University of Iowa as in the four Methodist-supported colleges in the state put together. If one includes the two other state-supported institutions of higher education in the state of Iowa, the figures become more impressive still. The total enrollment of Methodists in the four Methodist institutions (Cornell, Iowa Wesleyan, Morningside, Simpson) is approximately 1,290. The total number of Methodists in the three state-supported institutions of the state is over 6,082. (Figures for the academic year 1958-59.)

historically been particularly friendly toward religion. This has been especially true in some Great Plains and Western states where state constitutions are rather stringent in their prohibitions against public support of "sectarian" or religious teaching or of religion in any form.

Other publicly supported institutions of higher education have attempted, especially in recent years, to reflect the religious pluralism of American culture by permitting or encouraging religious activities on the campus under the sponsorship of all religious groups represented among the student body. Some have even attempted to reflect religious pluralism in their curricular programs in religion.

The first amendment to the federal constitution, prohibiting the establishment of religion by the federal government, has been of some importance in determining the pattern of relationship between religion and the publicly supported institutions of higher education. More important, however, have been state constitutions, local customs and practices, and the attitudes of university administrators and faculties. There have been no legal cases on the national level on the question of the state college's or university's approach to religion. There has been only one case on the state level directly concerned with this subject.[3]

Some Recent Developments

1. Work of the Religious Groups. One of the most significant developments in recent times has been the increasing amount of interest shown by the religious groups in their concern for religious education in the publicly supported institutions of higher learning. Seymour Smith reports that

contrasted to roughly 200 full-time professional workers employed by the churches for campus work in 1938, by 1953 the number had jumped to almost 1,000. In 1953 Catholics and Jews reported roughly 100 and 75 respectively; the remaining 825 were employed by the major Protestant denominations.

Smith goes on to point out that "the inclusion of the substantial number of local pastors and others giving part time to campus work would make these figures even more impressive. . . . Equally impressive increases in operating budgets and allocations for buildings and equipment have also taken place." [4]

Referring to the "rash of religious centers that has 'broken out' on or near the university campus," Glen A. Olds indicates that "the Catholics list 500, the Jews 200, the Lutherans 400, the Methodists 350, the Baptists 300, (and) the Episcopalians 200. . . . In values," Olds points out, "these centers range from modest 'homes' to multi-utility buildings worth upwards of $2,000,000." [5]

Most of the larger religious groups have created national organizations as means of co-ordinating and channeling their interest in the religious life and the religious

[3] Sholes vs. Board of Regents of the University of Minnesota, 1953. Mr. Sholes sought *mandamus* "to compel the University of Minnesota and its Board of Regents to adopt and enforce rules and regulations prohibiting the use of university property and facilities for aiding sectarian religious activities." The case was thrown out by the Supreme Court of the State of Minnesota on the grounds that Sholes had not exhausted available administrative remedies, i.e., that he had not taken his case directly to the Board of Regents. (*Minnesota Reports*, vol. 236, pp. 452 ff.)

[4] Seymour A. Smith, *Religious Cooperation in State Universities: An Historical Sketch* (Ann Arbor: The University of Michigan Press, 1957), p. 75. Used by permission.

[5] "Religious Centers," *Religion and the State University*, ed. Erich A. Walter (Ann Arbor: The University of Michigan Press, 1958), p. 226.

education of students in publicly supported institutions. Generally the work of these organizations is undertaken on the local campus through a religious foundation or center. The relationship of the religious center to the university varies from almost complete detachment to direct participation in the co-curricular or curricular work of the university. Activities range from those of a social nature to those concerned with serious study.[6]

2. The Work of Colleges and Universities. Paralleling and sometimes complementing the growth in church interest in religious education in publicly supported institutions has been the increasing concern shown for religious activities by the institutions themselves. This has been a long-standing concern, but with expanding enrollments since World War II it has been expressed in a "stepping up of the appointment of chaplains, coordinators and directors of religious activities employed by the universities themselves." Today about half of the state universities have some such officer.[7]

Institutions such as Ohio State University and the University of Minnesota have appointed co-ordinators of religious affairs who are attached to the office of student affairs. The primary function of these co-ordinators has been one of encouraging religious activities while not actually directing them. The co-ordinator works closely with the various religious groups and foundations in order to facilitate their work. He is appointed as an impartial representative of the university who will facilitate rather than originate or dominate religious activities. In many instances he will work through some sort of interreligious council. The appointment of such an officer represents the university's recognition of the importance of religious pluralism and also its limited responsibility for the religious life of the student.

The University of Michigan offers one of the most interesting case studies among the publicly supported universities. Interest in the religious life of the student has been vigorous at that university since its founding. A number of different approaches have been employed. With the creation of the Student Religious Association in 1937, the university took a direct hand in initiating religious activities. For various reasons this approach was considerably modified in 1954 with the appointment of a co-ordinator of religious affairs who is immediately responsible to the vice-president for student affairs. The co-ordinator heads a staff whose purpose is "to encourage the religious growth of students as an important part of educating the whole person." It is felt that this purpose can be carried out

through creating and facilitating relationships between the university and the religious resources available to it, including those provided by the churches and religious foundations, and through a program which 1) provides services to the instructional program of the university, and 2) builds attitudes which recognize religion as a valid area of intellectual inquiry and as an appropriate resource for the student's growth to responsible citizenship.[8]

At Pennsylvania State University, where there has been a chaplaincy since the nineteenth century, a major restructuring of the program in religious affairs has occurred in the recent past. This reflects, in part, the fact that an increasing number of Jewish and Roman Catholic students are attending the institution. It

[6] *Ibid*. Olds reports that the latter is on the increase.

[7] Smith, *op. cit.*, p. 76.

[8] C. Grey Austin, *A Century of Religion at the University of Michigan: A Case Study in Religion and the State University* (Ann Arbor: The University of Michigan Press, 1957), pp. 79-80.

is also an indication of the concern of the administration at Penn State to have an officer who would deal with religious affairs on its behalf. In addition to co-ordinating activities, the chaplain administers the university facilities for religion, including the Helen Eakin Eisenhower program center designed for use by groups of all faiths. Further, he is expected to "stimulate and maximize the religious life and affairs on the campus." In particular this means that

the chaplain's office is responsible for the administration of Sunday services in the University auditorium . . . and he takes initiative in developing and executing strategy for the total religious life in the university, represents the religious affairs of the university on official occasions, and performs religious counseling services.[9]

Like Penn State, a number of state institutions have developed a structure which indicates an interest going beyond co-ordination. In some instances chaplains function in much the same way that a Protestant chaplain would function in a church-related or independent college. In other cases a director of religious activities serves as an initiator and stimulator of religious activities. In still other institutions Y.M.C.A. secretaries have been designated as the institution's co-ordinator or director of religious activities.[10]

It is clear that although publicly supported institutions are in some sense "secular" institutions, an impressive amount of time and money is spent on religious activities in the majority of these institutions. Separation of church and State in America has not usually entailed antagonism between the two nor has it meant separation of religion from public education at the higher levels. If religious activities are accepted as symbolic of interest in God, any reference to the public institutions as "godless" is completely groundless.

Curriculum

While it may be part of the popular mythology that religion is not taught in state colleges and universities, it is quite evident that the opposite is so. Seymour A. Smith points out that "over ninety-five per cent of the major state universities, by one device or another, do make provision for courses in religion." [11]

At the same time, it is necessary to point out that the course offerings in these institutions vary from one or two courses offered in some department other than religion to more than thirty courses which form a full-scale curriculum in a single department or school of religion. Also, the patterns followed by the various institutions differ a great deal.

Generally six types of structure are evident: (1) Isolated regular courses listed in departments or divisions of the college or university but not specifically under the heading of religion. These courses usually appear in such fields as English literature, history, Oriental and classical languages, philosophy, psychology, and sociology. (2) A department of religion which operates generally as any other department in the college. (3) A department of religion and philosophy in which courses in both areas are taught under one departmental structure. (4) A depart-

[9] Smith, *op. cit.*, p. 92. Used by permission.
[10] *Ibid.*, p. 95. Smith points out that the use of Y.M.C.A. secretaries is especially common among Southern institutions.
[11] "Religious Instruction in State Universities: A Report of Recent Trends," *Religious Education*, LIII, 3 (May-June, 1958), 290. Smith's study included seventy of the larger state universities and colleges. He indicates that his sampling of additional state colleges "did not reveal an appreciably different over-all picture" (p. 293).

ment of philosophy which has a large number of offerings in the field of religion. (5) A school or institute of religion controlled and financed by one or more religious agencies but officially recognized by the college or university, credits being accepted either directly or approved for transfer. Schools and institutes of religion are usually incorporated and responsibilities are vested in a board of trustees. (6) Denominational courses sponsored by religious foundations and taught by direct arrangement with pastors. (In some institutions this pattern is designated by the rubric "Bible Chairs.") Each denomination is financially responsible for its own teaching personnel and for meeting certain conditions regarding facilities, equipment, and academic standards. A limited number of credits may be accepted by the college or university toward graduation requirements. Combinations of these types may be found in a number of institutions.[12]

Types of courses offered also vary greatly. Most commonly found are courses in Bible, ranging from a literary introduction to the Bible to a whole host of courses on various aspects of the Bible such as the prophets, the life and teaching of Jesus, the philosophy of the Old Testament, the early Christian Church, the theology of Paul, the archaeology of the Bible, and the like. Another common course is one that deals with some aspect of the living religions of the world, approached either historically or comparatively or both. Also quite common are courses in the philosophy of religion, the sociology of religion, and somewhat less common, the psychology of religion. Others include the history of Christian thought, religion in America, the history of Christianity, the Reformation, the Catholic faith, post-biblical Judaism, and the like. Courses specifically in the field of religious education are not common. For the most part the courses in religion offered in the publicly supported institutions are of a liberal arts nature and are not designed specifically to prepare the student for any type of professional service. While many public institutions offer a major in the field of religion or a program designed for pre-ministerial students, the majority of students who take courses in religion are non-majors or nonspecialists. Very few institutions offer advanced degrees in the field of religion. To my knowledge only one state university (Iowa) offers advanced work toward the Ph.D. degree in religion.

Patterns and Course Offerings in Specific Institutions

Twice in this century schools of religion have operated briefly at the *University of Michigan* (from 1908 through 1914 and from 1924 to 1926 with a series of lectures by scholars in religion for three years after that). More recently an interdepartmental degree program in religion and ethics has been initiated. The guiding principles of this program are as follows:

1) Religion is far too complex a fact of human life and history to fall fully within the academic competence of any one individual or department. 2) To understand the nature of the religious phenomena requires a multi-disciplinary approach. . . . 3) Theology has

[12] This typology was developed by Professor George W. Forell after he had spent the academic year 1951-52 making a nation-wide study of the teaching of religion in state colleges and universities. Dr. Forell's study was carried out under the sponsorship of the Division of Student Service of the National Lutheran Council and the Student Service Commission of the Lutheran Church Missouri Synod. The results of the study were privately circulated in a mimeographed report entitled *Survey of Credit Courses in Religion at Public Institutions of Higher Learning.* I am grateful to Forell for access to this report. It is the most thorough study of the subject that I have seen.

always traditionally been a normative discipline. The university in this country has not felt itself to be the proper platform to the presentation of religious norms as something which ought to be accepted by students. This does not, however, exclude the possibility that various theologies of importance in human history can and ought to be studied in the university. . . . This is best done within the existing framework of the university in the Department of Philosophy or History (especially intellectual history).[13]

The program of studies in religion at the University of Michigan is at present under the supervision of a committee appointed by the dean of the College of Literature, Science, and the Arts. This committee is responsible for recommending matters of policy with regard to the curriculum in religion, introduction of new courses, securing of new faculty members, and supervision of the concentration program in studies in religion. Eleven departments of the University of Michigan currently offer credit courses in the field of religion.

The rationale of the department of religion at the *University of North Carolina* is one which takes very seriously the role of the "Judaeo-Christian" tradition in our culture and, even more specifically, the nature and significance of Christianity. The major concern of the department is with "Biblical literature, the history of religious thought, and the implications of Christianity for current thought and practice." The department is informed by "the belief that Christianity is relevant to the whole of knowledge." For this reason, the department seeks to relate the study of the Bible and religion to the work of other departments, and courses in religion are also offered in related fields.

The catalogue statement points out various advantages to majoring in religion including the fact that students might gain "through their liberal arts education an aptitude for church leadership." The statement also indicates that "programs of study leading to M.A. and Ph.D. degrees are not presently offered but will be proposed in the future." [14]

The department of religion at *Oregon State College* is "non-sectarian in spirit and organization" and is committed to a "historical and critical approach to the literature and organization of religion." Courses are determined, for the most part,

to fit the needs of students who are preparing for service in the fields of Science, Engineering, Agriculture, Home Economics, Teaching, etc. Special attention is given to the religious education of those who anticipate lay leadership in churches of their local communities and those who plan to enter social service or religious vocations.[15]

The chairman of the department of religion at Oregon State is also chairman of the department of philosophy.

The *University of California* reports in its catalogue that

students interested in the study of religion either from the standpoint of liberal education, or of preparation for the ministry or some other phase of religious education, may select a major in one of the departments germane to the purposes of the student, or they may

[13] *The Teaching of Religion in State Universities,* a mimeographed document prepared for The First National Consultative Conference on Religion and the State University at the University of Michigan, November 16, 1958, compiled and edited by Milton D. McLean and Harry H. Kimber, pp. 32-33. Cf. Austin, *op. cit.,* pp. 24-25, 36-42.

[14] *The General Catalogue Issue,* The University of North Carolina, March 24, 1958, No. 589, p. 376.

[15] *Bulletin,* Oregon State College, 1958-59, p. 143.

propose an individual group major, or they may elect a suitable combination of courses under the general curriculum. Courses appropriate for such purposes may be found in a number of departments.[16]

A perusal of the California catalogue, however, indicates that there are very few offerings which relate specifically to the study of religion.

In contrast to the curricular offerings in religion at most state schools, those at *Oklahoma State University* are designed, in significant part at least, to prepare students for professional service. It is one of the few state universities which has a department of religious education within the College of Education. Among the courses offered in this department are church administration, methods of church school instruction, directing youth groups in the church, and religious organization leadership outside the church. There are also courses of a more general liberal arts nature.[17]

In 1948 a department of religion was established at *Michigan State University* within the division of social science of the College of Science and Arts. The basic principle upon which this department was founded and upon which it operates "is that religion is not only an integral part of a culture but is a field of knowledge, properly constituting, therefore, not only an appropriate but an indispensable area of teaching and inquiry in a university." It is stressed that courses within the department are taught descriptively and that the department has divorced itself from any official connection with campus religious activities in order to maintain the "principle of objectivity." Courses are offered at all levels some of which even carry graduate credit. There is no major in religion but a graduate minor may be taken in the field.

A noteworthy aspect of the department is the fact that the instructors include:

1) lecturers or chaplains of religious organizations who fulfill appropriate educational requirements and who are *invited* to participate in the program, 2) regular staff members who are on dual appointment with other departments of the university, and 3) at present one full-time staff member.

Courses include an introduction to religion offered in three sections by Protestant, Catholic, and Jew.[18]

The School of Religion at the *State University of Iowa* has been offering courses in religion since 1927. The school was founded on the assumption and conviction that "religion is inseparable from education, and that it therefore should be taught, in a tax-supported institution as well as in other institutions of higher learning, comprehensively and in line with the best educational practice." The primary goal of the School of Religion is to aid students in reaching a better understanding of the role of religion in human culture and experience. Major emphasis is placed upon the religions of Western culture. Courses are also offered in non-Western religions, however. Wherever possible an effort is made to afford students the opportunity to study a particular religion under an articulate representative of that religion who is also academically qualified to teach in the university. Thus the School of

[16] *Bulletin*, The University of California, Berkeley, 1958-59, p. 70.
[17] *Catalogue*, Oklahoma State University, 1958-59, pp. 92, 220.
[18] McLean and Kimber, *op. cit.*, pp. 13-17.

Religion staff is interreligious in nature with Jew, Catholic, and Protestants included. These men have full faculty status being appointed both by the Board of Trustees of the School of Religion and the Board of Regents of the State of Iowa. Salaries of the teachers come from non-state (private and denominational) sources. The state meets the administrative expenses of the school including the salary of the administrative director. The school offers such courses as Old Testament, New Testament, introduction to Catholicism, Christian ethics, Protestant faith, Catholic faith, post-biblical Judaism, living religions of mankind, and religion in America. At the same time the school welcomes and encourages the study of religion by the various disciplines in the university which can and do legitimately have an interest in this field.

The School of Religion offers an undergraduate major and programs leading to the M.A. and Ph.D. degrees in religion. Graduates are required to be well grounded in the thought and practice of Judaism, Roman Catholicism, and Protestantism, to gain a degree of competence in other major religions of the world, to have a strong minor in a field related to religion, and to specialize in a particular area of religious or theological studies.[19]

Courses at the *University of Illinois* are offered through the various denominational centers. The university approaches each foundation as a separate educational institution from which it accepts or transfers credit for courses offered in that foundation. These courses, however, are submitted to a university committee for approval and a university representative investigates the course and the adequacy of the instructor. Courses are currently offered by a United Protestant program and by Southern Baptist, Lutheran, Episcopal, Roman Catholic, and Jewish Foundations.[20]

Conferences and Projects

The role of religion in publicly supported institutions of higher education has been the subject for a number of studies and conferences in recent years. Just ten years ago (1949) a significant major interreligious conference was held on this subject at the University of Minnesota. Several sessions have been held at the same university since that time, including a conference of faculty and administrators of state colleges and universities of the Upper Mississippi Valley in 1955. Out of this conference came a continuing committee which has developed a number of significant study projects in the area of religion in the state university.

The most significant recent conference was The National Consultative Conference on Religion at the State University held at the University of Michigan in November, 1958.[21]

Other conferences in related areas include the Allerton Park (Illinois) Conference

[19] M. Willard Lampe, *The Story of An Idea*, Bulletin No. 740, State University of Iowa, March 1, 1958. State University of Iowa Publication, *Catalogue 1958*, pp. 52 and 126. McLean and Kimber, *op. cit.*, pp. 36-40.

[20] McLean and Kimber, *op. cit.*, pp. 54 ff.

[21] See Henry E. Allen, *Religion in the State University: An Initial Exploration*, Minneapolis, 1950; "The Place of Religion in the Curricula of State University," *Religious Education*, L, 5 (September-October, 1955); "Religion and the State Universities: A Report," *Religious Education*, LIV, (March-April, 1959); and the special issue of *The Journal of Higher Education* on "Religion and the State University" (April, 1959).

in 1956 on Religious Activities and the State University, the Conference on Religion in State Teachers' Colleges held at Yale in 1951; and the Conference on Religion in Junior Colleges held at Southern Methodist University in 1955.[22]

Significant developments of a somewhat different nature include the five-year study of teacher education and religion carried on by the American Association of Colleges for Teacher Education with the assistance of a grant from the Danforth Foundation and the program of the Danforth Foundation designed to assist colleges and universities in establishing new departments of religion. Although neither of these programs is concerned solely with publicly supported institutions they do have much relevance for such institutions.[23]

Problems and Conclusion

Perhaps the problem that bulks largest in the minds of the layman is the legal question raised by the principle of separation of church and State. It seems quite fair to say that this problem has been overemphasized, and that the principle of separation of church and State has been treated in a doctrinaire fashion as if it were entirely clear that this principle meant that there should be no teaching of religion in the state or publicly supported institutions. The facts indicate that there is teaching on a very broad scale and that this teaching has rarely been legally challenged. The opinions of legal experts vary on this issue. Most agree that the university is on perfectly safe grounds so long as it is seeking to live up to its responsibilities as an educational institution and so long as religion is presented in an academically acceptable manner and in accordance with the principle of voluntaryism.[24]

From the standpoint of the faiths possibly the most pressing and significant question is that of being relevant in the context of the "secular" college or university. It is quite possible that future developments will raise serious doubts about the relevance of the foundation or center which has become a standard fixture on most campuses. It is my personal impression that the religious groups might be wiser to put less money into buildings and more into the finding and training of men and women well qualified to "speak" to the needs of the intellectual community, less time and energy into building-centered activities and more exertion and ingenuity meeting the students where they are.

In the area of teaching one of the chief questions concerns the place of religion in the curriculum. An increasing number of college and university administrators are taking a direct interest in curricular programs in religion. We shall probably see more committees, programs, and chairs in religion but not a significant increase in the number of departments or schools. There is an understandable reluctance among university administrators and faculties to develop a full-scale program in the form of a department or school. This is likely to create more

---

[22] See "Religious Pluralism on the Campus" in *Religious Education*, LI (November-December, 1956) and "Religion in State Teachers Colleges," Yale Divinity School, 1952.

[23] See *Teacher Education and Religion*, A. L. Sebaly, editor, published by the American Association of Colleges for Teacher Education (Oneonta, New York, 1959).

Thus far seven institutions have been assisted in establishing new departments of religion by the Danforth Foundation program. Four of these are publicly supported.

[24] See Paul G. Kauper, "Law and Public Opinion," *Religion and the State University, op. cit.,* p. 83.

administrative, financial, and, possibly, legal problems than something more modest. Also there is a commendable desire to avoid the isolation of the study of religion from other areas.

This attitude does create a problem, however. Most areas or disciplines considered worthy of study in the modern university are structured in such a fashion as to provide for specialization, research, and graduate study. Nearly all programs in religion currently operating in the public colleges and universities are weak at these points. This means that religion is not getting the attention that other areas are and that scholars and teachers are not being prepared in this area. It would seem very desirable that in the future a few institutions would push on into a full-scale program in religion which would offer not only courses for the nonspecialist but a well-rounded program in advanced study and research for the specialist.

A related problem is that of qualified faculty. Most men now available have been trained in a seminary or seminary-related institution and are prepared primarily for the ministry or for teaching in seminary. Furthermore, the college or university program or department is in keen competition for qualified men with the churches and the seminaries, as well as the church-related and private colleges and universities.

Who, then, is qualified to teach religion (or to teach about religion)? Should "commitment" be added to scholarly competence? It is quite likely that future developments will include a stronger emphasis on both scholarly competence and some type of religious orientation. At any rate we have reached the point of quite general recognition that scholarly competence is not confined to either the non-religious or the religious individual.

It would be desirable if the religious groups could give increasing attention to the question of teaching religion in publicly supported institutions. A few of these groups have developed programs and materials for this purpose and are giving attention to the selection of personnel. However, much more could be done to find and train people to teach religion in the secular college and university. Furthermore, the religious groups could contribute significantly by subsidizing advanced study and research in religion in the public institutions.

Chapter 29

Evaluation of Religious Education

Ernest M. Ligon
William A. Koppe, Leonard A. Sibley, Jr.

THE REVEREND J'S CHURCH WAS IN A TURMOIL. BOARD MEETINGS WERE PITCHED
battles filled with bitterness and anger. The morale of the board of religious
education and the church-school staff was at its lowest point. Dissension permeated the whole congregation, reaching even the children and youth, and the
Reverend J was at the point of resigning. No one understood the source of these
tensions, nor their solutions. Then the Reverend J turned to modern and evaluative
methods. Among them he found the techniques of pro-con lists and characteristic
differences—remarkably simple but incredibly powerful. As he used it much of the
antagonism in his church disappeared. People's differences became sources of
strength, and he gave thanks daily for having learned something new and useful—
scientific evaluation.

As the reader explores even the simple methods described in this chapter, he will
sense that there *is* something new under the sun—evaluative techniques, for meeting
just such practical situations as the tensions in the Reverend J's church. This was
not always so. The early efforts at evaluation in religious education were difficult
and the dividends small. When Goodwin Watson did pioneering work in measurement of religious education, many churches found his methods difficult to use and
the results even more difficult to interpret.

The highly significant achievements of the Character Education Inquiry also
made an indelible impression on the field of religious education.[1] Many of the tests
and techniques used in that research are still valid and often used in other research
investigations. As one reads *Studies in Deceit*, he will be intrigued by the ingenious
devices used to measure honesty in children. Such techniques require considerable
skill, complex experimental set-ups, careful control of possible errors, and no
little deceit on the part of the experimenter himself. Nevertheless, an examination
of the three-volume report of these studies will be an interesting and highly
profitable experience for the student; one in which he will be convinced that such
qualities as honesty, helpfulness, and self-control can be measured.

One of the finest pieces of research of this type was done by Vernon Jones. His

[1] Hartshorne and May, *Studies in the Nature of Character*, 3 volumes.

public-school study is a masterpiece in research design.[2] The techniques used in the study are complex and require careful scientific training. No matter how "unscientific" one is, however, he will thoroughly enjoy reading Jones's two principal publications.[3]

Genetic Studies of Genius is, in the estimation of some, the finest single research study ever done in the field of psychology.[4] Volume II especially will be interesting.[5] It includes more than three hundred brief biographies of the great men of history. The findings are interesting, but the evaluational techniques will be even more intriguing. As one learns how the intelligence and character traits of these great men were estimated, he will be convinced that historical measurements are quite possible.

Robert J. Havighurst is well-known among religious educators. The methods used to build his developmental tasks theory are valuable for everyone. Most of them, again, are suited only to professional use in well-endowed research.[6]

Extensive research in this field has also been done in the Character Research Project. A great many research techniques are described in *Dimensions of Character.* Of particular importance are the use of open-end material, of small sample statistics, and of the concept of lay scientists—all recent developments in scientific evaluation which open vast new areas for research in religious education. Some techniques, which even a church-school teacher can use, are described, along with techniques demanding the trained personnel and elaborate equipment resources of the large laboratory. In this book are included the simple yet powerful techniques referred to in the opening paragraph of this chapter.

Many other names could be added to those already mentioned. If sufficient interest has been aroused to lead the reader into exploring this field more fully, refer to the bibliographies at the end of *Dimensions of Character* and Vernon Jones's definitive chapter in the *Manual of Child Psychology*. The long search for effective methods of evaluation is marked by many thrilling experiences. However far one may wish to go in mastering these methods, he will enjoy his explorations of them and will do his work in religious education much more intelligently because of having done so.

"Not every one who says . . . 'Lord, Lord,' shall enter the kingdom of heaven," nor is everyone who talks about evaluation doing it. To some people the word "criteria" is synonymous with "my opinion"; a "tested curriculum" is one that has not been changed for twenty years; it is "validated" when it is passed on by an important committee; and "analysis" consists in outlining some data under three headings. Unfortunately, the Lord's will is nowhere more rigid than in the use of the scientific method. The scientist above all others must say, "Thy will be done" to the third and fourth decimal places.

---

[2] *Character and Citizenship Training in the Public Schools.*

[3] Vernon Jones, "Character Development in Children—An Objective Approach," Leonard Carmichael (ed.), *Manual of Child Psychology* (2d ed.; New York: John Wiley and Sons, Inc., 1954).

[4] Lewis M. Terman (editor).

[5] Catherine M. Cox, *The Early Mental Traits of Three Hundred Geniuses* (Stanford: Stanford University Press, 1926).

[6] R. J. Havighurst, *Human Development and Education* (New York: Longmans, Green and Company, 1953); R. J. Havighurst and H. Taba, *Adolescent Character and Personality* (New York: John Wiley and Sons, Inc., 1949).

A Starting Point

Anyone will sense the flavor of scientific evaluation best if he actually carries out a "scientific investigation." Here is a very simple technique, but one which is astonishingly powerful. It does not have the precision of the more technical methods but is unsurpassed in discovering general trends and thus setting forth fruitful hypotheses to be explored more fully. When a judgment is made and evidence is sought to support it, this is not scientific evaluation. If, however, one sets forth a tentative judgment and then gathers an unbiased body of evidence in the light of which to evaluate it, he is a scientist. All the rest, even the higher mathematics, is commentary. Here is how you may proceed:

1. Consider some problem you are trying to solve—as an individual, as a teacher or parent, as a minister, or in any area in which you need to make significant decisions.

2. Write out a definite proposal for a course of action which you think might solve this problem.

3. Then make two columns, headed "pro" and "con." Under the first column (pro), list all of the evidence or arguments you can think of or discover which favor this course of action. Then do the same for the "con" column, listing all of the evidence or arguments against it.

4. Now look for characteristic differences between the two sets of items. These characteristic differences will constitute the basic principles you are seeking. A church which uses this procedure in board meetings, for example, will find that its decisions will be much wiser and usually unanimous.

The Potential of Research and Evaluation

"How can we measure the effectiveness of our methods?" This is the notion most religious educators have as to the role of evaluation. It is true that evaluation can accomplish this. If that is the extent of our vision for its possibilities, however, we are blind to many of its most significant values. Research can be creative as well as critical. Critical research can help discover whether or not present objectives are being achieved. Creative research makes it possible to use objective evidence in progressing from objectives based on personal opinion to objectives which are more basic in the universe itself. In traditional trait theory, men used to sit around a conference table and decide on some trait objectives which they wanted to inculcate in growing children. Today, no competent scientist would dream of deciding upon objectives in that way. The formulation of personality objectives is determined with the help of research. In fact, curricula and objectives can hardly be evaluated unless this is the case.

Research in secular education has told us much about individual differences and age-level characteristics. These findings, however, are only partially valid for the field of religious education. Research materials are now available by which we can spell out comparable differences and characteristics in the moral and spiritual area, and build curricula which take them into consideration. This list could be extended much further. One of the most difficult areas in religious education is communication. People hear what they listen for, not what the speaker says. Two people can read the same paragraph and understand it in widely different ways. The same person interprets the same statement differently at different times, depending on his emotional mood. Such problems require extensive research, and scientific methods are now available for dealing with many of them.

Some Useful Evaluational Methods

"I am not a scientist," almost everyone says. But before abandoning the possibility of using the scientific method in our work, let us look at some recently developed techniques. These are quite within the range of the intelligent layman and yet are remarkably effective in solving difficult problems. One simple way of collecting objective evidence on both sides of a question is called the *pro-con method*. Its use in making group decisions has already been described. It is even more powerful, however, in the search for underlying principles and dimensions by which to understand complex data.

Here are some ways in which it has been used: A church-school staff trying to decide whether to continue using its present curricular materials listed all of the good things about the curriculum (pro) and all of its weak points (con). Families seeking happier mealtime experiences listed their pleasant mealtimes (pro) and their unpleasant mealtimes (con). Curriculum writers asked a number of teachers to use a simple check list for some weeks, reporting which parts of each lesson they used successfully and which parts they used unsuccessfully or did not use at all. Parents have described successful and unsuccessful experiences in teaching religion to their children. In all of these cases, the first step was to put this evidence into pro-con lists: successful—unsuccessful, happy—unhappy, used—not used. Good evaluation depends first of all upon unbiased evidence—finding as many of the facts as possible on both sides. The unbiased evidence collected by using the pro-con method will help anyone to be more objective in making decisions and evaluating.

The *method of characteristic differences* is a companion to the pro-con technique, and is designed to discover underlying principles. Pro-con lists describe specific elements. One should then look for the characteristic differences between these lists, and it will be discovered that general patterns and trends run through successful and unsuccessful experiences.

For example, make two lists of "good intentions" which you can remember—things which you wanted to do because you thought they would be "good." Call one list "pro's," and list here the good intentions which you actually carried out—about half a dozen, if you can remember that many. Call the other list "con's," and list some others which you never got around to doing. Most of us find this the easier list to make.

This is all the evidence you need! Examine your two lists carefully. Do you see any characteristic differences between them? Are there some qualities which tend to be characteristic of your "pro" list but not of your "con" list, and vice versa? If you can persuade someone else to examine your lists, he will probably see differences which you did not notice. They are likely to be significant ones, too.

Why do we carry out some of our good intentions? The answer is, because they fit our motivations. Your characteristic differences are clues to your own pattern of motivations. All you have to do is to set up these same motivating conditions for any of your good intentions—including religious education! You will be amazed at how many of them will then come to life for you.

The key to this method is to seek the characteristic differences between two groups of data which differ in some definite way. This method has been used with pro-con lists, essays, rankings, "three wishes," test scores, descriptions of behavior, sociograms, and critical incidents. New uses are constantly being found. You can look for these differences yourself, but if you invite additional people to do so, they are likely to see differences which have escaped you. This method is particularly powerful in creative research where we are concerned not so much with identifying successes and failures as with discovering principles by which to build more effective programs.

"How can you measure a mother's love? How can you measure a teen-ager's moral and spiritual maturity?" Those untrained in science often ask such questions in a tone of incredulity. Science progresses in proportion to the accuracy of its measurements. Nevertheless, in religious education we have already begun to measure when we can say, "This mother loves her child more than that mother. This teen-ager is more mature than that teen-ager."

Ranking is a way of achieving this kind of measurement. Ranking is done by asking judges to put a set of items (for example, people, essays, situations) in order from the best to the worst, the most adequate to the least adequate, the most successful to the least successful. To do this, you must first state your criteria; that is, what evidence you will accept that one item is to be ranked above another. Give each judge a statement of these criteria and a set of the materials to be ranked. Ask him to put them in order, giving the best item a rank of "1," the next best a rank of "2." Several judges are usually used in order to cancel out individual prejudices and biases, and the final rank order is based on their pooled judgments. If you wish to be confident of this pooled-rank order, ask about five judges to do the ranking independently. If there is a fair measure of agreement among them, their pooled-rank order is likely to be reliable. Any standard statistics text will explain how to estimate the agreement among the judges.[7]

This process is not difficult. If you become familiar with it, you will find a great many situations in which you can use it for reasonably accurate measurement and evaluation. For example, if you wish to discover how well your church is achieving its objectives, ask children in your church and in a comparable church using a different curriculum to write statements answering some question relevant to your church's goals. Rank all of the statements from the two churches together. If your church's program is successful, on the average the children in your church should stand higher in the ranking than those from the other church. The method of characteristic differences can be used to provide a qualitative analysis of how the children in the two churches differ.

Statistics provides a group of powerful tools for evaluation. There is terror in mathematics for many people. To them, the word "statistics" suggests frightening visions of complex formulas and massive computers. As a matter of fact, statistics is not essentially a matter of mathematics; it is mostly objective thinking. Many useful statistical techniques can be mastered by anyone who has studied high-school algebra.[8] The research methods described so far will help you to solve many evaluational problems. If, however, you can add to these methods a working

[7] E. M. Ligon, *Dimensions of Character*, p. 331; Siegel, *Nonparametric Statistics for the Behavioral Sciences*, pp. 202-13, 229-38.

[8] Helen M. Walker, *Mathematics Essential for Elementary Statistics* (Rev. Ed.; New York: Henry Holt and Company; 1951).

knowledge of a few basic statistical tools, your evaluations will be far more accurate and insights will be found which would never have been discovered without such tools.

In most research evaluations, you will be looking either for differences between things or relationships between things. The tools of statistics are designed to tell you how to find differences and relationships and how large they must be before you can be confident that they are not accidental.

There are two relatively simple statistical tools which you can use to carry out evaluational studies with confidence and skill. Master them, and you will be able to answer many questions in religious education. The first is known as *chi square*.[9] It is one of the most versatile of all statistical tools, and answers the question, "How well do my data fit my theories?" The other is known as *rho* or the *rank-difference correlation*.[10] It is used with data which have been put in rank order. It makes it possible to measure with some accuracy the interrelationships among the forces we study in religious education and makes possible the development of reliable scales for measurement.

New statistical techniques are being developed every year. Many of these developments are in what are known as *small sample and non-parametric statistics*.[11] These tools are particularly useful for the kinds of problems encountered in the evaluation of religious education. A working knowledge of such basic statistical methods and concepts is not difficult to achieve. It is a necessity for anyone who hopes to become skillful in evaluation.

Design for Evaluation

Decisions made without evidence are rarely good decisions. Palmists, astrologers, and fortunetellers have not yet demonstrated their ability to make valid predictions. The evidence obtained from planned evaluation is far more fruitful than the evidence obtained from haphazard evaluation. For example, it is possible to evaluate a curriculum after you have used it. Your evidence and your findings will be much more meaningful, however, if the plan for evaluation is made in advance and the evidence of effectiveness is gathered systematically as the curriculum is being used. Good evaluation must be designed. There are many ways of doing this, but the four steps now to be described have been found to constitute the basis of good design.[12]

1. *State your objectives* in such a clear-cut and specific manner that you can find evidence to test them.

2. *Gather a body of unbiased evidence* concerning these objectives. In science, the word "unbiased" has no emotional connotation. It means that all of the relevant data have an equal chance of being included in your evaluation.

3. *Analyze this evidence.* This is the point at which you will use the evaluational methods described in the preceding section. They will help you to observe the significant characteristics of the evidence.

4. *Interpret your findings and formulate new hypotheses.* Consider what con-

[9] Ligon, *op. cit.,* pp. 312-316; Siegel, *op. cit.,* pp. 42-47, 104-11, 175-79.
[10] Ligon, *op. cit.,* pp. 329-31; Siegel, *op. cit.,* pp. 202-13.
[11] See especially Siegel, *op. cit.*
[12] John E. Anderson, "Methods of Child Psychology," Leonard Carmichael (ed.), *Manual of Child Psychology, op. cit.*

clusions you can draw as a result of your analysis of the evidence. It will then be possible to reformulate your original hypothesis and revise your objectives.

Let us describe in more detail each of these parts of a basic design for evaluation.

1. *Objectives:* Here are three principles for formulating good objectives.

a) Are these objectives meaningful in terms of what you want to achieve? Our ultimate objective in religious education is religious learning. Too often, however, our immediate objectives become attendance at church school and interest in its program. Success in achieving these goals must not mislead us into thinking that we have thereby achieved our ultimate objective.

b) Do these objectives take human nature into account? Are they realistic and achievable? Religion has at times tried to make all sexual behavior sinful. It is clear, however, that God has created human beings in such a way that sex is normal, and any objective which does not take this into account cannot be achieved.

c) Can these objectives be evaluated? In other words, can you find evidence to indicate whether or not you have made progress toward your objectives? It is not enough to assume that good-sounding objectives automatically produce good results. One woman tried to teach her child truthfulness by punishing him whenever she caught him lying. Her intentions were good, but the child actually learned to lie more cleverly so that he would not get caught. Her good intentions were not enough because she had no way to evaluate how well her method was accomplishing her objective.

These three principles for selecting an objective can help you to grow continually in whatever effort you undertake. Outline some of the objectives you are trying to achieve now—good reading and study habits, for example. Clarify your objectives in terms of these three principles. Then use the following steps to evaluate how well you are achieving your objectives.

2. *Unbiased Evidence:* Many methods have been developed for collecting good evidence.

a) Questionnaires and interviews are highly popular ways of gathering evidence. At the same time, they are among the most difficult methods for gathering unbiased evidence. G. Stanley Hall did monumental work in describing children's age-level characteristics for the first time. However, his findings were not complete because he based his entire study on questionnaires. Therefore he described only that peculiar variety of persons who returns questionnaires. Moreover, the questions on his questionnaire, brilliant as they were, did not mean the same thing to everyone who answered them; and therefore the answers were difficult to interpret. Anthropologists did research for years by interviewing natives of primitive cultures and rewarding them with trinkets or money. Then they found out that the natives were telling the interviewers whatever brought the best rewards.

You might think that such experiences would make people reluctant to use questionnaires, rating scales, and interviews to get unbiased evidence. However, the May-June, 1959, issue of *Religious Education* contained reports of 174 evaluational or research efforts. About 30 per cent of these studies involved some form of questionnaire and another 15 per cent involved interview methods. Some of these are excellent studies. Their results are both valid and reliable. This does not detract from the fact that almost half of all the studies reported that year involved the most difficult methods of obtaining objective evidence for evaluation.

There are a number of good books on developing questionnaires and others on the difficult skills of interviewing.[13] Unless you want to be fooled by your information, get one or more of these books and study them carefully before you blithefully suggest, "Let's send out a questionnaire!"

b) Another 20 per cent of these studies was based on *standardized personality, attitude,* or *intelligence tests,* some of which were designed for the purpose. This approach can be very fruitful, but it must be understood that standardizing a test is a highly technical procedure and should not be attempted without expert guidance.

c) *Direct observations of classes* and *pilot efforts* in the use of program or curricular material are the next most popular sources of information. It is difficult to anticipate all of the possible factors in a program in advance. On-the-spot observations and trial efforts provide data in their total setting. However, it is correspondingly difficult to avoid biasing findings in the direction of your wishes.

d) Some studies simply *describe* the characteristics (e.g., age, income, education) of particular populations. Such studies involve the difficult problem of obtaining representative samples. One investigator for a large magazine made a disastrously wrong prediction because he used the telephone directory in obtaining a sample. This sample was not representative because many of the people in the group he was studying did not have telephones.

e) One fruitful way to obtain unbiased evidence is by the use of *open-end questions*—questions which can be answered in a variety of ways rather than in terms of two or three alternatives such as true-false, yes or no, multiple choice. Such answers reveal far more about the personality of the person answering than do closed-end questions. The use of such data in scientific research and evaluation is a relatively new development.

Ask five women and five men to describe the same person. Record their answers verbatim. Study the difference between the men's and the women's answers. This difference is due to the fact that, given an opportunity, people tend to respond in terms of their personalities. With very little training you can develop skills in the use of open-end data. With considerable training you can learn the intricacies of projective tests, which are a highly developed form of open-end material.

f) One of the more generally useful open-end data-gathering methods is the *critical incident technique* in which the persons being studied report characteristic incidents relevant to the problem being investigated. Another is the use of *sociograms* and their variations. Have each child in a group choose privately the best leader, his best friend, and the person with whom he would most like to do various activities. A study of the interpersonal relations revealed by these choices will indicate a great deal about the characteristics of the group which you are studying.

Unbiased evidence is indispensable to any progress in religious education—but beware! This is the time to stay on the straight and narrow path. The most common error made by novices in evaluation is to gather far more evidence than they can handle. It is a good rule of thumb to allow about 25 per cent of the time and effort for collecting evidence and 75 per cent for analysis and interpretation of the evidence.

3. *Analysis of the Evidence:* This consists of putting the evidence in such form

[13] Payne, *How to Ask Questions*

that you can see what it tells you. The most common type of analysis is some form of *categorization*. We logically conceive a sensible scheme of things and then try to classify our evidence to fit. People are not logical, however; they are psychological. They almost never fit these neat schemes. One method to circumvent this is *content analysis* in which you let the categories develop from the data. The method of *characteristic differences* is a form of categorization which goes a step further. It helps uncover principles which contribute to differences among people and situations.

There was a time when the words "experimental design" and "control group" were almost synonymous. If people were as simple as chemical reactions or even rats, this happy marriage would have gone on for eternity. However, it is difficult to obtain useful control groups in religious education. Mothers are particularly reluctant to raise their children under experimentally controlled conditions, especially if they are in the less-favored control group.

The answer to this problem is the concept of creative evaluation. Control group research asks, "Is this method good or bad?" Creative research asks, "In which circumstances does this method work best?" or "Which methods seem to be associated with success?" To answer questions like these, methods have been developed to measure the interaction of forces involved. Simple statistical tools such as chi-square, ranking, and rank correlation have already been discussed and can be mastered quickly, even by those with little mathematical background. Of course, the more complex methods of analysis of variance and of factor analysis require considerably more training. In any case, how you make your decisions may well depend on at least a simple analysis of your evidence.

4. *Interpretation of Findings and Formulation of New Hypotheses:* What will you now do as a result of what you have learned? Here is where the common sense, practical experience, and intuitive judgment of the experimenter come into play. Analysis of the evidence gives you the facts, but you must interpret these facts and discover their implications for your program. The ultimate purpose of research and evaluation is to discover more effective methods and practice. Research findings have no value until the experimenter has used these findings to improve his program.

If your evaluation raises more questions than it answers, sing the Doxology. You are on the way to discovering more of the will of God. A final answer cannot be the will of an infinite God. Every evaluation should result in insights which in turn become new hypotheses to be tested.

A Look at the Future

Almost everyone knows how to lie with statistics. Our evaluations of our homes are quite different when we talk to the tax assessor than when we talk to a prospective buyer. Most of us are completely duped when others use statistics to lie to us. To some statistics are sources of fear, to others boredom, and to others mystery. Many people in America today are more influenced by the persuasive statistic of the advertiser than by the preaching from our pulpits.

Within another twenty-five years a person who does not know the basic principles of statistical reasoning may well be regarded as being as ignorant as one who cannot read and write. New developments in statistics are not only numerous but full of hope for the preservation of our western civilization. Statistics consists of a body of methods for making wise decisions in the face of uncertainty. We live in a world full of interacting forces. Each of us experiences directly only a small fraction of those forces. On the basis of that small sample, we must judge the whole. As the world grows smaller, the future of democracy depends more and more on accurate judgments on the part of its citizens. Only some competence in statistical reasoning will make this possible. Read through some elementary statistics text to convince yourself of this fact.[14]

It is even possible to look into the future of man's ability to solve objectively his increasingly complex problems. One of the new areas for statistical development is known as "Decision Theory." [15] It is still a decade away from practical use, but when it has been more completely developed we shall be able to put even our biases and prejudices into our equations and make decisions more wisely and objectively than ever before in history.

This is a very brief statement of evaluation in religious education. The bibliography offers fruitful adventures for those who wish to go further. We have no choice but to proceed into this field. Otherwise the world will soon leave us far behind instead of in the forefront of those who would make religion the power it ought to be in men's lives.

Bibliography

Bross, Irwin D. J. *Design for Decision.* New York: The Macmillan Company, 1953.

Character Education Inquiry. *Studies in the Nature of Character.* Three Volumes.

    I. Hugh Hartshorne and Mark A. May. *Studies in Deceit.* New York: The Macmillan Company, 1928.

    II. Hugh Hartshorne, Mark A. May and Julius B. Maller. *Studies in Service and Self-Control.* New York: The Macmillan Company, 1929.

    III. Hugh Hartshorne, Mark A. May and Frank K. Shuttleworth, *Studies in the Organization of Character.* New York: The Macmillan Company, 1930.

Festinger, Leon and Katz, Daniel. *Research Methods in the Behavioral Sciences.* New York: Dryden Press, 1953.

Jones, Vernon. *Character and Citizenship Training in the Public Schools.* Chicago: The University of Chicago Press, 1936.

Ligon, Ernest M. *Dimensions of Character.* New York: The Macmillan Company, 1956.

Payne, Stanley L. *How to Ask Questions.* Princeton, N. J.: Princeton University Press, 1951.

Siegel, Sidney. *Nonparametric Statistics for the Behavioral Sciences.* New York: McGraw-Hill Book Company, 1956.

Terman, Lewis M. (ed.). *Genetic Studies of Genius.* Stanford: Stanford University Press. This series included several volumes, the first appearing in 1925.

[14] Oliver L. Lacey, *Statistical Methods in Experimentation* (New York: The Macmillan Company, 1953); Helen M. Walker and J. Lev, *Elementary Statistical Methods* (Rev. Ed.; New York: Henry Holt and Company, 1958).

[15] Bross, *Design for Decision.*

Part IV

Agencies and Organizations

Chapter 30

State and Local Councils of Churches and Religious Education

John B. Ketcham

ONE OF THE CHIEF PRECURSORS OF ECUMENICAL EFFORTS WAS THE SUNDAY-school movement. Organized in 1824, the American Sunday School Union held numerous national conventions in the ensuing decades,[1] and there was a simultaneous interest in the organization of state and local associations, with nineteen being established by 1869. Many councils of churches trace their origin to these associations. The goal of the International Sunday School Association (successor to A.S.S.U.) was a council in every district, county, and state; and by 1893 only three states remained unorganized, while eleven had achieved the objective of total organization at every level.[2] The movement continued to grow in the early twentieth century, until by 1917 there were sixty-three state and provincial associations.[3] These were chiefly lay led, providing opportunities for undenominational fellowship and work.

The latter quarter of the nineteenth century and early years of the twentieth witnessed increasing denominational interest in Christian education, with the organization of numerous boards and departments. In 1910 the denominational leaders formed the Sunday School Council of Evangelical Denominations to promote interdenominational activities. The new council not only paralleled but actually challenged the leadership of the International Sunday School Association, which represented state and local associations, resulting in direct conflict between

[1] See ch. 1, pp. 17-23, for details of the Sunday-school movement's historical development.

[2] Ross W. Sanderson, "A History of State and Local Councils of Churches," an unpublished monograph. Used by permission of the author.

[3] "Half a Century of Growth and Service," an undated report of the International Sunday School Association.

the two from 1910 to 1922.[4] In this latter year the two bodies were merged to form the International Council of Religious Education. Provision was made in this new council for official representation of both denominations and state organizations. This merger had a marked effect on the structure of state and local organizations, for now there began to be carried down to state organizations the principle of unified guiding of field program. A new era had begun, but unresolved problems still remained in connection with the functions of interdenominational agencies for Christian education.

Formation of Other National Organizations

During the same decades in which the foregoing organizations for religious education were appearing, churchmen were also developing other phases of their interdenominational efforts. The interests of these organizations constitute the strands that today are woven into programs of local, state, and national councils of churches. The one year, 1908, saw the establishment of the Federal Council, the Home Missions Council and the Missionary Education Movement (Friendship Press). The Foreign Missions Conference, begun in 1893, was reorganized in a more functionally significant body in 1911. This foreign missions strand was to have more immediate effect on the co-operative work of world evangelization overseas. However, the first Missionary Conference at Edinburgh in 1910 and the other great world ecumenical conferences which followed were to contribute to the growing climate of co-operation among the denominations and their churches from the world level to the local level.

The Federal Council of Churches, ecclesiastically oriented, grew out of concerns for Christianizing the social order and was closely related to "Life and Work." Its contribution provided for district offices and local branches, the state and local federations, but the federal controls were denominational. Local church federations antedated the Federal Council, the first being organized in 1895. By 1915, there were many state, city, and county federations, with twelve salaried executives, some part time. In the 1920's many more were organized, but the Federal Council faced, in a different setting, the problems of relationship of state and local federations to the national body. After many years of exacting discussion the Federal Council came to the conclusion that the term "local branches" was wholly inappropriate and that state and local federations were autonomous bodies.

The Home Missions Council sponsored numerous state home-missions councils seeking to work with the denominations to avoid wasteful competition in the use of church extension funds.[5] Other agencies to perform other functions had likewise come into existence. One was the United Stewardship Council, another the Missionary Education Movement, a third the Council of Church Women. "Within a few decades it became evident that the varied functions of these national organizations had one common origin—the church itself." Pressures were mounting "to unite all these national phases of church cooperation into one comprehensive body. This was enthusiastically accomplished, after long and careful planning, at Cleveland in 1950. Once consummated, the National Council of Churches of Christ in the U.S.A. drew to itself additional functional agencies." [6]

[4] See ch. 1, pp. 20-21.
[5] *Growing Together,* chapter 1.
[6] *Ibid.*

One Task

Reference has already been made to the fact that most of the early co-operative work in the United States began because of the interest of laymen and a few clergymen in some aspects of the church's work. Most early co-operative organizations were thus undenominational, composed of laymen and clergy who saw a need and sought to meet it. As the denominations developed various boards and agencies to strengthen the work of their local churches it was inevitable that efforts would be made to make these organizations interdenominational in practice as well as in theory, with their policy making boards composed of official representatives appointed by the denominations. This happened nationally in the formation of the National Council in 1950. Since then, it has been reflected in the rewriting of constitutions and refining of the structures of state and local councils.

This process has not been without its struggles and difficulties, for there had developed in states and cities Sunday-school associations, councils of religious education, federations of churches, home missions councils, stewardship councils, councils of weekday religious education, student organizations, and church women's federations. The period of the 1920's and '30's, retarded in the early '30's by the depression, was a period of slow growth and change. Pressures were becoming stronger for the unification of functions in these various organizations at state and local levels. Mergers of councils of religious education and federations of churches were being effected. Some councils of religious education and some federations of churches expanded to include other interests. The 1940's marked the height of this merger and expansion process.

During the 1940's and early 1950's there was a phenomenal growth in state and local councils of church women. By 1959, 2,137 local and 50 state councils of church women had been established. In some cases they function as general departments of councils of churches. There are, however, councils of church women in every state and in more communities than have councils of churches.

At the national, state, community, and local levels these co-operative forces were discovering that the task of the Church and the churches was one task. The results of this growing appreciation are reflected in the unified structure of state and local councils. Councils are becoming inclusive at all levels, concerned with the total mission of the church in its various functions.

In 1959 there were 47 state councils,[7] and at the county and city level 872 organized councils with paid and volunteer leadership.[8] With the 2,187 councils of united church women and over 2,500 ministerial associations this totalled some 5,600 channels of co-operative activity in the states, counties, and cities of the United States.

Denominations and local churches are increasingly recognizing the importance of their corporate witness through these councils they have created. Active participation in their councils' deliberations, programs, services, and the financial support they are providing from their own budgets reveal this. With the development of denominational responsibility in and for their councils, however, there

[7] Six state councils have volunteer leadership—Alaska, Nevada, New Mexico, South Carolina, Utah, Wyoming.

[8] Of these fifty-three were councils of weekday religious education (fifty in Virginia alone) with paid teachers or supervisors, thirty-eight councils of religious education, and forty-four Sunday-school associations led by volunteers.

persists the perplexing problem of the relationship of local councils to state councils and state councils to the National Council. Within the framework of official denominational responsibility a major question is how to recognize the place and representation of the community, city, county, and state councils which the local churches and the denominational judicatories have helped create and support, in the next larger geographical council. Attempts to solve this problem of structure are being discussed at the world, national, state, and metropolitan levels. The concept of the nature of the church held by some denominations makes this a difficult problem. The growth of the conciliar movement at all levels points to the need for further careful delineation of these relationships and patient seeking toward solutions.

Basic Principles [9]

Councils of churches provide a groundwork of Christian co-operation; they are the response of Christians with a desire to work together, to express their unity in Christ. Certain principles provide the philosophical foundation that in turn supplies the framework over which the structure of the council can be built. These principles tend to shape the course of Christian co-operation throughout the ecumenical movement.

1. THE REPRESENTATIVE PRINCIPLE: The Council and its departments should be composed of official representatives of the co-operating denominations or local churches. Policies and program should be determined by these representatives acting together. It is thus that a council of churches and its subdivisions is the representative agent of its constituent membership. The program that results becomes the program of the bodies represented.

2. THE EVANGELICAL PRINCIPLE: Evangelical churches adhere to that interpretation of Christianity that emphasizes man's weakness to sin, Christ's saving power, and the need of a new birth and redemption through faith. The doctrinal phrase "Jesus Christ as Divine Lord and Savior" is generally incorporated in the preamble of councils of churches. This indicates that the member churches seek clearly to establish the fact that they are partners in a Christian fellowship that is striving to witness to its faith.

3. THE PRINCIPLE OF AUTONOMY: Each council of churches is autonomous. No authority or control is exercised by one council over another. This applies to city, county, trade area, state, and national councils. Structurally councils of churches are self-governing bodies. "Togetherness of purpose" is expressed, however, through voluntary ties of fellowship among councils of churches that are functional, experiential, and spiritual.

4. THE FUNCTIONAL PRINCIPLE: The structure of a council should be determined by its function—by its reason for existence, not the reverse. The basic purposes, the needs for action and service that the churches experience in their ministry in their communities, become the determining factors in their organizational growth and development.

5. THE PRINCIPLE FOR COMMITTEE MEMBERSHIP: Committees should consist

---

[9] Adapted from (a) A pamphlet—*Criteria for Self-Evaluation and Measurement by Councils of Churches.* (b) *Growing Together.* (c) J. Quinter Miller, *Christian Unity: Its Relevance to the Community.*

of competent people designated by the constituent churches or denominations, to whom the member churches have entrusted similar responsibilities. Modification may be necessary at local levels where many local churches constitute a council.

6. THE PRINCIPLE OF FINANCIAL INTEGRITY: Since the council is the joint possession of its constituent membership and a projection of their ministry, they share mutually in its cost. The financial integrity of the constituent membership is measured, at least partly, by the degree to which they bear their share of the cost of their co-operative work.

7. THE PRINCIPLE OF CO-OPERATIVE RESPONSIBILITY: The co-operative work of the council belongs to them. It is not independent, extra, or competitive; it is a mutual responsibility of their own creation. This shared responsibility through voluntary co-operation is a fundamental principle of all co-operative endeavor.

Churches—denominations—are not made one by any man or group. "But Christ has made us his own, and He is not divided." In him denominations and local churches find that "oneness" to which they witness through the structure of a council of churches based on these principles.

What Is a Council of Churches? [10]

A council of churches constituted on these principles should be understood in these terms:

1. A council of churches is an officially approved and constituted agency of a group of churches at the local level or of a group of denominations at the state level, desiring to forward certain phases of their own work in co-operation with other churches. A council of churches is not a church. It does not presume to have a creed. It does not determine theology. It does not administer the sacraments.

2. A council is a part of "The Church." It is established to help forward and demonstrate the will of God as revealed through Jesus Christ.

3. A council has the official endorsement of its member churches. It is constituted by official action of the local churches at the local level—i.e., by official boards, vestry, session, trustees of the local congregation—by official action of denominations at the state level—i.e., the denominational judicatories.

4. A council is representative of the churches. It is their organization through which they carry on those tasks they decide to do together. It is not just another community or religious organization. Since the council is representative of the churches at the local level, of denominational judicatories at the state level, and is the channel through which they carry on phases of their own work, then each local church or each denominational judicatory should include in its *own* regular budget an amount sufficient to pay for their own work which they carry on in co-operation with other churches. A council does not affect the autonomy of its member churches, but it should help a denomination or a local church re-evaluate the way it carries on parts of its program in co-operation with other churches to Christianize their community. However, the churches which constitute a council have by their own act signified their intention to do together those things which they believe can be done well or better together than could be done separately.

[10] John B. Ketcham, "What Is a Council of Churches?" mimeographed folder issued by National Council of Churches. Adapted and used by permission.

The Role and Function of a Council of Churches [11]

The role of a council of churches in the ecumenical movement is to witness to our oneness in Jesus Christ. Since a council of churches is created by a group of congregations, judicatories, or national plenary bodies of communions that desire to work together, the primary clue to its role is found in the purpose of the church itself, which is to bring all men into a saving relationship to Christ and to "increase among men the love of God and neighbor."

A council program is not always directed primarily toward witness to the total community; some programs should serve the particular needs of and be carried on within the churches or denominations themselves.

The functions through which councils seek to serve local churches or judicatories and the community are as follows:

1. To encourage and strengthen the co-operative work of the churches in each neighborhood, city (local council), and county within the state (state council).

2. To enable the member churches and/or judicatories to plan together and co-ordinate phases of their work in evangelism, Christian education, Christian life and work, Christian missions, and public relations.

3. To conduct research studies that will furnish a factual basis for church extension and church adjustment.

4. To help establish, encourage, and maintain, wherever needed, chaplaincy service in public and private institutions.

5. To represent Protestant-Orthodox Christians of
   a. a given state in legislative matters emerging at the state capitol;
   b. of a given city in those significant matters of community organization and relationships that may affect the moral and spiritual tone of the community.

6. To help provide a religious ministry to specialized groups including students, migrants, foreign-language groups, and American Indians.

7. To support and encourage the development of Church World Service, C.R.O.P., and resettlement of refugees.

8. To conduct ecumenical worship services and promote observances of the great common festivals of the Christian church year.

9. To sponsor and encourage policies in support of weekday religious education.

10. To assist the member judicatories in long-range program planning and co-ordination.

11. To foster the spirit of teamwork and professional growth among the inter-denominationally employed staff members of councils of churches within the state.

12. To develop and conduct, in co-operation with member churches or judicatories and related local councils of churches, an effective program designed to proclaim the gospel and interpret the significance of the churches through radio, television, films, car cards, printed literature, and the public and religious press.

13. To extend Christian fellowship among ministers, churchmen, church women, and young people on a city- or state-wide basis.

14. To help in relating the student work of the churches in colleges and universities, particularly state-supported institutions, with the religious life of the communities in which the said colleges and universities are located.

[11] "The Role and Function of Local, State and National Councils of Churches in the Ecumenical Movement." A study committee report of the Association of Council Secretaries, approved June, 1957. Adapted from the report and used by permission.

These areas of need are descriptive of functions or types of work the churches have found to be rewarding as they establish their agencies for interdenominational co-operation.

Christian Education Committee Organization

There are two general types of committee organization for Christian education within the structure of councils of churches. The first, found at both the state and local levels, is the Christian education division or department with sub-committees for each specialized phase of Christian education. There is a chairman of the entire division and subcommittee. The chairman of the division represents the total interests of Christian education on the executive committee. In the second type, each special phase of Christian education, such as children's work, youth work, leadership and administration, family life, vacation church school, and weekday religious education is planned and administered by a separate committee responsible directly to the executive committee or council. In this type each phase of Christian education is represented directly on the executive committee. In larger councils the trend is toward the division or department. This facilitates co-ordination of related activities and gives more visibility to the total educational function of the council.

The number of specialized committees within any given division or department varies from council to council. No two councils are exactly alike. It will depend on the recognized needs and desires of the official representatives of the denominations or local churches. Small volunteer councils have one committee with each member, or two members, responsible for a special phase of Christian education.

The following tabulated from listings of councils in the *Yearbook of American Churches*,[12] will give some idea of these specialized concerns and the frequency with which they occur.

41 State Councils		*266 City and County Councils*	
Leadership and Administration	30	Weekday Religious Education	90
Youth Council (UCYM)	27	Youth	81
Youth Work	23	Leadership and Administration	56
Youth Council Advisory	4	Youth Council (UCYM)	52
Weekday Religious Education	21	Audio Visual	39
Vacation Church School	20	Children	37
Children	19	Vacation Religious Education	35
Audio Visual	16	Family Life	19
Committee on Use and Understanding		Scouting	18
of the Bible	15	Campus Ministry	18
Adult	11	Adult	15
Camp	12	Music	12
Campus Ministry	11	Young Adult	10
Family Life	10	Religion and Public Education	7
Scouting	9	Retarded Children	7
Directors' Fellowship	5	Church Agency	6
Observation-Demonstration Schools	8	Directors' Fellowship	4
Religion and Public Education	3	Camps and Conferences	4

[12] Benson Y. Landis (ed.), *Yearbook of American Churches* (New York: National Council of Churches, 1959).

Educational Evangelism	3	Missionary Education	4
Christian Teaching Mission		Youth Council Adviser	4
Young Adults	2	Superintendents' Council	2
Day Camping		Use and Understanding of the Bible	2
		Day Camp	2
		Alcohol Education	1
		Radio-Television	1
		Christian Teaching Mission	1
		Drama	1
		Aging	1
		Ecumenical Education	1
		Library	1
		Observation and Laboratory School	1
		Migrant Ministry	1

Not all councils gave details of committee organization. Of those which did, there are twenty-one divisions of Christian education, ninety-one departments, thirty-six with separate specialized committees of Christian education, and fifty-one are specifically councils of weekday religious education.

The Distinctive Role of Christian Education in a Council

The Committee on the Study of Christian Education of the International Council of Religious Education (appointed in 1944) created a subcommittee, the Committee Approach to Religious Education, which undertook to identify those activities which should be committed to co-operative agencies of Christian education. The following statement presents the heart of the committee's findings:

The total mission of the churches is a synthesis of several emphases, each complementary to all the others and fundamentally the same in both local church and in inter-church organizations. This mission, some believe, consists of fellowship, evangelism, education, worship, and social action. But whatever the definition, a council should mediate these basic emphases to the community. The council's distinctive role in this process is quite different from that of the local church, but the fundamental nature of its task is the same. The work of inter-church councils is not marginal or secondary in importance but is integral to the churches' mission to the whole of life.

This fact must be realized by the denominations before the council system can be harnessed fully to their corporate tasks. Inter-church councils are as indispensable to local churches and the denominations for winning community life to Christ as their foreign mission societies are to the winning of other nations. Their work is determined by the same comprehensive Christian strategy that determines the imperative of foreign missions, and they deserve support commensurate with their importance.[13]

Each and every state and local council's department of Christian education, officially constituted, will have to determine the collective or corporate educational tasks of the churches in their geographical community. Through the process of group thinking and planning each council will have to determine the educational functions of its council. However they may determine this, "the educa-

[13] Adapted from *The Study of Christian Education* (Chicago: International Council of Religious Education, 1946-47), pp. 21, 22; and *A Restudy of Christian Education at the Ecumenical Level*, prepared by a study committee of the Department of Christian Education of the Church Federation of Greater Chicago, Lemuel Petersen and John W. Harms (eds.). Used by permission.

tional phase of the total council movement should be developed in terms of (1) the fundamental functions of religion in community life, and (2) the inner needs of the churches as a Christian fellowship which has a corporate mission to the community."

Christian education is one of several basic functional units in a council—i.e., evangelism, Christian education, social welfare, social education and action, ministry in institutions, radio and television, community research and church development, comity and Christian missions. These functions are each related to the others in ways that make them a single fabric of strategy for interdenominational service and leadership.

However, Christian education has its own place in this larger strategy. Its methodology expresses the theological and democratic presuppositions of our faith. One of these is respect for the inherent, intrinsic worth of each individual person as a child of God when He is understood as a loving heavenly Father.

Another is the conviction that persons have the capacity for growth when they are involved in the redeeming fellowship of God's people in the Church of Jesus Christ. When people are involved with one another as brothers within this fellowship of transforming love they grow into the likeness of God as we understand Him through Jesus Christ.

These values are not alone the possession of Christian education. They are shared by all other functions of the Churches, but Christian education in a peculiar and particular sense emphasizes these values. When it functions on its highest level within an ecumenical frame of reference, Christian education shows how to make these values a reality in the intergroup relationships of the Churches.[14]

The creative processes of the Christian educational function should be at the heart of every function in a council. In other words, Christian education is not confined to a Department of Christian Education but is a basic spirit and method of each and every department or division. The reverse is likewise true; Christian education at its best is permeated by the spirit of evangelism; it uses modern media of communication such as the press, radio, and television; it is concerned for the unfortunate as well as people in normal and wholesome circumstances; it is concerned for church development and extension; and it is concerned about the reconstruction of moral values in the social order. The Department of Christian Education's role in the Christian education function is the same as the council's for the total relationship among the denominations or local churches. *The Study of Christian Education* puts it this way:

To *coordinate* the ongoing Christian educational activities of the cooperating denominations or local churches either in relation to services which should be coordinated in the interest of more efficient operation, or in relation to the corporate outreach of the communions to the corporate life of the community; *or*

To *unify* the Christian educational functions of the cooperating denominations or local churches where they are agreed that it is desirable to place full administrative responsibility for essential educational functions in the hands of a council's Department of Christian Education, either to secure efficiency in operation or because the function(s) can only be performed in this way; *or*

To perform a combination of these functions.

To provide leadership for the development of a mature collective vision of what the Christian educational task of the ecumenical forces should be; and to implement this

[14] *Ibid.*

334

planning with such creative leadership in the development of program services, organizational units and financial resources as the cooperating denominational units responsible for Christian education want to accomplish together.[15]

According to this philosophy of function of Christian education in a council, the department should be an instrument or channel through which the co-operating denominations at the state level and local churches at the community level may co-ordinate and unify their educational forces for teaching children, youth, and adults.

What then are some of the functions that are the responsibility of an officially constituted department to consider, and through which they discover the areas for co-operative program development? The function of a department of Christian education is based on the principles and philosophy so far reviewed in this chapter. These principles, in terms of function, are:

1. To witness to the oneness in Jesus Christ through a program of Christian education—a program of Christian education which seeks to further the acceptance and practice of the gospel in the community, should itself be a witness to this unity.

2. To develop the basic purpose and principle of a comprehensive program of and strategy for Christian education.

3. To operate under the representative principle—at the state level, official denominational representatives and local council representatives; at the city level, official local church representatives sit in counsel to review programs, to evaluate needs, to study, to plan, to project, and to administer together a co-operative program of Christian education in those areas which these representatives desire and decide to develop together. This process will include defining immediate and long-range needs and determining how they may be met in a well-defined schedule.

4. To discover the phases of the Christian education program which can be carried on more effectively co-operatively than by denominations or local congregations working separately.

5. To develop agreements (at the state level between denominations, agencies, and local councils; at the community level between local churches and agencies) which will define which aspects of the program will be carried forward denominationally, which co-operatively. Always being aware that Christian education is one task and that the council is one channel through which the denominations or local churches carry on parts of their own program. Such agreements will avoid duplication and insure more complete coverage of all the areas of emphases within one program of Christian education.

6. To administer those aspects of the total program of Christian education that are agreed upon by the denominations or local churches to be the corporate functions of the council.

7. To develop a co-operative program of Christian nurture basic to intelligent discipleship, faithful stewardship, and effective leadership for age-group and functional leaders and professional workers. Such a program must provide for the training of "leaders of leaders."

8. To seek to have the program undergirded, expanded, and deepened by a developing sense of responsibility on the part of the participating denominations or

[15] *Ibid.*, p. 5.

local churches so that they recognize that this is a part of their own total educational program.

9. To assemble information about the life, the needs, the changing cultural patterns, and the institutions of a state or a community for use by the representatives in determining a comprehensive program of Christian education.

10. To serve as a channel for the exchange of information among the official representatives for use by the denominations or local churches and within the co-operative program. Such an exchange would serve to broaden the understanding of program practices and emphases within the member denominations or local churches.

11. To create a climate for the work of Christian education that undergirds the entire program of Christian education within local churches, the denominations, and their councils.

12. To encourage, at the state level, Christian education committees of the denominations and local councils; at the community level, Christian education committees of local churches; to develop a comprehensive program of Christian education and through their council effectively strengthen such a program.

13. To create a vital fellowship among the professional workers in Christian education.

14. To co-operate as a department within the total program of the council, developing a program consistent with and related to the concerns of other departments or committees of the council and which will be in accord with the overall philosophy and purposes of the council.

15. To relate this program to the National Council of Churches' Division of Christian Education and to contribute to and draw from the National Council resources for the enrichment of program.[16]

Since the 1800's, Christian education has stressed co-operation on the community, county, and state levels. Co-operative Christian education has helped pave the way for and become a part of present council of churches structure. Today, Christian education activities represent an important integral part of the total concerns and services of these councils.

A review of the history of the Christian education movement reveals that there have been recurring problems of relationships between the denominations and the activities in Christian education carried on through councils of churches. This is to be expected in any growing movement. This is bound to be when the co-operative agencies of the churches often undertake exploration, experimentation, and development of program in new areas which eventually become accepted as a function of the Christian education program of the denominations themselves. It is inevitable as denominations and local churches through their councils periodically review how well they are meeting changing needs in Christian education. In spite of and because of our philosophy of co-operation there are two questions which must continually be faced by a department of Christian education in councils of churches. (This applies in like manner to all other departments of a council.) These two questions are, What phases of the educational services and functions shall be carried on solely by the denominations and local churches, and, What phases of the

[16] Adapted and expanded from a study paper "Backgrounds to Cooperative Christian Education Program," prepared by Robert Breth for the Division of Christian Education, New York State Council of Churches. Used by permission.

educational services and functions shall be carried on by the denominations and local churches through the channel of their council of churches?

Councils today are realistically seeking to answer these basic questions. As the denominations and their local churches more fully comprehend the nature of a council as their organization, which they have created, which they support and which they use as one channel for carrying on parts of their educational program, these problems of relationship will be seen in their proper perspective. The need for constant review of effective functioning of a total co-operative program of Christian education will always require frequent counseling together on the nature and details of that program.

Bibliography

Bower, William Clayton and Hayward, Percy R. *Protestantism Faces Its Educational Task Together.* Appleton, Wis.: C. C. Nelson Publishing Co., 1949.

Growing Together. A Manual for Councils of Churches. New York: National Council of Churches of Christ in the U.S.A., 1955.

Miller, J. Quinter. *Christian Unity—Its Relevance to the Community.* Available from National Council of Churches, 1957.

"Criteria for Self-Evaluation and Measurement." New York: Department of Field Operations, National Council of Churches of Christ in the U.S.A., 1955.

"The Role and Function of Local, State and National Council of Churches in the Ecumenical Movement." New York: Study report of the Association of Council Secretaries, 1957.

Sanderson, Ross W. "A History of State and Local Councils of Churches." Unpublished monograph.

"A Manual for Christian Education Committees in Councils of Churches." New York: Commission on General Christian Education and Office for Councils of Churches, National Council of Churches of Christ in the U.S.A., 1959.

Vieth, Paul H. *The Church and Christian Education.* St. Louis: Bethany Press, 1947.

Chapter 31

Christian Education and
the National Council of Churches

Gerald E. Knoff

THE NATIONAL COUNCIL OF CHURCHES IS A VERY YOUNG ORGANIZATION, ITS founding date being November 29, 1950. It came into operational existence a month later, on January 1, 1951. Its youth and comparative inexperience are sometimes forgotten as one is impressed, and dismayed, with its complicated structure and its tremendous national and world influence. While there are long traditions behind many of its units, the life of the units together in the inclusive organization has been brief, filled with change, and often accompanied by the growing pains of childhood. The Division of Christian Education within this latest of all interchurch councils in the United States is a program body which has played its role in the partial achievement of a fuller unity and in the process has savored both the accompanying satisfactions and frustrations.

A Uniting Within a Union

The observer of the work of the Division of Christian Education finds it difficult to understand the complexity of the structure. Skeptical doubts have arisen about the number and varieties of units within it and the seemingly tortuous paths which are followed in carrying to completion the phases of its educational task. It is often helpful to such a surveyor to have pointed out to him that as the Cleveland Constituting Convention on November 29, 1950 declared that the Council was then officially constituted and dedicated it "to the glory of God and to the service of mankind" the Division of Christian Education, one of its larger units, was about to begin its new life as a "uniting within a union."

That is to say, of the eight national interdenominational agencies which many years before had helped draft the organizational plans for the new Council, three were to be united within this single new division. One additional body voted to come into the division as the planning went ahead with its arduous work through the years. No one agency of the days before 1950, therefore, can properly be said to be the one antecedent of the division. It has a multiple, not a single, ancestry.

1. THE INTERNATIONAL COUNCIL OF RELIGIOUS EDUCATION. Formed in 1922, itself the result of a merger between the International Sunday School Association and the Sunday School Council of Evangelical Denominations, the International

Council (as it was popularly called) brought to the merger the loyalty and accumulated co-operative experiences of forty denominational boards and thirty-three state councils of churches. This dual membership was itself a heritage of the double rootage of the I.C.R.E., and it was at the insistence of that body that provisions were written into the constitution and bylaws of the Council in formation, providing that in the four divisions both denominational boards and state councils of churches might become constituent members. The work of the International Council of Religious Education was principally in local church, family, and community Christian education.

2. THE MISSIONARY EDUCATION MOVEMENT OF THE UNITED STATES AND CANADA. This agency, carrying forward the tasks of the churches in missionary education and operating in two nations, was founded in 1902. While leadership training, production of audio-visual materials and dramatic resources, the providing of inspirational summer conferences on missions, and the gathering of statistical materials had all been valued services to the churches, the M.E.M. was best known for its production of study materials on annual home and foreign mission themes, designed to create among the churches an informed laity and ministry. Effective relationships had always been sustained with church youth groups, the movement itself having been born out of a concern for the effective missionary education of the churches' young people.

3. THE NATIONAL PROTESTANT COUNCIL ON HIGHER EDUCATION. This agency, organized under an earlier name in 1912, had carried forward the interests of the churches for college and university work. It was primarily interested in fostering and deepening the relationships between the church-related colleges and their parent denominations, but it has had a strong concern for student work in privately and publicly supported institutions. Its headquarters had been in Washington, D. C., in earlier years, but with the merger it decided that it should be located in New York with most of the other operations of the Council.

These three bodies were numbered among the original "merging agencies" of the National Council.

4. THE INTERSEMINARY MOVEMENT. This movement's beginnings go back as far as 1880 with early sponsorship by the Federal Council of Churches and the National Student Committee of the Y.M.C.A. John R. Mott was one of its early patrons and its organizing genius, and through the years it had made possible encounters across denominational, regional, and racial lines among students in a wide variety of theological seminaries. By 1950 there were 125 schools participating in the movement, with students working through eight regional councils and meeting in triennial national conferences. During the time the eight merging agencies were perfecting their plans for founding the National Council of Churches, the Interseminary Movement decided to become a part of the Council and of its Division of Christian Education.

5. UNDERGRADUATE STUDENT CHRISTIAN MOVEMENTS. During the later years of planning for the National Council, negotiations were begun between representatives of it and of the two principal undergraduate student movements of the country—the United Student Christian Council, organized in 1944, and the Student Volunteer Movement for Christian Missions, dating from 1886. It took time, however, to find a satisfactory organizational formula which would allow for responsible association within the National Council, one which would allow

for responsible association along with desirable student autonomy. Eventually a status of "related movement" was agreed upon, with the United Student Christian Council to be related to one of the Departments of the Commission on Christian Higher Education, and the Student Volunteer movement to operate as a Department of Missionary Services in the same Commission. These additional affiliations took place in 1953.

Far from being an organizational unity, therefore, which passed from a single previous existence into the National Council, the Division of Christian Education carries within itself the interests of six separate church agencies, each with an individuality of its own, each with its own constituency, each with its honorable record of service.

Objectives of the Division and Its Principal Units

This multiple origin might lead one to think that there was little common purpose or objective among such diverse church bodies. This is not at all the case. While all these bodies were specialized institutions (some with narrower specializations than others) all were parts of a larger whole, the efforts of the American churches and Christians to fulfill more effectively their Christian teaching ministry. All have found ample freedom and their individualized roles cared for within the Division's general functions. The bylaws stipulate that it is to:

Serve as an agency of the churches of the United States and Canada, through which their educational, home and foreign mission boards, departments of missionary education, and other agencies for missionary education, and state councils may cooperate in maintaining and developing the most effective programs of Christian education and conduct such work as they desire to have conducted in their behalf and serve as the agency through which their leaders may:

(1) Enjoy the inspiration and self-education which come through Christian fellowship.

(2) Share convictions, ideas, and experiences.

(3) Evaluate their current plans and practices.

(4) Cooperate in examining areas of needed service.

(5) Carry on cooperative research.

(6) Carry on activities for enrichment of their denominational programs.

(7) Plan together religious education activities of a community nature.

(8) Cooperate in developing a public mind favorable to the conduct of Christian education.

(9) Unite in carrying on certain designated aspects of their work.

(10) Conduct joint experimentation in needed new fields vital to Christian education.

(11) Provide a means whereby two or more denominations may join in common endeavors of their own choice.

(12) Assist state and local councils of churches in their work of religious education.

(13) Join in such other plans and activities as may seem wise and helpful.[1]

In addition it is the announced aim of the Division to work co-operatively with other Council units, with other educational, missionary, and character-building agencies, with the corresponding department of the Canadian Council of Churches, and with three world organizations—the World Council of Churches, the World

[1] Division of Christian Education, Bylaws, Article II, Section 2b. Used by permission.

Council of Christian Education and Sunday School Association, and the International Missionary Council.[2]

The Commission on General Christian Education has defined its purposes as follows:

To serve as the medium of the Division for advancing its work in the field of general Christian education.

To aid the member boards and agencies in the development of a comprehensive Christian education service for persons of all ages in the home, local church, and community.[3]

The Commission on Higher Education has determined its purposes in the following corresponding statement:

To awaken the entire public to the conviction that religion is essential to a complete education and that education is necessary to the achievement of progress.

To foster a vital Christian life in college and university communities of the United States of America including those of tax-supported institutions.

To strengthen the Christian college, to promote religious instruction therein, and to emphasize the permanent necessity of higher education under distinctly Christian auspices.[4]

Similarly the Commission on Missionary Education is empowered to:

Prepare, publish and distribute missionary education materials.

Hold training schools and conferences.

Carry on any other activities which may be decided upon to further the cause of missionary education and carry out the desires of the constituent boards and agencies.

Cooperate or assist in the work of other groups in closely allied fields, such as radio, television, or audio-visual materials.[5]

Scope of Program Services

As has been suggested above the chief educational units of the Division are its three program Commissions—the Commission on General Christian Education, the Commission on Higher Education and the Commission on Missionary Education.[6] In addition there are certain program services related directly to the Division's chief administrative officer, the Executive Secretary.

In February 1959 the list of these services were as follows:

General Division Services
Department of the English Bible
Standard Bible Committee
Conference Point Camp, Lake Geneva, Wisconsin
Geneva Point Camp, Lake Winnipesaukee, New Hampshire
Literature Associates
Newspaper Lesson Syndication
Conference and Convention Arrangements

[2] *Ibid.*, Article II, Section 2c, d, e, and f.
[3] Bylaws, Article III, Sections 1a and 1b.
[4] Bylaws, Article III, Section 1.
[5] Bylaws, Article III, Section 2.
[6] Prior to December 1957 these latter two units were known as the Commission on Christian Higher Education and the Joint Commission on Missionary Education, respectively.

Commission on General Christian Education
Department of Children's Work
Department of Youth Work and United Christian Youth Movement
Department of Adult Work
Department of Family Life
Department of Administration and Leadership
Department of Curriculum Development
Department of Weekday Religious Education
Department of Religion and Public Education
Department of Audio-Visual and Broadcast Education
The International Journal of Religious Education

Commission on Higher Education
Department of Campus Christian Life
Department of the Ministry
Department of Christian Institutions
Interseminary Committee
The Christian Scholar
The United Student Christian Council (a related movement)
The Student Volunteer Movement (a related movement)
The Faculty Christian Fellowship (a related movement)

Commission on Missionary Education
Promotion Department
Department of Children's Work
Department of Youth Work
Department of Adult Work
Production Department
Order Department

The Division's Governing Bodies

As is the case with the sister units of the Council, the Division of Christian Education is thoroughly responsible to those who have called it into being and whose agency it is—the denominational boards of Christian education, the missionary education agencies, and the member state councils of churches. Its assembly is its ultimate governing body, a group of persons most of whom are appointed by the member denominations, boards, and state councils. It meets triennially in connection with the meeting of the National Council's General Assembly. San Francisco, 1960, and Philadelphia, 1963, were chosen as assembly cities and dates.

The governing body which meets between sessions of the assembly is called the executive board. Its membership is composed principally of representatives of the three program commissions. Its numbers have usually been about seventy-five persons. The board can exercise between sessions of the assembly all the powers of the latter, save that of amending the Bylaws and of determining the membership of the division. There is a budget and finance committee whose functions are described by its name, and also a business committee which in addition supervises the investments, the physical properties, the contracts, the publishing operations, and all the manifold business involvements of an ongoing body whose budget in 1959 was over $2,300,000.

Each of the three commissions has an administrative committee responsible for

342

its work. Their names are different but they are similarly constituted and have similar duties.

The Related Movements

A term—that of *Related Movement*—has been used in the listing of the several program departments and has not yet been explained. These units are specified, but not defined with any accuracy, in the division Bylaws. Perhaps a good working definition would be that they are units which: (1) have a recognizable constituency of their own, (2) have had a prior existence as a regularly organized educational body, (3) usually have staff chosen upon the initiative of the unit, (4) enjoy a relatively large amount of program autonomy in the carrying forward of their own work, and (5) raise a substantial portion of their own funds. The United Christian Youth Movement, lodged within the Commission on General Christian Education, is one such related movement. The United Student Christian Council, the Student Volunteer Movement, and the Faculty Christian Fellowship are the other three, all of them administratively related to the Commission on Higher Education.

A merger of the three student movements took place in September 1959, which resulted in a truly unified student Christian movement in this country. The name chosen was the National Student Christian Federation, a body which as now established brings together the former United Student Christian Council, the Interseminary Movement, and the Student Volunteer Movement.

Still in process of formation is a body to be called the Council of Protestant Colleges and Universities, which if finally consummated will also have the status of a related movement. Its offices will be in Washington, D. C., in order to make it of maximum usefulness to college and university presidents visiting often in that city in which are located the headquarters of most of the national educational bodies.

The Associated Sections

For many years the International Council of Religious Education had associated with it large groups of professional people, meeting annually at the time of the yearly meetings of the Council. These bodies were not tightly bound to the Council in any administrative way, nor it to them. They were responsible for their own programs and for their own financing. Through the years they proved to be of tremendous value as professional associations, and the plan was brought forward into the division as a major organizational contribution from the I.C.R.E. The list of these sections is as follows:

Administration and Leadership
Adult Work
Children's Work
City Executives
Directors
Editors
Missionary Education
National Denominational Executives
Pastors
Professors and Research

343

Publishers
State and Regional Executives
Weekday Religious Education
Youth Work

Staff services are provided by the Commission on General Christian Education for all these sections, save for the Missionary Education Section, which receives its services from the corresponding Commission.

Joint Educational Efforts with Other National Council Units

The structural plans set up to accomplish the work of the church have a certain artificiality about them at best, and it is not too surprising that many of the programs of the Division are shared in part with one or more of the other units of the National Council. Staff members and program committee members are in frequent consultation with their colleagues in other divisions, and frequently programs are jointly administered where close association of interests has made this kind of shared effort natural and useful.

The Division shares three such endeavors with the Central Department of Evangelism, for example. The National Christian Teaching Mission is a program to awaken local churches to the presence and the needs of unchurched people living in their very neighborhood and to deepen the level of evangelistic fellowship within the congregation so that these unreached persons may be led to the Lord of the Church. The University Christian Mission has guided campus programs of evangelism and witness on hundreds of college and university campuses, and in its guidance local campus religious organizations have been effectively enlisted. *Youth Looks Up,* an evangelistic television approach to young people, always fresh and often unconventional, has explored new ways of reaching the masses of young people unrelated, indifferent, and often antagonistic to the church. In each of these evangelistic endeavors the Division of Christian Education is deeply, officially, and administratively involved.

The missionary outreach of the church is also one which cannot be departmentalized without doing harm to it and to the broader work of the church. The Commission on Missionary Education and the Student Volunteer Movement are closely associated with the life and planning of the Divisions of Home Missions and of Foreign Missions. Indeed the relationships of these two educational organizations with the two mission boards are as creative and sustained as are their operations within educational circles. A now defunct "joint department" and "joint commission" structure attempted to symbolize this program involvement, but in the interests of simplicity it was abandoned in 1957. The reality is still there, however, though the sign has gone.

The United Church Men, a general department of the National Council, gave valuable assistance to the Commission on Higher Education through the creation of a jointly sponsored "National Committee of Church Men for Church Colleges." The United Youth Movement has worked closely with the Departments of International Affairs, of Racial and Cultural Relations, and others in the Division of Christian Life and Work. The Department of Curriculum Development worked with the Division of Home Missions in making available lesson materials for migrant workers and for Spanish speaking peoples within the U.S.A. Probably thirty or forty separate programs could be listed which needed and received the direct services of trained Christian education leaders, program activities which were for sound administrative reasons lodged with some other major unit of the National Council.

The World Agencies of the Division

The Christian education enterprise is a world-wide concern and the division attempts to play a responsible role in it. The chief agency through which the division works in these matters is the World Council of Christian Education and Sunday School Association.[7]

The Division of Christian Education and the Division of Foreign Missions are the two U.S.A. members of this world agency which is composed chiefly of national interdenominational councils of Christian education. Some of the elected officers in the one serve in other elected capacities in the other. The Executive Secretary of the Division of Christian Education serves as a member of the Board of Managers of the World Educational Services Committee and has performed additional services on behalf of the North American unit of the W.C.C.E. and S.S.A. Denominational staff people work on committees of both bodies. No duplication of effort is involved since the W.C.C.E. and S.S.A. is not an operating agency within the United States and Canada. As American and Canadian leaders serve other parts of the world it is almost always through the established outreach and accepted program of the W.C.C.E. and S.S.A.

An important co-operation with the World Council of Churches comes from the involvement of the North American youth leaders and young people with the work of the Youth Department and Youth Committee sponsored jointly by the World Council of Churches and the W.C.C.E. and S.S.A. Through the instrument of this committee, American young people make an important contribution to the Christian youth of the world, and are reciprocally blessed in their work.

The United Student Christian Council is the U.S.A. member of the World's Student Christian Federation. Indeed the relationship might almost be stated in the reverse; the W.S.C.F. exists in the U.S.A. as the United Student Christian Council. Through this Federation the American Christian student mind is brought to bear upon the needs of the church around the world, and the ecumenical encounter finds meaning and significance in the mind of the Christian student. In one project especially, the Ecumenical Voluntary Service Projects, the W.S.C.F., the U.S.C.C., and the U.C.Y.M. are all intimately involved with each one bearing a clearly designated portion of the common task.

The Revised Standard Version of the Bible

The appearance of the Revised Standard Version of the Bible on September 30, 1952, marked another milestone in the long history of English translations of the Holy Scriptures. The New Testament had appeared in 1946 and had received wide acclaim. As a result of a carefully laid-out program extending over a five-year period conceived and administered by Philip C. Landers, there were held on that single evening more than 3,200 community celebrations marking the introduction of this, the latest Bible in the great Tyndale-King James tradition. Luther Allan Weigle, Dean Emeritus of the Yale University Divinity School, has served since

[7] For a more complete description of the work of this Council and the World Council of Churches see ch. 32, pp. 350-58.

its establishment as chairman of the Standard Bible Committee and has had associated with him in recent years Millar Burrows as vice-chairman.

The sales of the R.S.V. have averaged well over a million copies a year since its appearance, and it is rapidly being accepted in all parts of the English speaking world. By the end of the year 1958, twenty-two denominations with a church membership of 29,282,449 had officially adopted the R.S.V. for all or nearly all of their church-school lesson materials; while five others with a membership of 446,-094 had adopted it for some of their basic curricular material. Ten denominations with 9,799,186 members were using the R.S.V. in parallel columns with the King James Version.

During the long years of planning for the version Roy G. Ross played a leading role and had it not been for his indomitable faith in the merits of the proposal this great version of the Bible would never have come to completion. Generations of Christians in the years to come will have reason to be grateful to the members of the Standard Bible Committee, all of whom donated their services and who are responsible for the scholarly excellence of the translation.

The appearance of an R.S.V. translation of the *Apocrypha* caused a new interest among Protestants in these little known books, and members and clergy of the Episcopal and Eastern Orthodox churches were especially glad to see the new translation, since the intertestamental books are used in the liturgies of both these communions. An overture from the National Council of the Episcopal Church was the occasion for the authorization of the beginning of work on this translation in December 1952.

A Responsible Expression of the Churches' Work

One will never understand the Division of Christian Education unless he understands it as a thoroughly representative agent of the educational forces of the Protestant and Orthodox churches of the United States and Canada. When one comes to appreciate this relationship then he is in a position to understand some of the handicaps and difficulties under which it labors. But he has come close also to understanding the effective manner in which it is privileged to operate in its chosen and appointed field.

It is not a free-wheeling agency with the freedom which independence makes possible. Therefore it seldom makes the headlines, and often its work, even to its best friends and to its own administrators, appears pedestrian. Yet this dependence has its advantages, for when a division program does get under way, it has behind it powerful educational boards and councils and the channels of communication to the local church and the individual college or campus group are swift, multiple, and free-flowing.

The launching of a thoroughly interdenominational national program takes time, and it is the curricular processes which are inevitably the slowest. Occasional educational bulletins are produced more quickly, but even with them a careful process of review has been found indispensable to later general acceptance.

The three commissions have each developed their characteristic patterns of work, accepted procedures which are not always uniform even within a single commission, depending upon the nature and point of origin of a program or document. The goal in view is the same, however, a steady determination to make sure that the end result is that which was intended by the member churches when the proposal was first envisaged. The Division's staff, officers, and members of its governing bodies are all devoted to this watchful, critical supervision of its work. Largely because of this alertness the Division has never become a rival of the churches' official educational programs.

The Publishing Activities of the Division

Inevitably an educational program involves the production of written materials and written materials have to be published and through publication reach their intended, primary constituencies in two nations, and a secondary constituency in a score of other countries. Across the years there have been worked out several patterns of publishing which are proving to be generally satisfactory. Precedents have been established and the particular route a document takes in order to emerge in printed pages depends chiefly upon two factors—the point of origin of the manuscript and the essential nature of its contents. The most familiar methods of publishing are as follows.

1. If the document is finally to be a Sunday church-school lesson, this material has probably originated in one of the two basic committees of the Department of Curriculum Development—the Committee on the Uniform Series or the Committee on the Graded Curriculum. Outlines of lessons only are produced by these division committees made up of responsible denominational editors and curriculum specialists. The outlines are then released to denominational editors and writers and to independent publishers for development into lesson materials and teachers' aids, according to the genius, educational insights, doctrinal positions, and ecclesiastical polities of each church.

2. If the material is of supplementary nature or in the form of an educational bulletin, a supplementary resource, a statement of basic educational theory or principles, a manual of community outreach, or any one of a dozen other categories, auxiliary to "main-line" curriculum, it has usually originated in one of the educational committees of one of the commissions, is reviewed by the governing body of the commission, and after approval is published, usually by the National Council's Office of Publication and Distribution, but sometimes by the department itself dealing directly with a printer or contractor.

3. Service and promotional materials not involving substantial educational content are often produced by the department's executive. They may or may not be reviewed by the department's governing committee and are almost never reviewed by the governing commission.

4. An exception to the general principle that the Division does not produce basic curriculum for the local church is to be found in the missionary education materials prepared by the Commission on Missionary Education. In this unit by long-standing agreement significant curriculum creation and publishing operations are carried on co-operatively. Controlling the policies and operations of this Commission are denominational representatives of foreign and home boards and of boards of Christian education. The chief retail outlets for the books and other educational materials are the denominational publishing houses.

5. A fifth process deals principally with curricular materials and with leadership education books intended for community leadership education schools, vacation church schools sponsored either by denominations or by community councils of churches, and for weekday systems of religious education, generally under inter-

denominational auspices. In such instances descriptions of needed materials arise in the appropriate educational committee of the Commission on General Christian Education and are referred to the Cooperative Publication Association.

This body is an independent organization in which denominational editors and publishers meet regularly twice a year, and to which come the involved National Council staff executives as advisors. In this body publication proposals are modified, ratified or rejected, writers suggested and assigned, and publication responsibility allocated, to be exercised on behalf of the Association as a whole. The actual publication processes are completely denominationally controlled.

6. Publishing arrangements for the Revised Standard Version of the Bible follow still another pattern. The firm of Thomas Nelson and Sons has had an exclusive contract with the Division, operative since the New Testament appeared in 1946 and the complete Bible in 1952. It runs for ten years from this latter date. On October 1, 1962 five additional firms by contractual agreement already executed will also become publishers. Thomas Nelson and Sons will continue, with these newly added firms, until the expiration of the copyright or any renewal thereof.

7. The two official periodicals of the Division, *The International Journal of Religious Education* and *The Christian Scholar,* are published as departmental operations with the two administering commissions exercising supervision in matters of policy. Separate contracts are effected with printing firms. The magazines are held responsible by their commissions for living within their earned income plus their agreed-upon subsidy.

8. Educational committees will sometimes agree that a particular article or series of articles is needed and will agree to pay a chosen writer for such a manuscript intended for as many denominational Christian education periodicals as may desire to use it. An *ad hoc* committee is formed to negotiate with the writer, to solicit orders for the article from the editors of periodicals likely to be interested in the product, to review the proffered manuscript, and to oversee the payment of small honoraria to the writer from each of the magazines which has bought his article.

9. The Division Year Book is an annual compendium of the work of all the departments and commissions of the division—a record of minutes and other official actions; a directory of the many responsible boards, committees, and other governing units; a device for the public reporting of the division's finances; and a general reference book for information about denominational and state council personnel in Christian education. It is sold to individual purchasers, the largest group of which are those belonging to *Literature Associates.* These persons receive it, together with all other publications of the division for the payment of a single annual fee. It is a production of the office of the executive secretary, who is responsible for its accuracy and usefulness. This book could have perhaps been classified under category "3" above as service and promotional material for that is what it really is. Because of its symbolic nature as representing and communicating all the educational program of the division through the entire year it is listed separately.

Officers and Leaders

Since the division was constituted in December, 1950, it has had only two chairmen. Paul Calvin Payne served as chairman until December, 1957, at which time Bishop Reuben H. Mueller succeeded him. Luther Wesley Smith, Harry Thomas Stock, and Richard Hoiland successively have been the chairmen of the Executive Board.

The Commission on General Christian Education has had as chairmen Harry Thomas Stock, Richard Hoiland, and Franklin I. Sheeder. John O. Gross and E. Fay Campbell have led the Commission on Higher Education. Corliss P. Hargraves, Miss Avis E. Harvey, and William J. Keech have been the elected chairmen of the Commission on Missionary Education.

The executive officers of the three commissions are known as general directors. These persons for the Commission on Higher Education have been E. Fay Campbell (part time), Raymond F. McLain, and Hubert C. Noble. Franklin D. Cogswell and J. Allan Ranck have headed the staff of the Commission on Missionary Education. A. L. Roberts succeeded Gerald E. Knoff as General Director of the Commission on General Christian Education in 1953.

Roy G. Ross, who had been the general secretary of the International Council of Religious Education, was the first executive secretary of the division giving half time to its administration and the remainder of his time to the National Council as Associate General Secretary. This initial arrangement proved to be unworkable, the demands of both offices being what they were, and Ross resigned his division position to give full time to the other task. Gerald E. Knoff succeeded him on July 1, 1952 as the second executive secretary and the first full-time administrative officer of the division.

Bibliography

Barstow, Robbins W. (ed.). *Christian Faith in Action*. New York: Central Department of Publication and Distribution, National Council of Churches of Christ in the U.S.A., 1951.

Bower, William C. and Hayward, Percy R. *Protestantism Faces Its Educational Task Together*. Appleton, Wis.: C. C. Nelson Publishing Company, 1949.

Brown, Arlo A. *A History of Religious Education in Recent Times*. New York: The Abingdon Press, 1923.

Lotz, P. H. (ed.). *Orientation in Religious Education*. Nashville: Abingdon Press, 1950.

Vieth, Paul H. *The Church and Christian Education*. St. Louis: Bethany Press, 1947.

Weigle, Luther A. *American Idealism*. New Haven, Conn.: Yale University Press, 1928.

Periodicals

The Christian Scholar.
The International Journal of Religious Education.
The National Council Outlook.
Yearbooks, Division of Christian Education.
Biennial Reports, National Council of Churches of Christ in the U.S.A., 1952, 1954, and 1957 (triennial).

Chapter 32

The World Council of Christian
Education and the World Council of Churches

Nelson Chappel

IT IS THE PURPOSE OF THIS CHAPTER TO GIVE A BRIEF DESCRIPTION OF THE RELA-
tionship between the World Council of Christian Education and Sunday School
Association and the World Council of Churches—to outline the history, structure,
and program of the W.C.C.E.S.S.A.—and to indicate the situation which Christian
education faces in today's world.

The Relationships of the W.C.C. and W.C.C.E.S.S.A.

The World Council of Churches is the newest of the major world Christian
ecumenical bodies, having been constituted in 1948 at Amsterdam. Nonetheless,
it carries forward streams of co-operative activity in the fields of Faith and Order
and of Life and Work which began years earlier. The World Council of Churches
draws its strength from the fact that it is the first world ecumenical body in
modern times to be created by the official action of the churches functioning
directly as denominations. At this writing more than 170 autonomous church
bodies in 53 countries hold direct membership in the World Council of Churches.

The World Council of Christian Education and Sunday School Association had
its origins in the activity of interested groups of Sunday-school workers, largely
composed of laymen, who organized the first World Sunday School Convention in
London in 1889. When the World Sunday School Association was formally
organized in 1907, its first member units were Sunday-school organizations which
were not usually officially representative of the churches. Today the great majority
of the 57 national member units of the W.C.C.E.S.S.A. are councils of churches,
councils of Christian education, or national Christian councils that are officially
representative of the churches.

When the World Council of Churches was established in 1948, the existence of
the other world ecumenical bodies was recognized. The following resolution was
presented at the first assembly of the World Council of Churches by one of its
committees:

The Committee express admiration for the work of the World Council of Christian
Education and recommend that the World Council of Churches welcome cooperation with

the World Council of Christian Education in the field of Christian education, and further recommend that the World Council of Christian Education be included among the world organizations invited to send representatives in a consultative capacity to the Assembly.[1]

When the World Council of Churches was establishing a youth department at that first assembly, it was recognized that the W.C.C.E.S.S.A., also, was active in youth work. It was, therefore, agreed that 75 per cent of the membership of the youth committees of the two youth departments (W.C.C. and W.C.C.E.S.S.A.) should be identical, and that the two committees would always meet together. Nine years later in 1957 the W.C.C. and the W.C.C.E.S.S.A. agreed to have one joint World Youth Committee that would represent both youth departments and to which both departments would report. The joint W.C.C.-W.C.C.E.S.S.A. Youth Committee sponsors certain co-operative activities, the most important of which is called "World Youth Projects." This is a plan by which youth organizations in Christian churches around the world may share prayers, leadership, materials, and financial assistance. All "World Youth Projects" must be for youth and must be interdenominational, partially self-supporting, and approved by the National Council of Churches or equivalent body concerned.

It is recognized that each youth department also has its own special functions in addition to those which are carried on in co-operation. The World Council of Churches Youth Department sponsors an extensive program of international ecumenical work camps and regional conferences to provide church youth with ecumenical experiences. These activities are performed by the Ecumenical Youth Services Committee of the W.C.C. The W.C.C.E.S.S.A. Youth Department is responsible for the organizing of youth groups in local churches around the world, together with the preparation of suitable program materials and of leadership for them. These functions are sponsored by the Educational Youth Service Committee of the W.C.C.E.S.S.A. Both of these committees report to the joint W.C.C.-W.C.C.E.S.S.A. youth committee.

In addition to this official relationship of their youth departments, the World Council of Churches and the World Council of Christian Education and Sunday School Association have a wide field of common interest and co-operate wherever possible. The W.C.C.E.S.S.A. has also co-operated closely with the International Missionary Council which in 1959 was in the process of merging with the World Council of Churches.

In the World Christian Youth Commission, the W.C.C. and the W.C.C.E.S.S.A. both have co-operative relationships with the World Student Christian Federation, the World Alliance of Y.M.C.A.'s, and the World's Y.W.C.A.

The History of the W.C.C.E.S.S.A.

In 1780 Robert Raikes, a layman, started the Sunday-school movement which taught boys and girls to read and write, emphasizing the Bible especially. This movement brought public attention to the need for free education for the masses in Britain, an interest which was later pioneered by the churches and finally accepted as a responsibility of the government. The Sunday-school movement soon spread to America, and here as in Britain it ran into criticism from some of the

[1] W. A. Visser t' Hooft, *The First Assembly of the World Council of Churches—Official Report*, p. 132.

clergy as an improper activity for Sunday. This criticism of the movement made laymen more determined to keep control of it. It is significant that when the American Sunday School Union was formed in 1824 it was stated in the constitution that no clergyman could be a member of its board. Both the National Sunday School Union (England and Wales) and the International Sunday School Association (Canada and the U.S.A.), which together organized the first world Sunday-school convention in London in 1889, were independent organizations largely sponsored and controlled by laymen.

At that first world convention two significant actions were taken. Funds were raised to help send a missionary to India to serve the India Sunday School Union, and a continuation Convention Committee was appointed to prepare for the next world convention. Subsequent conventions were held at St. Louis, 1893; London, 1898; Jerusalem, 1904; Rome, 1907; Washington, 1910; Zurich, 1913; Tokyo, 1920; Glasgow, 1924; Los Angeles, 1928; Rio de Janeiro, 1932; Oslo, 1936; Toronto, 1950; and Tokyo, 1958.

At each world convention some new missionary activity to promote Sunday-school work was started until in 1907 it became evident that a permanent organization would have to be set up to supervise these activities. At that time the World Sunday School Association was formally organized, "to promote Christian education, including Sunday School work, to encourage the study of the Bible, and to participate in the church's task of world evangelization." [2] An executive committee was established as the governing body of the World Sunday School Association. It consisted of twelve persons from Britain, twelve from North America, and ten from the rest of the world. The latter group was seldom able to meet because of travel difficulties except at the time of a world convention. The two former groups met regularly and provided the administrative leadership for the association. Thus a British committee and a North American committee later developed as adminstrative committees of the W.S.S.A. They divided the world between them for area responsibility. General policy was still determined by a central executive committee, which usually met quadrennially or whenever a world convention was held. Later the governing body came to be known as "the council," and still later as "the assembly." At the first world convention considerable attention was given to the question of the place of young people in the church, so that in addition to Sunday-school work the member units of the council were asking for help in other areas of Christian education, such as youth work, vacation schools, Christian education in the schools, and other areas. By 1947 it had become apparent that the name "World Sunday School Association" was no longer adequate to indicate the enlarged program of the world body. At a meeting at Birmingham, England, in that year, the name was changed to the "World Council of Christian Education" which still remains the legal title of the world organization, although in 1950 the words "and Sunday School Association" were added to the title "for operating purposes." Since most of the administrative responsibilities were carried by the British and North American committees, which provided the entire staff and almost all of the financial support for the world body, it became increasingly difficult for the W.C.C.E.S.S.A. to operate as a unified world body.

In 1953, after years of study, a plan of integration was adopted, establishing a

[2] Bylaws of the W.C.C.E.S.S.A.

world office to unify the planning, program, and budget of the W.C.C.E.S.S.A. under one general secretary and two associate general secretaries. Each associate general secretary serves as the secretary of one of the administrative committees. The Assembly of the W.C.C.E.S.S.A. is now its governing body and meets quadrennially to determine general policy and program. Each member unit is represented in the assembly. There are now fifty-seven national autonomous member units of the W.C.C.E.S.S.A. which are national Christian councils, councils of Christian education, or equivalent bodies having major responsibility for Christian education in their countries and "representing churches holding the evangelical faith." [3] In the U.S.A. there are two member units of the W.C.C.E.S.S.A.—the Division of Christian Education and the Division of Foreign Missions of the National Council of the Churches of Christ.[4]

The two administrative committees have been broadened to include individuals from all member units for which they have area responsibility. These administrative committees continue to operate through their offices in London and New York. The world office is also located in New York.

The Assembly of the W.C.C.E.S.S.A. elects a small executive committee, known as the "Board of Managers" which meets annually to act for the assembly between its quadrennial meetings.

The Program of the W.C.C.E.S.S.A.

1. GENERAL PRINCIPLES. The W.C.C.E.S.S.A. is not a centralized body which prepares a Christian education program for the whole world. There was a time in its early history when this was thought possible, since there was one gospel and one Bible which was used all over the world. An International Sunday School Lessons Committee was established by the World Sunday School Association to prepare teaching materials for Sunday schools all over the world, but it was soon discovered that the same teaching materials could not even be used in two such similar cultures as are found in North America and Britain. The British section of this International Committee reorganized as the British Lessons Council which prepares Sunday-school lessons for the United Kingdom alone. The North American section of the International Lessons Committee became the committee of the same name of the International Council of Religious Education, now the Division of Christian Education of the N.C.C.C.U.S.A., and prepares lesson outlines for North America alone. The W.C.C.E.S.S.A. is now a federation of autonomous member units and the Council is maintained by them as a channel through which they can experience a world-wide Christian fellowship and through which they may exchange ideas, information, experience, materials, leadership, and financial aid. Outside of the circle of its member units the W.C.C.E.S.S.A. seeks to help the churches in these areas and also to establish national or regional organizations to promote Christian education "with the ultimate goal that they shall become self-directing, self-supporting, and self-propagating under national leadership." As a rule the services of the W.C.C.E.S.S.A. are only given to the churches of a particular country or area after they have initiated the request for such service.

2. CONVENTIONS, CONFERENCES, AND INSTITUTES. World conventions, which were once the main purpose of this world movement, are now held at less frequent

[3] Bylaws of the W.C.C.E.S.S.A.
[4] Cf. ch. 31, p. 345.

intervals. The Fourteenth World Convention on Christian Education was held in Tokyo, Japan, in 1958, with 4,014 delegates present from 64 countries.

Regional conventions and conferences are held more frequently. (E.g., through its London office the W.C.C.E.S.S.A. sponsors annual meetings of Christian education leaders in Europe. In 1957 the New York office co-operated with the International Missionary Council in sponsoring a Caribbean Consultation.)

3. THE WORLD CHRISTIAN EDUCATION MAGAZINE. The quarterly magazine *World Christian Education* is another medium through which Christian education leaders from around the world may exchange ideas, information, and experiences. Most issues of the magazine will contain contributions from more than twenty countries and its circulation includes readers in ninety-nine different countries.

4. FIELD VISITATION. Members of the staff of the W.C.C.E.S.S.A. each year make field visits in many different countries, at the invitation of the Christian education organizations there. One member of the staff has visited forty-three different countries in five years, and some of them several times during that period. Such a field visit has often been the first occasion when representatives of the many denominations in a particular country or area have come together face-to-face to discuss their Christian education task.

5. CURRICULUM PROJECTS. An increasing number of countries or areas have become aware of the need for indigenous curriculum materials in recent years. In 1941 the services of the W.C.C.E.S.S.A. were made available to the churches of Latin America in a project which has resulted in the production of the new Latin American Curriculum (in Spanish) for the Sunday schools of that area. Following World War II the W.C.C.E.S.S.A. has given similar assistance to the churches in Japan, in the Philippines, in India, in the Near East, in West Pakistan, and in East Pakistan. It is currently giving this same support to the churches of Africa south of the Sahara, the British West Indies, and to the churches serving Chinese-speaking people in Southeast Asia. In each of these curriculum projects the major work is done by people who live in the country or area concerned, with W.C.C.E.S.S.A. providing experienced leadership through consultants and enlisting sufficient financial aid to launch each project. A "Christian Education Guide" on "The Preparation of Curriculum Materials" has also been prepared and published by the W.C.C.E.S.S.A.

6. LEADERSHIP TRAINING. The W.C.C.E.S.S.A., when requested to do so by the church organizations in a country or area, assists them to train nationals as leaders by:

a) Securing scholarships for outstanding leadership prospects.

b) Leadership training courses planned in co-operation with the Christian Councils or equivalent bodies in the countries of the younger churches with special outside leadership being provided by the W.C.C.E.S.S.A.

c) Making available the services of specialists in religious education who may wish to use their sabbatical leaves from seminaries or executive positions in this type of service to the "younger" churches (Dean E. G. Homrighausen of Princeton Seminary, Professor Paul Vieth of Yale Divinity School, and Professor Donald Maynard of Boston University School of Theology are among those who have served in this way).

d) "In-service" training. The W.C.C.E.S.S.A. enlists from mission boards in Britain, Canada, and the United States of America a group of nationals or missionaries who are invited one by one into a country to work for a period of not more than three years beside those nationals who have been assigned Christian education work. During that time they attempt to train the nationals by working with them on all kinds of Christian education projects and services.

e) Helping each country to prepare its own leadership training program. Even courses on leadership training must be indigenous to meet the needs of the people of the particular area and culture. The W.C.C.E.S.S.A. sponsors special study conferences where the key workers in Christian education come together and are given guidance in planning suitable courses in leadership training for their people. A "Christian Education Guide" on "Preparation for Leadership" has also been prepared by the W.C.C.E.S.S.A.

7. AUDIO-VISUAL EDUCATION. The W.C.C.E.S.S.A. through its audio-visual department seeks to assist the churches around the world to make wise and effective use of audio-visual materials. It also makes available evaluations of suitable audio-visual materials for Christian education, especially those which are usable in the "younger" church areas. These evaluations are distributed through a bimonthly publication in "Sight-Sound" and also in booklet form, both of which are published jointly by R.A.V.E.M.C.C.O. (Radio, Visual Education, and Mass Communications of The Division of Foreign Missions, National Council of Churches), and the W.C.C.E.S.S.A.

8. THEOLOGICAL EDUCATION. The W.C.C.E.S.S.A. has been reminded by many areas that the individual pastor or minister is the key man in the local church's program of Christian education. Even in the United States, 90 per cent of all ministers in parishes must be their own directors of Christian education. Hence they should be prepared for an educational ministry during their regular theological training. In 1958 the W.C.C.E.S.S.A. sponsored a world consultation on "Training Ministers for a Teaching Ministry" in Tokyo, Japan, to study this question. The report of that consultation is worthy of study.[5]

9. EMERGENCY MATERIALS. In countries where there is no adequate supply of curriculum materials or of Bible pictures, the W.C.C.E.S.S.A., with the help of children in the United States of America and in Canada, publishes and distributes Bible pictures (Old and New Testament series) under the title of "Pictures for Children Everywhere." Twenty million of such pictures—large and small—have been printed in four colors. These Bible pictures are especially valuable in teaching illiterates or semi-literates. The W.C.C.E.S.S.A. also publishes in more than twenty languages an illustrated booklet on the life of Christ, "Jesus, Friend of Children Everywhere." The churches in each language area are free to revise the stories on the life of Christ to meet their need, before they are printed. Over two million of these booklets have been distributed in more than one hundred countries.

The Status of Christian Education in the World

It is difficult for those who live in North America to realize that a world revolution has taken place since the end of World War II. In Asia alone half of the people who live on this earth had their whole world turned upside down. Six hundred and fifty millions of these live in China and now have a completely new world to live in under a Communistic dictatorship. An equal number in other countries of Asia have made the tremendous leap from dependence or colonialism to

[5] See bibliography at end of chapter.

complete independence and freedom from foreign control. The world for them also has undergone tremendous upheaval, and this has affected the four hundred million people living in India, and the millions living in Pakistan, Ceylon, Burma, Malaya, Indonesia, and the Philippines. In the Middle East and in Africa the revolution continues and more and more millions of mankind live in an entirely new world without the guidance or control of foreign governments.

The spirit of nationalism which has developed in the drive for independence and self-determination in countries of Africa and Asia has greatly affected the work of the Christian church in these areas. Christianity must now become an indigenous movement with native leadership and program, or it will find itself out of step with the new spirit of these countries.

Already great changes have taken place in the life and work of the church, especially in the field of Christian education. Missionaries who brought the gospel to Africa and Asia were interested in Christian education, but when they found that the masses had little or no educational opportunity, they set out to provide general education under Christian auspices. They built, staffed, and administered elementary and secondary schools and set up training colleges for teachers. In Africa south of the Sahara, it was estimated that 80 per cent of the Africans in school in 1945 were in Christian schools. This was a great opportunity for Christian education. Today that opportunity is rapidly disappearing. Each country as it becomes independent tends to take over the education of its younger generation under the secular government. In Indonesia today only a handful of schools remain under Christian auspices. In India the government is gradually assuming the control of schools from the church. In Africa and the Near East, the same process is evident. In 1952 when the Gold Coast and Nigeria were given some control of their domestic affairs by the British government, they both passed laws denying government assistance to new schools opened under church auspices. The Belgian government has notified the churches and missions in the Belgian Congo that it intends to provide free elementary education for all children of school age in that colony. In Southern Rhodesia the government has informed the churches of its intention to provide elementary education for all children of school age. Some competent observers estimate that by 1970 only a very small minority of the schools in Africa will be under the control of the Christian Church. For Americans, accustomed to a secular system of education, this seems to be not an unmixed tragedy, *if* the local church and the homes are awake to their responsibility in Christian education. In the "younger" church areas, however, the church and mission leaders have been so burdened with responsibilities for church-operated schools that they have not had the time, the personnel, nor the resources to build strong Sunday schools, youth programs, and other forms of Christian education in the local church. In many parts of Africa and Asia, the Christian education program in the local church is woefully weak. It is for this reason that the World Council of Christian Education and Sunday School Association finds itself almost overwhelmed by requests from such areas for help in building indigenous curriculum materials for Sunday schools and programs for youth groups in local churches. The best programs in the world will fail without adequate leadership, and the W.C.C.E.S.S.A. is being asked repeatedly for help in enlisting, motivating, and training leaders, especially the lay leaders who are necessary for a strong program of Christian education in the local church.

In the Western world of Europe and North America, there is a much better developed program of Christian education but even between these two areas there are great contrasts. In Europe there is usually an opportunity for Christian education in the curriculum of the State schools. In this situation the Sunday-school program does not seem to be so important and in many churches a "children's service," with or without any group discussion, is often substituted for the Sunday-school program. Where Sunday schools are carried on, they usually serve children only, fourteen years of age and under. There is a gap between the Sunday-school program and the youth program of the churches, which commences at about sixteen to eighteen years of age. These youth programs vary a great deal, some emphasizing Bible study as their major activity and others concentrating mostly on recreation activities.

In North America, the Canadian situation is a complex one. In some provinces religious instruction is a part of the regular curriculum in the schools, while in others there are only "released time" opportunities. The main emphasis in Christian education in Canada is still in the local church and the home. Youth group programs begin early and are related to the program of the Sunday school, and in recent years there has been a great upsurge of young adult and adult programs.

In the United States most Protestant children attend Sunday schools in areas where no religious education is permitted on public school property. "Released-time" religious education reaches a small minority with a valuable program of religious teaching. In some areas this is an interfaith program participated in by Protestants, Roman Catholics, and Jews. The local church and the home must carry the main burden of Christian education in America. There has been an increasing attempt to awaken parents to their responsibilities as teachers of religion. It is being realized that the home can be the most important center for Christian education, but in modern times the home has often failed in its responsibility in this matter. The local church must carry a great responsibility for Christian education, and American churches are rising to that challenge as never before. In 1959 more than forty million people were enrolled in Sunday schools and between ten and fifteen million in Christian youth fellowships in the Protestant and Orthodox churches in America. In recent years much attention has been paid to improving curriculum materials and to training the kind of leadership that is required for a strong program in the local church.

America, with two thirds of the world's Sunday-school enrollment and youth fellowship membership, must carry a great responsibility for the Christian education movement in the world of today. The rising tides of nationalism make necessary the continued study of how this help can be given in a way that will be acceptable to sensitive peoples with new-found freedom.

Bibliography

Ferguson, J. M. M. *Tokyo Calling—Report of the Fourteenth World Convention.* Religious Education Press, 1958.

Jung, Emanuel. *Sontagsschule Als Kindergertesdienst.* Zurich: Zwingli-Verlag, 1944.

"Report of the World Institute on Christian Education, *Nishinomiya.*" New York: World Council of Christian Education and Sunday School Association, 1958.

Smart, James D. *The Teaching Ministry of the Church.* Philadelphia: Westminster Press, 1954.

"Training for a Teaching Ministry—Report of the Tokyo Seminar on Theological Education," New York: World Council of Christian Education and Sunday School Association, 1958.

Visser 't Hooft, W. A., *The First Assembly of the World Council of Churches—Official Report.* New York: Harper and Brothers, 1949.

Periodicals

The Ecumenical Review, published by the World Council of Churches.

The International Missionary Review, published by the International Missionary Council.

World Christian Education, published quarterly by the World Council of Christian Education and Sunday School Association.

Chapter 33

The Religious Education Association

Herman E. Wornom

FOUNDED IN 1903, THE RELIGIOUS EDUCATION ASSOCIATION (R.E.A.) IS THE OLDEST of the national agencies in America for dealing with matters of religion and education across denominational and institutional lines. Its founding marked the birth of the "Religious Education Movement." [1] Since the Association was the organizational expression of the movement and has been closely identified with the various currents of thought therein for more than fifty years, it is important to understand something of the character and objectives of the Association from the beginning.

Formative Factors

At the turn of the century, there was widespread dissatisfaction among religious and educational leaders with the *revivalistic* approach of the Sunday schools to religious education. The founders of the Religious Education Association were committed to an *educational* approach, which would use the insights of psychology and the practices of modern pedagogy in dealing with the child, use the findings of critical and historical scholarship in teaching the Bible, correlate religious instruction with education in history, literature, and the sciences; and recognize that all institutions of society—home, school, youth societies, press, colleges, and universities—influence religious nurture, and that the roles of all of them should be explored and unified in a total educational effort. The Religious Education Association was organized to espouse this educational approach.

The reasons for creating the new organization were made explicit in the call for the Founding Convention, which expressed the views of those who signed it to be:

1. That the religious and moral instruction of the young is at present inadequate, and imperfectly correlated with other instruction in history, literature, and the sciences; and

2. That the Sunday school, as the primary institution for the religious and moral education of the young, should be conformed to a higher ideal, and made efficient for its work by the gradation of pupils, and by the adaptation of its material and method of instruction to the several stages of the mental, moral and spiritual growth of the individual; and

[1] James D. Smart, *The Teaching Ministry of the Church* (Philadelphia: Westminster Press, 1954), p. 56.

3. That the home, the day-school, and all other agencies should be developed to assist in the right education of the young in religion and morals; and

4. That this improvement in religious and moral instruction can best be promoted by a national organization devoted exclusively to this purpose.[2]

The *comprehensive* approach of the new organization to religious education is indicated by the departments provided for in its constitution, all of which were immediately set up, namely: (1) the council (to deal with general issues and directions affecting all religious education), (2) universities and colleges, (3) theological seminaries, (4) churches and pastors, (5) Sunday schools, (6) secondary public schools, (7) elementary public schools, (8) private schools, (9) teacher training, (10) Young Men's and Young Women's Christian Associations, (11) young people's societies, (12) the home, (13) libraries, (14) the press, (15) correspondence instruction, (16) summer assemblies, (17) religious art and music.

Institutional comprehensiveness, however, was only one of R.E.A.'s goals. The founders felt the need for a *new conception* of the nature of religious education. A new methodology, new materials, a new philosophy, a new understanding of the relation of religious formation to the total educational process, were needed. Through investigation, research, and speculation, R.E.A. would undertake to formulate a new system, theory, and practice of religious education. R.E.A.'s seventeen departments would work at these tasks.

William Rainey Harper, then president of the University of Chicago and chairman of the first Executive Board of the Association, in stating the purpose of the Association at its first convention, described some of the investigations the departments would undertake. He said:

> The Association, through its Departments, will propose to make new contributions to the cause of religious and moral education, and this will be done through the light of scientific investigations. Some of these will attempt to define more closely the true relation of religious and moral instruction to other branches of instruction, and to indicate the part which religion should perform in the development of the individual and of society. Others will undertake to correlate religious and moral instruction, and to set forth the best methods of using the Bible for this purpose. Still others will endeavor to point out the application of the established results of modern psychology, modern pedagogy, and modern Bible study, as these stand related to religious and moral instruction.[3]

In addition to the comprehensive and creative nature of the program which Harper proposed and the Association undertook, the basic and continuing character of R.E.A. is perhaps best revealed by the principles which were set forth and reiterated at the first and later conventions for guiding all undertakings of the Association: (1) It should be *universal in spirit*, inclusive of widely varying viewpoints, avoiding control by any single school of thought, looking at each subject in its entirety, considering the needs of the whole nation rather than of a few sections. (2) It should be *co-operative in spirit*, refusing to enter into competitive rivalries, and seeking to perform a general service which would make the work of all institutions more effective. (3) It should be *scientific in spirit*, in all its explorations, proceeding carefully on the basis of fundamental principles, seeking to observe

---

[2] *Proceedings of the First Annual Convention of the Religious Education Association* (Chicago: R.E.A., 1903), pp. 317-18. Used by permission.

[3] *Ibid.*, p. 237.

accurately the facts, and from these to make deductions. (4) It would be *pioneering in spirit*, always seeking new ways to extend and improve religious education.

The founders of R.E.A. were not professional religious educators in the present-day sense of the term. (Such a profession did not exist in 1903.[4]) It has been characteristic of R.E.A., however, that from the beginning and continuously it has been composed of educational and religious leaders with wide horizons. Such persons have been among its leaders even when in later years religious education became highly professionalized.

At the beginning the entire membership of R.E.A. was Protestant, for there was little awareness on the part of Protestants of the pluralistic religious character of America. However, in this context it is highly significant that R.E.A., *although initially Protestant, very early invited Catholic and Jewish religious and educational leaders* to participate in its programs. In line with R.E.A.'s policy to make the most inclusive approach possible to religious education, the Very Rev. Prof. Thomas J. Shahan of the Catholic University of America gave a paper at the Association's third National Convention in 1905 on the subject "What Cooperation Is Now Possible in Religious Education Between Roman Catholics and Protestants." Father Shahan presented five ways in which co-operation was possible. For example, his first point was:

> We can all help . . . to bring about the universal recognition that religion and morality are necessary elements of a proper education; that they must be taught from early childhood, and that both represent something positive and permanent, indispensable to the welfare of individuals and states.[5]

Rabbi Moses J. Gries of The Temple, Cleveland, Ohio, gave a paper at the fifth R.E.A. Convention in 1908, and Dr. Emil G. Hirsch, Rabbi of Sinai Congregation, Chicago, was on the program of the sixth Convention in 1909. The latter's paper was entitled "Religious Education and Moral Efficiency" and was addressed to two propositions:

> They are, first, that moral efficiency can be attained and sustained only through the sanctions and sanctifications of religion, and therefore religious education is indispensable if moral efficiency is desired and striven after, and, secondly, that religious education must be planned and carried into effect with this end in view.[6]

The participation of Father Shahan, Rabbi Gries, and Rabbi Hirsch in early conventions of R.E.A. adumbrated the multi-faith approach to religious education which was to become policy two decades later and a genuine reality by the time of R.E.A.'s Golden Anniversary Convention.

During the early years, the Association was concerned to stimulate immediate improvements in the over-all program, organization, method, and content of religious education as practiced in homes, churches, schools, colleges, and other institutions. This is illustrated by the general themes of the early conventions, such

---

[4] One of the early achievements of the Association was that it so strongly stressed the need for persons professionally trained in both religion and education that churches, seminaries and schools of education soon began to prepare men and women for a specialized ministry in religious education.

[5] *Proceedings of the Third Annual Convention of the Religious Education Association* (Boston, 1905), p. 105.

[6] Emil G. Hirsch, "Religious Education and Moral Efficiency," *Religious Education*, IV (May, 1909), 129.

as: "The Aims of Religious Education," "The Materials of Religious Education," "Religious Education and the Home," "The Church and Education," "Training Religious Leaders," "The Relation of Higher Education to the Social Order," "Religious Instruction and Public Education," "Community Organization," "Weekday Religious Education." These themes will appear to the student in the third quarter of the twentieth century to be commonplace, but in contrast to the prevailing Sunday-school approach at the beginning of the century, these convention themes, as R.E.A. developed them, meant new dimensions for religious education. If it be remembered that in 1903 the Sunday school and young people's societies were not even official agencies of the church but were separate lay organizations, then it will be clear that even such a theme as "The Church and Education" suggests a new center of responsibility for religious education.

The churches did, in fact, soon see that they had a primary responsibility for religious education. They set up national and regional boards of education to give guidance to local churches, to provide standards, textbooks, leadership training, and objectives for each age level in a graded program. By 1922, with the founding of the International Council of Religious Education as a general co-ordinating body for the denominations, church agencies had taken over the improvement in the practice of religious education on which R.E.A. had focused in the first two decades of the century.

Questions were now raised as to whether R.E.A. had finished its task and should dissolve. An objective survey of the situation, authorized by R.E.A. and made by the Institute of Social and Religious Research, concluded to the contrary. R.E.A. had achieved one broad objective, but new tasks for a pioneering agency were emerging in a rapidly changing society. Moreover, R.E.A. had not conceived its function as being limited to that of achieving immediate results in the practice of religious education.

From the beginning, R.E.A. had given major attention to questions of educational theory, to fundamental problems of religious formation (the nature of the child and his religious experience), to the interrelation of religious instruction and training in other disciplines, to the relation between cultural and social forces and religious education, to the meaning for religious nurture of the findings of biblical scholars, to changing moral attitudes and behavior of the American people, and to broad trends and needs in provision for religious training in various educational and cultural institutions. Members of R.E.A. did thinking, research, and writing in these areas, presented and discussed their views and findings in meetings of the Association, and published them in its journal, *Religious Education*, or in book form. R.E.A. provided the most inclusive fellowship for sharing such theoretical and research work and for disseminating the results thereof. R.E.A. was unique in performing this function in the 1920's, and it continues to be so.

By 1927 the departmental structure of R.E.A., embracing all the various institutions of education, had practically disappeared. How then, would it continue to influence the policies and practices of ecclesiastical and educational bodies which do the actual work of religious education? This becomes clear when one examines R.E.A.'s organizational independence and its relations with other agencies.

Individuals, not institutions, have composed the membership of R.E.A. during its entire history. It has never had nor wanted any control over the actions of other institutions. Conversely, R.E.A. has not been controlled by or been responsible to

other institutions (ecclesiastical, educational, professional) for its actions. Organizationally, it has been an entirely independent corporation responsible only to its own
members. This has meant that the Association has been free to pursue any lines
of thought or research which seemed of value to its members. It could pioneer
beyond the commitments of other institutions. It has not needed to go through
the cumbersome process of getting approval of other institutions for its programs.
Being alone responsible for its actions, those actions have not been an embarrassment
to other institutions, as might on occasion happen if they were officially represented
in R.E.A.

The only way in which R.E.A. could influence other institutions has been by
espousing projects and ideas which on their merits appealed to the leaders of those
institutions as valuable. As it has done so, leaders of a great many religious and
educational institutions have, as individuals, joined R.E.A. In so doing, these
leaders have become informed channels of mutual communication and influence
between the free-wheeling R.E.A. and the agencies in which they are professionally
employed. The potential of these relationships is indicated by the comprehensiveness of R.E.A.'s membership, as detailed below.

The foregoing review of the concerns and policies of R.E.A. in its early years
reveals its traditional character. Problems dealt with have varied, but R.E.A.'s
essential character has continued.

Current Characteristics

The Association today is *comprehensive* both as to membership and as to the
range of religious and educational institutions and concerns dealt with in its
programs and in its journal, *Religious Education*. In membership it is multi-faith,
multi-professional, and inter-disciplinary. It is composed of influential leaders
of education and religion and of a variety of professions in the United States,
Canada, and other nations. Most professors of religious education in seminaries
and schools of education belong. The membership includes ministers, priests,
rabbis, religious, missionaries, and eminent laymen. It includes physicians, lawyers,
engineers, journalists, social workers, experts on the mass media, and business and
labor leaders. All the major disciplines of learning are represented—theology, the
humanities, history, the social sciences, and the natural sciences. There are research
workers and practitioners. Many graduate students of religious education are
members.

All levels of education and many kinds of educational agencies are represented.
From higher education there are administrators, faculty members, and directors of
student religious work. The executive heads (and often many of their staff) of
all major national boards or departments of education of the Protestant, Catholic,
and Jewish faiths are members. There are leaders of local churches, synagogues,
and community programs, who are concerned to keep abreast of basic developments
in religious education. Public, private, and parochial school personnel are represented. Also included are chaplains in the armed forces, leaders of group-work
agencies, and editors and writers for religious and educational publications.

The extensive multi-faith, multi-professional, and inter-disciplinary participation in R.E.A. is one of its unique achievements in comprehensiveness. The variety
of interests represented and the high level of discussions among Protestant,
Catholic, and Jewish leaders, which is typical of R.E.A. meetings, was described

by James V. Mullaney, chairman of the Liberal Arts Program of Manhattan College (Catholic) of New York City, in giving his reactions to R.E.A.'s national convention held in November, 1957. He stated:

The personnel of the convention was the first impact made on the individual member of it. The large number of persons; the astonishing variety of professions represented; the eminence of very many of the persons present; the varied cross-sections of religious affiliations—all these factors made the convention an unusually rich experience.

The first and most precious bond uniting this large group of distinguished persons was the unselfconscious *caritas,* the genuine religious brotherhood under God, which permeated all personal and professional contacts. This deep bond made for respect, openness, candor, thoughtfulness, and personal warmth. It did away with suspicion and with any sense of walking on egg-shells in the forthright discussion of issues on which convention members might not agree. There was no need for kid gloves because it was understood on all sides that intellectual differences are perfectly consistent with unity within an inclusive religious *caritas.*

The second bond of union was the uniform commitment to an intellectual, rather than a propagandist, level of discussion at all meetings and in all seminars. No one was "selling" anything to anyone. Contacts were on the level of respectful and honest inquiry, not of "pitches." [7]

The Association continues to deal with religious education as carried on through all of society's major educational institutions. During the period 1952-58 there have been symposia in *Religious Education* on the family and religion; church and synagogue systems of religious education; religion and higher education; weekday religious education; and religion and the public schools. On the last theme there were annual symposia from 1953 to 1957. There have also been symposia on such perennial themes as "The Curriculum of Religious Education," "The Bible and Religious Education," "Teaching Religion to Children," and "Adult Education."

The *pioneering* character of R.E.A. has continued. Now as in 1903, it takes the lead in exploring new problems, new social forces, and new concerns in the entire field of religious and character formation. It continually reports the findings of research on a multitude of problems. The role of theology in religious education, which was of small concern in the early years, has been frequently treated in *Religious Education* since 1950. Also there has been much attention to the relation between philosophy of education and religious education. During 1957, 1958 and 1959 there were five symposia on the contributions of various disciplines to theology and religious education.

Through its journal and meetings, the Association has highlighted for religious educators problems of religious and character education for armed forces personnel, the causes of juvenile delinquency and the responsibility of educational institutions in this field, the problems of religious pluralism, and the meaning for religious education of depth psychology. *Religious Education* has pioneered in presenting reports on experiments in the religious education of exceptional children—the gifted child and the retarded child. There have been symposia or articles on such recent approaches to character formation as role playing, group dynamics, and creative rhythmic movements.

A *scientific* approach to certain problems of religious education was established

[7] "Evaluations of Chicago R.E.A. Convention," *Religious Education,* LIII (January-February, 1958), 5. Used by permission.

as a primary policy of R.E.A. in 1903. This emphasis has developed over the years. At mid-century R.E.A. recognizes that science cannot provide the goals of religious education but that it can be highly useful in determining the means and method. R.E.A. does not conduct research, but it does stimulate its members and other agencies to do so.

Since May, 1948, the journal has carried a column "Significant Evidence" by Ernest M. Ligon, reporting on research in the field of general psychology which bears on religious and character education. All the material in Ligon's column is excerpted from *Psychological Abstracts*.

Perhaps the most useful service to research workers has been the publication of "Abstracts of Doctoral Dissertations in Religious Education." This service was begun in the 1930's by the International Council of Religious Education. Beginning in November, 1943, with the fifth report on "Abstracts," *Religious Education* has continuously published them, biennially at first, and annually since 1949. The compiling of the abstracts is done in co-operation with the Bureau of Research and Survey of the National Council of Churches and with professors in colleges, universities, and seminaries. Since 1953 the reports have been much more complete because of the increased participation of Catholic and Jewish professors in R.E.A. activities. Hardly any candidate for a doctoral degree in religious education would think of choosing his dissertation theme without first studying the "Abstracts" and other research reports in *Religious Education*.

In 1958-59, in co-operation with the Character Research Project of Union College, Schenectady, New York, R.E.A. undertook a comprehensive survey of all research, other than doctoral dissertations, completed or in process in the entire field of religious and character education for all age levels and all types of institutions. Effort was also made to discover research in the social sciences and humanities which would have a direct bearing on religious and character education. Abstracts of all the substantial researches collected by the survey were published in the May-June, 1959, issue of *Religious Education*.

Although R.E.A. is independent organizationally and pioneering in its program, it is *co-operative* in spirit and services. R.E.A. initiates many program ideas and projects and independently develops them through its own committees, seminars, conferences and journal, *Religious Education*. There is always a concern, however, that programs and projects so developed will become resources for other agencies. Often such ideas are taken over and put to work in the program and publishing activities of other agencies.

Through correspondence or by personal conferences, R.E.A. provides consultative assistance in developing the programs of many other agencies—national church and synagogue boards of education, colleges and universities, theological seminaries, state departments of education, school boards of municipalities, the National Conference of Christians and Jews, the armed forces Chaplains Board.

In addition to programs and projects initiated and developed by the Association itself, R.E.A. also collaborates with other institutions in some major activities. Its co-operation with the National Council of Churches in making an annual report of Abstracts of Doctoral Dissertations and with the Character Research Project in making a survey of other research has been noted above.

Recognizing the need for closer co-operation between chaplains in the Armed Forces and civilian religious and educational leaders in meeting the moral and religious needs of American young men and women, R.E.A. co-operated in 1954 and 1956 with the Armed Services chaplains in holding several one-day conferences on "Our Mutual Moral and Spiritual Mission" in Boston, New York, Chicago, and Los Angeles.

Illustrative of R.E.A.'s co-operation with other agencies on problems of religion and public education, its general secretary participated in a three-day conference of sixty consultants called in 1957 by the American Council on Education to advise on the latter's policy in this field. R.E.A. subsequently published the major papers of the conference in *Religious Education*. In similar fashion it has participated in committees and conferences of the National Council of Churches, the Anti-Defamation League and the National Conference of Christians and Jews to help those agencies to formulate policy in this controversial field.

In the field of public higher education the Association co-operated with the University of Minnesota in 1955 in holding at that institution one of the five regional conferences referred to below in the section on higher education. For the conference and the work of the committees, the University of Minnesota provided facilities and financing, and the R.E.A. provided program personnel and direction.

Another illustration of R.E.A.'s co-operation is the role it played in the National Consultative Conference on Religion and the State University, held at the University of Michigan in November, 1958, on the occasion of that university's Centennial of Student Religious Activities. R.E.A. did not participate in planning that conference, but its general secretary gave the keynote opening address on "Critical Issues of Religion in Public Higher Education." A sixty-page report of the papers and findings of the conference was published in the March-April, 1959, issue of *Religious Education*.

Higher Education

R.E.A. has always had a major interest in the place of religion in higher education. Since 1952 the Association has been concerned not just with course offerings in religion or with student religious activities but with the effect of the intellectual and cultural climate of higher education on the Judaeo-Christian heritage and view of man and with the effect of the prevailing directions of higher education on the shaping of the life goals of students and faculty. Between 1954 and 1956 the Association sponsored five two-day regional round-table conferences on religion in higher education—in New York, Chicago, Minneapolis, Pittsburgh, and Cambridge. The central concern of these conferences was "The Responsibility of Higher Education for the Judaeo-Christian Heritage in American Culture." Some 350 persons representing over 100 institutions participated. The conferences were unique in the wealth of religious traditions and academic disciplines represented by participants. There was a balanced cross section of the academic life of the university at each conference.

From the standpoint of the Religious Education Association, the purpose of these conferences was exploratory; that is, to find out what are the major concerns and issues regarding the place of religion in higher education in the opinion of a representative cross section of administration and faculties of all types of colleges and universities. In each of the five conferences certain fundamental questions were recognized as requiring intensive exploration. Answers to them would provide a philosophy of higher education from the standpoint of the Judaeo-Christian heritage. Among these recurring questions were:

1. What is the *status* of religious truth and religious approaches to truth versus scientific truth and modes of thought in higher education? What are the roles and relative importance of the empirical, speculative, intuitional, and revelational roads to truth in higher education?

2. Does the cultural, philosophical, scientific outlook and technical orientation of higher education today undercut or weaken the status of religious truth and the Judaeo-Christian world view in higher education and so in American culture?

3. Is there an inevitable tension between the absolute claims of religion and the principle of *free inquiry* which is central to pursuit of truth in a university? How does one give due recognition to these two divergent principles in dealing with religion in the university.

4. What is the potential role of a religiously committed faculty in increasing responsibility of higher education for Judaeo-Christian values? What is the potential of the university as a community of scholars (faculty and students) committed to discovery of truth, as an expression of religious faith; or of such a group of scholars as a cell or community within the larger, more heterogeneous body? Has this community ideal failed to develop even in church-related schools? Why should they not take the lead in making it work?

There is need for eminent scholars of the Protestant, Catholic, and Jewish faiths to undertake the writing of a philosophy of higher education which would answer the above and many other questions about the role of higher education in preserving and developing the influence of the Judaeo-Christian heritage in our culture. Such a volume or volumes would make a contribution to American higher education comparable to that made to British higher education by Sir Walter Moberly's *The Crisis in the University*. R.E.A. has a grant of funds to undertake this project.

In its concern for religion in higher education, R.E.A. has given special attention to the need for more adequate provision for religion in the curriculums of public institutions of higher education. This special concern derives from (1) the failure of most such institutions to make the same full provision for religion as they do for other disciplines, and (2) recognition that now and in the future the public rather than the private institutions will enroll the larger proportion of the student population.

Since the above-mentioned conference at the University of Minnesota in 1955, R.E.A. has co-operated with the Executive Committee of the Commission on the Study of the Place of Religion in the Curricula of State Universities, an *ad hoc* body authorized by the Minnesota conference. R.E.A. has provided executive services for this body and for four subcommittees which have explored the problems of dealing with religion in state institutions, namely: (1) the legal status of curricular offerings; (2) designing tests of religious literacy and attitudes; (3) appraisal of the administrative and curricular patterns for offering religion in state institutions; (4) supply and training of teachers of religion in the pluralistic and secular environment of public higher education. This entire operation has resulted in a much better understanding of the problem of state universities in dealing with religion as an academic discipline.

Organization

R.E.A. is a nonprofit corporation authorized by the state of Illinois. Its executive headquarters are in New York City. It is primarily a professional association of individuals. They join R.E.A. because of their personal interest in its work, and not as official representatives of any ecclesiastical body or educational institution. All professionals in categories named in the section above on "comprehensiveness" are eligible. Also eligible are laymen who have a wide interest in religious education and who wish to give the Association moral and financial support.

The Association functions through (a) local chapters; (b) national conventions; (c) commissions and regional meetings on religion in public education, higher education, philosophy of education, the Armed Forces, the mass media, research, and the like; (d) a national office with a general secretary and staff who administer and co-ordinate work, approved by a board of directors or formulated by its standing committees; (e) a bimonthly journal, *Religious Education*.

The organizational structure of R.E.A. is much less complex than it was at the beginning. The initial division of its activities into seventeen departments proved too cumbersome, and by 1927 the departments had disappeared. In planning convention programs a variety of seminars (sixteen in 1957) has replaced departmental programs. The policies and major plans of the Association today are all determined by a board of directors. Plans and programs for research, higher education, and *Religious Education* are formulated by three standing committees. Major plans of these committees are brought to the board for final action, although the board may assign to these committees responsibility for certain tasks with full authority to act thereon. From time to time the board appoints *ad hoc* committees to work in some areas of special concern or on projects such as a national convention or membership promotion. An executive committee of the board functions to implement policies and plans of the board which do not fall within the province of any of its standing or *ad hoc* committees. Meetings of the Association as a whole usually take place at the time of national conventions, when officers and board members are elected.

The Association has a small employed staff—a full-time general secretary and a part-time editor. There is also a full-time assistant, who does triple duty as book-keeper, advertising manager, and membership secretary. This small staff can be effective only because many members of the Association contribute expert services as members of committees or of *ad hoc* workshops or seminars. The policy of co-operating with other agencies which have larger or more specialized staffs also greatly extends the range of undertakings in which the Association is influential.

The influence of the Association is extended regionally and locally through chapters in metropolitan centers. A local chapter is made up of members of the national organization who reside in a particular geographical region (county, city) small enough for the members to get together for regular monthly or quarterly meetings. Each chapter is self-governing, elects its own officers, and determines its own program and finances. Program suggestions may be given by the national office, but they are entirely optional. The national office also gives help in organizing local chapters and in helping them to develop programs reflecting frontier concerns of national scope or of special local interest.

National Conventions

During most of its early history the Association held annual conventions. However, it was soon a matter of debate whether large conventions with comprehensive programs and wide appeal could or should be held annually. After three such conventions, held in 1903, 1904, and 1905, it was decided not to have a convention in 1906. It was reasoned that more time was needed between meetings to digest and implement ideas already presented. This point of view has prevailed again since 1950. Moreover, present policy requires that national conventions deal with issues of transcending importance for the total enterprise of religious education. Convention themes are of concern to a wide range of religious, professional, and academic interests; and programs are designed to serve all these interests. For example, the 1953 subject was "The Place and Adequacy of Religious Education in Our Times." The 1957 theme was "Images of Man in Current Culture and Tasks of Religion and Education."

The scope of ideas and the breadth of appeal of an R.E.A. convention is well illustrated by the 1957 convention. In general sessions there were four symposia on: (1) Secular Images of Man; (2) Sacred Images of Man; (3) What Image of Man Should Education Foster? (4) Strategy of Religion for Nurturing Sacred Images of Man.

In addition to the general sessions, the 550 full-time delegates divided into 16 seminar groups to explore the problems and issues posed by the convention theme for delegates with specialized concerns in the following fields: (1) the home, (2) the school, (3) church and synagogue, (4) the armed forces, (5) the larger community and the social order, (6) higher education, (7) the humanities, (8) the social sciences, (9) the healing sciences and counseling, (10) the mass media of communication, (11) theories and methods of education and religious education, (12) forming sacred images of man in children and youth, (13) practitioners of religious education, (14) love and sex, (15) research, (16) business and industry; management and labor. These reports and the major addresses of the convention were published in the March-April, 1958, issue of *Religious Education.*

The Journal

The bimonthly journal, *Religious Education,* is the Association's most substantial and regular channel of communication with its members and with all persons doing advanced thinking or experimentation in religious and character education. It is the only American journal which regularly presents the views of scholars and the findings of research on basic problems of religious education, including the views of Protestant, Catholic, and Jewish educators. Each issue of the magazine carries articles on a variety of subjects and also a symposium on some major problem or field of religious education or on the relation of religion to American education and culture. For example, recent issues have had symposia on value patterns and effects of the mass media, research, moral character and religious education, images of man in current culture, the religious education of children, the Bible and religious education, religion and public education, religion and the curricula of state universities, religion in training for the professions, labor-management and religion, the humanities and religious education, and the social sciences and religion.

Impact and Outreach

The Association has had a large influence on religious education in America, and this influence is more vigorous now than ever. This happens in four ways:

1. *Widening perspectives.* Because of the wide diversity and inclusiveness of its members, they have, collectively, great knowledge and understanding of the total religious and educational enterprise in America. The Association provides a meeting ground for the sharing of this knowledge and of the varied insights of its members. Even more important, R.E.A. fosters a climate of mutual respect, candor, and intellectual honesty, which encourages free and forthright discussion of ideas and convictions. This helps R.E.A. members to gain wide perspectives on the problems of religion and education.

2. *Exploring frontier problems.* The Association pioneers in opening up discussions and fostering studies on new or basic problems in the culture and in the total educational enterprise as they affect religion and religious education. Because of the wealth of perspectives present in its inclusive membership, the Association has unique resources for doing this.

3. *Implementing ideas.* R.E.A. members are all in strategic positions of leadership as scholars, administrators, research workers, and practitioners. Whatever insights for policy or practice they gain through meetings of the Association or through its journal, which they individually believe to be valuable, they can implement through hundreds of national, regional and local religious and educational bodies which reach millions of people or through publications read by millions.

4. *Services of the National Office.* The national staff and journal are a source of information and consultation for many individuals engaged in research and for many agencies which are developing new programs and policies. The latter include national denominational boards of education, state departments of education, national educational societies and councils, local school boards, colleges and universities. R.E.A.'s journal, *Religious Education,* is constantly in demand by such bodies and is also widely used by professors in seminaries and schools of education as a personal resource and for student assignments.

Thus, the Religious Education Association enhances religious education as a whole and strengthens its impact on American life.

Chapter 34

Agencies Serving Children and Youth

A. Wilson Cheek

THE EXPANSION OF VOLUNTARY AGENCIES IN THE UNITED STATES DURING THE past half century has been phenomenal. The impersonal relationships which our citizens feel toward big government and big business point up the value of voluntary associations as a major factor in keeping our democratic processes vital. It is altogether to the good, then, that of more than 650 voluntary associations in our country more than half of them are devoted in whole or in part to the welfare of children and youth. Among these the majority are regarded as secular agencies without any expressed purpose related directly to religious education. Even so, their programs are often designed to develop good health, good comradeship, and good citizenship, and are thereby to be regarded as an ally of the religious educator.

For the most part the major secular agencies serving children and youth fall into two categories. There are those concentrated in the urban areas, many of which are federated into the Boys' Clubs of America. They are generally located in low-income areas and centered around a building which provides facilities for sports, crafts, and other forms of recreation. Small towns and rural areas are served by agencies such as Four-H Clubs, Future Farmers of America, and Future Homemakers of America. Organized through the high schools under the auspices of the United States Department of Agriculture, they help rural boys and girls develop desirable ideals and standards for farming, homemaking, community life, and citizenship. The churches' attitude toward such agencies, both rural and urban, is cordial and friendly. The values inherent in these programs for the development of a sense of community across religious lines are recognized and appreciated.

One of the paradoxes of the modern ecumenical movement is that denominations are more deeply concerned with a reaffirmation of their distinctive heritage and doctrines, while at the same time more firmly committed to work toward Christian unity. One reflection of this is seen in the current use of the term "Christian education" in preference to the more general term "religious education." It is felt that "Christian education" more accurately describes the concept and program of religious nurture for children and youth within Protestant and Orthodox churches. In consequence of this and other factors the churches are working more closely than ever with the agencies which have an explicit religious purpose that can be directed toward fulfillment within the framework of specific denominations. There are five organizations with origins primarily in the Protestant tradition having religious purposes which are consistent with the objectives of Christian education.

371

They are: Camp Fire Girls, Inc., Boy Scouts of America, Girl Scouts of the U.S.A., the Young Men's Christian Association, and the Young Women's Christian Association. The first three have clear-cut policies for local church sponsorship. The Y.M.C.A. has in recent years developed club programs which are available for church sponsorship, though the programs of both the Y.M. and Y.W.C.A. are more often than not related directly to their own buildings and subsidiary units. Both of these organizations are committed in their purpose to the furtherance of evangelical Christianity.

Insights of contemporary education and psychology have led Christian educators to become increasingly concerned that the program of Christian education for children and youth be integrated rather than compartmentalized. Accordingly, the functions of the home, the church school, and agencies with an avowed religious purpose are seen to be closely interrelated. The time when any one of these institutions could view another as an unwelcome and inappropriate competitor has for the most part disappeared.

There are many evidences of this, one of which is the place of importance which the Committee on Church and Agency Relationships in Work with Children and Youth has come to have in the Division of Christian Education of the National Council of Churches. This committee is composed of representatives from the five agencies along with persons responsible for work with children and youth in the denominations and councils of churches. It meets annually as a full committee and does much interim work through subcommittees, there being one for each of the five agencies. Through the work of this committee there have been a number of noteworthy developments—a manual on *Church-Agency Relationships*[1] has been published, pilot conferences on various aspects of co-operative planning and co-ordination have been held, and the guide lines for similar committees in state and local councils of churches have been established.

General Observations

Among the five agencies related to the National Council of Churches there are some important differences and practices regarding religion. These will be dealt with in the sections of this chapter which describe their respective programs. Before doing so, there are some general observations to be made which are applicable to all of them. The Committee on Church and Agency Relationships calls attention to five positive values common to the agency programs which make significant contributions to the total program of Christian education.

Values in Agency Programs

1. The agencies may help to broaden horizons and bring church boys and girls and young people into contact with other youth of the community, even of the world, through their wide contacts. It is important that young persons growing up in today's world get to know well other young persons of various denominations, faiths, nationalities, races, and countries. The agencies offer particularly fertile proving ground for democratic group living and Christian brotherly relations.

2. The agencies offer a tested plan by which the outreach of the church into the community can be implemented—particularly through reaching families

[1] *Church-Agency Relationships,* "A manual on guiding principles for churches and agencies in their cooperative character-building programs."

the church has not been able to reach. The agency program often presents a certain sparkle and attractiveness to some growing boys and girls who have not responded to the appeal of the other church programs. Then, having come into agency work and found its close relationship to the rest of the church program, they grow to understand and want to venture into other church activities.

3. The agencies offer avenues for the church to participate in a program that has a community, national, and world outreach. Festivals crossing denominational, class, and cultural lines may be sponsored in the home town. These serve as a bridge of understanding across all lines of division.

4. The agencies offer to the churches some excellent methods and materials for use in securing and training adult workers with children and youth. The agencies offer insights into the development of boys and girls as "whole persons." They have experience in the intermeshing of agencies in a community and the correlation of effort of group workers in church, agency, school, and home. They have developed methods for guiding recreation, camping, teaching, music, and crafts. Joint training enterprises can be held with great enrichment to both church and agencies. Particularly may church workers, prone at times to become discouraged, catch the enthusiasm of agency workers, and with a new zest for their work, seek training in new methods.

5. The agencies have pioneered in developing approaches to the home. The home-agency co-operation actually achieved by some of them is a glowing monument to the vision of the policy makers and the effectiveness of the local workers. In recent years the denominations have developed excellent materials for use by parents. A pooling of resources and methods in this field by churches and agencies can be helpful to both.

Local Church Responsibility

It has come to be generally understood by agency and church people alike that the agency programs utilized by any given local church should be related to that congregation's total program of Christian education *only* through the educational body—usually the board of Christian education—and not through any single organization within the church. This is usually accomplished in one of the following ways:

1. The board of Christian education of a church may be responsible for the relationship to the agency: for determining the needs of the boys and girls and its own program, selecting the agency which can most effectively aid its own boys and girls, and for integrating the program into the total Christian education work of the church.

2. An agency representative may be a member of the board of Christian education which is responsible for the entire program for children and youth.

3. Special committees may be appointed to deal with and support each agency program in the church.

Where the agencies have their own buildings and equipment, which is generally the case with the Y.M.C.A. and the Y.W.C.A., their facilities and programs are available to churches as extra or correlated resources. Here again co-operative planning between the local church's Board of Christian Education and the agency leaders helps to assure a well-balanced and integrated program.

Co-operative Leadership Development

It is generally recommended that leaders for the agency programs within a local church be drawn from the membership of the congregation. Training of these leaders for the agency program *per se* is provided by the agency. These training programs maintain high standards, the strength of them being readily seen in these characteristics: (1) Emphasis on continuous, step-by-step, year-round training; (2) Close, friendly supervision and counseling by qualified consultants; (3) Sensitivity to each leader's special needs; (4) Involvement of parents; (5) Use of good group procedures; (6) Emphasis on democratic behavior and imaginative methods of training; (7) Development of exact skills; and (8) Learning by doing.

These accents make for creativity and flexibility in program, and constant program evaluation and job review keep the activities from becoming static. The total life of the church benefits from leaders who have the benefits of these training programs. Conversely, the agencies have the benefit of leaders who are regularly a part of the church's program and who know something of the nature of the church, its missions, aims, and government. This dual approach to leadership development keeps the agency program integral to the total program rather than an isolated and specialized program.

Co-ordination

Co-ordination of the multiple programs of churches and agencies is absolutely necessary for effective working relationships. The guiding principles for co-ordination might be summarized as follows:

Leaders of other programs of children and youth need to be informed about the agency groups. Often there appear ways that leaders can correlate and supplement one another's efforts, and avoid conflicts in ideas and scheduling. It is not enough, though, that leaders simply clear schedules with each other. The place of the agency program in the whole life of the members will be sensed by the boys and girls most meaningfully if the leaders have discussed basic philosophy and goals together. There must come into being a deep awareness that the leaders are all on one team, working for the full development of the children and youth.[2]

The Agencies—Their Purposes and Programs

The following sections describing the purposes and programs of the agencies are not intended to be exhaustive but may well serve as a guide in determining which agency program is best suited to a given local congregation or community. Each of the agencies has guidance material for use of its program by Protestant and Orthodox churches. The National Council of Churches provides guidance material for establishing relationships which foster maximum integration of the respective programs with the ongoing program of Christian education. Addresses of the various agencies will be found at the end of this chapter.

Boy Scouts of America

The purpose of the Boy Scouts of America is to

promote, through organization and cooperation with other agencies, the ability of boys to do things for themselves and others, to train them in Scoutcraft and to teach them

[2] Ralph N. Mould, "Top Drawer Leadership Needed," *International Journal of Religious Education*, XXXV (September, 1958), 9. Used by permission.

patriotism, courage, self-reliance and kindred virtues, using methods which are now in common use by Boy Scouts, by placing emphasis upon the Scout Promise and Law for character development, citizenship training, and physical fitness.[3]

The Boy Scouts of America charters churches, schools, civic organizations, and service clubs of various kinds to use the scouting program and to operate their own scout units. When a church is chartered to operate scout units it agrees to provide a meeting room of the same quality as facilities provided for other youth activities; and to recruit and appoint its own leaders, institutional representative, committee men, and unit leaders. Further, the church determines the type of Scout unit it wishes to operate. It may decide to open its group to all boys in the neighborhood and thereby extend the outreach of its service to the whole community. If a church prefers to serve only its own boys it has the privilege of controlling the membership of the unit.

The local council and districts of the Boy Scouts of America have professional staff and volunteer leaders trained to help a church operate successful Scout units. The services include leadership training, tailor-made to the needs of the church, facilities for long-term and short-term camping as an extension of the church's program under its own leadership in the environment of a boy-scout camp, and program resources such as *Scouting Magazine,* Program Quarterlies, *Boy's Life,* handbooks, and manuals. In addition, a neighborhood commissioner makes regular visits to the church to help the leaders operate successful scout units, and committees on finance, health and safety, advancement, and special activities lend assistance to scouting through the church. Scouting programs are available to boys from the age of nine years old through high school according to their interests and needs.

Cub scouting is a home-centered program for boys nine to eleven years old. The boy's dad and mother take part in his program. Cub packs are usually started where there is already a boy-scout troop. The pack is composed of small groups called dens, each of which holds a weekly meeting under the leadership of a boy scout, called a den chief, and a den mother, who is the mother of one of the cub scouts.

The boy-scout program for boys twelve years of age and older emphasizes outdoor skills and activities, participation in group life, and personal growth. Recognition is given for the boy's accomplishments. Boys are organized into patrols under boy leaders. One or more patrols make a troop. The scoutmaster and assistant are the troop leaders, selected by the troop committee from the church membership.

The new Explorer program is for all high-school boys. A boy can register as an explorer if he is in the ninth grade or above and is fourteen years of age. At fifteen years of age he can register regardless of grade. He may continue through his seventeenth year or until completing full-time high school. An explorer post may be known for its interest in scientific exploration, ham radio operation, dramatics, or any of many other special interests. The post carries on a well-rounded program of social, vocational, outdoor, and service experiences.

Two other aspects of the scouting program of special interest to churches should

[3] See A. E. Iverson, "The Boy Scouts of America," *International Journal of Religious Education,* XXXV (September, 1958), 12-13, 39. Used by permission.

be noted. As an incentive toward religious experience scouts and explorers have opportunity to participate in the Religious Awards Program. This is a program of study, experience, and service, in which a boy engages under the direction of his own priest, minister, or rabbi. In the Protestant program a scout fulfills requirements in five areas of experience—Christian faith, Christian witness, Christian outreach, Christian citizenship, and Christian fellowship.

Co-operative relationships with scout movements in other parts of the world are maintained through the International Committee on Scouting. The international program includes correspondence with pen pals, exchange of scout visits, interchange of training experiences for scout leaders, and giving of literature, visual aids, and other resources for helping scouting in underdeveloped areas of the world.

Camp Fire Girls, Inc.[4]

Camp Fire Girls believes that spiritual development is essential to a healthy, wholesome personality—to the child's becoming a "whole" person. It recognizes the importance of the church and of religious experience and teachings in the life of a girl. Spiritual values are basic to the campfire girls' program and inherent in the campfire girls' Law—worship God, seek beauty, give service, pursue knowledge, be trustworthy, hold on to health, glorify work, be happy.

Each part of this law is related to ethical living, encouraging an appreciation of God's world, emphasizing the dignity of individual human worth and character, and recognizing that service to others is one of the essentials of full living. All parts of the law contribute to a spiritual atmosphere or climate for the whole of life.

Campfire girls seeks the co-operation of leaders of all religious groups, emphasizing not only the faiths we share, but encouraging an appreciation of differences in belief, observance, and heritage. Working in concert across lines of differences the concept of the brotherhood of man finds expression in the lives of girls and women and the men they influence.

Because the interests of girls vary with their growth, campfire girls program is flexible and adaptable. The Blue Birds—seven (or in the second grade), eight, and nine years old—enjoy an appeal to their awakening imaginations. The program includes a variety of constructive activities—music, games, dramatic plays, home crafts, excursions into the community, and guided social experiences within the Blue Bird group.

Campfire girls who are ten years old or in the fifth through eighth grades are at the age when they want to "belong" yet each wants recognition as an individual. The program developed for this age group gives girls the opportunity to work, play, explore and achieve things together as a group. At the same time a girl may develop to the fullest her individual talents and personality.

Built upon seven major areas of interest, the intermediate program consists of seven crafts—home creative arts, outdoors, frontiers of science, business, sports and games, and citizenship. There are countless things to do in each craft, and in the doing girls progress through four ranks: trail seeker, wood gatherer, fire maker, and torch bearer.

A recent addition for the older girl is the torch bearer in religious growth, which supplements the regular program field "My Religion." It is to be carried

[4] See Elizabeth W. Leslie, "Camp Fire Girls," *International Journal of Religious Education,* XXXV (September, 1958), 13-14.

out under the guidance of the girl's religious adviser or his designated assistant. There is no "award" as such upon completion of the requirements, but suitable recognition may be given locally at the discretion of the minister.

Girls in the ninth grade through high school find opportunities for more grown-up activities in Horizon Club—career exploration, personality development, community service, and other activities. There are conferences with horizon clubs of other cities, inter-group activities within their own community, and boy-girl programs in co-operation with other church-sponsored clubs or other organizations. Each offers new opportunity for widening horizons of friendship and service.

Blue bird and campfire groups may have up to twenty members. Horizon clubs may have as many as thirty. They meet in homes, churches, schools, or wherever the needs of the group can be met.

A love of the out of doors and skill in outdoor living are integral parts of the campfire girls program for all age groups. Simple hikes, nature walks, and back-yard camping serve to introduce the blue bird to the wondrous world out of doors. All age groups participate in day, group, and resident camping. In many councils, older campers with special training may enjoy the adventure of primitive camping.

The campfire girls program is a valuable resource for building deeper understanding and appreciation of religious teachings. While girls of all races and religions may belong to campfire girls, a sponsoring organization may limit the group to girls of its own membership if it so desires. In community groups which include girls of many denominations, girls are urged to participate in the activities of their respective churches.

Girl Scouts of the United States of America [5]

"The Girl Scout organization is dedicated to helping girls develop as happy, resourceful individuals willing to share their abilities as citizens in their homes, their communities, their country, and the world." The program aims to strengthen a girl's beliefs, channel her energies, give her an opportunity to be of service to others, stimulate her to think and plan for herself, and help her to learn to live and work harmoniously with other people. The laws say that she shall be honorable, loyal, helpful, friendly to all, courteous, friendly to animals, obedient, cheerful, thrifty, and clean in thought, word, and deed.

Within the seven through seventeen age range, there are three separate groupings. Girls from seven through nine, or the second through the fourth grades, are known as Brownies. Typical activities include making simple gifts to give to hospitals and shut-ins and learning helpfulness to others, "especially those at home." Girls from ten through thirteen are known as Girl Scouts; this usually means girls in the fifth through the eighth grades. These intermediates are helped to acquire proficiency in the various scout fields of interests, such as agriculture, arts, crafts, community life, health and safety, homemaking, international friendship, literature and dramatics, music and dancing, nature, and sports and games. Girls fourteen through seventeen, usually in the ninth, tenth, eleventh, and twelfth grades in school, are known as Senior Scouts. They are given responsibilities in keeping with the mature role for which their age and training equip them. They learn to run

[5] See Marion Amen, "Girl Scouts of the U.S.A.," *International Journal of Religious Education,* XXXV (September, 1958), 15-16.

their troops with little supervision and to give service wherever needed—at home, in their communities, and abroad.

Girl scouting is carried out in small groups—eight to thirty-two members—and is a partnership between young people and adults. Each girl-scout troop has at least one adult leader who volunteers her services. Because of her interest in young people she is able to fulfill their need for the friendly interest and advice of a grown-up friend outside their home and school. She guides her troop in planning and managing its own affairs, which includes the democratic prerogative of choosing those activities which are of greatest value to its members, depending on the maturity level, the interests, and the needs of each group.

A fundamental girl-scout belief is that girls of all faiths, all races, and all national heritages should have equal opportunity to participate fully in all aspects of the girl-scout program. Churches find girl scouting an effective means of extending their influence to girls throughout the community beyond their own membership.

On the other hand, a girl-scout troop can have a wealth of historical and inspirational resources by affiliating with a church, not only in the many service projects that are offered, but also in arts, crafts, and music as well. Religious holidays and festivals offer opportunities for integrating the girl-scout program with that of the church through staging religious plays, singing carols, or making Christmas gifts for missions overseas. A troop finds that sponsorship by a church gives it stability, with a favorable meeting place, leadership, and program resources.

The relationship between a girl-scout unit and a religious group can vary greatly from place to place. Sometimes a church offers a troop a meeting place without taking any further responsibility toward the program. When there is a real partnership this is called troop sponsorship. In such a relationship the troop not only meets in the church, but also receives help from the church with leadership and program resources. Sometimes the girl-scout troop is an integral part of the church program for youth. The troop members in turn give service to the church in a number of ways. A written agreement is important in the case of sponsorship since it defines clearly the responsibilities of the church and of the girl-scout council.

Religious institutions with worldwide ties have welcomed the ways in which girl scouts are given opportunities to take part in international friendship projects based on the interests of the religious groups with which they are affiliated. One aspect of the international character of girl scouting is the exchange program. Every year, several hundred girls and leaders travel across the oceans to visit their sister Guides around the world. An almost equal number of Guides come to the United States to visit in homes and girl-scout camps and to take part in community activities. Living in each other's countries, these girls come to know and understand the reasons for their differences and similarities.

Young Men's Christian Association [6]

The Young Men's Christian Association in the United States has been described in its essential genius as "a world-wide fellowship united by a common loyalty to Jesus Christ for the purpose of developing Christian personality and building a Christian society."

[6] See John A. Ledlie, "Y.M.C.A. Programs for Children and Youth," *International Journal of Religious Education,* XXXV (September, 1958), 16-18.

The Y.M.C.A. movement is a complex organization which covers a wide age range and includes, in addition to the well-known community associations, work with college students, military personnel, and railroad men. We are concerned here, however, only with those aspects of the program dealing with children and youth.

The local Y.M.C.A. is a voluntary organization providing its members with opportunities to engage in a wide variety of activities according to their interests; to share in satisfying experiences of study, play, religious worship, and community service; to associate with others in small, closely knit groups; to develop capacities for leadership through committee work; and to be of service to others throughout the nation and the world.

As one aspect of its services to children and youth, the Y.M.C.A. has developed club programs for four age groupings which are available for church sponsorship. These are Father and Son Y-Indian Guides, for boys six years of age and over; Gra-Y and Tri-Gra-Y for boys and girls of grade-school age; Jr. Hi-Y and Jr. Tri-Hi-Y for boys and girls of junior high-school age; and Hi-Y and Tri-Hi-Y for boys and girls of senior high-school age.

Because of the significance of the family in contributing to the individual growth and to the development of a strong society, the Y.M.C.A. is giving increased attention to the family in program organization and emphasis. It was the recognition of the family as the basic unit in religious, moral, social, and civic values that led the Y.M.C.A. to develop a home-centered program, known as the father and son Y-Indian guides, in which fathers and sons participate together as big and little braves in small units known as tribes. The purpose of the program is to multiply the number of things that fathers and sons can do together. The Y believes that comradeship of father and son has mutual advantages that strengthen the family and enrich the community. Tribes are composed of not more than nine fathers and sons.

As the name indicates, the program of Y-Indian guides is based upon the lore of the American Indian. Just as the colorful life of the Indian revolved around the wigwam or tepee, so the tribal meetings are held in rotation in the homes of the braves. Just as the Indian council opened with a reverent ritual, so does the Indian guide council begin and end with a short, impressive ceremony.

The Gra-Y (abbreviation for grade school and Y.M.C.A.) is a club program for boys, approximately nine to twelve years old. The Tri-Gra-Y is a similar program for girls. These clubs may meet in any place where grade-school boys and girls are found—in homes, in schools, in churches, in the Y. Their purpose is "to be strong in body, mind, and spirit, and to live in a Christian way in our homes, churches, schools, and neighborhoods." These clubs are sponsored by a committee of three or more parents or other interested adults. The comparable club programs for boys and girls in junior high school and for young people of high-school age, have purposes and programs in keeping with the maturity level of the age group.

Both day camping and resident camping are important features of the Y.M.C.A. program for children and youth. The church and the Y.M.C.A. have mutual interests and concerns and many common goals in the field of camping. It is a program area conducive to close co-operation.

The responsibility for determining the nature of co-operative relationships rests with the local Y.M.C.A. and the churches, working through the appropriate church board and the local Y.M.C.A. Youth Program Committee. The Y.M.C.A. assists in the organization, the training of leaders, and the supervision of the group work program. A full range of materials has been developed for each of the four club programs. These consist of a leaders' manual, monthly publications, training materials, and visual aids. A wide variety of co-operative relationships exists, depending upon local conditions, but all are directed toward strengthening the programs of both the Y and the churches and more effectively ministering to all the children and youth of the community.

Whatever the relationships and nature of the program, it is the policy of the local Y.M.C.A.'s to provide experiences that will help children and youth: (1) To understand, accept, and respect themselves as individuals. (2) To develop a faith to live by, based on the teachings of Jesus. (3) To form habits of health and physical fitness. (4) To grow as responsible members of their families. (5) To accept the privileges and responsibilities of Christian citizenship in their own groups and in community life. (6) To develop and work for interracial and intergroup understanding. (7) To develop a sense of world-mindedness.

Young Women's Christian Association [7]

The purpose of the Young Women's Christian Association is "to build a fellowship of women and girls devoted to the task of realizing in our common life those ideals of personal and social living to which we are committed by our faith as Christians. In this endeavor we seek to understand Jesus, to share his love for all people, and to grow in the knowledge and love of God." The Y-Teen clubs, composed mostly of junior and senior high-school girls from twelve through seventeen years of age, translate this purpose into these goals: "to grow as a person; to grow in friendship with people of all races, religions, and nationalities; and to grow in the knowledge and love of God."

In addition to the Y-Teen club program, a large number of boys—called associates of the local Y.W.C.A.—and girls are found pursuing particular interests through hobby groups, classes, drop-in lounges, coed recreation centers, and special events. Many, also, are engaged in the health and physical education activities of the Y.W.C.A., including camping.

Though Y.W.C.A. groups do not ordinarily meet in churches, many young people of churches participate in Y.W.C.A. groups in addition to activities in their churches. Close co-operation between churches and the Y.W.C.A. is helpful to both and to the young people.

There is no standardized procedure for developing Y.W.C.A. teen-age program but the following criteria have been stated as a guide. The program with youth in the Y.W.C.A. must:

Be based upon the questions of youth today, deal with their immediate personal concerns, and offer guidance as young people seek to understand their questions.

Take into account all phases of life situations that face youth.

Grow out of their own expressions, desires, and decisions.

Include fun, recreation, and a chance to make new friends.

Increase opportunity for social and civic outreach in individual groups and in co-operation with community groups.

[7] See Sara-Alyce P. Wright, "The Teenage Program of the Y.W.C.A.," *International Journal of Religious Education*, XXXV (September, 1958), 18-20.

Bring together youth and adults of the Y.W.C.A. and the wider community in mutually interesting and vital enterprises.

Give meaning to Y.W.C.A. membership.

Contribute knowledge and experience for adventuring into new realms of ideas, activities, and relationships.

Strengthen hope and faith in a meaningful universe and in mankind.

Produce some positive evidence of an individual's growth as a responsible person, in wider friendships and in the knowledge and love of God.

The churches are encouraged to help supply responsible adults who will volunteer their skills and time to work with Y-Teens. Volunteers are needed to serve as club leaders; hostesses for teen canteens and dances; instructors in dancing, sewing, cooking, crafts, and sports; song leaders; piano players; teachers of first aid, hospital-aide and child-care courses; leaders for hikes and picnics; dramatic coaches; supervisors of service projects; camp counselors; speakers on etiquette, personal relationships, travel, current events, and jobs; discussion leaders; committee members; and office assistants in mailing, typing, and filing.

Both as a backdrop and as a horizon for all of the activities of the Y-Teen club are the international aspects of the program. Active knowledge and support of the United Nations is encouraged. There are contacts with people of various backgrounds and experiences and a sharing of their hopes, fears, problems, and joys. Special World Fellowship Projects are developed to help strengthen the mutual friendship of Y.W.C.A. youth in this country with those in the seventy countries around the world where the Y.W.C.A. is at work.

Bibliography

Church—Agency Relationships. A Manual on guiding principles for churches and agencies in their co-operative character-building programs. New York: National Council of Churches of Christ in the U.S.A., 1954.

International Journal of Religious Education, Vol. XXXV (September, 1958). This is a special issue devoted entirely to Church-Agency Relationships. This topic is occasionally considered by additional articles included in other issues.

Data on particular agencies and their relationships with the churches are also available from the following:

National Council of Churches of Christ in the U.S.A., 475 Riverside Drive, New York 27, N. Y.

Boy Scouts of America, New Brunswick, N. J.

Camp Fire Girls, Inc., 16 East 48th Street, New York 17, N. Y.

Girl Scouts of the U. S. A., 330 3rd Avenue, New York 22, N. Y.

National Council of the Y.M.C.A.'s of the U.S.A., 291 Broadway, New York 7, N. Y.

National Board of the Y.W.C.A. of the U.S.A., 600 Lexington Avenue, New York 22, N. Y.

Chapter 35

Jewish Religious Education

Judah Pilch

Historic Background

The Role of Learning in Jewish Life

THE RABBINIC DICTUM, "v'TALMUD TORAH KNEGED KULAM" (MISHNAH, PEAH 1:1)—"and the study of the Torah[1] excels all ethical deeds"—is indicative of the place of learning in Jewish life during the millenniums of dispersion. Teaching the young the tenets of Judaism was paramount among all other social and cultural functions of the Jew at all times. The command, "Thou shalt teach . . . diligently unto thy children" (Deut. 6:7), has been a holy task for every father in Israel throughout history. For centuries Jews studied Torah with great zeal and devotion. To the average Jew study was more than pursuit of knowledge; it was the fulfillment of a religious duty. The Jews considered religious education a life-long process, and learning for learning's sake was an important pattern of Jewish conduct.

Transition from Religious to Secular Learning

The major goal of Jewish education, until the end of the eighteenth century was to impart to the young a knowledge of the sacred literature, and to bring up good and pious Jews. The curriculum, therefore, consisted of instruction in the reading of the Hebrew prayers, the Pentateuch, the Psalms, portions of the Prophets, the Talmud, and the Commentaries. This sort of education was uniform for all Jews in the world. Secular knowledge, such as natural sciences, art, history, and allied branches, was either unknown or neglected.

With the beginning of emancipation [2] and with the increasing social intercourse between Jew and non-Jew, secular education became a necessity. A strong urge for modern learning became manifest. The transition between religious training as the sole type of education, and instruction in secular subjects, was accompanied by great difficulties. Not only were the people generally reluctant to change an age-old tradition, but the orthodox rabbis manifested great resentment, fearing that secular studies would lead to the abandonment of traditional Judaism. The new environment, however, overwhelmed the opposition.

---

[1] Torah, literally the Pentateuch. Torah also denotes the totality of religious thought and writing.

[2] The period of Jewish emancipation began on September 28, 1791, when the Jews of France were declared to be equal with all Frenchmen and free citizens of the Republic of France. The Jews in the Netherlands were emancipated in 1796, in the German states in 1848, in Denmark in 1849, in England in 1858, in Italy in 1859, in Austria in 1860.

Simultaneously with the democratization of education generally, ushering in compulsory education for all citizens in a number of lands of Jewish domicile, the Jews exhibited a unique devotion to secular learning and an understanding of its need and utility. In the period before World War I, most of the Jewish children were already attending either the public schools or Jewish educational institutions where secular subjects were taught alongside the Jewish studies. In the post-war period, all resistance to secular education was broken. It became universal in scope.

Jewish Religious Education Becomes Supplementary Education

Indeed secular education has been espoused by the Jews to such a degree that Jewish religious education, especially in America, has been relegated to a secondary place. The chief concern of the Jew today is to afford opportunities for his children to acquire a secular and professional education. Modern conditions have perhaps necessitated such a change in educational orientation, which has made for such a wide gap between the Jewish educational standards of only a century ago and those of today. But this thirst for knowledge of secular subjects has not estranged the Jew from his Torah. While intensive Jewish studies are pursued by a minority, a curriculum of extensive Jewish learning has been devised to meet the needs of all children and adolescents. Some knowledge of Jewish religio-cultural values is being transmitted in one form or another to a major portion of children everywhere in the Jewish world.

In pre-Civil War America, formal Jewish education was confined to the private Hebrew schools and to those congregations whose leaders accepted the responsibility to provide a Jewish religious education for the children of their members. There developed in the middle of the nineteenth century a Jewish nonpublic school which provided secular and religious instruction under one roof and one administration. There were also attempts at the organization of Jewish Sunday schools, patterned after the Sunday schools of the Protestants, for those children who attended the public schools during the week. With the development of the public-school system, the Jews adjusted themselves readily to the law of the land and sent their children to these schools. As the scholastic standards of the public school rose, and as their nonsectarian nature became increasingly evident, the majority of the Jews accepted it as the educational institution for all Americans, Jews and Christians alike. Rapidly after 1865 Jewish religious education became supplementary to public-school education. The Jewish community, whose numbers had grown from 250,000 in the late 1870's to 4,000,000 in the late 1920's, finding in this land a haven in the true sense of the word, was eager to adjust to the American way of life. It accepted the public school with great enthusiasm and set out to develop a supplementary school system to meet its religious needs as Jews.

The increased immigration in the forty years between 1880 and 1920 brought with it a variety of religious philosophies and beliefs, ethnic backgrounds, and a proliferation of *mores* and rituals. For some time Jewish education was in a state of flux, as was all of Jewish life. Gradually the American Jewish community became of age and acquired a physiognomy of its own. The differentiation in religious and intellectual expression among Jews became in time a direct by-product of life in America—religious pluralism. In the course of time American Judaism branched out into several organized nation-wide religious groupings. Today there are four major denominations, each having its rituals and symbolisms, its specific religious doctrine and dogma, and each conducting institutions for worship and social fellowship, schools for higher learning, and a system of religious schools for the children and youth.

Religious Groups in American Judaism and Their Educational Philosophies

Orthodox

Orthodoxy is the historical religion of rabbinic Judaism. It is based on literal belief in the Torah, which came to mean the sum total of Jewish religious teachings of all ages. The theoretical foundation of Orthodoxy is the doctrine of Divine revelation. According to this doctrine, the Torah and an interpretation of it were simultaneously revealed to Moses on Mount Sinai. The Torah and its interpretations were handed down from Moses to Joshua, from Joshua to the elders, and through a succession of authorities to the rabbis, who collected this oral law and expounded the Torah in the Mishnah and Gemara, which together constitute the Talmud. Orthodoxy maintains that the Torah and Talmud contain divine elements and are fountain heads of our knowledge of God's will. Both of these sources, then, constitute the basic foundations of Jewish religious teachings. Judaism, according to Orthodoxy, is a way of life to be practiced and applied in everyday activity. Any reform or compromise in the underlying principles of Judaism is considered an offense. Orthodox or traditional Judaism implies, therefore, the obligatory fulfillment of all religious observances, the fixed belief in the 613 religious duties as specified in the *Schulkhan Arukh* (the code of Jewish law and life compiled by Joseph Caro in the sixteenth century), which consists of instructions of what to do or not to do. It is the individual's fulfillment of these instructions or Mitzvoth [3] that makes one an Orthodox Jew.

In view of the great gap between Orthodox doctrines and present-day actualities, modern Orthodoxy in America has been making extraordinary efforts to bring the people back to the venerable pattern. The Talmudic Academies and the Rabbinical schools of the Yeshiva University and the Chicago Theological College, the Orthodox Commissions on Jewish education—all aim to guide American Orthodoxy and to service Jewish religious schools. The Orthodox group is committed to Torah learning, which prompts them to uphold the principle of intensive Jewish education. As a matter of fact, most of the day schools,[4] and the weekday supplementary Talmud Torahs [5] are either directly sponsored by Orthodox-oriented lay leaders and rabbis or are aided substantially by them.

The educational philosophy of the Orthodox group is related, of course, to their view of the essence of Judaism. Its basic premise is that "Judaism is not a religion based upon speculation. Its major task is not to solve the ultimate question of the nature of God. Its Torah is rather the divine guidance to the right life. Jewish duty consists in the application of the Torah ideals to the hundred and one tasks of daily life." [6] The task of Jewish education is therefore "to teach Judaism as a

[3] Mitzvah (singular) means commandment. It also came to mean a pious act.

[4] Day schools are the institutions that combine Jewish and secular studies.

[5] Talmud Torah means "the study of the Law." It is the name given to the traditional Hebrew School.

[6] *A Model Program for the Talmud Torah* (New York: The Union of Orthodox Jewish Congregations, 1942), p. 13.

totality so that the interrelation between the various Mitzvoth, the Sabbath and the Holy Days, social justice and charity, dietary laws and decency, becomes clear." [7] All subject matter is to convey the "God directed form of life," and all courses are to be taught from the original texts, rather than *Ersatz* efforts. Hence the school curriculum calls for biblical and rabbinic studies, Orthodox religious convictions and observances (application of the code of law in one's daily conduct), in addition to the Hebrew language. The school program makes provisions for the study of history, Jewish civics, and Israel—all from the point of view of the divine purpose in shaping the destiny of the world and of Israel.

Reform

The Reform movement originated in Germany [8] in an attempt to meet the challenges which appeared to threaten the religious life of the Jewish people as a result of emancipation. It represented the first effort to adjust traditional Judaism to modern conditions. The theoretical basis for Reform was its interpretation of Judaism as a theological doctrine of ethical monotheism, as a religion of truth and justice. In line with this doctrine a revised liturgy was, therefore, composed, which introduced the vernacular, as the principal language of prayers, while retaining some of them in the original Hebrew, and eliminated references to the return to Zion, a personal Messiah, or Israel as a people in exile striving for redemption.

The *Schulkhan Arukh* (code of law) too was no longer adhered to, the second days of the Festivals were abolished and the dietary laws disregarded. Many significant rituals, such as daily prayer in the *talit* and *tefillin* [9] and the reading of the prayers and the Pentateuch in Hebrew, were eliminated.

In the last three decades, however, a renascence of traditional Jewish values has begun to manifest itself. Reform Judaism has modified its stand with regard to the upbuilding of the state of Israel, and its rank and file are as concerned with the welfare of the Jewish people everywhere as are the Orthodox and the Conservative Jews. The rabbinic leadership has brought back to the Temple many of the customs and traditional ceremonies, and Hebrew is being reintroduced into the services.

All Reform congregations are affiliated with the Union of American Hebrew Congregations, whose rabbinical school is the Hebrew Union College, established in 1875 in Cincinnati. The Commission on Jewish Education, organized in 1923— representing the lay organization (U.A.H.C.) and the Central Conference of American Rabbis—helped to foster Jewish awareness among the tens of thousands of religious-school students affiliated with the Union.

The fundamental form of Reform education is the Sunday school, and its aims as formulated in the official curriculum are as follows:

To inspire our children with positive and abiding faith in the Jewish religion according to the Liberal Reform tradition; to stimulate their sense of responsibility toward fellow-Jews in all parts of the world, with deep concern for the State of Israel and its people; to provide them with happy experiences in the practice of Judaism; to prepare them to utilize their religious faith . . . in meeting their personal problems, and to inculcate in

---

[7] *Ibid.*, p. 14.

[8] The first Reform Temple was organized in 1810.

[9] The prayer shawl, known also as the fringed garment, and the phylacteries.

them the universal ideal of Israel's prophets and sages, leading toward their dynamic involvement in the service for freedom, brotherhood and peace.[10]

The curriculum calls for a knowledge of the Hebrew Union prayerbook, a knowledge of general Jewish history and the history of the Jew in America, ability to know liturgical Hebrew and the "encouragement of those who have special language potential to the full mastery of the Hebrew language," [11] a knowledge of Jewish ceremonial observances, familiarity with the major Bible stories and selected utterances. For the higher grades the curriculum provides for the study of certain selections from post-biblical literature and a knowledge of the basic tenets of Reform Judaism. All subjects are to be taught in English, including the Bible. The Hebrew portions of the prayerbook, however, as well as Hebrew as a language and as a vocabulary of religious *mores,* are to be given, of course, in Hebrew.

Conservative

Conservative Judaism represents the middle path between Orthodoxy and Reform. It regards traditional rabbinic Judaism as an essential aspect of its religious philosophy and accepts modern methods for examination of the past and the adaptation of religious practices to modern needs. Conservative Judaism differs from the Reform orientation in that it does not wish to reduce Judaism to a creed and the Jewish people to a religious sect. Conservatism regards Judaism and the Jewish people as inseparable. The preservation of both, according to Conservative theory, is essential and desirable. It is also distinguished from Orthodoxy in its readiness to re-examine old Judaic values in the light of new developments and in its scientific approach to the study of biblical and rabbinic literatures.

In its rituals, too, the Conservative synagogue represents the middle course between Reform and Orthodox. Men and women are seated together. Some prayers are read in the vernacular. Hebrew, however, plays a significant role; not only are most prayers recited in it, but the weekly reading of the Torah is in Hebrew. Many of the customs have been preserved in a new and modernized form. Confirmation ceremonies, Sunday school, teaching of the Bible in English, and late Friday night services are deviations from the Orthodox way, but really constitute the modern application of old religious practices.

The Conservative group's spiritual stronghold is the Jewish Theological Seminary, organized in 1886. The congregations are federated in the United Synagogue whose Commission on Jewish Education, organized in 1946, is servicing religious schools conducted by the Conservative congregations. The basic educational objectives of Conservative Judaism are centered around four areas of instruction, which constitute the curriculum for their affiliated schools: (1) Judaism as a way of life, founded upon the belief in the existence and sovereignty of God; (2) Israel, the totality of the Jewish experiences as a people; (3) Torah, the heritage of the enduring Jewish values in Judaism and the experience of Israel as recorded in Jewish literature; (4) Hebrew, both as an integral part of the other three areas and as an area of learning in itself.[12]

[10] Emanuel Gamoran, *Curriculum for the Jewish Religious School* (New York: Union of American Hebrew Congregations, 1955), p. 3.

[11] *Ibid.* p. 4.

[12] Leon S. Lang, *A Curriculum for the Congregational School,* p. 12.

These units of study should attain the following goals:

To imbue the child with love of God and trust in His goodness; to provide opportunities for the child to develop keen spiritual and ethical sensitivity; to develop a desire and convey the skills to practice the Mitzvot and the traditions . . . in the synagogue and in the home; to enable the child to acquire increasing knowledge of the Hebrew language; to broaden and deepen the child's intellectual and spiritual life through knowledge of Jewish history, literature and culture; to strengthen the child's identification with his local community, Israel and World Jewry; to motivate the child to accept the study of Torah as a lifelong pursuit, and to explore the teachings of Judaism and the ideals of American democracy, for the reciprocal influence they should have on each other.[13]

Reconstructionism

The theory of Reconstructionism views Judaism as a religious civilization. The Reconstructionist philosophy, evolved by Mordecai M. Kaplan, himself a teacher at the Jewish Theological Seminary of the Conservative wing, advocates the "reconstruction" of Judaism by rethinking its fundamental ideas. The development of a unified Jewish philosophy adapted to conditions in America, in which all positive Jewish values will have their necessary place is the motto of this movement.

To make Judaism what it should be, we must learn to approach it neither as a super-naturally revealed law, nor merely as an ethical monotheism, but as a religious civilization. As a religious civilization, it embraces the entire gamut of social, creative, and spiritual self-expression. Nothing Jewish should be alien to the Jew, whether it be a National Homeland, the Hebrew language and literature, ethical ideals, legal codes, artistic productions or religious worship and observances. If Judaism is to render Jewish life worthwhile, its program should consist of community, culture and religion. Community is the social framework which would hold together all Jews, however diverse in their religious outlook, who are willing to help build the Jewish future. Culture is a common universe of discourse, habits and creative aspirations that enables a people to be like-minded. Religion is the affirmative world outlook as it finds expression in worship ritual. A Judaism in which these three elements interact organically must be the goal of all our strivings as a people.[14]

The Reconstructionist views on Jewish education are based on the premise that it too is subject to reconstruction. The desired goals of such a reconstructed Jewish education are the following: (1) acceptance of the idea of Jewish peoplehood, (2) motivating interest in Israel, (3) motivating participation in Jewish communal life, (4) promoting equality of all religions, (5) the revitalization of the Jewish religion, (6) the stimulation of Jewish literature and the arts, (7) participation in the movement for social betterment. [15]

The Reconstructionist movement has had some impact upon a number of leading Jewish educators. A number of schools, especially of those congregations affiliated with the Reconstructionist fellowship, set out to develop a curriculum which would be based upon these seven objectives of Jewish education.

[13] *Objectives and Standards for the Congregation's School* (New York: United Synagogue Commission on Jewish Education, 1958), pp. 7-8. Used by permission.

[14] Mordecai M. Kaplan, "The Meaning of Reconstructionism," *The Reconstructionist*, VI (February, 1940), 14. Used by permission.

[15] Michael Aler, *Reconstructing Jewish Education* (New York: The Jewish Reconstructionist Press, 1957), pp. 144-49.

The American Jewish Community—Diversity in Unity

Despite the divergence of views with regard to the nature of Judaism and despite the tendency of each of the religious groupings to strengthen its structural base, American Jewry constitutes *one* community. It is important to understand that in addition to the different current religious schools of thought, there exist within the community a variety of groupings which represent still other interpretations of Jewish life. To begin with, there are many unaffiliated Jews to whom a religious congregation is not the only core of Jewish identification. There are the secularists, the humanists, the Yiddish-culturists, and the secular-Zionists (some of whom sponsor Jewish school programs for their children). Then too, there are many affiliated Jews who find religio-cultural fulfillment in civic endeavors of all kinds. They are taking an active part in the work of agencies for aid to Jews overseas, in defense activities, in helping their brethren in the upbuilding of the State of Israel, in looking after the sick, aged, and underprivileged children, and in general welfare activities on behalf of Jews and non-Jews alike. Thus, despite the multiplicity of loyalties to one or another expression of Jewish life, there is a growing recognition of the oneness of the Jewish community. The *rapprochement* of religious views is made possible, on the one hand, by the age-old tradition that "All Jews are responsible for one another," and on the other, by the influences of the American idea. The efficiently organized program of community structure for co-ordinated philanthropic and cultural activities within the Jewish community enhances the possibilities for interaction among the different groupings. There is much more substance to that which unites Jews than to that which divides them.

As for the theories and practices in Jewish education it is important to note that the young parents of the new generation especially are not concerned with differences in theology or in ritual. They are interested in providing their children with a religious education indigenous to the American scene. They want a good school plant, a good staff, a functional program. They want Jewish schooling not to tax unduly the time and energy of their children, attending the public schools and engaging in recreational activities. From a careful study of the educational objectives of the different groups we see that there is a common core of content for all types of curricula. For all Jewish schools are part of the American Jewish community; all children live together, have a common past and a common faith and fate.

In the light of our contention that Jewish schools may differ from each other in form, content, and operation, but that they nevertheless have many elements in common insofar as aims and curriculum are concerned,[16] it is advisable to discuss the Jewish schools of America in terms of the intensity of their instruction rather than in terms of their ideological auspices and affiliation. By and large the intensive Hebraic education is given by Orthodox-oriented schools, the less intensive instruction, which is in many cases in the process of rapid intensification, is that of the Conservative movement; and, finally, the still less intensive education is provided in the Sunday schools of the Reform. The differentiation in the degree of intensity of the religious educational program runs parallel to the ideological view-

[16] Alexander M. Dushkin, "Common Elements in Jewish Education," *Jewish Education*, XXIII (November, 1945), 5-13.

point of the particular group under whose aegis the school functions. It is important to note, however, that all these schools together, including those of the a-religious groups, constitute the school system of the diversified yet united American Jewish community.

Types of Jewish Education

The Most Intensive Education—the Day School

The Jewish day school or the Jewish "complete" school, generally defined, is an educational institution in which a combined program of Jewish and general studies is offered. There are four types of institutions that are included in the category of Jewish day schools. These are the Talmudic day school, the modern day school, the integrated school, and the Hebrew-English private school. While educational approaches among these schools vary, they, nevertheless, approximate the designation of a school which provides the most intensive Jewish education in modern times.

The traditional day school makes provision for the study of the Pentateuch, major portions of the Prophets and Scripture in the original Hebrew, and places great stress on teaching of Talmud. The English studies meet the requirements of the city and state authorities. The school day ranges from eight to ten hours. The Hebrew studies are given in the morning hours and the English in the afternoon.

The modern day school stresses the study of Hebrew language and literature. In addition to Hebrew, there is the study of Bible, Jewish History, prayers, and selected portions from the Talmud. All instruction is in the Hebrew language. The English studies are given equal attention and equal time. As a rule, this school begins at nine o'clock and ends at four o'clock.

The integrated day school aims to integrate American and Jewish cultures and to achieve a blending of Judaism and Americanism. To attain this end "both curricula are offered departmentally throughout the school day." [17] The pupil may begin the school day with the study of Bible, go next to a lesson in arithmetic, then proceed to the study of the Hebrew language, then to geography, and so on. The idea of integration is also incorporated into the subject matter of instruction. The subjects taught are the same as in the modern day school, but with more stress on the mutual relationships between English and Hebrew studies.

The Hebrew-English integrated school lays stress on English subjects and provides opportunities for Jewish learning for only five hours a week. It is a modern and progressive school which satisfies those parents who seek private instruction of a high caliber and who are eager to solve the problem of a two-school system.

In recent years a number of day schools are also sponsored by Yiddish-culture groups. The program of these schools differs from the modern day school in that Yiddish language and literature are included as basic subjects of instruction.

The majority of day schools are sponsored by Orthodox groups. Some that fall in the category of modern day schools are conducted by the Conservatives. In 1959 there were 214 day schools with an attendance of about 43,000 in this country. This constitutes about eight per cent of the Jewish child population in attendance in any type of a Jewish school.[18]

[17] The description of this type of school was taken from Rabbi Joseph Lookstein's article on the Ramaz School of which he is principal, in *Types of Jewish Schools*, ed. Israel S. Chipkin (New York: American Association for Jewish Education, 1947), pp. 32-34.

[18] These figures are based on the 1958 census conducted by the Research Department of the American Association for Jewish Education, headed by U. Z. Engelman.

The Most Intensive Supplementary Education—the Talmud Torah

Next to the day school, the Talmud Torah offers an intensive Jewish education. Its program is geared to an appreciation on a child level of the totality of the Jewish cultural heritage, including religion—in many cases, especially religion. It meets daily after public-school hours for seven and a half to ten hours of instruction per week. The Talmud Torah is either affiliated with a synagogue—usually Orthodox, occasionally Conservative—or conducted by an association of laymen who are devoted to traditional Judaism. In the 1920's this was the predominant type of a weekday school. With the rapid growth of the congregational school in the 1930's and 1940's, however, the Talmud Torah declined. It is still in existence today either as intercongregational or as a community-supported Hebrew School. Its program is based on a six-year curriculum which includes the following areas of study: The Hebrew prayerbook, the Bible (a knowledge of the narrative and legalistic portions of the Pentateuch, and selections from the early prophets), the Hebrew language (an ability to understand, read, and write simple Hebrew), Jewish history, customs, and ceremonies (taught at present in English), and the Jewish arts (music, arts, and crafts). The number of pupils estimated to have attended these schools in 1958 was about 13 per cent of the entire Jewish school population.[19]

The Congregational Weekday School

The weekday congregational school is another institution for supplementary religious education. Its pupils attend classes after public-school hours, generally for an hour and a half or two hours a day, two days during the week and on Sunday. While there are variations in the pattern (some Orthodox and Conservative congregations maintain the Talmud Torah type of program four days a week), most Conservative and to some extent modern Orthodox synagogues conduct three-day schools. In many of these schools the children concentrate on Hebraic studies during the week and on Sundays join pupils who come only once a week for the study of those subjects that are taught in English. Among these are Jewish history, customs, and ceremonies; Jewish civics; Israel; and the Jewish arts. In recent years many conservative congregations enacted regulations calling for the elimination of the Sunday-school department for all children between the ages eight to thirteen. Thus the weekday department of their religious school has been strengthened in numbers and the study of Jewish classics accelerated.

The curriculum of most three-day programs is based upon five years of attendance. The children enter at the age of eight and graduate at thirteen, upon becoming Bar-Mitzvah (confirmants). They study selections of the Pentateuch in Hebrew, the prayerbook, the Hebrew language (as preparation for the study of Bible, as well as for an understanding of the prayerbook), Jewish history, religious practices in home and synagogue, and the Jewish fine arts. In the recently published survey of Jewish education in greater New York (qualitative studies), it was reported that "the data indicated that the curricula of Orthodox and Conservative congregational Weekday Schools were basically very similar. The differences that were revealed were

---

[19] "Minutes," Board of Governors, American Association for Jewish Education, December 15, 1958, New York.

390

minor in character." [20] According to the census conducted by the American Association for Jewish Education for the school year 1958-59, 18.3 per cent of all children attending Jewish educational institutions were in the three-day congregational schools, 7.6 per cent in the two-day institution, and 5 per cent in the four-day schools.

The One-Day-A-Week Type of Education

These schools are frequently referred to as Sunday schools because they conduct their classes on Sunday mornings. The Sunday school is the largest single unit in the American Jewish school system. The time of instruction in these schools averages two hours a week. The Sunday schools usually meet between thirty-two and thirty-five Sundays a year and provide a total of sixty-four to seventy hours of instruction. Their course of study is based on six to eight years of attendance.

The Sunday school is usually identified with the Reform movement, although in recent years Reform congregations have organized a number of two-and-three-day departments. Conservative and Orthodox congregations, too, operate one-day school units. There are many common elements in the programs of the Sunday schools sponsored by the three major religious groupings. The language of instruction in all the Sunday schools is English, and the core curriculum consists of Jewish history, customs, and ceremonies; Bible stories at the lower level; and some prayers in Hebrew. Moreover, in all these schools emphasis is placed on preparation for participation in the synagogue life of the respective groups and identification with the Jewish community. Practically all schools conduct certain co-curricular activities, and in the higher grades there are discussions on current events, reading of selections from the Bible in English, and instruction in religious and ethical values of Jewish literature. Some functional Hebrew is now being taught in many of these schools, especially those of the Reform congregations that do not have a weekday Hebrew department. During the school year 1958-59, 45 per cent of the enrollees attended the Sunday schools.

The Yiddish Schools

The early Yiddish schools were organized by immigrants who came to America at the beginning of the century. The basic elements of their curriculums were Yiddish language and literature and Jewish history. The orientation of these schools has undergone a considerable change in the last two decades. Their curriculums now reflect the historic importance of the millenniums-old Jewish culture and include the study of Hebrew language, selections from the Bible, and the observance of Jewish festivals. The number of Yiddish schools has considerably declined in recent years. In 1956 they constituted less than 3 per cent of the entire Jewish school population.

Secondary Schools for Jewish Education

The large congregations conduct high-school departments. The graduates from the elementary Sunday schools are encouraged to meet at least once a week for continued study. In the mid-size and large communities the children who graduate from the elementary Hebrew schools are directed to central high schools, where they continue their Judaic studies on a higher level for five to seven and a half hours of weekly study. Regrettably, the secondary schools attract only about 7 to 10

[20] *Survey of Jewish Education in Greater New York for 1951-1952, Qualitative Studies* (New York: Jewish Education Committee of New York, Inc., January, 1959), p. 28.

per cent of high-school age youth. The course of study in the one-day high schools includes the Old Testament, Jewish history, current events, religious and philosophic texts, and basic Hebrew. The language of instruction is English.

In the communal or intercongregational high-school departments, the course of study includes the Prophets, Scripture, selections from Talmudic texts, selections from medieval and modern Hebrew literature, Jewish history, and current events. The language of instruction is Hebrew.

Schools for Higher Jewish Learning

In addition to the theological seminaries maintained by the Orthodox, Conservative, and Reform movements, there are a number of other schools of higher Jewish learning whose aim is to promote Jewish scholarship and to afford opportunities for advanced Jewish studies for both professional and lay Jewish leaders. The nonrabbinic schools include The Dropsie College in Philadelphia, Yeshiva University in New York, the University of Judaism in Los Angeles, and the newly organized Jewish University in Chicago. There are also ten Hebrew teacher-training schools, offering degrees of Bachelor of Jewish Education and Master of Hebrew Literature, and a number of colleges of Jewish studies for advanced Jewish education maintained by the central agencies for Jewish education in twenty-two of the larger Jewish communities. It is also worth noting that many of the Jewish community centers conduct adult institutes for Jewish studies, as do many of the synagogues.

The Jewish Camp

In recent years the summer camp has become another important factor in the Jewish educational process. The three or four noncommercial camps in the 1920's designed for Jewish educational activity grew into seventy to eighty. The camp is an excellent means for the integration of Jewish education with a camp program. It is a unique opportunity for the utilization of the summer vacation period for Jewish "learning and doing."

Camping provides a continuous, integrated social environment as the natural milieu for the educational influence to be brought to bear upon the mind, character and emotions of the pupil-campers. At camp all activities can be integrated into a single harmonious process of normal (Jewish) living. At camp there is harmony, wholeness and naturalness of environmental influences.[21]

The growing acceptance of the camp idea for the development of Jewish cultural life for children and youth prompted national organizations and synagogal groups to establish summer camps. The Zionist youth organizations, the Reform group, the Conservative and the Orthodox, the Yiddish and Hebrew speaking groups, all maintain summer camps. The bureaus of Jewish education, the colleges of Jewish studies, and the day schools also operate camps.

Teachers

There is a serious shortage of qualified personnel to staff the Jewish religious schools. There are many reasons for the shortage of teachers, and they are related to

---

[21] Albert P. Schoolman, "The Jewish Summer Camp," *Types of Jewish Schools in America,* ed. I. S. Chipkin (New York: American Association for Jewish Education, 1947), p. 50.

one another. A few are: (a) the increase in enrollment, (b) the economic factor, (c) lack of professional satisfaction, (d) little if any social recognition, (e) limited opportunity for professional growth. The 10 recognized Hebrew teachers colleges graduate annually 150 students, and there is a need in the community for four or five times that number.[22]

There are approximately 9,000 teachers employed in the American Jewish schools. 3,000 are full-schedule teachers who work in the weekday afternoon schools and in the day schools; 2,500 are part-time teachers, who work from eight to ten hours a week; and approximately 4,000 are semiprofessional, voluntary teachers in charge of classes in the Sunday schools.[23] Earnest efforts have been put forth in recent years by the American Association for Jewish Education to solve the problem of teacher shortage.

Co-ordination of Jewish Educational Endeavor

Local Bureaus of Jewish Education

Local central agencies for Jewish education, known by the name of Bureaus, were organized in the past three decades in all major communities. The function of these community agencies is to render service to every element in the community with a positive attitude toward Judaism and Jewish life and "to help each element carry on its work in terms of its own ideology in accordance with the highest standards which conditions permit and to encourage each element to engage in experimentation and to seek new ways and new means for implementing its objectives." [24] There are forty-two such local agencies in the United States.

National Ideological Commissions on Jewish Education

The schools of the three major religious groups are being serviced nationally by their own ideological mentors—the national commissions on Jewish education. There are four such commissions for the Orthodox [25] groups, one for the Reform, one for the Conservative, and two for the Yiddish schools. Each commission prepares curriculums and syllabuses for their affiliated schools, reflecting the aims of Jewish education of their particular ideologies. They also publish textbooks and audio-visual aids and sponsor workshops for the teachers in service. These commissions have also organized the professional-school personnel into five associations corresponding to their counterparts among the lay groups.

The American Association for Jewish Education

The American Association for Jewish Education is the over-all national service agency. It relates itself to all elements of the American Jewish community, irrespective of ideological differences. It is dedicated to the principle of community responsibility for Jewish education, and strives to stimulate, promote, extend, and improve the status of Jewish education on all age levels and among all ideological

[22] Judah Pilch, "Teacher Shortage: Problem and Solution," *Congress Weekly*, XXIII (October 29, 1956).

[23] Minutes of meeting of the National Committee on Teacher Education and Welfare, sponsored by the American Association for Jewish Education, Atlantic City, May 23, 1957.

[24] Leo L. Honor, "Jewish Elementary Education in the United States (1901-1950)," Publication of the Jewish Historical Society, Vol. XLII, No. 1.

[25] There are at least three divisions in the Orthodox Community—Ultra-Orthodox, middle of the road Orthodox, and the Modern Orthodox.

groups. The A.A.J.E. offers services in the fields of educational research, community organization for Jewish education, pedagogics and curriculums, promotion and interpretation, personnel and teacher-training. It sponsors the National Board of License for the certification of full-time professional teachers, conducts a department on Jewish audio-visual materials, and co-operates with all national and local organizations in the advancement of the cause of Jewish education for children, youth, and adults. It is the parent agency of all local bureaus of Jewish education.

Trends in Enrollment and Financing

Trends in Enrollment

According to findings of the Research Department of the American Association for Jewish Education,[26] there were 485,000 Jewish children in attendance during the school year 1956-57. The Commission for the National Study for Jewish Education, which is sponsored by the A.A.J.E., conducted a Jewish school census and ascertained that the enrollment figures for 1958 were 553,600. The rise in Jewish school population has been continuous and constant. In 1942 there were 200,000 enrollees; in 1950, 266,609,[27] and in 1958, 553,600. It is estimated that 45 per cent of the total number of pupils are to be found in the Sunday schools and 55 per cent in the supplementary weekday schools and in the day schools. It is worth noting that the Jewish schools attract from 80 to 85 per cent of all Jewish children during their school career (ages five to fourteen).

Trends in Financing

In 1956, the cost of operating all the Jewish schools in the United States amounted to approximately $46,000,000.[28] For 1958 it was closer to the sixty million mark. The instructional and administrative expenses only are included in these figures. It is estimated that two thirds of these funds are derived from tuition fees and voluntary contributions of parents, lay committees, and congregational subsidies. Federations and welfare funds contributed in the neighborhood of four million dollars in 1957. The remainder is derived from other sources. The rise in the cost of the Jewish educational enterprise runs parallel to the growth of the school population. The strengths of these developments bespeak an ever-growing interest in and concern with Jewish education as the best guarantee for the creative survival of the Jewish community.

Conclusion

The function of Jewish education is to establish the continuity between the present and the past of the Jewish people and to transmit those aspects of the Jewish religio-cultural heritage which withstood the test of the ages. A concerted effort is being made by American Jewry to do so.

Bibliography

Berkson, I. B. "Jewish Education—Achievements and Needs," *The American Jew*. ed. Oscar I. Janowsky. New York: Harper and Brothers, 1942.

[26] *American Jewish Year Book, 1958*, pp. 124-39.

[27] Uriah Zevi Engelman, "Jewish Education in Facts and Figures," *Jewish Education Register and Directory* (New York: American Association for Jewish Education, 1951), p. 27.

[28] Uriah Zevi Engelman, "Jewish Education," *American Jewish Year Book*, ed. Morris Fine (Philadelphia: Jewish Publication Society, 1958), p. 134.

Chipkin, Israel S. *Jewish Education in the United States at the Mid-Century*. New York: American Association for Jewish Education, 1951.

Engelman, U. Z. *Trends and Developments in Jewish Education*. New York: American Association for Jewish Education, 1957.

Gannes, Abraham P. *Central Community Agencies for Jewish Education*. Philadelphia: Dropsie College, 1954.

Hertz, Richard C. *The Education of the Child*. New York: Union of American Hebrew Congregations, 1953.

Katzoff, Louis. *Issues in Jewish Education*. New York: Bloch Publishing Co., 1948.

Lang, Leo S. *A Curriculum for the Congregational School*. Philadelphia: Board of Jewish Education, 1951.

Pilch, Judah (ed.). *Jewish Education Register and Directory*. New York: American Association for Jewish Education, 1951.

Chapter 36

Roman Catholic Religious Education

Gerard S. Sloyan

CONTRIBUTIONS TO THIS VOLUME HAVE MADE IT CLEAR THAT THE SYNAGOGUE and the church have equally and immemorially had a concern for sacred learning. If God has addressed his word to man—as both are convinced is the case—and if he expects a loving response to this message of his conceived in everlasting love, then the "holy people" who receive the message must see to the widest diffusion possible among that people.[1]

For the Catholic, the end term of religious education is faith in the biblical sense—a movement of the soul, a commitment of the self involving the whole being, in response to God's unfailing word spoken in his Church. Abraham, David, Paul, and all the saints made a fitting response of faith—which was necessarily both intellectual affirmation and perfect trust—to the word addressed to them from on high.[2] They did this not simply as individuals divinely enabled but also as members of a believing community. This is the response which Catholics hope to make, through the mediation of Jesus Christ. In his role as head of that body which is the Church he dispenses the Father's gift of life. Christ's filial attitude toward his heavenly Father has its counterpart among his members in their lively, obedient faith.[3] This is not a cravenly submissive quality but a trustful one which knows it cannot be betrayed.

In light of all this, Roman Catholic religious education may be defined as *the unfolding of the terms of God's gift freely given—life—and of the response of free acceptance to that gift*. It is comprised of an objective element, sacred truth—"object of faith"—and a subjective one, the states of heart and mind necessary to come into possession of that truth—"virtue of faith." [4]

The roots of the religious instruction given by modern Roman Catholics lie, of course, in the catechumenate practices of the first five centuries, the monastic and episcopal schools of the Merovingian and Carolingian periods, and the require-

[1] Cf. Louis Bouyer, *Liturgical Piety* (Notre Dame, Ind.: University of Notre Dame Press, 1955), p. 29.

[2] Cf. Brother Alfred, F. S. C., "Teaching Religion," *Catholic Education*, V (October, 1958), 31, for a discussion of religious education as response to God's revealing word.

[3] Cf. Karl Adam, *The Christ of Faith*, The Christology of the Church (London: Burns and Oates, 1957), pp. 216-17.

[4] This distinction is well made by François Coudreau, P.S.S., "Introduction to a Pedagogy of Faith," Gerard S. Sloyan (ed.), *Shaping the Christian Message* (New York: The Macmillan Company, 1958), pp. 132-37.

ments laid down by medieval synods regarding regular pulpit instruction of adults in the *Credo, Pater, Ave,* and the various sacraments. The Middle Ages introduce the schoolmaster as a village fixture under the parish priest's direction. In this matter the heightened commercial interests of the crusading period were influential. Some rudimentary religious instruction undoubtedly went ahead as part of the village school's program. Another source of popular formation was the quizzing administered to penitents by the clergy on the occasion of the annual confession, from the eighth century onward. This resulted in the confessional booklets (*libelli*) containing lists of sins, a device that proliferated after the invention of printing. These questions or headings, put onto wall charts for use in the churches in the later Middle Ages, served as forerunners of the printed catechism. The usual subject headings were the creed, sacraments, commandments, and prayer. This was the era of rhymed couplets, placards, religious dramas, and images in every medium depicting events in the Bible and the lives of the saints. Catechizing took place largely within the family but was strongly augmented by the sacred art of the time, by shrines and pilgrimages, by the multitude of popular devotions, and in a restricted measure the sacred liturgy—unfortunately dethroned from its didactic eminence, in good part, with the replacement of Latin by the vernacular tongues and the substitution of literal realism for symbolic realism.[5]

The success of Martin Luther's catechism (1529) underlined the great need for well-formulated popular instruction. Except for its structure, in which the commandments came first, in order to impress upon man his total helplessness without grace, the catechism was not marked by any of the "new teaching" and was the product of medieval Christian thought. The Catholic response to the success of this *Büchlein* was immediate and not very effective. Beginning in 1535, with the *Catechismus Ecclesiae: Lere und Handlung des heiligen Christentums* of Georg Witzel, a series of Catholic catechisms began to appear in Germany from the pens of men like Dietenberger (1537), Gropper (1546), and Helding (1549).[6] They were too diffuse in style, too edifying and too numerous. Luther's principle of pedagogy was simpler and more effective:

> For the young and simple folk must be taught one definite text and version, else they will easily become confused, if today we teach thus and next year thus, as though we wanted to improve it, and so all our labor and toil is lost . . . we must always teach . . . in such a manner that we do not alter one syllable . . . If thou preachest to scholars or wise men . . . thou mayest vary these articles . . . But with the young keep always to one form . . . so that they may repeat them and learn them by heart.[7]

Such was the spirit of the times. Religious education consisted in sets of propositions for rote memorization derived from the great prayers, the decalogue, and the sacraments, far more than from the record of God's love upon the *sacra pagina,* which culminated in the good news of man's salvation in Christ. Catholics and

---

[5] Cf. Josef A. Jungmann, *Handing on the Faith* (New York: Herder and Herder, 1959), pp. 1-19.

[6] Chr. Moufang, *Katholische Katechismen des 16. Jahrhunderts in deutscher Sprache* (Mainz: F. Kirchheim, 1881); P. Bahlmann, *Deutschlands katholische Katechismen* (Münster: Regensbergesche Buchhandlung, 1894), gives full data on twenty-eight German catechisms between 1500 and 1582, ten in Latin from the same period, and the text of a late fifteenth century *Tafel des christlichen Lebens.*

[7] Martin Luther, *The Shorter Catechism,* quoted in Henry Bettenson (ed.), *Documents of the Christian Church* (New York: Oxford University Press, 1947), p. 287.

Reformers vied with each other to make pulpit preaching more effective, but the instruction of young and old alike was caught in the vice grip of certain stereotypes which neither group was successful in loosing for several centuries.

Catechisms of the Period After Trent

The *Catechismus Romanus* was produced in 1566 at the instigation of the recently completed Council of Trent, at the press of Paolo Manuzio in Venice. The final compilation was the work of three Dominican theologians (friars of the Order of Preachers) Foreiro, Foscarari, and Marini and two Latin stylists Calini and Poggianus, but it is unsigned.[8] B. J. Kidd has referred to this extensive theological manual for parish priests as "a classic both of theology and Latin." Its division was fourfold: the Creed, the Sacraments, the Decalogue ("the end whereof is charity"), and the Lord's Prayer. These headings, according to the authors, "comprise the whole force and doctrine of Holy Scripture." There is little reference to the religious differences of the times in the body of this four-hundred page work, though the Preface does speak of the pestilence of "new and strange doctrines" and "innumerable smaller books . . . which [have] deceived with incredible facility the simple and the incautious." [9] The spirit and tone of the remainder of this work are largely satisfying. The chief citations are from Scripture, the Fathers, and the Councils. There is little scholasticism, doubtless because of the low esteem in which it was held by the Reformers. There are certain unhappy emphases, for example, a juridical view of the redemption, which in teaching our rescue from the tyranny of the devil by a ransom price that far outweighs our indebtedness could easily mislead the reader about the true nature of divine love.

All in all, however, the volume is hearteningly biblical in its outlook and liturgical in the sense that sacramental life is central, even if the communal celebration of the mysteries is not especially adverted to. A tragedy of post-Reformation Catholic life is that various cullings from this volume for popular use pressed certain themes which it developed and neglected others, to the general impoverishment of Catholic religious formation. Thus, the treatment of the Eucharist with its stress on the symbolic signification which "renders us one mystic body" laid the foundations for a liturgical renewal. The times were not ready for it, however. This

---

[8] *Catechismus ex Decreto Concilii Tridentini ad Parochos Pii V Pontificis Max. et deinde Clementis XIII Iussu Editus* (Roma: Typis Sacr. Congr. de Prop. Fide, 1845). Trans. J. Donovan, *The Catechism of the Council of Trent* (Baltimore: Lucas Bros., n.d.).

[9] In a remarkable letter to *The Tablet* (London) dated April 18, 1959, Mary Cahill writing from Canterbury identifies the "pernicious booklets" which the Tridentine volume deplored with all compressed religious handbooks for the young. "The catechisms we speak of and use, those so condemned by this authority, are the booklets wherein the content of the faith, after being 'squeezed into academic shape,' dissected, desiccated, is reduced to tabloid form and embodied in stereotype questions and answers." Surely the writer proves too much. While the *genre* "catechism" has been under fairly consistent attack from one source or other within the Church for four centuries, on pedagogical grounds, it has never been identified as a form of presenting the faith which the authors of *Catechismus Romanus* or any more official authority meant to reprobate. Many have written in the spirit of Cardinal Mercier of Mechelen of these "booklets of abstract, frozen, formulas which have no connection with the vivid life of the Christian soul" (quotation the correspondent's), but the evidence of the acceptance and use of such booklets by Catholic bishops is overwhelming. They cannot be interpreted to have given positive sanction thereby to bad teaching.

spirit of corporate worship has been four centuries in coming to birth with something of the vigor of the church's "springtime."

The great catechist of Germany was Peter Canisius; of Italy, Robert Bellarmine; both were members of the Company of Jesus. The former produced an adolescents' catechism in 1555, *Summa Doctrina Christiana per quaestiones tradita et in usum Christianae pueritiae nunc primum edita*.[10] One year later an abridgement was published in both Latin and German. A medium-sized book was the last to appear, in 1558. This "Shorter Catechism" (*minor*), as it was called, had immense success in many languages. In 1566 Canisius made a definitive edition of his *Summa* to bring it into line with the catechism of Trent. One of his last acts before his death at the age of seventy-five was to syllabicate his "Shortest Catechism" (*minimus*). Bellarmine contributed *Dottrina Cristiana breve* in 1597 and *Dichiarazione piu copiosa della dottrina Cristiana*, a year later, both at Rome. In 1604 while Archbishop of Capua he produced for the use of his own clergy the *Dichiarazione del simbolo*.

The "Canisius of France," Edmund Auger, produced his catechisms in 1563 (Latin) and 1568 (French).[11] Jerónimo Martinez de Ripalda did a like service for Spain in 1616. The former introduced the element of the subject and his needs. No longer does Auger ask with Aquinas, "What things are necessary for a man to win salvation?" or with Canisius, "Who may be called a Christian?" but he asks "Why did God create us, and does he preserve us from day to day in this world?"

An examination of these books, all of which had great influence, will reveal the origins of the religious instruction made available to the American Catholic child. The questions and answers may have come to them through the German-language catechism of Josef Deharbe (1847) or that authorized by the Third Plenary Council of Baltimore (1885), which was revised in 1941, but the matter and manner will prove to be much the same. Theologically precise after the manner of Trent's formulation of Catholic theology, their sole concession to child nature was the abridgement of lengthy doctrinal formulas. More to the point, the sole method of theological argumentation and stress employed was that proper to the post-Tridentine period.

The Use of the Bible in Catechetics

A biblical framework for religious instruction had seemed ideal to the Church Fathers because God's revelation had been accomplished successively in history. The penchant for "clear ideas" in proposition form dislodged it in the medieval period. The sixteenth-century struggle over the correct interpreting of scripture

[10] Cf. J. Brodrick, *St. Peter Canisius, S.J.* (Baltimore: Carroll Press, 1950), pp. 223-52, for full citation on these works, especially F. Streicher, *S. Petri Canisii . . . Catechismi Latini et Germanici*, 2 vols. (Rome, Munich, 1933-36). Likewise cf. Brodrick, *The Life and Works of Blessed Robert F. Cardinal Bellarmine*, I (London: Burns, Oates and Washbourne, 1928), 389-98. W. Croce, S.J., has observed the failure of these great catechists to deal with the sacraments in their proper place in The Creed as part of the "heritage of the holy community" (*sanctorum communionem*), placing them rather in conjunction with the Decalogue as a means to insure the practice of loving obedience; also their failure to set aside "the various enumerations (mostly of moral content) inherited from the Middle Ages." Cf. "Contents of Catechesis: the Message of Salvation," *Lumen Vitae*, XI (October-December, 1956), 597.

[11] Cf. J. Dutilleiul, "Auger," *Dictionnaire d'Histoire et de Géographie Ecclésiastiques*, V (Paris: Letouzey et Ané, 1931), 379 ff.

meant that the Bible, except for the use of proof texts, returned to Catholic religious instruction very slowly. Claude Fleury attempted a *Catéchisme historique* (1683) in France which was Bible based. One of Bossuet's catechisms for his diocese of Meaux (1687) was along these lines, and likewise that of the Oratorian Pouget (1702).[12] In Austria the innovator was Felbiger, while the title in Germany goes to Bernard Overberg who published his *Biblische Geschichte des Alten und Neuen Testaments* in 1799.[13]

Felbiger and after him C. von Schmid (*Biblische Geschichte für Kinder*, 1801), Schuster (1847), Mey (1875), and Knecht (1907), were all concerned to tell children stories from the Bible, but they considered them merely examples of virtue which would illustrate and augment the catechism lesson. Overberg's had been a larger view. For him the Bible was "the history of God's gratuitous concern for man's salvation." [14] The same idea was central in the thought of Bernard Galura, Bishop of Brixen, in his *Biblische Geschichte der Welterlösung durch Jesum den Sohn Gottes* (1806).[15] Galura built everything around the theme of "the kingdom of God." This indeed may be considered basic to the "new catechetical movement" in the Catholic Church, which probably should be dated by the appearance of Otto Willmann's *Didaktik als Bildungslehre* (1909).[16] This pupil of a pupil of Herbart laid the groundwork for the efforts of Heinrich Steiglitz and the "Munich Method," which featured the three steps—presentation, explanation and application—in every lesson.[17] Far more important than the "method," which by now through disciples of Herbart, is the common property of all pedagogy, is the content of the catechetical presentation. The message of salvation is seen to be God's living design to lead us into the very life of the Trinity through Christ, our hope of glory.

This pedagogy is *theocentric* in its insistence on the idea of God and his sovereignty over the men who will find happiness in his will. It is *Christocentric* in that Jesus the Lord is the sole way to the Father.[18] The Old Testament must be studied because it is the tutor leading us to Christ (Gal. 3:24). God in Christ is the salvation of a sinful world. Profoundly biblical and liturgical in its orientation, this modern catechesis celebrates at altar and font the mysteries it proclaims, and mediates in the classroom the mysteries celebrated.

Religious Education in the Contemporary Period

Among the leading figures of Catholic religious education in this country must be named Thomas Edward Shields,[19] George Johnson,[20] John M. Cooper,[21] William

---

[12] Cf. Heinrich Kreutzwald, *Zur Geschichte des Biblischen Unterrichts* (Freiburg: Herder, 1957), pp. 15-29. The Bossuet catechism, the most available of the three, is well worth examining: *Oeuvres Complètes de Bossuet*, II (Paris: Lefevre, 1836), 348-55.

[13] Cf. Kreutzwald, *op. cit.*, pp. 37-68; 111-21.

[14] Theodore Filthaut, *Das Reich Gottes in der Katechetischen Unterweisung* (Freiburg: Verlag Herder, 1958), p. 163.

[15] Cf. Kreutzwald, *op. cit.*, pp. 129-31.

[16] O. Willmann, *The Science of Education*, tr. F. Kirsch, 2 vols. (Beatty, Pa.: Archabbey Press, 1922).

[17] Cf. Jungmann, *op. cit.*, pp. 181-93.

[18] *Ibid.*, pp. 388, 400-401.

[19] Cf. Justine B. Ward, *Thomas Edward Shields* (New York: Charles Scribner's Sons, 1947); also Shields' series of school readers, *Religion* (Washington, D. C.: Catholic Education Press, 1909-18).

H. Russell,[22] Walter Farrell, O.P.,[23] and Archbishop Edwin V. O'Hara.[24] All were theorists who either wrote widely or were influential as teachers. The last-named, who was bishop of Kansas City, Missouri, provided an exception. His genius lay in administering nation-wide programs of religious instruction, biblical translation, and social action. Joseph B. Collins, who has been very productive in catechetical writing, serves as National Director of the Confraternity of Christian Doctrine.[25] This confraternity of laymen under episcopal direction was founded in Milano and approved by Pope Pius V in 1571. Modern church law requires that every Catholic parish have a unit of this confraternity to carry on instruction at all levels. Other names prominent in catechetical activity in the United States in the last decades would include F. J. Connell, A. N. Fuerst, R. E. Bandas, Sister M. Rosalia, Ellamay Horan, and Leo Trese.

The slow blooming of excellence in religion teaching among American Roman Catholics has been occasioned, interestingly enough, by the vigorous development of parish and private schools.[26] These schools have received every professional attention in the secular branches of study in virtue of state requirements. The desire of Catholics to conduct schools no whit inferior to those supported by public funds has been the other factor in their progress. Many teachers in these schools have gone on to become specialists in reading readiness, science and languages; however, most of them remain at the level of "general practitioner" in the teaching of religion. Certain priests, sisters, brothers, and laymen have become expert as teachers of religion, but the far greater number are at the plateau of merely satisfactory performance. Part of the reason for this is that, through a variety of

[20] Cf. Frances M. Schaf, *A Bio-bibliography of Monsignor George Johnson* (unpublished Master's thesis, The Catholic University of America, Washington, D. C., 1954). Sister Mary Joan Smith, O.P., and Sister Mary Nona McGreal, O.P., *Guiding Growth in Christian Social Living*, 3 vols. (Washington, D. C.: The Catholic University of America Press, 1944-46) is a work by two of Johnson's students in the curriculum of the Catholic elementary school which grew out of his university lectures, the "campus school" which he directed, and the statement of policy *Better Men for Better Times* (Washington, D. C.: Commission on American Citizenship, 1943), written, though not signed, by Johnson and R. J. Slavin.

[21] John M. Cooper, *Religion Outlines for Colleges* (2d ed., revised; Washington, D. C.: Catholic Education Press, 1935-46); "Religion in the College Curriculum," in Roy J. Deferrari (ed.), *College Organization and Administration* (Washington, D. C.: The Catholic University of America Press, 1947), pp. 148-74. A fruit of the labors of college religious educators is the Society of Catholic College Teachers of Sacred Doctrine (Annual Proceedings from office of the Secretary, St. Mary's College, Notre Dame, Ind., 1955).

[22] Cf. William H. Russell, *Christ the Leader* (Milwaukee: Bruce Publishing Co., 1937); *Jesus the Divine Teacher* (New York: P. J. Kenedy, 1944); *Teaching the Christian Virtues* (Milwaukee: Bruce Publishing Company, 1952).

[23] Cf. Walter Farrell, O.P., *A Companion to the Summa* (New York: Sheed and Ward, 1938-42), 4 vols. This work has occasioned widespread popular study of the teaching of St. Thomas Aquinas.

[24] Cf. J. G. Shaw, *Edwin Vincent O'Hara* (New York: Farrar, Strauss and Cudahy, 1955).

[25] Cf. Joseph B. Collins, S.S., *Teaching Religion* (Milwaukee: Bruce Publishing Co., 1953); also *The Confraternity Comes of Age* (Paterson, N. J.: Confraternity Publications, 1956).

[26] Cf. Sister Marie Carolyn Klinkhamer, O.P., "Historical Reason for Inception of Parochial School System," *Catholic Educational Review*, LII (February, 1954), 73-94; Sister M. Laurina Kaiser, O.S.B., *The Development of the Concept and Function of the Catholic Elementary School in the American Parish* (Washington, D. C.: Catholic University of America Press, 1955).

circumstances, the clergy never came to acquire special skill in a field that is traditionally theirs.[27]

This has meant that the bulk of literature in religious instruction has consisted in aid books concerned chiefly with ingenious explication of the traditional catechisms, but without new insights. No thoroughly satisfactory journal of theory was available until the appearance of the international quarterly *Lumen Vitae* in 1946, again in good part because of priestly unfamiliarity with the actual work of catechizing.[28] An absence of profundity in doctrinal, biblical, and liturgical orientation has marked certain otherwise excellent efforts, both because the expanding need for pastoral care has hampered American Catholic theological scholarship, and because catechetical specialists themselves have been inadequately prepared in the sacred sciences. There is consistent improvement, however, owing in no small part to contemporary progress in Scripture study and the liturgical renewal, with which catechetics and preaching go hand in hand.[29] The competently edited journal *Worship* (formerly *Orate Fratres*, 1926) has been of inestimable assistance to religious educators.[30] The labors of American Catholic teachers have also received strong confirmation from the appearance of the official German national catechism [31] in English and the writings of the Austrian theologian, Johannes Hofinger.[32]

It usually comes as a surprise to the American Protestant to learn that his Catholic brother experiences approximately the same difficulty in administering Confraternity of Christian Doctrine programs as he does in his Sunday school or other Christian education effort. The disclosure that the Catholic school has not, by the very fact of its existence, solved all questions of religious education for those who attend it normally meets with incredulous response.

The Origin of American Catholic Schools

No mistake should be made about the general satisfaction of American Catholics with their schools. Although the Code of Canon Law (promulgated in 1918) requires that bishops establish elementary and "intermediate" schools where they are lacking (Canon 1379, §1), and national or regional universities as well (§ 2), all of which the faithful Catholic must support (§ 3),[33] one can be reasonably certain that the vigor of the schools in this country results more from the private convictions of thousands of individuals than from the coercive force of law. That,

[27] This matter is examined by J. Hofinger, S.J., "The Formation Our Catechists Need," in Sloyan, (ed.), *op. cit.*, pp. 228, 238-42.

[28] *Lumen Vitae: International Review of Religious Education*, 14 vols. (through 1959); published at 184 rue Washington, Brussels, Belgium.

[29] For a discussion of this fruitful interrelation, cf. Paul B. Marx, O.S.B., chap. 8, "Liturgy and Religious Education," *Virgil Michel and the Liturgical Movement* (Collegeville, Minn.: Liturgical Press, 1957), pp. 219-54.

[30] Published ten times a year at St. John's Abbey, Collegeville, Minn.

[31] *A Catholic Catechism* (New York: Herder and Herder, 1957; revised American edition, 1959).

[32] Johannes Hofinger, S.J., *The Art of Teaching Christian Doctrine* (Notre Dame, Ind.: University of Notre Dame Press, 1957).

[33] Cf. *Codex Iuris Canonici* (Romae: Typis Polyglottis Vaticanis, 1918). Also Conrad Humbert Boffa, *Canonical Provisions for Catholic Schools (Elementary and Intermediate)* (1939) and Alexander F. Sokolich, *Canonical Provisions for Universities and Colleges* (1956). Both, Washington, D. C.: Catholic University of America Press.

at least, is the way things have come to be. Whereas the canons cited are theoretically universal in their application, the seat of church government at Rome willingly points to the success which has uniquely attended the efforts made in the United States over the last century and a half.

A question commonly debated in periodical literature in the field of education is whether the Catholic schools of this country consider themselves "protest schools." Whatever the answer to the question as a contemporary one (and surely it is a fact that parental consciences seek satisfaction through them as they could not do through public schools), the historical data seem to show that the parochial school was not a spontaneous development but was "devised in answer to situations in the United States which were unique—and uniquely demanding." [34] When John Carroll, first Catholic Archbishop of Baltimore (then the whole U. S.), made the appeal he is credited with for parish schools in 1790, he estimated that there were 35,000 Catholics in the country. The situation had changed vastly both for Catholics and other religious groups by the time the agitation for universal free education—a thing previously undreamed of as possible—began in the mid-nineteenth century. Carroll's first pastoral letter (1792) had made no mention of Catholic schools other than to suggest that the sons of Catholics patronize "George Town" College so as to return from it to their "neighbourhoods" as instructors of others who could not be sent from home. [35]

The earliest canonical enactment with regard to schools came in 1829 with the thirty-fourth decree of the First Provincial Council of Baltimore that "schools be instituted, in which the young might be instructed in the principles of faith and morals, at the same time they were being taught letters." [36] This proposal came chiefly as a response to the flourishing anti-Catholic movement organized in the 1820's, in which tract and Sunday-school societies and home and foreign mission groups grew in influence. It was likewise a time when the deism of certain thinkers active in public affairs resulted in efforts to secure control of the schools in order to free them from Protestant influence and secularize them thoroughly. [37] Billington describes the activities of the "Public School Society" of New York which regularly read Protestant prayers and the King James version of the scriptures, sang hymns, gave religious instruction at variance with Catholic belief, and used textbooks "blatantly Protestant in sympathy and . . . openly disrespectful of Catholicism." [38] A letter from Rome to Bishop Flaget of Bardstown, Kentucky, in 1820, strongly urged him to establish schools and place them under the supervision of clergymen. [39]

At first, not every parish was required to erect a school. A letter following a provincial council of 1833 speaks of the "success and permanence" of colleges and schools as something that rests with the people, but it is by no means clear that

[34] Klinkhamer, *op. cit.*, p. 75.

[35] Peter Guilday (ed.), *National Pastorals of the American Hierarchy, 1792-1919* (Washington: National Catholic Welfare Council, 1923), p. 4.

[36] *Ibid.*, *A History of the Councils of Baltimore* (New York: The Macmillan Company, 1932), p. 94. Translation from the Latin is my own.

[37] Klinkhamer, *op. cit.*, pp. 78-81, cites studies which describe the struggle in New York, Connecticut, Massachusetts, and Kentucky, as does Roy Allen Billington's informative *The Protestant Crusade, 1800-1860* (New York: The Macmillan Company, 1938).

[38] Billington, *op. cit.*, p. 142.

[39] John Lancaster Spalding, *Life of the Most Reverend M. J. Spalding, D.D.* (Baltimore: John Murphy and Company, 1873), p. 154, as given in Klinkhamer, *op. cit.*, p. 79.

parish schools are being referred to.[40] Academies or free schools that were not parochial (i.e. under the auspices of the parish), already existed in good numbers by this time. The fourth provincial council of Baltimore (1840) warned against "the grave risks the public or common schools held for the faith of Catholic boys and girls" because of their distinctive Protestant character, which in that unfortunate period included sermons against the Roman Church.[41] A spirited controversy in New York in the next year resulted in the abolition of all religious instruction, as a means for the public schools to get control of the common school fund.[42]

By 1840, 454 Catholic churches existed, of which at least 200 had parish schools, though whether these were truly parochial in their patterns of control and support is impossible to know.[43] A series of ten diocesan synods between that year and 1852, including one in San Francisco, gave cumulating encouragement to the church-school idea. It was not until the latter year, however, that a decree of the first plenary council of this country (i.e., made up of all those having ecclesiastical jurisdiction) urged bishops to set up schools connected with each church in their dioceses.[44] A pastoral letter which followed this legislation called the founding of schools "the discharge of a duty," and described it as acting upon the suggestion of Pope Pius IX (Nov. 21, 1851) "to provide for the religious education of youth." [45] Subsequent provincial councils (e.g., Cincinnati) and diocesan synods (Newark) stressed parish schools. At the latter in 1856 the terminology was put beyond all doubt for the first time: "Sacerdotes . . . scholas catholicas in suis Paroeciis constituendas curent," [46] "let priests see to the establishment of Catholic schools in their parishes." The acts of the Second Plenary Council (Baltimore, 1866) gave extensive treatment to education and to parish schools, as do those of the Third Plenary Council (1884), the last to have been held. According to the pastoral letter of this council, "No parish is complete till it has schools adequate to the needs of its children, and the pastor and people of a parish should feel that they have not accomplished their entire duty until the want is supplied." [47]

It is to be observed throughout all this that the pastoral care of souls was uppermost in the minds of the bishops. Consequently, anyone who maintains that Catholic schools exist as an "arm" of the Roman Church for its purposes of faith and worship will be quite correct. It was assumed and occasionally said in the debates and correspondence of the time that the training of an upright citizenry was likewise a purpose of Catholic schools. Had there been, however, no threat of perversion in faith or religious indifferentism it is doubtful that the schools

---

[40] Guilday, *Pastorals*, p. 74.

[41] Guilday, *Councils*, p. 125.

[42] Billington, *op. cit.*, p. 149. Cf. Henry J. Browne, "Public Support of Catholic Education in New York, 1825-1842: Some New Aspects," *The Catholic Historical Review*, XXXIX (April, 1953), 1-27.

[43] Klinkhamer, *op. cit.*, p. 85.

[44] *Concilium Plenarium Totius Americae Septentrionalis Foederatae, Baltimori habitum, anno 1852* (Baltimore: John Murphy and Company, 1853), p. 47, cited in Klinkhamer, p. 87.

[45] Guilday, *Pastorals*, p. 191.

[46] *Statuta Novarcensis Dioceseos . . . 1856* (New York: Edward Dunigan, 1857), p. 32, cited in Klinkhamer, p. 88.

[47] Guilday, *Pastorals*, pp. 246-47; *Councils*, pp. 238-39.

would have come into being on the same terms. There do not seem to have been any pangs among Catholics over failure in discharging a public duty, namely, the support of common schools, for it was widely felt that any such claim on their civic allegiance had been forfeited by the course common-school education had taken. A few bold spirits felt that the solution attempted could be improved upon, notably, Archbishop John Ireland of St. Paul, Minnesota.[48] The thought of such men was that by withdrawing, Catholics would be serving the life of the young nation badly; besides, the innate sense of Americans for tolerance and fair play would probably right the situation before long, when they came to recognize in the support of religious schools the logical response to the demands of conscience.

At this distance it is easier by far to report on what did happen than on what might have happened. It should be observed that although, in fact, a system of schools emerged, the Catholic Church does not identify religious education with religious schooling. In modern times, uniquely in human history, universal education has been realized in many parts of the world. The church requires in such a period that the Christian learnings of her children should keep pace with secular knowledge. That this should happen in the same classroom is not an absolute requirement. What is demanded is that the school should not be hostile to or completely disinterested in the integration of sacred and secular. The last-named state of affairs is not so much essential to the concept of religiously neutral public education as it is to the dogma of a philosophical creed regarding it. This total unconcern with religion causes a tension in the consciences of believers. This tension the Roman Catholic Church continues to resolve by conducting her own schools.

Catholic School Populations and Teaching Staff

At no time has it been possible to enroll every Catholic child in a Catholic school. Even in the vigorous contemporary period, only about 50 per cent of all those of school age are enrolled.[49] Factors which keep the figure low are expense, the unavailability of schools, mixed marriages in which the non-Catholic parent holds out for public or non-church education as the last "right" he may exercise, and occasionally dissatisfaction shown by Catholic parents with the quality of Catholic school education available.[50] This complaint, still valid in certain areas three and two decades ago, is seldom based on fact nowadays, although crowded

---

[48] Daniel F. Reilly, O.P., *The Catholic School Controversy, 1891-93* (Washington, D. C.: Catholic University of America Press, 1944); Frederick J. Zwierlein, *The Life and Letters of Bishop McQuaid*, 3 vols. (Rochester, N. Y.: Art Print Shop, 1926-27). A good summary of the entire unpleasantness is to be found in John Tracy Ellis, *The Life of James Cardinal Gibbons*, I (Milwaukee: Bruce Publishing Co., 1952), 653-707.

[49] These figures were taken from the Official Catholic Directory for 1958 (New York: P. J. Kenedy and Sons). There are 783,155 children listed as enrolled in Catholic secondary schools while the pastors of the country report 780,330 Catholic children of high-school age in public schools. The elementary school populations recorded are 3,921,522 Catholic students in Catholic schools and 1,945,252 in public schools. The latter figure is so low that it may be supposed that only those under religious instruction are tabulated. Another 44,370 pupils are in protective institutions, most of which provide schooling, but on which no breakdown between elementary and secondary levels is available. The population totals of nonchurch schools depend entirely on the reliability of parish census techniques and is made further ambiguous by the question familiar to religious sociologists of every church group, "Who is a Catholic?"

[50] For an empirical study on the question, cf. James Reddington Curtin, *Attitude of Parents toward Catholic Education* (Washington, D. C.: Catholic University of America Press, 1954).

classrooms, undifferentiated high-school programs, and inadequacy of equipment continue to be a trial to parents who have a good educational ideal. Others who are in search of "status" and its tokens have no difficulty in finding the religious school too plebeian. Paradoxically, convent-school education becomes a status item for non-Catholics.

In far more cases esteem for the moral and spiritual benefits available in Catholic schools makes parents avid proponents of Catholic education. This occasionally results in the parental mentality, "Better eighty students in a classroom with a Sister than twenty-five in a room without one." Such a loyalty to religious women who have become competent educators has its drawbacks. It has resulted, for instance, in the thoughtless attitude—born of respect—of both clergy and laity alike which sanctions impossible classroom situations so that children may be "taught by the Sisters." The physical and emotional health of these teachers often breaks after a number of years with classroom populations of sixty and seventy. Another result of the mentality is the illusion that only Sisters are capable of giving a thoroughly Christian education. The rapid increase of lay teachers in Catholic schools, often graduates of Catholic colleges and as much at ease in their religion lesson as in any other, is dispelling this misconception. Many of the women teachers are mothers of families who have already served as the primary religious educators of their children, and they bring this experience to the children of others.

The Aims of Catholic Education: Certain Hazards

Writing in 1929 on Christian education, Pope Pius XI described its purpose as "cooperating with divine grace in forming Christ in those regenerated by baptism." Since the rebirth of man in the Spirit is total, his Christian education will necessarily look to all of his faculties—intellect, will, emotions, aesthetic nature, and bodily make-up. Although hopefully the first products of Catholic education will be saints, the system is not unconcerned with pupils as scholars and citizens. Attempts are frequently made to "Christianize" the whole curriculum, including textbooks, courses of study, and methods of presenting material. This avowed emphasis places upon teachers the heavy burden of seeing to it that the independent value of learnings is preserved. In other words, they must be on their guard that the order of nature is not subverted to the point where everything becomes merely a means to a religious end.

A second delicate matter is the danger that teachers and pupils alike may become an "in-group" of the larger national culture, having limited contacts with other segments of the population and tending to see everything through the prism of its own patterns of response. Catholic education readily acknowledges that this constitutes a hazard. The Roman Church tolerates the "segregation" of its students only because it does not know how to achieve the important ends it has in view otherwise. By every device possible Catholic education hopes to minimize the isolation. It counts heavily on academic and athletic competitions, Red Cross, CARE, and other service programs; likewise the daily interchanges at the neighborhood level which are inevitable, yet in need of intelligent encouragement in our society.

Coupled with these contacts, there is the insistence in Catholic education that the individual has special obligations to his fellows in a racially, economically, and politically diverse society. In the religious sphere positive bigotry is nonexistent in the Catholic school. While the identification of the Roman Catholic Church with the Church of Jesus Christ is assumed throughout, no unpleasant corollaries are ever drawn from this doctrinal proposition which would place those who believe otherwise in a second-class position as friends and fellow citizens.

In Catholic schools, the idea that "one religion is as good as another" provided the believers are in good faith is described as religious indifferentism. An apostolic outlook, one of working with the Holy Spirit to share the treasure of faith, is inculcated in students, but it is never let degenerate to the level of proselytism.

The Administration of American Catholic Schools

The concluding portion of this chapter should fittingly contain some mention of the organization of Catholic schools, as well as extra-school programs of religious education. The chief school officer of each diocese, after the bishop, is that priest who serves as vicar of the bishop for all educational affairs. He is usually termed the diocesan "superintendent of schools" or "secretary for education." The great majority of these men hold graduate degrees in education. In larger dioceses they will have one, two, and three assistants. The tasks of the diocesan school office are, as those of county and state systems, a mixture of administration and the supervision of instruction. The chief school officer locally is the pastor in elementary and secondary situations which are truly parochial. Normally he defers to the judgment of the Sister or Brother principal in educational matters, but he does not relinquish all control because the ultimate responsibility both to parents and to the bishop is his. Nonparochial schools (academies, secondary schools conducted by members of clerical and nonclerical religious congregations, e.g., Franciscan Fathers, Brothers of Christian Instruction) are equally under the jurisdiction of the bishop and his educational representative.

The Third Plenary Council (Baltimore, 1884) decreed diocesan school boards as a means to achieve the improvement of systems. At first these boards flourished, but they gradually fell away to the role of advisory bodies as the office of school superintendent gained in force. Such boards still exist; they have their chief efficacy in counseling the bishop on the location of diocesan high schools and the financing of diocesan wide and inter-parochial ventures. In a few dioceses, usually where the office of school superintendent has been very well developed by a series of incumbents, they serve as a truly advisory body in educational questions.

Diocesan superintendents of schools usually rely heavily on the services of Sisters and Brothers as direct supervisors of the instructional process, whether they are in the employ of the diocese or of the religious community which conducts schools in several dioceses. In larger diocesan systems there will be subject-matter supervisors in music, art, language arts, and the like. The Department of Education founded at the Catholic University of America in 1905 is the seed ground of training for many, though by no means all, diocesan superintendents of schools. Dozens of other universities and teacher-training colleges provide for the professional preparation of teachers and supervisors. A noteworthy development is the Sister Formation section of the National Catholic Educational Association, incorporated into that group in 1958 after a previous history of some four or five years. The purpose of the section is to insure the religious and professional advancement of the Sisters before whom are seated about 75 per cent of the 4,500,000 children enrolled in Catholic elementary and secondary schools.[51]

Mention of the N.C.E.A. focuses attention on this voluntary, dues-paying organization which is the chief organ for the professional improvement of Catholic education. Its executive secretary, since 1944, has been the Right Reverend Frederick G. Hochwalt, who has been responsible for its success in no small measure. Offices are at 1785 Massachusetts Avenue, N.W., Washington 6, D.C. The following "departments" are found in the association: major seminary, minor seminary, college and university, school superintendents, secondary school, elementary school, and special education. "Sections" likewise exist devoted to teacher-education, Sister-formation, priestly and religious vocations, and Newman Club chaplains. The association, founded in 1904, publishes a *Bulletin* in four numbers annually, of which the third, the August issue, contains the proceedings and addresses of the annual meeting held in Easter week. Monsignor Hochwalt likewise serves as director of the Department of Education of The National Catholic Welfare Conference, in which position he reports to a committee of bishops annually on the condition of all the schools, not just member schools of N.C.E.A. His work here is a development of the pioneer work of his predecessor, the Right Reverend George Johnson. In 1953 Monsignor Hochwalt prepared a descriptive report on the state of school programs at all levels and the Confraternity of Christian Doctrine, which is remarkable for its breadth and comprehension.[52] Interested readers of this essay could consult few articles with greater profit.

At the present writing there are 9,653 Catholic elementary schools, parochial and private; 2,434 secondary schools; 260 colleges and universities; 91 diocesan seminaries; 425 religious seminaries and scholasticates; and 331 schools of nursing. The total of students under Catholic instruction is 7,783,462; their teachers total 147,330, of whom 95,919 are sisters; 35,124 laymen; 10,412 priests; 4,568 brothers; and 1,302 scholastics (clerical students).

The constant increase of the Catholic population is providing the church with the greatest challenge in religious education it has known up until now. The possibilities of expansion are limited severely by modern construction costs and by the legitimate salary demands of lay teachers, who are constantly on the increase. The schools are supported entirely by the nonpublic funds of the Catholic faithful, except for relatively small gifts from industry and the foundations at the college level. While the ability to supply schools and teachers is limited, the demands of parents for such services are limitless by comparison. Many who grew up with the "Catholic school idea" are now receiving the unwelcome information that in the parish where they reside there will not be room for their children to enroll as they come along; that the entrance of these children into secondary school will be determined by their qualifying for a limited number of places through examination.

[51] Cf. Sister Ritamary, C.H.M. (ed.), *The Mind of the Church in the Formation of Sisters* (New York: Fordham University Press, 1956); *Spiritual and Intellectual Elements in the Formation of Sisters* (Fordham, 1957); *Planning for the Formation of Sisters* (Fordham, 1958).

[52] Frederick G. Hochwalt, "Catholic Education in the U. S. A. in 1953," *Religious Education,* XLVIII (September-October, 1953), 3-19; as a supplement to this report, it is suggested that readers refer to Joseph Fichter, *Parochial School: A Sociological Study* (Notre Dame, Ind.: University of Notre Dame Press, 1958).

More and more, Catholic parents are discovering that religious education and religious schooling cannot be identical terms in their lifetimes. This adversity is proving a blessing on other fronts; for example, that of the weekday school of religion, whether through released time or otherwise. Until recent decades, 95 per cent of the church's teaching efforts and 99 per cent of its funds have been devoted to anywhere between one half and three quarters of its children. The very success of the schools led to the disregard—unconscious in many cases—of children not enrolled in them. Often where school facilities were available, the children not enrolled were pastoral "problems" for a variety of reasons. It was easy to identify their parents with slackness or an unco-operative spirit of some kind. Often they were the "semi-Catholics," on their way into the Church or on their way out.

Now, however, apostolic movements such as the Legion of Mary, Our Lady's Sodality, and specialized Catholic Action groups are joining forces with graduates of Catholic colleges and the zealous parents of children who have no Catholic schooling in prospect, to form vigorous parish units of the Confraternity of Christian Doctrine. Functioning as officially specified, it is a thoroughly lay movement except for the training of teachers by the clergy. There is a lay executive board—both for the diocese and each parish—and there are teachers, "fishers" (home visitors), and helpers. There are adult discussion clubs, a parent-educator section for preschool children, and an apostolate of good will to non-Catholics.

All of this activity is causing lay religious educators to cast a keen glance of scrutiny at the teaching materials proposed to them for their use. Unsupported by the oral traditions of a teaching congregation, they are pioneering for better methods because they have received little legacy of teaching methods, good or bad. Young teachers, lay and religious alike, formed in a Christian spirit by the power of the liturgy, are shocked to discover its total absence in catechisms and aid books. Persons formed in biblical wisdom through their study clubs, their recent seminary training, or Sister-Formation college are necessarily transmitting these insights and others doctrinal in character to their students.

For all of these reasons Roman Catholic religious education finds itself at this time in a crisis situation. Larger than ever before and, to outward appearances, more successful, it threatens to be more inadequate to the challenge than ever before because of the sheer weight of numbers. But it is at the same time at a flood tide of the Spirit in its aims and its apostolic determinations. Protestant, Orthodox Christian, and Jew may hope to find in their Catholic brother in the decades that lie immediately ahead a zealous but not an embattled worker in the vineyard of our God who is the Lord.

Chapter 37

The National Conference of Christians and Jews

Dumont F. Kenny

RELIGIOUS EDUCATION, CONSIDERED EITHER IN TERMS OF ITS PRINCIPLES AND practices or of its administration and organization, cannot fail to relate to a basic characteristic of American society, cultural pluralism. Within our boundaries are the races of the world, the peoples of nearly every culture, and the faithful of major religious denominations: 64,000,000 Protestants, 36,000,000 Catholics, 5,500,000 Jews. Religious pluralism is a fact of life in twentieth-century America.

As a result, the citizens of this country are the inheritors of the values of a rich religious and political heritage. Yet, the religious virtues of love and charity and the political ideals of justice and democratic process have sometimes succumbed to human failings and passions. Fear and pride have played their destructive roles in nurturing prejudicial attitudes and discriminatory actions against members of groups who differ because of race, religion, or national origin. On occasion, these breakdowns in human relations have been alarmingly widespread. One of these waves of religious and racial hatred, paced by such organized effort as that of the Ku Klux Klan, led to the establishment of the National Conference of Christians and Jews (N.C.C.J) in the election year of 1928.

A handful of concerned and far-sighted citizens under the leadership of former Chief Justice Charles Evans Hughes, former Secretary of War Newton D. Baker and S. Parkes Cadman, Past President of the Federal (now National) Council of the Churches of Christ in America, founded in that year an organization to make the moral concept of brotherhood part of the *mores* of our society and to rally in American communities the forces of resistance to prejudice, bigotry, and intolerance. To establish the pattern of Protestants, Catholics, and Jews standing and working together for those principles which they hold in common, these founders were joined by industrialist Roger W. Straus and Carlton J. H. Hayes as the first national co-chairmen. Everett R. Clinchy was selected as director of the National Conference and later served as its president until 1958 when he was succeeded by Lewis Webster Jones.

This first systematic step to combat anti-Catholicism, anti-Semitism, and anti-Protestantism in the United States had its genesis in the "good will" movements of the early 1920's among American religious groups. Noteworthy among these efforts was the organization in 1924 of the Committee on Good Will between Jews and

Christians by the Federal Council of the Churches of Christ in America. Such early attempts placed chief reliance on exhortation and verbal expressions of good will. Gradually and increasingly, the evidence indicated that a larger and more inclusive program should be inaugurated than was possible under specifically Protestant or other denominational auspices.

Nature and Purposes

The statement of purposes of the National Conference of Christians and Jews written by the organization's founders has been incorporated into the bylaws with little modification:

Believing in a spiritual interpretation of the universe and deriving its inspiration therefrom, the Corporation exists to promote justice, amity, understanding and cooperation among Protestants, Catholics and Jews, and to analyze, moderate and strive to eliminate inter-group prejudices which disfigure and distort religious, business, social and political relations, with a view to the establishment of a social order in which the religious ideals of brotherhood and justice shall become the standards of human relationships.

Toward these high objectives, often through trial and error methods, this unique adventure in brotherhood took on an organizational approach and conceptual base which has permitted continuous expansion of its program over the years. Gradually it became clear that the nature of the N.C.C.J. must be civic, not religious, quasi-religious, or even interfaith. The distinctive quality is that it is a civic organization of religiously motivated persons. Its members strive for the brotherhood of man under the fatherhood of God, endeavor to promote civic co-operation and mutual understanding among men of good will of all religious, racial, and nationality groups without compromise of religious beliefs, and seek through education to secure in principle and in practice for members of all religious, racial, and nationality groups the dignity, rights, and freedom inherent in the moral law, in religious faith, and guaranteed by the Constitution of the United States.

The National Conference, a nongovernmental and nonpolitical organization, is an association of individuals, not of official representatives of religious, educational, or other organizations. N.C.C.J. does not officially represent nor attempt to speak for any religious organization. It does not aim at any sort of amalgamation of religious bodies or at modifying any of the distinctive beliefs of its members, but rather it aims to promote affirmative co-operative action among Protestants, Catholics, and Jews in areas of common civic concern. Hence, it is not its function to compose theological differences, establish a least common denominator of belief among those who accept divine revelation, or engage in common worship.

It engages in an educational program to the end that people will be impelled to recognize and to grant to others the same dignity and rights they seek for themselves. In its educational efforts to aid in the establishment or in the protection of the peace of our communities and our nation, it emphasizes the moral imperatives upon which this objective depends. It seeks in all of its work to guard against the dangers of religious indifferentism. The National Conference, a civic organization, is undergirded by the spiritual strength of men of faith.

Growth of Program Efforts

During its formative years, programs emphasized the sponsorship of seminars which brought together prominent Protestants, Catholics, and Jews in discussions of mutual problems. These seminars held at various eastern universities developed interesting techniques to cope with group differences and built bridges of understanding across religious lines. In these same early years the "trio" idea was adopted and trio teams of minister, priest, and rabbi spoke at thousands of meetings in hundreds of cities across the nation. In succeeding years, as the N.C.C.J. began to deepen its program and widen its organization, it established a number of professionally staffed regional offices and an augmented national headquarters in New York. Today over sixty N.C.C.J. regional offices, several divisional offices, and hundreds of voluntary chapters serve an ever-increasing number of American communities.

In widening its scope of operations the N.C.C.J. established in 1934 the Religious News Service (R.N.S.). It is the only world-wide news agency furnishing spot news of all denominations to the church press, secular newspapers, nationally circulated magazines, and radio and television stations. R.N.S. Daily News Reports of both foreign and domestic religious news, its fifteen-minute religious news script for radio "The Religious News Reporter," its photo service, and several weekly features are made available to local newspapers and religious publications at moderate subscription rates. It was in this same year that N.C.C.J. began to make brotherhood a household word by sponsoring, at the suggestion of Monsignor Hugh McMenamin, a Catholic priest of Denver, the first celebration of Brotherhood Day. In 1940 the observance was lengthened to an entire week—the week in February in which the birthday of George Washington occurs. Now a permanent part of the American scene, Brotherhood Week provides each year an opportunity for people to rededicate themselves as individuals to the basic ideals of respect for persons and human rights, to dramatize the practical things which people can do to promote an understanding and realization of these ideals, and to enlist the support of greater numbers of people in the year-round activities to build brotherhood.

The rise of various forms of dictatorship such as Nazism, Fascism, and Communism gave new impetus to the program of the National Conference which stresses the dignity and worth of the individual, strives for good relations among all groups comprising the nation, and seeks to fulfill the American dream of liberty and justice for all citizens. During World War II the organization joined wholeheartedly in the campaign for national unity and sent out hundreds of teams to help in achieving this goal. N.C.C.J. trios were sent to hundreds of Army camps and military installations from Attu to the Canal Zone.

Following the war, the N.C.C.J. used some of its resources and personnel to widen the movement for better intergroup relations in areas of need outside the United States. In 1946 it placed trained staff at the disposal of military government in Germany to inaugurate Councils of Christians and Jews in major cities of that country. In 1947 N.C.C.J. was instrumental in fostering the creation of the Canadian Council of Christians and Jews. In 1950 its leadership joined at a meeting in Paris with 150 representatives of 15 free nations of Europe and North America in organizing World Brotherhood, which now exists as a separate and legally distinct corporate body for carrying on a similar program in other parts of the world.

The historical realities of a culturally pluralistic society with its attendant intergroup problems present a tremendous challenge to all religious educators and to all citizens concerned with justice and democracy. Statesmen and scholars have long recognized religious animosity, group hostility, and prejudice as a major barrier to the full realization of democratic processes and our Judeao-Christian ideals. Current situations of religious, racial, and ethnic inequalities and discriminatory actions remind us of the need of bringing our practices more in line with the ideals of getting increasing numbers of citizens to recognize, secure, and protect the inherent dignity and worth of all individuals and of getting all citizens to appreciate the rich value to our country of unity without uniformity.

Program, Philosophy, and Structure

To effect real change toward the stated objectives of N.C.C.J. is a difficult task in a huge and complex society. One effective and economical way to accomplish this, and the basic rationale for N.C.C.J.'s program efforts, was the decision to program with and through existing institutions of society which have an important influence on social change. Recognizing that man has always sought to educate the young, has aspired to the highest values religiously, has used his leisure time for individual recreation and social recreation, has had to earn a living, and has found it necessary to communicate with others, N.C.C.J. took functional advantage of these "trunk-line" institutions by organizing national commissions of outstanding lay leaders and their regional counterparts along these lines. A permanent national commission of leading American educators was created in 1939 as the Commission on Educational Organizations. N.C.C.J. thereby became a pioneer organization in the new field of intergroup education. The Commission on Religious Organizations was established in 1942 to secure additional leadership and impetus in a key area of N.C.C.J. program. In 1946 the Commission on Community Organizations was created to enlist the hundreds of voluntarily joined civic, social, and fraternal organizations in America. In 1948 the Commission on Labor-Management Organizations was organized, and in 1951 the Commission on Mass Communications. To apply the resources of the various Commissions in an integrated fashion to major problem areas, such as racial integration, several inter-Commission Committees were subsequently developed.

Thus, working with and through schools and universities, and in co-operation with the American Council on Education, N.C.C.J. initiated and underwrote three major projects in intergroup education. First was a study of prejudice in textbooks, conducted by Howard E. Wilson and a staff of nine experienced teachers and research workers. This three-year study, from 1944 to 1947, was reported in the volume *Intergroup Relations in Teaching Materials* (1948). Beginning in 1945, Lloyd Allan Cook and his staff began four years of field studies with twenty-four selected colleges for teacher education. The work of this project is reported in two volumes, *College Programs in Intergroup Relations* (1950) and *Intergroup Relations in Teacher Education* (1951). Simultaneously, the American Council on Education, with N.C.C.J.'s financial support, initiated the three-year (1945-1948) Project in Intergroup Education in Cooperating Schools, under the direction of Hilda Taba. A separate project, in a sense a continuation of the first, was financed and sponsored by the N.C.C.J. until 1951. The Cooperating Schools Project conducted more than 250 studies in 72 schools and community groups involving approximately 2,500 teachers, school administrators, and community leaders. This Project produced nine volumes in the field of intergroup education, the summary report entitled *Intergroup Education in Public Schools* (1952).

In 1944 the National Conference convened a group of leading educators and religious leaders at Princeton to discuss the relation of religion to public education. Following this conference, and with an initial grant of funds from N.C.C.J., the American Council on Education created its important Committee on Religion and Education. This committee has issued three influential reports, *The Relation of Religion to Public Education* (1947), *The Function of the Public Schools in Dealing with Religion* (1953), and *The Study of Religion in the Public Schools* (1958).

As a continuing activity in teacher education, the N.C.C.J. co-operates each summer with approximately forty-five colleges and universities in offering workshops in human relations. Over 1,250 teachers and school administrators attend these workshops annually, approximately 50 per cent receiving scholarships from the regional offices of the National Conference. Developing human relations is a major program effort of the Commission on Educational Organizations. The workshops have done much to bring knowledge, sound motivation, and skills to educational leaders who face challenges involving intergroup relations in their own schools and communities. Augmenting this work, the Commission has published and made available at moderate cost a variety of educational materials, notably the Intergroup Education Pamphlet series which at present comprises ten booklets.

The United States, a country of religious and cultural diversity, is likely to remain so in the foreseeable future. How to learn to live with difference and how to create constructive working relationships between members of our varying religious groups is a task as difficult as it is important. It is not to be expected nor is it necessary that we agree on such issues as religion and public education, religious censorship, temperance legislation, birth control legislation, Sunday closing laws, problems of adoption, posting of religious symbols on public property, observance of religious holidays and festivals, and the cluster of problems involved in church-state relationships. It is basic, however, to a free society that we keep lines of communication open in friendly and frank exchange of ideas and viewpoints. If, as a result, the best we can achieve is to agree to disagree agreeably, this is still positive gain.

To support this process of dialogue—another way of saying communication around important subjects—the Commission on Religious Organizations has several national committees at work attempting to set standards, provide clarification, stimulate research, and create and distribute needed materials. It encourages through local N.C.C.J. offices involvement of clergy and laymen in dialogue groups meeting on a regularly scheduled basis. A unique function of the National Conference is its role as a conferring agency in which it takes no organizational position on controversial issues but does provide a context for ameliorative discussion. A participant in one such dialogue effort sponsored by the Fund for the Republic noted in *The Christian Century* that those attending "learned enough about the current climate on matters of religion and secular culture to rise from their chairs with new enthusiasm," and that "the values which emerge in the dialogue center around the air-clearing which will enable us all to see better than before just where we are and what can be our reasonable expectations in church-state affairs." [1]

[1] Martin E. Marty, "A Dialogue of Conspirators," *The Christian Century*, LXXV (May 28, 1958), 638-39.

"Man is not an isolated individual living in a social vacuum, but a social being destined to live and to work out his salvation in association with his fellow beings," said the Administrative Board of the National Catholic Welfare Conference in 1940. "He is a member of a community and he has, in consequence, duties of social justice and duties of charity which emerge from this relationship. On no other foundation can man build that good society which is desired so ardently by the great mass of mankind." [2]

The Institute for Religious and Social Studies of the Jewish Theological Seminary of America noted that

The problem of group relations in our country is basic to the survival of civilization. The moral influence of America is indispensable to the establishment of world understanding and this influence can be exerted only if America sets its own moral house in order. American failure to overcome infringement of minority rights compromises our standing in the world and makes our pleas for cooperation among men of different cultures seem hypocritical. [3]

In assisting churches and synagogues in their work for the brotherhood of man under the fatherhood of God, N.C.C.J. has recently begun to extend its workshop program to involve clergy and seminarians at selected university divinity schools and seminaries. The members of its Campus Interreligious Committee became the leadership nucleus of the first National Consultative Conference on Religion and the State University held at the University of Michigan in 1958. Publications in the area of religion and education and religious liberty do much to open up all facets of key issues, call attention to narrow bias and provincialisms, and analyze problems in the interests of ameliorative discussion and study. Confrontation of certain civic problems such as the current difficulties in the area of integration often provide an opportunity for Catholics, Protestants, Eastern Orthodox, and Jews to work together in applying common religious sanctions. The by-product inevitably is increased understanding and respect for the unique contribution of others across religious lines. Obviously religious educators, since they have a stake in the enterprise, are making a contribution in these two major program areas of N.C.C.J. activity. Indeed, a two-day Institute program designed specifically for religious educators was initiated in Pittsburgh during the years 1952-54.

Methodological Assumptions and Findings

It is generally recognized that there are at least two distinct approaches to building brotherhood in our type of society. One road which may be followed is that of direct social action and law. The legislative program, the picket line, the propaganda barrage, the law suit, have their place and certainly have accounted for much social advance. Yet it is also true that attitudes cannot be legislated nor compelled. A second road is available as well, the educational process, specified in some of its aspects above. The approach N.C.C.J. has chosen, the educational approach, recognizes the validity and importance of direct social action. Education for better

[2] National Catholic Welfare Conference, "Statement of the Archbishops and Bishops of the Administrative Board, N.C.W.C. on the Church and Social Order," February 7, 1940, cited in Raphael Huber (ed.), *Our Bishops Speak* (Milwaukee: Bruce Publishing Co., 1952), p. 324.

[3] Louis Finkelstein, "Three Paths to the Common Good," in *Unity and Difference in American Life*, ed., Robert M. MacIver (New York: Institute for Religious and Social Studies, 1947), p. 5.

human relations may be defined to mean the patient, quiet, constructive effort to get people to see the desirability of social change in line with stated objectives. Education in this sense is not dramatic fire fighting; it is rather the more fundamental task of fire prevention. By no means, however, is this a passive process, for it involves activity of the mind and heart which tends to close the gap between what we profess and what we do, between the ideals of our Judaeo-Christian heritage and the practices of a secularistic world. Such an educational program must be based on research, receive its dynamism from religious values, make use of educational techniques and philosophic insights, and profit from advances in social analysis and psychological findings.

Some of this research in recent years has indicated that sustained educational programs can have four main effects: (1) supply accurate information to replace misinformation, myths, and stereotypes that distort intercultural perceptions and understanding; (2) develop the capacity to feel with people whose cultural backgrounds are different from one's own; (3) develop the personal and social skills required to make one's knowledge and sensitivity in intercultural relations functional; (4) acquire ways of thinking about intercultural relations that lead to the formation of rational and ethical generalizations and forestall stereotype and cynicism. The concept of cultural pluralism, especially its interreligious aspects, requires additional study. The field of endeavor remains hampered by a paucity of empirically validated research in the area of interreligious group relationships, especially when contrasted with such other areas as research in interracial relations.

The causes of group prejudice are many and vary with individuals. It follows, therefore, that the methods of combatting such prejudice must be similarly multiple for an organization conducting programs designed for the broad purpose stated in its bylaws. For example, exhortation and appeals to conscience may be powerful means to lessen prejudice in a given case. But in others, these methods may be inadequate. Nor is the imparting of information enough, any more than is mere contact between persons and groups. N.C.C.J. programming cannot be limited, it has been found, to the descriptive and the factual. Imaginative, creative methods must be encouraged, the so-called "social inventions" in programming—e.g., sociodrama, role playing, projective educational methods, discussion techniques—with due regard to the strength and limitations of such methods. In general, it has been found best in programming to focus first on areas of agreement and then, as the group matures, to move into more emotionally charged areas of disagreement.

In conducting its programs N.C.C.J. has learned that prejudice toward religious, racial, nationality, or other groups must be seen in a total community context and in relation to the realities of the individual himself. A multiple approach to the intergroup situation in the community via all the important opinion-making and opinion-influencing forces is desirable. Teachers, for example, cannot be expected to work at this task alone. Religious leaders, community organization leaders, leaders in mass media, labor and industrial leaders, all have their share of the responsibility. This is a basic methodological assumption of N.C.C.J. programming.

For religious education the task is one of renewed dedication not only to love of God but also to love of neighbor. The present unhappy state of human relationships in our modern society can be effectively and permanently influenced only by those who are prepared and willing to co-operate in its organization and institutions. To those religiously motivated men of good will who believe that spiritual values may be detached from the relatively unimportant things of time, it may be suggested that we need to work at making a good world for bad men just as much as making good men for a bad world. The values of order, of charity, and of love, all too often exiled from the area of intergroup relations by those whose nervous anxiety prevents them from making any value judgments at all, must come back into their own once again. Religious educators, eminently qualified to accept this challenge, can contribute in no better way to the brotherhood of man under the fatherhood of God.

Bibliography

Allport, Gordon. *The Nature of Prejudice*. Reading, Mass.: Addison-Wesley Publishing Company, 1954.

————. *The Individual and His Religion*. New York: The Macmillan Company, 1950.

American Council on Education. *Reading Ladders for Human Relations*. Revised Edition. Washington: American Council on Education, 1955.

Catholicism in America. Edited by Commonweal Magazine. New York: Harcourt, Brace and Company, 1954.

Eakin, Mildred and Frank. *The Sunday School Fights Prejudice*. New York: The Macmillan Company, 1953.

Ellis, John T. *American Catholicism*. Chicago: University of Chicago Press, 1956.

Finkelstein, Louis; Ross, John E.; and Brown, William A. *The Religions of Democracy; Judaism, Catholicism, Protestantism in Creed and Life*. New York: The Devin-Adair Company, 1941.

Herberg, Will. *Protestant, Catholic and Jew*. New York: Doubleday and Company, 1955.

Kane, John J. *Catholic Protestant Conflicts in America*. Chicago: Henry Regnery Company, 1955.

Kenny, Dumont F. (ed.). *Research in Inter-Religious Group Relationships*. New York: National Conference of Christians and Jews, 1959.

Intergroup Education Pamphlet Series. New York: National Conference of Christians and Jews, 1948-59.

Rosten, Leo. (ed.). *A Guide to the Religions of America*. New York: Simon and Schuster, Inc., 1955.

Simpson, George and Yinger, J. Milton. *Racial and Cultural Minorities: An Analysis of Prejudice and Discrimination*. Revised Edition. New York: Harper and Brothers, 1958.

Taba, Hilda; Robinson, John; Hall, Elizabeth; and Vickery, William. *Diagnosing Human Relations Needs*. Washington: American Council on Education, 1951.

Underwood, Kenneth. *Protestant and Catholic: Religious and Social Interaction in an Industrial Community*. Boston: Beacon Press, 1957.

Williams, Robin M. *The Reduction of Intergroup Tensions*. New York: Social Science Research Council, 1947.

Walter, Erich A. (ed.). *Religion and the State University*. Ann Arbor: University of Michigan Press, 1958.

Yinger, J. Milton. *Religion, Society and the Individual: An Introduction to the Sociology of Religion*. New York: The Macmillan Company, 1957.

A Selected Bibliography

Compiled by the Editor

PERHAPS THE MOST IMPORTANT WORD IN THE FOREGOING TITLE IS "SELECTED," for this will be immediately apparent to the reader. Each year a vast array of books appears on the scene, and the inclusion of even a generous sampling of them would have been impossible within the limitations of available space. Hence, it will probably be helpful to list the factors which have determined the selections and their organization.

1. The outline is an adapted version of the excellent one provided by Leonard Stidley for *Orientation in Religious Education*, Philip H. Lotz, editor (Nashville: Abingdon Press, 1950).

2. The selections have been gleaned from the bibliographies submitted by the thirty-seven contributors to this volume and from the editor's acquaintance with contemporary literature.

3. Recent publications have been stressed, with the great majority having appeared in the past decade. A very small percentage of older books is included, in almost every case, because of abiding value and/or the absence of more recent replacements.

4. Not all the listed volumes are in print. However, their ready availability in libraries made inclusion seem justified.

5. Variety has been a fundamental goal, especially variety in viewpoint. This variety has also resulted in listing both the more scholarly textbook and the briefer, more popular book within almost every category. Hence, it is hoped that the bibliography will serve the needs of the seminary or college student as well as the local church, volunteer worker.

6. In many instances only one or two books of a particular type or on a particular subject could be listed. It should not be concluded that these are the only volumes available, or even that they are the "best." Rather, inclusion here reflects the fact that these publications have been valuable to the compiler and one or more of the contributors. Other persons would undoubtedly make alternate suggestions. However, it is hoped that these selections will prove similarly valuable to the reader.

7. While many books from denominational publishers are included, items with a specifically denominational emphasis have generally been omitted. It must be admitted that this factor excluded numerous fine volumes, but it was judged to be more important to confine selections to materials with general interest.

I. NATURE, PRINCIPLES, AND HISTORY OF RELIGIOUS EDUCATION

1. Nature, Philosophy, and Principles of Religion and Religious Education

Bower, William C. *Christ and Christian Education.* Nashville: Abingdon-Cokesbury Press, 1943.

Bushnell, Horace. *Christian Nurture.* New Haven, Conn.: Yale University Press, 1947.

Butler, J. Donald. *Four Philosophies and Their Practice in Education and Religion.* Revised Edition. New York: Harper and Brothers, 1957.

Chave, Ernest J. *A Functional Approach to Religious Education.* Chicago: The University of Chicago Press, 1947.

Christian Education Today. Chicago: International Council of Religious Education, 1940.

Coe, George A. *What Is Christian Education?* New York: Charles Scribner's Sons, 1929.

Cully, Iris V. *Dynamics of Christian Education.* Philadelphia: Westminster Press, 1958.

Davies, Rupert E. (ed.). *An Approach to Christian Education.* New York: Philosophical Library, 1956.

Elliott, Harrison S. *Can Religious Education Be Christian?* New York: The Macmillan Company, 1940.

Fuller, Edmund (ed.). *The Christian Idea of Education.* New Haven, Conn.: Yale University Press, 1957.

Gable, Lee J. (ed.). *Encyclopedia for Church Group Leaders.* New York: Association Press, 1959.

Grimes, Howard. *The Church Redemptive.* Nashville: Abingdon Press, 1958.

Gutzke, Manford G. *John Dewey's Thought and Its Implication for Christian Education.* New York: King's Crown Press, 1956.

Hordern, William. *A Layman's Guide to Protestant Theology.* New York: The Macmillan Company, 1955.

Howe, Reuel L. *Man's Need and God's Action.* Greenwich, Conn.: Seabury Press, 1953.

Jaarsma, Cornelius R. (ed.). *Fundamentals in Christian Education: Theory and Practice.* Grand Rapids, Mich.: W. B. Eerdmans Publishing Company, 1953.

Lotz, Philip H. (ed.). *Orientation in Religious Education.* Nashville: Abingdon Press, 1950.

Mason, Harold C. *Abiding Values in Christian Education.* Westwood, N. J.: Fleming H. Revell Company, 1955.

Miller, A. O. *Invitation to Theology.* Philadelphia: Christian Education Press, 1958.

Miller, Randolph C. *The Clue to Christian Education.* New York: Charles Scribner's Sons, 1950.

————. *Education for Christian Living.* Englewood Cliffs, N. J.: Prentice-Hall, Inc., 1956.

Munro, Harry C. *Protestant Nurture.* Englewood Cliffs, N. J.: Prentice-Hall, Inc., 1956.

Murray, A. Victor. *Education into Religion.* New York: Harper and Brothers, 1954.

The Objective of Christian Education for Senior High Young People. New York: National Council of Churches, 1958.

The Objectives of Christian Education: A Study Document. New York: National Council of Churches (n.d.).

Price, J. M.; Chapman, J. H.; Carpenter, L. L.; and Yarborough, W. F. *A Survey of Religious Education.* Second Edition. New York: Ronald Press, 1959.

Sherrill, Lewis J. *The Gift of Power.* New York: The Macmillan Company, 1955.

Smart, James D. *The Teaching Ministry of the Church.* Philadelphia: Westminster Press, 1954.

Swearingen, Tilford T. *The Community and Christian Education.* St. Louis: Bethany Press, 1950.

Vieth, Paul H. (ed.). *The Church and Christian Education.* St. Louis: Bethany Press, 1947.

Williams, Daniel D. *What Present-Day Theologians Are Thinking.* Revised Edition. New York: Harper and Brothers, 1959.

Wyckoff, D. Campbell. *The Gospel and Christian Education.* Philadelphia: Westminster Press, 1959.

———. *The Task of Christian Education.* Philadelphia: Westminster Press, 1955.

2. The History of Religious Education

Bower, William C. and Hayward, Percy R. *Protestantism Faces Its Educational Task Together.* Appleton, Wis.: C. C. Nelson Publishing Company, 1949.

Butts, R. Freeman. *A Cultural History of Western Education.* Second Edition. New York: McGraw-Hill Book Company, 1955.

Dunn, William K. *What Happened to Religious Education?* Baltimore: Johns Hopkins University Press, 1958.

Eby, Frederick and Arrowood, Charles. *The History and Philosophy of Education: Ancient and Medieval.* Englewood Cliffs, N. J.: Prentice-Hall, Inc., 1940.

Lankard, Frank G. *A History of the American Sunday School Curriculum.* New York: Abingdon Press, 1927.

Mulhern, James. *History of Education.* Revised Edition. New York: Ronald Press, 1959.

Sherrill, Lewis J. *The Rise of Christian Education.* New York: The Macmillan Company, 1950.

Sloyan, Gerard S. (ed.). *Shaping the Christian Message.* New York: The Macmillan Company, 1958.

Smith, William A. *Ancient Education.* New York: Philosophical Library, 1955.

II. RELIGIOUS GROWTH AND THE LEARNING-TEACHING PROCESS

1. Moral and Religious Growth

Allport, Gordon W. *Becoming: Basic Considerations for a Psychology of Personality.* New Haven, Conn.: Yale University Press, 1955.

———. *The Individual and His Religion.* New York: The Macmillan Company, 1950.

Clark, Walter H. *The Psychology of Religion.* New York: The Macmillan Company, 1958.

Gesell, Arnold. *The First Five Years of Life.* New York: Harper and Brothers, 1940.

Gesell, Arnold and Ilg, Frances L. *The Child from Five to Ten.* New York: Harper and Brothers, 1946.

Gesell, Arnold; Ilg, Frances L.; and Ames, Louise B. *Youth: The Years from Ten to Sixteen.* New York: Harper and Brothers, 1956.

Hildreth, Gertrude H. *Child Growth through Education.* New York: Ronald Press, 1948.

Johnson, Paul E. *Personality and Religion.* Nashville: Abingdon Press, 1957.

———. *Psychology of Religion.* Revised Edition. Nashville: Abingdon Press, 1959.

Ilg, Frances L. and Ames, Louise B. *Child Behavior.* New York: Harper and Brothers, 1955.

Manwell, Elizabeth M. and Fahs, Sophia L. *Consider the Children How They Grow.* Revised Edition. Boston: Beacon Press, 1951.

Merry, Frieda K. and Ralph V. *The First Two Decades of Life.* Second Edition. New York: Harper and Brothers, 1958.

Oates, Wayne E. *Religious Dimensions of Personality.* New York: Association Press, 1957.

Sherrill, Lewis J. *The Struggle of the Soul.* New York: The Macmillan Company, 1951.

———. *Understanding Children.* Nashville: Abingdon Press, 1939.

Stone, Lawrence J. and Church, Joseph. *Childhood and Adolescence.* New York: Random House, 1957.

Yeaxlee, Basil A. *Religion and the Growing Mind.* Greenwich, Conn.: Seabury Press, 1952.

2. The Learning Process

Bernard, Harold W. *Psychology of Learning and Teaching.* New York: McGraw-Hill Book Company, 1954.

Bowman, Clarice M. *Ways Youth Learn.* New York: Harper and Brothers, 1952.

Cantor, Nathaniel F. *Dynamics of Learning.* Third Edition. Buffalo: Henry Stewart, Inc., 1956.

——. *The Teaching-Learning Process.* New York: The Dryden Press, 1953.

Crow, Lester D. and Alice V. *Human Development and Learning.* Cincinnati: American Book Company, 1956.

Guthrie, E. R. *Psychology of Learning.* Revised Edition. New York: Harper and Brothers, 1952.

Hilgard, Ernest. *Theories of Learning.* Revised Edition. New York: Appleton-Century-Crofts, Inc., 1958.

Kingsley, Howard L. and Garry, Ralph J. *Nature and Conditions of Learning.* Second Edition. Englewood Cliffs, N. J.: Prentice-Hall, Inc., 1957.

Learning and Instruction. Forty-ninth Yearbook of the National Society for the Study of Education. Part I. Chicago: University of Chicago Press, 1950.

Little, Sara. *Learning Together in the Christian Fellowship.* Richmond, Va.: John Knox Press, 1956.

Meadows, Thomas B. *Psychology of Learning and Teaching Christian Education.* New York: Pageant Press, 1958.

Morse, William C. and Wingo, Glenn M. *Psychology and Teaching.* Chicago: Scott, Foresman and Company, 1955.

Prescott, Daniel A. *The Child in the Educative Process.* New York: McGraw-Hill Book Company, 1957.

Thorpe, Louis P. and Schmuller, Allen M. *Contemporary Theories of Learning.* New York: Ronald Press, 1954.

Trager, Helen G. and Yarrow, Marian R. *They Live What They Learn.* New York: Harper and Brothers, 1952.

3. The Teaching Process

Brogan, Peggy and Fox, Lorene K. *Helping Children Learn.* Yonkers, N. Y.: World Book Company, 1955.

Brubacher, John S. *Modern Philosophies of Education.* Second Edition. New York: McGraw-Hill Book Company, 1950.

——. *Modern Philosophies and Education.* Fifty-fourth Yearbook of the National Society for the Study of Education, Part I. Chicago: University of Chicago Press, 1955.

Dewey, John. *Experience and Education.* New York: The Macmillan Company, 1938.

Edge, Findley B. *Teaching for Results.* Nashville: Broadman Press, 1956.

Garrison, Noble L. *Improvement of Teaching.* New York: The Dryden Press, 1955.

Johnson, Earl A. and Michael, Ruby E. *Principles of Teaching.* Boston: Allyn and Bacon, Inc., 1958.

Muldoon, Mary. *Learning to Teach.* New York: Harper and Brothers, 1958.

Reed, William W. *Teaching the Church's Children.* New York: Morehouse-Gorham Company, 1958.

Ryburn, William M. *Principles of Teaching.* Third Edition. New York: Oxford University Press, 1958.

Simpson, Ray H. *Improving Teaching-Learning Processes.* New York: Longmans, Green and Company, 1953.

Smith, Henry P. *Psychology in Teaching.* Englewood Cliffs, N. J.: Prentice-Hall, Inc., 1954.

Temple, William. *Teaching.* Philadelphia: Westminster Press, 1951.

4. Character Education

Ashley-Montague, M. F. *Helping Children Develop Moral Values*. Chicago: Science Research Associates, 1953.

Backus, Ramona *et al. Character Education in the Summer Camp*. New York: Association Press, 1948.

Betts, George H. *Foundations of Character and Personality*. Indianapolis: Bobbs-Merrill Company, 1937.

Künkel, Fritz and Dickerson, Roy. *How Character Develops*. New York: Charles Scribner's Sons, 1940.

Ligon, Ernest M. *Dimensions of Character*. New York: The Macmillan Company, 1956.

————. *A Greater Generation*. New York: The Macmillan Company, 1948.

5. Group Work and Group Dynamics

Blumenthal, Louis H. *Administration of Group Work*. New York: Association Press, 1948.

Bonner, Hubert. *Group Dynamics: Principles and Applications*. New York: Ronald Press, 1959.

Coyle, Grace L. *Group Work with American Youth*. New York: Harper and Brothers, 1948.

Dimock, Hedley S. and Trecker, Harleigh B. *Supervision of Group Work and Recreation*. New York: Association Press, 1949.

Douglass, Paul F. *The Group Workshop Way in the Church*. New York: Association Press, 1956.

Douty, Mary A. *How to Work with Church Groups*. Nashville: Abingdon Press, 1957.

Strang, R. M. *Group Work in Education*. New York: Harper and Brothers, 1958.

Sullivan, Dorothea F. (ed.). *Readings in Group Work*. New York: Association Press, 1952.

Thelen, Herbert A. *Dynamics of Groups at Work*. Chicago: University of Chicago Press, 1954.

Understanding How Groups Work. Chicago: Adult Education Association, 1955.

Workshop on the Dynamics of Work Groups. Chicago: Adult Education Association, 1953.

6. Counseling and Religious Education

Blum, Milton L. and Balinsky, Benjamin. *Counseling and Psychology*. Englewood Cliffs, N. J.: Prentice-Hall, Inc., 1951.

Brayfield, A. H. (ed.). *Readings in Modern Methods of Counseling*. New York: Appleton-Century-Crofts, Inc., 1950.

Doniger, Simon (ed.). *Religion and Human Behavior*. New York: Association Press, 1954.

Hiltner, Seward. *The Counselor in Counseling*. Nashville: Abingdon Press, 1952.

————. *Preface to Pastoral Theology*. Nashville: Abingdon Press, 1958.

Hulme, William E. *Counseling and Theology*. Philadelphia: Muhlenberg Press, 1956.

————. *How to Start Counseling*. Nashville: Abingdon Press, 1955.

Maves, Paul B. (ed.). *The Church and Mental Health*. New York: Charles Scribner's Sons, 1954.

Morris, E. C. *Counseling with Young People*. New York: Association Press, 1954.

Sherrill, Lewis J. *Guilt and Redemption*. Richmond, Va.: John Knox Press, 1945.

Shostrom, Everett L. and Brammer, Lawrence M. *Dynamics of the Counseling Process*. New York: McGraw-Hill Book Company, 1952.

Zerfoss, Karl P. (ed.). *Readings in Counseling*. New York: Association Press, 1952.

7. Leadership Education

Campbell, Donald T. *Leadership and Its Effects upon the Group*. Columbus, Ohio: Ohio State University, 1956.

Gwynn, Price H. *Leadership Education in the Local Church*. Philadelphia: Westminster Press, 1952.

Leadership Education Handbook. New York: National Council of Churches. Frequently revised and reissued to aid leadership schools.

McKibben, Frank M. *Guilding Workers in Christian Education*. Nashville: Abingdon Press, 1953.

Ross, Murray G. and Hendry, Charles E. *New Understandings of Leadership*. New York: Association Press, 1957.

Stogdill, Ralph M. *et al*. *Leadership and Role Expectations*. Columbus, Ohio: Ohio State University, 1956.

Wittenberg, Rudolph M. *Art of Group Discipline*. New York: Association Press, 1951.

III. THE HOME, THE CHURCH AND RELIGIOUS EDUCATION

1. The Church and the Home

Bailey, Derrick S. *The Mystery of Love and Marriage*. New York: Harper and Bros., 1952.

Barrett, T. Van B. *The Christian Family*. New York: Morehouse-Gorham Company, 1958.

Duvall, Evelyn R. M. *Family Living*. New York: The Macmillan Company, 1950.

Fallaw, Wesner. *The Modern Parent and the Teaching Church*. New York: The Macmillan Company, 1946.

———. *Toward Spiritual Security*. Philadelphia: Westminster Press, 1952.

Feucht, Oscar E. (ed.). *Helping Families through the Church*. St. Louis: Concordia Publishing House, 1957.

Maynard, Donald M. *Looking Toward Christian Marriage*. Nashville: Abingdon Press, 1958.

———. *Your Home Can Be Christian*. Nashville: Abingdon Press, 1952.

Peterson, James A. *Education for Marriage*. New York: Charles Scribner's Sons, 1956.

Thompson, W. Taliaferro. *Adventures in Parenthood*. Richmond, Va.: John Knox Press, 1959.

Westcott, Regina H. *The Family Lives Its Religion*. Revised Edition. New York: Harper and Brothers, 1954.

Winter, Gibson. *Love and Conflict*. New York: Doubleday and Company, 1958.

Wynn, John C. *How Christian Parents Face Family Problems*. Philadelphia: Westminster Press, 1955.

2. Sex Education

Bibby, Cyril. *How Life Is Handed On*. New York: Emerson Books, Inc., 1947.

Child Study Association of America. *Facts of Life for Children*. Indianapolis: Bobbs-Merrill Company, 1954.

Dickerson, Roy E. *So Youth May Know*. Revised Edition. New York: Association Press, 1948.

Eckert, Ralph G. *Sex Attitudes in the Home*. New York: Association Press, 1956.

Hulme, William E. *God, Sex and Youth*. Englewood Cliffs, N. J.: Prentice-Hall, Inc., 1959.

Mooney, Belle S. *How Shall I Tell My Child?* New York: Garden City Publishing Company, 1947.

Pittenger, W. Norman. *A Christian View of Sexual Behavior*. Greenwich, Conn.: Seabury Press, 1954.

Short Guide to Christian Sex Education. New York: Morehouse-Gorham Company, 1949.

Strain, F. B. *New Patterns in Sex Teaching*. New York: Appleton-Century-Crofts, Inc., 1951.

IV. ORGANIZATION AND ADMINISTRATION OF RELIGIOUS EDUCATION

1. Organization in the Local Church

Cummings, Oliver deW. *Christian Education in the Local Church.* Revised Edition. Philadelphia: Judson Press.

Gable, Lee J. *Christian Nurture Through the Church.* New York: National Council of Churches, 1955.

Heim, Ralph D. *Leading a Sunday Church School.* Philadelphia: Muhlenberg Press, 1950.

Leach, William H. *Handbook of Church Management.* Englewood Cliffs, N. J.: Prentice-Hall, Inc., 1958.

Lobingier, John L. *The Better Church School.* Boston: Pilgrim Press, 1952.

Miller, Randolph C. *Education for Christian Living.* Englewood Cliffs, N. J.: Prentice-Hall, Inc., 1956.

Vieth, Paul H. *The Church School.* Philadelphia: Christian Education Press, 1957.

2. Religious Education and the Public Schools

American Council on Education. *The Function of the Public Schools in Dealing with Religion.* Washington, 1953.

——. *The Study of Religion in the Public Schools.* Washington, 1958.

Barker, Ernest. *Church, State and Education.* Ann Arbor, Mich.: University of Michigan Press, 1957.

Butts, R. Freeman. *The American Tradition in Religion and Education.* Boston: Beacon Press, 1950.

Hartford, Ellis F. *Moral Values in Public Education.* New York: Harper and Brothers, 1958.

——. (ed.). *Public Schools, Religion and Values.* Lexington, Ky.: University of Kentucky Press, 1956.

Henry, Virgil. *The Place of Religion in Public Schools.* New York: Harper and Brothers, 1950.

Johnson, F. Ernest (ed.). *American Education and Religion.* New York: Harper and Brothers, 1952.

Martin, Renwick H. *Our Public Schools, Christian or Secular.* Pittsburgh: National Reform Association, 1952.

McCluskey, Neil G. *Public Schools and Moral Education.* New York: Columbia University Press, 1958.

Moore, J. M. *The Place of Moral and Religious Values in Programs of General Education.* Hazen Foundation, 1952.

Moral and Spiritual Values in the Public Schools: Washington: Educational Policies Commission, National Education Association, 1951.

O'Neill, James M. *Religion and Education under the Constitution.* New York: Harper and Brothers, 1949.

Riehl, G. M. *Technique and Theories for Teaching Moral and Spiritual Values in the Public Schools.* Eugene, Ore.: University of Oregon, 1956.

Sebaly, A. L. (ed.). *Teacher Education and Religion.* Washington: American Association of Colleges for Teacher Education, 1959.

The State and Sectarian Education. Washington: National Education Association, 1957.

Thayer, Vivian T. *Attack upon the American Secular School.* Boston: Beacon Press, 1951.

3. Weekday and Vacation Church Schools

Butt, Elsie M. *The Vacation Church School in Christian Education.* Nashville: Abingdon Press, 1957.

Schultz, Florence. *Summer with Nursery Children.* Boston: Pilgrim Press, 1958.

Shaver, Erwin L. *Weekday Church School.* Boston: Pilgrim Press, 1956.

4. Camping and Religious Education

Backus, Ramona *et al. Character Education in the Summer Camp.* New York: Association Press, 1942.

Bowman, Clarice M. *Spiritual Values in Camping.* New York: Association Press, 1954.

Burns, Gerald P. *Camp Organization for Program.* Chicago: American Camping Association.

———, *et al. The Program of the Modern Camp.* Englewood Cliffs, N. J.: Prentice-Hall, Inc., 1954.

Ensign, John and Ruth. *Camping Together as Christians.* Richmond, Va.: John Knox Press, 1958.

Goddard, Carrie L. *Living with Others.* Nashville: Abingdon Press, 1959.

Goodrich, Lois. *Decentralized Camping: A Handbook.* New York: Association Press, 1959.

Jobe, Mabel L. *Handbook of Day-Camping.* New York: Association Press, 1949.

Reimann, Lewis C. *The Successful Camp.* Ann Arbor, Mich.: University of Michigan Press, 1958 .

5. Religion and Higher Education

Aubrey, Edwin E. *Humanistic Teaching and the Place of Ethical and Religious Values in Higher Education.* Philadelphia: University of Pennsylvania Press, 1959.

Brown, Kenneth I. *Not Minds Alone.* New York: Harper and Brothers, 1954.

Fairchild, Hoxie N. (ed.). *Religious Perspectives in College Teaching.* New York: Ronald Press, 1952.

Ferré, Nels F. S. *Christian Faith and Higher Education.* New York: Harper and Brothers, 1954.

LeFevre, Perry D. *The Christian Teacher.* Nashville: Abingdon Press, 1958.

Meland, Bernard E. *Higher Education and the Human Spirit.* Chicago: University of Chicago Press, 1953.

Reddick, DeWitt C. (ed.). *Church and Campus.* Richmond, Va.: John Knox Press, 1956.

Smith, Seymour A. *The American College Chaplaincy.* New York: Association Press, 1954.

———. *Religious Cooperation in State Universities.* Ann Arbor, Mich.: University of Michigan, 1957.

Snavely, Guy E. *The Church and the Four-Year College.* New York: Harper and Brothers, 1955.

Von Grueningen, John P. (ed.). *Toward a Christian Philosophy of Higher Education.* Philadelphia: Westminster Press, 1957.

Walter, Erich A. (ed.). *Religion and the State University.* Ann Arbor, Mich.: University of Michigan Press, 1958.

6. Building for Religious Education

Adair, Thelma and McCort, Elizabeth. *How to Make Church School Equipment.* Philadelphia: Westminster Press, 1955.

Atkinson, C. Harry. *Building and Equipping for Christian Education.* New York: National Council of Churches, 1956.

Planning Schools for the Use of Audio-Visual Materials. Three booklets, Washington: National Education Association.

Kramer, E. J. *Equipment and Arrangement for Children's Groups in the Church.* Nashville: Board of Education, The Methodist Church, 1946.

Shear, John K. (ed.). *Religious Buildings Today.* New York: F. W. Dodge Corp., 1957.

V. CURRICULUM FOR RELIGIOUS EDUCATION

Bower, W. C. *The Curriculum of Religious Education.* New York: Charles Scribner's Sons, 1925.

A Guide for Curriculum in Christian Education. New York: National Council of Churches, 1955.

International Curriculum Guide. Chicago: International Council of Religious Education, 1931.

VI. METHODS IN RELIGIOUS EDUCATION
1. General Considerations of Method

Foster, Virgil E. *How a Small Church Can Have Good Christian Education.* New York: Harper and Brothers, 1956.

Lobingier, John L. *If Teaching Is Your Job.* Boston: Pilgrim Press, 1956.

Wiles, Kimball. *Teaching for Better Schools.* Englewood Cliffs, N. J.: Prentice-Hall, Inc., 1952.

Youngman, Bernard R. *Teaching Religious Knowledge.* London: University of London Press, 1953.

2. Age-Group Methods
(A) CHILDREN

Anderson, Phoebe M. *Religious Living with Nursery Children in Church and Home.* Boston: Pilgrim Press, 1956.

Bro, Margueritte H. *When Children Ask.* Revised Edition. New York: Harper and Brothers, 1956.

Carlson, J. B. *The Nursery Department of the Church.* St. Louis: Bethany Press, 1958.

Clark, Marjorie A. *Methods of Teaching Religion to Children.* London: Society for Promoting Christian Knowledge, 1956.

Dillard, Polly H. *Church Kindergarten.* Nashville: Broadman Press, 1958.

Fahs, Sophia L. *Today's Children and Yesterday's Heritage.* Boston: Beacon Press, 1952.

Fenner, Mabel B. *Guiding the Nursery Class.* Philadelphia: Muhlenberg Press, 1950.

Heaton, Ada B. *The 3's at Church.* Philadelphia: American Baptist Publication Society, 1953.

Heron, Frances D. *Kathy Ann, Kindergartner.* Nashville: Abingdon Press, 1955.

Hill, Dorothy L. *Working with Juniors at Church.* Nashville: Abingdon Press, 1955.

Hunter, Edith F. *The Questioning Child and Religion.* Boston: Beacon Press, 1956.

Keiser, Armilda. *Here's How and When.* New York: Friendship Press, 1952.

Kemp, C. F. *The Church: The Gifted and the Retarded Child.* St. Louis: Bethany Press, 1957.

Reed, William W. *Teaching the Church's Children.* New York: Morehouse-Gorham Company, 1958.

Roorbach, Rosemary K. *Religion in the Kindergarten.* New York: Harper and Brothers, 1949.

Whitehouse, Elizabeth S. *The Children We Teach.* Philadelphia: Judson Press, 1950.

(B) YOUTH

Baruch, Dorothy W. *How to Live with Your Teen-Ager.* New York: McGraw-Hill Book Company, 1954.

Bowman, Clarice M. *Ways Youth Learn.* New York: Harper and Brothers, 1952.

Cummings, Oliver deW. *Youth Fellowship.* Philadelphia: Judson Press, 1956.

Griffiths, Louise B. *The Teacher and Young Teens.* St. Louis: Bethany Press, 1954.

Jones, G. Curtis. *Youth Deserves to Know.* New York: The Macmillan Company, 1958.

Landis, Judson T. and Mary G. *Teen-Ager's Guide for Living.* Englewood Cliffs, N. J.; Prentice-Hall, Inc., 1957.

Miller, Haskell M. *Understanding and Preventing Juvenile Delinquency.* Nashville: Abingdon Press, 1958.

Roberts, Dorothy M. *Partners with Youth*. New York: Association Press, 1956.

Tani, H. N. *Ventures in Youth Work*. Philadelphia: Christian Education Press, 1957.

Wittenberg, Rudolph. *On Call For Youth*. New York: Association Press, 1955.

Wyckoff, D. Campbell. *In One Spirit*. New York: Friendship Press, 1957.

(C) ADULTS

Adult Education for Everybody. New York: Adult Education Council, 1954.

Bergevin, Paul E. and McKinley, John. *Design for Adult Education in the Church*. Greenwich, Conn.: Seabury Press, 1958.

Clemmons, Robert S. *Dynamics of Christian Adult Education*. Nashville: Abingdon Press, 1958.

Donahue, Wilma T. *Education for Later Maturity*. New York: Whiteside, Inc., 1955.

Gleason, George. *Single Young Adults in the Church*. New York: Association Press, 1952.

Havighurst, R. J. and Orr, Betty. *Adult Education and Adult Needs*. Chicago: Center for Study of Liberal Education for Adults, 1956.

How to Teach Adults. Chicago: Adult Education Association, 1955.

Howe, Reuel L. *The Creative Years*. Greenwich, Conn.: Seabury Press, 1959.

Kempfer, Homer. *Adult Education*. New York: McGraw-Hill Book Company, 1955.

Knowles, Malcolm. *Informal Adult Education*. New York: Association Press, 1950.

Lindhorst, Frank A. *Teaching Adults*. Nashville: Abingdon Press, 1951.

Little, Lawrence C. (ed.). *The Future Course of Christian Adult Education*. Pittsburgh: University of Pittsburgh Press, 1959.

Powell, John W. *Learning Comes of Age*. New York: Association Press, 1956.

Sheats, Paul; Jayne, C. D.; and Spence, R. B. *Adult Education*. New York: The Dryden Press, 1953.

Zeigler, Earl F. *Christian Education of Adults*. Philadelphia: Westminster Press, 1958.

3. Use of the Bible in Religious Education

Abba, Raymond. *The Nature and Authority of the Bible*. London: James Clarke and Company, 1959.

Anderson, B. W. *The Unfolding Drama of the Bible*. New York: Association Press, 1953.

Bouquet, Alan C. *Everyday Life in New Testament Times*. New York: Charles Scribner's Sons, 1954.

Bower, William C. *The Living Bible*. Revised Edition. New York: Harper and Brothers, 1946.

Carlyon, James T. *Interpreting the Bible to Youth*. Nashville: Abingdon Press, 1954.

Fairly, John L. and Arleen G. *Using the Bible to Answer Questions Children Ask*. Richmond, Va.: John Knox Press, 1958.

Gettys, Joseph M. *How to Teach the Bible*. Richmond, Va.: John Knox Press, 1949.

Goodspeed, Edgar J. *How to Read the Bible*. Philadelphia: John C. Winston Company, 1946.

Love, Julian P. *How to Read the Bible*. Revised Edition. New York: The Macmillan Company, 1958.

Miller, Madeleine S. and John L. *Harper's Bible Dictionary*. New York: Harper and Brothers, 1952.

Miller, Randolph C. *Biblical Theology and Christian Education*. New York: Charles Scribner's Sons, 1956.

Niles, Daniel T. *Reading the Bible Today*. New York: Association Press, 1955.

Smither, Ethel. *The Use of the Bible with Children*. Cincinnati: Methodist Book Concern, 1935.

Wright, George E. and Filson, Floyd V. *The Westminster Historical Atlas to the Bible*. Revised Edition. Philadelphia: Westminster Press, 1956.

4. The Arts and Religious Education

Bailey, Albert. *Christ and His Gospel in Recent Art*. New York: Charles Scribner's Sons, 1948.

Ferguson, George. *Signs and Symbols in Christian Art*. New York: Oxford University Press, 1954.

Rest, Friedrich. *Our Christian Symbols*. Philadelphia: Christian Education Press, 1954.

Smith, Jean L. *Great Art and Children's Worship*. Nashville: Abingdon Press, 1948.

Stafford, Thomas A. *Christian Symbolism in the Evangelical Churches*. Nashville: Abingdon Press, 1942.

5. Drama and Religious Education

Durland, F. C. *Creative Dramatics for Children*. Yellow Springs, Ohio: Antioch Press, 1952.

Eastman, Fred. *Christ in the Drama*. New York: The Macmillan Company, 1947.

Ehrensperger, Harold. *Conscience on Stage*. Nashville: Abingdon Press, 1947.

Holroyd, George H. and Ratcliff, Nora. *Drama in Schools and Youth Centers*. London: Macdonald and Company, 1949.

Lobb, Kenneth M. *Drama in School and Church*. Toronto: Clark, Irwin and Company, 1955.

Plays for the Church. New York: National Council of Churches, 1957.

Siks, Geraldine B. *Creative Dramatics: An Art for Children*. New York: Harper and Brothers, 1958.

6. Play and Recreation in Religious Education

Bauer, Lois M. and Reed, Barbara A. *Dance and Play Activities for the Elementary Grades*. New York: Chartwell House, 1951.

Corbin, Hayman D. *Recreation Leadership*. Englewood Cliffs, N. J.: Prentice-Hall, Inc., 1953.

Danford, Howard G. *Recreation in the American Community*. New York: Harper and Brothers, 1953.

Fitzgerald, Gerald B. *Leadership in Recreation*. New York: A. S. Barnes and Company, 1951.

Harbin, Elvin O. *The Recreation Leader*. Nashville: Abingdon Press, 1952.

Hartley, Ruth E. *et al. Understanding Children's Play*. New York: Columbia University Press, 1952.

Hartley, Ruth E. and Goldenson, Robert M. *The Complete Book of Children's Play*. New York: Thomas Y. Crowell Company, 1957.

Millen, Nina. *Children's Games from Many Lands*. New York: Friendship Press, 1943.

Page, Hilary F. *Playtime in the First Five Years*. Second Revised Edition. Philadelphia: J. B. Lippincott Company, 1954.

Recreation Activities for Adults. National Recreation Association. New York: Association Press, 1950.

Ward, Winifred. *Playmaking with Children from Kindergarten through Junior High School*. Second Edition. New York: Appleton-Century-Crofts, Inc., 1957.

7. Audio-Visual Materials and Techniques
in Religious Education

Audio-Visual Materials of Instruction. Forty-eighth Yearbook of the National Society for the Study of Education. Part I. Chicago: Univeristy of Chicago Press, 1949.

Audio-Visual Resource Guide. Fourth Edition. New York: National Council of Churches, 1958. This guide is frequently revised and new editions issued. During interims between editions, supplements are published—usually annually.

Bachman, John W. *How to Use Audio-Visual Materials*. New York: Association Press, 1956.

Dale, Edgar. *Audio-Visual Methods in Teaching*. Revised Edition. New York: The Dryden Press, 1954.

Haas, Kenneth B. and Packer, Harry Q. *Preparation and Use of Audio-Visual Aids*. Second Edition. Englewood Cliffs, N. J.: Prentice-Hall, Inc., 1950.

Kinder, James S. *Audio-Visual Materials and Techniques*. New York: American Book Company, 1950.

Parker, E. C. et al. *Film Use in the Church*. New York: National Council of Churches, 1955.

Planning Schools for Use of Audio-Visual Materials. Washington: National Education Association.

Rumpf, Oscar J. *Use of Audio-Visuals in the Church*. Philadelphia: Christian Education Press, 1958.

Sands, Lester B. *Audio-Visual Procedures in Teaching*. New York: Ronald Press, 1956.

Tower, Howard E. *Church Use of Audio-Visuals*. Revised Edition. Nashville: Abingdon Press, 1959.

Wittich, Walter A. and Schuller, Charles F. *Audio-Visual Materials: Their Nature and Use*. New York: Harper and Brothers, 1953.

8. Discussion Techniques

Auer, John J. and Eubank, Henry L. *Handbook for Discussion Leaders*. Revised Edition. New York: Harper and Brothers, 1954.

Bergevin, Paul E. and Morris, Dwight. *Manual for Discussion Leaders and Participants*. Bloomington, Ind.: Community Services in Adult Education, 1954.

Cantor, Nathaniel F. *Learning Through Discussion*. Buffalo: Human Relations for Industry, 1951.

Keltner, John W. *Group Discussion Processes*. New York: Longmans, Green and Company, 1957.

Shull, W. R. *Techniques of Discussion with Teen-Agers*. Chicago: National Forum, Inc., 1951.

Wagner, Russell H. and Arnold, Carroll C. *Handbook of Group Discussion*. Boston: Houghton Mifflin Company, 1950.

9. Music in Religious Education

Ingram, Madeline D. *Organizing and Directing Children's Choirs*. Nashville: Abingdon Press, 1959.

Kettring, Donald. *Steps Toward a Singing Church*. Philadelphia: Westminster Press, 1948.

Morsch, Vivian S. *The Use of Music in Christian Education*. Philadelphia: Westminster Press, 1956.

Shields, Elizabeth. *Music in the Religious Growth of Children*. Nashville: Abingdon Press, 1943.

Thomas, Edith L. *Music in Christian Education*. Nashville: Abingdon Press, 1953.

Toney, H. G. *Music Levels in Christian Education*. Wheaton, Ill.: Van Kampen Press, 1952.

Whittlesey, Federal L. *A Comprehensive Program of Church Music*. Philadelphia: Westminster Press, 1957.

10. Activities in Religious Education

Lobingier, Elizabeth M. *Activities in Child Education*. Boston: Pilgrim Press, 1950.

Mendelowitz, Daniel M. *Children Are Artists*. Stanford: Stanford University Press, 1953.

More Than Fun: Creative Activities for All Our Children. A Report to the mid-century White House Conference on Children and Youth. New York, 1951.

Pearson, Ralph M. *New Art Education.* Revised Edition. New York: Harper and Brothers, 1953.

Rice, Rebecca. *Creative Activities.* Boston: Pilgrim Press, 1947.

VII. PRAYER AND WORSHIP

1. The Nature of Prayer and Worship

Abba, Raymond. *Principles of Christian Worship.* New York: Oxford University Press, 1957.

Davies, Horton. *Christian Worship.* Nashville: Abingdon Press, 1957.

Edwall, Pehr; Hayman, E.; and Maxwell, W. D. (ed.). *Ways of Worship.* New York: Harper and Brothers, 1951.

Hedley, George. *Christian Worship.* New York: The Macmillan Company, 1953.

Horton, Douglas. *The Meaning of Worship.* New York: Harper and Brothers, 1959.

2. Prayer and Worship for Age Groups

Bays, Alice A. *Worship Services for Junior Highs.* Nashville: Abingdon Press, 1958.

Bowman, Clarice M. *Worship Ways for Camp.* New York: Association Press, 1955.

Brown, Jeanette P. *More Children's Worship in the Church School.* New York: Harper and Brothers, 1953.

Gebhard, Anna L. and Edward W. *Our Family Worships At Home.* Nashville: Abingdon Press, 1958.

Lee, Florence B. *Worshiping God at Church.* Philadelphia: Judson Press, 1958.

Little, Gertrude. *Worship Programs for the Small Sunday School.* Anderson, Ind.: Gospel Trumpet Company, 1952.

Williams, John G. *Worship and the Modern Child.* New York: The Macmillan Company, 1958.

Biographical Index of Contributors

THE FOLLOWING BRIEF BIOGRAPHICAL SKETCHES ARE INCLUDED TO ASSIST THE reader. The data recorded comprise church membership, educational background, professional history, and major publications of each contributor. If additional information is desired, it is recommended that the reader consult such standard biographical works as *Who's Who in America* or bibliographical resources, such as *Education Index*.

ATKINSON, Charles Harry
> American Baptist Convention; Acadia University, A.B. (1922); Andover Newton Theological School, B.D. (1926); Assoc. Minister, Clarendon Street Church, Boston, 1922-24; Minister, First Church, Livermore Falls, Me., 1924-28; Minister, First Baptist Church, Medford, Mass., 1928-38; Minister, Brunswick Street Baptist Church, Fredericton, New Brunswick, Canada, 1938-41; Secretary, Edifice Funds and Building Counsel, American Baptist Home Mission Society, New York, 1941-53; Executive Director, Bureau of Church Building, National Council of Churches, New York, 1953-56; Editor, *Protestant Church Buildings and Equipment*, 1956 to present. Publications: *Building and Equipping for Christian Education* (1956); contributor to *Religious Buildings Today* (1957).

BAILEY, Albert Ernest
> The Presbyterian Church in Canada. University College (Toronto), B.A. (1948); University of Toronto, M.A. (1951); Knox Theological College, Diploma (1951); Princeton Theological Seminary (doctoral study). Minister, Dundalk, Ontario Presbyterian Church, 1947-53; Teaching Fellow, Princeton Theological Seminary, 1954-56; Assistant Editor of Church School Publications, The Presbyterian Church in Canada, 1956 to present; Lecturer in Christian Education, Knox College (Toronto), 1957 to present.

BONE, Maurice David
> United Presbyterian Church in the U. S. A. University of Illinois, B.S. (1928); McCormick Theological Seminary, B.D. (1931). Minister of McIntosh and Morristown, S. D. Presbyterian Churches, 1931-34; Lamour, Cottonwood and Grand Rapids, N. D. Presbyterian Churches, 1934-37; First Presbyterian Church, Aberdeen, S. D., 1937-46; Grace Presbyterian Church, Council Bluffs, Iowa, 1946-49; Assoc. Dir. of Youth Work, Board of Christian Education of the Presbyterian Church in U. S. A., 1950-55; Counselor in Camping, Board of Christian Education, Presbyterian Church in U. S. A., 1955 to present.

BUTLER, Rosa May
> Methodist Church. Oklahoma City University, B.F.A. (1932); Scarritt College, B.A. (1934); Union Theological Seminary (New York), S.M.M. (1953). Chmn. Music Dept., Virginia School, Huchow, China, 1935-37; McTyeire School, Shanghai, China,

1937-39; 1940-43; and 1946-48; Ginling College, Nanking, China, 1948-51; Assoc. Prof., Scarritt College, 1944-46, 1952 to present.

CASE, William F.
Methodist Church. Ohio Wesleyan University, B.A. (1940); Boston University School of Theology, S.T.B. (1945); Columbia University, M.A. (1948); Columbia University and Union Theological Seminary, Ed.D. (1953). Assoc. Exec. Sec'y, Bd. of Ed. of Ohio Annual Conference, Methodist Church, 1945; Ass't. Prof., Baldwin-Wallace College, 1946-48; Lecturer, Westminster Theological Seminary, 1949; Professor, Garrett Biblical Institute, 1949-59; Dean and Professor, National Methodist Theological Seminary, 1959 to present.

CHAPPELL, Nelson Thomas
The United Church of Canada. University of Alberta, B.A. and B.D., (1927, 1932); University of Chicago, M.A. (1929); Indiana Central College, D.D. (1958). Minister, St. Paul's United Church, Grande Prairie, Alberta, 1930-35; Crescent Heights Church, Calgary, Alberta, 1935-37; Westminster Church, Saskatoon, Sask., 1937-41; Chaplain, Royal Canadian Air Force, 1941-45; Secretary, Dept. of Christian Education, Canadian Council of Churches, 1945-50; General Secretary, John Milton Society for the Blind, 1950-53; General Secretary, World Council of Christian Education and Sunday School Association, 1953 to present.

CHEEK, A. Wilson
The United Church of Christ. Catawba College, A.B. (1936); Theological Seminary of the Evangelical and Reformed Church, B.D. (1939). Minister, Trinity E. and R. Church, Conover, N. C., 1939-44; Faith E. and R. Church, Brookford, N. C., 1939-47; Macedonia E. and R. Church, Hickory, N. C., 1945-47; Director of Youth Work, E. and R. Church, 1947-50; Director of Youth Work and Executive Secretary of the United Christian Youth Movement, National Council of Churches, 1950-57; Director of Adult Work, National Council of Churches, 1957-59; Associate General Secretary, World Council on Christian Education and Sunday School Association, 1959 to present.

CLARK, Walter Houston
Protestant Episcopal Church. Williams College, A.B. (1925); Harvard University, M.A. (1926), Ed.M. (1935), Ph.D. (1944). Lenox School, Lenox, Mass., 1926-45; Instructor, Bowdoin College, 1945-47; Associate Prof., Middlebury College, 1947-51; Dean and Prof., Hartford School of Religious Education, Hartford Seminary Foundation, 1951 to present. Publications: *The Oxford Group: Its History and Significance* (1951); *The Psychology of Religion* (1958).

CULLY, Iris Virginia
Protestant Episcopal Church. Adelphi College, A.B. (1936); Hartford Seminary Foundation, A.M. (1937); Garrett Biblical Institute, B.D. (1954); Northwestern University, Ph. D. (1955). Director of Religious Education, Hollis, N. Y. Presbyterian Church, 1937-39; Director of Curriculum Laboratory and Visiting Instructor, Garrett Biblical Institute, 1957 to present. Publications: co-author of *Two Seasons: Advent and Lent* (1954); *The Dynamics of Christian Education* (1958).

CULLY, Kendig Brubaker
Protestant Episcopal Church. American International College, A.B. (1934); Hartford Seminary Foundation, B.D. (1937), M.R.E. (1938), Ph.D. (1939); Seabury-Western Theological Seminary, S.T.M. (1953). Minister, Melrose (Mass.) Highlands Congregational Church, 1941-46; First Congregational Church, Haverhill, Mass., 1946-51; Minister of Education, First Methodist Church, Evanston, Ill., 1951-54; Lecturer, Assistant Professor and Professor, Seabury-Western Theological Seminary, 1953 to present. Publications: *We Can Live Together* (1950); *Christianity Changes Things* (1951); *The Bible and the Christian Life* (1954); *Sharing Our Religion*

(1955); *Your Christian Vocation* (1958); co-author of *Two Seasons: Advent and Lent* (1954); contributor to *Distinguished American Jews* (1945); *Unused Alibis* (1951).

DIRKS, John Edward

United Presbyterian Church, U.S.A. University of Dubuque, B.A. (1940); Yale University Divinity School, B.D. (1943); Columbia University, Ph.D. (1947). Counselor to Protestant Students, Columbia University, 1945-49; Professor, Lake Forest College, 1949-55; Stephen Merrell Clement Professor of Christian Methods, Yale University Divinity School, 1955 to present. Publications: *Critical Theology of Theodore Parker* (1948); contributor to *Toward a Christian Philosophy of Higher Education* (1956).

FALLAW, Wesner

Furman University, A.B. (1927); Columbia University, M.A. (1936), Ed.D. (1944). Y.M.C.A. Secretary, Charleston, S. C., 1927-33; Alumni Secretary, Ass't Professor and Ass't to the Dean, Furman University, 1933-34, 1937-39; Director of Religious Education, Winnetka, Illinois, 1940-46; Professor, Andover Newton Theological School, 1946 to present. Publications: *The Modern Parent and the Teaching Church* (1946); *Toward Spiritual Security* (1952).

GABLE, Lee Jay

United Church of Christ. Franklin and Marshall College, A.B. (1928), D.D. (1953); Lancaster Theological Seminary, B.D. (1931); University of Pennsylvania, M.A. (1940). Minister, Dallastown, Pa. Evangelical and Reformed Charge, 1931-39; Director of Leadership Education, Penna. State Council of Christian Education, 1939-44; Director of Leadership Education, Board of Education of Evangelical and Reformed Church, 1944-46; Director of Administration and Leadership, National Council of Churches, 1946-52; Professor, Lancaster Theological Seminary, 1952 to present. Publications: *Christian Nurture Through the Church*, (1955); *Encyclopedia for Church Group Leaders* (1959).

GODDARD, Alice L.

United Presbyterian Church, U. S. A. Auburn Seminary, B.R.E. (1932); Graduate Study at Wayne State University; Graduate of Chaffee Noble School of Expression. Director of Religious Education, Fort St. Presbyterian Church, Detroit, 1939-41; Director of Religious Education, Detroit Council of Churches, 1941-46; Director of Children's Work, National Council of Churches, 1948-57; Director of Weekday Religious Education, National Council of Churches, 1957 to present.

HAM, Howard Miller

Methodist Church. Sterling College, A.B. (1943); Iliff School of Theology, Th.M. (1946), Th.D. (1947); University of Chicago, Ph.D. (1954). Newspaper work in Missouri and Kansas, 1935-40; Field Executive, Boy Scouts of America, 1944-45; Minister of Methodist Churches in Kansas, Colorado and Illinois, 1940-51; Professor, Iliff School of Theology, 1951 to present.

HEIM, Ralph D.

United Lutheran Church in America. Wittenberg University, A.B. (1919); M.A. and B.D. (1923); D.D. (1948); Northwestern University, Ph.D. (1929). Professor, Thiel College, 1927-32; Professor, Hartwick College, 1932-39; Dean, Hartwick College, 1934-39; Professor, Lutheran Theological Seminary, Gettysburg, Pa., 1939 to present. Publications: *Workbook for Old Testament Study* (1938); *A Harmony of the Gospels for Students* (1947); *Workbook for New Testament Study* (1948); *Leading a Sunday Church School* (1950); *Youth's Companion to the Bible* (1959).

HULME, William Edward

American Lutheran Church. Capital University, B.S. (1942); Evangelical Lutheran Seminary at Capital University, B.D. (1945); Boston University, Ph.D. (1948).

Minister, Clinton Heights Lutheran Church, Columbus, Ohio, 1946-49; Chaplain and Professor, Wartburg College, 1949-55; Professor, Wartburg Theological Seminary, 1955 to present; Lutheran Tutor and Chaplain, Mansfield College, Oxford University, Oxford, England, 1958-59. Publications: *Face Your Life with Confidence* (1953); *How to Start Counseling* (1955); *Counseling and Theology* (1956).

HUNT, Rolfe Lanier

Methodist Church. Millsaps College, B.A. (1924); George Peabody College for Teachers, M.A. (1927), Ph.D. (1937). Superintendent, Bassfield, Miss. Consolidated Schools, 1927-29; Assistant and Associate Editor, Methodist Episcopal South, Board of Christian Education, 1930-36; Superintendent of Schools, Louise, Miss., 1937-42 and Magnolia, Miss., 1942-45; Editor-in-chief, *Phi Delta Kappan*, 1945-52; Chief of Editorial Section, U. S. Office of Education, 1952-53; Executive Director, Department of Religion and Public Education, National Council of Churches, 1953 to present. Publications: *A Study of Factors Influencing the Public School Curriculum of Kentucky* (1939); *Methodist Men at Work* (1948); *A Primer for Christian Living* (1951); *High School Ahead* (1952).

KENNY, Dumont Francis

Roman Catholic Church. Fordham University, B.S. (1940); Graduate Study at Columbia University, Teachers College (1940-41); University of Chicago, Ph.D. (1953). Head, Educational Department, P. J. Kennedy and Sons, 1938-40; Specialist Officer, Education and Religious Affairs, U. S. Army, 1943-45; Chief of Religious Affairs, Office of Military Government, Hesse, Germany, 1945-48; Professor, Lewis College, 1949-52; Vice-President for Program Development, National Conference of Christians and Jews, 1952 to present. Publications: co-author, *Technical Manual for Education and Religious Affairs* (1945); *The Citizen and Resources for Group Understanding* (1955); editor, *Research in Inter-Religious Group Relations* (1959).

KETCHAM, John B.

American Baptist Convention. Colgate University, B.A. (1928); Union Theological Seminary, B.D. (1932). Associate Director of Religious Education, Brooklyn Federation of Churches, 1930-34; Director of Christian Education and Associate Executive, Rochester Federation of Churches, 1934-38; Director of Field Administration, International Council of Religious Education, 1938-49; Associate Director Field Administration, National Council of Churches of Christ, 1950-53; Executive Director, Office for Councils of Churches, N.C.C.C.A., 1954 to present.

KNOFF, Gerald Everett

Methodist Church. Florida Southern College, B.A. (1930); Yale University, B.D. (1933), Ph.D. (1936); Rikkyo (St. Paul's) University, Dr. Humanities (1958). Minister, South Meriden, Conn. Methodist Church, 1934-36; Clinton, Conn. Methodist Church, 1936-38; Director of Religious Activities, Iowa State Teachers' College, 1938-44; Director of Educational Program (1944-45) and Associate General Secretary (1945-51), International Council of Religious Education; Associate Executive Secretary (1951-52) and Executive Secretary (1952 to present), National Council of Churches of Christ, U. S. A.

KOPPE, William Aram

Reformed Church in America. Yankton College, A.B. (1948); University of South Dakota, M.A. (1949); University of Kansas, Ph.D. (1954). Assistant Instructor, University of South Dakota, 1948-49; Research Associate, University of Kansas, 1950-53; Assistant Professor, University of Minnesota, 1953-54; Character Research Project, Union College, 1954 to present.

LIGON, Ernest Mayfield

National Convention of Christian Churches. Texas Christian University, A.B. (1921), M.A. (1921), LL.D. (1948); Yale University, B.D. (1924); Ph.D. (1927). Assistant

Instructor, Yale University, 1924-27; Assistant Professor, Connecticut College, 1927-29; Professor and Chairman Department of Psychology, Union College, 1929 to present; Founder and Director of Union College Character Research Project, since 1935. Publications: *The Psychology of the Christian Personality* (1935); *Their Future Is Now* (1939); *A Greater Generation* (1948); *Dimensions of Character* (1956).

LITTLE, Lawrence Calvin
Methodist Church. Davidson College, A.B. (1925); Duke University, M.A. (1929); Adrian College, D.D. (1931); Yale University, Ph.D. (1941). Teacher and Assistant to Superintendent, Winn Parish, La. Public Schools, 1917-20; All-South Field Secretary, International Society of Christian Endeavor, 1920-21; Minister, Methodist Protestant Churches, Concord, N. C., 1923-24; Grace Church, Greensboro, N. C., 1924-25; General Secretary for Youth Work, Methodist Protestant Church, 1926-32; Professor, Western Maryland College, 1932-45; Professor, University of Pittsburgh, 1945 to present. Publications: editor, *Religion and Education for Professional Responsibiltiy* (1956); editor, *Charting the Future Course of Christian Adult Education in America* (1958); editor, *Formulating the Objectives of Christian Adult Education; The Future Course of Christian Adult Education* (1959).

MAVES, Paul Benjamin
Methodist Church. Nebraska Wesleyan University, A.B. (1936); Drew University Theological School, B.D. (1939); New York University (1945-46); Drew University, Ph.D. (1949); Harvard University Divinity School, (1957-58). Associate Minister, Trinity Methodist Church, Albany, N. Y., 1940-42; Minister, Middlebury, Vt., 1942-45; Research Associate, 1946-48, and Acting Executive Secretary, Department of Pastoral Services, Federal Council of Churches, 1948-49; Assistant, Associate and Professor, Drew University Theological School, 1949 to present. Publications: co-author, *Older People and the Church* (1949); *The Christian Religious Education of Older People* (1950); *The Best Is Yet to Be* (1951); *The Church and Mental Health* (1954); *Understanding Ourselves As Adults* (1959).

MICHAELSEN, Robert Slocumb
Methodist Church. Cornell (Iowa) College, B.A. (1942), D.D. (1954); Yale University, B.D. (1945), Ph.D. (1951). Assistant Professor, State University of Iowa, 1947-52; Assistant Professor, Yale Divinity School, 1952-53; Professor and Director, School of Religion, State University of Iowa, 1954 to present. Publications: contributor to *Work and Vocation* (1954), *The Ministry in Historical Perspective* (1956), and *Faith and Ethics: The Theology of H. Richard Niebuhr* (1957).

MOORE, Raymond Soul
Seventh-Day Adventist Church. Pacific Union College, A.B. (1938); University of Southern California, Ed.M. (1946), Ed.D. (1947). Teacher and Assistant Principal, Artesia, Calif. Public Schools, 1938-40; Principal, Hermosa Beach, Calif. City Schools, 1940-41; U. S. Army, 1941-45; Superintendent of Schools, Artesia, Calif., 1945-46; Associate Professor and Professor, Pacific Union College, 1947-51; President, Japan Missionary College, 1951-56; Professor, Potomac University, 1957 to present. Publications: *Organization and Administration of Teacher Education in California* (1947); *Science Discovers God* (1953); *Michibiki, the Leading of God* (1956).

NELSON, Carl Ellis
Presbyterian Church, U. S. Austin College, Sherman, Texas, B.A. (1937); Austin Presbyterian Theological Seminary, B.D. (1940); University of Texas, M.A. (1944); Columbia University, Ph.D. (1955); Austin College, D.D. (1955). Minister to Presbyterian Students, University of Texas, 1940-42; Instructor, Austin Presbyterian Seminary, 1942-44; Director of Youth Work, Board of Christian Education, Presbyterian Church, U. S., 1944-48; Professor, Austin Presbyterian Seminary, 1948-57;

Professor, Union Theological Seminary, New York, 1957 to present.

NEWBY, Donald Orville

Disciples of Christ. Joplin Jr. College, A.S. (1945); Drury College, B.A. (1947); Disciples Divinity House, Federated Theological Faculty, University of Chicago (1947-50). Director of Youth Work, First Christian Church, Maywood, Ill., 1948-50; Director of Youth Work, Missouri Council of Churches, 1950-52; Associate Executive Secretary, United Christian Youth Movement and Associate Executive Director, Youth Department, National Council of Churches, 1952-57; Exec. Sec'y, U.C.Y.M. and Exec. Dir., Youth Dep't, N.C.C.C.A., 1957 to present.

PILCH, Judah

Jewish. University of Chicago, B.S. (1932); Columbia University, M.A. (1946); Dropsie College, Ph.D. (1951). Instructor, College of Jewish Studies, Chicago, 1930-39; Dean, Rochester Institute for Adult Jewish Studies, 1939-44; Director, Bronx Council for Jewish Religious Education, 1944-47; Executive Director, American Association for Jewish Education, 1949 to present; Visiting Lecturer, Yeshiva University, 1952 to present; Visiting Lecturer, Dropsie College, 1956 to present. Publications: *Jewish Life in Our Times* (1943); *Teaching Contemporary Jewish Life* (1948); *The Heder Metukan: Emancipation of Jewish Education, 1882-1914* (1951); *Jewish Education Register and Directory* (1952).

SIBLEY, Leonard A., Jr.

Reformed Church in America. Hope College, B.A. (1946); New Brunswick Theological Seminary, B.D. (1947). Minister, the Reformed Church, Colts Neck, N. J., 1946-48; Minister of Education, First Reformed Church, Schenectady, N. Y., 1948-51; Character Research Project, Union College, 1951 to present.

SLOYAN, Gerard

Roman Catholic Church. Seton Hall University, B.A. (1940); Seminary of the Immaculate Conception, (1940-43); Catholic University of America, S. T. L. (1944), Ph.D. (1948). Assistant pastor, Diocese of Trenton, 1947-50; Instructor, Assistant Professor, Catholic University, 1950 to present. Publications: editor, *Shaping the Christian Message* (1958).

TAYLOR, Marvin J.

Methodist Church. Olivet Nazarene College, B.Th. (1943); McCormick Theological Seminary, B.D. (1946); University of Chicago, A.M. (1949); University of Pittsburgh, Ph.D. (1954). Assistant Professor, Olivet Nazarene College, 1948-54; Minister of Education, Mt. Lebanon Methodist Church, Pittsburgh, 1954-56; Assistant Professor, University of Pittsburgh, 1956 to present. Publications: editor, *Religious Education: A Comprehensive Survey*.

TOWER, Howard E.

Methodist Church. DePauw University, A.B. (1929), Litt.D. (1954); Boston University School of Theology, S.T.B. (1931). Minister in various Massachusetts Methodist churches, 1930-37; Executive Secretary, Board of Education, New England Southern Methodist Conference, 1937-45; Director of Audio-Visual Education, Methodist General Board of Education, 1945-52; Associate Secretary and Director of Program and Production for Methodist Television, Radio and Film Commission, 1952 to present. Publications: *Church Use of Audio-Visuals* (1950), Revised Edition (1959).

VIETH, Paul Herman

United Church of Christ. Central Wesleyan College, Warrenton, Mo., A.B. (1917); Yale University, B.D. (1924), Ph.D. (1928); St. Paul's University, Tokyo, Japan, Hum.D. (1958). Superintendent of Administration and General Secretary, Missouri Sunday School Association, 1917-22; Director of Religious Education, Church of the Redeemer, New Haven, Conn., 1923-24; Director of Research and editor of the

International Journal of Religious Education, 1924-31; Visiting Professor, Duke University, 1931; Director of Field Work and Horace Bushnell Professor of Christian Nurture, Yale University, 1931 to present; Adviser, SCAP, Tokyo, Japan, 1947-48. Publications: *Teaching for Christian Living* (1929); *Objectives in Religious Education* (1930); *Improving Your Sunday School* (1930); *How to Teach in the Church School* (1935); co-author, *Visual Aids in the Church* (1946); editor, *The Church and Christian Education* (1947); *The Church School* (1957).

WARREN, James Herndon
Methodist Church. University of North Carolina, B.A. (1947); Northwestern University, M.A. (1948); Scarritt College for Christian Workers, M.A. (1950). Instructor, Athens College, 1950-52; Assistant Professor, Scarritt College for Christian Workers, 1952 to present.

WILLIAMS, Daniel Day
United Church of Christ. University of Denver, A.B. (1931); University of Chicago, M.A. (1933); Chicago Theological Seminary, B.D. (1934); Columbia University, Ph.D. (1940). Minister, First Congregational Church, Colorado Springs, Colo., 1936-38; Dean of Chapel and Instructor, Colorado College, 1938-39; Professor, Chicago Theological Seminary and Federated Theological Faculty, University of Chicago, 1939-54; Associate Director, Survey of Theological Education, 1954-55; Professor, Union Theological Seminary, New York, 1954 to present. Publications: *The Andover Liberals* (1941); *God's Grace and Man's Hope* (1949); *What Present Day Theologians Are Thinking* (1952), Revised edition (1959); co-author, *The Advancement of Theological Education* (1957).

WORNOM, Herman Eskridge
United Church of Christ. Randolph-Macon College, A.B. (1923); Columbia University, M.A. (1924); Graduate Study at Columbia University and Union Theological Seminary (1936-39). Director of Religious Education and Student Work, Central Congregational Church, Worcester, Mass., 1925-29; Director of Religious Education, Congregational Church, Glen Ridge, N. J., 1929-37; Minister of Education, Chevy Chase Presbyterian Church, Washington, D. C., 1939-40; Supervisor of Field Work, Springfield College, 1940-41; Director of Field Work and Professor, Pacific School of Religion, Berkeley, Cal., 1942-46; Executive Secretary, Department of Christian Education, Protestant Council of the City of New York, 1946-52; General Secretary, Religious Education Association, 1952 to present.

WYCKOFF, DeWitte Campbell
United Presbyterian Church, U. S. A. New York University, B.S. (1939), A.M. (1941), Ph.D. (1948). Teacher and Community Worker, Alpine, Tenn. for Presbyterian Board of National Missions, 1939-41; Director of Youth Division, Greater New York Federation of Churches, 1941-42; Staff Assistant and Assistant Secretary, Rural Church and Indian Work Units, Presbyterian Board of National Missions, 1942-47; Assistant, Associate, and Professor, New York University, 1947-54; Thomas W. Synnott Professor of Christian Education, Princeton Theological Seminary, 1954 to present. Publications: *The Task of Christian Education* (1955); *In One Spirit: Senior Highs and Missions* (1958); *The Gospel and Christian Education* (1959).

ZIEGLER, Jesse H.
Church of the Brethren. Bridgewater College (Virginia), A.B. (1935); Catholic University of America, M.A. (1937), Ph.D. (1942); Bethany Biblical Seminary, B.D. (1944); Chicago Institute for Psychoanalysis, Certificate in Child Care, (1959). Minister, University Park Church of the Brethren, 1935-41; Professor, Bethany Biblical Seminary, 1941-59; Associate Director, American Association of Theological Schools, 1959 to present. Publications: *The Broken Cup: A Socio-psychological Study of a Changing Rural Culture* (1942).

Index

439